John Dewey
and Daoist Thought

SUNY series in Chinese Philosophy and Culture

Roger T. Ames, editor

John Dewey and Daoist Thought

Experiments in Intra-cultural Philosophy

Volume One

Jim Behuniak

Front cover: Roofline image taken by John Dewey in China.

Back cover: Image of John Dewey (Peking, July 5, 1921), courtesy of the Morris Library, Special Collections Research Center, Southern Illinois University Carbondale.

Published by State University of New York Press, Albany

© 2019 State University of New York

All rights reserved

No part of this book may be used or reproduced in any manner whatsoever without written permission. No part of this book may be stored in a retrieval system or transmitted in any form or by any means including electronic, electrostatic, magnetic tape, mechanical, photocopying, recording, or otherwise without the prior permission in writing of the publisher.

For information, contact State University of New York Press, Albany, NY
www.sunypress.edu

Library of Congress Cataloging-in-Publication Data

Names: Behuniak, James, author.
Title: John Dewey and Daoist thought / Jim Behuniak.
Description: Albany : State University of New York, [2019] | Series: Experiments in intra-cultural philosophy ; volume one | Series: SUNY series in Chinese philosophy and culture | Includes bibliographical references and index.
Identifiers: LCCN 2018033271 | ISBN 9781438474496 (hardcover : alk. paper) | ISBN 9781438474502 (pbk. : alk. paper) | ISBN 9781438474519 (ebook)
Subjects: LCSH: Dewey, John, 1859–1952—Knowledge—Taoist philosophy. | Dewey, John, 1859–1952—Travel—China. | Taoist philosophy. | Philosophy, Chinese. | Philosophy, Comparative. | East and West.
Classification: LCC B945.D44 B393 2019 | DDC 191—dc23
LC record available at https://lccn.loc.gov/2018033271

10 9 8 7 6 5 4 3 2 1

For Anna

Contents

List of Illustrations	ix
Prelude	xi
Dewey's Chinese Friendships	xi
Dewey and Chinese Thought	xv
Acknowledgments	xxi

Part I

1. John Dewey and Intra-cultural Philosophy	3
Philosophy East and West	3
Comparative Situations	10
Culture and the Comparative Philosopher	17
Experiments in Intra-cultural Philosophy	22
Connecting Strains of Culture	28
2. Forms and Nature	37
Philosophy Out of Gear	37
Mystery and Form	45
De 德 and Directional Order	57
Habits and *Dao* 道-Activity	64
Form (*xing* 形) and Environment	70
3. Orders and Spontaneity	75
Dewey's Metaphysics	75
Embracing the One (*baoyi* 抱一)	80
1-2-3 and the Great Continuum	87
Attaining the One (*deyi* 得一)	93
Forms and Types	100

4. Rhythms and Energies — 109
    The Chinese Landscape — 109
    Forms, Rhythms, and *Qi* 氣 — 116
    Types and Potentials — 125
    Nature and *Xing* 性 — 136
    Wuwei 無為 and Observing the Small — 142

Part II

5. Methods and Intelligence — 155
    Theory and Ordinary Activity — 155
    Method and *Dao* 道-Practice — 162
    The Virtues of Individual Method — 168
    Knowledge and Intelligence — 179
    The Man from Song — 186

6. Knowledge and Technology — 193
    Knowledge Wanders North — 193
    The Primitive Mindset — 201
    Knowledge and Wholeness — 210
    The Tool of Knowing — 216
    The Monopoly of Knowledge — 223

7. Bodies and Artifacts — 233
    Dewey's Body-Practice — 233
    Animal Bodies and Rival Anthropologies — 240
    Language and the Human Difference — 250
    Imitation and Human Selfhood — 256
    The Great and Venerable Teacher — 261

8. Problems and Inquiry — 269
    Autumn Floods — 269
    Nature and Valuation — 275
    Dismissing Market Daoism — 282
    Intelligence and Prognostication — 292
    Destiny Unbound — 300

Notes — 311

Works Cited — 359

Index — 379

Illustrations

Figure 0.1	John Dewey with Sing-nan Fen, date unknown.	xiii
Figure 1.1	One of John Dewey's "Green Ink Pages," written February 1951 while he was visiting Hawai'i.	35
Figure 2.1	John Dewey with goat in 1946.	60
Figure 4.1	Wang Shimin (1592–1680). Hanging scroll. *Mountain with River, Bridge, and Building.*	111
Figure 4.2	Pair of traditional landscape scrolls that John Dewey obtained in China.	151
Figures 5.1–5.4	L. J. Bridgman's original 1888 illustrations for Charles Lamb's *A Dissertation Upon Roast Pig.* Top (left to right): "Ye Delightful Pig" and "Bo-Bo Playeth with Fire." Bottom (left to right): "Ye First Taste" and "Ye Family Rejoiceth."	190
Figure 7.1	F. Matthias Alexander works on John Dewey's posture, date unknown.	263

Prelude

> John Dewey retained a keen and personal interest in young Chinese students even after his retirement from Columbia. Consequently, his influence on the Chinese people is deep-rooted because it is two-fold—through his teachings and through his personal contact with hundreds of young Chinese who pride themselves on being his friend.
>
> —Meng Chih 孟治 to William H. Kilpatrick, September 16, 1949

Dewey's Chinese Friendships

When John Dewey died in 1952 at the age of 92, few people knew that he had adopted a Chinese son. Sing-nan Fen 樊星南 (1916–2011) was born in Suzhou, one of the oldest cities in the Yangzi basin and one known for its lovely flowered gardens, elegant canals, and stone bridges. While a student in China, Fen became a self-taught specialist in American philosophy. He translated Josiah Royce's *The Spirit of Modern Philosophy* into Chinese along with several of Dewey's articles. As Dewey later remarked, "He read some of my philosophical works for translation into Chinese while still in China and all on his own got a much more adequate idea of their purport and tenor than most college students here."[1] Fen earned a Boxer Indemnity Fellowship in 1946 and came to the United States to study at the University of Chicago. Unhappy with his classes at Chicago, he spent most of his time reading Dewey instead, using hundreds of index cards to organize his notes. Fen wrote to the world-famous philosopher, expressing his admiration and sending him some of his own philosophical essays. Dewey was instantly impressed, and wrote back to Fen encouraging him to transfer to Columbia.

When Dewey learned that his good friend, Joseph Ratner, would be in Chicago, he asked him to pay a visit to Sing-nan Fen. Ratner advised him on transferring to Columbia, which Fen did the following year. Upon his arrival in New York City, Dewey invited the young man to a dinner party at his home. Fen can relate what happened next:

> My first visit to Dewey's apartment was a disaster. The Dewey's served cocktails before dinner. I was physiologically allergic to hard liquor. To be polite, however, I took all the drinks they offered. Gradually I felt dizzy, sick, ran to bathroom and became unconscious until the next morning on the sofa in the living room. When I woke up, the sweet old man sat beside me and offered me breakfast. I thought that was the end of our beautiful friendship. But that was the beginning of my being adopted to Dewey's family.[2]

The two would remain like father and son for the rest of Dewey's life. Their surviving letters convey the depth of their communion. Dewey would address Fen as his "Son" and sign his letters, "With Love, Father," and "Pa Dewey." Johnny and Adrienne, Dewey's legally adopted children, took to calling Fen their "Brother." He became part of the family.

Dewey supported and mentored Sing-nan Fen during his years at Columbia. Fen visited Dewey regularly, went on country outings with the family, visited ice cream parlors with the kids, and vacationed with the family at their Maple Lodge retreat in Pennsylvania. Dewey read and commented on Fen's PhD dissertation, *An Examination of the Socio-Individual Dichotomy as it Relates to Educational Theory*, which was submitted to Teacher's College in March 1949. The work was primarily concerned with restoring continuity between nature and culture—a concern that Dewey shared with Fen. This was the period in which Dewey had come to see "culture" rather than "experience" as the natural context in which human behavior is expressed. Culture, Dewey realized, *is* nature. As Fen would argue in his dissertation: cultural behaviors are "objectively natural—as a tree grows, as a volcano erupts, as a stone falls, as a dog runs."[3]

Dewey sought out opportunities for Fen, wrote him letters of support for his job applications, and suggested to him topics for papers. "Something about Chinese [philosophy] in relation to Chinese culture would be good," Dewey proposed, "an article on how American—or more generally Western philosophy strikes a [Chinese student] would hit a popular note."[4] Fen focused mainly on issues relating to his study of American philosophy, educational psychology, and pragmatic naturalism, and he produced a series of original articles. Alain Locke took notice of the quality of his work and hired Fen to his first teaching job at Howard University in 1950.

Prelude / xiii

Figure 0.1. John Dewey with Sing-nan Fen, date unknown. Courtesy of Ruth Fen.

Sing-nan Fen is one of many Chinese students that Dewey established friendships with over the years, and there are several important figures among them. Dewey directed the dissertations of luminaries such as Hu Shih 胡適 (PhD 1917) and Feng Youlan 馮友蘭 (PhD 1923), and several more of his graduate students would rise to become prominent names in the Chinese world. His contact with Chinese students, however, went beyond those whose studies he directed. Chinese students attended Dewey's classes no matter which department they belonged to.[5] Even before his visit to Asia, the Chinese connection seemed to be there. "Dr. Dewey, you talk like Confucius," they would tell him. With a bashful smile, the philosopher would reply that he often heard that from his Chinese students.[6]

Dewey's affinity with Chinese students was more than academic. He genuinely enjoyed having Chinese company and went out of his way to make Chinese friends. In 1922, he and his first wife, Alice, invited a group of Chinese students to join them for Easter weekend on their farm in Long

Island. The students picked sweet corn in the morning and buttered it for breakfast. As one student remembers, Dewey "treated us tenderly, just like his own children."[7] Such affections were mutual. In the winter of 1928, a group of forty Chinese students at Columbia hosted a dinner for Dewey at the "China Garden Restaurant" on 125th Street. Dewey spoke, and the students were "very much impressed by his love for China, of Chinese culture, of the Chinese people, and of Chinese students." On this occasion, Dewey remarked that, "if he could take on a second citizenship, he would certainly choose China."[8] As his daughter Jane relates, China would always be "the country nearest his heart after his own."[9]

Throughout his life, Dewey committed himself to the improvement of US–China relations. His fellow Americans, he believed, understood too little about Chinese culture. As Meng Chih 孟治 remembers, "Dewey was troubled by this absence in the Columbia community of a reciprocal understanding of China." This concern led Dewey to cofound the China Institute in 1926. Today, it remains the oldest non-profit organization in the United States devoted to fostering cross-cultural understanding with China. Its original mission remains an important one: "to disseminate information concerning Chinese and American education; to promote a closer relationship between Chinese and American educational institutions through the exchange of professors and students; to assist Chinese students in America in their educational pursuits; to help American students interested in the study of things Chinese; and to stimulate general interest in America in the study of Chinese culture."[10] The China Institute stands as a concrete manifestation of Dewey's commitment to the improvement of Chinese-American relations, evidence of which is found throughout his mature life.[11]

Dewey's affection for China and its people became fortified during his own journey to China in 1919–1921. He and his wife Alice, and for a time their adult daughter Lucy, lived in China for over two years. Dewey's itinerary is remarkable even by today's standards.[12] Over his two years, two months, and ten days in China, Dewey delivered nearly 200 talks and lectures, covering dozens of topics, and he acquired an enormous amount of firsthand experience. "I prize highly the unusual opportunity to get some acquaintance with [Chinese] thought and conditions," he wrote.[13] That much he certainly did. Dewey was a keen observer of the Chinese world, penning essays on scenes and situations throughout the country that, in the words of Walter Lippmann, were "models of what political reporting ought to be."[14]

The China trip was a genuine pivot in Dewey's life—easily among the two or three most formative experiences that he ever had. In her fine study, *John Dewey in China: To Teach and to Learn*, Jessica Ching-Sze Wang reminds us that Dewey did not only *teach* while he was in China. He came away with a deep understanding and a life-long appreciation for Chinese culture as a "result of his own observations, assisted by his conversations with various people—his own students and translators, travel guides, missionary friends, academic acquaintances, and institutional hosts—and, most important, by his own study of Chinese history."[15] Over the course of his career, Dewey became moderately well versed in the history of Chinese thought. His private library grew to contain several volumes—including Feng Youlan's 1931 translation of the *Zhuangzi*, Lionel Giles' translation of the *Mencius*, and volumes on the history of Chinese philosophy.[16]

Dewey and Chinese Thought

In the pages ahead, there will be opportunities to consider Dewey's visit to China and to explore its significance to his life and work. The present study, however, is not primarily about Dewey's trip to China. It is equally about the final phase of Dewey's philosophical career—the period in which his "cultural turn" was being realized alongside his friendship with Sing-nan Fen. Germinal in this late-period turn, but not fully realized, was a new way of thinking about cross-cultural philosophy. "Culture," for Dewey, had come to represent the context in which human life-activities take place, including the activity of doing philosophy. Thus, to encounter the philosophy of another culture—to "compare," say, Chinese thinking with some other tradition—became for him an activity already situated within the larger matrix of culture, and thus shaped by modes of activity characteristic of human life-activities in this broader sense. Dewey was not so much interested in "comparative philosophy" as a primary activity, but rather in why different cultural strains of philosophy came to be related and how this occurred within the warp and weft of culture. Thus, one of the principal objectives of the present study is to develop such an "intra-cultural philosophy" as the next logical step in Dewey's philosophy, an extension of what came to be known as his "cultural turn."

This more methodological work is undertaken in the opening chapters of each volume, respectively. The remainder of the work is conceived as an extended experiment in doing such intra-cultural philosophy, bringing specific concerns into play as connections between Dewey and Chinese thought are made. The purpose is not simply to observe such philosophical connections, but to *use* them to help reconstruct intellectual habits that are impediments to improving how we currently think. Following Dewey's lead, the present work identifies specific inadequacies and anachronisms in our commonsense view of things—especially with respect to the pre-Darwinian, essentialist, and teleological habits of mind that continue to shape the way we think about organic form, human nature, and ethics. In turn, these volumes argue that seriously engaging classical Chinese thought can help us to correct such shortcomings in our approaches to both natural and cultural phenomena.

To that end, these volumes will be critical on multiple levels. They will engage readings of early Chinese philosophy with which they disagree, while drawing widely from research that supports their findings. For those new to Chinese philosophy, it should be understood that it is a sometimes-contentious field that features distinct interpretative approaches. Given its aim, the present work will be particularly interested in challenging approaches in which essentialist and teleological inferences are made central to the understanding of classical Chinese philosophies. Such approaches remain influential among a prolific subset of researchers in the field. In volume two, *John Dewey and Confucian Thought*, this line of critique will culminate in challenging a set of positions associated with the "Heaven's plan" reading of early Confucianism, one that is corollary to a particular "virtue ethics" reading of the tradition. Here, the work of Philip J. Ivanhoe will be critically assessed as the prime example of such an approach. I will argue that the "Heaven's plan" reading of early Confucianism is both weakly defended and, as Donald J. Munro argues, detrimental to advancing Chinese philosophy in the modern academy.[17]

Some readers may wonder what such argumentation has to do with John Dewey. Actually, the connections are quite important. Among the larger theses in the present work is that the Chinese tradition is best able to serve as a contemporary resource in philosophy when our readings are liberated from certain Greek-medieval assumptions. Dewey was tireless in encouraging us to liberate philosophy in general from such assumptions, especially when they are manifestly "out of gear" with contemporary scientific understandings. Thus, interpretations of Chinese thought that are based on such assumptions will be critiqued where it can be demonstrated that textual and philosophical evidence runs against them.

Let me clarify at the outset what is meant by "Greek-medieval" in the context of such argumentation. When Dewey uses this phrase, he has in mind a distinct set of ideas that comes to characterize the mainstream features of pre-modern Western thought: final causes, unchanging truths, discrete substances, fixed ends, and essential natures. As Raymond D. Boisvert notes, Dewey has a "penchant for gliding over significant details" in his treatment of such Greek-medieval ideas, resulting often in their "oversimplification."[18] As Thomas M. Alexander observes, however, such generic treatments are necessary to what is an "underlying sophisticated, subtle, and profound reading of the history of Western civilization" in Dewey's works.[19] Without question, notions such as the fixed end (*telos*) and essential nature (*natura*) are prioritized in the Greek-medieval tradition, and such ideas factor enormously into its development. This is not to say that alternative ways of thinking are not operative straight through the tradition. One need only recall Heraclitus' observation that "everything flows" (*panta rhei*), remember John Scotus Eriugena's treatment of "analysis" (*analytike*), or consider the implication of Nicholas of Cusa's "knowing ignorance" (*docta ignoratia*) to recognize that Greek-medieval thinking is not a monolithic entity. Plato and Aristotle themselves contain enough counterpoints and ambiguities to complicate such an assertion. Dewey, as we will see, appreciates the internal complexity of the world's philosophical traditions and refuses to treat them as "block-like" entities. He also recognizes, however, the need to isolate and identify *specific* strands of philosophical thought for explicit critical purposes. Here, the phrase "Greek-medieval" will be loosely employed for such purposes without further qualification.

Similarly loose phrases will be employed on the Chinese side. Terms like "Chinese cosmology" and "Chinese natural philosophy" will come to mean something in these volumes. Edward Slingerland has recently argued that such designators are indicative of a tendency to treat Chinese thought as "monolithic and timeless," "uniform and eternal"—a way of thought that is "normatively superior" to Western thought. He identifies this as the "neo-Orientalist" stance.[20] Most readers would not make such inferences; but if my style leaves any ambiguity, let me state at the outset that making such culturally essentialist claims is never my intention. There are, in truth (*pace* Slingerland), characteristics that *do* come to define mainstream Chinese thinking; but these are impossible to understand without taking into consideration the Chinese alternatives. Here, referents for terms like "Chinese cosmology" and "Chinese natural philosophy" will be carefully formulated and defended based on specific textual, historical, and philosophical evidence. That such orientations are "normatively superior" to their alternatives (be they "Chinese" or "Western") is not simply assumed but defended.

"Dewey" and "Daoist Thought" (and in volume two, "Confucian Thought") represent oceans of philosophical material, so the following will hardly be an exhaustive survey of their connections. Each chapter explores some general topic to a finite extent. The problems that motivate the following inquiries are primarily problems with which Dewey struggled, as these strike me as most urgent in our own time and serve well to illuminate important connections to Chinese thinking. Students of the Chinese tradition will find much to identify with in this approach. As Bryan W. Van Norden observes: "Students of Chinese philosophy should find Dewey especially interesting because he wrestled with the same problems that have drawn many of us to the study of Chinese philosophy."[21] Indeed, the interests of Dewey and of early Chinese thinkers range from "nature" to "culture" and generate rich insights into how these domains overlap and relate to one another. Each tradition is interested in illuminating the connections between humans-and-nature and identifying problems that arise at their intersection. Students of Dewey should find Chinese thinking interesting for the same reason. As these volumes argue, the Chinese tradition provides tremendous insight into philosophical topics and questions that preoccupied Dewey. For those interested in American philosophy more generally, there will be occasions to consider connections between Chinese thought and that of Dewey's philosophical associates as well: Charles Sanders Peirce, William James, and George Herbert Mead—further adding to the intra-cultural mix.

The volume of primary materials catalogued under "Dewey" and "Daoist/Confucian Thought," along with the wide range of topics these materials cover, results in this being a two-volume work. Volume one covers topics such as the nature of organic form, teleology, cosmology, knowledge, the body, and technology—engaging Dewey with themes conventionally labeled "Daoist," and volume two considers topics such as education, tradition, ethics, the family, human nature, and religiousness—engaging Dewey with themes conventionally labeled "Confucian." These are not hard-and-fast categories, but sufficient to furnish a basic structure for the work. Sinologists will note the sketchy nature of terms like "Daoist" and "Confucian," but they will be used here in their conventional sense as serviceable-enough categories for what lies ahead.

The work proceeds in four parts. In the present volume, part I focuses on issues that pertain mainly to the *Daodejing* 道德經 and part II focuses mainly on the *Zhuangzi* 莊子. In the second volume, part I focuses mainly on the *Analects* (*Lunyu* 論語) and part II concentrates on the *Mencius* (*Mengzi* 孟子) and related texts. These are also not hard-and-fast divisions but clear enough to serve as a general organizing framework. Dewey's ideas and experiences will be parsed accordingly.

There are no unusual conventions to observe. The names of Chinese authors are presented in whatever Romanization form they typically use, with classical Chinese terms presented in traditional form throughout, except in "Works Cited" when appropriate. Chinese texts are cited both by their location in a standard, English translation (when available) and by their location in the Chinese original from which I worked (if the former is not bi-lingual). The one exception is the *Daodejing*, which is referenced according to chapter numbers using the standard Wang Bi 王弼 edition. Unless stated otherwise, all Chinese translations are my own. Like much contemporary research in Chinese philosophy, what follows has benefitted tremendously from Donald Sturgeon's editorial work and continued maintenance of the on-line "Chinese Text Project" (http://ctext.org). What once took hours now takes minutes thanks to Sturgeon.

Citations of Dewey's works contain the title of each work along with reference to its location in the *Collected Works of John Dewey*: "Early Works" (EW), "Middle Works" (MW), and "Late Works" (LW), accordingly. See "Works Cited" for bibliographical details. Passages from *The Correspondence of John Dewey (1871–1952)* in electronic format are cited simply as "*Correspondence*" with the article number, date, and correspondents provided. Again, see "Works Cited" for details. Each volume has its own index and "Works Cited" apparatus. Readers interested in particular subject matter should consult both indexes.

When quotations of any kind go un-cited, they are from the same source cited in the next footnote in the same paragraph. At the time of writing, the preparation of Dewey's "China lectures" for electronic publication through the Intelex "Past Masters" series has been initiated but suspended indefinitely. In the present volumes, each reference is cited according to its location in whatever hard copies were available at the time. Should the Intelex version become realized, it will be easy to find entries through the Intelex search engine and the citations here will be obsolete.

In Dewey's "China lectures," I took the liberty of rendering his language gender-neutral. Since these are back-translations from the Chinese, I felt that it was permissible to grant Dewey the benefit of the doubt. I also took the liberty with all materials of substituting the word "Chinese" for Dewey's more antiquated term "Oriental" whenever it was clear that Dewey was referring to something specifically Chinese. Such in-text substitutions appear in brackets.

Acknowledgments

As Alfred North Whitehead once said, "There is always more chance of hitting upon something valuable when you aren't too sure what you want to hit upon."²² In philosophical writing, I have always found this to be the case. This project began without any fixed end in mind—certainly not two volumes. When I started out, I figured that my two oceans, "Dewey" and "Daoist/Confucian Thought," held enough currents and eddies to move something along. The project grew in volume and complexity over time, and my outlook on several issues changed in the process of research and writing. Engaging in such philosophical exploration is a luxury, and I am indebted to many for having had the opportunity.

First, I thank the Fulbright U.S. Scholar Program for awarding me one year at National Taiwan University to teach and conduct research in its Department of Philosophy. Much of this project was conceived in Taiwan, and I am grateful to Chairperson Lee Hsien Chung 李賢中 for his generous support and kindness, and to the entire philosophy department for welcoming me and my family to Taipei. My graduate students at NTU, in seminars on both Chinese and American philosophies, assisted me in gaining insight into many of the topics presented here. They have my sincere gratitude. I also wish to thank everyone at Fulbright Taiwan, who under the leadership of William Vocke (who retires this year) provide an outstanding support network for American scholars working in Taiwan. Over the past seven decades, the success of the Fulbright program worldwide demonstrates that modest appropriations in federal budgets show huge returns when they enable private citizens to conduct research in the Arts and Sciences. Such investments in the public good are the main function of any government funded by taxpayers, and this remains the metric by which its functionality is assessed.

I also wish to thank my home institution, Colby College, for affording me academic leave and for granting me a sabbatical to complete the work that I started in Taiwan. I am especially grateful for the generosity of my colleagues in the philosophy department, who adjusted their schedules to mine on short notice with nothing but encouragement and support. I am also indebted to the Center for Dewey Studies, and especially to Paula McNally and Harriet Simon, who made my research in Carbondale both a pleasure and fruitful. Thanks also to Doug Berger and Tom Alexander for their hospitality during my visit, and a big thanks to Nick Guardiano at Morris Library for his help with reproductions and permissions. Sadly, at the time of writing, the Center for Dewey Studies has been defunded and is now unstaffed—one among many recent victims of a flawed conception of what it means for public bodies and institutions to serve the public good. Let us remember that in a representative democracy such flaws in governance are ultimately correctable, but this requires concerted public engagement.

Certain sections of what follows appear in alternate forms elsewhere. Part of chapter 1, first section, has been published as Behuniak (2017); chapter 3, second section, is a reformulation of Behuniak (2009a); chapter 5, sections two and three, expands upon Behuniak (2010); chapter 5, section five, appears elsewhere as Behuniak (2016); and chapter 8, section three, is a version of Behuniak (2015). See "Works Cited" for more information. I thank the University of Hawai'i Press, Springer, and Bloomsbury for permissions accordingly.

There are a number of people who kindly agreed to review various parts of these manuscripts while they were still in preparation. In no particular order, I thank Steve Angle, Ralph Weber, Alexus McLeod, Geir Sigurðsson, Roger Ames, Ray Boisvert, Amy Olberding, Bob Neville, Zhu Hong, Joe Haroff, Richard Bernstein, and Sor-hoon Tan. I also thank my anonymous referees for SUNY Press who read both volumes in their entirety and provided candid criticisms. Any errors that remain are due (as usual) to my own intransigence. I also wish to thank everyone at SUNY Press, and everyone whose name appears in the "Works Cited" to these volumes (especially my contemporaries). Without the information, insight, and provocation that I derive from your work, the present work would be diminished.

Finally, I wish to thank my family—Connie, Anna, and Anton—for the love and support that they give me. I dedicate each volume to one of my two remarkable children. In order of composition, of course.

VOLUME ONE

Part I

1

John Dewey and Intra-cultural Philosophy

> The world today is a very special world. Cultures and civilizations are coming into contact to a degree that has never before been possible. Humans have known for a long time that the earth was round. Now we are discovering that knowledge, as it circulates about the world, can also be thought of as being round.
>
> —John Dewey, Guangdong Educational Association, July 1921

Philosophy East and West

The first two East-West Philosophers' Conferences at the University of Hawai`i constitute an important chapter in the history of comparative philosophy. Wing-tsit Chan recalls the first meeting in 1939 as a "very small beginning," one that served primarily as the impetus for F. S. C. Northrop's thesis that East and West represented two contrasting styles of thought. As Chan remembers, "We saw the world as two halves, East and West." Accordingly, in his subsequent 1946 work, *The Meeting of East and West*, Northrop "sharply contrasted the entire East, as using doctrines out of concepts by intuition, to the [entire] West, as constructing its doctrines out of concepts by postulation."[1] The purpose of the second meeting in 1949 was to study the possibility of achieving a "world philosophical synthesis" between East and West. This broader perspective would be cognizant of similarities as well as differences. Areas of agreement on issues in metaphysics, ethics, and social theory were duly noted at the conference.[2] But since there could be no "orchestrated unity" composed of identical principles alone, differences were refined and preserved, these being important as the "basis of the synthesis."[3] Pursuant to the goal of achieving this world philosophical synthesis, Charles A. Moore founded the journal *Philosophy East and West* in 1951.

It is unlikely that John Dewey ever read *The Meeting of East and West*. Friends had advised him against it. "That Northrop book I mentioned the other day is not worth looking at," Arthur Bentley told him.[4] "Full of sweeping statements, more stimulating than reliable," is what Albert Barnes had learned.[5] Dewey saw reviews of the book, and suggested to Sing-nan Fen that a "critical account of [Northrop's book] might be a good jumping off place for publication."[6] But it was Dewey who would contribute to East-West philosophy at this juncture. In 1950, he wrote a letter to Moore in which he had some "complimentary things" to say about the forthcoming journal.[7] Moore wrote back, asking permission to include parts of Dewey's letter in the "News and Notes" section of the first issue. Moore stated his preference, however, that Dewey write a fresh statement "expressing [his] conviction about the specific philosophical relationship between Oriental and Occidental philosophy or, perhaps, stating [his] ideas as to the best philosophical approach to a substantial synthesis of East and West."[8] In response, Dewey composed what would become the first article ever to appear in *Philosophy East and West*—a short piece entitled "On Philosophical Synthesis."

Fittingly, the article was written in Hawai`i. Hoping to improve his declining health, Dewey sailed with his family for Honolulu just weeks after receiving Moore's letter. When the *SS President Wilson* docked on January 17, 1951, a delegation from the University of Hawai`i came to receive them at the pier.[9] Dewey's "valuable article" would be written seaside on Waikīkī beach, under a canopy of palms in the breeze-swept cottages of the Halekulani resort.[10] Though modest in length, the vision it relates is remarkable for its clarity, sophistication, and foresight. It is also noteworthy as a bold rejection of Northrop's thesis that "East" and "West" are discrete and separable entities. In its entirety, this is what Dewey wrote:

> I think that the most important function your journal can perform in bringing about the ultimate objective of a "substantial synthesis of East and West" is to help break down the notion that there is such a thing as a "West" and "East" that have to be synthesized. There are great and fundamental differences in the East just as there are in the West. The cultural matrix of China, Indonesia, Japan, India, and Asiatic Russia is not a single "block" affair. Nor is the cultural matrix of the West. The differences between Latin and French and Germanic cultures on the continent of Europe, and the differences between these and the culture of England on the one hand and the culture of the United States on the other (not to mention Canadian and Latin American difference), are extremely important for an understanding of the West. Some of the elements in Western cultures and Eastern cultures are so closely allied that the problem of "syn-

thesizing" them does not exist when they are taken in isolation. But the point is that none of these elements—in the East or the West—is in isolation. They are all interwoven in a vast variety of ways in the historico-cultural process. The basic prerequisite for any fruitful development of inter-cultural relations—of which philosophy is simply one constituent part—is an understanding and appreciation of the complexities, differences, and ramifying interrelationships both within any given country and among the countries, East and West, whether taken separately or together.

What I have just said might at other times and under other circumstances be considered so obvious as to be platitudinous. But at the present time and in the present circumstances, I venture to think that it is far from being such. Under the pressure of political *blocs* that are now being formed East and West it is all too easy to think that there are cultural "blocks" of corresponding orientation. To adapt a phrase of William James, there are no "cultural block universes" and the hope of free men everywhere is to prevent any such "cultural block universes" from ever arising and fixing themselves upon all mankind or any portion of mankind. To the extent that your journal can keep the idea open and working that there are "*specific* philosophical relationships" to be explored in the West and in the East and between the West and the East you will, I think, be contributing most fruitfully and dynamically to the enlightenment and betterment of the human estate.[11]

The motive behind Dewey's comments can be understood on different levels. On one level, they reflect his alarm at the emerging Cold War.[12] On a deeper level, however, they reflect his current thinking on "the intimate connection of philosophical systems with culture," a preoccupation that absorbed him during the final years of his life.[13]

This latter dimension is now better understood thanks to the recent recovery of the manuscript, *Unmodern Philosophy and Modern Philosophy*.[14] This remarkable work, one that Dewey considered "the summation of his philosophical beliefs throughout the years," was never finished and then reportedly lost in 1947.[15] Dewey conceded before the manuscript went missing that he was not satisfied with its progress, and expressed frustration that the project "never would jell." Significant drafts, however, have now been recovered from the Dewey archives, and despite their fragmentary nature, there are clear objectives driving the book.

The intent of the project was twofold. First, Dewey wanted to establish "culture" as the irreducible context in which everything human occurs. According to Phillip Deen, Dewey intended in this work to make culture "the most inclusive category within which various regions of human life interact." Second, Dewey sought to trace the sociocultural history of Western philosophy and to contextualize its problems accordingly. "The purpose of this book," Dewey writes, "is to discover the cultural source and context of problems and distinctions which have taken on technical philosophical meaning."[16] To this end, the work was divided into two parts. The first part was devoted to the analysis of Western intellectual history, especially the role that Greek-medieval assumptions played in the modern period. The second part was a critical treatment of certain dualisms that persisted as a result: "Things/Persons," "Mind/Body," "Theory/Practice," "Material/Ideal," and "Nature/Human."

Had the manuscript been fully realized and published in 1947, it likely would have impacted the East-West Philosophers' Conference in 1949. Dewey regarded the project as one with direct relevance to East-West philosophy. He had come to recognize that certain puzzles that occupied Western philosophy "played no particular role in [Chinese] systems." This suggested to him that such problems had their sources in the "cultural history of the European world rather than in the factual subject matters" under consideration.[17] He thus notes in his drafts that one of the wider ends served in *Unmodern Philosophy* would be the "realization that a problem that appears to be the same problem when it is stated in general terms . . . has, in fact, different contents and directions according to the cultural situation in which it is bred and nourished." Such differences, he notes, are "of utmost import for the hardly as yet commenced comparative study of the course taken by philosophers in China and India in their contrast with the European tradition."[18]

Such sensitivity to the cultural situation of world philosophies was not universally shared at the 1949 conference. The Sinologist Herrlee C. Creel, for instance, laments the treatment of Chinese philosophy at the Second East-West Philosophers' Conference, where scholars "too seldom tried to analyze Chinese thinking on its own grounds and in its own terms."[19] As Moore relates, one of the noteworthy achievements of the 1949 conference was to establish that, "the philosophy of China must not be overlooked . . . nor must it be considered similar to or identical with the philosophy of India simply because both are Oriental."[20] The Hawai`i conference helped to change such simplistic thinking, and Dewey furthered this process with his article in *Philosophy East and West*. Among those helping to pave the way in Honolulu was Cornelius Krusé, a Wesleyan University philosopher who admired Dewey as the "inveterate foe of all dualisms" and who was probably the first American to deliver a lecture connecting Dewey's educational theories with Confucian philosophy.[21] Krusé is credited with stressing that, "There is great complexity of philosophical doctrines and methods in the East, and it may be added that this complexity exists, not only *among* the various countries of the East, but also *within* each of the several countries, and frequently within particular systems of one given country or philosophy."[22] As Moore reports, this would become the consensus view by the time that East-West philosophers met for a third time in 1959.[23]

It is hard to know whether the completion of Dewey's lost work would have altered the course of East-West philosophy. One thing, however, we do know. The rediscovery of this work now provides us with a fuller context in which to understand his inaugural statement in *Philosophy East and West*. That statement, despite its prominent place in the journal, has never really been examined. How, after all, *should* comparative philosophers respond to the uncomfortable irony that the opening sentence in their flagship journal, *Philosophy East and West*, is one that rejects the very distinction between East and West? With an important link now restored, we can better understand what prompted Dewey to say what he did.

The year that Dewey's comments appeared in the journal was the same year that he returned to writing his "Re-Introduction" to *Experience and Nature*. This is the juncture at which Dewey famously wrote, "Were I to write (or rewrite) *Experience and Nature* today I would entitle the book *Culture and Nature*," explaining that the term "culture" could now "fully and freely carry my philosophy of experience." The rationale for replacing the term "experience" with "culture" was foreshadowed in the 1949 version of the "Re-Introduction." Here, Dewey explains that "experience," as he used it in 1925, was meant to designate "all which is distinctively human." He came to realize, however, that it is a "fitting name for the special way in which humans, at least in the Western world, have shaped their participations in and dealings with nature," an insight which, "entails the recognition of philosophy's variability in different cultural eras and areas." Dewey was not alluding to non-European philosophies in this instance. Rather, he was referring to the "cultural historic period and geographical area" of Western Europe, wherein modern philosophy struggled to break free from the Greek-medieval inheritance in its midst.[24] This is a theme that had long motivated Dewey and that dominated his thinking in the final period of his life. The essay, "Modern Philosophy" for instance, which appeared just three months after Dewey's death, was devoted to chronicling the burdens placed on modern philosophy that were "imposed by cultural conditions of earlier periods."[25]

This concern was to guide what would have been Dewey's crowning book, *Unmodern Philosophy*. For Dewey, the holdover of old assumptions in the modern period accounted for a "failure to carry the application of the standpoint and methods proper to science—in its modern sense—all the way through."[26] Specifically, he meant that the failure of Western Europe to overcome its devotion to the "fixed" and "unchanging" continued to block its assimilation of a more dynamic worldview. "What I have in mind," he explains, "is the fact that devotion to the immutable and hence to that which could not be affected by the tooth of time nor be hemmed in by any spatial location led the philosophers in sympathy with the *new* to feel that they could strengthen it by providing an underpinning of the eternal and universal."[27] As Dewey saw it, in one of the "most striking cases of confusion resulting from admixture of the old and new," modern-era scientists, while they had begun to substitute "events" for substances, and "connections of changes" for the immutable, proceeded to theorize the former in terms of static regions and fixed laws. Modern-era philosophers were no less diverted in their undertakings. New methods of inquiry had come into their possession, but they proceeded to tangle themselves in a maze of anachronistic dualisms. Dewey referred to this unfortunate admixture of old and new as a "Wandering Between Two Worlds," explaining that it was "wandering not so much *between* two worlds as *in* two worlds, taking our direction now from a chart of *that* world and now from a chart of *this* one."[28]

As Dewey saw it, the two worlds that overlapped in the modern period did not await any wholesale reconciliation into some higher unity. "What is wanted," he wrote, "is not a 'synthesis' [between them] . . . but *specific* studies of intercommunication, and of blocks and arrests that have unduly exaggerated one phase of human behavior and minimized other phases."[29] Dewey felt that Greek-medieval thought needed to be critically assessed so as to preserve those elements that continue to serve us well while reconstructing those elements that were blocking or arresting our intellectual growth. The argument of the book, as Dewey related to a friend, was to be that such blocks and arrests "prevented the development of a synthesis which *actually corresponds* to the vital conditions and forces of the present."[30]

This was the issue that occupied Dewey's mind when the invitation to comment on the prospects for "East-West Synthesis" crossed his desk. Naturally, his first response would be "*What* East?" "*What* West?" and "*What* synthesis?" Dewey was already engaged in a comparative study of distinct cultures *within* the European tradition. The notion that there was a single "West" directly contradicted that study. As Dewey saw it, there was no integrated "West" in operation. As he wrote in his manuscript: "We [in the West] do not enjoy the benefits that would accrue from integrated organization of beliefs, either ancient or modern."[31] Furthermore, "synthesis" for the sake of synthesis did not interest him. It mattered greatly to Dewey that the purposes that motivated philosophical synthesis were *intelligent*. He made no secret of his own allegiances. He stood with the traditions that he deemed "scientific," and for Dewey, "scientific" denoted practices in which "*process* is seen to be the 'universal' in nature and in life," and continuity "*the* regulative principle of *all* inquiry."[32] Scientific cultures organize themselves around on-going discoveries in the physical and biological sciences, those that are bringing process-oriented conceptions to the fore. Modern cultures will continue to lag as long as they "wander" in the pre-Darwinian, Greek-medieval world—that now antiquated land of unchanging truths, discrete substances, fixed ends, and essential natures.

Even though Dewey lost the penultimate draft of his masterwork, the thesis he had developed remained fresh in his mind in 1951. He offered *Philosophy East and West* the most constructive advice that he could in light of his current thinking. The task of East-West philosophers, he thought, should be to parse out the different strands of philosophy that world cultures had to offer, and then to establish "*specific* philosophical relationships" for intelligent purposes. While Dewey regarded certain strains of thinking to be practically incompatible—some in the Modern and Greek-medieval traditions, for instance—the more contemporary problem of incommensurability never occurred to him. Retrospectively, his critique of "cultural block universes" was an advance response to that challenge.

In preparing an argument against cultural incommensurability at the Sixth East-West Philosophers' Conference in 1989, Richard J. Bernstein essentially remakes Dewey's point for that purpose. Bernstein writes:

> We must always strive to avoid a false essentialism when we are trying to understand the traditions to which we belong or those alien traditions that are incommensurable with "our" traditions. For frequently discussions of East-West lapse into such a false essentialism where we are seduced into thinking that there are essential determinate characteristics that distinguish the Western and Eastern "mind." This false essentialism violently distorts the sheer complexity of overlapping traditions that cut across these artificial simplistic global notions.[33]

Dewey recognized the "East/West" dichotomy as the sort of false essentialism that results from the "fallacy of intellectualism," whereby distinctions are fashioned from concrete relations and then converted into essences that no longer stand in those relations. Such intellectualism first regards "all experiencing as a mode of knowing," and then requires that its subject matter be reduced and transformed into self-contained objects for *episteme*.[34] Converted into such objects, "East" and "West" (or for that matter, "Daoism" and "Platonism," or "Greek" and "Chinese") become monolithic schemes that permanently house finite traits and stationary truth tables. Between such "block-like" objects, radical incommensurability might be imagined to obtain, thus resulting in the problem of comparing them.

Such a "problem," however, takes its place among those that exist in purely theoretical space. As David L. Hall and Roger T. Ames suggest, the persuasiveness of arguments for radical incommensurability are of the type "possessed by arguments to the effect that bumble bees cannot fly."[35] When motivated by a genuine purpose, the human mind is capable of connecting anything to anything. That is among its principle functions. This helps to explain why Dewey encouraged East-West philosophers to keep the idea open and working that there are "*specific* philosophical relationships" to be discovered between cultural traditions. He thought that it was important to establish an environment in which such connections could be made as intelligent purposes arose, and he believed that *Philosophy East and West* could help us to do that.

Comparative Situations

Dewey's recommendations in "On Philosophical Synthesis" did not accord neatly with the "Sameness/Difference" rubric that had guided comparative philosophy to that point. In fact, his vision remains a genuine alternative in a field still dominated by assessments of sameness and difference, one in which progress is attempted and then watchfully scrutinized in those terms. At this juncture, sameness and difference have become the Scylla and Charybdis through which comparative philosophers must cross. Steer too close to *sameness* and one risks what Martha C. Nussbaum calls "descriptive chauvinism," the act of understanding what is unfamiliar by "recreating the other in the image of oneself."[36] Steer too close to *difference* and one risks what Edward Slingerland calls "*neo*-Orientalism," the claim of radical otherness.[37] Either transgression sinks the comparative project. Descriptive chauvinism annuls one's claim to have made a comparison, while *neo*-Orientalism precludes one from actually making it. Those who would make philosophical comparisons must somehow chart a course between sameness and difference without succumbing to either criticism. Sailing these waters can be unforgiving, leaving one to wonder if there is any safe passage at all.

Prolific comparative philosophers like Roger T. Ames provide good case studies. Some argue that Ames reads Dewey into Chinese philosophy—the transgression of *sameness*.[38] Others claim that Ames believes that "the Chinese and Western philosophical traditions are essentially incommensurable"—the transgression of *difference*.[39] Erin M. Cline is noteworthy for criticizing Ames from both angles, suggesting in separate discussions that he reads Dewey into Chinese philosophy (i.e., the Scylla of *sameness*) while also rendering Chinese philosophy incommensurable with Western thinking (i.e., the Charybdis of *difference*).[40] Thus, she complains of a "tension" in Ames' work that prevents her from resolving his view into one or the other standpoint. She wishes to know "which side Ames ultimately comes down on."[41]

Such binary, "Sameness/Difference" ultimatums present a genuine challenge to comparative philosophy. They expose the fact that every comparison, without exception, *must* violate the terms of sameness and difference. Zhang Xianglong regards this predicament as one that is inherent to comparative philosophy, and he addresses it in terms of a "comparison paradox" that traces back to Plato. For Plato, comparison involves detecting sameness and difference between two or more discrete objects. "A is the same size as B" expresses a comparison, and "A is larger than B" another. If one subscribes to a rigid understanding of formal properties, as Plato does, then such comparisons are paradoxical. In the first instance, the relation of "sameness" is not a relation at all. If two objects are the *same*, then we are not really talking about two objects but *one*. Accordingly, relations of sameness require relations of difference. The relation of "difference," however, is attended by its own problems. If two things are really different, then under what category can they be held together for comparison? Zhang summarizes the resulting paradox as follows: "Any comparison will demand the *simultaneous presence* of 'sameness' and 'difference.' [But] this will negate the common measure [i.e., sameness] or the pivot of comparison [i.e., difference] . . . and thus make comparison impossible."[42]

Plato's *Timaeus* describes the "World Soul" as two rings rotating in opposite directions in the heavens: the orbits of the "Same" and "Different." Within these rings are ribbons circling in counter rotation upon which ride the sun, moon, and planets against the zodiacal firmament.[43] The human soul is fashioned and calibrated within these astronomical movements, thus determining its basic cognitive judgments: *Sameness* and *Difference*. These two judgments participate in the celestial operations of the "World Soul," thereby providing the foundation for rational thought and language (*logos*). As Lloyd P. Gerson observes, in providing this account of human cognition, Plato "sees the need to incorporate principles of identity and difference into the soul's very fabric." The paradox of this admixture, however, haunts Plato. He finally confronts the problem directly in the *Parmenides*. Gerson explains that the cogency of Plato's philosophy ultimately "rests upon the successful distinction of sameness and identity" in this context.[44] Whether or not Plato resolves this puzzle is a matter of debate. Regardless of how the matter is decided, however, the prevalence of Scylla and Charybdis analysis in comparative philosophy suggests that the human mind indeed operates as Plato suggests, and that overcoming our binary judgments of "Sameness/Difference" is difficult if not impossible.

But does this mean that the act of comparison is itself impossible? As Zhang Xianglong sees it, the problem with Plato's account of the comparison paradox is that it is negated by actual experience. Comparisons *are* possible. We make them all the time. Thus, some assumption in the comparison paradox must be wrong. Of course, the prime suspect is Plato's assumption that "Sameness" and "Difference" are eternal forms that transcend concrete relations between particular things. As Plato sees it, comparative relations evoke "Sameness" and "Difference" *themselves*, and such universals are incompatible and cannot be instantiated in any single instance, as comparison itself requires. One might regard this as merely a semantic point, depending on how one feels about Plato. Zhang insists, however, that comparative philosophy succumbs to dangers related to the comparison paradox whenever it reports on how cultural objects *themselves* are the same or different. For such judgments always entail conceptual rigidity in the form of a universal standard that "provides common measure for the compared sides."[45] It is always with respect to some idealized standard that such objects are regarded as either the same or as different. Regardless of whether such standards are tacit or explicit, the result is a fixed paradigm in which comparisons are made. As long as comparative philosophy generates such fixed paradigms, the two horns of the comparison paradox remain.

Zhang Xianglong's solution to the comparison paradox is noteworthy in its own right. Most relevant for our purposes, however, is how strongly it resonates with aspects of Dewey's own thinking on this issue. Zhang resolves the paradox by shifting attention away from the *terms* of comparison and focusing instead on what he calls the "comparative situation." He introduces the notion with a concrete example:

> When I see some dates on a high tree and several bamboo rods lying at the foot of the tree, I take the longest rod to get the dates without any kind of idealized thinking. In such an act, I successfully accomplish a comparison. The so-called "successful comparison" refers to those comparative acts that produce the meanings or have the effects that would not have appeared in unilateral or non-comparative acts. I call the structure which makes the comparison successful a *"comparative situation."*

Zhang regards the successful comparison as one that occurs without the mediation of "idealized thinking." Such thinking refers to the stipulation of a fixed measure—that conceptual rigidity which invites the comparison paradox. Comparisons, Zhang argues, occur naturally enough without such interventions. When we actually compare things, we are not dealing with isolated terms in need of superordinate measures. Instead, we are simultaneously seeing A, B, and . . . "The ellipsis," Zhang continues, "is indispensable and more important than what is explicitly said." The ellipsis represents the situation itself, "the mechanism of meaning-production that functions in a non-universalistic and anonymous way."[46] Such a mechanism prompts the perception of meanings or connections that would not have surfaced had that particular situation not arisen. For Zhang, the normal comparative act is a function of such situations, such that situations themselves decide the terms for comparison. When terms are instead prefigured within a fixed paradigm, comparison easily succumbs to the "comparison paradox" and becomes something other than comparison.

Dewey arrived at a similar point in his own thinking. Defining the word "Comparison" for the 1911 edition of the *Cyclopedia of Education*, he writes the following: "In the first place, since any and every object is like any other object in some conceivable regard, intelligent comparison always implies [a] specific end or purpose. We would not ordinarily compare an elephant and justice, a square and a rose, not because no points of similarity can be found, but because there is no purpose to be [served] by discovering such points." Dewey thus understands comparison pragmatically. Comparison is an operation informed by practical ends, one whose terms and outcomes emerge in the process of doing it. He notes that pedagogically it would be absurd to ask students to identify similarities and differences between things for no purpose whatsoever—and here, Dewey stresses, any practical purpose will do: "erosion, the principle of gravitation, navigability, supply of energy for manufacturers, or whatever."[47]

Dewey is essentially in agreement with Zhang Xianglong. *Some* comparative situation must be operative if one is to make comparisons. Crucial here is not mistaking Dewey's appeal to purposes for what Zhang calls "idealized thinking." By introducing a practical concern such as navigation, Dewey does not mean to evoke the abstract principles of "Navigation." Instead, he underscores his position that "active occupations should be concerned primarily with *wholes* . . . the completeness of appeal made by a situation." For Dewey, there is no "Navigation" *itself*. Rather, there are situations that require navigation—reaching for dates with a bamboo pole, for instance. Such purposes are inseparable from whatever distinctions the situation demands. As Dewey sees it: "The unity of purpose, with the concentration upon details which it entails, confers simplicity upon the elements which have to be reckoned with in the course of action. It furnishes each with a *single* meaning according to its service in carrying on the whole enterprise."[48]

We need to consider the more elusive aspects of "situation" before understanding how this relates to comparative philosophy specifically. The "situation," for Dewey, serves as a corrective to more atomistic versions of empiricism. We never experience discrete objects or qualities in sheer isolation as the latter suggests, but always within some contextual whole. Such wholes are "situations." For Dewey, as for Zhang Xianglong, "situations" refer to the ontological context in which thought occurs and distinctions are made within fields that are both discursive and continuous.[49] Were there no such binding qualities to lived experience, "activity would be a meaningless hop-skip-jump affair," Dewey writes.[50]

Richard Shusterman provides the clearest and most comprehensive description of how "situations" operate in Dewey's thinking, providing five such functions. To paraphrase Shusterman:

1) *Thinking is always contextual.*
   The "situation" provides the context.

2) *Thinking identifies and employs objects.*
   The "situation" determines their distinctions and relations.

3) *Judgment requires standards of adequacy.*
   The "situation" decides what level of detail, complexity, or precision is deemed sufficient.

4) *Inquiry requires sustained and directional thinking.*
   The "situation" provides the needed sense of unity, continuity, and direction.

5) *Thinking involves the association of ideas.*
   The "situation" determines which associations are relevant.[51]

Thus described, the "situation" is elusive by nature. Operative situations cannot become "objects" of thought, for they *establish* the objects of thought. As Dewey puts it: "a quart bowl cannot be held within itself," meaning that a situation cannot become an element in a proposition the terms of which it is setting.[52] As Philip W. Jackson notes, "As soon as we begin to offer a description of the situation we are in, we have exited that situation (by transforming it into an object) and entered another one."[53]

Shusterman warns that by postulating "situations" Dewey risks sliding into a "foundational metaphysics of presence," but that the slide is avoidable because "[Dewey] provides the means to avoid it."[54] Thoughts and actions for Dewey are shaped by the habits, purposes, and needs of organisms-in-environments. That ought to be the final analysis. As Shusterman sees it, introducing the term "situation" as a quality *uniting* such factors adds nothing to their descriptions. While I see the point, I am less concerned than Shusterman about "situations" and more willing to allow Dewey his terminology—letting it stand for whatever tertiary features permit the intersection of such habits, purposes, and needs in particular environments. In chapter 3, such features (treated in terms of "Thirdness") will be taken up in a more detailed manner when we consider the work of Charles Sanders Peirce. For present purposes, the important point is that such operations have phases that routinely occur below the level of consciousness. These phases can become objects of conscious thought when the situation changes.

Dewey is well aware that it is difficult to give a positive, non-reifying account of what a "situation" actually is. He suggests that the term is most readily indicated by a negative statement: "What is designated by the word 'situation' is *not* a single object or event or set of objects and events. For we never experience nor form judgments about objects and events in isolation, but only in connection with a contextual whole. This latter is what is called 'situation.'"[55] Situations, as such, are ubiquitous: "To live in a world [is to] live in a series of situations."[56] As Sing-nan Fen explains, "We live in one situation after another, [and] even this *afterness* is in a situation, not between situations."[57] For Dewey, while present situations cannot become objects of thought within themselves, situations can do so "in connection with some *other* situation to which thought now refers," just as a quart bowl might be "contained in another bowl."[58] When this occurs, one becomes conscious of how certain habits, purposes, and needs intersect and give rise to particular sets of objects, associations, inferences, comparisons, etc. Such connections had not been objects for thought in the prior "situation."

Criticism in comparative philosophy relies almost entirely on such transpositions. Scylla and Charybdis analyses surface only when comparisons made in situation (A) become terms in situation (B), such that propositions made about them in (B) also contain (A) as a term. In other words, specific comparisons are exposed to scrutiny under "Sameness/Difference" categories only *after* they have been made in whatever "situation" decided those terms. Typically, the situations undergoing transposition are those of other comparative philosophers.

Again, Roger T. Ames provides a good example. Ames' broader oeuvre focuses on how tacit assumptions shape the way that others read the Chinese tradition. By "assumptions," Ames means "those usually unannounced premises held by the members of an intellectual culture or tradition that make communication possible by constituting a ground from which philosophical discourse proceeds."[59] The fact that Ames has his *own* assumptions animates critics like Eske Møllgaard, who point out how "ironic" it is that Ames' work "falls into the very trap it rightly advises others to avoid."[60] Ames critiques those in situation (A) from his own situation (B). Møllgaard then criticizes situation (B) from his own situation (C). The point here is that such critical transpositions have no natural terminus. Sing-nan Fen understood Dewey's insights into this dynamic particularly well. The idea is that any "one universe [of discourse] may be a term of discourse in another universe," and provide "criteria with which to criticize any specific universe of discourse." Meanwhile, at each point in the process, one's own universe of discourse is "traceless"—it resolves invisibly into its own background "like a solution of salt and water."[61]

This is why comparative philosophers are inordinately busy directing their criticisms toward one another, such that, as Robert W. Smid observes, "It would seem that setting oneself up as an exemplar for comparative philosophy is not limited to any particular approach to comparison but is rather endemic to the task of comparative philosophy itself."[62] Given how comparative situations operate, we never see the ground of our comparative judgments as we make them. We are thus guaranteed to notice the speck in our neighbor's eye before recognizing the plank in our own.

As Mark Johnson explains, Dewey's description of how situations operate in human cognition is more than just idle speculation. "There is empirical evidence from brain science suggesting that Dewey was correctly describing the process of a developing thought," reports Johnson, "which moves from felt pervasive quality [a situation] to higher-level conceptual discrimination and inference." The core-shell architecture of the human brain ensures that the more densely connected, core limbic system is already active beneath the higher neocortical regions that are responsible for abstract and discriminative judgments, such as those ascribing "Sameness/Difference" to objects. Instincts, emotions, and drives invariably establish the situation in which such judgments occur. As Johnson maintains, the architecture of the brain "[makes] sense of Dewey's claim that our experience always begins with a pervasive unifying quality of a whole situation, within which we then discriminate objects, with their properties and relations to one another."[63]

This being the case, a rare degree of humility and self-awareness is required of comparative philosophers. John H. Berthrong states the matter plainly: "One must start *somewhere* in the task of making comparisons and, if we are honest, we will confess that we start from where we ourselves are."[64] Comparative assertions and critiques are always embedded in pre-reflective situations, and these situations include the cultural, biographical, and temperamental profiles of those who do the work.

This dynamic, while an impediment to self-criticism, does not entirely rule it out. For Dewey, the more that we become aware of our own "situations," the better able we are to achieve what he regarded as one of the central objectives of philosophy: the "critique of prejudices." While we never completely rid ourselves of our own prejudices, such reflection can result in a kind of "intellectual disrobing." As Dewey explains: "We cannot permanently divest ourselves of the intellectual habits we take on and wear when we assimilate the culture of our own time and place. But intelligent furthering of culture demands that we take some of them off, that we inspect them critically to see what they are made of and what wearing them does to us."[65]

Culture and the Comparative Philosopher

These considerations take on special significance with respect to Dewey's project in *Unmodern Philosophy*. On the one hand, the project was an attempt to uncover certain "principles" of Greek-medieval and Modern cultures, with the express purpose of arguing that we needed to overcome the former principles. Generating complexity, however, was Dewey's implicit acknowledgment that "principles" were also guiding the kind of work that *he* was doing in his treatment of the cultural material. As Dewey writes:

> The philosopher is first and last a human being with his own intellectual and emotional habits who is involved in a concrete scene having its own color of tradition . . . A *contemporary* philosopher . . . comes to his work, protected and perhaps muffled by an immense intervening apparatus. He carries in his head a vast body of distinctions previously made . . . the two variables: himself as a thinker and the cultural material thought about, are insofar technalized, if I may venture the word, for him in advance.

Such considerations, Dewey suggests, "reach deeper than the particular interpretation [here] offered," which even in its "bare outline," affords recognition of "the underlying conditions of philosophy."[66]

In the culminating chapter of *Unmodern Philosophy*, "Experience as Life-Function," we learn what Dewey is talking about. He had indicated elsewhere that phrases such as "life-function" would be implicated in his transition from "experience" to "culture." In the crowning chapter of his lost work, he would make the transition.[67] In the final decade of his life, Dewey was preparing to identify the "critical and constructive effort [that] constitutes philosophy" with four newly developed postulates. What follows is a paraphrase:

1. *Experience* is a synonym for *life-functions*.

2. *Life-functions*, as here used, means *human living*, which is *sociocultural*.

3. *Psychology* is concerned with *human behavior* in the above respects.

4. *Experience*, as defined above, is the means or agency for the constructive projection of *sociocultural* activities for systematic criticism.

That this constitutes "philosophy," Dewey writes, "is not so much a separate postulate as it is the focal point of the four postulates just set down."[68] As the sequence of postulates suggests, experience is both what human life *is* and what it *does*. Dewey intended here to establish "culture" as the overarching context in which this obtains.

In this connection, philosophy, like experience, takes on a "genetic-functional" character. It is both situated *in* a culture as well as being the critical and constructive mode *of* that culture. The term "genetic-functional" is one that Dewey had previously used in his review of Alfred North Whitehead's philosophy. On that occasion, he identifies genetic-functional operations with the inherently active nature of situations.[69] He stresses a similar dynamic in *Unmodern Philosophy*, explaining that "what goes before—a genetic reference—and what comes after, a functioning reference," but *not* a distinction that is discretely sequenced—rather, one that is "inherently temporal and temporally continuous."[70]

The "genetic-functional" category is a subtle one. Dewey struggles to formulate it with clarity in his late-period writings. In unpublished papers, he is keen to distinguish it from what is commonly referred to as the "genetic method"—i.e., the history of how we have arrived at our understanding of some subject matter. Rather, Dewey means for it to indicate an "understanding of continuity in the subject matter investigated."[71] In *Unmodern Philosophy* he explains that: "In short, the phrase 'genetic-functional method' is a way of indicating, first, that philosophic inquiry gets ahead by placing the material of its problems in a *context*, and secondly, of announcing that this context consists of the material of prior and subsequent life-functions as interactivities." Also: "The method is *genetic* in that it attempts to place the subject matter dealt with in the context of the conditions under which it comes into existence . . . [and it] is *functional* in that it indicates what the factual subject matter under examination *does* specifically when it comes into existence."[72]

Another way to approach this is to reflect again on the role of the "philosopher" as Dewey now understands it. Philosophical inquiry is behavior that emerges in the context of life-functions: cultural, biographical, temperamental, etc. For human beings, this entails a *sociocultural* situation that is part of a temporal continuum (i.e., "genetic"). Once philosophy begins, however, its "two variables," the philosopher and the cultural material treated, become "technalized" in that context (i.e., "functional"). One is *trying* to do something and philosophical subject matter is taken up instrumentally in the attempt. Such activity is holistic—for as Dewey sees it, "consideration of genetic processes and of functions cannot be separated from each other."[73] Philosophical activity consists irreducibly of *some* one doing *some* thing *some* where for *some* reason. Such operative situations (i.e., "quart bowls") of philosophy cannot themselves become transparent objects of thought as we are in them. However, given the temporally continuous nature of genetic-functional activity, we are able to perform such observations as we *move* from situation to situation, and this is what makes progress in philosophy possible.

This has major implications for cross-cultural philosophical research. Whereas to *study* another philosophical tradition involves acquaintance with the "situations which have to do with problems that have played an influential part in the history of [that] philosophical discourse," to *be* a philosopher is simultaneously to be "involved in a concrete scene having its own color of tradition," one that conditions the way in which such cultural material is being apprehended. There is no method by which to avoid this "double-barreled" condition. Philosophy, given its genetic-functional nature, is both *shaping* and *shaped by* the situations in which it operates along with other life-functions on a temporal continuum. With reference to experience, Dewey explains what this means for philosophical discourse:

> "Experience" as the most inclusive category of philosophical discourse is a warning that every distinction and relation that figures needs to be placed where it emerges in the set and system of ongoing life-functions and with respect to the way it operates in this connection. In its comprehensive function, *experience* denotes organic-environmental interactivity, and as a "double-barreled" term, [it stands] for both modes of experienc*ing* and that which is experienc*ed* . . .

From this standpoint, Dewey finds it "almost beyond belief" that anyone who knows much about the history of Western philosophy would regard its material as open to "uncolored and uncoloring inspection or introspection and report."[74] He would find it equally if not more unbelievable that Western comparative philosophers would consider the objects of *non*-Western philosophies to be available for such neutral consideration. By now, it must be understood that, as genetic-functional activity, philosophy is a *product* of cultural conditions even as it *produces* its interpretations of cultural materials. Because the overarching context for this is "culture," that term was set to replace "experience" in Dewey's thinking.

It is fascinating that Dewey held such a position, complete but unexpressed, when he wrote his comments for *Philosophy East and West*. This places them in an entirely new light and again underscores how forward-looking they were. Dewey's article speaks, in fact, more directly to issues facing comparative philosophers *today* than to issues that concerned his readers in 1951.

The field, for instance, currently grapples with what is called the "third of comparison" (*tertium comparationis*) and how it functions in the act of comparison. Ralph Weber contributes the most to articulating the scope of this problem. Weber argues that every act of comparison, be it similarity, family resemblance, analogy, or something else, is informed by a *tertium* that enables comparison to occur. "The third of comparison," he argues, plays a crucial role "in the *determination* of the *comparata* which one then sets out to compare in one or another respect."[75] As an example, Weber uses the comparison of *Mengzi* 孟子 and *Xunzi* 荀子 on the topic of "human nature." In order to establish such a comparison, one must already identify the *comparata* as "two" of something, and that could mean any number of things: *two* Confucians, *two* philosophers, *two* texts, *two* theories, and the list goes on. As Dewey remarks, "There are as many meanings of identity and identification as there are types of operations by which they are determined."[76] Each type of identification influences the range of possible conclusions that a comparison might result in. As Weber observes, comparative philosophers "are not very strict when it comes to specifying the 'pre-comparative' *tertium* of their *comparata*," and thus seldom discuss how such choices influence their results.

Comparative philosophy generally regards "culture" itself as a *tertium*. In comparisons of Greek and Chinese thought, for instance, it is usually assumed that Greece and China are two "cultures" and that, as such, they will produce two "philosophies" (now a double assertion). On the basis of representing "two" of these things, Greek and Chinese thought can be compared. Weber observes that, "Any double assertion of cultural and philosophical difference hence presupposes a *tertium* in the sense that both *comparata* are said to be 'cultures with a philosophy of their own' (or to be relatable to such a notion). It remains to be determined in each such comparative study what precisely is understood by the terms 'culture' and 'philosophy.' " Weber raises a number of provocative points here. He adds another in observing that: "The problematic of the *tertium* leads one to the role of the person who makes the comparison," meaning "[there are] *purposes* that go into comparisons, and focusing on the problematic of the *tertium* might be helpful to make clear just what purpose is at play."[77]

With reference to Weber's concerns, Dewey's approach in *Unmodern Philosophy* is remarkable in at least two respects. First, there is little question as to Dewey's purpose. He states clearly that his intention is to draw a comparison between certain aspects of the Greek-medieval and Modern "worlds" in order to critique the continuing influence of the former. Second, over the course of executing his comparison, Dewey recognizes and openly constructs the categories of "culture" and "philosophy" that both genetically furnish—and functionally operate—as his *tertium*. He thereby implies within his argument that its philosophical subject matter is already conditioned by the cultural situation in which it is set.

This makes Dewey's approach in *Unmodern Philosophy* something other than comparative philosophy. Had his comments in *Philosophy East and West* been understood in this context, it might have been recognized that Dewey was not really advocating cross-cultural comparison at all, but rather something more "intra-cultural" in nature. The phrase "intra-cultural philosophy" more clearly announces that its own activities occur *within* the cultural matrix, and that its own genetic-functional character conditions the *tertium* of its own comparisons. "Culture," for Dewey, is the source of every *tertium*. It stands for the developing situations in which comparisons are made and in which their results become amenable to our purposes. The phrase "comparative philosophy" leaves room for the false impression that one can step outside of culture and reflect on cultural objects from an un-biased position for *no* reason whatsoever, which violates the genetic-functional nature of philosophy itself. By including a more explicit reference to culture in its own self-description, "intra-cultural philosophy" stands a better chance of remaining aware of its own nature and purpose—of "knowing what it's about," as Dewey liked to say.

The reasoning behind "On Philosophical Synthesis" now makes better sense. Since every operation of comparison and synthesis is undertaken for some reason, Dewey refuses to endorse either "comparison" or "synthesis" as a general goal and speaks instead of "*specific* philosophical relationships." His point is that it is easier to reflect intelligently on what is done for a specific purpose rather than allow such generic activities to masquerade as ends-in-themselves. Meanwhile, Dewey's critique of "cultural block universes" indicates his desire to liberate cultural elements from fixed sets (or *tertium*) that would limit their potential to serve instrumentally in other connections. Dewey anticipated that intra-cultural philosophy would change over time as cultural needs and interests changed. Important to remember in this connection is that, while cultural elements can be synthesized "in isolation," "*none* of these elements—in the East or in the West—is in isolation," but rather "all interwoven in a vast variety of ways in the historico-cultural process."[78] The act of isolating, comparing, and synthesizing cultural objects, Dewey realized, was an act that proceeded from within culture already—and since cultural situations change, so too will our understanding of the world's philosophical heritage.

Restored now to its proper context alongside Dewey's late-period work, this inaugural statement in *Philosophy East and West* can be regarded as a still-unrealized vision of what "intra-cultural philosophy" might look like. It is a vision that was ahead of its time in 1951, but perhaps one whose time has come.

Experiments in Intra-cultural Philosophy

That "On Philosophical Synthesis" can be read as "paving the way toward some important developments in intercultural philosophy" is recognized by Lenart Škof, whose recent work puts Dewey to good use in furthering "intercultural philosophy" as practiced in contemporary continental and Indian philosophical circles.[79] The "intra-cultural philosophy" developed here is distinct from this tradition. As presently envisioned, intra-cultural philosophy is original to and co-extensive with the American tradition. Ralph Waldo Emerson, who engaged with Chinese, Indian, and Islamic philosophies, lies within its lineage. William James' interest in Buddhism and his treatment of Swami Vivekananda are included. Works in the "pragmatist and process traditions" in comparative philosophy, as outlined by Robert W. Smid, are important expressions in this lineage.[80] The latter are sophisticated examples of intra-cultural philosophy in its more refined, methodological and comparative form, one closely associated with the history of the East-West Philosophers' Conferences.

In the present sense, however, intra-cultural philosophy embraces more than just what professional philosophers have done. As essentially pragmatic and inclusive in its orientation, it does not exclude cultural figures whose credentials are more eclectic. It matters not from what quarters Gary Snyder, Thomas Merton, or John Cage gained their insights into non-Western philosophies. *Passion may have whispered it or accident suggested it*. Their contributions still push the total drift of American culture toward greater assimilation of non-Western traditions, and such legacies matter. Such figures are not to be arbitrarily excluded from what is here regarded as "intra-cultural philosophy."

As broad as the present designation is, however, its relationship with analytic philosophy is somewhat complex. In the postwar period, classical American and non-Western philosophical traditions suffered simultaneous displacement from the American academy through the force of the analytic wave. After a period in exile, each tradition rebounded simultaneously, resumed their histories intertwined, and have enjoyed resurgences since the 1980s. There are, accordingly, deep attitudinal affinities and shared experiences between non-Western philosophies and classical American philosophy *as traditions*, and this is simply not the case with analytic philosophy as a tradition. In fact, many analytic philosophers remain antagonistic toward non-Western and classical American philosophies. Such attitudes, unfortunately, continue to shape the landscape of philosophy in the United States.[81]

Intra-cultural philosophy in the American sense does not exclude *any* subfield within world philosophy—Anglo-American analytic, European continental, Indian *darśana*—all philosophical methods are welcomed. In this respect, it is pluralistic in nature and gladly embraces all. It does, however, understand itself as "experimental" in its use of any *particular* philosophical method. Dewey defines experiment as "the art of conducting a sequence of observations in which natural conditions are intentionally altered and controlled in ways which will disclose, discover, natural subject-matters which would not otherwise have been noted."[82] Experimental inquiry, Dewey writes, is a uniquely intentional form of activity: "*doing something* which varies the conditions under which objects are observed and directly had [by] instituting new arrangements among them."[83]

Consciously or not, this is what comparative philosophers are already doing. If one compares, say, Aristotle's *Nicomachean Ethics* and the Confucian *Analects*, two cultural objects are identified and brought into contact in a controlled setting. Hypotheses are tested. Conclusions are drawn. The scholar observes results that issue from the interaction and juxtaposition of elements. If one is fortunate, connections once unnoticed are revealed and future lines of inquiry become suggested. Such experimental inquiry qualifies as "intra-cultural" if one remains aware of the context in which it occurs. The scholar's own situation furnishes such experiments with meaning and purpose and "technalizes" the objects under consideration. As cultural instruments, Aristotle's writings and the Confucian *Analects* will not be taken up to serve the exact purposes for which they were instrumental in the past (assuming this were even possible). Rather, each will be taken up to satisfy the contemporary interests of the scholar in the context of her discipline and her life. Intra-cultural philosophers understand that their work is *always* so situated. They understand that each of us operates within a "quart bowl" and that our situations "confer simplicity upon the elements . . . furnishing each with a *single* meaning according to its service in carrying on the whole enterprise."[84]

In the field of Chinese philosophy, recent monographs have compared Confucius with Western thinkers as diverse as Aristotle, Dewey, Rawls, and

Wittgenstein, and in each instance the "Confucius" that emerges is a compellingly fresh character.[85] Such variability in outcome signals neither defect nor deficit. It expresses both the complexity of Confucius and the distinct backgrounds of the authors who conducted those studies. One might be tempted to think that by eschewing comparison altogether and by focusing directly on the *Analects* and on traditional commentaries, one might encounter greater unanimity through stricter fidelity to Confucius himself. These days, such thinking is regarded as hermeneutically naïve and is known to be empirically false. There is tremendous insight to be gained from traditional commentaries, and nothing substitutes for reading the text, but this only begs the question. *Who* is reading the text and its commentaries and *why*? Within what cultural situation is such an experience being had? As Dewey once observed, "One cannot decline to *have* a situation for that is equivalent to having no experience."[86] In the wake of twentieth-century hermeneutics, such views are commonly accepted and intra-cultural philosophy embraces them.

Intra-cultural philosophy, however, has no historical connection to continental hermeneutics. It inherits its hermeneutical spirit directly from Concord—*'Tis the good reader that makes the good book*. "One must be an inventor to read well," says Ralph Waldo Emerson. "When the mind is braced by labor and invention, the page of whatever book we read becomes luminous with manifold allusion."[87] For the intra-cultural philosopher, books serve as an elemental catalyst for original thinking—just as they do in the classical Chinese tradition.[88]

Before this approach is mistaken for an "anything goes" attitude toward reading world philosophies, let it be noted that there are fixed standards to observe. Translations of ancient texts must be defensible at a minimum. As for understanding the *ideas* that are expressed in those texts, Dewey suggests that we strive to understand the "general *properties* of situations which have to do with problems that have played an influential part in the history of [that] philosophical discourse" in order to "reconstruct the environment sufficiently to know what problems its needs imposed upon [a thinker]."[89] Progress is definitely possible in this area, and such research is invaluable to intra-cultural philosophers.

The ideal of reconstructing the past, however, is regulative only. One cannot reconstruct the past but in the present, and the present is always culturally situated. In the case of pre-Qin Chinese philosophy, the challenges we face in reconstructing its historical context are great. We know that many pieces to the puzzle are missing: texts, thinkers, whole lineages lost to time. We know that "texts" in early China are rarely single-authored works and that they exhibit uncertain time depths. Archeological finds present us with earlier versions of core texts that differ from our received versions—and now the field is inundated with newly unearthed texts that no one knew existed. *Perfect fidelity and accuracy in our interpretations* . . . Doubtless very fine ideals to play with, but where on this moonlit and dream-visited planet are *they* found? Rather than pretending to achieve perfect fidelity, intra-cultural philosophers hone their skills, learn as much as they can about an intellectual milieu, and then follow their instincts—testing interpretations and looking for connections that are important and that make sense.

In coming to understand the fundamentally "experimental" attitude of intra-cultural philosophy, it is helpful to review Dewey's "three outstanding characteristics" of inquiry as outlined in *The Quest for Certainty*. Paraphrased, these characteristics are as follows. First, "all experimentation involves overt doing," thereby *changing* our relation to the objects that we apprehend. Second, "experiment is not random activity," but rather *directed* by conditions set by the problems that prompt inquiry. Third, "the outcome of the directed activity is the construction of a new empirical situation," resulting in objects that have the property of being *known*.[90] Accordingly, the features that strike one as important in a text like the *Analects* emerge operationally in the context of whatever experiment one might be engaged in. Philosophical theories amount to tools in such inquiries; they are *instrumental*. Western virtue ethics, pragmatic naturalism, consequentialism, humanism, the *gongfu* 功夫 method—each theory operates in disclosing relations not otherwise apparent. At bottom, the features that *are* important in a philosophical text are those that are *discovered* to be important in a specific inquiry. This is axiomatic in intra-cultural philosophy.[91]

Given that our readings are products of whatever experimental inquiries we have chosen to engage in, arguments in favor of particular readings are never *only* arguments about the truth and accuracy of an interpretation; they are also arguments about *importance* and *meaning*—claims about what is at stake, and why anyone outside of a limited academic circle should care. This has always been a feature in the finest "comparative" studies. Intra-cultural philosophy regards this feature as normative and makes it explicit.

This prompts us to reflect on how texts like the *Analects* assume such enduring relevance and meaning across multiple cultural situations. What makes texts like the *Analects* so consistently *important*? Dewey once observed that, "Continuity of culture in passage from one civilization to another as well as within [a] culture, is conditioned by *art* more than by any other one thing."[92] Great philosophical works share with great artworks the hallmark of the aesthetic, something that Dewey refers to as "quality." The *Analects*, for instance, surely contains the thoughts of individuals other than Confucius, and its compilation owes itself to anonymous editorial hands. As a complex vision of the human experience, however, the text assumes an appreciable quality as a whole. This singular feature is what enables it to inspire readers across the generations. What William James observed about individual people is also true of great philosophical works: the most important thing about them is their *vision*. However imperfectly captured, each great work of philosophy expresses a "sense of what life honestly and deeply means."[93]

For Dewey, such aesthetic expressions strike us "below the barriers that separate human beings from one another." In this way, our experience with a classic text from a remote culture is much like our experience with a remote artwork. It feels very direct, even though the features of its original context were "transient" and "do not exist now." While our contemporary experiences with such works will never be identical to some past experience, there is a felt connection deeper than any surface comparisons. As Dewey sees it:

> [Experience] is a matter of the interaction of the artistic product with the self. It is not therefore twice alike for different persons even today. It changes with the same person at different times as [he or she] brings something different to a work. But there is no reason why, in order to be aesthetic, these experiences should be identical. So far as in each case there is an ordered movement of the matter of the experience to a fulfillment, there is a dominant aesthetic quality. *Au fond*, the aesthetic quality is the same for Greek, Chinese, and American.[94]

With this mention of "the same," are we turning back towards the straits between the Scylla and Charybdis of comparison? No. In describing the aesthetic encounter, Dewey is not describing an event that by occurring leads inevitably to comparison. The ordered movement between the viewer and an artwork, or between the reader and a text, culminates in something that Dewey calls "assimilation." As he explains: "*de facto* assimilation comes first and need not eventuate in the express conception of resemblance."[95] The artwork has a pervasive quality, and each aesthetic experience with the work culminates in a further pervasive quality. The work thereby becomes assimilated into what Dewey calls "*an* experience."[96] "'Assimilation,'" Dewey writes, "denotes the efficacious operation of pervasive quality; 'similarity' denotes a *relation*. Sheer assimilation results in the presence of a single object of apprehension."[97] In this core respect—i.e., *au fond* and genetically—the contemporary Sinologist's experience with the *Analects* is identical to that of Zhu Xi 朱熹 in the twelfth century. Each encounter involves an object that possesses its own pervasive quality, and each encounter culminates in the experience of having that object assimilated in a particular situation. Each beholder, Dewey explains, must *create* this form of experience, and the work fulfills it.[98]

As Sing-nan Fen reminds us, "There is an old Chinese saying that a great teacher is like a spring breeze and a seasonal rain." The same can be said for great works of art and literature. "The charm or power of personalities like Confucius [or the Confucian *Analects*]," Fen suggests, "builds up situations in the medium of their own personality."[99] Such situated encounters result in assimilations that are, in the first instance, singular and incomparable. Deep down, each of us knows this. "If symbols are at hand," Dewey suggests, "[such assimilations] may lead to a further act—a judgment of similarity."[100] Only then does comparison begin.

Unlike projects in comparative philosophy, "experiments in intra-cultural philosophy" prioritize *assimilation* over comparison. The difference is easy to observe in conspicuous cases. Thomas Aquinas assimilates Aristotle's *Metaphysics*, Ralph Waldo Emerson assimilates the *Bhagavad-Gītā*, Nishida Kitarō assimilates *Essays in Radical Empiricism*, and Feng Youlan assimilates *The Critique of Pure Reason*.[101] Comparisons occur in each case, but they are the byproducts of each philosopher coming to incorporate the latter material into his own vision of things. The genuine broadening and deepening of the thinker's *vision* is where the intra-cultural encounter actually occurs. In Sing-nan Fen's words, the experience "lifts us beyond what we already know and already are."[102]

Again, such encounters share many of the same features that Dewey identifies with our cross-cultural aesthetic experiences:

> The moving force is genuine participation, in some degree and phase, in the type of experience of which primitive, [Chinese], and early medieval objects of art are the expression . . . at their best they bring about an organic blending of attitudes characteristic of the experience of our own age with that of remote peoples . . . Their enduring effect upon those who perceive and enjoy will be an expansion of *their* sympathies, imagination, and sense.

Participation as the expansion of "sympathies, imagination, and sense" is what distinguishes intra-cultural philosophy from our academic day jobs—which is to reconstruct the original context of a remote text or manuscript as best we can. As for actually *assimilating* that work, "we understand it in the degree in which we make it a part of our own attitudes," explains Dewey, "not just by collective information concerning the conditions under which it was produced."[103]

As Dewey reminds us, the actual work of art "is what the product does with and in experience."[104] Intra-cultural philosophy is thus *experiential* while being *experimental*, and Dewey is known for stressing the connection between the two. In absorbing Dewey's late-period shift from "experience" to "culture," it is crucial not to lose sight of the fact that Dewey never renounces the importance that he places on *experience*. There is no way to understand what experiments are without a solid understanding of this notion.

For Dewey, experience is an "active-passive affair," a balance between "doing and undergoing" that is struck in a particular way.[105] Not all activity qualifies as "experience." Much of the time, experience is not being had because the proper balance is not being struck. "Excess on the side of doing or [excess] on the side of receptivity, of undergoing," explains Dewey, can interfere with the assimilation of subject matter into experience.[106] As already indicated, experiments involve an "overt doing" upon materials that render those materials *known*. In order for such experiments to register as *experiences*, these activities must circle back upon a "return wave" of consequences. "When an activity is continued *into* the undergoing of consequences," Dewey writes, "when the change made by action is reflected back into a change made in us, the mere flux is loaded with significance. We learn something."[107]

The same "return wave" circuit can be observed in our experiences with artworks. Reflecting on how we behave in museums, Dewey distinguishes aesthetic perception from the mere "recognition" of an artwork, the former being akin to assimilation and the latter to a simple act of identification or labeling.[108] One might, for instance, tour an art gallery in a single afternoon, but one cannot *experience* every artwork on a single visit. Each piece requires time and energy to assimilate. The same holds true for philosophical texts. One might read the *Analects* dozens of times before certain passages are assimilated into experience—and even then, one's encounter with the text does not come to an end. Future experiments bring fresh experiences born of new connections.

Connecting Strains of Culture

The discussion up to now has involved individual encounters with cultural works. It remains to be seen if such encounters change as broader historical and cultural processes are considered. Can one culture "assimilate" elements from *another* culture? Common sense answers in the affirmative and examples abound. As Sing-nan Fen observes, artists have always been competent in assimilating elements from other cultures, "whether in gardening, architecture, irrigation, bookbinding, breeding, folk-dancing, painting, music, or lyric poetry, the East and West do meet, and meet on a high and equal level of intelligence and intelligibility."[109]

Such facts prompt deeper reflection. In "On Philosophical Synthesis," Dewey argues that East and West should not be regarded as "cultural blocks," since this overlooks the sheer complexity of cultures: "Latin," "French," and "Germanic" distinctions, for instance. There are, Dewey maintains, "complexities, differences, and ramifying interrelationships" both *within* and *among* the cultures of the world. With that said, do we *need* to determine where one culture ends and another begins? It seems that cultures converge and diverge on multiple levels simultaneously. There is a pronounced elasticity, for instance, between the cultures of Christianity, France, French Catholicism, and *Chapelle Royale* during the age of Louis XIV. How do we distinguish such cultures? In "On Philosophical Synthesis," Dewey refers to the world as a "cultural matrix," one in which its myriad elements are "all interwoven." As Ralph Weber suggests, a specific *tertium* is required to determine the boundaries of any given culture. For Dewey, the generation of such a *tertium* would itself be an act within culture.

Since this evokes the problem of the one and the many, the ontology of culture may never be resolved to our complete satisfaction. We may, however, arrive at some provisional understanding. In making their case against radical incommensurability, David L. Hall and Roger T. Ames suggest that cultural systems are related to one another against an indeterminate background. As they see it: "Many of the paradoxes involved in attempting to interpret across boundaries are dissolved when one recognizes that there is but a single field of significances which serves as a background from which individual cultures and languages are foregrounded." Such a "background," for Hall and Ames, is not a standing ground of perennial human meanings, but rather a "vague field of significances open to articulation for this or that purpose, but existing primarily *in potentia*."[110] Dewey would agree with such a proposition.[111] On this basis, intra-cultural philosophers can use labels such as "French Catholic," "Aristotelian," "Appalachian," "Buddhist," or "Minoan" as needed to indicate whatever common elements such referents internally sustain, so long as each label responds satisfactorily to its purpose. If all goes well, there is no material difference between the reality of the label and the satisfaction of the purpose.

Individual cultures, rather than being "block-like" entities fixed by solid boundaries, are complex and elastic objects. They are composed, however, of real elements—material, historical, spiritual, and linguistic. With respect to the realism of distinct cultures, Dewey writes that, "Each culture has its own individuality and has a pattern that binds it together." Each possesses its own "collective individuality" and "veridical significance." As anyone would, Dewey identifies artistic styles with specific cultures in *Art as Experience*. In this context, he stresses that the art product is a "strain in experience rather than an entity in itself."[112]

In light of Dewey's eventual shift from "experience" to "culture," we should pause to consider this statement. As Joseph Margolis observes, direct discussions of culture in *Art as Experience* are "remarkably rare," as in this work Dewey "avoids admitting the primacy of the cultural" in discussing the relationship between aesthetic experiences and artworks. Such a subordination of culture, Margolis submits, is indicative of Dewey's "biological exuberance" in the 1920s and '30s.[113] By the mid-1940s, however, Dewey's shift toward "culture" was underway, and he would likely have wanted to reformulate his aesthetic theory in terms of *Art as Culture* rather than *Art as Experience*. Addressing the need to update Dewey's position accordingly, Russell Pryba suggests that the ontological status of the artwork in Dewey's framework needs to be modified so that its status no longer equates simply to experience. It must be established that its "existence is already secure in virtue of the cultural environment in which it is indissolubly embedded and in which aesthetic experience takes place." According to Pryba, this would help to "[provide] a more general metaphysics of culture which could accommodate the kind of comprehensive vision for philosophy that Dewey saw as necessary towards the end of his life."[114]

Intra-cultural philosophy settles for a provisional sketch of this vision, one that will account for how arts and philosophies operate at the cultural-level and how assimilation between particular cultures takes place. Philosophies, like artistic works and styles, can be considered "strains of experience" *within* cultures, strains that both genetically define and functionally direct those cultures. Philosophical strains, as Dewey says, would "[sustain] the closest connection with the history of culture," to the extent that "philosophy not only *has* a role, [but] *is* a specifiable role in the development of human culture."[115] Each strain is culturally situated, and when cultures come into contact with one another, new situations arise in which strains of experience stretch and cross into other strains organically—within and among the intersecting cultures. Such transmissions go a long way in accounting for the resulting identity of cultures. As Dewey writes: "Cultures are in many respects individual or unique, and their manifestations are 'explained' by correlations with one another and by borrowings due to chance contacts. The chief, even if not the sole, law of their changes is that of transmission from other individualized cultures."[116] For Dewey: "When the art of another culture enters into attitudes that determine our experience genuine continuity is affected. Our own experience does not thereby lose its individuality but it takes unto itself and weds elements that expand its significance."[117]

Again, Dewey's late period thinking on this topic begins to crystallize in what was intended to be the final chapter of his lost work. It is a vision consistent with what he would eventually propose in *Philosophy East and*

West—one in which cultures are "all interwoven in a vast variety of ways" within a matrix of "complexities, differences, and ramifying interrelationships."[118] Dewey was preparing to inaugurate a new term—*Togetherness*—to describe this emerging vision. In his unfinished draft, he writes:

> Because everything experienced is determined by interactivity of organic-ongoing conditions, everything inquired into and discussed belongs in a field or situation. Fields and/or situations possess spatial and temporal *togetherness* of the existences and events which constitute them. They are extensive and enduring. "*Togetherness*" as used here covers what is often named by the words connections and relations, and interconnections and relationships. I have employed a word derived from the word "together" because I want to avoid as far as possible prejudgment regarding the kind of way or ways in which things go and come together in forming situations. The notion of "relations" has often been played with dialectically . . . [for instance] to justify the necessity of some kind of monistic scheme and block universe. The word *together* involves denial of the existence of any such thing as complete isolation, and in so far points to a highly [*ill.*] property of every experience as field [or] situation. But it leaves room for every kind of connection that observation discloses without the necessity of forcing them all into the Procrustean bed of some preferred type.[119]

Within such a framework, cultures are not simply "related" to one another in some Procrustean bed of "Sameness/Difference." They are more importantly always *together*. The field in which individualized cultures (e.g., the Christian, the French, and the French Catholic) come into focus is extensive and enduring in its *togetherness*, but also plastic and indefinite—capable of coming together in a variety of ways based on the interests of the situation. Such togetherness is inherently *dynamic*—such that the postulation of any "cultural block universe" threatens to impede the realization of *new* connections as fields of inquiry grow and as cultural relations change.[120]

David L. Hall and Roger T. Ames appear, then, to have anticipated what becomes Dewey's mature position on the ontology of culture. For Hall and Ames, "a productively vague model of cultures would construe them as local distortions of a general field which is itself without specifiable boundary conditions," but allowing for "a vague complex of significances [to be] focused in accordance with a variety of interests."[121] Equally for Dewey, each cultural situation is understood as *indefinite*—if we "include in 'indefiniteness' the vague shading off that occurs at the edges, which may contain things and connections that will be focal and, so to say, bright and clear in other situations of experience."[122]

The logic of "On Philosophical Synthesis" thus expresses the final phases of Dewey's thinking. In doing so, it suggests a point of departure for understanding a more "intra-cultural" form of philosophy, one that encourages creative experimentation with new connections between the myriad "strains" of human experience—experiments that establish from *within* the matrix of culture "*specific* philosophical relationships" for genuine purposes. It thus retains what Dewey regards as the "imaginative" function of philosophy: "bringing to a focus of unity and clarity the ideas that are at work in a given period more or less independently of one another, in separate cultural streams."[123] Such activity entails imagination in that it strives to make cultural connections that have yet to be made.

It is important for civilizations to create and sustain such opportunities not only for their philosophers but also for their general populations. In China, Dewey reflects on the importance of this function in describing what it means to be a good citizen. "A good citizen must be a creative contributor to his culture," he explains to his Beijing audience. This means to "benefit from the past and present culture" and to "contribute to the development of the emerging culture by initiating new experiences of [one's] own which may influence others." As Dewey observes: "The main reason we want to conserve and teach the culture of the past is that we need to relive it, to infuse life into it, to use it, and make it applicable to present-day social situations and conditions."[124] Becoming a good "intra-cultural" citizen requires such creative imagination, commitment, and effort.

Dewey was aware that "imagination" is a suspect term in philosophy, owing to its frequent association with "fantasy or doubtful reality."[125] Imagination is an equally dubious faculty in Sinology, where it is associated with taking interpretive liberties with a text.[126] There will be no apology, however, for the inclusion of imagination in intra-cultural philosophy. The reason is simple: the limits of our imaginations set limits to what we think it is possible for a philosophical text to be saying. If progress in understanding is to continue, such limits cannot be fixed. "The healthy imagination," Dewey writes, "deals not with the unreal, but with the mental realization of what is suggested. Its exercise is not a flight into the purely fanciful and ideal, but a method of expanding and filling in what is real."[127] By their very nature, philosophical writings from other cultures challenge us to *activate* and *expand* our philosophical imaginations, not to disable or constrict them. Doing the latter only narrows the margins for insight.

Brook Ziporyn relates candidly how rare it is for Sinologists to make it through their careers with imaginations intact. Pressure to "integrate this initially strange system into accepted habits, linguistic forms, cultural theories" is exerted from the outset. One's initial wonder is "ground down" as one is "chastened and taught to rein in his exuberance." Whatever imagination one initially brings to the prospect of generating novel interpretations of classical Chinese texts is "systematically made into an object of opprobrium."[128]

Surely, the fact that imagination is not a virtue in Sinology is not among Sinology's own virtues. As Holmes Welch observes, it is more like a plain reality. Contemporary Sinology is a rigorous and exacting vocation. The "crushing demands" of its training and research expectations leave little opportunity for scholars to exercise their philosophical imaginations. "If there is any *métier* designed to smother the imagination," Welch submits, "it is Sinology."[129] Set conventions get established out of necessity. Terms with complex semantic values are converted into currencies that are instantly recognizable, widely understood, and easily exchanged. Within the borders of Sinology, general purpose terms like "The Way," "Heaven," "Fate," "Virtue," and "Benevolence" become coin of the realm in a stable economy.

Sinology needs philosophy, and philosophy needs Sinology. Both activities, in performing their functions, need imagination. For the intra-cultural philosopher, studying the ideas of other cultures is fundamentally an exercise in imagination. It is an expression of what Dewey calls the "perennial adventure of the human spirit," one that requires "the creative work of the imagination in pointing to the new possibilities."[130] This is especially true when the object of concern is a philosophical text. As Dewey observes, the enduring quality of all great works is their "renewed instrumentality for consummatory experiences." If a work like the *Analects* is prevented from serving as instrumental to new experiences, then it "turns in time to the dust and ashes of boredom."[131] Sinology and philosophy become equally *boring* when not animated by fresh perspectives on their subject matters. Accordingly, intra-cultural philosophy is not satisfied with simply "recovering" the past. Its task is to re-imagine the *relevance* of the past. "The junction of the new and old is not a mere composition of forces," Dewey writes, "[but] a re-creation in which the present impulsion gets form and solidity while the old, the 'stored,' material is literally revived, given new life and soul through having to meet a new situation."[132]

Such engagement is never severed from cultural history or tradition. Philosophy, as one strand within culture, never ceases to maintain continuity with its own past. Periodically, in fact, it must carefully revisit that past in making its future. "Philosophy," Dewey states, "sustains the closest connection with the history of culture, with the succession of changes in civilization. It is fed by the streams of tradition, traced at critical moments to their sources in order that the current may receive a new direction."[133]

The future of philosophy, as Dewey says, is something that is "simply bound to change," and its evolution "needs to be seen and reported in terms of the distinctive features of culture."[134] "On Philosophical Synthesis" provides a point of departure for this vision, one that regards philosophy as an intra-cultural enterprise—an imaginative attempt to make new connections between various "strains" of human experience and thus establish from *within* the matrix of culture "*specific* philosophical relationships" for genuine purposes. Such a vision represents the final stages of Dewey's thinking; and by all indications, he was prepared to go further in this direction.

The evidence for this is tantalizing. Buried in the Dewey archives at Carbondale, there are two sheets of paper upon which are scrawled the general outline for a book that Dewey would never write. The first sheet of paper is stationary from "American President Lines," the ocean liner that brought Dewey to Honolulu in 1951. The second sheet is from the Halekulani resort in Waikīkī, where Dewey wrote his piece for *Philosophy East and West*. These items are catalogued under "Assorted Manuscripts" as two pages in "Green Ink," so named for the unusually striking color of the ink that Dewey uses. Accordingly, the original "Halekulani" page is a much more vivid object than the reproduction provided on the right.

The "American President Lines" page designates chapter 1 of the book as "Pre-Human Animal Life," chapter 2 would be "Cultural Transformation," chapter 3 would be "Failure to Understand in Cultural Terms," and chapter 4 would be "Communication." The "Halekulani" page reproduced here sketches the outline for this fourth and final chapter. It is terse and oblique—full of abbreviations, torn and repaired, and obscured by water damage. Here, however, is a tentative reconstruction of what it says:

> Communication. It's what culture achieves [,] outcomes in process of *trans*-mission sent across and over, thereby cancelling [the] separation of organic processes-operations *qua* physical and giving communication [,] . . . making a leap towards a *new* status—as cultural *dispositions*. Give them the *function* of communicating and transmitting. Permanence of the [*ill.*] . . . is the *miracle* [*ill.*] . . . representing cognitive content—the cumulative aspect of culture. . . . [*ill.*][135]

Obscure, yes. Made more so by the fact that Dewey's green ink is running dry, its once verdant color disappearing as he attempts to resuscitate his pen. These pages are dated February 18, 1951—one week before Dewey left Hawai`i to be hospitalized on the mainland.

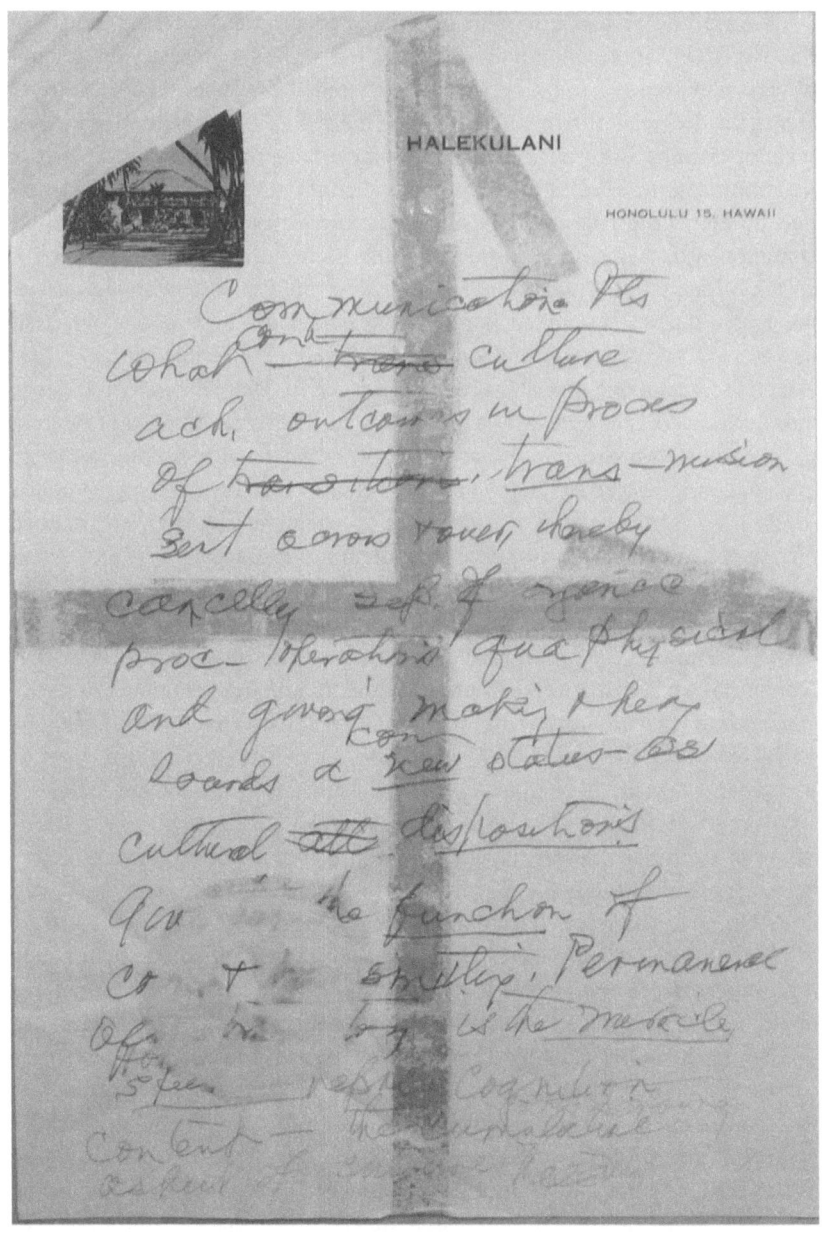

Figure 1.1. One of John Dewey's "Green Ink Pages," written February 1951 while he was visiting Hawai`i. John Dewey collection, Special Collections Research Center, Morris Library, Southern Illinois University Carbondale.

Anything said about such fragments is speculative. Alongside "On Philosophical Synthesis" and other late-period writings, however, the general direction of Dewey's thinking can be surmised. Dewey believed that it was a mistake to treat different cultures as "block-like" objects that reduce to their operations *qua* physical in geographical isolation. The miracle that is "communication" enables different cultural strains to leap "across and over" one another. Each cultural disposition communicates and transmits cultural content as it transforms, such that thinking itself is the cumulative aspect of culture. The resulting continuity of culture is underscored with the use of the prefix *trans-*. Envisioned is an East-West-North-South philosophy that moves past the dialectics of "Sameness/Difference," one that embraces the essential *togetherness* of cultural experience. What Dewey had in mind is a more self-aware alternative to the allegedly disinterested exercise of making philosophical comparisons. What he proposes to the readers of *Philosophy East and West*, accordingly, is the establishment of a richly de-centered philosophical environment, one that facilitates engagement with the world's entire philosophical heritage in response to contemporary needs.

Dewey glimpsed this future from the crossroads of the Pacific—Oʻahu, the island that kānaka ʻōiwi still refer to as "The Gathering Place." There, for close to a century, the philosophy department at the University of Hawaiʻi at Mānoa has sustained a doctoral program that is uniquely multicultural in its constitution. Before a gathering in Hawaiʻi recently, Peter D. Hershock, co-organizer of the Eleventh East-West Philosophers' Conference, explained to participants that the hyphen in "East-West" is meant to signify mutuality and two-way implication.[136] Dewey likewise recognizes "the hyphen" as a mark of dynamic interrelatedness.[137] Hyphenated terms are, in some sense, spherical in nature—and so too is the togetherness of East-West. Go far enough in one direction, and one returns again to the beginning.

At the start of his stay in China, Dewey expressed wonder at the cultural prospect before him. He had come from America, "the newest culture of all," to give lectures in China, "the oldest culture in the world." Speaking in Beijing, he observed how interconnected the world had become: that culture itself, "having undergone innumerable mutations and metamorphoses," had made its journey around the world and was now circling back to its beginnings. "We can say that our culture is something like a sphere, just as the earth is physically spherical," he observed. This rounded-out cultural heritage, Dewey hoped, "all nations of the earth will share."[138] Intra-cultural philosophers believe with Dewey that fostering access to such a global heritage is possible, and that experiments working toward this goal continue to lend themselves "most fruitfully and dynamically to the enlightenment and betterment of the human estate."[139]

2

Forms and Nature

> Westerners have typically regarded the people of China as being extremely conservative noting that the latter have been subjected to classical patterns of thought for some two thousand years or more . . . But these people overlook the fact that Aristotle dominated Western thinking for fully as long a time as classical thinking has prescribed the pattern for China. It was only about three hundred years ago that revolutionary currents in Western thought began to challenge the domination of Aristotle, and it was even more recently that Aristotle's fundamental concepts were superseded by others more appropriate to our time.
>
> —John Dewey, National Peking University, November 1919

Philosophy Out of Gear

In the only extant draft of "Wandering Between Two Worlds" (chapter 6 of *Unmodern Philosophy*) Dewey indicates that the subtitle of that chapter would be "Philosophy Out of Gear."[1] Dewey had used this phrase before. It appears in a 1945 article entitled, "Dualism and the Split Atom: Science and Morals in the Atomic Age."[2] In this article, Dewey addresses an issue of terrifying proportions, "the greatest threat to security that human imagination can encompass"—the atomic bomb. Here, he repeats the argument that was to drive his ill-fated manuscript: namely, that the principles upon which we have organized Western cultures are "out of gear" with those represented by our best scientific understandings. As Dewey saw it, our confused reaction to the atomic age revealed once again the "tragic split" between what we regard as merely scientific on the one hand, and what we esteem as truly human and spiritual on the other. This tragic split, which originates with the Scientific Revolution and endures through the Industrial Revolution, stems again from the fact that modern science has progressed beyond the Greek-medieval notions of unchanging essences and fixed ends whereas our moral and religious imaginations have not. As Dewey explains to a Beijing audience, "The greatest weakness of Western civilization is the lag of social and ethical science far behind the rapid progress being made in the natural sciences."[3] The result is anachronism and ineptitude in ethical reasoning, cultural confusion, and a lack of coordination in human affairs—all signs of a "drifting" and "wandering" between two worlds.

Religious fundamentalism remains our most prominent example of such a split-up condition, principles in one area of life "out of gear" with those in another. In *A Common Faith*, Dewey observes that:

> The fundamentalist in religion is one whose beliefs in intellectual content have hardly been touched by scientific developments. His notions about heaven and earth and man, as far as their bearing on religion is concerned, are hardly more affected by the work of Copernicus, Newton, and Darwin than they are by that of Einstein. But his actual life, in what he does day by day and in the contacts that are set up, has been radically changed by political and economic changes that have followed from applications of science.[4]

Medical technologies illustrate well Dewey's point. One would think that most Creationists would elect to receive the most effective antibiotic for a life-threatening infection. Such treatment, however, is based on evolutionary science, the assumptions of which directly contradict Creationism with respect to the nature of organic life. Most liberal societies would defend the Creationist by arguing that one's medical decisions and religious commitments are entirely separable, and that one may believe however one wishes in either domain. The resulting wall of separation between science and religion thus preserves *liberty*—but only at the expense of failing to achieve harmony between fundamental human needs.

"The result is mental confusion," Dewey submits. "The 'split' inevitably reacts upon the mind to blur its insight and weaken its firmness of grasp; no one can use two inconsistent mental standards without losing some of his mental grip."[5] One thus lives in a "divided world," one whose "parts and aspects do not hang together." Such splitting-up is both the cause and symptom of an increasingly disintegrated human personality. As Dewey observes: "When the splitting-up reaches a certain point we call the person insane. A fully integrated personality, on the other hand, exists only when successive experiences are integrated with one another. It can be built up only as a world of related objects is constructed."[6]

Classical pragmatists are not univocal with respect to how tightly one's world must "hang together." William James is less stringent than Dewey, and

Charles Sanders Peirce is more stringent than both. Dewey is closer, however, to Peirce than to James. As Dewey sees it, there is "but one sure road of access to truth," and it is the road of "patient, cooperative inquiry operating by means of observation, experiment, record and controlled reflection"—in other words, that which is "conveyed by the word 'scientific' in its most general and generous sense."[7] For Dewey, modern science makes possible societies founded on the "expanding community of cooperative effort and truth," those in which "everything discovered belongs to the community." When revolutionary changes occur in scientific understanding, such societies prepare themselves for "nothing less than a revolutionary change in morals, religion, politics and industry."[8]

Private retreats into fantasy, "noble lies," willful ignorance, and dogmatisms cripple the development of such communities and prevent their "world of related objects" from being realized. Like Peirce, Dewey's ultimate faith lies in communities of open inquiry and their eventual success. The antibiotic-taking Creationist who maintains self-refuting assumptions about organic nature lives in manifest contradiction and exhibits defiance toward such communities. He insists upon operating under competing rules of action. However infrequently such rules conflict, Dewey sides with Peirce who maintains that such behavior is untenable in the "long run."

Dewey thought it was untenable already. The separation of scientific considerations from moral and religious interests was preventing science from "[operating] within, not just outside of and against, the moral values and concerns of humanity."[9] For as long as Western civilization maintains its cleavage between science and religion, conditions are fostered for one or the other to be relegated to second-rate status. Dewey especially feared that such a split would lead to a disregard for modern science and to a dismissal of its seemingly alien domain.

Such fears remain legitimate. Facing once again "the greatest threat to security that human imagination can encompass," we are confronted in the United States with an appalling disregard for scientific evidence regarding climate change and other issues.[10] Such disregard is not limited to isolated cultural pockets, but is evident in the most prominent sectors of U.S. politics, industry, business, and religion. The denial of climate science is a complex phenomenon, with commercial interests and political ideologies playing important roles. Research also shows, however, that many are simply not prepared psychologically to accept the reality of climate change. Kari Marie Norgaard's work on the social and cognitive factors that influence such denial underscores the power of "ontological security" in fueling resistance to climate-related facts.[11] In this respect, climate denial is not unlike the continuing denial of Darwinian evolution. In each case, it is the radical impact of *change* that is the object of resistance—the thought that we are not immune from degrees of change that Greek-medieval principles assured us that we *were* immune from.[12]

Ontological security is indeed a core human need, but it is not achieved simply by adopting a metaphysics that denies the reality of change. Just as it was in 1945, the state of our world is "so fearful, so frightful . . ." but for Dewey, "to look to some unreal solution to its problems which is essentially reactionary—going back to the ideas of Greek or medieval times" is only to "adopt a method of escape."[13] It is an attempt "to find something so fixed and certain as to provide a secure refuge."[14] There is no such refuge. Given the severity of our climate crisis, Dewey's dire warnings about the atomic age remain painfully relevant. As he wrote then: "[If this fails] to teach us that we live in a world of change so that our ways of organization of human interrelationships must also change, the case is well-nigh hopeless."[15]

Such concerns drove Dewey to insist upon the integration of science and ethics. His appeal takes many forms, and it is easily caricatured and often misunderstood.[16] In its most basic form, Dewey's appeal is simply that moral philosophy must begin to generate approaches that are better informed by findings in the natural sciences. The Darwinian revolution, with its denial of extra-temporal forms and fixed ends, was foremost on Dewey's mind in making such a suggestion. In his 1948 "Re-Introduction" to *Reconstruction in Philosophy*, he explains:

> [Natural] science is forced by its own development to abandon the assumption of fixity and to recognize that what is actually "universal" is *process*; but this fact of recent science still remains in philosophy, as in popular opinion up to the present time, a technical matter rather than what it is: namely, the most revolutionary discovery yet made. The supposed fact that morals demand immutable, extra-temporal principles, standards, norms, ends, as the only assured protection against moral chaos [can, therefore] no longer appeal to natural science for its support. . . .[17]

Dewey here equates scientific understanding simply with "process," just as he had in his then recently lost manuscript. Insofar that the word "scientific" for Dewey denotes practices in which "*process* is seen to be the 'universal' in nature and in life," then the integration of the "scientific" with other concerns simply means the development of process-oriented approaches in more areas of human concern.[18]

Nowhere is this more pressing than in the moral sphere, which continues to be deeply informed by "out of gear" conceptions. For us, developing a more empirically minded, scientifically viable moral outlook is not an optional philosophical project. It is a cultural necessity. As Dewey explains: "A culture which permits science to destroy traditional values but which distrusts its power to create new ones is a culture which is destroying itself."[19] Darwinian logic requires us to rethink the status of our values and to devise new approaches to generate and secure them. It requires, Dewey suggests, that we shift attention from "an ultimate goal of good to the direct increments of justice and happiness that intelligent administration of existent conditions may beget and that present carelessness or stupidity will destroy or forego."[20] Such proposals sound deflated, even blasphemous to the unreconstructed mind; but the choice is one of either appealing to empirical reality and working *within* nature to secure human goods or ignoring empirical reality and thus refusing to do so. For Dewey, the choice is clear.

With this in mind, the present chapter begins to chart a conceptual route around our outmoded Greek-medieval assumptions—drawing from both Dewey's philosophy and Daoist thought. The goal is to establish a philosophy of nature that can withstand empirical scrutiny and also provide a viable framework in which to reconstruct our value inquiries. Such a complex project can only be pursued incrementally, and the present chapter is only the beginning stage in this process. Its results will not be known until experiments are conducted in subsequent chapters.

The difficulty at this preliminary stage cannot be underestimated. Dewey, after all, regarded the project of changing common sense in the "popular mind" from a pre-Darwinian to a post-Darwinian outlook to be the "intellectual task of the twentieth century."[21] He knew that it would be difficult to complete. "Probably most educated people thought the conception of biological evolution had [already] been accepted as a commonplace," he observes in *A Common Faith*—but the Scope's Trial "revealed how far that was from being the case."[22] Dewey pushed on, with the reconstruction of Greek-medieval assumptions a centerpiece of his philosophical agenda.

He received his share of cultural backlash along the way, and such reactions continue to reverberate today. The National Catholic Alumni Federation regarded Dewey as "Atheistic" and "Un-American" for portraying a universe "without final ends, forms, or assignable limits."[23] He received postcards from Texas telling him that he was "going straight to hell."[24] It was publicly implied that he was a "manifestation of Satan."[25] Strangers reached out to Dewey offering prayer, asking how he could be such a kind and gifted person and still not accept Jesus as his Lord and Savior.[26] Toward the end of his life, Dewey had reason to suspect that Christian fundamentalists were responsible for systematically distorting his positions in the popular press.[27] Such distortions continue into the present, as Dewey remains an active target of religious and cultural conservatives in the United States.[28]

Dewey understood that teleological and essentialist assumptions were deeply embedded in common sense and that changing them would be an uphill battle. "The doctrine that nature does nothing in vain, that it is directed by a purpose, was not engrafted by scholasticism upon science," Dewey notes, "it formulates an instinctive tendency."[29] Recent findings in developmental psychology confirm this. Barbara Kelemen presents strong evidence that young children are "broadly inclined to view natural phenomena as intentionally created" and that they have a congenital bias toward "[treating] objects and behaviors as existing for a purpose."[30] Ironically, our tendency to see agency and purpose in nature is most likely an outcome of natural selection. The intuitive assumption that unfamiliar objects have agency and (possibly malicious) intent carries obvious survival value, one worth any number of false positives. Children inherit such basic teleological assumptions and employ them "promiscuously," reports Keleman, applying them to virtually every object in their worlds.[31]

Essentialist thinking, equally advantageous to survival within variable conditions, is also ubiquitous in early childhood. Susan Gelman finds that preschool children "from a variety of cultural contexts expect members of a category to be identical in non-obvious ways," and that, "for some categories, children are more nativist than adults."[32] With essentialist and purpose-driven reasoning so deeply engrained in human thinking, it is no surprise that Darwinian theory meets resistance. As Edward Slingerland observes, "we are evolved in such a way as to be incapable, at some level, of believing in evolution."[33]

Additional cognitive factors contribute to our inability to assimilate the truth about issues like climate change. The human species is not well equipped to respond to matters that are so remote in nature. As Graham Parkes reminds us, we have survived because "our ancestors developed effective physical responses to immanent threats of harm," whereas the risks of climate change are "incremental and not directly perceptible by the senses."[34] Such gradual and largely deferred consequences boggle our innate response patterns. From a cognitive psychology standpoint, it is hard to envision a crisis more conducive to paralysis.[35]

Philosophical insight is indispensable to breaking such impasses, but philosophy does not consistently escape our cognitive limits either. David Hume's skepticism with respect to how reliable our insights are into the "two eternities, before and after the present state of things" is well founded.[36] In such instances, as Immanuel Kant demonstrates in his "Antinomies," we are inclined to indulge our cognitive limits even when it defies both reason and understanding to do so.[37] There are, however, philosophers in every age who think their way beyond the confines of common sense and generate more penetrating insights into reality. Unfortunately, says Dewey, "common sense too often has been confused and hampered instead of enlightened and directed by the philosophies proffered it."[38] Given the fact that some articles of common sense now threaten our very survival, we need desperately to generate insights that guide us beyond them—insights to get us "back in gear."

As a series of "experiments in intra-cultural philosophy," of interest here are the "*specific* philosophical relationships" between Dewey's insights and those available in the Chinese tradition. There are good reasons, in fact, to turn to China for assistance in overcoming the anti-scientific biases that plague American culture. While the roots of human resistance to evolution and climate science point toward stubborn cognitive predispositions, there are social, cultural, and historical factors that determine the readiness with which adults in any given society overcome such predispositions and embrace the legitimacy of science. One recent study of the teleological stance in China, for instance, confirms that teleology is a deeply entrenched cognitive bias. It also finds, however, that Chinese respondents, when not cognitively taxed, endorse scientifically unwarranted teleological statements at a significantly lower rate than their Western counterparts—suggesting that, "Chinese culture may attenuate baseline tendencies to be teleological."[39] Research also suggests that the convictions of cultural authorities influence the degree to which adults are able to overcome adolescent biases and accept a more scientific outlook.[40] In the United States, it is not uncommon for political, religious, and cultural authorities to embrace and promulgate anti-scientific views with respect to evolution and climate change. In China, fewer authorities do this.

Such has been the case for well over a century. When Darwinism was first introduced to China there was little controversy over its truth. Indeed, as James Reeve Pusey relates, Darwinism was "the first Western theory that most Chinese intellectuals thought true."[41] As Jerome Grieder writes, "The virtually universal appeal of Darwinism to the younger generation in China just after the turn of the century is one of the more intriguing phenomena of modern Chinese intellectual history."[42] Dewey's most famous Chinese student, Hu Shih (whose pen name *shi* 適 was inspired by the phrase "survival of the fittest"), represents the "wave of enthusiasm" for evolutionary theory that swept through China from the nineteenth century forward. For Hu, as for other Chinese intellectuals, evolution was readily assimilated and "easily linked up with the naturalism of some of the ancient Chinese thinkers."[43] For the Chinese, there was nothing to fear or to deny in Darwinian theory. Even middle-school students in China were reading T. H. Huxley's *Evolution and Ethics* when it came out in translation.[44]

The ongoing, mainstream controversy over the *fact* of evolution in the United States reveals that U.S. cultural authorities sustain significantly different convictions, and that evolution is not so "easily linked up" with philosophical assumptions in North America. This would help to explain the pronounced statistical differences in science denial among adult populations in China and the U.S.—the starkest disparity among major industrialized countries. According to studies in 2011 and 2014, China places in the top three among countries whose citizens identify themselves as "evolutionists"—64 percent. The U.S. comes in second to last in this category—28 percent. China is also at the top of the list among those whose citizens believe that climate change is real and caused by human activity, and that human behavior must now change—94 percent and 91 percent, respectively. The U.S. ranks dead last on both of these questions—54 percent and 57 percent.[45]

Cultural difference may also factor into variations found in essentialist thinking across adult populations in East Asia and elsewhere. Research into essentialist assumptions in Asian populations suggests that there are cross-cultural similarities among children, but a "difference in the level of essentialism among adult participants," implying that culture "[plays] a role in the developmental trajectory" of essentialist thinking in East Asian and Western societies.[46] This is part of a growing body of evidence showing that "far from being universal, essentialist beliefs vary dramatically across cultures."[47] Given such differences in general outlook—on evolution, climate science, and other issues—any philosophical resource that helped to shape East Asian cultures in this respect is one that American culture should assimilate.

This presents Dewey's century-old admonition to the Chinese in a new light. "I am trying to make you aware of the great responsibility for the development of human culture that rests on your shoulders," he explained to Chinese educators in 1919. "[Your] efforts must be directed towards the evolution of a culture which will be the common possession of all humanity." Dewey's hope was for the Chinese to recognize that "out of their heritage they can help the rest of the world be on the alert for crises in human culture, that they can supply some of the things that are lacking in Western culture, and that they can contribute richly and creatively to the development of a new world culture."[48]

Within China's philosophical heritage, the Daoist tradition is especially proficient at identifying and articulating the environmentally embedded, non-purposive, and non-essentialist nature of organic form (xing 形)—features that correspond to how natural science currently knows the world to be. As we will see in future chapters, Daoism goes further and develops prescriptive accounts of human flourishing based on such features—accounts that might lend themselves as substitutes for those based on our lingering pre-Darwinian assumptions. Again, this larger argument can only be established incrementally. In the remainder of this chapter, we will review the salient features of Dewey's philosophy and begin to establish "*specific* philosophical relationships" with the Daoist tradition. These first steps are perhaps the most difficult. Thinking past commonsense presuppositions about organic form and teleology is not an easy intellectual exercise. As a result, what follows will at times be dense and slow going; but it will establish some of the basic philosophical connections between Dewey and Daoism.

Mystery and Form

As William James observed: "All are beggars before the ontological question." Why and whence this world, or *any* world? "Absolute existence is absolute mystery," James writes, "for its relations with the nothing remain unmediated to our understanding."[49] James invites us to imagine shutting ourselves in a dark closet, and to "think of the fact of being there, of one's queer bodily shape in the darkness . . . of one's fantastic character at all . . . not only that *anything* should be, but that *this* very thing should be, is mysterious!"[50]

For James, mystery attaches itself to the very "thisness" (*haecceitas*) of things. Not all thinkers, however, are so taken by this quality. To Aristotle, "*this* very thing" is simply a primary substance and it is completely knowable in principle. The ontological question of "Why?" it exists does not arise for Aristotle. Maintaining that, "there cannot be generation either of everything or in an absolute sense of *anything*," the ontological "Why?" does not arise in his thinking.[51] Anything that exists is generated from something that already exists, and it emerges according to principles that are open to our understanding. The "whatness" (*quidditas*) of a thing, i.e., the formal properties that distinguish it as a member of a species and characterize its orderly operations, is all there is to *know* about any primary substance and such things are fully knowable. The species-forms that enable such understanding inspire deep admiration and aesthetic appreciation in Aristotle.[52] But nature's works participate in no ontological mystery. For Aristotle, the question of "Why?" something exists is properly a question of "What?" and "How?" and these questions are answerable. There is no inherent strangeness to existence for Aristotle. He is unmoved by "the mystery of *fact*."

The *Daodejing* represents a different view. Its opening chapter observes a twofold character in the nature of things: that which is named (*youming* 有名) and that which is unnamed (*wuming* 無名). Alternately, the text allows us to read *ming* as a verb, such that what is here (*you* 有) designates the "mother" of things, whereas nothing (*wu* 無) designates their "beginnings."[53] In determining the names of things that are here (*you*), humans organize things into categories and thus "name" them according to their "whatness." The act of naming is identified in the *Daodejing* with desire (*yu* 欲).

As Aristotle rightly observes: "All humans by nature desire to know."[54] There is nothing inherently wrong with such a desire. As the *Daodejing* says: "Through desire, one observes the boundaries of things." Such observations enable us to mark out distinctions and to navigate the world accordingly. Naming (*ming* 名), however, does not address what James calls the "mystery of *fact*." Naming has its limits, and so too should our desire to name. "In the absence of desire, one observes the mystery of things," the *Daodejing* teaches. When something goes unnamed (*wuming* 無名) it is allowed to stand forth in its "thisness"—not in any functional relation to what is already here but rather foregrounded in its sheer presence before nothing (*wu* 無).

To neglect this feature of the world is to pass over the mysterious existence of things. Aristotle does so by coupling "*this* something" with the categories that render it commensurable with our desire to know. For the *Daodejing*, however, the distinction between a thing so named (*youming* 有名) and that which is unnamed (*wuming* 無名) is nothing more than a function of this desire. Things *are* knowable for the Daoist, but they are not primarily and exhaustively knowable. "Names" are present, but they do not account for the primary, "nameless" quality that prompts existence. As Chapter 1 concludes: "These two spring from the same source and differ *only* in name. This is the murky depth of things. The depth within the depth is the gateway to all mystery."

Like Aristotle, Dewey was curious about living things and committed to inquiry into their natures. Here, we find significant affinity between Dewey and Aristotle. Like the *Daodejing*, however, Dewey was equally sensitive to the ineradicable mystery of existence, and this reflects a significant difference between Dewey and Aristotle. Acknowledging such mystery is a recurrent theme in Dewey's writings and it does important philosophical work. "There is doubtless a great mystery as to why any such thing as being conscious should exist," Dewey observes.[55] "The mystery is that the world is as it is," and it is the "mystery that anything which exists is just what it is."[56]

Dewey's appreciation for the "mystery" of things is not generally noted, but it is one of the earliest features of his philosophy, tracing back to his very first writings in 1886.[57] It is also among the most persistent features of his philosophical outlook. In his lost manuscript, Dewey returns to "mystery" in discussing brain functions:

> The mystery that attends the matter is that such things as [organisms] with brain structures exist at all. But this mystery is identical with that of anything at all existing just as it does . . . the *mystery* is that the world is what it is, and that applies to the wing

of a bird, the occurrence of thunder and lightning, the existence of stones that are heavy and gases that are light as well as to the function of the brain.[58]

Such appeals to "mystery" are often associated with a departure from scientific analysis, but for Dewey the opposite is the case. Allowing things to stand forth in their sheer presence (or *you* 有) prior to any functional analysis serves to interrupt certain common sense habits of thought with respect to forms, natures, and ends. As such, mystery is not a barrier but an *invitation* to analysis that is more adequate to contemporary scientific understandings. Aristotle was never mystified by the presence of birds, thunder, stones, or gases because he assumed that each thing had its purpose (*telos*) fixed within a universal scheme, one of a finite number of eternally existing species-forms. "Chance" was tightly circumscribed, and it was not properly the cause (*aitia*) of anything. Aristotle questions those like Empedocles who believe that "parts of animals came to be by chance," and Democritus who believe that "chance is a cause, but that it is inscrutable to human intelligence, as being a divine thing and full of mystery."[59] According to Aristotle, such mystery offers no account that explains "Why?" something is what it is—i.e., "What?" and "How?" For him, appeals to mystery only divert attention from the four accounts that *do* explain things: the material, efficient, formal, and final.[60]

Reintroducing the "mystery" of things serves as a corrective to Aristotle's natural philosophy on multiple levels. First, it reinstates the contingency of form. Like Dewey, we ought to be genuinely mystified to find birds and other organisms as we do, because the world might have been completely different. At the phylogenetic level, we know that organic forms and functions evolved largely by chance and that they have done so without superordinate ends or goals. The results are genuinely incredible and worthy of our astonishment.

But even now, as we behold such forms, we remain prone with Aristotle to mistake their functions for "causes that operate for a purpose."[61] Modern science requires us to move beyond this assumption. Causes do not have purposes. Dewey's thinking here invites another correction. Organic functions do not operate *for* anything (e.g., the heart does not pump blood *in order* to circulate it through the body). Instead, such functions operate in a manner consistent with what Ernst Mayr describes as "programs," or "coded or prearranged information that controls a process (or behavior) leading it toward a given end."[62] As currently understood, programs that are native to an organism are inherited in the DNA of the cell nucleus; programs that are acquired are incorporated through the establishment of pathways in the brain and central nervous system.[63] The result at any juncture is a discursive process the ends of which are displayed *immanently* in the functioning of the organism. From this perspective, the heart is one member of an integral form that achieves, among other things, the circulation of blood. It is not in any primary sense an isolatable organ that operates *in order* to do so. While it can be said that the heart *causes* blood to circulate, this does not reflect the operation of any "final cause" in the standard Greek-medieval sense. Nor does it represent any "formal cause" in that sense. From the standpoint of evolutionary biology, form is not any kind of cause—rather, it is a *result*. Specifically, it is the result of successful responses to selection pressures over time.

Darwinian theory requires us to revise Aristotle in specific ways. Identifying these ways and revising accordingly, however, has proven to be a challenging and controversial assignment. Generally speaking, Western philosophers have sought to revise Aristotle from the side of modernity by reducing final causation to mechanistic explanations based on efficient causation.[64] Such efforts, yet to be decisively achieved, are abetted by arguments that teleology is simply an illusion.[65] Philosophers sensitive to the autonomy of the biological sciences challenge the legitimacy of such eliminativist strategies. As Mark Perlman submits:

> While it is perhaps not so surprising that philosophers would go against common sense in rejecting teleology (indeed some take it as an essential part of philosophy to oppose common sense), it is surprising that analytic philosophers, with their strong focus on science, would reject a notion that is so central to some areas of science, most notably, biology and the engineering sciences.[66]

Aristotle remains indispensable until this matter is resolved. Final causation continues to serve as the last line of defense against the reduction of biology to mechanistic physics. As Marjorie Grene argues, something like the final cause *must* be preserved, for what it indicates is something that "is lacking in the modern concept of adaptation, or better, of the organism as a pure aggregate of adaptive mechanisms."[67]

Ernst Mayr is known as a strident defender of the autonomy of the biological sciences.[68] The extent to which his "programs" render organic form something *other* than an aggregate of matter in motion, however, is debatable. Despite his best efforts, "prearranged information" that "guides a process" still sounds like mechanistic causality to many ears. Mayr indeed intends for his programs to be "consistent with a causal explanation," and thus identifies them as "something material" that exist "prior to the initiation" of a goal-directional process.[69] The program is then "causally responsible" for the nature of the process.[70] But as Menno Hulswit observes, "Mayr fails to explain what he means by 'causal.' [And we] can only interpret him as follows: a program is an efficient cause, which in combination with other efficient causes . . . completely determines the end state of a process of behavior."[71]

Despite this difficulty, Mayr's work lends considerable clarity to the issue. First, he alerts us to the fact that the word "teleological" is very loosely applied in philosophical literature.[72] It continues to be applied indiscriminately to multiple phenomena: those conventionally understood to be either "purposeful or goal-directed."[73] Purposeful and goal-directed, however, are materially different classes. All purposeful activities are goal-directed, but not all goal-directed activities are purposeful. The beating of the heart is goal-directed, in that it functions *directionally* toward the end-state of keeping an organism alive. It does not, however, do so *purposefully*—it does so because it is "programmed" to do so.

Mayr secures this clarification by introducing a distinction between end-driven processes that are properly teleological (i.e., *purposeful*) and those that are simply *goal-directional*, "seemingly or genuinely." Processes that are "seemingly" goal-directional are termed "teleomatic"—covering processes such as water flowing downhill or metal becoming molten. These are "end-directed only in a passive, automatic way, regulated by external forces or conditions." Processes that are "genuinely" goal-directional are termed "teleonomic"—covering processes such as the beating of the heart or hens setting on eggs. These "owe their goal-directedness to the operation of a program," and are thus *genuinely* goal-directional.[74]

Dewey uses similar reasoning in classifying natural "ends" somewhere between automatic "results" and purposeful "aims," but he is keener to avoid the reductionism and dualism that Mayr's distinctions introduce.[75] For Dewey, wind blows sand around the floor and the positions of the grains are changed. "Here is a result, an effect," Dewey explains, "but not an *end*. For there is nothing in the outcome that completes or fulfills what went before it." Consider now the activity of bees. "The results of the bees' actions may be called ends not because they are designed or consciously intended, but because they are true terminations or completions of what has preceded. When the bees gather pollen and make wax and build cells, each step prepares the way for the next." Honeycombs are built, the queen deposits larvae in the cells, and the bees then brood them for hatching. The essential characteristic in such end-driven activity, Dewey observes, is "the significance of the temporal place and order of each element." Properly speaking, such "ends" are also "results," but they are results with the pronounced quality of being consummatory.

The next level of complexity entails "aims," and these are *purposeful* in nature. The beekeeper, for instance, introduces partitioned comb hives with removable trays so that the honey can be harvested for human consumption. Such "aims" are also "ends," in that the activity implies "an orderly and ordered activity, one in which the order consists in the progressive completing of a process." The quality that distinguishes the beekeeper's "aim," however, is "foresight in advance of the end or possible termination."[76] This is what makes her "result" genuinely purposeful. Note that there are no sharp, ontological distinctions that emerge between "aims," "ends," and "results" in Dewey's analysis—all three are present wherever "aims" exist and no one kind of process reduces to another.

Dewey's most sustained attempt to reconstruct organic form accordingly is made in the "Nature, Ends, and Histories" chapter of *Experience and Nature*. Here, Dewey formulates a metaphysical context in which the "ends" of natural forms operate without reduction to either purpose-driven "aims" or purely mechanical "results." In establishing this framework, Dewey first moves to neutralize the "eulogistic" ends of Greek-medieval teleology. Final ends are not, as they were for Aristotle, "*that for the sake of which*" something occurs.[77] Still less are they inherently *good*, as they were for medieval thinkers like Thomas Aquinas—for whom "goodness implies the aspect of an end" and "*God is the last end of man and of all other things*."[78] As Dewey sees it: "A natural end which occurs without the intervention of human art is a terminus, a *de facto* boundary, but it is not entitled to any such honorific status of completions and realizations as classic metaphysics assigned them."[79]

With ends in the honorific sense replaced by such "terminals, arrests, or enclosures," Dewey appeals to the sequential order of the end-driven process as an integrated *unit*. As such, the isolation of any single term, "as if it had an inherent generative force" that supersedes the first and final terms, is an unwarranted postulation. Both mechanistic and teleological reasoning tends to assert one or more terms in the series as the "cause" (either efficient or final) of some segment of the sequence. "But in fact," Dewey writes, "causality is another name for the sequential order itself; and since this is the order of a history having a beginning and end, there is nothing more absurd than setting causality over against either initiation or finality."[80] Since sequential order presents itself as a "whole" in the first instance, efficient and final causal analyses amount to second order descriptions of discursive units taken up through human intelligence as select orders of connections.

Dewey now proceeds to reconsider both "final ends" and "efficient causes" within this reconstructed framework, wherein organic form represents not an event *causally* end-driven but simply the "order of a history." The problem with traditional teleological and mechanistic views is that each one "[isolates] an event from the history in which it belongs and in which has its character." Re-envisioning sequential orders as *units* with specifiable *histories* corrects this error and renders the natural world a scene of "temporal episodes," thus allowing new conceptions of end and mechanism to emerge. As Dewey explains: "It enables thought to apprehend causal mechanisms and temporal finalities as phases of the same natural processes, instead of as competitors where the gain of one is the loss of the other."[81] Dewey's reconstructed framework meets the requirements of physical science by affirming the instrumentality of organic orders as mechanical sequences that are capable of redirection for the purposes of control. This traces the connection of changes in natural sequences with an eye toward intervention in the series. It also serves the traditional taxonomic function of Aristotelian teleology by allowing for the definition of organic forms with respect to their characteristic orders as historical sequences with consummatory ends. This distinguishes forms with respect to their functional operations as wholes. These two accounts are rendered compatible and neither is reducible to the other.[82]

Dewey's theory relies on the abandonment of the old, honorific conception of final ends. In replacing this conception with the more neutral notion of ends as "terminations, arrests, or enclosures," Dewey renders organic form a unit of organization that exhibits nothing but sequential order. Since "all directional order resides in the sequential order," there is no *causal* role for final ends to play.[83] This does not mean that there are no directional orders in nature. Organic sequences *are* directional. Each sequence is marked by the orderly co-adaptation of means toward a single result. For living organisms, this result is survival—continued *growth*. Organisms that are here (*you* 有) achieve this particular outcome in some determinate way. With respect to organic forms, their endurance is "a function, a consequence, of changes in the relations [that such forms] sustain to one another, not an antecedent principle." In other words, structural endurance is not *caused* by anything within the form. As we will see in chapter 3, it is the continuity (*yi* 一) of the world system that makes endurance its outcome.[84] As a scene of enduring structures and forms, nature does not produce "ends" that magically activate their own antecedents. That would be backwards causation. Instead, nature produces stable directional orders that actively move toward their own consummations (*cheng* 成). For living organisms, such consummations are measured as *growth*. What are mistaken for final causes in nature are the "qualities" (or *de* 德) of these directional sequences.

To rediscover the "mystery" of things is to appreciate such qualities. "We are given to forgetting, with our insistence on causality, that things exist as just what they qualitatively are," Dewey writes.[85] Again, to focus on the "thisness" of organic form redirects analysis away from traditional teleological thinking. Dewey explains:

> In the old dispute as to whether a stag runs because he has long and slender legs, or has the legs in order that he may run, both parties overlook the natural descriptive statement; namely that it is of the nature of what goes on in the world that the stag has long legs and that having them he runs . . . [The] wonder and mystery do not seem to be other than the wonder and mystery that there should be such a thing as nature, as existential events, at all, and that in being they should be what they are. The wonder should be transferred to the whole course of things.[86]

The teleological puzzle of the stag's legs—are they the *means* for running or is running the *end* for which they exist—overlooks the sheer "thisness" of running stags. *Running stags.* Good heavens, "*Why?*" The sheer presence of running stags is something that is too astonishing to provoke analysis in the first instance. It is a blinding miracle that such a population exists, and our first reaction should be "*Wow,*" "*Oh,*" or "*How beautiful.*"

Such reactions apprehend organic form (*xing* 形) prior to any reasoning about its essential nature or purpose (*telos*). As such, they are examples of what Dewey calls "qualitative thought." "'How beautiful,'" he explains, "symbolizes neither a state of feeling nor the supervening of an external essence upon a state of existence but marks the realized appreciation of a pervading quality that is now translated into a system of definite and coherent terms." Confusion and incoherence, by contrast, "are always marks of lack of control by a single pervasive quality." Apprehended in qualitative thought, running stags present neither confusion nor incoherence with respect to how running relates to their legs. *Stags run.* Period. Apprehending *that*, without further analysis, points us directly to the status of "form" in Dewey's philosophy. "Form is not one isolated element among others," he explains, "but is an arrangement or pattern of elements." Elements function within wholes, while "the quality of the whole permeates, affects, and controls every detail."[87]

With respect to stags and other living organisms, "quality" expresses their *organization*. Here, "organization" is to be understood as an active verb. As organisms evolve, they *organize* themselves. In developing *organs*, they become *organized*. "Organization is a fact," Dewey observes, "though it is not an original organizing force."[88] As Sing-nan Fen suggests, organic wholeness is something that is "built up" over time, such that "the word 'whole' stands for the sequentiality, the consistency, and the continuity—in one word, the *organization* of [actions]."[89] In the case of living things, it is not their organizations that become organized; rather, it is their *life-activities* that become organized. "Quality," for Dewey, is an immediate feature of the organized *result* of such life-activities—not to be confused with the discursive order of the resulting organization. Organization as *order* registers sequentially as a series of operations open to causal analysis. Organization as *quality* registers all at once.[90]

Consider again the organization of stags. *Stags will eat grass or acorns that are masticated using strong molars against a hard plate at the roof of their mouths. They have no upper teeth. As herbivores, they must chew their food long enough to release adequate amounts of cellulose for digestion. As ruminants, their digestion occurs in a four-chambered stomach. Partially chewed food is swallowed into one chamber, and later regurgitated and re-chewed in preparation for the next chamber. This enables them to utilize bacterial agents in digestion and to store large quantities of nourishment quickly, thus avoiding long periods with their heads down.* Thus might begin one description of the stag's life-activities in sequential "order." This organization also registers immediately as a pervasive "quality"—*Wow!* How could one not be amazed that such creatures are here (*you* 有)? As Walt Whitman knew, even a field mouse is "miracle enough to stagger sextillions of infidels."[91] Familiarity alone, or simple indifference, blinds us to this fact.

This brings into focus one of the central, but more elusive tenets in Dewey's philosophy—one that Thomas M. Alexander calls the "thread through the labyrinth."[92] In *Experience and Nature*, Dewey refers to this feature as the "denotative method." What it entails is that empirical philosophy always uses the "refined, secondary" elements of analysis "as a path pointing and leading back to something in primary experience"[93]—i.e., something with the quality of "thisness." Dewey first outlines this method in his 1905 article, "The Postulate of Immediate Empiricism." Here, he explains that things "*are* what they are experienced *as.*" The stag is experienced *as* a unified whole—as *that*. Subsequent analysis is then *about* this pre-theoretical quale that registers first in qualitative thought. "There are two little words," Dewey explains, "through explication of which the empiricist's position may be brought out—'*as*' and '*that*.'" By these little words, Dewey writes, "I want to indicate the absolute, final, irreducible, and inexpugnable concrete *quale* which everything experienced not so much *has* as *is*." Experience, Dewey says, "is always of *thats*."[94] In its immediate presence (*you* 有), the stag is not an object that is "known" (*zhi* 知) through discursive reasoning about its organization. It is simply *that*. The denotative method sets out by first "finding and pointing to [such] things in the concrete contexts in which they present themselves." Subsequent inquiry, Dewey explains, "can review the starting point when it is found necessary."[95] Otherwise, things simply *are* what they are experienced *as*. Non-empirical philosophies routinely overwrite qualitative thought by generating *ex post facto* analyses that presume to "know" things through categories and relations not operative in the first instance.[96]

It is important to recognize at this juncture that apprehending "this-ness" in its qualitative dimension does not thwart or detract from scientific-quantitative analysis. Coming to know "How" things occur and "What" their organization entails still involves measuring forms quantitatively, as stable directional orders alongside other natural occurrences. Procedurally, the mysterious "thisness" of things does not block this line of inquiry. As Dewey explains: "Under exactly what conditions does organization occur, and just what are its various modes and their consequences? We may not be able to answer these questions satisfactorily; but the difficulties are not those of a philosophical mystery, but such as attend any inquiry into highly complex affairs."[97] In order to engage in such inquiries, scientific-quantitative procedures are designed. Qualitative thought does nothing to conflict with such procedures. In fact, such thinking naturally accompanies them. Scientific-quantitative thinking, according to Dewey, "never gets away from qualitative existence," nor does it need to.[98]

Dewey understood that this was a debatable assertion. Among the aims of his 1938 work, *Logic: A Theory of Inquiry* was to better articulate the continuity between qualitative thought and scientific-quantitative analysis. At the time, Dewey was carefully observing Myrtle McGraw's on-going experiments in psychology and neuroanatomy at Columbia University.[99] He wished to observe scientific-quantitative procedures in person as he completed what were "the hardest [chapters] in the whole book," those on mathematical and quantitative judgment. Dewey was also receiving extensive feedback from Ernest Nagel, who carefully read and responded to drafts of these chapters.[100] Dewey did everything he could, in other words, to get his account right.

The resulting treatment centers on the subordination of the act of quantitative measurement to that of comparison—or at least, a recognition of the "equipollence of comparison and measurement." As we saw in chapter 1, "comparison" for Dewey is an act that is always undertaken in some "situation," for some purpose, and with the help of some *tertium quid*. As such, "comparison obviously involves selection-rejection, for objects and events cannot be compared *in toto*."[101] Subject matter for comparison must be converted into "parts," and such parts belong to "wholes." As Dewey points out, in certain respects whole-part thinking is "entirely qualitative." As he writes: "To be a whole is to be complete, finished; to be of a seamless quality throughout. If *parts* are mentioned in connection with such a whole, nothing separable or removable is denoted."[102]

As Dewey had already postulated, the presence of some "dominant and pervasive quality, is the background, the point of departure, and the regulative principle of all thinking."[103] This principle informs thinking in its scientific-quantitative mode as a matter of course. Genetically speaking, the act of taking measurement thus "assumes a qualitative form" from the outset. Accordingly, judgments such as "long/short," "scanty/much," represent measurements in their primary form. Such judgments are not made absolutely or in some kind of vacuum; rather, they are made in specific *comparative situations* with respect to some *means-end relation*.[104]

As Zhang Xianglong suggests, the bamboo rod is "long" or "short" compared to some other rods for the purpose of reaching dates on a tree. Dewey intends to begin with such qualitative assessments and to naturalize the development of quantitative measurement from there.[105] With the invention of enumerated homogenous units, he notes, "the relatively qualitative *long* and *short* are refined into terms of *so* long or *so* short." Quantitative measurements thus enable "unlike qualitative things [such as the rod and the tree] to be indirectly compared with respect to one another." Such procedures, in themselves, do not constitute a radical break from qualitative thought. As Dewey explains: "The negation of quality or indifference to it which is sometimes ascribed to quantity and number (and a ground made for their disparagement) is not final but, on the contrary, *positive* means for controlled construction of new objects and institutions of new qualities."[106]

Western intellectual and cultural history is burdened by an unusually sharp dualism between "Qualitative/Quantitative" modes of thought.[107] Rather than explore this history, we focus here on the logic of Dewey's reconstruction of their relation. His reconstruction involves two main premises. First, the qualitative dimensions of experience are practically bottomless. For Dewey, as Thomas C. Dalton explains, "the possible range that phenomena may vary qualitatively extends beyond and is never fully exhausted by or reduced to deductive propositions based on discrete quantitative measurements."[108] Second, the simple act of enumeration, i.e., adding "1" to *n*, like any single operation (Dewey uses chopping wood as an example), is "indefinitely recurrent or non-terminating," meaning that it can be done *over* and *over* again until it is intercepted by an opposing operation or set of conditions.[109] Together, these two premises imply the following: Since no one is going to attend to *every* quality, and no one is going to count to *infinity*, the indeterminate range of qualities and the indefinite measurement of quantities become settled into units that are *ipso facto* limited.

The question is this: *what provides the limit?* For Dewey, the answer is some "situation" that is populated with qualitative wholes/parts that are being compared or measured for some particular purpose. Scientific-quantitative methods and mathematical operations are indeed generic enough to determine a wide range of human purposes in all kinds of "situations"—but they have no function *outside* of such "situations."

In subordinating "Qualitative/Quantitative" distinctions to the "situation," Dewey manages to open up a middle ground between two extreme Western approaches that stem from a shared confusion: these being the "romantic" approach that resists the scientific, and the "positivistic" approach that asserts its supremacy. As Dewey says, there are those who "deplore the reduction by the scientist of all materials to numerical terms on the ground that it seems to [destroy] value which is qualitative." Meanwhile, there are those who "insist that every subject-matter must be reduced to numerical terms." As Dewey sees it, "both are guilty of the same logical error." Each party fails to recognize that quantified propositions have an instrumental reference. The fact that Zhang Xianglong's bamboo rod is 90 inches long means that it is good for getting dates. As such, "propositions about magnitude are based upon an *underlying* pervasive quality, and are indifferent only to differences *within* this basic quality." It does not matter, for instance, where his bamboo rod falls within the 495–570 nanometers that make it green. The "situation" as a whole determines its own subordinate wholes-and-parts and sets limits with respect to what qualities matter and which measurements are relevant. The qualitative whole sets "the limits or 'ends' from which and to which propositions are means," Dewey writes. As such, "they provide the criteria by which the relevancy and force of propositions of measurement, qualitative and quantitative, are measured."[110]

Such understandings are important as we establish connections with early Chinese thought, particularly as these relate to science and logic. More "romantic" readings of Chinese thought tend to celebrate its "aesthetic" or "intuitive" dimensions. More "positivistic" assessments (in response, perhaps, to the romantic readings) tend to regard the Chinese tradition as lacking in scientific rigor. There are long standing confusions involved in this dualistic approach, which manifest themselves in Northrop's *The Meeting of East and West*. Helping to set the record straight, Joseph Needham is responsible for sweeping away the nineteenth-century illusion that Chinese culture is somehow congenitally deficient or backwards technologically. He is also responsible, however, for raising the question of why modern scientific advances stalled in China just as they began to accelerate in the West—the so-called "Needham Question."[111] Addressing this question goes beyond the scope of the present discussion (we will return to it in chapter 4 of volume two). For present purposes, it is important to note that early Chinese sciences, as Nathan Sivin argues, were specific rather than unified, and quantitative-and-qualitative in nature. Scientific inquiry, for the Chinese thinker, "was an activity in which the rational operations of the intellect were not sharply disconnected from what we would call intuition, imagination, illumination, ecstasy, aesthetic perception, ethical commitment, or sensuous experience."[112] Dewey would say that the Chinese approach is the more balanced one, while those reliant on sharp "Quantitative/Qualitative" distinctions create unnecessary rifts in culture.

It is prudent at this juncture to say little more about ancient Chinese sciences, especially as they relate to early Daoist thinking. As Lisa Raphals reports, "New research and the evidence of recently excavated texts are transforming our understanding of the scientific aspects of Daoist thought."[113] While findings are not yet conclusive, early indications are that scientific-quantitative inquiries in ancient China were more sophisticated than we originally thought. As recently as 2014, it was announced that the oldest known decimal-based calculator in the world (dating to 310 BCE) was unearthed in China.[114] Who knows what might be discovered next?

The larger point, gleaned from Dewey, is that there is nothing that prevents scientific-quantitative inquiries from thriving alongside a tradition like Daoism, one that is keenly aware of the "mysterious" nature of things. For while scientific-quantitative inquiry into the *occurrence* of a thing does not concern itself with such mysteries, Dewey reminds us that: "We forget in explaining its occurrence that it is only the *occurrence* that is explained, not the thing itself. We forget that in explaining the occurrence we are compelled to fall back on other individual things that have just the unique qualities they do have. Go as far back as we please in accounting for present conditions and we still come upon the mystery of things being just what they are."[115]

We may never be able to reconstruct perfectly how ancient thinkers arrived at their ideas about the natural world, nor fathom how they structured their scientific-quantitative inquiries. What we do know, however, is that some of the results in early China stand up quite well alongside what the natural sciences currently tell us. This is particularly true with respect to the nature of organic form. Keeping "qualitative thought" in mind, we turn now to establish "*specific* philosophical relationships" with Daoist theories of form (*xing* 形). Such experiments enable us to better appreciate how the latter might serve in getting our own thinking "back in gear."

De 德 and Directional Order

One of the most striking features about the *Daodejing* is how boldly it challenges teleological common sense. The text repeatedly states that purposes do not direct forms and functions in their natural state. One of the most often used phrases is *weierbushi* 為而不恃: "acting without presumption (with respect to outcome or aim)."[116] The phrase is employed both as a description of natural occurrences and a prescription for optimal human behavior. With respect to the former, the *dao* 道 of nature is said always to act without doing anything *for the sake* of something (*daochangwuwei* 道常無為).[117] This is consistent with the contemporary idea that organic forms and functions are neither the products of superordinate purposes nor driven by final causes. As a result, the *Daodejing* provides a natural philosophy significantly different from those most prominent in the Judeo-Christian and Greek-medieval traditions. In this respect, the *Daodejing* is more contemporary in its philosophical implications. Its account of organic nature is subtly drawn, but it continues to provide remarkably keen insights into the nature, origin, and behavior of living things.

Chapter 51 is important in this respect, providing what can be regarded as a direct account of organic form (*xing* 形). The chapter reads:

> *Dao* 道 produces them. *De* 德 rears them. Other things shape (*xing* 形) them. The propensity of circumstances (*shi* 勢) matures them. Therefore, the myriad beings cannot do other than to honor *dao* and prioritize *de*. Honoring *dao* and prioritizing *de* are not commands (*ming* 命) but rather normal (*chang* 常) for things just as they are (*ziran* 自然). Hence, *dao* produces them, and *de* rears them: grows them, nurtures them, structures them, matures them, nourishes them, and protects them.[118] Things are generated but are not beholden (*buyou* 不有). They act but without presumption (*bushi* 不恃). They grow but without being directed by any outside force (*buzai* 不宰). This is what is referred to as their mysterious *de*.

According to this chapter, organisms emerge within the course (*dao*) of nature and exhibit an obscure momentum or power (*de*) that lends integrity to their development. *De* would seem then to be a good candidate for what Aristotle describes as a final cause: that *for the sake* of which a mature, functioning organism results. Chapter 51, however, strongly resists the notion that such a "power" transcends the directional order itself. An organism, being just what it is, prioritizes (*gui* 貴) a specific developmental sequence. That is all. The only *causal* force involved is the propensity of circumstances (*shi*)—and as we shall see, this notion differs significantly from final causality.

Let us try to better understand *de* 德.[119] One way to understand the meaning of this term in the present context is to explore its relationship to *dao* 道. The prioritization of *de* is coupled with the honoring of *dao*, each being an expression of living things in their natural, unforced state. Chapter 21 describes the relation between *de* and *dao* in the following manner:

The greatest expression of *de* proceeds directly from *dao*. When *dao* does something, it is elusive and intangible. So intangible! So elusive! In the midst of it appears some vague outline (*xiang* 象). So elusive! So intangible! In the midst of it appears some living creature (*wu* 物). So profound! So obscure! In the midst of it appears some life force (*jing* 精). This life force is utterly genuine. In the midst of it appears something authentic (*xin* 信). From the ancient past to the present moment, its name has never been dispensed with. Through it, the source of multitudes can be observed. Through what do we recognize the manifestation of this source of multitudes? Through this (*yici* 以此).

Dewey's thought can help us make sense of this account and to conceptually connect it to Chapter 51. Dewey suggests that each organic form has a twofold nature. First, each form is an organization of life activities exhibiting a stable directional order. Second, each form is an expression of qualitative wholeness standing forth in its own mysterious presence. With respect to the first feature, Chapter 51 teaches that *de* 德 is what rears (*xu* 畜) a living thing. Here, *de* represents the directional order of an organic form: that which nourishes it, structures it, matures it, and so on. In this context, one might say that *de* amounts to the particular *dao* 道 of an organic form. Chapter 51 also teaches, however, that there is a broader *dao* of nature that produces (*sheng* 生) each organic form. This is the *dao* that in Chapter 21 is described as the source of multitudes. How, then, do we come to recognize this broader, more elusive *dao*? We do so through apprehending organic form *not only* as a stable directional order, but also as an integral whole mysteriously present as *just what it is*—i.e., as one distinct unit of possibility realized (*deyi* 得一). What Dewey refers to as "quality" is akin to what *de* signifies when it is considered in the context of this broader, more elusive *dao*.

The remarkable thing about *de* 德 is that it manages to bridge Dewey's twofold description of organic form. Dewey did not intend any sharp bifurcation between directional orders and their mysterious qualities—and in the *Daodejing*, there is no such bifurcation. That which can be named (*youming* 有名) and that which is unnamed (*wuming* 無名) spring together from the same murky source. *De* emerges as a complex notion in Chinese thought because it proceeds directly from this source, reflecting both the *power* of a directional order as well as the mysterious *allure* of its immediate presence (*you* 有). This dual feature exemplifies a central point—namely, that if mystery is once again to exist alongside order, then "chance" must be reinstated at the ontological level. Stable directional orders are indeed what the broader *dao* 道 of nature produces; but the *specific* orders that emerge are the results of novelty in the world system. Such novelty is what ultimately lends *de* its mysterious quality. Again, it is a sheer "mystery of *fact*" that any particular living thing exists at all. Shaped by supporting conditions, the *Daodejing* describes such forms as emerging in a sort of embryonic outline, appearing as living creatures, and then maturing as life forces (*jing* 精) standing forth in utter self-possession and authenticity.

This should not be difficult to appreciate. Picture the Asian elephant (*Elephas maximus*), the red-eyed tree frog (*Agalychnis callidryas*), or even the domestic goat (*Capra aegagrus hircus*). What modern science tells us about these forms does not diminish our astonishment in the slightest. Such forms, as Dewey reminds us, are *events* with unrepeatable histories. Thus understood, they are not themselves causes but rather the *results* of those histories. Each animal would be something different—or *nothing at all*—were conditions even slightly altered. The near-miracle status that animal forms appear exactly as we find them is rudimentary knowledge in evolutionary biology. The chances that any organism is here (*you* 有) rather than not here (*wu* 無) is *vanishingly small*—a likelihood that, as Daniel C. Dennett makes clear, is astronomically remote.[120] As Richard Dawkins reminds us: "Every animal owes its existence to an astonishing list of contingencies that might not have happened."[121]

Figure 2.1. John Dewey with goat in 1946. JHU Sheridan Libraries/Gado/Getty Images.

If we are to properly update our understanding of organic forms as exceedingly rare, unrepeatable events, we must clarify what is meant by an "event." For Dewey, the "indispensable character of anything which may be termed an event" is the "qualitative variation of parts with respect to the whole which requires duration in which to display itself."[122] In this sense, the stag with its multi-stage digestive process is an *event*—a variety of parts dynamically organized through time with respect to a specific result. Dewey calls such an organization dynamic because "it takes time to complete it."[123] Such discursive events, however, are simultaneously *wholes* with a "phase of brute and unconditioned 'isness,' of being just what they irreducibly are."[124] Apprehended in qualitative thought, the stag has a pervading "thisness" that registers immediately—meaning that, "the *form* of the whole [is] present in every member [of the organization]."[125] In this respect, the organization of the stag's digestive system is a single, unified result in the vast history of ruminant digestion in mammals. As such, "[it] is final; it is at once initial and terminal; just what it is as it exists." In each such result, Dewey says, there is "something obdurate, self-sufficient, wholly immediate, neither a relation nor an element in a relational whole, but terminal and exclusive."[126]

In speaking of the nature of events, Dewey makes important qualifications as needed. One such qualification is outlined in his 1931 essay, "Context and Thought." Questioning the enthusiasm with which some of his contemporaries were reducing all modes of existence to "events," Dewey offers the following caution:

> That all existences are *also* events I do not doubt. For they are qualified by temporal transition. But that existences as such are *only* events strikes me as a proposition that can be maintained in no way except by a wholesale ignoring of context. For, in the first place, every occurrence is a *con*currence. An event is not a self-enclosed, self-executing affair—or it is not save by arbitrary definition. One may easily slip down a hill, but the slipping is not a self-contained entity . . . The actual slide depends upon an interaction of several things, very many in an adequate account. Yet, unless I am mistaken in my interpretation, there is evidence that some contemporary writers tend to treat every existence as if to *be* an existence were to be a slide or a slip . . . [By] implying that the context of an event is simply other events is suspiciously like assuming that by putting enough slides together you can make a hill.[127]

Dewey's critique is in line with his insistence on the role of "situation" in anything that amounts to experience. Organic form, from an evolutionary perspective, is the result of *experience*. As such, it cannot be reduced to any number of "events" without reference to the situations in which such events have taken place. It goes without saying that the digestive system of the stag did not emerge in a vacuum. It needs to be stressed, however, that any confluence of circumstances that shaped such a form (*xing* 形) is one that exhibited structured relations *already*. This is another reason to resist the suggestion that we ought to reduce the tertiary element that "situations" hold in place to the events being held together. Again, the cosmological implications of this (treated in terms of "Thirdness") will be taken up in the next chapter.

In anticipation of that discussion, it is worth recalling briefly the larger context of life on our planet. Our current understanding is that the universe began 13.8 billion years ago. Before that there was absolutely nothing—a silent, empty void. The universe initially appeared as a tiny dot that contained everything in a state of potential. That dot burst open, creating space and time while expanding at incredible speeds. Within the first second, energies were configured into two distinct forces: electromagnetism and gravity. Still within the first second, energies congealed to form the elementary particles of matter. After about 380,000 years of swirling, simple atoms of hydrogen and helium emerged from the soup of primary particles. Clouds formed. Density increased. After 200 million years, stars appeared. The universe needed another 8 or 9 billion years of cooling before solar systems began to form. Another billion years after that, the first single-celled organisms appeared on Earth.[128] About 600 to 800 million years ago, these organisms evolved into multi-celled organisms. In time, fungi, plants, fish, amphibians, reptiles, and dinosaurs evolved. Then, 65 million years ago, an asteroid struck the Yucatan peninsula and set in motion a series of events that destroyed the dinosaurs and many other life forms. Our mammalian ancestors flourished in the niches created by these radically altered conditions. *Homo sapiens* came onto the scene about 200,000 years ago. As large-brained language users, we were able to out-smart our terrestrial adversaries and create complex civilizations that have flourished for nearly 10,000 years. Throughout this entire process, the elementary forces of matter and energy have remained constant.

Let this suffice for context. In general orientation, early Chinese thinkers fare quite well alongside the current understanding of our origins. In fact, we are only now in possession of one of the most interesting documents pertaining to early Chinese views on the matter. The recently recovered *Hengxian* 恆先 manuscript recounts the origin of the universe, the rise of organic life, and the development of human institutions in a remarkably illuminating manner.[129] The language of this document mirrors Chapter 16 of the *Daodejing*, even using the same obscure phrase to refer to "organic growth" (*yunyun* 芸芸). The title of the work, *Hengxian*, means something like "Constancy as the Antecedent." It begins with a description of "constancy" as the original state of the universe—an utter stillness and emptiness wherein nothing existed. Space arises, and then in rapid succession energy (*qi* 氣), matter, and the passage of time. After this burst of activity, things remained "muddled and murky" for some interval. The text is careful to explain that, over the course of this process, energy (*qi*) was not created but rather spontaneously being generated (*zisheng* 自生). In the midst of such emergence, over an unspecified span of time, a multitude of forms took shape.[130]

With respect to how things arose in general, the *Hengxian* describes emergence and proliferation in a thoroughly concurrent manner: "differentiation (*yi* 異) gave rise to [*more*] differentiation, returning [to a course] (*gui* 歸) gave rise to [*more*] returning, departures (*wei* 違) gave rise to divergences (*fei* 非), divergences gave rise to departures, and dependence (*yi* 依) gave rise to [*more*] dependence." With respect to organic form specifically the text could not be more direct: "organic growth was mutually engendering" (*yunyunxiangsheng* 芸芸相生). Such growth proceeded to fill up every available niche in "Heaven and Earth."[131]

As for "*Why?*" organic life emerged, the *Hengxian* does not reveal any primordial secret. It does, however, give us something to think about. It states the following: "That things emerge together but differ in how they are engendered is because things are engendered according to what they desire (*yu* 欲)."[132] Erica Fox Brindley alerts us to the unusual nature of this statement. The term *yu* is rarely used in this manner, and its meaning is quite unclear. As Brindley suggests, it may just be a metaphorical usage of the term and nothing remarkable. She encourages us, however, to entertain the term literally and to consider its implications. As Brindley reports, other early connotations of *yu* encompass "not just the affective states of desiring, yearning, and wanting, but also conditions of needing and feeling at ease, at rest, at peace (*an* 安)."[133] Thus, in the sense of having to satisfy the "designated needs, parameters, and potentials" of a thing, Brindley submits that *yu* might be envisioned as something like a genetic code. *Yu* would then be the active *need* for an organism to satisfy its own directional order.

This would make perfect sense to Dewey. Dewey identifies need as "the most obvious difference between living and non-living things."[134] He also identifies need with the advent of serial order in organic form. For living things, he explains: "There are needs (in the sense of existential tensions); these needs can be satisfied only through institution of a changed objective state of affairs. Effectuation of this close, or consummatory state, demands an ordered series of operations so adapted *to one another* that they are co-adapted to arriving at the final close."[135] In their entireties such processes, both existentially and modally, express a "need" (*yu* 欲).

Dewey uses plant life as an example. A plant needs water, carbon dioxide, to bear seeds, etc. This state of "need" is neither an affective psychic state *within* the plant nor a preliminary state that gives way to a state of *not* needing such things. Thus, need denotes the "concrete state of events" for the plant. The history of this need is situated within an environment, such that the plant "acts differently upon the environment and is exposed to different influences from it" depending on its own stage of development. Rather than saying that "need" somehow operates *within* the plant, it would be more accurate to say that the plant *is* the need being expressed within its environment. *The plant is a series of operations co-adapted in satisfying the need.* "The reality," Dewey submits, is "the growth-process itself." Each "need" expresses itself *completely* through its serial operations *as a whole*. To mentally isolate one operation and present it as occurring "for the sake" (*wei* 為) of a need that operates as a superordinate *cause* of the whole series amounts to what Dewey calls a "silly reduplication." As he observes: "The real existence is the history in its entirety, the history as just what it is. The operations of splitting it up into two parts and then having to unite them again by appeal to causative power are equally arbitrary and gratuitous."[136]

"Need" thus provides a path around teleological common sense. Just as "desire" (*yu* 欲) can encompass "rest" (*an* 安), organic need encompasses its own satisfaction in being met. As Dewey suggests, organic activity is best understood as a compound notion: "need-demand-satisfaction," all at the same time.[137] Simply by *existing*, organisms are in the modal state of *needs being met*. As long as something continues to live, existence is "attained" (*de* 得) in a directional order with its own inherent quality and momentum (*de* 德).[138] To say that this directional order exists *for the sake* of its own attainment is a meaningless statement, while to suggest that it is *caused* by its own attainment is simply incoherent. Such thinking does little to reveal what organic forms (*xing* 形) are and how they operate.

Habit and *Dao* 道-Activity

Having now established some "*specific* philosophical relationships" between Dewey's notion of the organism and the Chinese conception of organic form (*xing* 形), the next step is to consider *dao* 道-activity alongside Dewey's teachings on "habit." For Dewey, understanding "habit" is the key to overcoming the "Organism/Environment" dualism that persists in Western thinking. His analysis results in a view that not only concurs with evolutionary biology, but also aligns with premises that several early Chinese thinkers regarded as true: *viz.*, that organic form (*xing*) is environmentally embedded, that it is not teleologically-driven, and that it is not static in nature.

The publication of Dewey's 1896 article, "The Reflex Arc Concept in Psychology" was a watershed moment in his career. This article prefigures themes that would guide his thinking for the rest of his life. The article's main objective is to overcome the dualism in the standard, "Stimulus/Response" account of organic behavior. Dewey aims to replace the "Cause/Effect" notion of the reflex arc (i.e., stimulus: *cause*, response: *effect*) with a more holistic notion of an organic *circuit* in which the organism is continually reconstructing its relationship with its environment. In the standard "Stimulus/Response" account, "stimulus" is regarded as an *external* pressure coming from the environment, whereas "response" is an *internal* reaction from the organism. Therein lies the dualism. Dewey maintains instead that both stimulus and response are "always inside a coordination and have their significance purely from the part played in maintaining or reconstructing the coordination." Such coordinations are not a "series of jerks," whereby the environment does one thing and then the organism does another. Rather, stimulus-*and*-response represents "one uninterrupted continuous redistribution" of energies [or *qi* 氣], "a change in the system of tensions" in a single unbroken context [or *yi* 一].[139]

Among other breakthroughs, this article anticipates the formulation of directional order as Dewey's replacement for conventional teleology. The move is preliminary, but it is clearly evident. In the "Reflex Arc" essay, Dewey is not denying that "stimulus" and "response" are useable categories. He wants only to clarify their actual status in relation to the scope of their use. Stimulus and response, Dewey writes, "are not distinctions of *existence*, but teleological distinctions, that is, distinctions of function, or part played, with reference to reaching or maintaining an end." For instance, in observing a hen setting upon contact with her eggs, it is natural for us to identify one element of this behavior as "stimulus" and another as "response." This is because we *already* identify the behavior of the hen as driven by a teleological purpose (*telos*). Dewey explains:

> It is only when we regard the sequence of acts *as if* they were adapted to reach some end that it occurs to us to speak of one as stimulus and the other as response. Otherwise, we look at them as a *mere* series . . . [We can say] that it is only the assumed common reference to an inclusive end which marks either member off as stimulus or response, that apart from that reference we have only antecedent and consequent; in other words, the distinction is one of interpretation.

Dewey hastens to add that, "I am not raising the question as to how far this teleology is real," adding that, "my point holds equally well" in either case.[140] That is true. He has, however, now set the stage for the eradication of final cause (*telos*) as conventionally understood and for its replacement with something other than mechanistic causality.

In the case of the setting hen, "there is simply a continuously ordered sequence of acts, all adapted to themselves and in the order of their sequence, to reach a certain objective, end, the reproduction of the species, the preservation of life, [etc.]." This sounds like conventional teleology, but Dewey's reasoning is subtler. In identifying stimulus-and-response in the setting of the hen, we forget that we are not indexing separate moments, but rather a *single continuous circuit* in which an accomplished adaptation or "organization" has already been attained (*de* 得). There is a discrepancy, then, between our identifications and what they actually represent. As Dewey explains: "The end has got thoroughly *organized into* the means. In calling one stimulus, another response we mean nothing more than that an orderly sequence of acts is taking place. The same sort of statement might be made equally well with reference to the succession of changes in a plant, so far as these are considered with reference to their adaptation to, say, producing seed."[141]

Keep in mind that the signature contribution of the "Reflex Arc" essay is that it dissolves the "Organism/Environment" dualism. In *Democracy and Education*, Dewey's position receives clearer treatment. "Environment," he writes, denotes not merely the surroundings of an organism, but "the specific *continuity* of the surroundings with [the organism's] own active tendencies." Organic functions are thus the historical results of biological organization within specific environments. The jawbone and digestive chambers of the stag, for instance, are "what they are *because* of the material with which their activity is engaged." They are "more truly ways in which the environment enters into experience and functions there than they are independent acts brought to bear upon things." Organism and environment do not represent two separate histories. Instead, organism-and-environment indexes a "single continuous interaction of a great diversity (literally countless in number) of energies."[142] Again, Dewey's insights align closely with evolutionary biology. Today, we understand much better how natural selection operates and how populations undergo the reconstruction of genotypes as adaptations occur within specific environments over generations.

As outlined in chapter 1, one of the central objectives in intra-cultural philosophy is to establish "*specific* philosophical relationships" for explicit purposes. With the aim of recovering Daoist thought as a contemporary resource in natural philosophy, I propose that organic "adaptation" is one key to understanding what Daoist thinkers regard as *dao* 道-activity. Adaptation occurs both in populations and in individuals. Each type of adaptation results in a directional habit, one that is either *native* to an organism or *acquired* in the course of its own lived experience. As for acquired habits, Dewey explains that environments operate steadily to "call out certain acts" in an organism, resulting in "habits [being] formed which function with the same uniformity as the original stimuli." Over time, "there is an adaptation of the stimulus and response to each other." Such results can be regarded in two compatible ways. On the one hand, an established habit is goal-directional in nature: "Habit means an ability to use natural conditions as means to ends. It is an active control of the environment through control of the organs of action." On the other hand, the established habit is spontaneous directional behavior: "Adequate control means that the successive acts are brought into a continuous order; each act not only meets its immediate stimulus but helps the acts which follow."[143]

With respect to our familiar habits, it is difficult to improve upon William James' treatment in the *Psychology*. Each of us develops a "definite routine manner of performing certain daily offices" connected with such things as tying our shoes or brushing our teeth. Such operations are habitual in that each phase takes place "in its appointed order" below the level of consciousness.[144] In such behaviors, an initial stimulus triggers an ordered sequence of acts *as a whole*. The moment one's fingers touch the laces, the operation arrives in its entirety. There is no gap between its phases since they are adapted to one another in the order of their sequence toward the end. The resulting habit becomes a way (or *dao* 道) of tying one's shoes, one that reflects the organization of tendencies built up over time. One might "aim" to tie one's shoes on purpose in order to keep them snug; the activity in its existential performance, however, is *weierbushi* 為而不恃: "done without presumption (with respect to outcome or aim)." It is performed without foresight in advance of an end. Such activity is *dao*-activity.

Dao 道-activity expresses one of the hallmarks of organic life: the formation of *habits*. All organisms form habits—through them, we literally *in*-habit our habitats. The structural difference between population-level adaptations and personal habits does not change the fact that each involves the integration of organism-and-environment and the coordination of stimulus-and-response. Thus, on both the phylogenetic and ontogenetic levels, organic forms exhibit holistic integrity as a matter of course. They are instances in which means-and-end exhibit continuity (*yi* 一). In other words, organic forms (*xing* 形) exhibit instances in which, as Dewey says, the "end has got thoroughly organized into the means."[145]

Such continuity is what distinguishes *dao* 道-activity from more purely mechanical and teleological activities. Here's how. In mechanical activity, there is an *accidental* relationship between means and end. *A breeze blows into the room and grains of sand change position on the floor.* This exhibits a "result"—the sand might have just as easily been moved as a result of children running through the room. In teleological activity, there is an *instrumental* relationship between means and ends. *A broom is taken up and sand is swept toward the center of the room.* This exhibits an "aim"—the broom is taken up with the purpose of producing (*wei* 為) a specific outcome. In *dao*-activity, there is neither an accidental nor an instrumental relation between means-and-end. Rather, there is a *necessary* one. *The stag is startled by a predator and runs away.* That's it. There is no further analysis. Stags are here (*you* 有) and running away is their *dao*.

When the stag runs, its legs perform a function that is directly and necessarily related to their existence. Running is not simply one possible function alongside other mechanical functions that the legs might otherwise perform. Those legs *run*. Are the legs then instrumental to the running, *there* for the sake of running? No. This imputes teleological purpose such that the object of "running" operates as it would for human cognition—i.e., as a separate "aim" in relation to which the legs are instrumental. Stags do not have such aims, and neither do legs. The legs are *there* and they run because over the course of inhabiting a specific environment they have taken on that form (*xing* 形). Such forms are *weierbushi* 為而不恃—"produced without presumption (with respect to outcome or aim)," and operate as such. Dewey regards the consequent phases of such operations not as "results" or "aims" but as *ends*—in the non-eulogistic sense of a "terminal, arrest, or enclosure."[146] In such activity, the end is not a separable force that somehow *drives* its respective organization either causally or purposefully. The end is inseparable from its own *organization*—it is, as Dewey says: "significant not by itself but as the integration of the parts. It has no other existence."[147]

In connection with *dao* 道-activity, Dewey's discussion of habit and adaptation results in a conception of organic form (or *xing* 形) that preserves what is useful in Aristotle's thinking while revising the picture accordingly.[148] The most important revision is in re-thinking the relationship between organism-and-environment. "To see the organism *in* nature," Dewey writes, means for it "to be *in* [nature], not as marbles are in a box but as events are in a history, in a moving, growing, never finished process."[149] As we will see in the next section, this is one of the hallmarks of Chinese natural philosophy. Evolutionary biology requires us to recognize that environments play a constitutive role in determining the ongoing histories, functions, and activities of organisms embedded within them. As Jonathan Lear observes, for Aristotle, "the environment only supplies a backdrop against which an organism acts out the drama of its life. The environment may be benign or hindering, but beyond that it plays no significant role in the development and life of the organism."[150] Aristotle thus offers insufficient resources with which to conceptualize the continuity between organic life and changes in environmental conditions.

Here, it is pressing for us to get our thinking "back in gear." Among the most readily observable effects of global warming (especially here in Maine) is climate tracking. Changes in fish distribution, for instance, are key indicators of rising temperatures in marine environments.[151] The situation is not as simple as Aristotelian-style common sense would suggest. Not all organisms move with the same conditions simultaneously. Transactions on all levels: ecological, genetic, behavioral, and physiological each play complicated roles.[152] As organisms redistribute, predators are separated from prey and parasites lose their hosts. Certain organisms abruptly escape their evolutionary histories and behave unpredictably. The transactions that ensue produce changes in overlapping *circuits* in which organic form is but one phase, meaning that the change is bi-directional (*xiang* 相) in nature.

Suppose, for example, that the life cycle of an herbivore accelerates with the earlier arrival of food plants. Is this event occurring *inside* the organism or *outside* in the environment? Let us assume that genetic variation factors into fitness-related traits such as phenological timing.[153] This transaction now amounts to a segment in a history that is shared by *both* the evolving organism and its environment. If the life cycle of the herbivore fails to adapt to its new conditions, it is deselected and phases out of the history that it shares with its food plants. If it evolves so as to consume the plants earlier in the season, the environment undergoes the change.

That common sense refuses to graduate from its Greek-medieval assumptions is part of what makes it difficult for the complex manifestations of climate change to serve persuasively as "evidence" in the court of public opinion. America, after all, is a nation in which a sitting U.S. Senator once brought a snowball into the Senate chamber as evidence that global warming is a "hoax."[154] Greek-medieval assumptions about the relationship between organism-and-environment are simply wrong, and for philosophers to continue to perpetuate such errors in any form retards civilization. Dewey understood that environments consist of "the sum total of conditions that enter in an active way into the direction of the functions of any living being. Environment, therefore, is not equivalent merely to surrounding physical conditions." Further breaking down this commonsense dualism, Dewey affirmed that organic activity itself is a modification of environmental conditions, such that "the evolution of life, the increase in diversity and interdependence of life functions, means an evolution of new environments just as truly as of new organs."[155] For Dewey, "every overt activity changes, to some extent, the environing conditions which are the occasions and stimuli of further experiences."[156] This occurs at every level of organic life. As Dewey notes:

"Even a clam acts upon the environment and modifies it to some extent. It selects materials for food and for the shell that protects it. It does something to the environment as well as has something done to itself."[157]

Again, it is the shared *history* of organism-and-environment that Dewey is keen on establishing and that Greek-medieval thinking leads us to overlook. Elizabeth Kolbert, reflecting on the threat of mass extinction in our century, summarizes the shortcomings of Greek-medieval thinking in this connection rather succinctly. As she writes: "Aristotle wrote a ten-book *History of Animals* without ever considering the possibility that animals actually had a history."[158] Such errors can no longer underwrite commonsense assumptions about the natural world. We *know* that Dewey and the Chinese are correct in identifying organic form (*xing* 形) with historical, mutual (*xiang* 相) transactions within organism-and-environment circuits.[159] In the effort to reorient imagination and common sense in this general direction, Dewey and Chinese thought offer resources that we cannot afford to ignore.

Granted, it is difficult to adequately reconstruct natural philosophies in early China. Texts do not consistently outline their basic assumptions. Plus, there is no reason to assume that all texts converge on a single "Chinese" understanding of the natural world. Still, the presence of a more dynamic, environmentally embedded view of organic form is plain to see.

Form (*xing* 形) and Environment

One of the most noteworthy features of biotic taxonomies in early China is that they are not morphological in nature. Often they are geographical. For instance, if one wishes to learn the names of plants and trees in ancient China, Confucius suggests that one read the *Songs* (*Shijing* 詩經).[160] This collection of poetry serves as a botanical compendium of sorts, with dozens of references to specific types of vegetation.[161] What one finds in the text is a recurrent grammatical construction through which plants and trees are organized according to which environments "have" (*you* 有) them. The taxonomy is locative. The south "has" trees with curved drooping branches. The hills of the south "have" mulberry trees, medlar trees, *kao* 栲 trees, and the *tai* 臺 plant. The northern hills "have" willow trees, plum trees, *niu* 杻 trees, and the *lai* 萊 plant. The valleys "have" motherwort. Mountains "have" lofty pine, thorny elms, bushy oaks, sparrow plums, mulberry trees, and varnish trees—which are also "had" on hillsides, along with turtle foot and thorn fern. The marshes "have" lotus flowers, rushes, valerian, and *Polygonum amphibium*. The moor "has" creeping-grass. The wet lowlands "have" white elm, mulberry, chestnut, willow, carambola fruit, and pear trees. The central plains "have" pulse.[162]

As Sarah Allan reminds us, there is no radical distinction between plants and animals in early Chinese thinking—both are understood as "living things" (*wu* 物).[163] Thus, it makes sense that animals would also be sorted according to the territories that "have" them.[164] The *Shuowen* 說文 lexicon routinely indexes animal classifiers according to the environments they inhabit. For example, *yu* 魚 (fish) are "water animals," *hu* 虎 (tigers) are "mountain animals," and *shu* 鼠 (rats) are "crevice animals." The *Huainanzi* 淮南子, a Daoist-inspired text from the early Han dynasty, catalogs animal types through correlation with wider ambient phenomena. The resulting taxonomy does not treat animal morphology in any great detail—for no such taxonomy exists in early China.[165] Animal sorting is instead treated within the framework of "Earth Topography" (*dixing* 地形).[166] The rationale is stated: "Earthly regions, each according to its type, produce life."[167]

Accordingly, the energies (*qi* 氣) of various regions and their elements are correlated with an array of congenital and acquired characteristics in living things. The *Huainanzi* notes the obvious: "The myriad living things are born, each of a distinct type."[168] These types, however, are historicized through a compact account of biological evolution. Humans trace their origins back to "Oceanman" (*hairen* 海人). Hairy animals trace back to horses, and then to dragons. Other dragons serve as the progenitors of turtles, fishes, and birds. Earth's present diversity is accounted for on the basis of hybridization among these primitive types: "The five types mingled seed and flourished outwardly, coming to resemble their [present] forms and proliferations."[169] Biological evolution is plainly affirmed.

The "Earth Topography" chapter of the *Huainanzi* can be regarded as representative of mainstream views about the natural world in early China. As John S. Major notes, much of its content is corroborated elsewhere, and it is formed into "self-contained units [that] were probably copied verbatim or nearly so from now-lost sources."[170] Its assumptions about the natural world are operative in parts of the *Zhuangzi* as well. In the "Ultimate Happiness" (*zhile* 至樂) chapter, we find an account of evolution that corroborates the idea that organic forms are extensions of their environments. In Burton Watson's rendering, this account explains that the seeds of things have "mysterious workings" (*ji* 機). These mysterious life-initiators produce hereditary lineages depending on where they "get" (*de* 得). If they get into the water, they become Break Vine. If they get to the water's edge, they become Frog's Rope. On the slopes, they become Hill Slippers. If manure is introduced to the Hill Slippers, they become Crow's Feet. These will eventually become maggots, then butterflies, insects, snakes, and birds. The saliva of the birds then produces another lineage of bugs (!). These bugs eventually produce the Green Peace plant, which in turn produces leopards, horses, and human beings. This fanciful account concludes with a more circumspect observation: "Human beings in time return again to the mysterious workings (*ji*). So all creatures come out of the mysterious workings and go back into them again."[171]

Here, the term *ji* 機 denotes a trigger-like mechanism that initiates pulses of activity in the organism. As A. C. Graham suggests, it is "the thing which makes it go."[172] The idea is that, once the mysterious engine of life-activity "gets" (*de* 得) into some environment, it is shaped (*xing* 形) into whatever form the environmental conditions will "have" (*you* 有). The resulting "presence" (*you*) of each form expresses the quality of its own allure (*de* 德) while manifesting the directional order (*de*) of its growth. There exists a conceptual link between *de* and this mysterious trigger (*ji*) of organic activity. As Sarah Allan maintains, *de* retains the sense of a "seed that gives life," encompassing "what we would call the genetic makeup" of a population or individual, as well as what she terms its "unusual presence."[173]

Allan builds upon Roger T. Ames' presentation of the philological evidence.[174] In the *Shouwen* lexicon, *de* 德 is defined as an "arising" or "presencing" (*sheng* 升). As Scott Barnwell observes, it is unclear how Xu Shen 許慎 acquires this association.[175] It is more generally accepted that *de* is a later variant of *de* 悳, which also appears abbreviated as *zhi* 直, a term commonly used in its derivative sense as "upright" or "vertically straight."[176] In another sense, *zhi* 直 means "to grow straight without deviation" in the context of organic issuance. This is evident in its cognate terms, "to sow" (*zhi* 種) and "to plant" (*zhi* 植). *De* thus retains a semantic association, however obscure, with arising and organic growth. This association likely informs its' meaning in the *Daodejing*.

Recall that Chapter 51 presents a concise, four-part description of what organic forms are like. It states that: "*Dao* 道 produces them. *De* 德 rears them. Other things shape (*xing* 形) them. The propensity of circumstances (*shi* 勢) matures them." The first three parts have been discussed: first, organic forms issue from the elusive *dao* of nature; second, each form has its own "quality" and directional order (*de*) of growth; and third, environing conditions actively shape (*xing*) the evolving contours of each form. Their maturation (*cheng* 成) is now attributed to the propensity of circumstances (*shi*). What does this fourth component signify?

François Jullien has done the most comprehensive work on *shi* 勢, a term that can be translated variably as "position," "power," "circumstances," and "propensity."[177] As Jullien argues, the term indicates the operation of a spontaneous efficacy in nature that cannot be explained in terms of either final or efficient causality. It is rather an efficacy that "results from the very disposition of things." Jullien presents the "logic" of *shi* as indicative of what he sees as an "indifference to any notion of a *telos*, (or) final end for things."[178] Jullien demonstrates that *shi* is a ubiquitous notion in early China and that it represents something other than final causality in the Greek-medieval sense. What's more, the notion operates in contexts in which one might expect to find conventional teleological reasoning.

One way to reconstruct this idea is to begin with the Chinese militarist tradition. In the *Art of War* (*Sunzibingfa* 孫子兵法) there is a close relationship between the notion of propensity (*shi* 勢) and the mysterious workings (*ji* 機) of things. This association is explained by analogy with a crossbow ready to fire and birds of prey poised to attack. *Shi* is likened to the tensional state of the drawn weapon and *ji* to the release of its trigger mechanism. This release—a pulse-like "node" (*jie* 節) of activity—is likened to the precise timing of the bird, who descends upon her victim when conditions are exactly right, with instantly lethal results. *Shi* is also compared to the velocity of water crashing down a steep gorge, which in turn is equated with the efficacy of the strategic form (*xing* 形) in which troops in battle stand positioned and ready for action.[179]

The "art of war" is to discern the conditions that "shape" (*xing* 形) the battle situation as it happens, so as to utilize the efficacy resident in the situation to one's strategic advantage. As Jullien notes, the notions of "shape" (*xing*) and "propensity" (*shi* 勢) are closely linked and lie at the heart of this philosophical vision. It is assumed that wherever there is any shape or configuration (*xing*) there are mysterious workings (*ji* 機) present and the propensity (*shi*) for them to be instantly triggered. Such triggering does not rely upon any superordinate power or agency. As Jullien puts it: "the situation is itself the source of [the] effect."[180]

Such thinking is co-extensive with Chinese natural philosophy, especially as it pertains to assumptions about the behavior of living things. Wherever there is organic form (*xing* 形)—or more precisely, wherever there is an environment that "shapes" (*xing*) organic form—conditions exist for organic, trigger-like mechanisms (*ji* 機) to discharge instantly given the propensity (*shi* 勢) in the environment. This is what Chapter 51 of the *Daodejing* means by *shi* completing or maturing (*cheng* 成) organic form. As an organization of adaptive habits, organic form exhibits *dao* 道-activity to the extent that it exists as a phase in the integrated circuit between organism-and-environment. Existentially, its maturation cannot be separated from the environment in which this occurs.

This principle is related vividly in the *Annals of Master Yan* (*Yanzi Chunqiu* 晏子春秋) when it observes that "Orange trees planted south of the Huai River produce mandarin oranges (*ju* 橘), but those planted north of the river produce bitter-fruited oranges (*zhi* 枳). The foliage of the trees looks exactly the same, but their fruits are different. Why? Because the climate (*shuitu* 水土) is different."[181] As it does for Dewey, the environment in this case denotes "the specific *continuity* of the surroundings with [the organism's] own active tendencies."[182] The Daoist thinker assumes such continuity, providing in this context an understanding of how *dao* 道-activity issues from organic form without recourse to efficient or final causality. In this connection, *de* 德 represents the directional order or "power" latent in organic form itself, which is a deposit of tendencies accumulated over time that "nourish, structure, and mature" the organism in its environmental transactions.

As we will see in chapter 4, such ideas are strikingly compatible with contemporary systems-oriented approaches in biology. Giuseppe Longo and Maël Montévil's work on developing a systems theory of the organism suggests that natural philosophies such as the Chinese can play a role in reconstructing our current understandings. "In our view," they write, "there is currently no satisfactory *theory* of biological organization as such, and in particular, in spite of many attempts, there is no theory of the organism."[183] Much of this stems from two large errors in Western thinking. First, there is the Aristotelian error of theorizing the trajectory of organisms according to their "inner" vitalistic ends. Next, there is the Cartesian error of theorizing the trajectory of organisms according to their "outer" physical laws. Systems approaches in biology attempt to untangle the considerable confusion that each error generates by attempting to theorize and quantify the complex interactions (or, as Dewey would stress, *transactions*) within biological systems. Going forward, the findings of Longo and Montévil will be considered alongside early Chinese natural philosophy and later (in volume II) alongside Confucian theories of human development. This will further suggest ways in which early Chinese thought can help to get us "back in gear."

Before going forward, however, we need to dig deeper. The *Daodejing* tells us that there is an elusive *dao* 道 that produces (*sheng* 生) each thing. This is the *dao* that in Chapter 21 is described as the "source of multitudes." This *dao* reveals itself whenever organic form is considered *not only* as a directional order but also as an integral whole mysteriously present as just what it is. The "Earth Topography" chapter of the *Huainanzi* is sensitive to the presence of this more elusive *dao*. As the text observes: "Human beings, birds and beasts, the myriad beings, and the tiny organisms—each is present (*you* 有) and thereby living (*sheng*). Some are utterly peculiar and others have their counterparts. Some fly about and others go on foot. But no one understands their actual essence (*qing* 情). Only one who understands and has fathomed *dao* is able to get to the root and source of this."[184] Arriving at this "root and source" will require another round of experiments. This time we ask: How does one account for order in the world? What traits of existence explain organic life? What is "potential" and how does it become actualized? Such questions are taken up in chapter 3.

3

Orders and Spontaneity

> The question of whether the universe is monistic or pluralistic is no longer really a problem. The only real problem is the determination of the circumstances which call for application of the principle of unity, and of other circumstances which require application of the principle of pluralism.
>
> —John Dewey, Beijing, March 1920

Dewey's Metaphysics

Ralph Waldo Emerson describes the process by which nature educates mind as one of mutual growth. Nature and mind "proceed from the same root; one is leaf and one is flower." For Emerson, mind takes shape together with nature by establishing connections, "discovering roots running underground whereby contrary and remote things cohere and flower out from one stem."[1] Dewey provides a similar account of how experience relates to nature. For Dewey, "experience is *of* as well as *in* nature," and the depth and breadth that it reveals puts it directly "into possession of some portion of nature [that renders] other of its precincts open."[2] Nature's precincts, according to Emerson, are expansive in range: "system on system shooting likes rays, upward, downward, without center, without circumference."[3] For Dewey, experience burrows into this web of connections. As he explains: "it tunnels in all directions and in so doing brings to the surface things at first hidden—as miners pile high on the surface of the earth treasures brought from below." Among the bounties of nature are the "generic traits of existence" revealed through experience, and Dewey means to identify and assemble these in his metaphysics. As he sees it, "the traits possessed by the subject-matters of experience are as genuine as the characteristics of sun and electron. They are *found* . . . When found, their ideal qualities are as relevant to the philosophic theory of nature as are the traits found by physical inquiry."[4]

The cogency and purview of "Dewey's Metaphysics" have long been debated.[5] Rather than enter into these debates, the goal here is to gather from Dewey whatever serves our needs. The aim remains to assimilate early Chinese thought and to get our selves "back in gear" in the process. There is plenty to consider. Dewey's initial suggestion that metaphysics has a place in contemporary thought relates directly to his concern with revising certain inadequate commonsense notions about organic form. Specifically, he is concerned with an either/or stalemate in our post-Darwinian reconstructions—namely, the choice between either reducing organic behavior to mechanistic causation (i.e., *materialism*) or introducing some invisible agency as an animistic force (i.e., *vitalism*). Neither option, Dewey contends, provides a satisfying account of what living things actually are.

Daoist thinkers likewise recognize this stalemate and the confusion that it signals. In the *Zhuangzi*, the figure of "Vast Impartial Accord" relates the following:

> Chickens squawk and dogs bark. This much, humans understand. Yet no matter how great our understanding, we are not able to theoretically explain *why* such things naturally come to be. Moreover, we are not able to make sense of what [animals] might do next. We can pick apart and analyze [animal behavior] until the subtlety reaches a point where no more divisions are possible, or the question becomes so large that it cannot even be encompassed. But whether we say "something causes it" (*shi* 使) or "nothing makes it happen" (*mowei* 莫為), we have not yet gotten past the living thing (*wu* 物). So, in the end, we falter. "Cause" implies something material (*shi* 實). "Nothing makes it happen" implies some void. What can be named and is material is the lodging place of the living thing. What cannot be named and is immaterial is the void inside. We can argue about this and try to make sense of it, but the more we talk about it the further away it gets . . . The theories that "something causes it" or "nothing makes it happen" are merely crutches for our own perplexity.[6]

As the one-legged creature in the "Autumn Floods" (*qiushui* 秋水) chapter learns, living beings have no idea what causes their trigger-like mechanisms (*ji* 機) to operate as they do. The one-legged creature asks a millipede how it causes (*shi* 使) its myriad feet to glide along in such well-ordered syncopation. "You don't understand!" replies the millipede: "All I do is activate my natural mechanisms (*tianji* 天機). I have no idea how it happens."[7] As the *Daodejing* teaches, according with *dao* 道 and prioritizing *de* 德 are what living things do just as they are (*ziran* 自然). Materialistic explanations are inadequate in accounting for *why* this is so, and musings about immaterial forces appeal to nothing but an empty void. And yet, *chickens squawk and dogs bark*. Why do they behave in such ways? The answer is simple: Because chickens and dogs are here (*you* 有) and doing such things is their *dao*-activity. If the case were otherwise, there would be no chickens and dogs.

The recently discovered pre-Qin document *All Things Flow in Form* (*Fanwuliuxing* 凡物流形) opens with a series of questions that probe into this issue—namely, what shapes the behavior of living things and lends them their organic integrity? The author asks: "All living things flow in form, what have they attained (*de* 得) in order to reach maturity (*cheng* 成)? Flowing in form, reaching maturity in bodily structure (*ti* 體), what have they attained in order not to die? Having reached maturity, being alive, how do they look around and call out?" Similar questions prompt Dewey's own metaphysical reflections. Are life functions due to something physical? Are they due to some animistic force? "What do grasses and trees attain in order to live?" asks the author of *All Things Flow in Form*.[8] Evoked here is the most fundamental question in all of natural philosophy: *What explains life?*

Dewey's response begins to take shape in his 1915 article, "The Subject Matter of Metaphysics." Here, he encourages us to bypass transcendental metaphysics in taking up this question.[9] Both the mechanistic and vitalistic approaches postulate a "cause" of life activities—be it material or immaterial—and regard this cause as temporally original in generating organic form. Such discrete causes, however, never surface in experience. They are eclipsed by a more fundamental "mystery." Recall that, for Dewey, even though scientific inquiry helps to explain the occurrence of a thing, "it is only the *occurrence* that is explained, not the thing itself . . . Go as far back as we please in accounting for present conditions and we still come upon the mystery of things being just what they are."[10] In the *Zhuangzi*, "Vast Impartial Accord" agrees—our causal analysis can "reach the point where no more divisions are possible," and still the living thing (*wu* 物) stands there just as it is. Postulating an ultimate cause *behind* the living thing sets us on a path to nowhere. It is the kind of metaphysics against which Kant warned—that which is "deceived and led to the childish endeavor of catching at bubbles."[11]

As Dewey sees it, contemporary metaphysics should "raise the question of the sort of world which *has* such an evolution [of organic form], not the question of the sort of world which *causes* it." The question of cause, for Dewey, "appears either to bring us to an *impasse* or else to break up into just the questions which constitute scientific inquiry." Thus, "with reference to [the] evolution of living beings, the distinctive trait of metaphysical reflection would not then be its attempt to discover some temporally original feature which *caused* the development, but the irreducible traits of a world in which at least some changes take on an evolutionary form."[12] Dewey is interested in describing the "generic traits" of such a world, not in accounting for the origins of particular things nor for the origin of the whole.

Dewey signals at this juncture that he is "not concerned to develop [such] a metaphysics." As R. W. Sleeper observes, however, Dewey proceeds to advance significant metaphysical claims in this 1915 article.[13] Most notably, he submits a list of three "generic traits" of existence: *change, specificity/interaction*, and *diversity*.[14] This assemblage is best understood as a variant of Charles Sanders Peirce's three categories: Firstness, Secondness, and Thirdness. Let us review Peirce's categories alongside Dewey's three traits—i.e., those that Dewey regards as characterizing the sort of world in which organic forms exist.

For Peirce, the category of Firstness refers to the state of sheer potential from which something occurs, that aspect of its being "positively such as it is regardless of aught else."[15] This is the most elusive of Peirce's three categories—for as he cautions: "Stop to think of it, and it has flown." Firstness has the character of being what the Daoist calls "spontaneous" (*ziran* 自然). "It must be initiative, original, spontaneous, and free," explains Peirce, "otherwise it is second to a determining cause." Dewey refers to this category simply as *change*, which designates possibility just on the verge of realization. As Peirce relates, "[Firstness] is full of life and variety. Yet that variety is only potential; it is not definitely *there*."[16]

Firstness only becomes *actualized* in what Peirce calls Secondness, or what Dewey refers to as *specificity/interaction*. As Carl R. Hausman explains, Secondness is the mode by which "Firstness itself has a link with the world."[17] Secondness is the presence of a *specific* thing, interacting among other specific things. "Secondness," Peirce submits, "is the easiest to comprehend, being the element that the rough-and-tumble of the world renders most prominent."[18] "Pure" Secondness, according to Peirce, amounts to "thisness" (*haecceitas*).[19] Within the Daoist framework, this would be the sheer presence (*you* 有) of a thing foregrounded against its potential absence (*wu* 無).

Thirdness, or what Dewey calls *diversity*, stands for the generic types that characterize the variety of Seconds in the world. Peirce attributes this characteristic to the tendency of nature to form "habits" and thereby to exhibit general traits and predictabilities. It must be supposed, writes Peirce, "that there is an original, elemental, tendency of things to acquire determinate properties, to take habits."[20] As he observes, "five minutes of our waking life will hardly pass without our making some kind of prediction," and predictions are based upon the existence of diverse types that have the habit of being fulfilled. Thus, "it must be that future events have a tendency to conform to a general rule." This general character, which consists in the fact that "future facts of Secondness will take on a determinate general character," is what Peirce calls Thirdness.[21] Within the Daoist framework, this is the feature that enables us to make distinctions and to name (*ming* 名) things.

There will be more to say about Peirce's categories and their connections to Daoist thought. The next order of business, however, is to make some adjustments to our vocabulary. By the mid-1940s, Dewey had grown wary of the word "metaphysics." As he relates to Sing-nan Fen: "I don't care so much for the word 'metaphysical' because it has [received] a sort of 'out of the world' meaning."[22] By the end of the 1940s Dewey came to positively regret that he ever used the words "metaphysics" or "metaphysical." He realized that critics were assuming that he was "[treating] metaphysics as a name for that part of philosophy that is concerned with the relation of experience to existence" as this plays out in the Western tradition. "Nothing could be farther from the facts of the case," Dewey insists, admitting that, "I now realize that it was exceedingly naïve of me to suppose that it was possible to rescue the word from its deeply engrained traditional use. I derive whatever consolation may be possible from promising myself never to use the words again in connection with any aspect of any part of my own position."[23] In deference to this commitment, made by Dewey as a nonagenarian, the words "metaphysics" and "metaphysical" will no longer be used to describe his philosophy.

The need remains, however, to designate what Dewey meant by these words and to distinguish this from other philosophical terms. Dewey primarily wanted to distinguish metaphysical descriptions from those that were being generated in the special sciences. For Dewey, "any intelligible question as to causation seems to be a wholly scientific question." Scientific inquiry begins with a given existence and asks *how* it came about. Such questions concern its *occurrence*, and the lengths to which inquiry will go is an entirely practical matter. Such analysis is *diachronic* in nature: "[tracing] back a present existence to the earlier existences with which it is connected."[24]

Metaphysics, Dewey thought, was different. It produces not a description of the *genesis* of any existence or group of existences, but rather of the "ultimate or irreducible traits" of a world in which at least some diachronic changes take on such form. Such analysis is *synchronic* in nature: "[obtaining] indifferently whether a subject-matter in question be dated 1915 or ten million years BCE." This feature prevents metaphysical inquiry from being confused not only with science but with inquiries into "ultimate origins and ultimate ends—that is, from questions of creation and eschatology."[25] Dewey thus regarded metaphysics as an account of nature *just as we find it*. Synchronic in character, it does not attempt to account for the ultimate origins or ends of the events whose generic traits it seeks to describe.

The best replacement for "metaphysics" is the word "cosmology," one that Dewey did not employ to any significant extent. "Cosmology" has two distinct advantages. First, in Dewey's mind it already suggests a broader "Philosophy of Nature" in which the special sciences are unified.[26] Second, the word has a rich history in American philosophy already. Robert C. Neville establishes in 1981 that the task of cosmology is to "single out the *important* features of the world" and to "provide an interpretation of everything in the world while excluding that which is not found in the world." Neville does this with the assimilation of Chinese traditions specifically in mind. For him, an adequate cosmology may well require more nuance than any single set of cultural resources can provide, thus "Chinese philosophical systems [can] provide categories by which a cosmology can be sensitive in these areas."[27] With this precedent in mind, the word "cosmology" now replaces "metaphysics" in the present study.

One additional designation, however, is still needed: that for which Dewey calls inquiry into "ultimate origins and ultimate ends." For this referent, the designation "cosmogony" will suffice. Like scientific inquiry, cosmogony is diachronic in nature. It is concerned with the moment of creation, but also with whatever precedes that moment and necessarily follows from it. Henceforth, "cosmogony" is so used.

There are still two questions standing to be considered. First, there is that posed in *All Things Flow in Form*, which asks: "What do living things attain (*de* 得) in order to reach maturity (*cheng* 成)?" Second, there is that posed in "The Subject Matter of Metaphysics," which asks: "What are the generic traits of a world in which at least *some* changes exhibit organic form and functioning?" Considered together, Daoism and classical American philosophy generate provocative answers to these questions, establishing insights that further challenge our Greek-medieval assumptions about the nature of organic form and prompt us to get our thinking "back in gear."

Toward such insights we continue to make our way. Turning again to the Daoist tradition, the next step is to formulate a cosmology and cosmogony inspired by the *Daodejing*. Given the complexity of this assignment, the following two sections require considerable digression and more detailed Sinological analysis than have most discussions up to this point. Again, the reader is asked to exercise some patience. The vision that is reconstructed in the next two sections will be informing the entirety of what follows.

Embracing the One (*baoyi* 抱一)

As suggested in chapter 1, the field of early Chinese philosophy is undergoing a revolution. It is being inundated with newly recovered documents.[28] Considered as a whole, this influx amounts to a sea change. It is difficult to remain current with everything that is happening, and it will require generations to absorb what it all means. For now, bamboo manuscripts lost for millennia are being downloaded onto our laptops—challenging received understandings, posing new possibilities, and galvanizing our philosophical imaginations.

How does one philosophize with such documents? As already outlined, intra-cultural philosophy follows Dewey's counsel in striving to understand the "general properties of situations which have to do with problems that have played an influential part in the history of [a particular] philosophical discourse" in order to "reconstruct the environment sufficiently to know what problems its needs imposed upon [a thinker]."[29] This has always been difficult to do in classical Chinese philosophy, and in some respects recent discoveries add to the difficulty. For instance, while archeological finds open new directions for research into the *Daodejing*, they also demonstrate conclusively that the text evolved gradually into its received form: the Han-era Wang Bi edition. In other words, we now know that the *Daodejing* belongs to what Gerald L. Bruns calls a "manuscript culture," one in which texts remain open to successive modifications, rather than to a "print culture," in which texts are composed once and then closed.[30] The *Daodejing*, like other early Chinese texts, was hand-copied by individuals for specific purposes, and it could be (and was) occasionally modified to fit those purposes.

With this being the case, how does one "reconstruct the environment sufficiently" to understand the *meaning* of the text? Is there a single, correct meaning that stands to be recovered? The answer must be "No." There is no single meaning to the text. There are, however, concrete situations in which the text *was* actually interpreted and mobilized for specific philosophical purposes.[31] Fortunately, variants in terminology and editorial structure in newly restored versions provide insights into the various situations in which the meaning of the text was understood. Chapter 22 of the Mawangdui version shows evidence of being edited for a purpose, and through the analysis of its variants I hope to recover a *specific* historical reading for our use. I am not claiming that the following analysis reveals *the* meaning of the *Daodejing*—but I do maintain that it reveals one way in which the text was actually understood in ancient China.

In the received Wang Bi version of the *Daodejing*, Chapter 22 describes the activity of the sage in the following terms: "The sage embraces the one (*baoyi* 抱一) to become model (*shi* 式) to the world." The Mawangdui versions of Chapter 22 (both A and B), while similar to the Wang Bi in many other respects, contains the following variant: "The sage holds to the one (*zhiyi* 執一) to become shepherd (*mu* 牧) to the world." Some scholars do not find *baoyi* and *zhiyi* to be importantly different. Harold D. Roth, for instance, in his study of breath meditation in the "Inner Training" (*neiye* 內業) tradition, finds that the two phrases in that context "imply the same thing."[32] The two phrases, however, appear significantly different at first glance. The verb *zhi* 執 has the extended meaning of "to grab, to seize, or to manage." The verb *bao* 抱 has the extended meaning of "to embrace, to cherish, or to hug." *Zhi* means "holding to" in the manner that a law is followed. *Bao* means "to hold" in the manner that an infant is cradled in the arms. *Zhi* carries the negative connotation of holding on to something by force or as a stipulation. Mencius, in fact, uses the phrase *zhiyi* to represent an attitude that he despises: "What I detest about those who hold to the one (*zhiyi*) is that they cripple *dao* 道. One thing is taken up and a hundred others go by the wayside."[33] The verb *zhi* carries this negative connotation even in the *Daodejing* itself. On two occasions we read that to forcibly hold to (*zhi*) something causes it to slip away.[34] In light of such cautionary statements, the notion that the sage *ought* to hold to the one (*zhiyi*) reads like an aberration.

The most plausible explanation of the Chapter 22 variant is that the phrase "holding to the one" (*zhiyi* 執一) is Legalist in nature and that, in this context, it reflects the assimilation of the *Daodejing* by the Legalist-minded Huang-Lao 黃老 school.[35] Robert G. Hendricks acknowledges this possibility, noting that the term "shepherd" (*mu* 牧) is a "known reference to the ruler in the political writings of the time," making the Mawangdui version "seem to have a specific, political focus instead of a general one."[36] The specifically Legalist meaning of "holding to the one" (*zhiyi*) is conveyed in the *Annals of Lü Buwei* (*Lüshichunqiu* 呂氏春秋), which states: "The king who holds to the one (*zhiyi*) rectifies the myriad beings . . . Where there is unity (*yi* 一) there is order. Where there is duality, there is chaos."[37] In a Legalist context, "holding to the one" thus stands for the seizure of political control and the establishment of order by positive law (*fa* 法). Rules are posited by a supreme ruler and enforced by heavy punishment. Other texts reiterate this basically coercive understanding of the phrase.[38] *Zhiyi* results in a zero-sum game: diversity and novelty lose while top-down order prevails.

This Legalist-minded preference for unity over difference is one of the hallmarks of the later Huang-Lao tradition. In his analysis of the difference between the Huang-Lao and Daoist thinking, R. P. Peerenboom utilizes to good effect what David L. Hall and Roger T. Ames call the "logical" vs. "aesthetic" conceptions of order.[39] Briefly, "aesthetic" orders are those that begin with the uniqueness of the "one" particular as it collaborates with other particulars in an emergent complex of relatedness, resulting in an order that is site-specific and reflective of the achieved togetherness of just that diversity of particulars. "Logical" order, on the other hand, begins with a pre-assigned pattern of relatedness—it begins with the "one" of unity. The constituents of such an order are then recognized not in their particularity but for their ability to satisfy a pre-designated function in a precedent order. Peerenboom argues that Huang-Lao thought diverges from Daoist thinking in that it understands *dao* 道 itself as a "pre-configured natural order," one that is "characterized by a constant, pervasive unity, and hence deemed *the* 'One' (*yi* 一)."[40] Tu Wei-ming concurs and writes: "The method by which the unalterable standard of the One is obtained becomes the main focus of the Huang-Lao texts."[41] While the Huang-Lao tradition is distinct from the more draconian legacy of Legalism, it builds off that legacy by embracing a strictly transcendent, top-down approach to order.

In embracing such a "logical" conception of order, Huang-Lao dispenses with the idea that *dao* 道 facilitates the emergence of novel, unforced orders that begin, in Peerenboom's words, "with the uniqueness of the *one* particular." Thus, whereas in Daoism "there is always an element of spontaneity, a potential for novelty," this element is "negligible if not completely lacking in the world of Huang-Lao."[42] If Peerenboom is correct, and if the Chapter 22 variant indicates a Huang-Lao substitution of the verb "hold" (*zhi* 執) for the verb "embrace" (*bao* 抱), then we can deduce with some likelihood what the phrase "embracing the one" (*baoyi* 抱一) means in the context of philosophical Daoism. Unlike *zhiyi* 執一, which represents a disregard for spontaneity in favor of a more top-down instantiation of a preexisting order, *baoyi* represents the opposite: a preference for unforced, spontaneous orders—an association that the Legalist-minded editors of the Mawangdui version meant to dispense with. If this interpretation is correct, then it can be noted that the term "one" (*yi* 一) undergoes significant change in meaning once modified by *zhi* in the Mawangdui variant. The substitution amounts to replacing the "one" of novelty with the "one" of law-like generality. It signals, in other words, a *complete shift in cosmological emphasis*.

This difference registers in the first line of Chapter 42 in the Wang Bi version of the *Daodejing*: "*Dao* produces one" (*daoshengyi* 道生一). Chapter 42 has rightly been called "the crux of early Daoist ideology and cosmology."[43] As here understood, it furnishes a statement in which "embracing the one" (*baoyi* 抱一) is affirmed as a uniquely "Daoist" attitude, one that insists that the roles of diversity and novelty be preserved and cherished in any cosmological account of order. It is in relation to such Daoist thinking, here to be defended, that Huang-Lao thinking is opposed.[44]

As it stands, the opening stanza of Chapter 42 has inspired a long, illustrious tradition of commentary. Such an enigmatic formulation makes commentary hard to avoid. The chapter begins: "*Dao* 道 produces one; one produces two; two produces three; and three produces the myriad beings." What is this supposed to mean? The most influential commentaries on this passage were written in the third century of the Common Era. By that time, the decision had been made to read the sequence as *cosmogony*. However, as Alan K. L. Chan observes, "there is no clear indication that the generation of things is to be taken in the past tense," and it is only later in the tradition that "the ambiguity is clarified" by interpreting Chapter 42 as "referring to the coming to be of the constituent forces of the world."[45]

The archeological finds at Guodian now compel us to reconsider the relationship between early Chinese cosmogony and Chapter 42—to ask even whether Chapter 42 is rightly understood as cosmogony at all. The Guodian manuscript unearthed in 1993 was not only the earliest extant version of the *Daodejing* (one without a "Chapter 42"): it came with its own distinct cosmogony, a work entitled *The Great Continuum Produces the Waters* (*Taiyishengshui* 太一生水). This document describes the emergence of the world-system in some detail. According to its account, the waters were the first to be produced, then the heavens, earth, spirits, *yin* 陰 and *yang* 陽, the four seasons, hot and cold, wet and dry, and finally the annual cycle.[46]

Considerable interest has been paid to the identity of the "Great Continuum" (*taiyi* 太一) from which these elements are said to emerge and to which they are said to return. Hendricks reports the consensus view: in pre-Qin philosophical texts, the phrase "Great Continuum" appears to be another name for *dao* 道. He goes on to suggest that while the phrase "Great Continuum" is absent from the *Daodejing*, the term "one" (*yi* 一) "[also] seems to be used to mean the Way (*dao*) in several chapters," citing Chapter 42 as one example.[47] There is an obvious tension in this analysis. If the Great Continuum (*taiyi*) and one (*yi*) each mean *dao* and are semantically interchangeable even in the context of Chapter 42, then the first line of that chapter can be glossed as "*dao* produces *dao*." As I have already suggested, the term "one" (*yi*) can mean different things in different contexts according to how it is modified by different adjectives and verbs. Where "ones" (*yi*) are concerned in classical Chinese, there is not necessarily a "one-to-one" correspondence in meaning.

As it now stands, the relationship between the *The Great Continuum Produces the Waters* and Chapter 42 is a matter of considerable uncertainty. Some suggest that the latter is related to the former as either its recapitulation or its development. Others suggest that the two texts represent very different views. Sarah Allan maintains that the two accounts of world production might be linked in some general manner given the presence of the number one (*yi* 一) in each, but as she observes, the two accounts "cannot be reconciled as numerical sequences."[48] If we accept the consensus view that the Great Continuum (*taiyi* 太一) is a style-name for *dao* 道, then at issue in determining the relationship between these two formulations is the nature of the relationship between the "products" of two primary, generative equations. In both *The Great Continuum Produces the Waters* and Chapter 42 something is "produced" (*sheng* 生). If the two sources of production overlap in meaning, and consensus remains that they do, then their respective primary products should also overlap in meaning. But in order to sustain this line of reasoning *and* answer Allan's concern, we must drop the assumption that the ones (*yi*) in these two equations correspond in meaning. If we refuse to drop this assumption, then we are indeed faced with an irreconcilable numerical sequence.

There is a simple two-step solution to this problem, one that renders these two formulations different yet philosophically consistent. *First*, allow the "one" of the Great Continuum (*taiyi* 太一) to mean the "one" of continuity and non-differentiation. Meanwhile, allow the "one" of Chapter 42 to mean the "one" of discontinuity and difference. *Second*, regard *The Great Continuum Produces the Waters* as cosmogony and Chapter 42 as cosmology. The difference then becomes what Dewey regards, respectively, as the difference between accounts of the "ultimate origins and ends" of the world and of the "generic traits of the world" as we find it. One would expect such descriptions to be philosophically consistent, but not identical.

The Great Continuum Produces the Waters is clearly a cosmogony—as Scott Cook notes: it is a "specific type of cosmogony hitherto unseen among early Chinese texts" and stands "among the earliest detailed cosmogonies of any type."[49] According to its account, the Great Continuum produces the waters, and the waters are said to have then assisted the Great Continuum in producing the heavens. Earth was cooperatively produced in kind, then so too the spirits, and so forth, in what is most easily envisioned as a diachronic sequence of events.

Once a thing is born into this world, however, it immediately changes and grows. The text explains that the cooperative evolution of the myriad beings continues beyond the moment of creation. The waters continue to flow, and the Great Continuum becomes "stored" (*zang* 藏) in the waters, "moving through each temporal phase, completing a cycle only to begin anew: making itself the mother of the myriad beings."[50] At this very moment, the Great Continuum continues to operate in the waters. Such a cosmogony naturally leads into the cosmological question: "What *are* the generic traits of this world, so produced and still on-going?"

Chapter 42 provides an answer. The never-ending waters (*shui* 水) continue to introduce novelty into the world-system. "*Dao* produces one" (*daoshengyi* 道生一) describes this feature of the world as we find it. "*Dao* exists *because* it produces," writes Isabelle Robinet.[51] What it produces is what Peirce calls "Firstness"—that which is "present, immediate, fresh, new, original, spontaneous." *Dao* gives birth to the unprecedented, the newly possible—that which is always forthcoming and emerging. Such a reading makes good sense given how the term *dao* is normally understood in scholarly literature.⁵² As Edmund Ryden suggests in his recent translation of the *Daodejing*, Chapter 42 begins by stating that, "The Way generates the Unique."⁵³

Franklin Perkins provides additional support for the claim that the phrase "*Dao* produces one" (*daoshengyi* 道生一) in Chapter 42 stands in favor of spontaneity and novelty over opposing views—in this case, the view that appears in *All Things Flow in Form*. As Perkins observes, the latter text contains a numerical account that differs markedly from that in Chapter 42. This newly discovered account goes as follows: "One produces two, two produces three, three produces the mother, and the mother matures the bonds."⁵⁴ As Perkins sees it, this account presumes that there is a fixed presence (*you* 有) that serves as a pre-established source for order: the "one" (*yi* 一) at the beginning. According to him, positioning *dao* as antecedent to the "one" in the Chapter 42 sequence is meant to affirm "the progressive differentiation of the one within a more fundamental account in which things emerge from *dao* or no-being (*wu* 無)."⁵⁵ Since anything that emerges from "no-being" is novel by definition, this reading supports the idea that the "one" represents the introduction of novelty in the Chapter 42 sequence.

The alternative, more static account to which Chapter 42 is opposed entails a top-down vision of a preexisting "one" that the Legalist-inspired Huang-Lao thinkers intended to affirm. Such a tradition needed to repudiate the novelty-driven cosmology of Chapter 42, and so it does at the very beginning of the Mawangdui *Canon Law* (*Jingfa* 經法) document. The first line reads: "*Dao* produces law" (*daoshengfa* 道生法). In what amounts to a keynote statement, the novel "one" of Chapter 42 is eclipsed by law (*fa* 法). Made plain in the "Assessments" (*lun* 論) section of the same document is that this substitution entails the "one" of a static, transcendent order. In what appears to be a calculated reversal of the Chapter 42 cosmology, the Huang-Lao author declares: "Heaven holds to the one (*zhiyi* 執一), makes clear the three, and determines (*ding* 定) the two . . . The one of heaven (*tianzhiyi* 天之一) is something that does not lose its constancy (*chang* 常). Heaven holds to the one and thereby makes clear the three."⁵⁶ Here, the top-down conception of order is unmistakable. The "three" (*order*) issues from a transcendent "one" (*yi* 一) which in turn determines the "two" (*relations*). Novelty is absent because the process of "*Dao* giving birth to one" (*daoshengyi* 道生一) is nowhere to be found. Spontaneity thus plays no role in the advent of order or in the patterning of relations among things.

Instead of establishing law from the top-down, the *Daodejing* describes *dao* 道 as the source from which orders spontaneously emerge through dynamic relations that things have with one another. The phrase "*Dao* models itself on spontaneity" (*daofaziran* 道法自然) expresses this, and thus appears in the earliest known edition of the text (the Guodian version) as well as in Chapter 25 of the Wang Bi edition. As Wang Zhongjiang maintains, this phrase has nothing to do with "any form of manipulation or control over the myriad beings" but rather "indicates that *dao* honors and goes along with the natural self-expression of the myriad beings," allowing each one to grow freely according to its own directional order (*de* 德).[57]

This is what philosophical Daoism ultimately stands for. *Dao* 道 displays boundless generosity in that it sponsors *any* order on the cusp of emergence and refuses none. As Chapter 34 teaches: "The myriad beings depend on [*dao*] in order to live and it does not refuse them." As Wang Zhongjiang sees it, such ceaseless enablement is the "most beautiful virtue" of *dao*.

Later, this virtue reemerges as the central theme of the "*Dao* as Source" (*yuandao* 原道) chapter of the *Huainanzi*. Here, Liu An explains that the myriad beings—"creatures that walk on hooves and breathe through beaks, that fly through the air and wriggle on the ground"—rely on *dao* 道 to live and grow, "yet none of them understand its power [*de* 德]." According to Harold D. Roth, this "power" is expressed through the "subtle guiding force in all phenomena that enables them to spontaneously act in accord with their unique natures."[58] Chapter 42 of the *Daodejing* provides a triadic account of what Dewey calls the "generic traits" of the world in which this occurs, one in which the myriad beings emerge and are sustained in growth amidst a constant influx of novelty—not randomly or discontinuously, but along courses (*dao*) with directional orders (*de*) that express an underlying continuity.

1-2-3 and the Great Continuum

As we have seen, the cosmology of Chapter 42 describes how an influx of novelty results in relations among particulars, and how order emerges from such relations, forming patterns that enable the myriad beings to proliferate and be as they are. The notion of an ever-transforming energy (*qi* 氣) informs this vision, and it reads in full:

> *Dao* 道 produces one; one produces two; two produces three; and three produces the myriad beings. The myriad beings shoulder *yin* 陰 and carry *yang* 陽; their energies blend to create harmonies (*he* 和).

Reminded by Alan K. L. Chan of the ambiguity of tense in this passage, I follow Hans-Georg Moeller in resolving this ambiguity into a present tense, cosmological reading. As Moeller writes: "What is envisioned [in Chapter

42] is not really a 'historical' process of linear causation or generation, not a diachronic development, but rather a process in which all elements combine into a synchronic order. Oneness, twoness, threeness, and multiplicity do not follow each other in a sequence, they rather go along with each other."[59]

Read in conjunction with *The Great Continuum Produces the Waters*, which is a diachronic cosmogony, the "one" (*yi* 一) in the phrase "*Dao* 道 produces one" is the cosmological (and thus synchronic) mark of the primordial waters that began flowing at the dawn of creation and *continue to run*. As long as *dao* keeps producing "ones," time and change are inescapable. Heraclitus' dictum remains in effect: "On those stepping into the same rivers, other and other waters flow." This is the keynote statement in Daoist cosmology: the feature that makes it a fundamentally process-driven view of the world.

Be that as it may, one *can* step into the same river twice. Any cosmology that stalls at the level of novelty overlooks the colossal fact that stable relations obtain in the world. Thus, the account must continue: "One produces two." In a novelty-driven world, each "one" gives way to another "one." Suddenly there are *two* and relations obtain. Let moments of time serve as an example. Each moment is utterly discrete and unprecedented, an irreducible "one." Yet, each moment assumes a qualitative profile in relation to other moments. Characteristics of earlier/later, for instance, are assumed at once. Thus, each moment bears its novel singularity and its relational profile simultaneously. As synchronic traits of anything that exists, novelty and relationality are always encountered together. Here, Dewey concurs.[60] In Daoist cosmology, the "two" that marks such relations stands for the correlative bipolarity of *yin* 陰 and *yang* 陽.[61] *Yin* and *yang*, however, signify correlative qualities that emerge only together and in relation among concrete particulars. Earlier/later moments provide one example, but every qualitative relationship, light/dark, hard/soft, masculine/feminine, etc. exhibits the same correlative trait. There is not a characteristic in existence that does not entail its own compliment on the spectrum. Such spectrums do not swing free of the particulars that manifest them. All qualities are borne entirely by *things* in concrete relationships. Thus: "The myriad beings shoulder *yin* and carry *yang*."

To end our account here would be to leave off at a discordant relativism: each thing takes for its qualities what another is not, and there is no framework within which any relation might become functional in a larger whole. This is not how our world operates. Thus, the account must continue: "Two produces three."

At the level of "three," order arrives. The tendency of natural objects to achieve equilibrium and to endure is an obvious general feature requiring treatment in any cosmology. Chinese thinkers develop a cluster of terms to describe the endurance of orders in nature. *Li* 理 is the most general term, and it eventually comes to mean "pattern," "coherence," or "wholeness." Chapter 42 uses the term "harmony" (*he* 和). Suggested here is that fluid-like energies (*qi* 氣) blend and infuse (*chong* 沖) and when they do, they have the tendency to coalesce in orderly ways. Such harmonies resemble steady-state systems, such that they mark suspensions of flux without entailing the negation of novelty. Novelty persists, but it now manifests itself in determinate, qualitative forms that larger harmonies promote and proliferate. As such orders overlap and intersect they become procreant.

In the Chinese tradition, the four seasons provide the classic example of how such harmonies are procreative in nature. The four seasons proceed with regularity, and major transformations are normally slow. Myriad beings are produced and become stabilized within their orderly patterns. The "Seasonal Rules" (*shize* 時則) chapter of the *Huainanzi* presents an account of seasonal regularities and their life cycles in remarkable detail, all in order to assist humans in correlating their own activities within them.[62] The manner in which the seasonal order engenders and sustains a multitude of living processes illustrates perfectly the third element in Daoist cosmology: "Three produces the myriad beings."

Charles Sanders Peirce's triadic cosmology provides a powerful heuristic with which to engage this Daoist vision. As Ellen M. Chen sees it, Peirce's system is "particularly attractive to the Daoist" because it is "strikingly similar to what is presented in the *Daodejing*."[63] Peirce's "firstness" captures that element of pure spontaneity that attends the production of each "one" in the ongoing creative process (*daoshengyi* 道生一); "secondness" is mirrored in the determinate, qualitative nature that each thing assumes as it relates to other things (*yinyang* 陰陽); and "thirdness" represents the diverse orders that take shape as the interlocking habits of things form dynamic harmonies (*he* 和) at broader levels.

While there are indeed parallels between Peirce's categories and the 1, 2, 3 of Chapter 42, the most intriguing connections are at the level of fundamental ontology. Reading Peirce alongside Daoist reflections on "nothing" (*wu* 無) is an experiment that returns profound results. Peirce's conception of the "nothing, pure zero" from which all things emerge evokes the state that Chapter 25 of the *Daodejing* describes as being "indeterminate and complete, before heaven and earth emerged, silent and empty, standing alone and not changing." Such is not a state of *negation*, submits Peirce: "This pure zero is the nothing of not having been born. There is no individual thing, no compulsion outward nor inward, no law. It is the germinal nothing, in which the whole universe is involved or foreshadowed. As such, it is absolutely undefined and unlimited possibility—boundless possibility." This state of "pure zero" accords with how the Great Continuum (*taiyi* 太一) is understood in Daoist thought.

As Peirce suggests, the only bridge from such an indeterminate "nothing" to a determinate *something* is spontaneity (or *ziran* 自然)—and the *Daodejing* concurs with such reasoning.

Peirce offers the following: "The logic of freedom, or potentiality, is that it shall annul itself . . . unbounded potentiality became potentiality of this or that sort—that is, of some *quality*, thus the zero of bare possibility . . . leapt into the *unit* of some quality."[64] So things commenced at the start. Creation, however, is not finished. As Peirce explains, it is "going on today and will never be done."[65] Within a Daoist cosmology, "*dao* 道 producing one" represents the ongoing creative process by which bare possibility continues to be steadily "annulled," giving birth to units of determinate possibility for events (*wu* 物) to realize. This process reflects the endless generosity of *dao*, which continues to yield indeterminate regions within the nothing of bare possibility (*wu* 無) so that events may occupy those regions and thereby exist (*you* 有).

Chapter 40 describes this process as follows: "Annulment (*fan* 反) is the movement of *dao* 道 and yielding (*rou* 弱) is its function. The myriad beings of the world are born from what exists (*you* 有) and what exists is born from nothing (*wu* 無)." Chapter 25 describes the annulment of bare possibility as a process in which primordial indeterminacy "turns back" (*fan*) upon itself as it issues into *dao*.[66] Such an oddly recessive forthcoming is only barely discernable from this side of its occurrence. The author of Chapter 25 struggles to find the words to describe such an elusive process, one by which actuality is furthered through the *retreat* of bare possibility. "I do not know its name, so I style it '*dao*.' If pushed, I would call it 'immense' (*da* 大). 'Immense' is to say that it is going away. 'Going away' is to say that it is advancing further. 'Advancing further' is to say that it is 'turning back' (*fan*)."[67]

The broader coherence of the Daoist vision now comes into view. The concept of annulment or "turning back" (*fan* 反) provides the conceptual link between Chapter 42 and *The Great Continuum Produces the Waters* cosmogony. The primordial state that Chapter 25 refers to as "standing alone, silent and empty" is another way of describing the Great Continuum, the zero-state of continuity in which every possibility resides. Against such a perfectly continuous "one" (*taiyi* 太一), the event of creation is a flash of sheer *dis*continuity in which bare possibility is annulled and a discrete possibility is suddenly realized. This can only be conceived as a moment of spontaneity (*ziran* 自然)—one upon which *dao* 道 then models itself. Peirce envisions the process as follows: "Out of the womb of indeterminacy we must say that there would have come something, by the principle of Firstness, which we may call a flash . . . Then there would have come other successions ever more and more closely connected, the habits and the tendency to take them ever strengthening themselves, until the events would have been bound together into something like a continuous flow."⁶⁸ According to the *The Great Continuum Produces the Waters*, the Great Continuum gives birth to this flow, which it describes as that of the "waters" (*shui* 水). Each drop in the stream consists of *dao* giving birth to one more unit of possibility (*deyi* 得一). Together, the juxtaposition of continuity and *dis*continuity illuminates the nature of order as understood in the Chapter 42 cosmology.

To get a clearer sense of this reasoning, imagine the Great Continuum as a continuous field like an empty blackboard. Peirce proposes the following: "I draw a chalk line on the board. This discontinuity is one of those brute acts by which alone the original vagueness makes a step towards definiteness. There is a certain amount of continuity in this line. Where did this continuity come from? It is nothing but the original continuity of the blackboard which makes everything upon it continuous."⁶⁹ Peirce's chalk line emerges with a "step towards definiteness," a *flash* of spontaneity. This breach of continuity is one unit of possibility suddenly afforded on the surface of the board. As such, it is a "First." Realized through the actual contrast of black and white, it is a "Second." The finitude of the line now expresses a definite character, an ordered togetherness that is identifiable and persists. As such, it is a "Third."

This latter characteristic *grows*, becoming richer and more discernable as additional lines appear on the board. As these lines spontaneously arrive (*one*), relations are formed (*two*), and larger generalities take shape (*three*). The condition for the possibility of this latter, tertiary quality is the continuity (*yi* 一) of the blackboard itself, upon which every *dis*continuity is invariably bound by its own *continuity*. Such continuity affords each unique line numberless opportunities to share in and express general characteristics with other lines as they arrive. As this happens, units of possibility ("ones") are steadily realized (*deyi* 得一).

Among the notable features of Daoism's process-oriented approach is that the Great Continuum (*taiyi* 太一) is never diminished, even as it is steadily annulled (*fan* 反) in the process of giving birth to discrete units. To understand why, imagine the Great Continuum as itself a line. Upon this line, the store of possible points is infinite. Any infinitesimal that is realized as a point still leaves infinite points unrealized. Infinitesimals thus represent the constant *potential* for breaks in the continuum. Since infinitesimals are not individuals as such, they do not constitute any "collection" that will ever decrease in magnitude.⁷² Western thinkers like Nicholas of Cusa recognize the same. The "Maximum" endures even as division erupts on its surface. Within each point in the line, explains Nicholas: "only the Maximum is to be found," such that the Maximum "envelops all" even while being segmented.⁷³ Given this feature, it is impossible to exhaust the possibilities of the Great Continuum—its potential to produce new points can never be depleted or even abridged.

From such an inexhaustible "no-thing" (*wu* 無) where *no* individuals reside, units of possibility issue through *dao* 道 into a world which will "have" (*you* 有) them. Accordingly, the unique character (*de* 德) of each unit is born on *this* side of the process, from *within* the existing world system. As Chapter 1 of the *Daodejing* states: "What is no-thing (*wu*) refers to the *beginning* of the myriad beings, and what is here (*you*) refers to the *mother* of the myriad beings."[74] In this formulation, the beginning (*shi* 始) represents the spontaneity that attends creativity *as such*, while the mother (*mu* 母) represents the proximate conditions that shape each event as it happens.

Since this discussion has become rather abstract, let us turn closer to shore by considering again the status of organic form (*xing* 形). Fourteen billion years ago, when the universe was in its zero-state, the likelihood that the Red-eyed tree frog (*Agalychnis callidryas*) would become a reality was infinitesimal in nature. It was a possibility with no content—entirely unthinkable! As order emerged and organisms evolved, conditions took shape that gave birth to the realization of such a possibility. Pure chance found its way there, and conditions gave birth to the frog. Having now been realized, the frog is unequivocally here (*you* 有)—standing forth in the power (*de* 德) of its own remarkable character. Its presence, however, leaves numberless other forms *un*realized. In fact, the presence of the Red-eyed tree frog does not diminish the power of the recumbent continuum in the slightest.

While what is here (*you* 有) and what is not here (*wu* 無) can be considered separately, they in fact constitute a single dynamic in the advent of possibility. As the flow of actuality proceeds, *The Great Continuum Produces the Waters* suggests that the Great Continuum remains "stored" (*zang* 藏) in the waters. Each finite achievement becomes a vehicle that "turns back" (*fan* 反) to "assist" (*fu* 輔) the Great Continuum in liberating further possibilities from the bottomless reserve.[75] Thus understood, each unit of possibility that is realized, owing to the continuity that it inherits upon the Great Continuum, is like an evolving shell that "contains" (*zang*) its own continuum of possibilities to annul.

Again, animal forms provide a concrete example. As Daniel C. Dennett observes, "there might have been a time, in the very distant past, when the possibility of six-limbed mammals on Earth had not yet been foreclosed."[76] At one stage in evolution, there were organic forms vague enough with respect to limb configuration to "store" (*zang* 藏) this as a distinct possibility. Over time, the chances that a "six-limbed mammal" *would* emerge on Earth were negotiated down through historical transactions between such primitive forms and their environing conditions. At this point, the prospects for a "six-limbed mammal" on Earth are not looking good. The possibilities that *are* stored in present forms, however, remain numberless. In the infinite long run, *anything* is possible. It is accurate then to say that *dao* 道 is not the only thing that is "immense" (*da* 大) in this world. As Chapter 25 teaches: "The heavens are immense, the earth is immense, humans are immense, and the ruler is immense." Countless possibilities are stored in each of these "four immensities" (*sida* 四大). Each reserve of possibility is shelled within its next largest order, with its possibilities graded accordingly.

In this respect, as the *Daodejing* teaches: "Humans follow the earth, the earth follows the heavens, and the heavens follow *dao* 道," such that each order establishes conditions within which subordinate possibilities are arrayed and made accessible. To "follow *dao*," however, does not mean following a process that models itself on some pre-ordained order or end. *Dao* follows spontaneity (*ziran* 自然). This means that even the most enduring orders will eventually change and liberate untold possibilities.

Attaining the One (*deyi* 得一)

The foregoing analysis enables us to revisit our standing questions with greater nuance. First, we have the question posed in *All Things Flow in Form*, which asks: "What do living things attain (*de* 得) in order to reach maturity (*cheng* 成)?" Second, we have that posed in "The Subject Matter of Metaphysics," which asks: "What are the generic traits of a world in which at least *some* changes exhibit organic form and functioning?" Our first question, in fact, is readily answered in the Chinese tradition. The *Annals of Lü Buwei* answers it directly. "As a general rule," we learn, "the myriad forms reach maturity (*cheng*) as a result of attaining the one (*deyi* 得一)."[77] What does this mean? As we have seen, the meaning of this statement might differ according to how the term "one" (*yi* 一) is being understood.

This gives us a chance to test our interpretative hypothesis. According to the present reading, we should expect to find at least two distinct ways of approaching this statement: a more top-down, politically minded "Huang-Lao" way, and a more novelty-friendly, organically minded "Daoist" way. Variants observed in Chapter 39 of the *Daodejing* surface as predicted. Among the phenomena that "attain the one," the Wang Bi version includes the myriad beings (*wanwu* 萬物)—the multiplicity of living things whose lives depend upon the sheer generosity of *dao* 道. "The myriad beings 'attain the one' and thereby live/grow (*sheng* 生)," explains the author. "If the myriad beings lacked that through which they live/grow they would go extinct." These lines are absent in the Mawangdui version, while those with overt political content are retained. "Rulers and kings 'attain the one' and bring order to the world," we read. "If they were not by this means noble and high they would stumble and fall."⁷⁸ The latter statement does not present any interpretative challenge to the Huang-Lao editor, whereas identifying the "one" (*yi* 一) with the spontaneity of organic life/growth (*sheng*) certainly does.

Thus, in the present context, understanding the "one" in terms of our Chapter 42 cosmology continues to recommend itself as an interpretive strategy—in this case, one for understanding what "attaining the one" (*deyi* 得一) means in philosophical Daoism. In a novelty-driven cosmology, *deyi* would mean coming forth from nothing (*wu* 無) to become one unit of possibility, something realizable in the world. As Charles Sanders Peirce explains, unbounded potentiality becomes "potentiality of this or that sort—that is, of some *quality*." The zero of nothingness thus "[leaps] into the *unit* of some quality."⁷⁹ This "leap" prepares the way for a discrete individual, one bearing what Dewey identifies as the "secondness" trait of *specificity/interaction*. Thus, by virtue of "attaining the one," each thing becomes distinct in having its own characteristic "qualities" (*de* 德) in relation to other things.⁸⁰ As Chapter 39 relates: "The sky 'attained the one' and became clear; the earth 'attained the one' and became calm." If such qualitative integrity were lacking, the sky would "fall to pieces" and the earth would "burst into bits." The fact that the world does *not* fall to pieces or burst into bits indicates that units of possibility are being steadily realized in things just as they are (*ziran* 自然). Simply by being here (*you* 有), each unit expresses a power (or *de* 德) that lends integrity to its qualities, direction to its movements, and momentum to its growth.

The fact that this occurs without teleological "aims" is made explicit in Daoism's refusal to equate *de* 德 with "virtue" as understood in rival philosophies. While sharing some features with such notions, *de* in the *Daodejing* does not refer to anything that is not already attained (*de* 得) simply by existing. In fact, striving to attain a secondary form of "virtue" (*de* 德) in addition to one's natural, spontaneous (*ziran* 自然) integrity obscures this "higher" *de* and introduces end-driven operations where they do not belong. Chapter 38 explains:

> Higher *de* 德 is not "virtue." Thereby, it keeps its *de*. Secondary "virtue" cannot let go of "virtuosity." Thereby, it loses its *de*. Higher *de* does not act for the sake of anything (*wuwei* 無為). There is nothing for which it acts. Secondary "virtue" *does* act for the sake of something. There *is* something for which it acts.

As Philip J. Ivanhoe suggests, the actions of the higher *de* are "spontaneous and natural: like the flowing of water or the falling of timely rain."⁸¹ Such phenomena occur without any purpose, aim, or final end (*telos*).

The fact that this higher *de* 德 does not act for the sake of anything (*wuwei* 無為) underwrites Daoism's normative stance against human institutions that pursue so-called "virtuous" outcomes through clever agendas and fixed objectives. Such excursions into knowing (*zhi* 知) limit the furthering (*yuan* 遠) of things by restricting their freedom to annul (*fan* 反) their own store of possibilities as they go along. Those who govern with "profound" *de* refuse to forecast fixed ends for this reason. As Chapter 65 explains: "Those who consistently realize this style [of governance] are said to be profoundly *de*. Profound *de* goes deeper and advances further. It goes with things as they annul (*fan*). Only when this happens is the great flowing accordance (*dashun* 大順) reached." Before going deeper into this prescriptive outlook, the alternative to teleology that informs it needs to be better understood.

Having addressed the *All Things Flow in Form* question, let us turn to that which Dewey poses in "The Subject Matter of Metaphysics"—namely, "What are the generic traits of a world in which at least *some* changes exhibit organic form and functioning?" Dewey's answer to this question is deceptively simple. He offers the following observation: "While metaphysics takes the world irrespective of any particular time . . . time itself, or *genuine change in a specific direction*, is itself one of the ultimate traits of the world irrespective of date."[82] This trait, "genuine change in a specific direction," encompasses all three of Dewey's other traits: *change, specificity/interaction*, and *diversity*. First, it is *change*; second, it is *specific*, and third, it is *directional*—in that diverse types have an end state toward which they move. Thus contained within this single, *meta*-trait is Peirce's triadic cosmology in its entirety. Unpacking its implications alongside the teachings of Daoism helps to bring into focus the alternative to conventional teleology that it presents, an alternative that does not reduce to efficient causation.

It is fitting that Peirce contributes at this juncture. Dewey recognized no thinker "more calculated than Peirce to give emancipation from the intellectual fortifications of the past and to arouse fresh imagination."[83] Peirce's notion of "habit" is especially profitable to read alongside the *Daodejing*. For as we have seen, "habit" and *dao* 道-activity are closely related ideas. Plus, each concept assumes there to be continuity between cosmological traits and the behavior of organic form. As Dewey observes, "even the casual reader of Peirce should be aware that habit on his view is first a cosmological matter and then is physiological and biotic—in a definitely existential sense. It, habit, operates in and through [organic form], but that very fact is to him convincing evidence that the organism is an integrated part of the world in which habits form and operate."[84]

A world in which habits form and operate—how did such a world ever come about? Peirce submits that a deep-seated principle of continuity (or *taiyi* 太一) is the only thing that can explain it. He arrives at this hypothesis by transcendental deduction. *How is it possible* that there are uniformities in nature? As Peirce sees it, "Conformity with law is a fact requiring to be explained; and since Law in general cannot be explained by any law in particular, the explanation must consist in showing how law is developed out of pure chance, irregularity, and indeterminacy."[85] Peirce's triadic cosmology is a "guess" at this riddle. From the zero-state of primordial nothingness there must have come a *flash* of spontaneity (*one*), then another (*two*), and then another (*three*). Presumably, this occurred within the Planck epoch, when the universe was between zero and 10^{-43} of a second old and there were no observable laws in operation. The third flash established the habit of flashing, thus realizing the infinitesimal chance that "habit-taking" would ever take hold. Once the habit of taking habits was formed, the zero-state of nothingness became functionally a continuum against which novel asymmetries became individuals (*two*) of some type (*three*). With this, the conditions for the possibility of the world were established.

"[It] is clear that nothing but a principle of habit," writes Peirce, "itself due to the growth by habit of an infinitesimal chance tendency toward habit-taking, is the only bridge that can span the chasm between the chance medley of chaos and the cosmos of order and law."[86] How, then, does habit now function? "[It] is a generalizing tendency, and *as such* a generalization, and *as such* a general, and *as such* a continuum or continuity."[87] In the present world system, each habit exhibits one form of continuity: one that serves a mediating function between subsidiary elements in the realization of one unit of possibility (*deyi* 得一). In this way, "uniformities in the modes of action of things have come about by their taking habits."[88] Such continuities are what Peirce refers to as "Thirds."

From this standpoint, attaining the one (*deyi* 得一) entails more than simply being novel (*one*) and becoming a discrete individual (*two*)—it also entails being an individual of some general type (*three*) with a tendency to mature (*cheng* 成) in predictable ways. Accordingly, *de* 德 represents not only the allure of a thing but also its "directional order"—its momentum, power, or potential to grow. The trick is coming to understand how such directional growth occurs without any operative *purpose*, i.e., without being for the sake of something (*wuwei* 無為)—without having what Dewey calls an "aim." This is the question that vexes common sense.

It is common sense, however, that *asks* the question—and the very asking obscures the solution. In most natural cases, means-and-ends are inseparable, continuous (*yi* 一). Seeds *sprout*, wings *fly*, milk *nourishes*. In such achieved adaptations between organism-and-environment, how could one element in the unit exist for the sake (*wei* 為) of the other? *What* other? Dewey's strategy, as presented in chapter 2, is to dissolve the dualism that obscures this insight. He re-envisions directional orders as *units with specifiable histories,* thus enabling us "to apprehend causal mechanisms and temporal finalities as phases of the same natural processes, instead of as competitors where the gain of one is the loss of the other."[89]

Dewey's cosmological *meta*-trait: "genuine change in a specific direction," anticipates this philosophical move. It assumes that each event, by its very nature, contains all three of Peirce's traits: Firstness, Secondness, and Thirdness. Thus, each event displays *some* chance, *some* efficient causation, and *some* goal-directedness, without these becoming adversaries that threaten to subsume one another. The modern tendency, again, is to reduce goal-directedness to efficient causality. For Dewey, however, "aims," "ends," and "results" grow out of one another. They are not discrete ontological species, but rather different degrees to which "genuine change in a specific direction" becomes *organized*—simple as that.[90]

Dewey did not entirely fathom Peirce's thinking.[91] Dewey's *meta*-trait, however, implies that what Pierce calls "Thirdness," or the exhibition of a general type, is a feature of *every* event no matter how obscure or ephemeral. Like Aristotle, Peirce was unable to envision a world in which "efficient" and "final" causes did not operate together in every instance. As Peirce observes, "final causation without efficient causation is helpless . . . Efficient causation without final causation, however, is worse than helpless . . . it is mere chaos; and chaos is not even so much as chaos without final causation; it is a blank nothing." Peirce's "final cause," however, is something other than what Aristotle had in mind. For Peirce, final causation is simply "that mode of bringing facts about according to which a general description of result is made to come about." Such generality is essentially *vague*, in that it is "quite irrespective of any compulsion for it to come about in this or that particular way." The end result, Peirce says, "may be brought about at one time in one way, and at another time in another way."[92]

To illustrate, Peirce appeals to the behavior of gases. When left undisturbed, gas molecules tend irreversibly toward the result of being uniformly distributed. This end-state depends only to a slight degree upon efficient causality, since whatever forces the molecules impose on one another are weak and more or less random in their distribution.[93] Accordingly, the possible routes by which the end-state of the gas might be reached are immense (*da* 大). In the case of organic functioning, it is more difficult to observe such immensity because means-and-ends have been so closely adapted to one another. The "chance" element in stag digestion, for instance, appears more restrained due to the latter's organization. According to the logic of infinitesimals, however, the possibilities stored (*zang* 藏) in the digestive process are no less immense (*da*) than those in the gas canister. There are minute indeterminacies at every stage (and at the subatomic level, certainly) as the organic process comes to term (*cheng* 成) and exhibits a type.

The leap just made, between gas distribution and stag digestion, triggers the modern objection that a boundary in nature has been crossed. According to Ernst Mayr, gas distribution is "teleomatic" and only *seemingly* goal-directed, whereas stag digestion is "teleonomic" and thus *genuinely* goal-directed (i.e., determined by a "program"). From a Peircean perspective, however, each phenomenon exhibits the same basic cosmological feature: *the tendency of nature to form habits*. The laws of mechanics and those of digestive systems are different in manifold ways, but they are similar in that each "tends asymptotically toward bringing about an ultimate state of things." Peirce suggests that, "If teleological is too strong a word to apply to them, we might invent the word *finious*, to express their tendency towards a final state."[94]

As Dewey observes, Peirce's notion of *finious* "habits" is at once cosmological and physical while being physiological and organic.[95] Chinese thinkers exhibit a similar ambivalence to such domain distinctions when speaking of *dao* 道-activity. Mencius speaks of the *dao* of water and compares human tendencies to "water flowing downward," suggesting that a single manner of tendency applies.[96] When the *Huainanzi* speaks of the "spontaneous propensity of things" (*ziranzhishi* 自然之勢) it proceeds seamlessly from "metal becomes molten under heat" and "round things spin," to "trees give bloom" and "birds hatch eggs" without ever indicating that these are disparate kinds of phenomena.[97] What can be said generically about each is that it "attains the one" (*deyi* 得一) such that it exhibits *some* degree of chance, *some* degree of efficient causality, and *some* degree of goal-directedness.

Dewey recognizes that Peirce's triadic cosmology answers the need for a vision adequate to the science of evolution. He observes that, for Peirce, "the idea of evolution is one form of the principle of continuity." The notion that everything has a 1-2-3 about it "points to the conclusion that all things can be explained only on the basis that they *grow*." As Peirce observes: "Even laws themselves are evolutionary growths. Wherever there is genuine diversification, there must be spontaneity and contingency."[98] Daoism represents an elegant, intuitive, and accessible tradition in which to make sense of this. As such, it contributes a cosmological-cosmogonic vision that, unlike the Judeo-Christian tradition, easily accommodates evolution by natural selection. As we have seen, organic ends in Daoism are coterminal with the environments in which forms take shape (*xing* 形). Accordingly, the procreant mother (*mu* 母) of the myriad beings is that which is already here (*you* 有), bracing things as they continue to evolve. Included in what is "here" are the patterns, harmonies, cycles, and conditions that mediate between an indeterminacy that is latent in change and ends that are consummatory in nature.

For Peirce, "Thirds" perform this mediating function. "By the Third," he writes, "I understand the medium which has its being or peculiarity in connecting the more absolute first and second," meaning that, "every process, and whatever is *continuous*, involves thirdness."[99] Peirce's notion of "thirdness," alongside the Daoist notion of the "three" (*san* 三), keeps our thinking squarely "in gear." Such theories of dynamic, emergent order succeed by not reinstating what Stuart A. Kauffman, in his landmark work on the origin of biological order, refers to as "nonsensical medieval ideas about 'types' based on an outmoded essentialism."[100] As Dewey notes, "Peirce understands by the reality of a 'general' the reality of a way, habit, disposition, of behavior; and he dwells upon the fact that the habits of things are acquired and modifiable." In fact, Peirce "virtually reverses Aristotle in holding that the universal always has an admixture of potentiality in it."[101] In so doing, Peirce doubts that events of a perfectly identical "type" ever occur twice. The "summer" and "winter" cycles, for instance, never identically reoccur because the chance element in their realization virtually ensures statistical deviations greater than zero. "The odds are infinity to one that it is not zero," he surmises, "and we are bound to think of it as a quantity of which zero is only one possible value . . . one of an infinity of values in that neighborhood."[102] The basic cosmological premise behind Kauffman's notion of emergent order within complex systems is not far different.[103]

Philosophical Daoism concurs in maintaining that "chance" elements modulate systems in which order grows. As we know, "*Dao* models itself on spontaneity" (*daofaziran* 道法自然). The operation of chance ensures that patterns (*li* 理) and harmonies (*he* 和), while remaining steadily operative, evolve with the influx of novelty. The Daoist vision invites us to consider organic form (*xing* 形) accordingly: as an intersection of working "habits" embedded in dynamic environments that evolve as conditions change. Moreover, in accounting for the goal-directedness of such forms, the Daoist tradition enables us to bypass the "Mechanistic/Animistic" stalemate—the choice between "something causes it" (*shi* 使) or "nothing makes it happen" (*mowei* 莫為). The living thing exists in constant transaction with its environment. In the process, the propensity (*shi* 勢) shored up in the environment triggers *dao*-activity commensurate with the ongoing organization of the form. There is no separable "aim" or purpose (*telos*) that *causes* this to happen, and it does not happen for the sake (*wei* 為) of any future end. As Dewey suggests, growth/maturation (or *cheng* 成) is an "ever-present process" in living things.[104] Activities of "fulfilling, consummating, are continuous functions," he explains, "not mere ends, located at one place only."[105] Better understanding how this dovetails with Daoist thinking and differs from Greek-medieval reasoning should enable us to update our notion of "types" accordingly. Testing this will be our next experiment.

Forms and Types

As Dewey suggests, Peirce "virtually reverses Aristotle in holding that the universal always has an admixture of potentiality in it."[106] What this means is that forms become actualized *over the course* of their instantiation and remain open to modification as the process continues. According to Dewey, one of the greatest fallacies in philosophy is to wrongly conceive this fact as it pertains to organic form. In the "Reflex Arc" essay, Dewey identifies this as the "historical fallacy," whereby "a state of things characterizing an outcome is regarded as a true description of the events which led up to this outcome; when, as a matter of fact, if this outcome had already been in existence, there would have been no necessity for the process." The "Stag," for example, is the current *outcome* of an ongoing historical process. If there had been no such process, there would be no such outcome. Stags are here (*you* 有) because stags have, over time, adapted successfully to their environment and continue to survive within it. To regard the "Stag" as somehow prefigured in its own past, as the cause of its own present, or as the aim of its own future, obscures what stags actually represent. As Dewey explains, such interpretations transfer a "set of considerations which hold good only because of a completed process [and reads them back] into the content of the process which conditions this completed result."[107] From an evolutionary standpoint, the "Stag" is an ongoing *event*. It retains an "admixture of potentiality" because its existence amounts to the history of a population that remains open to further development as the event continues.

In *Experience and Nature*, Dewey reformulates the "historical fallacy" into what he calls "*the* philosophical fallacy." This fallacy consists in converting an *eventual* outcome into an antecedent existence and then postulating that existence as the *reason* or *cause* that explains its eventual outcome. The circularity is obvious. Its most deleterious effect is that it devalues the process through which a given result is achieved. By reducing a concrete process to that which occurs "for the sake" of its own end, the fallacy "escapes the need (and salutary effect) of taking into account the operations and processes that condition the eventual subject-matter." As Dewey explains, "the fallacy converts consequences of interactions of events into causes of the occurrence of these consequences—a reduplication which is significant as to the *importance* of the functions, but which hopelessly confuses understanding of them."[108] As Larry A. Hickman observes, Dewey regards this fallacy as "both ubiquitous in the history of philosophy and devastating in terms of its consequences," leading to gratuitous metaphysical postulations and misleading hypostatization in several instances.[109]

Aristotle, unfortunately, commits this fallacy systematically in his treatment of organic form. He does so by drawing his initial reasoning from artifice. "*Why do saws have sharp teeth that are made of iron?*" Aristotle asks. "To effect so-and-so and for the sake of so-and-so," he replies. If saws are to exist, then they *must* consist of such-and-such material in such-and-such an arrangement. This is what Aristotle calls a "hypothetical necessity."[110] In the case of such artificial instruments, their "aim" or "purpose" (*telos*) determines the materials and arrangements that come to be so organized. Aristotle transposes this reasoning directly onto organic form. For as he asserts: "Now exactly the same way with the body, which like the axe is an instrument—for both the body as a whole and its several parts individually have definite operations for which they are made—just in the same way, I say, the body, if it is to do its work, *must of necessity* be of such and such a character, and made of such and such materials."[111] According to this reasoning, the digestive system of the "Stag," both in its material composition and its functional arrangement, exists *for the sake* of the "Stag." For if stags did not have the digestive system that they *do* have, then there would be no "Stags." Proceeding from this tautology to the premise that "Stags exist" invites the circularity.

Aristotle's keenest insight is that, in the case of living things, the formal and final causes are "pretty much . . . one and the same."[112] This assertion underscores his commitment to the immanence of ends in nature. This notion: that "the final cause has been completely identified with the formal," is thought by some commentators to secure what modern biology needs in the face of mechanistic physics—namely, something *other* than an aggregate of adaptive mechanisms to explain directional order.[113] Jacob Rosen, however, has recently questioned the degree to which Aristotle's statement results in a "picture very similar to the outlook of today's evolutionary biology," a reading that he regards as "highly misleading." As Rosen explains, "Aristotle is not saying that the *role* of formal cause is ever the same as the *role* of final cause. He is only saying that, often, the same thing has both of these roles in relation to something."[114] This observation in fact underscores the problem of using Aristotle to secure our post-Darwinian needs. Aristotle's equation of the formal and final causes is a double-edged sword—for it also serves as the conceptual link between the "nature" of a thing and its unchanging species-essence.[115] As Dewey reminds us, "Aristotle absolutely denied any evolution of forms, species, and ends," and thus "confined change within certain absolutely fixed limits."[116]

So, while a single power might serve as both the formal and final cause in a living thing, this does not introduce any genuine dynamism in Aristotle's system. It may be true, as André Ariew explains, that the *telos* operative in the explanation of functional arrangements in the organism, "whereby an item is explained in terms of its usefulness," (i.e., its final cause) *is* for Aristotle the same *telos* that determines growth in the maturing organism (i.e., its formal cause). This identification, however, rather than render organic form thereby more dynamic, cements its changes into place. While Aristotle's "ends" are rightly understood as "non-purposive, non-rational, non-intentional, and immanent, residing in an inner principle of change," they entail no potential for change in forms or functions *themselves*.[117] As Dewey observes, such potential never results in the "origin of new forms [or] a mutation from an old species, but only the monotonous traversing of a previously plotted cycle of change."[118]

This is where the Chinese tradition offers a genuine alternative. It has already been shown that evolutionary thinking was common in early China, and that cosmogonies like the *Hengxian* regard the emergence of organic form as a gradual and concurrent development. It has also been shown that early Chinese understandings of organic form tended to be locative in nature, grouping forms according to the dynamic environments that "have" (*you* 有) them. What is more, when Chinese thinkers do organize animals more formally into "types" (*lei* 類), the process looks nothing like the Aristotelian or Linnaean procedures. As Roel Sterckx explains, the Chinese "integrated animals within correlative schemes guided by extra-biological sets of principles such as time or season, space or biotope, color, and human activity."[119] The *Huainanzi* engages extensively in this practice, building upon the *Book of Changes* (*Yijing* 易經)—a tradition to which Liu An ascribes great authority as a model for discerning patterns in the natural world.[120] According to this tradition, the ancient sage Fuxi was the first to observe such patterns. Among other things, "He observed the patterns of the birds and animals, and how they had adapted (*yi* 宜) to the land." Assumptions tracing back to these primitive observations include that: "directional trends can be sorted by type" (*fangyileiju* 方以類聚), "living beings can be divided by groups" (*wuyiqunfen* 物以群分), and "organic forms mature on earth" (*zaidichengxing* 在地成形).

Aristotle also observes as much; but Fuxi observes more, *viz.* that "movement and equilibrium are constants" (*dongjingyouchang* 動靜有常) and "change and transformation are manifest" (*bianhuajianyi* 變化見矣).[121] Organic forms adapt (*yi* 宜) to conditions *as they change*, and the possibility for them to transform (*hua* 化) in the process was understood. As John S. Major explains: "Transformation is the key to the total conceptual framework of the *Huainanzi* . . . Such ceaseless transformation instantiates the intrinsic dynamism of the [*dao* 道] that brought the phenomenal world into being and that continues to compel it to evolve."[122]

What then are "types" (*lei* 類) in early China? The notion that organic forms might eventually *change* requires us to distinguish their "types" from

Platonic forms or Aristotelian essences as traditionally understood. Such a challenge is not unique to those working in Chinese philosophy. The task of developing a species concept consistent with evolutionary biology occupies contemporary biologists and philosophers as well. Today, there are several competing accounts of "species" in the scholarly literature.[123] Among them, M. T. Ghiselin and David L. Hull are recognized for making groundbreaking progress with the radical approach of considering species as *individuals* rather than classes.[124] By "individuals," they mean entities that are "spatiotemporally localized, well-organized, cohesive at any one time, and continuous through time."[125] As Maureen Kearney explains, such reasoning "precludes viewing species as classes or natural kinds because classes and kinds are tied to an essentialism that is inconsistent with an evolutionary worldview." In contrast, "individuals are particulars with spatiotemporal extension; they are not subject to a membership relation but to a part-whole relation."[126]

Debate over the viability of the "species-as-individual" approach continues, with considerable discussion about how criterion such as spatial localization, temporal boundary, continuity, and cohesion are satisfied at the species level. Ernst Mayr and others resist the word "individual" for a variety of reasons, one being that "individuals" (*individuus*) by definition cannot be "divided down" as biological taxa can be. The term "population" is thus preferable as a unit term on the species level. As Mayr sees it, there is "no real conflict between the terms individual and population, for a biopopulation [also] has the spatiotemporal properties, internal cohesion, and potential for change of an individual."[127]

Recent work in classical Chinese language and logic demonstrates that Chinese philosophers have something to contribute to this effort. Chad Hansen inspires ample debate with his thesis that classical Chinese nouns function as "mass nouns" (as opposed to "count nouns") in that they lack plural forms, do not take definite articles, and are understood to denote collections defined by *part-whole* relations rather than *member-set* classifications. Hansen further maintains that ancient Chinese theories of language are thoroughly nominalist: that Chinese philosophers are "not committed to any entities other than names and objects," and that the tradition as a whole exhibits a form of "behavioral nominalism," one that regards mind "not as an internal picturing mechanism which represents the individual objects in the world, but as a faculty that discriminates the boundaries of the substances or stuffs referred to by the names."[128] If Hansen is on the right track, then early Chinese thinking recommends itself as a resource for generating species concepts more adequate to contemporary needs. For according to Hansen's thesis, classical Chinese does not employ general terms like "Stag" to denote static universals such as "Stagness." Instead, it uses "names" (*ming* 名) to denote mereological wholes with spatiotemporal extensions—e.g., collections of "stag-stuff" for which the mass-noun "Stag" (*zhu* 麚) is a proper name. Strictly speaking, there are no classical Chinese "kinds" in Hansen's view. There are only spatially extended populations cohesive enough to bear a name.

This pertains to how the notion of "type" (*lei* 類) is understood in the Mohist *Canons*. Hansen maintains that it is not premised on the notion that universal or abstract properties are ontologically real in the Platonic sense. Rather, it rests on the premise that "the world controls projections of linguistic expressions from the outside," i.e., according to "stuff" (*shi* 實) that is actually out there. Formulating "types" commits us to certain behaviors accordingly. The Mohists thus "embed their realistic theory [of "types"] in a pragmatic framework."[129]

A. C. Graham largely agrees with Hansen in maintaining that, "Chinese philosophy is concerned not with essences but with the fitting of names to objects (*mingshi* 名實)."[130] According to Graham, the Mohist *Canons* teaches that this process demands consistency in identifying similarities and differences, thus obliging us to treat certain things in certain ways—but it does not involve postulating abstract "classes" with individual members.[131] Things actually *do* resemble one another in countless "kinds" of ways. Generating a "type" (*lei* 類) requires only that we fix some standard (*fa* 法) by which to measure sameness and difference. "The choice of standard is a matter of discretion," Graham observes.[132] There is no collection that is predefined as a "type."[133] As Graham notes: "the Mohist seems to have no other word for definition than 'standard.'"[134] Thus, establishing "types" is basically a constructivist process of "analogical grouping," as Kurtis Hagen maintains. For Hagen, so ordering the world is an "ongoing process that has no final or perfect articulation."[135] In the *Huainanzi*, "types" (*lei*) are assembled according to their practical utility. The text itself is the result of a project undertaken for the purpose of orienting human activity productively in the world.

There is plenty here that lends itself to the "species problem" as currently set in the philosophy of biology. Hansen's mass-noun hypothesis, however, has been subject to decisive critique over the years. Research has established that classical Chinese *does* in fact employ count nouns, and this seriously challenges Hansen's argument.[136] Rather than dismiss Hansen's contributions entirely, Chris Fraser advances them in part by liberating the "mereological worldview" and "behavioral nominalism" hypotheses from Hansen's mass-noun hypothesis. "Both of these [former] hypotheses are highly plausible," Fraser argues, but not for the reasons that Hansen thinks. As Fraser observes, Canon A78 of the Mohist *Canons* clearly distinguishes general terms from singular terms when it categorizes three distinct sorts of names (*ming* 名): (1) reaching (*da* 達) names like "Thing," (2) kind (*lei* 類) names like "Horse," and (3) personal (*si* 私) names like "Jack."[137] Chinese thinkers are perfectly capable of distinguishing general terms from proper nouns—and they are hardly oblivious to "kinds," without which, as Plato suggests, human thought and communication is impossible.[138]

On this basis, Fraser proceeds as follows. Instead of positing "wholes *instead* of kinds," he argues that Chinese thinkers posit "kinds *as* wholes," a thesis that swings free from Hansen's mass-noun hypothesis. Chinese nominalist semantics is *not* the consequence of Chinese grammar as Hansen contends; rather, it is "based on the notion of similarity between particulars, as determined by practices for comparing and grouping them into kinds." In Fraser's view, the double-inference that Hansen makes, from the mass-noun hypothesis to mereology, and then from mereology to nominalism, is unnecessary and ultimately unsound. The notion that Chinese thinkers entertain a "mereological worldview" is plausible on its own account, and "behavioral nominalism" is quite sturdy—"overwhelmingly likely to be a correct interpretation of ancient Chinese philosophy of language."[139] Neither of these hypotheses *needs* to be grounded in Hansen's claims about the status of Chinese nouns.

At this point, the live question becomes how do sameness and difference operate in a world dynamic enough to *really* give rise to overlapping "types" (*lei* 類). David L. Hall and Roger T. Ames contribute importantly to this inquiry. They distance themselves from Hansen early on, distinguishing their "process" ontology from his "stuff" ontology and replacing the "part-whole" model with their own "focus-field" model.[140] Joining the general consensus, they also maintain that Chinese "types" (*lei*) are "not understood by appeal to a shared essence or 'natural kinds,' but by a functional similarity or relationship that obtains among unique particulars." Such relationships, envisioned within the focus-field model, are neither "established by the presumption of 'essences' or 'natural kinds' defining membership in a set of such kinds, nor by the presumption of the contextually defined mereological sets wherein the parts constitute the whole in an additive or summative manner." The idea of bringing orders into "focus" presumes nothing ontologically but a vague, unbounded "field" of potential orders that might become so focused. According to Hall and Ames, the result is neither a "one-many" model nor a "nominalized version of the part-whole" model. The focus-field approach results instead in a "this-that" model.[141]

Building upon the insights of Graham, Hansen, and Hall and Ames, Brook Ziporyn has more recently undertaken a comprehensive reconstruction of Chinese thought based on the notion of "coherence" (*li* 理). While "coherence" is a term that enters only gradually into the Chinese philosophical lexicon, Ziporyn demonstrates that its associations are foreshadowed in patterns of thought that precede its emergence as a central philosophical term.

One of Ziporyn's main insights is that early Chinese thinkers are not easily divided along "Realist/Nominalist" lines. Rather, there seems to be a common assumption, i.e., "[that] things are neither the same nor different; they can be made as much really one and the same as it is possible to be, or as really different as it is possible to be, by connection with another real thing that connects up with them in a particular situation: that other real thing is human action, designed for human purposes." Rather than being "nominalists" or "realists" with respect to the ontological status of "objects," Chinese thinkers display "ironic" or "non-ironic" attitudes toward the applicability of "coherences." Ziporyn thus departs from what he sees as the default nominalism that both Hall and Ames and Hansen ascribe to early Chinese thinkers. For Ziporyn, "the actual approach taken by Chinese thinkers to the question of kinds and categories is neither strictly nominalist nor strictly realist in the Western sense." The notion of coherence (*li*) underwrites this unique approach, which Ziporyn finds significantly different from the nominalism that usually results when Western philosophers deny universal essences.

In exploring possible avenues towards this Chinese approach, Ziporyn briefly considers the classical American tradition. He notes that Peirce's realism and James' nominalism were both regarded as necessary consequences of the pragmatic method. "This would suggest," he writes, "that pragmatist methodology as such does not supersede the problem of a dichotomy [between realism and nominalism] so much as postpone it; it remains unresolved." Ziporyn mentions Dewey in passing, only to identify him with James—they are "both nominalists."[142]

This is incorrect. It is well established that Dewey is not a nominalist.[143] "The defect of nominalism," Dewey says, "lies in its virtual denial of interaction and association . . . [It] ignores organization, and thus makes nonsense out of meanings."[144] Ziporyn's aim, to articulate an approach that factors in "human agency and participation in *creating* continuities," such that there are natural qualities that "[emerge] from their coherence with the totality of experience, in a way that evades a dichotomization of nominalism and realism," is one that Dewey shares.[145] Dewey's critique of nominalism and partial embrace of Peircean realism positions him squarely in that elusive middle that Ziporyn seeks. The relevance of Dewey's thinking in this connection will be taken up in the next chapter. That discussion will not require the ontological analysis initiated here. For as Dewey sees it: "The problem of the relation of universals to individuals is a logical rather than ontological one."[146] What Ziporyn identifies as "that other real thing"—*viz.*, "human action, designed for human purposes," is what ultimately sets the problem of universals for Dewey.

That "other real thing" needs to be held in mind as we review positions in early Chinese ontology. The extent to which "part-whole" or "focus-field" thinking operates is important in specific instances of interpretation. Each approach has its merit. Most likely, however, there is no generalizable Chinese "ontology" that is operative in every context. As Chris Fraser notes, "the Mohist texts provide our strongest grounds for attributing mereological views to classical Chinese thinkers. Outside of Mohist thought, the evidence for such views is sparse and mainly suggestive rather than explicit."[147] David L. Hall and Roger T. Ames argue that the "focus-field" model is *more* suggestive, and they open new avenues of understanding through its use. What is clear, however, is that Daoism is strongly committed to the principle of continuity (*yi* 一). Precisely how one "divides down" from the Great Continuum (*taiyi* 太一) might legitimately vary in different contexts—part-whole, focus-field, one-many, this-that. As Ralph Waldo Emerson says, nature enables the human mind to burrow into such possibilities: "discovering roots running underground whereby contrary and remote things cohere and flower out from one stem."[148] Such inquiry, as Dewey suggests, brings new connections into view—as miners pile high on the surface "treasures brought from below."[149] The principle of continuity (*yi*) reminds us that the value of each treasure lies in how well it works in connecting things on the surface.

Moving to chapter 4, our philosophical experiments are well underway. It should be clear by now that Chinese thought has a lot to offer us as we update our understandings of the natural world. The connections between Daoism and American philosophy are numerous and deep, and forging such connections helps us to assimilate Chinese thinking in light of our contemporary needs. Scholarship in Chinese philosophy has improved significantly in recent years, aided by recent archeological finds and more sophisticated hermeneutical approaches. The fact that early Chinese cosmology is process-oriented—i.e., that the "ultimate is creativity" expressed within a "universe of constant change"—has been common knowledge in Western Sinology since the early 1960s.[150] Hall and Ames have since contributed to ensuring that our understanding of the Chinese tradition remains grounded in such an orientation, even as our own assumptions lure us elsewhere.[151] Work remains to be done, however, in *assimilating* such a process-oriented vision in numerous topic areas—and this is where intra-cultural philosophy is concerned. Contemporary physics and evolutionary biology assure us that the early Chinese picture of nature is, in many respects, more accurate than the Greek-medieval picture. While the latter has its own cultural value, elegance, and coherence, there are specific ways in which it is "out of gear" and now abetting forces that threaten civilization.

Antiquarians can and should preserve every treasure that the Greek-medieval world contains. The role and responsibility of the philosopher, however, is different. As Sing-nan Fen reminds us: "That we as human beings are environmentally bound is a factual lesson learned by philosophers from scientists. As far as the lesson is factual, there is little which a philosopher can argue about."[152] As Dewey sees it, philosophers need to begin with the facts. After that, their cultural role is to serve as the custodians of meaning between science and common sense. Given that organism-environment continuity and evolution by natural selection reflect the way things really are, the question becomes how we are to conceptualize organic forms, directional orders, natural species, etc. accordingly. Only when such reconstructions are undertaken can there be intelligent inquiries into how such concepts affect our values and purposes. Culturally, these are urgent questions that demand our philosophical energies. Philosophers working in the Chinese tradition should understand that they are poised to contribute important work in this area, and that their conceptual resources are particularly well suited to the task. In chapter 4, we see that locating organic form (*xing* 形) in a dynamic world of rhythmic energies (*qi* 氣) is another advantage that the Chinese tradition brings.

4

Rhythms and Energies

Where space is available, there should be a school garden where children can plant and tend flowers and trees, and learn by direct observation and experience how things grow.

—John Dewey, Peking Women's Teachers College, May 1921

The Chinese Landscape

While living in China, Dewey paid a visit to K. J. Koo. Koo was a co-manager of the *Eastern Times* newspaper in Shanghai, which was in publication from 1914 to 1921. Koo also produced high-quality lithographs of Chinese paintings, a number of which Dewey acquired.[1] "I have long been a great admirer of Chinese paintings," Dewey told him, "and I cannot tell you what a great pleasure it is to know that the masterpieces are available in reproduction." Dewey felt that he would be "doing Americans a great favor" by introducing them to such artworks, so he offered to serve as a liaison for Koo should he wish to expand his sales into the American market.[2] Days after writing Koo, Dewey was in Jiangsu and bought a beautiful landscape painting, "said to have been created in the Ming dynasty." Dewey indeed secured provenance for a painting by the Ming dynasty artist Wu Bin 吴彬 (1573–1620).[3] Dewey loved the work and "couldn't take his eyes off it."[4] Later in Beijing, Dewey would see even more: "some of the best old Chinese paintings still remaining in China, Song dynasty and in perfect condition." Again, the landscapes impressed him the most. "I don't believe the world has anything finer to show than two or three of these paintings we saw," he wrote to Albert Barnes.[5] In terms of art, "the Chinese at the present time appear to have the world beat."[6]

Dewey considered making a significant investment in Chinese paintings in order to move the work at auction in the United States. He soon realized that being a Westerner (and a non-specialist) put him at a disadvantage in a

Chinese market flooded with imitations. So, he abandoned the idea.[7] Still, he purchased a number of works for his private collection. One of these works would eventually hang on the wall of his library in his Manhattan apartment, opposite a carved Chippendale chair. As S. J. Woolf relates, Dewey's eyes would sometimes rest on the painting as he paused to gather his thoughts.[8] A popular interviewer and gifted illustrator, Woolf met with Dewey several times in the 1920s and '30s (he sketched Dewey's portrait for the cover of *Time* magazine in 1928). Dewey admired Woolf's ability to relate in just a few words the "background" of a person's thinking—his "power to convey the intangibles, the atmosphere in which men live and do their work."[9] In conveying Dewey's "intangibles," Woolf relates his material connection to the Chinese world: "this Yankee philosopher, sitting in his library surrounded by his books and his Chinese curios," thoughts coming together in the Chinese landscape before him.[10]

Woolf was not the only visitor struck by the "precious Chinese art" and the "lovely scrolls" in Dewey's New York City apartment.[11] Such work provided the philosopher with a concrete link to Chinese sensibilities. Along with his contemporaries, Dewey had limited access to in-depth scholarship on East Asian philosophy. He was aware, however, that Chinese art was "indissolubly connected" with the Daoist tradition.[12] The salient features of Daoist cosmology would be embodied in Dewey's paintings, just as they are in any classic landscape in the "mountains and waters" (*shanshui* 山水) style.

Wang Shimin's 王時敏 (1592–1680) *Mountain with River, Bridge, and Building* can serve as a reference as we review these features. According to Daoist cosmology, "*dao* produces one" (*daoshengyi* 道生一), resulting in a continuous stream of novelty that animates the cosmos. These waters arrive in a flowing river that gushes into the scene at the heart of the composition. Tracing the river back to its source leads us into the mountains, toward the misty emptiness, or to nothing (*wu* 無). Our eyes wander from place to place. Each element is interrelated: banks and river, trees and leaves, cliffs and valleys, plays of light/dark, soft/hard, high/low, all without a vanishing point perspective. Above, there are imposing mountains: emblems of persistence and stability. But how long do such mountains last? "A mountain lasts longer than a cloud," Dewey observes, "but we know that mountains had an origin and that they will, given a sufficiently long time, decay and pass out of existence."[13] Even now, in the encroaching distance, the mountains are fading into the mist—the same mist that shrouds the headwaters of the river.

The scene is emblematic of our world-system: an emergent order of possibilities (*one*), relations (*two*), and harmonies (*three*), woven together against an indeterminate background. The composition is embedded within the Great Continuum (*taiyi* 太一), but it also turns back (*fan* 反) as the scene

Figure 4.1. Wang Shimin (1592–1680). Hanging scroll. *Mountain with River, Bridge, and Building.* © The Trustees of the British Museum.

spills forward toward the viewer. The work forces no single perspective. There are multiple distinct avenues into the composition, yet the work sustains itself as a coherent whole (*li* 理).

How does one approach the Chinese landscape? Does one cherish the freedom to move between different perspectives, allowing the eyes to travel freely in the harmony (*he* 和) that they mutually sustain? Or does one resist such lack of uniformity and aim to eliminate inconsistencies by fixing each element into a single, unified perspective? Such responses would reflect the divergent attitudes toward the "one" (*yi* 一) observed in Daoism and Huang-Lao, respectively. The latter preference for a more unified perspective is reflected in other painterly traditions. During the European renaissance, for instance, it was not uncommon for artists to pencil in geometrical ratios before the brush even hit the canvas. This was to ensure a unified, single-point perspective. Meanwhile, Chinese painters took to composing their landscapes horizontally on long scrolls, a continuous medium that would literally recede in the process of viewing the work. This renders the single-point perspective impossible to secure.

Dewey did not deny the legitimacy of either convention. As he observes: "Chinese rendering of perspective is as perfect in one way as that of Western painting in another."[14] He had, however, what he describes as "a very deep appreciation" for the Chinese approach.[15] He recognizes that an "emphasis upon spaciousness is a characteristic of Chinese paintings," and that such openness of perspective defies any rigid limit. Such perspectives "move outwards," Dewey observes, "while panoramic scroll paintings present a world in which ordinary boundaries are transformed into invitations to proceed." Such works "express space as opportunity for movement and action"—and live creatures, Dewey thought, were "always after larger scope of movement." "Movement, action, and doing" are what living is all about.[16]

How does the "spaciousness" of the Chinese landscape function? According to the *Hengxian*, the emergence of space (*yu* 域) precedes all movement in the universe. Such space, however, is not the empty, "absolute space" of Newtonian physics. In fact, the term for "space" in this instance is not written as *yu* 域 but as *huo* 或, a common substitute which means both an unspecified "something" as well as the conjunction "perhaps."[17] As Liu Jing observes, there are important conceptual overlaps between *yu* and *huo*. Each term suggests indeterminacy and open possibility—the field of potential in which experience might continue.[18] In the "Autumn Floods" chapter of the *Zhuangzi*, human foolishness is identified with confusing the space of utmost immensity (*zhidazhiyu* 至大之域) with boundaries that we have already set, such as "the tip of a hair is the smallest thing possible."[19] Such boundaries overlook the fact that space (*yu*) is the region of *further* possibilities—an opening toward the "perhaps" (*huo*). As Chapter 25 of the *Daodejing* explains, the possibilities housed within the "four immensities" reside entirely within this borderless space (*yuzhongyousida* 域中有四大). In our present world system, human possibilities are shelled within those of the earth (*di* 地) and those of the earth are shelled within those of the heavens (*tian* 天). *Everything*, however, proceeds spontaneously from *dao* 道 in the broader field of wide-open space (*yu*).[20]

"Spaciousness" in the Chinese landscape serves as a visual reminder that this world emerges from the field of sheer potential, and that its myriad orders evolve continuously within this field. In fact, continuity (*yi* 一) is the only operative principle of such orders. As Aristotle observes, "[things are] 'continuous' when their limits touch and become one and the same and are contained in each other; so that it is clear that continuity belongs to things out of whose mutual contact a unity naturally arises."[21] Given that each unit of possibility achieved (*deyi* 得一) proceeds from within the Great Continuum (*taiyi* 太一) order naturally arises from each set of limits. Such orders are continuous with all other orders—whether these orders are prior or subsequent, super- or subordinate, simple or complex. While *some* order is captured from the finite, vanishing-point perspective, order *itself* cannot be captured from such a perspective. Thus, the aim of the Chinese landscape painter is not to present any single order, but to capture instead the coherence (*li* 理) in which multiple orders are simultaneously sustained.

As Tsung Pai-hwa observes, this was the primary criterion that Shen Kuo 沈括 (1031–1095) employed during the Song dynasty in his criticism of landscape paintings. The main purpose of this criticism, Tsung writes, was to "elucidate the fact that the painter of landscapes, unlike the ordinary observer standing on a fixed point on ground level and viewing mountains from below, should with the eyes of the heart [*xin* 心] cover the scene in its totality and conceive the part as bound to the whole. He should integrate the total scene into a rhythmical and harmonious object of art." Perfecting the "spaciousness" of the Chinese landscape was crucial to portraying the world accordingly—as a living, growing coherence (*li* 理) of rhythmic processes. "The empty space—the void—of Chinese painting is not a dead nothing, offering merely a background to bring out the movement of matter," Tsung writes. "[It] is the very essence of life; all rhythms of life grow from it."[22] As Sherman E. Lee explains, the rhythmic divisions of space captured in Song landscape paintings are "rendered to produce an inner rhythm that dominates the whole composition." Such works, as he says, have "major philosophical implications."[23]

In *Art as Experience*, Dewey explores the dynamics of rhythms as they relate to the stabilization of form in nature. His frame of reference is not

Chinese painting, but modern physics. Aiming always to keep his thinking culturally "in gear," Dewey sought to generate theories that comported well with current scientific understandings. In the 1890s, he became interested in the work of James Clerk Maxwell.[24] Maxwell had developed a mathematical framework that synthesized the findings of Hermann von Hemholtz and Michael Faraday along with others. Hemholtz established in the 1840s the modern formulation of the "law of conservation," stating that energy is neither created nor destroyed but remains constant through transformations in form. Meanwhile, Faraday had demonstrated that "transactions" between particles liberated potential energy that converted into the kinetic energy necessary to accelerate mass to a reference velocity.[25] Maxwell's path-breaking synthesis prepared the way for relativity and field theories in the twentieth century.

These two theories—that of the conversion of energy and the energy-converting transactions between physical events—informed not only Dewey's aesthetics but his entire philosophical orientation. Defending his use of the term "transaction" in the 1940s, Dewey notes that it was "indeed, used by Maxwell himself in describing physical events."[26] By aligning himself with modern physics, Dewey hoped to arrive at a more plausible description of organic life and to generate philosophical hypotheses accordingly.

Ernest Nagel, somewhat uncharitably, once remarked that, "Dewey's physics and even mathematics was at best second-hand." Nagel acknowledges, however, that Dewey's comments on physical science "were often full of insight."[27] As it happens, Dewey was not as far removed from modern physics as Nagel suggests. Dewey's daughter Jane was a professional physicist and conducted post-doctoral research with Niels Bohr, Werner Heisenberg, Erwin Schrödinger and others at the Institute for Theoretical Physics in Copenhagen in the 1920s. Dewey visited her at the Institute, and they discussed current happenings in the field.[28] Dewey was not personally involved in such research, but he reached out to those who were and did everything he could to render his ideas commensurable with their best understandings. He offered his own theories in the scientific spirit, exhibiting a "willingness to go where evidence points instead of putting first a personally preferred conclusion; [using ideas] as hypotheses to be tested instead of as dogmas to be asserted."[29] Citing Maxwell in support of the notion of "transaction" was not meant to "give support to one's own form of generalization," Dewey said, but rather an attempt to keep his ideas grounded in current scientific understandings—even as inquiry remained open to "whatever wide-ranging treatment in this field may in the course of time succeed in establishing itself, whosesoever it may be."[30]

Dewey's project in *Art as Experience* was also conceived, in part, as an attempt to formulate an aesthetic theory consistent with modern physics. His

"Wandering Between Two Worlds" thesis furnished the rationale: "From one point of view the problem of recovering an organic place for art in civilization is like the problem of reorganizing our heritage from the past and the insights of present knowledge into a coherent and integrated imaginative union," Dewey writes. "Science is here," he continues, "and a new integration must take account of it and include it."[31] Just as in other areas of human concern, we must keep our theories of art and aesthetics "in gear" in order to fully appreciate what such modes of experience mean.

Modern physics, for Dewey, does not demand any revision of artistic content.[32] For now, such findings require only that we recognize the ways in which past aesthetic theories have distorted the manner in which existing art *already* expresses principles arrived at through modern physics. Contemporary physicists, for instance, are now compelled "in virtue of the character of their own subject-matter to see that their units are not those of space *and* time, but of space-time." The artist, Dewey submits, "made in action if not in conscious thought this belated scientific discovery from the very beginning." In other words, artists understood such things before science had the means to verify them. Similarly, the dynamics of rhythm and form have been operative in aesthetic perception and production since time out of mind. Only now, however, do we appreciate in modern scientific terms the manner in which "rhythm is a universal scheme of existence, underlying all realization of order in change."[33] Form, accordingly, is no longer identified with static essences in the natural sciences. Instead, it expresses the "organization of energies" in dynamic, growing relations. This is how form has always operated in the arts. Thus, Dewey uses the term "energy" all through *Art as Experience* (130+ times, in fact) to demonstrate that aesthetics is compatible with such modern understandings.

"Perhaps insistence upon the idea of energy in connection with fine art seems to some minds out of place," Dewey writes. "Yet there are certain commonplaces that it is proper to utter in connection with art that cannot be intelligible unless the fact of energy be made central: its power to move and stir, to calm and tranquilize."[34] For Dewey, the principles that govern aesthetic experience and its production involve the same "energies" that operate in the physical world. "Art releases energy and focuses and tranquilizes it," he observes. "It releases energy in constructive forms."[35]

While "energy" is an elusive term in Dewey's writings, it is an important one philosophically in that it helps him to foreground qualitative relations in dynamic systems—a function without which his philosophy would remain "out of gear." In Dewey's mind, "energy" serves to index certain optimal features that prevail when systems sustain "order, rhythm, and balance." The resulting harmonies mean that, "energies significant for experience are acting at their best."³⁶ As we see presently, this elusive category of "energy" has a well-developed correlate in the Chinese tradition.

Forms, Rhythms, and *Qi* 氣

The idea that energies (*qi* 氣) pervade and coalesce within the world is a mainstay of Chinese thinking. As stated in Chapter 42 of the *Daodejing*: "the myriad beings shoulder *yin* 陰 and carry *yang* 陽; their *qi* blends to create harmonies." The idea that energies have, as Dewey says, the power "to move and stir, to calm and tranquilize" is a central tenet in Chinese thought—it informs not only Chinese aesthetics, but also Chinese medicine, psychology, natural philosophy, martial arts, and ethics. In fact, the notion that *qi* animates the world is probably the most common assumption in the Chinese tradition. It serves as a sort of metaphysical vernacular and its associations broaden over time.

The *Zuozhuan* 左傳 teaches that *qi* 氣 in its different phases and permutations gives rise to various sets of qualities: the "five flavors," the "five colors," the "five modes of music," and when out of balance, the "six illnesses."³⁷ As the qualities of taste, sight, and sound, *qi* refers to the conversion of ambient energies into sense experience: "[It] is supposed to make possible speech in the mouth and sight in the eyes . . ." Kwong-loi Shun explains, "[it] can grow when the mouth takes in tastes and the ear takes in sounds."³⁸ As the measure of health and well-being, *qi* represents the energies that animate the live creature: the vitality derived from environing conditions that cause physical growth and sustain life. *Qi* concentrates in living things as a kind of vital fluid, and in the natural world as a kind of vapor. It constitutes both the emotional and the meteorological environment of life as the prevailing "atmosphere" or "weather."³⁹

Understanding *qi* 氣 presents certain challenges. First, there is no single description that covers every account that is available. The *Zuozhuan* teaches that there are six phases of *qi* representing three sets of correlative qualities: *yin/yang* 陰陽, wind/rain, and darkness/light. Some chapters in the *Zhuangzi* refer to these six *qi*, while others describe *qi* as "continuous throughout the world" (*tiandizhiyiqi* 天地之一氣).⁴⁰ By the Han dynasty, it is described as taking on two primary forms: *yinqi* 陰氣 and *yangqi* 陽氣. These energies coalesce into the "five phases" (*wuxing* 五行)—Earth, Fire, Water, Metal, and Wood—in the cosmic process.⁴¹

As Jane Geaney argues, *qi* 氣 is not to be understood as a "permanent substrate of reality" in such formulations, since it is "context dependent" and "changes according to its context."⁴² Unlike Aristotle's notion of matter (*hyle*), descriptions of *qi* routinely defy any sharp distinction between "Form/Matter" or "Being/Modality." *Qi* is not the bare material of a thing, for it is hylozoistic, dynamic, and identified with a variety of qualities. Such qualities take on myriad expressions—biological, emotional, meteorological, spiritual, and so on—according to how it is harnessed, blocked, released, or lost. A thing immediately manifests qualities by virtue of how its *qi* flows in relation to surrounding conditions. There is no primary "Form/Function" distinction to be made in such descriptions. Qualities are discharged and undergone immediately by virtue of configurative dispositions that are always formal-and-functional. As Judith Farquhar observes, "*qi* is both structural and functional, a unification of material and temporal forms that loses all coherence when reduced to one or the other 'aspect.'"⁴³

Whether or not *qi* 氣 stands up to scientific scrutiny is an interesting question, but as a philosophical concern it is misplaced. Some claims made about *qi* are clearly dubious.⁴⁴ The function of *qi* in Warring States thought, however, is rarely speculative or overtly metaphysical. Rather than being presented as an independent postulate, *qi* is part of a largely non-technical vocabulary that helps to describe observable patterns and changes in a variety of practical contexts. In this respect, *qi* is useful in everyday discourse just as the English term "energy" is useful. As Dewey argues, the surrender of "metaphysical and *extra*-scientific [notions] . . . does not mean that search for broad generalizations has been given up." Maxwell's doctrine of the conservation of energy is useful to us precisely as "an exceedingly comprehensive generalization," notes Dewey, one that functions pragmatically in the generation of "formulae for effecting transformations from one field to another, the qualitative difference of the fields being maintained."⁴⁵ In a like fashion, *qi* is useful in discussing function-states that are materially dependent and structurally embedded within multiple fields simultaneously.

The "Inner Training" chapter of *Guanzi* 管子, for example, uses the term to discuss the mutual influences of skeletal alignment, eating habits, and emotion in the human experience. These are qualitatively different fields of activity, but transactions between them do occur and they have concrete results. In fact, as Harold D. Roth observes, the early Chinese assumption that there is "full integration" between physiological and psychological systems is a "remarkably modern notion."⁴⁶ The proper philosophical (as opposed to scientific) concern is whether common sense registers such influences and communicates them effectively. In the Chinese tradition, *qi* 氣 is central to the establishment of such common sense.

The focus, then, is not so much on what *qi* 氣 *is* or whether it can be observed under an infrared microscope. As Dewey reminds us, even Maxwell's "conservation of energy" does not entail any actual "force which is at once electrical, mechanical, thermal, etc., and yet none of them, but a kind of non-descript Thing-in-itself back of all of them."[47] Our attitude toward *qi* should be similarly "pragmatic" in the Peircean sense, such that "knowing what the effects of [*qi*] are, we are acquainted with every fact which is implied in saying that it exists, and there is nothing more to know."[48] Further descriptions are both unverifiable and unnecessary. By the same token, one should remember that, as William James says: "The term 'energy' does not even pretend to stand for anything 'objective.'"[49] The sole empirical fact to which "energy" refers is that force operates qualitatively across multiple fields—electrical, mechanical, thermal, etc. As Dewey notes, in actual scientific procedure the term "energy" represents formulae "for converting any one of these forms of energy into any other, provided certain conditions are satisfied."[50] Physicists like Richard Feynman describe the conservation of energy in similar terms.[51]

So, rather than being a metaphysical *thing*, "energy" (*qi* 氣) signals that continuity, relationality, and change are taken seriously. Inquiries are then structured accordingly. This has consistently been the case in Chinese thought, but such a dynamic approach emerges only recently in the Western tradition. As Dewey tells his Chinese audience, "Our [Western] ancestors paid more attention to the static aspects of the universe, such as its substance. The development of modern science has [now] made explicit the concept of energy . . . The significance of this concept lies in its emphasis on the dynamic aspects of the universe rather than on its static aspects."[52] According to such thinking, relations are primary and discrete agency is secondary. As Dewey observes: "There is no such thing physically as manifestation of energy or effective power by one thing except in relation to the energy manifested by other things."[53] Accordingly, "energy" requires that we revise our substance ontologies and generate more process-oriented understandings of structure-and-function. Dewey offers the following:

> By *process* is meant the manifestation of energy in a change; by *structure* the arrangement of energies in a relatively static or enduring form; by *function*, the consequences that give meaning or significance to processes and structures . . . Processes refer to the (relatively) dynamic factor; structure to the (relatively) static, and function to the "ends" maintained and sub-served—the phase of use and purpose.[54]

Such formulas help us to identify what needs to be reconstructed in Aristotle's system and why. First and foremost, identifying energy with *change* means reversing Aristotle's identification of *energeia* with activity actualized—as that which is *not* in the process of coming to be. Aristotle is keen on distinguishing the actual activity (*energeia*) of a thing from its change (*kinēsis*) since, for him, the latter represents "an incomplete actuality of the movable."[55] As Aristotle sees it:

> [Every *kinēsis*] takes time and is for the sake of an end, and is complete when it has made what it aims at. It is complete, therefore, only in the whole time or at that final moment. In their parts and during the time they occupy, all movements are incomplete, and are different in kind from the whole movement and from each other.[56]

Motion (*kinēsis*) is thus regarded as a lower order of being—something incomplete in relation to its invariant end state. Aristotle maintains that, "This is why it is hard to grasp what motion is."[57]

For Dewey and for Chinese thinkers, change is easier to grasp. Motion (*kinēsis*) is ontologically on par with form and generative of its own energy (a.k.a. kinetic energy). Energies coalesce in structures that are only *relatively* fixed, and "ends" depend upon functions that give "meaning or significance to the processes and structures." None of these elements are entirely predetermined or frozen in place. "Ends" are functional in that they *use* existing structures and energies in reaching their outcomes, whatever those outcomes turn out to be. "Process may be compared to the energy of a stream," Dewey writes, "(itself constituted of an immense number of unit-processes), and structure to the banks, the bed, etc."[58] The prevalence of *qi* 氣 in Chinese discourse signals that Chinese thinkers are equally sensitive to the dynamic balance that structures-and-energies represent. Since their elements are in flux, Chinese thinkers become attuned to the practical interest that we have in attending to such balances. The eventual formulation of two complementary energies—*yinqi* 陰氣 and *yangqi* 陽氣—is the logical result of thinking that takes *rhythmic motion* to be what lends structure to change.

In discussing the resulting nature of "balance" in Daoist philosophies, Steve Coutinho stresses this essentially "rhythmic" conception of change. He writes:

> Our first reaction may be that balance requires equality, but in fact, the Daoist conception of natural balance is complex and dynamic. Imbalance is not merely inequality, but is heading toward one extreme to an excessive degree. Equality presupposes a static conception of balance that would not allow for natural cycles of change. *Dynamic* balance requires leaving the center

and constantly returning; only through such mutually balancing *processes* can organic phenomena thrive.[59]

Coutinho uses walking as an example. Walking is a kind of "controlled falling," whereby we throw ourselves off balance then recover only to redirect our fall to the other side. As such, "balance is a balancing," suggests Dewey, "a matter of distribution of weights with respect to the way they act upon one another."[60] Balance is not obtained by mechanically flopping to each side an equal number of times. Instead, balance occurs in the rhythmic succession of *re*-balancing that takes place in dynamic intervals over time.

Here, as Dewey notes, "There is a wealth of suggestion in the phrase 'takes place.'" There is "no rhythm when variations are not placed," for rhythm itself is an "ordered variation of changes" in time-and-space. In order to sustain rhythm, Dewey says:

> There must be energies resisting each other. Each gains intensity for a certain period, but thereby compresses some opposed energy until the latter can overcome the other which has been relaxing itself as it extends. Then the operation is reversed, not necessarily in equal periods of time but in some ratio that is felt as orderly. Resistance accumulates energy; it institutes conservation until release and expansion ensue. There is, at the moment of reversal, an interval, a pause, a rest, by which the interaction of opposed energies is defined and rendered perceptible.[61]

Qi 氣 discourse is concerned chiefly with those "intervals, pauses, rests" in which energies become perceptible in relation to the rhythmic balance of form. Such concerns alert one to the importance of returning (*gui* 歸) to states that enable balance, which in turn enables the continued growth and vitality of organic form (*xing* 形). For Dewey too, "living may be regarded as a continual rhythm of disequilibrations [sic] and recoveries of equilibrium," resulting in the vicissitudes and recalibrations that steadily shape organic life.[62] It would be a mistake, as we have seen, to locate this process "inside" the organism or "outside" in the environment. "In part," Dewey writes, "environmental energies constitute organic functions; they enter into them."[63] Accordingly, for Dewey, "direct experience comes from nature and [humans] interacting with each other. In this interaction, human energy gathers, is released, damned up, frustrated and victorious."[64] The "natural energies of the environment," Dewey teaches, "sometimes carry the organic functions prosperously forward, and sometimes act counter to their continuance."[65] Conditions change, and living things fall in and out of rhythm. Chinese thinkers understand the dynamics of maintaining equilibrium in terms of whatever complimentary energies are involved: *yinqi* 陰氣 and *yangqi* 陽氣. Such terms must be understood squarely within the framework of Chinese natural philosophy. To understand them within a Greek-medieval framework subjects classical Chinese philosophy to serious distortion.

Dewey knew that such complementary thinking and its implications were already established in Daoist philosophies. "[The] concept of the necessary complementarity of opposites," he explains to his Chinese audience in 1920, ". . . holds that [human] destiny, happiness, and the goodness of [human] nature, are inevitable concomitants of changes which occur in the universe. This kind of determination is similar to the philosophy of Laozi and Zhuangzi, both of whom asserted that only a fool could regard the world as unchanging, or suppose that either his happiness or his misery would continue forever."[66] In *Experience and Nature*, Dewey expands upon these insights. He cites Laozi 老子 as a philosophical forerunner in doing so. The legendary author of the *Daodejing*, Dewey explains, was among those who celebrated facts that were "fundamentally significant for the formation of a naturalistic metaphysics."[67]

In the second chapter of *Experience and Nature*, "Existence as Precarious and Stable," Dewey establishes these facts, and they are wholly in keeping with Daoist philosophy. "We live in a world which is an impressive and irresistible mixture" of the precarious-and-stable, flux-and-form, process-and-structure, fluency-and-fixity. "We may recognize them separately but we cannot divide them," Dewey writes, "[for] unlike wheat and tares they grow from the same root."[68] For the Daoist thinker, such binaries are indeed mutual (*xiang* 相). As Chapter 2 of the *Daodejing* says: "What is here (*you* 有) and what is not here (*wu* 無) are mutually generated. Difficult-and-easy are mutually established. Long-and-short are mutually exhibited. Tone-and-sound are mutually composed. Back-and-front are mutually sequenced. This much is constant (*hengye* 恆也)."

It is not difficult to appreciate the Daoist sensibilities in *Experience and Nature*. Wu Jingxiong 吳經熊 (John C. H. Wu), noted jurist, scholar, and translator of the *Daodejing*, read *Experience and Nature* soon after it came out and was deeply impressed with its cosmic vision. He recommended the book to his friend and correspondent, Oliver Wendell Holmes. Holmes' subsequent comments are legendary. "It is like shavings of jade—subtle, sometimes epigrammatic, emancipated, seeing the world and man as fluid."[69] Such responses are not unlike those normally reserved for the *Daodejing*. *Experience and Nature*, Holmes wrote, "seemed to me to feel the universe more inwardly and profoundly than any book I know."[70] Holmes expressed agreement with Wu's own assessment, observing that Dewey had "more of our cosmos in his head" than any other philosopher[71]—one exception, perhaps, being Laozi himself.

Dewey did not think that Aristotle was far behind Laozi. The former came close to recognizing the fundamental Daoist insight: the mutual implication of binaries in nature. Aristotle, however, "did not go far on the road, though it may be used to suggest the road which he failed to take." As Dewey sees it, "[Aristotle] acknowledges contingency, but he never surrenders his bias in favor of the fixed, certain and finished. His whole theory of forms and ends is a theory of the superiority *in Being* of rounded-out fixities."[72] This was his Achilles' heel.

Aristotle was not alone in holding this bias. At the dawn of Greek philosophy, the ontological contest between Parmenides and Heraclitus involved the separation *in Being* of two realms: Appearance and Reality. From the Platonic synthesis forward, this split resulted in tendencies to relegate either stability or flux to a lesser ontological status—and most often, flux was subordinated. Once again, considered from an evolutionary standpoint, this might not be so surprising. *Homo sapiens* may well retain some congenital impulse to remove flux by sequestering it to a harmless domain. Survival prospects are poor for animals not immediately suspicious of novelty in their surroundings; thus we might be more inclined toward removing it.

In our philosophies, however, the elimination of change and flux results in an imbalanced view of reality. By way of compensation, twentieth-century thinkers such as Henri Bergson sought to reverse its prospects. As Dewey observes, Bergson "deified change by making it universal, regular, sure." Thus, in contrast to fixity, "flux [was] made something to revere, something profoundly akin to what is best in ourselves, will and creative energy."[73] Dewey was wary of such reactionary philosophies, just as he was suspicious of those who would reduce all occurrences to "events"—i.e., those who would treat every existence as if it were a "slide or a slip" and then imply that "by putting enough slides together you can make a hill."[74] Dewey does not regard flux as ontologically more primary than stasis. Instead, he maintains that flux-*and*-stasis, novelty-*and*-order, are mutual (or *xiang* 相) and operate together in a rhythmic fashion. He evokes Laozi accordingly.[75]

The rhythmic nature of complementary energies (*qi* 氣) further illuminates the nature of organic form (*xing* 形). Recall that, according to the logic of the Great Continuum (*taiyi* 太一), each *dis*continuity is invariably bound by its own *continuity*. Every flash of novelty (*one*) enters into *yin-yang* 陰陽 relations (*two*) and thus takes on form (*three*). Dewey's thinking helps underscore the importance of "two" in this equation. "Polarity, or opposition of energies," he writes, "is everywhere necessary to the definition, the delimitation, that resolves an otherwise uniform mass and expanse into individual forms." Form does not take shape simply because there is something called "coherence" (*li* 理). Form takes shape because concrete relations have the tendency to *become* coherent. "Form is arrived at whenever a stable, even though moving, equilibrium is reached," Dewey explains. "Changes interlock and sustain one another. Wherever there is this coherence there is endurance." The balance attained through organic form expresses the specific harmony (*he* 和) sustained in interlocking energies (*qi*). It does not descend upon these energies from somewhere else. As Dewey puts it: "Order is not imposed from without but is *made* out of the relations of harmonious interactions that energies bear to one another."⁷⁶ For Dewey as for Daoism, form has an element of flux woven right into it. In fact, "form" and "flux" are two aspects of what is primary—*rhythm*.

In the *Zhuangzi*, the rhythmic nature of organic form is portrayed in the image of the "Potter's Wheel of Nature" (*tianjun* 天均). "The myriad beings all have their seed-types," the text relates, "and their different forms (*xing* 形) make way for one another. They begin and end as a single ring. None can attain such an orderly arrangement. This is what we refer to as the 'Potter's Wheel of Nature.' The potter's wheel is what natural operations are."⁷⁷ As Brook Ziporyn explains, the image of the potter's wheel brings together elements of stability-*and*-instability, form-*and*-flux. "[The] even distribution of clay [is] made possible by the constant spinning of the wheel: the potter's wheel's very instability, its constant motion, is what makes things equal." Somewhere, at the very centermost midpoint of the circle, there is *rest*—"the unmoving center of the spinning wheel, the stability that exists in the midst of this instability without eliminating it."⁷⁸ As Dewey sees it, "all interactions that effect stability and order in the whirling flux of change are rhythms. There is ebb and flow, systole and diastole: ordered change." In the spinning of the potter's wheel, the balance and counterbalance of its constant return ensures that there is *rhythm*. The stillness at the center ensures that there is *symmetry*. "Symmetry and rhythm are the same thing felt with the difference of emphasis that is due to attentive interest," explains Dewey. Symmetry involves "the equilibrium of counteracting energies," while rhythm involves movement "spaced by places of rest." Wherever rhythm and symmetry take hold there is *balance*. The *Shuowen* lexicon glosses the "potter's wheel" (*jun* 均) accordingly—it is *pingbian* 平徧, "balance all around."

Dewey's main concern is that rhythm and symmetry are misconceived when they are interpreted in overly static terms. Rhythms involve *recurrence*, but recurrence is too often thought of mechanistically. "Mechanical recurrence is that of material units," he writes, "aesthetic recurrence [which he identifies with natural rhythms] is that of *relationships* that sum up and carry forward." Such natural rhythms are "vital, physiological, functional. Relationships rather than elements recur, and they recur in differing contexts and with different consequences so that each recurrence is novel as well as a reminder."⁷⁹

Were it true that all rhythms proceeded *mechanically*, then there would be no organic life—not because machines are inanimate, but because they cannot escape the law of entropy. Mechanical systems are isolated, and according to the Second Law of Thermodynamics the entropy of isolated systems increases over time. Organic forms are remarkable in this respect. As Daniel C. Dennett explains, "They are things that defy this crumbling into dust, at least for a while, by not being isolated—by taking in from their environment the wherewithal to keep life and limb together."[80] In sustaining the balance of life/growth (*sheng* 生), living organisms convert potential energies in their environments into the means of their own furtherance. Life is thereby *extended*—this due to the inherent power (*de* 德) of organisms to activate kinetic phases that use environing conditions to their own advantage. To become increasingly *organized* to do this, without exceeding the energy budgeted by the Second Law of Thermodynamics, is what makes life the wonder of the world.

Chinese common sense guides us well in teaching that *qi* 氣 is being steadily converted and stored as long as life continues. As the *Guanzi* states: "Where there is *qi* there is life, where there is no *qi* there is death. What lives does so by virtue of its *qi*."[81] The rhythmic pulsations that allocate energies on the "Potter's Wheel of Nature" are not static, mechanical recurrences—rather, each recurrence marks a functional return (*gui* 歸) to the center of balance. As Dewey reminds us, organic life exists always in the state of *need*. Thus, "every movement of experience in completing itself recurs to its beginning, since it is a satisfaction of the prompting initial need." Each cyclical recurrence occurs, then, "with a difference; it is charged with all the differences the journey out and away from the beginning have made."[82] Such rhythmic cycles gather and contain energies (*qi*) as they proceed.

Through each cycle of living, a fresh relationship with one's environment is initiated and equilibrium is renewed, thus beginning another round of adjustment between organism-and-environment. "There is no such thing as a final settlement," Dewey writes, "because every settlement introduces the conditions of some degree of a new unsettling."[83] For the live creature, becoming perfectly *settled*—purely *static*—is to be instantly *dead*: to fly off the "Potter's Wheel of Nature." It would be a mistake then to understand the idea that "the myriad beings live/grow (*sheng* 生) by attaining the one (*deyi* 得一)" in static terms. "The definition of symmetry in static terms," Dewey warns, "is the exact correspondent of the error by which rhythm is conceived to be recurrence of elements."[84] The "one" (*yi* 一) in this context refers to the organic integrity that a live creature realizes in order to continue living in rhythmic symmetry. This is not a fixed state or unchanging condition—it is a process of *balancing energies*, one of sustaining equilibrium (*jing* 靜) in the midst of movement (*dong* 動).

It is within such a dynamic framework that we need to reconstruct our commonsense notions of potentiality and natural kinds. More so than many others, these notions remain beholden in the modern mind to outmoded Greek-medieval assumptions. Accordingly, our thinking in these areas needs badly to be updated. Early Chinese thought is well prepared to assist us as we bring these notions more in line with empirical reality. The next round of experiments will be concerned with doing just that.

Types and Potentials

The idea that life involves a quantum of *qi* 氣 evokes the idea of potentiality, which in the Greek-medieval tradition is bound up with the idea of teleology. The idea of teleology, in turn, is bound up with assumptions about natural kinds. With respect to how natural kinds are regarded in early China, Brook Ziporyn argues that the Chinese position lies somewhere between realism and nominalism. As Chad Hansen, A. C. Graham, Chris Fraser and others maintain, early Chinese logic tends not to postulate abstract categories above and beyond the aggregates that belong to them. The formulation of types (*lei* 類) according to standards of sameness and difference, however, play an important role in Chinese thinking. Having now considered *qi*, we are in a better position to understand the qualities through which types are designated and the status of those qualities in the world.

The *Huainanzi* maintains that phenomena of similar types "resonate" (*ganying* 感應) with one another through what John S. Major and others describe as "dynamic influences exchanged through the energetic medium of *qi* 氣."[85] Such resonance becomes the dominant concept through which relations between disparate phenomena are understood by the early Han dynasty. Its philosophical antecedents, however, as Major says, trace back to the Warring States period.[86] The concept of resonance (*ganying*) thus brings Chinese causal assumptions into focus and illuminates how potentiality was understood in the broader tradition.

Because Greek-medieval assumptions align so closely with untutored common sense, they naturally serve as a baseline from which to approach the vision that early Chinese thinkers eventually developed. For Aristotle, potential (*dunamis*) is an "internal principle" operative within each member of a natural kind. Change is then "the fulfillment of what exists potentially, in so far as it exists potentially" in the thing.[87] In order for potentiality to be fulfilled, something prior "in order of generation and of time" must act upon it, and that something serves in the mode of actuality (*energeia*).[88] It is crucial for Aristotle that each account of change (*kinēsis*) identifies actuality and potentiality in a linear order of explanation—one thing is "mover," another is "moved."⁸⁹

Resonance (*ganying* 感應) is distinct in that it presupposes neither linearity nor the distinction between actuality and potentiality. When things of the same type (*lei* 類) "move" (*dong* 動) one another, efficacy between them is considered mutual (*xiang* 相). "Root and twig mutually respond to one another," the *Huainanzi* explains.⁹⁰ Changes do not so much *cause* one another as *correlate* with one another. In this manner, things are conceived as embedded in dynamic matrices of mutual interaction on multiple levels simultaneously. In such a world, actuality (*energeia*) is not required to put change into motion. *The world is already in motion*—and where movement is primary, there is no need for any "Prime Mover." Accordingly, each transformation indexes a whole situation with the propensity (*shi* 勢) to trigger ongoing changes as they are happening. As Carine Defoort observes: "Events [in early China] were not seen as caused by one powerful and preceding event, but as woven in a network of interdependent nodes, a colossal pattern in which things reacted upon each other by a kind of mysterious resonance rather than mechanical impulsion."⁹¹ Scholars who look closely into causal thinking in early China tend invariably to reach similar conclusions.⁹² Such findings are of more than antiquarian interest. Empirical studies suggest that such thinking continues to have an influence in how East Asians view the world. Cognitive psychologists Ara Norenzayan and Richard E. Nisbett find that, even today, "East Asian and American causal reasoning differs significantly."⁹³

The fact that there is no exact equivalent in early Chinese thought to "potential" (*dunamis*) in the Greek-medieval sense is not a deficit. As Bertrand Russell suggests, "when potentiality is used as a fundamental and irreducible concept, it always conceals confusion of thought. Aristotle's use of it is one of the bad points in his system."⁹⁴ Arthur Waley, however, senses that the meaning of *de* 德 in Chinese thinking is "bound up with the idea of potentiality . . . a latent power, a 'virtue' inherent in something."⁹⁵ The tendency to imagine or project such a virtue as residing *within* a thing is a strong one, but there is nothing that actually warrants such an interpretation. "[We] have an unfortunate tendency," Dewey observes, "to conceive a fixed state of affairs and then appeal to a latent or potential something or other to effect change. But in reality the term ["potentiality"] refers to a characteristic *of* change."⁹⁶

Daoist thinking helps to straighten this out. As change takes place, *de* 德 amounts to the extension of something's influence *into* its surroundings—both through its kinetic energies that convert potential energies into means for its own development and through its intersection with other processes that channel its potential energies in various directions. As such, potency (*de*) is synergetic rather than self-contained; it always involves interactions *between* things. *De* is thus associated with the release of energies generally—not only those that are stored as possibilities *within* a given thing but also those stored as possibilities in the surrounding world. As Roger T. Ames explains, *de* "encompasses both participating agency and its effects," thus suggesting that it is similar to "virtue" (*virtus*) is the archaic sense of "having inherent virtue or power to produce effects."[97] In this way, *de* is consistent with resonance (*ganying* 感應) in that it does not easily reduce to any sharp distinction between "Mover/Moved" or "Inner/Outer" (*neiwai* 內外).

Interestingly, *de* 德 is associated with the state of the newborn infant in the *Daodejing*. As Chapter 28 says: "When *de* is constant and not abandoned, one returns to the state of the newborn child." As Chapter 55 says: "One who is steeped in *de* is like an infant . . . its bones are tender and its sinews soft. But its grip is firm." Dewey likewise understands infancy as a state of unassuming power. Too often, he explains, immaturity is assessed *comparatively* rather than intrinsically. Infancy is seen as a state of privation (or *mere* "potential") in relation to the traits of some matured form. Such thinking, for Dewey, is yet another example of "*the* philosophical fallacy." The process of growth is subordinated to an already fixed end. "The fulfillment of growing is taken to mean an *accomplished* growth," he writes, "that is to say, an Ungrowth, something which is no longer growing." As Dewey sees it, immaturity exerts a power all its own: it designates "a positive force or ability—the power to grow."[98]

For Dewey, such growth involves two distinct traits: *dependence* and *plasticity*. Dependence is normally thought of as a deficit rather than a power, but it is the dependence of infants on others that equips them with attachment behaviors (such as being adorable) and proximity signaling (usually crying) that instantly stimulate maternal behavior. Few forces command attention like the allure (*de* 德) of the wide-eyed infant—her raw charisma compensating for a nearly complete physical incapacity. As human infants grow, there are direct correlations between interdependent sociability and cognitive performance.[99] As toddlers, they continue to both radiate and gather up the energies (*qi* 氣) that surround them. As Dewey observes: "Few grown-up persons retain all of the flexible and sensitive ability of children to vibrate sympathetically with the attitudes and doings of those about them."[100]

Plasticity is a second trait that defines the understated power of immaturity. Plasticity, as both Dewey and William James stress, is not an inert attribute. It does not, as Dewey says, "signify a mere passivity to be shaped from without."[101] Rather, plasticity is the *active* ability to grow from experiences—"the power to *develop dispositions*," without which "the acquisition of habits is impossible."[102] Infancy teaches us that, where *de* 德 is abundant, there is tremendous power for growth. As one ages, this power steadily diminishes.

Thus, from the perspective of those who value the absolute (as opposed to the relative) qualities of growth, reaching maturity can be overrated. As Chapter 15 of the *Daodejing* suggests: "Those who stay with *dao* 道 do not want to become full. By not becoming full, they remain like hidden sprouts not rushing to early ripening."[103] Recognizing the importance of prolonged infancy in the human experience, Dewey notes that "early perfection and high specialization of function are unfavorable to further development, and that they render practically impossible the acquisition of *new* powers."[104] Throughout the *Daodejing*, power is attributed to that which remains soft (*rou* 柔) and pliant (*ruo* 弱). Traits that seem to render their bearer vulnerable to injury in fact represent the opposite. As Chapter 76 says, living things are born soft and pliant (*rouruo* 柔弱) and as death approaches they become rigid and stiff. As we know, the hardening of the heart muscle is a disease that arrives with maturity, and the reduction of plasmablasts responsive to infection is a feature of an aging immune system. Accordingly, that which preserves its pliancy and flexibility (*shourou* 守柔) exhibits the most strength (*qiang* 強).[105] Nothing lives forever, but the Daoist focuses on prolonging the power (*de* 德) that exists at its height in infancy. That power is the power to continue growing.

Again, the Daoist maintains that the possibilities stored (*zang* 藏) within the world are immense (*da* 大). There is bottomless potential resting in the Great Continuum (*taiyi* 太一) ready to be annulled (*fan* 反) in the process of growth. "Here" (*you* 有), on *this* side of the process, units of possibility are steadily realized in rhythmic cycles of organic transformation, as mutual influences circulate and return on the "Potter's Wheel of Nature." As things change, the meaning of "potentiality" refers to the qualities of particular *transactions* between things rather than to qualities that inhere strictly "within" any single entity on the wheel. "To say that an apple has the potentiality of decay," explains Dewey, "does not mean that it has latent or implicit within it a causal principle which will some time inevitably display itself in producing decay." Instead, "its existing changes (in interaction with its surroundings) will take the form of decay, *if* they are exposed or subjected to certain conditions not now operating upon them." Potentiality, for Dewey, thus "signifies a certain limitation of present powers, due to the limited number of conditions with which they are in interaction plus the fact of the manifestation of new powers under different conditions."[106] In this way, the entire world "assists" (*fu* 輔) in the liberation of potential, shepherding new properties into being in the process.

Making good logical and ontological sense of potentiality remains a philosophical challenge. We feel compelled to ask *what* potentiality is and *where* it is located. Dewey attempts to clear up the confusion by using the logical and ontological status of "food" to illustrate his point:

[With] the emergence of animal life certain materials became *foods*. We may then say that these materials *were* foods all the time and even that they are intrinsically or 'by nature' *foods*. Such a view confuses potentiality with actuality. Looking back, we can validly confirm that these materials were *edible*. But they are not foods in actuality until they are *eaten* and *digested*, i.e., until certain operations are performed that give crude materials those new properties which constitute them of the special kind *foods*.[107]

Aristotle might have agreed with this reasoning. For him, lumber has the "potential" to become a building, but "the actuality of the buildable as buildable is the process of building."[108] Looking back, Aristotle would agree that the lumber was *buildable*. But it is not a "building" until it becomes built, i.e., until certain operations are performed that give those crude materials the properties of a building. So, how does Dewey's thinking differ?

There are two differences, and each one is important. First, Dewey would regard the act of building to be a single event, a situation in which the builder *and* the lumber realize new properties simultaneously. As the lumber becomes a building, the laborer becomes a builder. Aristotle also recognizes that change is a two-way street in such cases, and that "the road from Thebes to Athens is the same as the road from Athens to Thebes." He is unable to surrender, however, the causal reasoning that makes of such a *single* event an episode with two distinct ontological descriptions. There is "nothing to prevent the operation of two things being one and the same," Aristotle maintains, "provided the actualizations are not *described* in the same way, but are related as what can act to what is acting."[109]

Dewey regards such thinking as a gratuitous duplication. There is but a *single*, continuous interaction between the builder and the building, and "the two principles of continuity and interaction are not separate from each other. They intercept and unite."[110] Aristotle's separate descriptions are true as propositions of ordered sequences. But for Dewey, "ordered sequences are the subject-matter of propositions in which the succession of gross qualitative events [can be] resolved into the constituents of a *single continuous event*." Causation as an ordered sequence is a *logical* category, not an *ontological* one. In the event of building a house, there are an "indefinite number of antecedents and consequents with which it is connected, since every event is existentially connected with some other event without end." Consequently, Dewey argues, "the only possible conclusion upon the basis of an existential or ontological interpretation of causation is that everything in the universe is cause and effect of everything else."[111] As the Chinese say, such influences are mutual (*xiang* 相). This locates Dewey squarely in the vicinity of East Asian views of causation.

The second difference with Aristotle is subtler, but equally important. When Dewey states that, by being eaten, edible materials become the "special kind *foods*," he is establishing the criteria for identifying "types." His thinking diverges from Greek-medieval reasoning about natural kinds while avoiding the sharp "Realism/Nominalism" dichotomy that Brook Ziporyn finds absent in the Chinese tradition.[112] Let us consider Dewey's treatment.

The point of departure for understanding Dewey's position on types is his appreciation for Charles Sanders Peirce's approach to universals. "Peirce understands by the reality of a 'general' the reality of a way, habit, disposition of behavior," Dewey notes, "and he dwells upon the fact that the habits of things are acquired and modifiable."[113] As Peirce sees it, every generality involves a description of what *may* happen but is not necessarily happening now—as such it involves "potentiality." The capacity of a food plant to nourish, for instance, lies dormant until it is actualized on particular occasions in transaction with herbivores. Thus, giving nourishment is a genuine "*way*" that the food plant behaves under specific conditions. "So," Dewey notes, "[Peirce] criticizes the nominalists for denying, by implication if not explicitly, that things have *ways* of behaving." Things really *do* have ways of behaving, and such realities provide "the cosmological or physical basis for logical possibilities or universals." Such universals, for Peirce, take the form of "leading principles" that we carry over into the field of inquiry—"modes that with respect to actualization are potential and general, being actualized only under individualized conditions of interaction with other things."[114] Edible materials thus become the "special kind *foods*," and such universals can guide us in drawing inferences. As Dewey sees it, "realism is correct in insisting upon universals and upon the fact that they enter in some way into the determination of known and knowable existences."[115]

The problem with realism, Dewey suggests, is linguistic. In coming to know "what" something is, we classify it under a common noun like "food." Such nouns inevitably become "things," and are then understood to exist in a constant or uniform manner as universals. Such common-noun "things," however, are not what actually exist in a general way. What exists in a general way are the *verbs* that describe the operations of the common nouns; "for what is designated by a verb is a *way* of changing and/or acting," explains Dewey. Such "ways" are what provide the realist a basis for positing logical possibilities or universals in the form of leading principles—nouns as such do not do this. "*A* footrace or *a* fire," Dewey points out, is a singular occurrence expressed in noun form; "but racing and burning are *ways* of acting and changing," and such verbs indicate that which *really* carries the possibility of recurrence.[116]

Nouns have a tendency to obscure the dynamic nature of what is real. Terms such as "white," for instance, give no clear indication of their true nature—unless, Dewey observes, they are expressed with endings such as *-ity*, *-ness*, and *-tion*. In the physical sciences, color "stands for a definition; it formulates a relation of characters of the nature of periodic vibrations to other characters of radiation and absorption." Thus, "*Whiteness* is the functional correlation of the radiating-absorbing capacity of certain vibrations combined in certain proportions."[117] In other words, terms like "white" also index *ways* of acting and changing and not static objects or entities. "Nominalism is thus on the right track," Dewey submits, "as far as it insists upon the necessity of *symbols*," which are essentially common nouns—"standing in" for a number of different instantiations. Beyond that, common nouns have no special ontological status. "But," Dewey adds, "nominalism has always been guilty of ignoring the operational basis and function of the symbols upon which it [places] its sole emphasis, and in most cases in consequence it [ignores] their functional and prospective reference."[118]

Dewey thereby establishes a position that "agrees with the 'realistic' interpretation of generals in affirming that *ways* of acting are as existential as are singular events and objects," while also "[agreeing] with 'nominalism' in holding . . . that the logically general, whether generic or universal, has necessarily the character of a *symbol*."[119] Dewey thus avoids the sharp "Realism/Nominalism" dichotomy that Ziporyn discusses.

What, then, are "types" (*lei* 類) from such a standpoint? Operationally speaking, universals amount to *if-then* propositions that "are not about the individuals of the kind, but about a relation of characteristic traits which determine the kind."[120] Assuming the verb-form nature of such traits, "types" are determined by the characteristic *ways* that things behave as a rule (*ze* 則) in interaction with other things. As Dewey and Chinese thinkers suggest, everything in the universe is causally implicated with everything else. Thus, "types" represent truncated sets of such traits based on practical considerations and observational constructs. Everyone knows, for instance, that "acorns become oak trees" under favorable conditions. This *way* of behavior can be stated in propositional form: *if* an acorn is provided with adequate soil, nourishment, light, water, and so on, *then* it becomes an oak tree.

Logically speaking, the "type" is a conditional. *Ontologically* speaking, for the acorn, becoming an oak tree is not an optimal or intended trajectory but a *possible* one, for many other propositions are true of acorns. As Dewey notes, "concrete things have *ways* of acting, as many ways of acting as they have points of interaction with other things."[121] *If* an acorn is put in a blender with 4:1 parts water, *then* it becomes a liquid that falls within a specific viscosity index. One might determine this viscosity range as a standard (*fa* 法) and construct another type (*lei* 類) that includes other things that behave in the same way. The point is that the type-determining proposition in the second case is as true as that in the first—i.e., that under different conditions, "acorns become oak trees." Dewey's point, in either case, is that "potentialities cannot be *known* [until] *after* the interactions have occurred."[122] Acorns might become something else (like squirrels) and in the future even something else (like biofuels). The potentiality (*de* 德) of the acorn in *every* case implies a "progressively increasing diversification of a specific thing in a particular direction" and not, as Dewey maintains, "a causal force immanent within a homogenous something and leading it to change."[123] "Common sense," Dewey observes, "is given to ascribing these consequences to some 'power' inherent in things themselves (an ingredient of the popular notion of substance), and to ignoring *inter*action with other things as the determining factor."[124] Common sense misleads us here.

Again, the thinking behind a text like the *Huainanzi* is more amenable to modern, systems-oriented understandings. Despite the fact that many of its correlations sound unusual to our ears, its core assumptions together underwrite the positions thus far discussed. The central idea in the text is that certain events occur simultaneously due to ambient conditions operative across intersecting fields. Such events can be organized into types (*lei* 類) that serve to indicate the nature of those conditions and what behaviors one should expect when they prevail. Granted, certain correlations might sound odd to us—e.g., "when the east wind blows, wine turns clear; and when silkworms secrete silk in fragments, strings on the lute break." Considered as seasonal occurrences attended by changes in temperature and atmospheric pressure, however, such correlations are plausible. The philosophical focus, in any case, is on the mysterious, nonlinear nature of causal conditions that trigger such disparate behaviors simultaneously.

That such thinking defies common sense is what makes it so alluring. "That things of a certain type (*lei* 類) mutually respond (*ying* 應) to one another is a dark, mysterious, obscure, and subtle thing," the author writes. Still, "*something* stimulates (*gan* 感) them."[125] Notably absent is any attempt to isolate discrete elements as the "causes" of correlated phenomena. The assumption is that there *are* no isolatable "causes," but rather various resonances occurring across entire fields of energy (*qi* 氣) simultaneously. Such thinking is consistent with the form-propensity (*xing-shi* 形勢) dynamic observed previously in the militarist tradition, where it operates in various ways.[126]

To repeat, such ideas dovetail with contemporary systems thinking; and for the intra-cultural philosopher, this indicates the potential for Chinese thought to lend itself with credibility to getting us "back in gear" with more scientific understandings. Some of the most intriguing recent work in the area of systems theory is in the field of biology. In pursuit of a new "theory of organism," Giuseppe Longo and Maël Montévil have initiated a project to formulate a mathematical model that extends from physics into biology, thus encompassing both the inert and the living within a framework informed by modern theoretical physics. This is an ambitious project, and now is not the time to probe deeply into it. Its basic components, however, are easy to relate. The systems theory of organism has four features: *biological temporal organization, extended critical transitions, enablement,* and *anti-entropy*. Each feature tracks on to a key assumption in Chinese natural philosophy.

As Longo and Montévil observe, there are differences between physical and biological objects and their trajectories. In the case of physics, "objects" are generic and "trajectories" are specific, whereas in biology the opposite is the case. "That is, a rat, a monkey, or an elephant are the *specific* results of *possible* (generic) evolutionary trajectories of a common mammal ancestor—in other words each of these individuals is *specific*. They respectively are the result of a unique constitutive history, yet a possible or *generic* one."[127] Biological processes are thus "general" in the Peircean sense but also irreversible, non-iterable, and resolutely historical. Thus, a systems theory of organic form must include *biological temporal organization* as a feature. Life is temporally paced by *rhythms* within-and-without, conceived by Chinese thinkers as *yin-yang* 陰陽 cycles on the "Potter's Wheel of Nature." The wheel only spins in one direction and it never stops. Organic events that occur on its surface thus possess that "*meta*-trait" that Dewey formulates in "The Subject Matter of Metaphysics," namely: "*genuine change in a specific direction*."[128]

Longo and Montévil recognize that physical (linear) time is unable to register the rhythmic "returns" (or *gui* 歸) that ensure the continuity of such processes in the midst of their constant flux. Such time-scapes "do not seem to have a counterpart in the mathematical formalization of physical clocks."[129] Recall that, for Dewey, "each recurrence is novel as well as a reminder."[130] Biological time must therefore be mathematically represented through a two-dimensional circular helix in order to account for variegated biological rhythms, metabolic evolution, aging, and so forth. The "living being," as Longo and Montévil argue, "is a true 'organizer' of time" and must be quantified as such.[131]

The agency involved in such temporal structuring is one that exhibits *extended critical transitions*, the second element in a systems theory of organism. This is a feature that Chinese natural philosophy is especially adept at satisfying. "Critical" states in physics refer to those in which the properties of a system spontaneously change. Such dynamics involve "tipping points" at which stable equilibriums are broken and new equilibriums secured. It is understood that in biology, as in physics, changes occur in phase space such that "order precisely means that a specific 'direction' has been 'chosen'" irrespective of initial conditions. "Closer to the scale of biology," Longo and Montévil write, "materials like water or iron are able to show different properties in different situations. Depending on the temperature and pressure, water may be a solid, a liquid, or a gas."[132] Since organic symmetry is also *rhythmic*, as Dewey also knows,[133] Longo and Montévil maintain that, "the critical transitions we look at [in organic form] are to be analyzed as taking place through an interval, not just a point, with respect to each control parameter." Accordingly, "living entities are not 'just' processes, but something more: they are lasting, *extended critical transitions*, always transient toward a continually renewed structure."[134]

In Brook Ziporyn's analysis of Chinese thought, "coherence" (*li* 理) is serviceable here while also obviating the need for non-empirical teleological reasoning. Rather than "essentialism," what we have is a world in which "several alternate, even incompatible, sets of instructions might be not only applicable but indeed built in," Ziporyn writes, "with the full authority of objectivity, as it were."[135] Such an idea is central to refocusing organic trajectories in the systems approach. "We consider living systems as 'coherent structures' in a continual (extended) critical transition," Longo and Montévil explain. "The permanent state of transition is maintained, at each level of organization, by the integration/regulation activities of the organism, that is by its global coherent structure."[136]

The fact that such activity does not—and indeed, *cannot*—occur in a vacuum brings us to the third feature of the theory, *enablement*. That environmental "niches," some contingent and others constructed, enable organic forms to exist is well understood in evolutionary biology. The difficulty, however, is presenting this postulate in a formal, mathematically rigorous way. The challenges are manifold. As treated by Thomas Kuhn, the history of the physical sciences serves as a reminder that determining a field of observable influences in a system establishes a "paradigm."[137] Key observables are designated as relatively invariant, and trajectories are then measured against them. Along with Ziporyn, Longo and Montévil recognize that mathematically constructed phase spaces "are not 'already there,' as absolutes underlying phenomena: they are our remarkable and very effective invention in order to make physical phenomena intelligible."[138] Ziporyn is keen to stress (and Longo and Montévil would agree) that such "human agency and participating in *creating* continuities" does not automatically evoke *anti*-realism.[139] The assumption that things have definite *ways* of responding (*ying* 應) in different configurations underwrites the realist component of types (*lei* 類) in Chinese thinking. Of course, things exhibit a range of responses under all sorts of conditions. Thus, establishing types is an exercise in human discretion—something undertaken for a *purpose*. A text like the *Huainanzi* grounds itself in such practicality at every turn.

But again—organizing the world according to human purposes does not automatically result in *anti*-realism. As Ziporyn points out, human purpose is "another real thing" that enters into situations that result in types. As he puts it: "The act of judging things to be the same or different, the human act of naming itself, must be included in the Chinese understanding of what is real."[140] This is wholly in keeping with what Dewey calls "naturalistic humanism." For Dewey, the notion that human experience, language, inference, purpose, etc. are things "extraneous which [are] occasionally superimposed upon nature, but [form] a veil or screen which shuts us off from nature," is among the most insidious assumptions in philosophy, one that renders the human being "an unnaturalized and unnaturalizable alien in the world." Dewey insists that "all modes of [human] experiencing are ways in which some genuine traits of nature come to manifest realization," and this includes the formulation and use of general objects of knowledge.[141] "Nature *has* intelligible order as its possession in the degree in which we by our own overt operations realize potentialities contained within it," Dewey argues.[142]

At this juncture, philosophers can leave the mathematical challenge of quantifying overlapping fields of coherence to the mathematicians. More pertinent to us is that the notion of niche-based "enablement" requires a new theory of causation. The key here, as Longo and Montévil explain, is that a "niche *enables* the survival of an otherwise incompatible/impossible form of life, [but] it *does not cause* it . . . niches enable what evolves, while evolving with it."[143] Greek-medieval options are inadequate here. Attributing "efficient causality" to such niches is a philosophical non-starter. Common sense responds by attributing "final cause" (*telos*) to the organism, which is a philosophical dead end. For outside of our more antediluvian schools of virtue ethics, the Greek-medieval *telos* has been dislodged from respectable philosophy centuries ago. Thus, we find ourselves at a conceptual impasse.

Chinese natural philosophy has the tools to assist us and we should use them. Like systems-level causal analysis, Chinese natural philosophy reduces causality neither to organic "form" (*ala* Aristotle) nor to external "force" (*ala* Descartes). The Chinese approach, instead, allows us to split the difference by understanding organic processes as (1) form (*xing* 形), (2) power (*de* 德), (3) configuration (*shi* 勢) and (4) trigger (*ji* 機) all at the same time—non-reductively and synchronically. Such dynamic transactions are what Longo and Montévil hope to quantify. If such researchers (or computer programmers) *do* manage to model such transactions, the diagnostic applications would be incredible, especially in the field of disease etiology and prevention. As it happens, Longo and Montévil already appeal to the early Chinese treatise *Classic on the Pulse* (*Maijing* 脈經) as an example of how systems-level thinking modifies heart rhythm diagnostics.[144]

As Sing-nan Fen suggests, it is not the job of philosophers to determine the facts in matters such as these. Scientists are the ones to do that.[145] The cultural role of the philosopher is to listen to the scientist and then assist common sense in "getting its head around" how the world actually is, so that societies can make intelligent decisions and adjudicate good and bad from an informed standpoint. As Dewey says, the natural sciences now point toward "process" as the fundamental trait of reality.[146] Thus, working philosophers need to become more-or-less "process philosophers" or else contribute to throwing civilization further "out of gear." Those who work in the field of Chinese philosophy are well positioned in this regard. As Brook Ziporyn notes, the postulate that "process orientations are closer to what Chinese thinkers tend to have in mind" is by now "rather uncontroversial" in the field. The odd commentator who denies this perhaps doesn't fully understand what "process philosophy" means.[147]

The kind of process thinking encountered in Chinese natural philosophy is especially congruent with the final feature of the systems theory of organism: *anti-entropy*, which underscores the inescapable novelty at the base of organic phenomena. Biological evolution, which is premised on descent with modification, is process-driven by definition. For Longo and Montévil, it is important to recognize that *change*, understood as critical transition, occurs at every level of the life process. "It is crucial," they write, "that this applies at each individual cellular mitosis," which as they stress is *"never an 'identical' reproduction."*[148] Change is thus *the* engine driving biological organization, and any account of the orders that such organizations assume must begin from there and work its way up.

As a vague, heuristic framework in which to think about organic form in systems-oriented terms, it is hard to improve upon Chapters 42 and 51 of the *Daodejing*. Within such a framework, organic form (*xing* 形) exhibits *biological temporal organization* as each living thing (*wu* 物) emerges through *extended critical transitions* from its inception (*shi* 始) to maturity (*cheng* 成). Given the fact that *anti-entropy* is the essence of life, organic trajectories are realized spontaneously (*ziran* 自然) through *enablement* shored up in environmental conditions (*shi* 勢). There is no need for superordinate material causes or vitalistic forces to explain such occurrences, as everything is implicated in the dynamic nature of organic form. Another Chinese concept that merges easily into a systems approach in biology is *xing* 性, a term that is routinely misunderstood by commentators given how entrenched our teleological assumptions are. What follows is the first of several philosophical experiments in these volumes that will involve the term *xing*.

Nature and *Xing* 性

To understand *xing* 性 in Warring States philosophy roughly along Aristotelian, pre-Darwinian lines—simply as the "nature" of a thing—will always be tempting because such an understanding demands little philosophical effort or imagination. As we know, essentialist and teleological assumptions are deeply engrained in human cognition, so why would early Chinese thinkers *not* assume that each thing has a species-essence? Is that not an article of common sense? As the tradition develops, *xing* becomes increasingly understood in this manner. Dai Zhen 戴震 (1724–1777), for instance, glosses the term with perfect confidence, observing that: "For thousands of years, the differences among the various species have remained the same, all simply following what is inherent in them."[149] Enough has been said, however, about Chinese natural philosophy to suggest that the notion of species-essence is not to be taken for granted in early Chinese thought. There are, in fact, instances in Warring States literature in which *xing* most certainly does *not* refer to a species-essence. Mencius uses the term as a verb to describe how the sages Yao and Shun acquired and exercised their ethical virtues. They *xing*-ed them.[150] Zhuangzi relates a story about an expert swimmer who, born on dry land, acquires his *xing* by spending lots of time in the water.[151] There are also instances in which *xing* sounds very much like what is conventionally thought of as the "nature" of a thing—but do such instances automatically evoke a species-essence?

The suggestion that early Chinese thinking displays more nuance on this topic than Greek-medieval thinking is philosophically exciting, for it means that Chinese thinking holds more than antiquarian interest on the subject. Today, we know that things do not have teleological "natures." To assume that the proposition, "acorns become oak trees," means that acorns, by virtue of some immutable "species-essence" or "purpose," are *meant* to become oak trees is a completely antiquated mindset.

After all, what *is* an oak tree—really? Terrestrial plant life crept out of the waters some 430 million years ago. Coniferous (cone-bearing) trees appeared about 130 million years later, and Angiosperms (leaf-bearing) trees evolved some 100 million years after that. Angiosperms managed to outmaneuver and outnumber Conifers by having shorter reproductive cycles and because insects came along to facilitate the spreading of pollen. Insects and Angiosperms evolved together, side-by-side (*bing* 並), accelerating diversification and contributing to the propagation of countless species of each. Oak trees are unique members of the Angiosperm family because they are especially prone to interspecific hybridization. Oaks are wind pollinated, and their pistils have unusually weak internal barriers to fertilization by other oak species (hundreds of species of oak have been identified worldwide). The kind of tree that comes from an acorn depends largely on which spores were carried on the breeze. Different oaks in the same population might share half of their genetic data while exhibiting considerable morphological diversity.[152]

Acorns, left to their own devices, have small futures. They are too heavy to be dispersed by the wind, and if they fail to escape from under the canopy of their parent tree they cannot grow. Lying in the shade, they become ideal homes for the larvae of moths and weevils. So, how *do* acorns manage to become oak trees? One answer is *squirrels*. Acorns are brimming with nutrients—proteins, carbohydrates, and fats—and they support several species of birds and mammals. Squirrels survive by hoarding acorns in caches *away* from their source. Sometimes, they drop one. More often, they die before finishing their troves. Acorns that are fortunate enough to be harvested by a squirrel but *not* converted into food have the chance to become an oak tree—thus provisioning the next generation of squirrels. Now wait, what is the "purpose" of acorns again?

Dan Robins is one of a growing number of Sinologists who recognize that the early Chinese notion of *xing* 性 is not a near-equivalent to species-essence in its Greek-medieval sense. His argument rests largely on an analysis of how the term is used in predication. According to Robins, when Warring States writers use *xing* to attribute characteristics (e.g., "It is the *xing* of water to be clear," *shuizhixingqing* 水之性清),[153] *xing* is not the subject of predication. Rather, "it is the water and not its *xing* which is said to be clear, and the point of attributing its clarity to its *xing* is to say something about how or why it is clear."[154] If it is the *xing* of water to be clear, then this means that water has that particular *way* of behaving when not disturbed. As the *Zhuangzi* observes: "It is the *xing* of water that, if not stirred, then it is clear."[155] According to Robins, "There is no basis in any Warring States text for thinking of the concept of *xing* as essentially tied to species natures or specific differences."[156] In other words, *xing* does not serve as the equivalent of the Greek-medieval species-essence upon which "types" (*lei* 類) are then based in Warring States philosophy.

Based on a thing's *xing* 性 one can certainly *formulate* types. Mencius does so when he designates barley seeds as a "type" based on their tendency to sprout when given adequate nourishment.[157] For Robins, however, the meaning of *xing* in such instances is precise:

> [According] to Warring States texts it is a thing's *xing* to have some characteristic just in case the thing has the characteristic naturally, and it is a thing's *xing* to behave in some way only if it behaves that way spontaneously. A characteristic is natural in the relevant sense just in case it is either innate or the result of spontaneous development (*sheng* 生). A development or a way of behaving is spontaneous in the relevant sense just in case it occurs of itself (*ziran* 自然), without interference. It follows that it

can be a thing's *xing* to behave some way only if it actually does behave that way when not interfered with.[158]

Nowhere in such an account are species-essences necessarily postulated, let alone *immutable* species-essences. According to early Chinese logic, terms like "Barley" (*mou* 麰) represent the behavior of a mass of concrete, real things—not any fixed "nature."

A. C. Graham carefully considers the meaning of *xing* 性 in Warring States texts. Succumbing initially to the spell of common sense, he claims that *xing* can be thought of along "lines rather suggestive of Aristotelian teleology," and that the term "nature" is a "very close English equivalent."[159] Ironically, he wavers almost immediately on the latter claim, noting that *xing* confirms "one's general impression when groping towards an understanding of early Chinese concepts, that often they tend to be more dynamic than their nearest Western equivalents, and that English translation freezes them into immobility."[160] He proceeds to qualify his position to such a degree that his opening thesis is one that is hardly defensible based on the evidence he provides. By 1991, Graham reverses his view, claiming that the English word "nature" in fact "predisposes us to mistake [*xing*] for a transcendent origin, which . . . would also be a transcendent end." He comes to realize that *xing* is more accurately conceived "in terms of spontaneous development in a certain direction rather than of its origin or goal." Accordingly, the maturity (*cheng* 成) of an organic process is one that involves "the interdependent becoming integral rather than the realization of an end."[161] Graham thus abandons teleology as he comes to better understand the Chinese term.

Roger T. Ames chronicles the evolution of A. C. Graham's understanding of *xing* 性 in greater detail.[162] Graham's final view is consistent with the general ideas forwarded here, and it is close to Dan Robins' own understanding of *xing*. For Robins, *xing* is likewise the spontaneous activity of a thing in a particular direction rather than its origin or goal. As he puts it: "We might say not that it is the *xing* of a seed to be a plant, but that it is the *xing* of a seed to grow into a plant—for this is something that the seed is *currently doing*."[163] In this way, *xing* amounts not to a fixed "essence," but simply to whatever a thing is doing when it behaves without interference. This modest, more flexible definition allows for a thing's *xing* to be improved upon, preserved, extended, changed, violated, diminished, lost, and so on—all of which factor importantly into Warring States debates. It also allows one to propose that things can be categorized as types based on similarities in their *xing*, as Mencius famously does not only with barley seeds but with human beings.

One point, however, continues to imply that *xing* 性 aligns more closely with the Greek-medieval notion of "nature" than Robins suggests—namely, the fact that *xing* and "nature" have similar etymologies. The word for "nature" in Greek (*phusis*) comes from *phuō*, "I grow." The word for "nature" in Latin (*natura*) comes from *nascor*, "I am born." The case is similar in classical Chinese. *Xing* is closely related to the term for both "birth" and "life," *sheng* 生, and all of these ideas come to define one another.[164] "Life is called *xing*," declares Gaozi.[165] Xunzi offers a more nuanced definition, maintaining: "That by which something is so-and-so at birth/during life (*sheng*) is called *xing*. The harmony (*he* 和) by which it remains alive; the exact coincidence of its stimulus-response (*ganying* 感應) behaviors, and that which, without effort, it spontaneously does (*ziran* 自然)—these are [also] called *xing*."[166]

Robins maintains that the grammar at the beginning of Xunzi's definition clearly indicates that *xing* 性 is *not* what something is "at birth" but rather "during life." Eric L. Hutton disagrees, and argues that the grammar is "not obvious" and he prefers "at birth."[167] In reality, the point is moot. It goes without saying that live creatures exhibit spontaneous behaviors (*xing*) at birth. The Moro reflex, for instance, (also known as the "startle reaction") is present for the first 4 to 5 months in normal human infants. It begins to disappear, however, as other fear responses are developed. The sucking reflex, common to all nursing mammals, is triggered when objects come into contact with the roof of the mouth. This reflex also diminishes over time. Meanwhile, other congenital reflexes persist throughout the course of a normal human life (the knee jerk, stretch, and gag reflexes, for instance). Some common reflexes surface only *after* other mechanical and neurological adaptations have occurred, such as those involved in walking. For humans this is conditioned through voluntary effort, normally between 8 and 12 months of age. Once walking is mastered it becomes second nature.

Accordingly, whether or not Hutton is correct about Xunzi's first sentence makes no difference to Robins' argument. Whether they are present "at birth" or surface "during life," *all* of the above reflexes qualify as *xing* according to Robins' definition, but they need not qualify *at the same time*—nor must they qualify forever.[168]

Dewey's position on the topic follows from his notion of "habit." Recall that, for Dewey, habits are both *native* and *acquired*. While analytically separable, each type involves the complete integration of organism-and-environment and stimulus-and-response. This accounts for its philosophical connection to *dao* 道-activity. Habit, like *dao*, exhibits perfect continuity between means-and-end. Unlike mechanical behavior (which is *accidental*) and teleological behavior (which is *instrumental*) habitual behavior is *spontaneous* in that the "end has got thoroughly organized into the means."[169]

The philosophical subtleties that surround Dewey's position on the development of "habit" can easily generate confusion. "*As organized activities,*"

Dewey explains, habits are "secondary and acquired, not native and original."[170] As for habitual behavior that *is* native and original, Dewey uses the terms "impulse" or "instinct." As he says, "[Impulse and instinct] will assert themselves if they get any chance at all. They are spontaneous."[171] However, while they are "primary" in a linear sense, impulses and instincts are *not* primary in actual behavior. "In conduct the acquired is the primitive," Dewey writes. "Impulses although first in time are never primary in fact; they are secondary and dependent."[172] Such thinking sounds paradoxical.

The fact behind the paradox is that *behavior never stands still*. As Dan Robins and A. C. Graham each recognize, *xing* 性 refers to what something is *currently doing*—not to what it once did (its *origin*) nor to what it might someday do (its *end*). Native impulses turn into habits in real time, and what qualifies as *xing* are those habits that are *currently operative*. As such, they retain continuity with native impulses. "[Habit] has its wellspring within our own makeup," Dewey explains, "[they] are simply the organization of one's natural powers and tendencies—powers which are native but imperfect."[173] Spotting native impulse or instinct in the *raw* would be like spotting the first few flashes of existence within the Plank epoch. It cannot be done, because habit is already there. Impulse *becomes* habit, and habit in turn becomes impulsive. Impulse and habit evolve together in organic development.

Again, the problem as Graham notes is that English words like "nature" have the unfortunate tendency to freeze Chinese terms like *xing* into place. It thus becomes a fixed species essence or "nature." Careful reflection, however, reveals that whether it is present at birth (as Hutton says), emergent over the course of a life (as Robins says), or both (as Dewey says), the concept of *xing* does not warrant the species-essence inference—not at all.

Rather than species-essence being the corollary of *xing* 性, its corollary is individual "allotments" (*ming* 命)—the spontaneous tendencies that each individual is fated to experience during its own natural lifespan (*xingming* 性命). Such tendencies include not only the evolutionary inheritances that others share, but also those of one's family history, genetic quirks, and other preexisting conditions specific to the individual organism. As *Focusing the Familiar* (*Zhongyong* 中庸) suggests, conditions such as these are "commanded" (*ming* 命) by the forces of Nature (*tian* 天) and there is little one can do to change them.[174] As Lisa Raphals points out, there is a semantic field crossed between such "commands" (*ming*) and the "allotments" (*ming*) that result from them.[175] They are similar enough ideas, however, in terms of their irrevocability. The good news for living things is that life (*sheng* 生) is the most resilient force on earth. Each allotment of a lifespan (*ming*) expresses a power (*de* 德) that can be relied upon to spontaneously extend its own growth and development to the *utmost* degree possible under the conditions.

The "Short Preface" (*xiaoxu* 小序) to the *Songs* describes this force succinctly: "The myriad beings attain the emergence of their ways (*dao* 道) . . . [each] attains the extremity (*gao* 高) of its immensity (*da* 大) . . . [and] the life/growth (*sheng* 生) of each one attains its own adaptive fit (*yi* 宜)."[176] The not-so-good news is that, in the struggle for existence, *dao* plays no favorites. The cholera germ has its power (*de* 德) just as any human being does, and *dao* will generously yield to the *de* of the bacteria when the situation is right. As Chapter 5 of the *Daodejing* reminds us: "Heaven and earth are not humane (*ren* 仁), they treat the myriad beings as straw dogs."

Wuwei 無為 and Observing the Small

Since the term *xing* 性 does not appear in the *Daodejing*, it can be set aside for later discussions. One idea that *does* carry over into the text is the corollary idea that living things have allotted lifespans (*ming* 命) that are non-negotiable. This is generally understood to be the quantity and quality of one's *qi* 氣 as prenatally configured.[177] Daoist practitioners believe that through intelligent bodily practices one can extend life and energy to the maximum degree afforded by one's allotment. Over the centuries, the tradition has experimented with some questionable methods for doing so, but the core idea is that organic life is best lived in its normal (*chang* 常) state, meaning that any activities superfluous to physical health detract from the power (*de* 德) inherent in organic form. Accordingly, the Daoist tradition recommends a practice of cognitive readjustment, whereby one reconnects with the rhythms and energies of organic life.

Up to this point, our experiments have focused largely on factual considerations with respect to how early Chinese thought might get us "back in gear" with empirical reality. As we prepare to enter part II of this volume, the range of our experiments will extend to include more prescriptive and normative considerations. Since, empirically speaking, the Daoist tradition presents a relatively accurate picture of the natural world, its prescriptive dimensions should be carefully understood and taken seriously. In this, the final section of part I, we will begin to establish Daoism's prescriptive outlook in preparation for future applications.

In approaching this aspect of Daoist philosophy, it is crucial to preserve the ground already covered. As we have seen, the most important difference between Chinese and Greek-medieval thinking is that the latter is resolutely teleological and the former is not. For Aristotle, "Nature, like mind, always does whatever it does for the sake of something, *which* something is its end." This obtains at every level of organic behavior: "This is true of [*animas*] that enter into the constitution of plants as well as those which enter into that of animals," writes Aristotle.[178] Such teleology informs normative thinking throughout the Greek-medieval tradition. Chinese natural philosophy begins with the opposite premise. *Dao* 道 is understood as *weierbushi* 為而不恃: "acting without presumption (with respect to outcome or aim)," such that the *dao* 道 of nature does not act *for the sake* of anything (*daochangwuwei* 道常無為).[179] This is a central feature of Daoist philosophy, and it needs to be remembered as we move from the descriptive features of Chinese natural philosophy to the more prescriptive dimensions of the Daoist tradition.

This feature, as central as it is to Daoist philosophy, is easy to forget. Treatments of Chapter 16 in the *Daodejing*, for instance, illustrate well how teleological concepts creep back in as we make philosophical connections with normative approaches that are more familiar. Chapter 16 prescribes the following:

> Become completely empty. Maintain quiet equilibrium. The myriad beings arise side-by-side (*bingzuo* 並作).[180] We observe them being restored (*fu* 復). With respect to things that grow organically (*fuwuyunyun* 夫物芸芸), each is restored by returning to its root and source (*gen* 根). Returning to the root and source is called equilibrium (*jing* 靜). This is called restoring the course of an allotted lifespan (*fuming* 復命). Restoring the course of an allotted lifespan is called normalcy (*chang* 常). Realizing normalcy is called intelligence (*ming* 明).

It is not uncommon for commentators to render *ming* 命 as "destiny" in this passage and then drift into teleological reasoning. Philip J. Ivanhoe exhibits this tendency.[181] Such readings depart sharply from early Daoist thinking. In classical Chinese, the term equilibrium (*jing*) instantly evokes its inseparable partner, movement (*dong* 動). When confronting changes in its environment, the live creature needs to restore itself (*fu*) in order to continue growing. Understanding the prescriptive message in Chapter 16 requires focusing squarely on the power of growth without introducing the notion of a destined end (*telos*). Such ends are explicitly rejected in the *Daodejing*.

Fu 復 is a term that recent archeological finds help us to better understand.[182] Its manner of growth entails returning (*gui* 歸) to a root and source (*gen* 根). *Gen* in this context can be thought of as the live creature's still center on the "Potter's Wheel of Nature." Thus understood, to "return" to equilibrium means neither leaping backward toward an *origin* nor forward toward an *end*. Either movement, in fact, derails normal growth patterns. What *gui* means by "returning" is instead a *resuming* of unforced growth along parameters resident in the organism-environment circuit. Equilibrium (*jing* 靜) thus entails restoring symmetry through rhythmic adjustment. In other words, it is the re-balancing of *qi* 氣 energies. The word "normalcy" (*chang* 常), which can also be translated as "constancy," draws attention to what organic life is constantly doing—namely, cycling in and out of equilibrium. As Dewey says, organic life is in a constant state of *need*. "Need," he explains, is a "condition of tensional distribution of energies such that the body is in a condition of uneasy or unstable equilibrium."[183] When equilibrium is disturbed, the "need" is to restore it. When it is regained, the "need" is to maintain it. The "need" in not to leapfrog backwards or forwards to any origin or end, but instead to prolong and enrich the life/growth process (*sheng* 生).

One of the curious things about the appearance of the term "need" (*yu* 欲) in the *Hengxian* is that in the *Daodejing* the term stands for something different: the "desire" (*yu* 欲) that results in various calamities when overextended. Hans-Georg Moeller's treatment of desire in the *Daodejing* helps us to reconcile these seemingly disparate meanings. As Moeller suggests, Daoist teachings about controlling desires (*yu*) are "paradoxically grounded in their fulfillment."[184] Desire, he explains, is a state of agitation—a state of not being satisfied. When an organism is hungry, for instance, it desires food. When it has eaten enough (*zu* 足) the desire goes away. One desires periodically to engage in sexual intercourse. When one has had enough, the desire goes away. The mastery of desire, explains Moeller, is really a "mastery of satisfaction," or the "mastery of fulfillment." As Chapter 44 teaches: "Knowing what is enough (*zu*) is to avoid degradation. Knowing when to stop is to avoid peril. Only then can one endure for a long time." Daoism does not advocate denying or suppressing one's desires for things like food and sex—we *need* such things. Instead, the idea is to identify what is enough (*zu*) and to satisfy *that*. As Chapter 46 says: "One who realizes what is enough will always have enough." The problem is that, when desire is undisciplined by the realization of what is enough, it grows into unnecessary and insatiable *wants*.

As Dewey observes, "Primary needs may be few and simple, [but] *wants* may become indefinitely diversified and complex."[185] With such diversification, Moeller understands the danger to be the emergence of a "self-perpetuating state of desire that continuously projects satisfaction into the future"—a constant state of not "needing" but of *wanting*.[186] Humans are particularly (if not exclusively) susceptible to this problem. From a cognitive science standpoint, its future-orientation is the key component. Not all animals have the cognitive ability to *want* things in the future. The diversity and complexity that Dewey identifies as distinguishing the states of want from that of need is marked by the ability to slot *specific* objects into linear temporal series as future desirables. Such cognitive activity requires event-independent temporal representations.[187] As John Campbell argues, non-human animals generally do not have the concept of a particular time in which a *specific* object may or may not be procured. They do, however, have the ability (both innately and learned) to identify temporal phases in which objects may appear with respect to recurrent cycles, patterns, and rhythms both circadian and seasonal.[188] This is enough to satisfy their "needs."

Such temporal orientations differ from those that enable us to *want*, for instance, a specific leather jacket by next Saturday night. Considerable planning and forecast goes into securing *that* particular object by *that* particular time. Most animals secure their needs at closer range when the time comes around. Our ability to break free from such intimate temporal horizons enables us to project specific desires into more abstract futures. However, as Chapter 3 of the *Daodejing* warns, there are social perils that come with projecting "valuable goods that are difficult to procure," while Chapter 12 notes that psychological perils follow in the wake of doing so: "the dashing and hunting that make a person's mind crazy." Since being in a constant state of *wanting* is not a normal (*chang* 常) way to live, such anxieties deplete *qi* 氣 and shorten one's lifespan (*ming* 命).

The normal way to live, according to Daoism, is *wuwei* 無為—not doing/making things to be thus or so. As Edward Slingerland explains, the term *wei* 為 has a broad semantic range in classical Chinese. In addition to "doing" and "making," it also means "regarding" things in a certain way. Thus, *wuwei* means "not regarding" things as such. To be "without regard" or "non-regarding" (*wuyiwei* 無以為) is to resist attributing undue worth to *specific* objects or outcomes. "Such regarding causes a person to value one thing over another, and therefore provides ulterior motives for action," explains Slingerland.[189]

The notion that human beings ought *not* to regard one thing over another, however, strikes one as *prima facie* absurd. Could it be that the *Daodejing* advocates a world in which *no* improvements are ever considered or pursued? If so, then what Bryan W. Van Norden grimly imagines would be true: "Most of the children in [the Daoist] 'utopia' will die from diseases before they reach maturity."[190] Dewey, however, provides a more nuanced interpretation of *wuwei* 無為 as a Daoist principle. "It is something more than mere inactivity," he observes, "it is a kind of rule of moral doing, a doctrine of active patience, endurance, persistence while nature has time to do her work."[191] The "ulterior" motives that stem from doing (*wei* 為) are those that project ends beyond what *present* conditions make possible—specific ends that are so highly "regarded" that they in fact *dis*-regard the means through which they might be realized. Thus, *wei* represents a failure to work with conditions intelligently (*ming* 明).

To rush ahead and insist upon a specific outcome without regard for the play of conditions is to ignore the active propensities (*shi* 勢) in a given situation. This (as we will see in chapter 5) is a recipe for stupidity.

"Active patience," as Dewey calls it, recovers the element of *timing* (*shi* 時)—which accounts for the elegance and efficacy of most animal behavior. While projecting future goals, humans can still align their activities with natural rhythms and thereby maximize success. For as Mencius observes, "One might be clever, but it is better to make use of the propensity of things (*shi* 勢). One might have a garden hoe, but it is better to wait for the season (*shi* 時) to arrive."[192] Dewey likewise associates the principle of *wuwei* 無為 with Chinese agrarian practices. China's "unparalleled human achievement," he observes—to go on tilling and tilling while safeguarding the health of the soil—"for thousands of years [the Chinese] have been conserving the resources of nature, nursing, preserving, patiently, obstinately." In this way, "the Chinese have learned to wait for the fruition of slow natural processes." The lesson that Daoism has to teach us, writes Dewey, is that "active doing and striving are likely to be only an interference with nature."[193]

Daoism, accordingly, is not about having *no* objectives. Rather, it teaches that great achievements are only incrementally secured and that patience is a virtue. As Chapter 63 of the *Daodejing* says: "The greatest things in the world can only arise from what is small. Thus, ultimately, sages do not make (*wei* 為) great things happen. This is why they can bring great things to fruition (*cheng* 成)." Chapter 64 provides the classic imagery: "A tree the width of a person's embrace springs from the tiniest shoot," and "a tower nine stories high rises from one basketful of earth." The wisdom of such an approach is that it avoids what Dewey calls "*the* philosophical fallacy." Ends are not postulated at the outset, i.e., they are not treated in abstraction from the *processes* through which they become realized. Daoism thus avoids subordinating processes to pre-conceived ends. This is what *wuwei* 無為 means in actual practice—being attentive to minute opportunities to intelligently change course in the midst of an on-going process.

Such practice is called "observing the small" (*jianxiao* 見小). As Chapter 52 teaches: "To observe the small is called intelligence (*ming* 明). To preserve flexibility is called strength. Using such lights, restoring (*fu* 復) and resuming (*gui* 歸) such intelligence, one does not lose oneself to calamity. This is to make habitual what is normal (*chang* 常)." Because humans remain fundamentally organic creatures, such an intelligence is to be "restored" and "resumed"—not acquired or learned. Our nonhuman relatives, animal and vegetable, exhibit such intelligence "normally" (*chang* 常) because their *dao* 道-activities continue to preserve continuity between means-and-ends. The fact that we can technologically separate and thus manipulate means and ends is both our supreme advantage and our curse. If not tempered with intelligence (*ming*), it presents us with genuine opportunities to destroy ourselves.

This, however, does not have to be our fate. Dewey and Daoism hold out hope that we humans can recover, even augment, our animal intelligence. The requisite ideals of *wuwei* 無為 and "observing the small" merge naturally with Daoism's 1-2-3 cosmology. The sage embraces the one (*baoyi* 抱一) and thereby attends to the subtle ways in which small variations (*one*) grow through dynamic relations (*two*) into large-scale orders with cascading results (*three*). This connection is further suggested in subsequent Daoist-related works, such as the *Wenzi* 文子. Long regarded as a medieval forgery, archeological digs in 1973 have recovered bamboo fragments of the *Wenzi* dating from about 55 BCE, making the text considerably older than once thought. While much about the history and pedigree of the text remains unknown (it is highly syncretic), the contents of the newly recovered, "proto-*Wenzi*" strips are suggestive. Asked how the sages of old governed the world, the text replies that, "They held to the one (*zhiyi* 執一) and were *wuwei*." Another fragment relates that, "When sages hold to the one they observe the small, and thus are *wuwei*." And finally, "By observing the small [sages] accomplish great things."[194] The received text further teaches that effective governance entails "observing the small and thus preserving flexibility (*rou* 柔)," and "being flexible and yielding to micro-subtleties (*weimiao* 微妙) is to observe the small."[195]

Recalling previous discussions, it is curious that the *Wenzi* employs the Huang-Lao phase, "holding to the one" (*zhiyi* 執一) rather than the Daoist phrase, "embracing the one" (*baoyi* 抱一). In virtually every other respect, the teachings of the *Wenzi* are diametrically opposed to Huang-Lao.[196] This oddity confirms Arthur Waley's observation that *baoyi* and *zhiyi* "[have] a curious history, very typical of the way in which the various schools, while retaining the same time-hallowed watchwords, adapted them to their own needs."[197] Huang-Lao editors moved to abandon the "one" of novelty by replacing the *bao* 抱 with *zhi* 執. The *Wenzi* then usurps the Huang-Lao vocabulary, refutes its worldview, and reinstates the novelty.

In any case, however these Daoist texts came to be written, they contain remarkably subtle insights into the nature of the world and how to live productively within it. Chapter 10 of the *Daodejing* provides what is perhaps the most comprehensive prescriptive statement in the entire corpus of early Daoism. This chapter encompasses many of the ideas discussed thus far, and it underscores the close connection between "embracing the one" and *wuwei* 無為. Chapter 10 goes as follows:

> Nourishing the soul and embracing the one (*baoyi* 抱一), can you not depart from these?[198] Concentrating the *qi* 氣 and making it

pliant, can you be like an infant? Cleansing and purifying the profound mirror, can you be without blemish? Caring for the people and ordering the state, can you be without knowledge (*wuzhi* 無知)? Opening and closing the gates of Nature (*tian* 天), can you play the part of female? . . . Apprehending things clearly in all directions, can you be without coercive action (*wuwei*)? Produce things (*shengzhi* 生之). Nurture them. Produce, but do not possess. Act, but do not be presumptuous. Enable growth, but do not dictate (*changerbuzai* 長而不宰). This is called profound efficacy (*de* 德).[199]

Along with "observing the small," "embracing the one" emerges as an ideal habit or attitude that involves attentiveness to change and particularity. Prescribing such habits is consistent with the non-teleological orientation of the tradition. Sages join in the production (*sheng* 生) of things, but they do not take ownership of them; they nourish the growth of things, but do not dictate their development. This is to cherish and defer to the spontaneity of each thing—i.e., to "embrace the one" (*baoyi*).

The Daoist sage refuses to set preconceived limits to the immensity (*da* 大) of the world's possibilities. He or she works patiently toward a goal without predetermining the exact form in which it will be realized. In this way, means-end continuity is preserved and energies are allowed to gather momentum and to reach their consummations (*cheng* 成) naturally. Again, Daoism is not about *doing nothing*—rather, it is about realizing optimal outcomes in specific sets of circumstances. The path of sagely activity is not to establish some "grand scheme" at the outset; it is rather to appreciate the manner in which each detail contributes dynamically to an emergent result, and then to attend to such details while adjusting course accordingly. The sage thus "observes the small" and allows the vastness of space (*yu* 域) to do its work. This is what it means to go along with *dao* (*shundao* 順道).

∾

In closing out part I, volume one, let us take stock of where we are and look ahead. Dewey's "On Philosophical Synthesis" stands as the keynote statement in a journal devoted to broadening dialogue in East-West philosophy. Rather than seeing such dialogue as an invitation to make comparisons, Dewey envisions it as primarily an opportunity to make experimental connections—to forge "*specific* philosophical relationships" for explicit purposes aimed at the betterment of the human estate. While it is crucial that we present ancient traditions accurately, and it is useful to understand where they stand in terms of "Sameness/Difference" with our own traditions, such projects are ultimately subservient to what is genuinely important to intra-cultural philosophy: the *assimilation* of different traditions in order to enlarge and improve our own outlooks. Intra-cultural philosophy acknowledges that it operates for such a purpose and realizes that this occurs within a larger cultural context.

As an American currently living in the United States, my immediate concern is with the anti-scientific biases that pervade American society. Such attitudes feed our worst tendencies: moral absolutism, climate change denial, cultural chauvinism, religious fundamentalism, and so on. Dewey's understanding of the problem makes sense to me. To varying degrees, Western societies are stuck "Wandering between Two Worlds," living in a world profoundly transformed by advancements in the natural sciences while harboring moral and religious sensibilities that, vaguely or explicitly, appeal to postulates belonging to the Greek-medieval world: unchanging truths, discrete substances, teleological ends, essential natures, and so on. The resulting moral and cultural confusion is a symptom of being "out of gear" with empirical reality.

Philosophers have a central role to play in turning this around. Our task is to pay attention to what science knows and to help update common sense accordingly, observing how values and purposes become reconfigured in the process. The point of philosophy is not to leave things dangling in the aftermath of "deconstruction." Dewey's focus is always on *reconstruction*, meaning that philosophers must continue working to secure our values on empirical grounds and to reorient our purposes intelligently. Ultimately, philosophy serves as but one strand within culture—the comprehensive interest of which is to optimize social, aesthetic, scientific, moral, and religious experiences by establishing working connections within the nature-culture circuit. Philosophy does not work alone, but it has a unique office through which it contributes to this general human aim.

The foregoing presentation of Daoist thinking is designed to serve the interests just expressed. It focuses primarily on those aspects of the Daoist tradition that might assist us in updating our outlooks with respect to the natural world. Organic form, teleology, and cosmology are topics that call forth subtle analyses in both the Chinese and Western traditions. The argument here is that early Chinese analyses are generally more adequate with respect to what science tells us than are Greek-medieval analyses. The Chinese analyses recommend themselves to us on that basis. There remains much work to be done, however, as we have only begun to explore the prescriptive dimensions of this tradition. In part II, experiments will focus on the *Zhuangzi* and on some of the topics that it treats: e.g., knowledge, the body, technology, and so on. Here, we begin to see normative considerations emerge more distinctly as the text engages polemically with alternative viewpoints.

We also continue in part II to establish "*specific* philosophical relationships" between Dewey and Daoism. Reading Dewey alongside the *Zhuangzi* on topics like knowledge, the body, and technology proves to be a remarkably profitable exercise. Dewey's personal experiences and intellectual influences suggest connections in areas that he is not typically associated with—e.g., body practices, primitivism, and mysticism—each of which factors significantly in the Daoist tradition. As for topics that Dewey is more regularly associated with—e.g., intelligence, methods of learning, and instrumentalism—each of these resonates with the Daoist tradition in surprising ways. The intra-cultural experiments in part II aim primarily at reconstructing our understanding of how humans relate to Nature (*tian* 天), an understanding that is vital for us to update in light of current scientific knowledge.

Indeed, perhaps no general cultural condition has changed more dramatically in recent times than the human-nature relationship—yet, Greek-medieval assumptions in this area continue to operate. Here, getting ourselves "back in gear" will require considering empirically what it is that makes humans unique in the natural world. It also involves identifying how human knowledge (*zhi* 知) relates to *dao* 道-activity generally, as an instrument that can either disrupt means-end continuity or restore it according to how it is regarded and used. All of this will be considered in part II of the present volume.

Let me close part I with an anecdote. Long stored away in Special Collections at Morris Library in Carbondale are two remarkable landscapes that Dewey brought home with him from China. When these items were retrieved in October 2016 (after being finally located; they had been mislabeled in storage!), it became evident to the librarians and to us at the Dewey Center that they had never before been retrieved from the archive. Opening these neglected cases and lifting out the protective wrap to reveal the sleeping artwork was an experience those assembled will never forget. These scrolls were hidden treasures. Given their classic composition, their open perspective, and their expert use of shading, they stand up well alongside similar works in their style.

The reproductions provided here, however, conceal the true nature of these scrolls—just as we were initially deceived when first laying eyes on the originals. *These are not Chinese landscape paintings.* Nor are they among the less-expensive reproductions that Dewey acquired from Mr. Koo in Shanghai. In reality, these are exquisite silk embroideries stitched with the very finest of threads. Even in their presence, this is not immediately apparent. Every element is woven—the scenes, the Chinese characters, the red chops. The thread is *ultra*-fine. Some ethereal needle, the size of which is unimaginably small, worked each weft of thread carefully and patiently into each warp of silk. The net effect is stunning. Indeed, the greatest things arise from

Rhythms and Energies / 151

Figure 4.2. Pair of traditional landscape scrolls that John Dewey obtained in China. John Dewey collection, Special Collections Research Center, Morris Library, Southern Illinois University, Carbondale.

what is small, and trees the width of an embrace spring from the tiniest of shoots.

As Dewey observes, "It is not so easy in the case of the perceiver and appreciator [of the artwork] to understand the intimate union of doing and undergoing as it is in the case of the maker." Standing before these works, however, the viewer is pulled directly into the process of creation, such that "taking in involves activities that are comparable to those of the creator."[200] One cannot help but follow the tiny trails of the individual threads, "observing the small" as they weave themselves into the emergent whole. One can imagine Dewey sitting in his library, marveling at the inclusive end to which each strand contributes.

VOLUME ONE

Part II

5

Methods and Intelligence

> Planting is an active undertaking. It can engage students' instincts for activity and can orient them towards society in such a way that their behavior will be of social benefit. This apparently minor activity can be made a primary means of education . . . I could have chosen any one of a large number of other examples—preparing food, raising silkworms, spinning silk, or weaving cloth.
>
> —John Dewey, National Peking Academy of Fine Arts, May 1921

Theory and Ordinary Activity

The incandescence radiated by drift and uncertainty is what sages use as their guide. They have no use for taking (*wei* 為) things to be thus or so—instead, they rely on ordinary activity (*yong* 庸). This is what it means to use intelligence (*ming* 明).[1]

With this, Zhuangzi distinguishes his approach from those reliant on knowledge (*zhi* 知). The *Zhuangzi* is then replete with stories about craftspeople gaining insight and developing efficacy by engaging in ordinary activities—mundane tasks not unlike those that Dewey lists, "raising silkworms, spinning silk, or weaving cloth." Ordinary activity stories in the *Zhuangzi* comprise what Joseph Needham calls the "knack passages."[2]

The most famous story is that of Cook Ding. Cook Ding, we learn, was carving an ox for the ruler, Wenhui. With a "zip and a whoosh," his blade whizzed through the carcass as if he were "dancing the Mulberry Grove or keeping time with the *Jingshou* chorus." Wenhui exclaims, "Ah! So good! That skill (*ji* 技) can reach such heights!" Cook Ding lays aside his knife and says, "All I care about is *dao* 道, which goes beyond skill." He then explains: "When I first started carving oxen, I perceived nothing but oxen. After three years, I still had not perceived the entire ox. These days, spirit carries me through and I no longer use my eyes to see. My faculty of knowing (*guanzhi* 官知) recedes and my spirit impulses (*shenyu* 神欲) take over. I rely on natural patterns, strike at the biggest openings, and direct [the blade] through the largest hollows. I go with how things actually are (*guran* 固然). Thus, I never have to cut through ligaments or tendons, let alone any main joint." Such expertise, he explains, lends longevity to his instrument: "Good cooks change their knives once a year because they *cut*. Average cooks change their knives once a month because they *hack*. I've had this knife for nineteen years, and I've carved thousands of oxen with it. The blade remains as sharp as it was fresh from the whetstone."³

The idea is that, when one carves in accord with the natural contours of the carcass, no resistance is met. As Cook Ding explains: "Any given joint has space within it, and the blade of the knife has no thickness. When something with no thickness enters into something with space, it is vast and open and the blade has plenty of room to move about. This is why after nineteen years the blade remains as sharp as it did fresh from the stone." There are intervals, however, when problems do arise. "I sometimes hit knots," he explains, "and I sense how difficult it is to execute." His trepidation at once becomes caution—his gaze settles, his activity slows, and he moves his chopper with micro-precision (*wei* 微). Then all at once—*plop*—the flesh comes "crumbling apart like clumps of earth falling to the ground." He stands there, knife in hand, beholding his work with satisfaction before wiping off his knife and putting it away. On hearing Cook Ding's account, Wenhui replies: "How wonderful! From hearing the teachings of Cook Ding I have learned how to nourish life (*yangsheng* 養生)!"⁴

This episode has received more than its share of philosophical attention, especially among Western commentators. This is not surprising. The notion that an ordinary activity like carving oxen (or as Dewey suggests, preparing food or spinning silk) might provide valuable insights into how to live is no less provocative today than it was among the ancient Greeks. As the Greeks asked, how can practical activity alone deliver the kind of guidance that theory provides? How can a mere "knack" (*empeiria*) for doing something give one the "wisdom" that knowledge (*episteme*) brings?

Among Western commentators, Robert Eno has challenged the *dao* 道 of Cook Ding on this basis. As he notes, the Mohist tradition of rational argument "made it possible for China to embark on a philosophical enterprise similar to that of the Greeks, one based on the connection between reason and certainty and taking theoretical knowing to be the basis for wisdom and behavioral excellence." The Cook Ding episode represents Zhuangzi's rejection of this emerging philosophical enterprise and signals his endorsement of *dao*-learning as the ideal form of human activity. According to Eno, Zhuangzi "takes the ethical position of advocating that people make a sustained effort to reform themselves through the acquisition of a *dao*" rather than pursue theory knowledge. The substance of Zhuangzi's critique is presented in the "On the Parity of Things" (*Qiwulun* 齊物論) chapter of the *Zhuangzi*. Here, according to Eno, Zhuangzi establishes himself as a "thorough skeptic on the possibility of attaining fact or theory knowledge, that is, certain understanding based on the powers of language and reason."[5]

What puzzles Eno is how *dao* 道-learning can be claimed as a cardinal value given such a thorough disregard for theory. "On the Parity of Things" is so dismissive in this respect, he writes, that it "resists any temptation to lay groundwork for a theory that would allow us to transform this valuation of skill mastery into a coherent ethical theory."[6] Such disregard for theoretical grounding, he argues, makes *dao*-learning impossible to justify—and without the guidance of theoretical knowledge, the mastery of ordinary activity (*yong* 庸) might lead to anything. As such, Cook Ding's *dao* is completely *a*-moral. Whatever value it might have is "not an ethical value," Eno writes. It lacks even the minimal features through which it might "disassociate itself from positive valuation of complex skill systems based on torture or mass murder."[7] As Eno sees it, "*dao*-practices can be adapted to any end: the *dao* of butchering people might provide much the same spiritual spontaneity as the *dao* of butchering oxen . . . [Cook Ding's *dao*] makes no selection among the goals to which it might apply." Such an approach, in Eno's estimation, is "ethically inadequate." In order to correct such inadequacy, one must go beyond the *dao* of ordinary practice (*yong*) and establish some theory (*yan* 言) that will guide the selection of ends. As it stands, Zhuangzi's world is a "field of flux," one that provides a "changing array of opportunities [for *dao*-learners] to engage their powers for the ends they envision."[8] Eno poses the standard ethical-theoretical question: "Yes, but what ends *should* they envision?" Here, Zhuangzi offers us nothing.

The present chapter is an extended response to Eno, and its experiments will take some time to unfold. First, we will see that Eno's criticisms of the *Zhuangzi* are similar to critiques that are often directed at Dewey. Philosophically this is not surprising, because the manners in which Dewey and Zhuangzi conceive of learning through "ordinary activity" overlap and connect. We will see that, for Dewey, there are distinct virtues to be derived from such learning. These virtues, I hope, will mitigate some of Eno's concerns with Cook Ding.

On a more fundamental level, however, the following argument will question the actual cogency of Eno's critique of *dao* 道-learning. If, as Hans-Georg Moeller argues, the moment "one begins to look at the world and oneself in moral terms, this is already a turning away from the *dao*,"[9] then Eno may be asking the wrong questions. I will argue that Eno's critique of Cook Ding's *dao* indeed misfires, both structurally and conceptually. It misfires structurally because it bifurcates the means-end continuity that defines *dao*-activity, and it misfires conceptually because rather than evaluate *dao*-activity in terms of "Good vs. Evil" one should evaluate it in terms of "Intelligence vs. Stupidity." The classical Chinese corpus provides ample insight into this latter evaluation, most notably in its "Man from Song" stories. There will be more to say about this later. As I said, these experiments will take some time to unfold.

To begin, it needs to be established that critics see in Dewey the same troubling omission that Eno sees in the *Zhuangzi*. Dewey tells us *how* we should do things, but he never tells us *what* we should be doing. Lewis Mumford argues that this leaves us with nothing more than the "apotheosis of actualities; it is all dressed up with no place to go."[10] Richard Hofstadter's critique is typical. "The child's impulses [according to Dewey] should be guided 'forward'—but in which direction?" Dewey produces an educational *method* without furnishing any criteria for choosing ends. The result, in Hofstadter's estimation, is quite valuable in providing an understanding of method as *means*, but it is "quite unclear, often anarchic, about what these methods *should* be used to teach."[11] William Ernest Hocking's critique of Dewey's theory of knowledge reflects a similar concern. Dewey claims that philosophy must be "willing to abandon its supposed task of knowing ultimate reality and to devote itself to a proximate human office."[12] But "this can never happen," Hocking insists, "for philosophy can never perform the second function without the first." Activity without knowledge, Hocking insists, is blind. "Knowing and doing are not the same thing," he writes, "nothing but confusion can be got from identifying them, for in that case activity itself could not be known."[13] When activity is not "known," anything can happen.

Such is the thinking behind Robert Eno's critique of Cook Ding's *dao* 道. The latter offers no theoretical guidance as to *ends*, and actions cannot be morally sanctioned if we do not "know" what we are doing. The omission of such features, according to Eno, is a "distressing lapse for anyone for whom ethics is a cogent enterprise."[14] Such thinking is anticipated in Greek philosophy. Plato makes the operative distinction in the *Gorgias*, one between "arts" (*technē*) that are guided by theoretical content and "knacks" (*empeiria*) that accrue their results simply by trial and error. The former is likened to medicine, and the latter to baking pastries. Activities like baking pastries "impersonate" medicine by presenting themselves as "arts," i.e., as activities that rely upon knowing the nature of their subject matters. But baking pastries is really just a "knack." As Socrates explains: "It has no account of the nature of whatever things it applies [and] by which it applies them, so it's unable to state the cause of each thing." Socrates "refuses to call anything that lacks such an account an 'art' (*technē*)." That term is reserved for practices that treat their objects as universals and thus lend themselves to a rational account (*logos*) that can be taught. Without appeal to such objects and their application, there is no way to know if the outcome of an activity is really "good" or merely pleasing. "There are some practices that concern themselves with nothing further than pleasure and procure only pleasure, practices that are ignorant about what is better or worse," explains Socrates, "while there are other practices that *do* know what is good and what is bad. I place the 'knack' of baking pastries among those that are concerned with pleasure, and the 'art' of medicine among those concerned with the good."[15]

Plato suggests in the *Philebus* that productive activities lie on a continuum. At one end is a knack like flute playing, which progresses by "hit or miss training," and as such will have "a lot of imprecision mixed up in it and very little reliability." On the other end of the spectrum is an art like building, with its "frequent use of measures and instruments, which give it a high degree of accuracy." As Socrates explains, "It employs straightedge and compass, as well as a mason's rule, a line, and an ingenious little gadget called the carpenter's square."[16]

Such building tools—the plumb line (*shengmo* 繩墨) and the carpenter's square (*guiju* 規矩)—are ubiquitous images in early Chinese philosophy. As they do for the Greeks, they represent technologies of "knowing" that are transferrable from one practitioner to another. As Mencius says, "When the master carpenter instructs others, he must use the compass and square, and the students must also use the compass and square."[17] As the *Huainanzi* relates, "Being able to make things level and true *without* using the carpenter's square and plumb line to center them is a method (*shu* 術) that cannot be shared."[18] It is generally understood, however, that such technologies alone do not impart the skills necessary to use them intelligently. "A woodworker or a wheelwright can give a person a compass or square," Mencius explains, "but he cannot make him skillful at using them."[19] Appealing directly to the story of Cook Ding, the *Huainanzi* explains that "the compass, the square, the angle rule, and the plumb line are the tools of the skillful, but they do not make one skilled." As Liu An explains, Cook Ding's knife was allowed to wander in the spaces between the joints, and "that which wanders in the spaces between the mind and the hand is not in the realm of things, and this is something that even fathers cannot teach to their sons."[20]

As Dewey notes, the student of carpentry requires firsthand experience. "Nobody else can see for him," he writes, "and he can't see just by being 'told,' although the right kind of telling may guide his seeing and thus help him see what he needs to see."[21] The ultimate goal of *dao* 道-learning, similarly, is something that lies beyond theoretical instruction alone, because *dao* itself is beyond all objects of *technē*. As the *Huainanzi* explains: "the ultimate subtlety of *dao* is without standard or measure. The roundness of Nature (*tian* 天) cannot be obtained through the compass, and the squareness of earth cannot be obtained through the carpenter's square."[22]

However sharp the "*Technē/Empeiria*" distinction tends to be, the relative priority of each term remains an open question. Even for Plato this is not completely fixed. In the *Euthydemus*, Socrates points out that the art of hunting extends no further than pursuing and capturing its object—for having secured this end, the hunters prove "incapable of using it." They have no choice but to "hand over their prey to the Cooks."[23] In this instance, it is the cook who has the knack for converting the raw end of a technical operation into something genuinely worthwhile. In this episode, the "art" (*technē*) of hunting is subordinated to the "knack" (*empeiria*) of cooking, which alone turns its subject matter to good effect.

Dewey's approach, in the context of early childhood education, is to allow ordinary activity (or *yong* 庸) to determine how these elements ought to be balanced. Activities like cooking "enable [students] to formulate [their] experience more definitely and accurately," and such formulations determine the relative status of theory and ordinary practice. The latter activities, he maintains, "involve ability to use tools and utensils in cooking, the carpenter shop, and the laboratory, and to pursue a continuous line of work until it accomplishes definite results."[24] Theoretical formulations (*yan* 言) are among the "tools" that students use.

As Louis Menand reminds us, cooking was among Dewey's "curricular obsessions" at the Lab School: the children cooked and served lunch once a week. As Dewey saw it, preparing and serving a meal (as opposed to, say, reciting the alphabet or memorizing the multiplication table) was an ordinary, goal-directed activity continuous with life outside of the classroom.[25] In the course of their culinary activities, the children would come to incorporate the more abstract principles of arithmetic, chemistry, and biology, and engage in a variety of technical operations as the menu warranted. Cooking, Dewey found, worked as "a most natural introduction to the study of chemistry, giving the child here also something which he can at once bring to bear upon his daily experience."[26] Such instruction introduces and uses tools in their natural setting, as agencies for bringing about consummatory ends. "Fortunate for us is it that tools and their using can be directly enjoyed," notes Dewey, "otherwise all work would be drudgery."[27] By engaging in ordinary activities in the classroom, students learn to use tools to reorganize problematic situations in which they together invest their interests and efforts. Dewey believed that this furnished more than mere technological training—it would have concrete ethical dividends in a democratic society, preparing children to think and work together effectively.

This is likely not yet sufficient to answer critics like Mumford, Hocking, and Hofstadter. Plus, Eno's criticism of Cook Ding still stands. How does a theory-deprived *dao* 道-practice like that of Cook Ding ensure that the "skills" and "tools" at his disposal will not be used for evil purposes? What guiding method (*shu* 術) is in place for avoiding such an outcome and ensuring that the ends of Cook Ding's activities are the right ones?

As we address these concerns, it must be recognized that Eno's queries, like those of Mumford, Hocking, and Hofstadter, proceed from assumptions that are explicitly Greek in nature. Eno is interested in a form of "discursive certainty" that becomes dominant in Greek philosophy but appears only briefly in the Mohist tradition.[28] His reading of "On the Parity of Things" reflects this interest. Ultimately, Eno's assessment is more comfortably housed in the Greek philosophical context (wherein arguments such as Zhuangzi's would be more marginal than mainstream) than in the Warring States context (wherein Mozi's arguments would be more marginal than mainstream). The inferences that Eno makes reflect this philosophical orientation. The notion that without an object of rational thought (*logos*), which is presumed to have a different ontological status than that of our knacks (*empeiria*), activity is irrational and thus prone to "evil" is a distinctly Greek-medieval idea. No philosopher in early China thinks exactly this way. This does not negate Eno's concerns, but it does foreground the cultural context in which they are set.

This is why answering Eno's critique requires experiments in juxtaposing the values of mainstream Greek and Chinese philosophies. It is a fortunate opportunity in fact, because it helps us to zero in on an important set of issues. First, observe that Eno's main assumption (*viz.* that without a stable object of knowledge, evil is permissible) is "out of gear" by contemporary standards. As Dewey explains in "The Influence of Darwinism on Philosophy," the theory of evolution by natural selection "cuts straight under" such Greek-medieval assumptions. As he writes: "The conceptions that had reigned in the philosophy of nature and knowledge for two thousand years, the conceptions that had become the familiar furniture of the mind, rested on the assumption of the superiority of the fixed and final; they rested upon treating change and origin as signs of *defect* and *unreality*."[29] Such perceived deficiencies, for Eno, are what open the door to moral perversity.

Darwinian theory challenges such a worldview, because what the Greeks identified as "forms" and "ideas" (*eidos*) the Scholastics identified as *species*. To know one meant knowing the other. Given the teleological assumptions in this tradition, this is significant because knowing such objects meant knowing the "good way for something to be." By observing that species have a temporal origin and are subject to change, Darwin challenges the entire edifice of Greek-medieval knowledge, because as Dewey observes: "the conception of *eidos*, species, a fixed form and final cause, was the central principle of knowledge as well as of nature."[30] The fact that such "knowledge" was marginal in early China allows us to observe how Daoism fares as Eno's assumptions come under the scrutiny of more contemporary approaches.

Again—while Eno's critiques are based on "out of gear" assumptions, this does not mean that his concerns are illegitimate. One of the most important functions of philosophy is to identify where errant assumptions becloud the expression of legitimate concerns and then to translate such concerns into terms that track on to empirical reality. Only then can such concerns be effectively addressed. Here, what needs to be understood is how theory (*yan* 言) relates to ordinary activity (*yong* 庸) in the absence of any transcendent *eidos*. Next, we need to understand how normative concerns are properly addressed in such a framework. Dewey is ready to assist. The "Nature of Method" chapter in *Democracy and Education* enables us to take strides in sorting through these issues while providing a valuable heuristic for understanding what Cook Ding's *dao* 道-practice entails. To such a treatment we now turn.

Method and *Dao* 道-Practice

The first thing to note about Dewey's treatment in the "Nature of Method" chapter is his insistence that method (*meta-hodos*) always means the arrangement of subject matter in ongoing activity. "Never," writes Dewey, "is method something outside the material." He uses eating as an example. "When a man is eating, he is eating *food*. He does not divide his act into eating *and* food." In any well-formed, smooth-running activity, there is no separation between method and subject matter. They are continuous (*yi* 一).

Thus, when the "Method/Subject Matter" distinction arises, it is derivative rather than primary. It emerges into consciousness only when a situation becomes problematic. If there are stones in my rice, a conscious distinction between my "method" of eating and the "subject matter" in my mouth obtains. As long as eating remains problematic, the distinction between method and subject matter pertains. Such distinctions, however, can be misleading. Dewey maintains that such a distinction is "so natural and so important for certain purposes, that we are only too apt to regard it as a separation in existence and not as a distinction in thought." For Dewey, such mental distinctions do not correspond to ontologically separate entities. In terms of what is actually happening, "there is simply an activity which includes both what an individual does and what the environment does." Whether it is done consciously or not, eating rice is fundamentally an *activity*. The degree to which it is engaged in reflectively is the degree to which it requires intelligent direction to execute: the degree to which it presents some kind of problem.[31] The word "problem" should be understood broadly here. Reflective thought is occasioned by situations that are "disturbed, troubled, ambiguous, confused, full of conflicting tendencies, obscure, etc."[32]

Like Dewey, Cook Ding also understands reflective awareness to be something that emerges only when a smooth-running activity becomes problematic. When he encounters a knot the complexity of which supersedes his mastered skill, his trepidation becomes conscious concentration, re-engaging his faculties so as to direct the next phase of activity. In this connection, Zhuangzi introduces the distinction between spirit impulses (*shenyu* 神欲) and the faculty of knowing (*guanzhi* 官知). Cook Ding's spirit impulses represent a "type of congruence with his environment," notes Eno, while his faculty of knowing emerges only as he encounters difficulty and falls out of such congruence.[33]

Another knack passage helps to fill in the larger picture. Carver Qing was an expert at carving bell-stands. In preparing himself for the activity, he would meditate to calm his mind and thus free himself from all considerations extraneous to carving bell-stands. Once properly attuned, he would enter the forest and "observe the natural dispositions" (*guantianxing* 觀天性) of each tree until he found one in which a bell-stand could be "completely seen" (*chengjian* 成見). Unmediated then by second-order considerations, his carving was perfectly suited to the requirements of the specific subject material. Qing describes his activity as "bringing the natural into congruity with the natural" (*yitianhetian* 以天合天). Since his carving method fit (*shi* 適) the subject matter perfectly, there was never any obstacle or impediment. He denies, in fact, that he used any method (*shu* 術) at all. As the narrator says: "When the shoe fits, you forget the feet."[34] Cook Ding, however, unlike Carver Qing, must carve whatever ox comes before him "just as it is" (*guran* 固然). Thus, there *are* phases in which his method and subject matter will not be entirely congruous (*he* 合). As Cook Ding says, there are "difficult places." When his activity becomes reflective, his "gaze settles" and his "movements slow," and a more theoretically informed knowledge (*guanzhi* 官知) emerges to direct the moves necessary to restore his spirit-like activity.

Dewey is keen to stress that "activity does not cease in order to give way to reflection." The same is true for Cook Ding. When the latter runs into trouble, his movements slow but his activity does not *stop*. This is a significant point. For Dewey, reflection involves an imaginative rehearsal of possible lines of action until one line is hit upon that "furnishes an adequate stimulus to the recovery of overt action . . . Then energy is released. The mind is made up, composed, unified." Even as deliberation proceeds, the organism never *stops* interacting with its environment. As Dewey notes: "The primary fact is that man is a being who responds in action to the stimuli of the environment. This fact is complicated in deliberation, but it is certainly not abolished."[35] Dewey explains that, even when "reflection terminates, through a definitive overt act, in another non-reflectional situation," it is not as though activity suddenly stopped and then started up again. "I am here exaggerating by condensing into a single decisive act an operation which is continuously going on," writes Dewey.[36]

A. C. Graham, in his analysis of spontaneity and choice in the *Zhuangzi*, describes Daoist deliberation in similar terms. "One hits in any particular situation on that single course which fits no rules but is the inevitable one," explains Graham, then a response "spring(s) directly from the energies inside us."[37] The entire operation remains "inside nature," he says, and it is consistent with concepts "resembling those of stimulus and response." According to Graham, the Daoist does not "depart from the spontaneity of the rest of nature to make choices between alternatives."[38] As in Dewey's analysis of deliberation, Cook Ding's activity does not *cease* in the deliberative mode of knowing. Cook Ding never *stops* to decide his next move. Rather, he moves right along, "like dancing the Mulberry Grove or keeping time with the *Jingshou* chorus," making whatever adjustments are necessary in the moment. His activity reaches its natural culmination when—*plop*—the meat falls away.

Thus, insofar that Cook Ding's *dao* 道-activity entails an "end," it entails what Dewey calls an "end-in-view." Dewey describes ends-in-view as ends "employed as plans within the state of affairs," and distinguishes them from ends as "objects of contemplative possession and use," which he associates with Greek-medieval thinking.[39] Ends-in-view are *coterminous* with their means, they arise out of activity and guide it as it goes along. As such, and as we have already seen, there is no resulting bifurcation between means-and-ends in *dao*-activity.

Additional knack passages reiterate this point. Artisan Chui, it is said, could fashion arcs freehand that could "match the lines of the compass and carpenter's square." He could do so because his "fingers transformed along with the subject matter" as he worked it. Chui no longer thought about what he was doing—all of his movements fit (*shi* 適) perfectly. "When things come together into a fit," he explains, "the internal (*nei* 內) is not adjusted and the external (*wai* 外) is not followed."[40] In other words, the distinction between "Means/Ends" dissolves.

This non-dual feature of *dao* 道-activity bears directly on the structural cogency of Robert Eno's criticism of the Cook Ding episode. For Eno, *dao*-

activity can be adapted to any end—it makes "no selection among the goals to which it might apply."[41] According to the present reading, this criticism is confused. Cook Ding's *dao*-practice cannot be treated as a means to some end *outside* of its own activity. Ends-in-view, as Dewey says, are "turning points *in* activity." In the case of Cook Ding, when reflection intervenes to redirect his movements, the end he arrives at arises "in the course of activity . . . to direct its further course," and such ends, as Dewey says, "are in no sense ends *of* action . . . they are redirecting pivots *in* action."[42] Eno treats *dao*-activity as a means to some end *of* action—but this violates the very essence of *dao*-activity, which entails continuity between means-and-ends *in* action. Thus, as formulated, Eno's critique misfires. For the moment that he criticizes *dao*-activity as a means only, he is no longer criticizing *dao*-activity at all.

As discussed in chapter 2, the continuity of means-and-ends displayed in activities such as the growth of a plant or the running of the stag is what distinguishes *dao* 道-activity from more purely *mechanical* or *teleological* forms of activity—those in which "Means/Ends" are separable. Hence, as Dewey explains, there are two kinds of means: "One kind is external to that which is accomplished; the other kind is taken up into the consequences produced and remains immanent in them."[43] This point is crucial to understanding Zhuangzi's position in "On the Parity of Things." As Eno observes, Zhuangzi is critical of an increasingly "philosophical" approach to human conduct, one that takes "theoretical knowing to be the basis for wisdom and behavioral excellence." More specifically, Zhuangzi is critical of the tendency of knowledge (*zhi* 知) to fix in advance the ends of human activity. According to the schools that he criticizes, the Mohist and Confucian, there is already a "right" and "wrong" way to live. If such ends are indeed fixed and regarded as "objects of contemplative possession and use," then this indicates, as Eno says, a "generic similarity to Greek philosophy."[44] Zhuangzi's rebuttal, in that case, is that such "Necessarily So/Necessarily Not" (*shifei* 是非) stipulations are arbitrary when abstracted from the context of ordinary activity. Ends-in-view are not objects to be "known" apart from such activity—rather, they are as Dewey says: "redirecting pivots *in* action," just as "knowing" itself is a "pivot of readjusting behavior" *within* activity.[45]

Zhuangzi thus counters the philosophers in his midst with what he calls the "Pivot of *dao*" (*daoshu* 道樞), a position from which one can respond intelligently (*ming* 明) to the endless "ends" that arise in the ever-changing context of ongoing activity.[46] In thus responding, Zhuangzi would agree with Dewey in maintaining that, "ends are, in fact, literally endless, forever coming into existence as new activities occasion new consequences. 'Endless ends' is a way of saying that there are no ends—that is no fixed self-enclosed finalities."[47] The kind of knowledge introduced by the more doctrinaire schools in early

China (and championed in the Greek-medieval tradition) suggest that there *are* fixed, self-enclosed finalities that can be captured in theories (*yan* 言). This assumption is fatal to *dao*-activity and that is why Zhuangzi rejects it.

While "On the Parity of Things" calls into question the epistemological and ontological status of such theoretical objects and their ends, the message of the "knack passages" is not that generalized content has no role to play in human activity. That is an unsustainable position. The critique is that, apart from ordinary activity, generalized content is divorced from the source of its meaning and value. This is a long-standing issue in Chinese education. As Dewey explains to an audience of educators in Fuzhou, "I have not been in China very long, but I am told that almost everywhere students memorize and recite the Chinese classics without having even a remote understanding of their meaning."[48] The *Zhuangzi* recognizes a similar cultural tendency and seeks to set the tradition straight. "Books are nothing but model sayings," the text explains. "Model sayings carry value (*gui* 貴), and their value derives from their meaning (*yi* 意). Meaning, however, has something to which it must be adapted (*sui* 隨). Theories (*yan* 言) cannot be used to transmit (*chuan* 傳) such pertinence."[49]

Following this statement is another knack passage. Duke Huan is found reading the classics in the upper (*shang* 上) part of the hall, while Wheelwright Bian is engaged in his craft below (*xia* 下). The craftsman takes a break from his work and goes upstairs to accuse the Duke of "reading the dregs of the sages." The wheelwright defends his criticism of the Duke in terms of his own knack for making wheels. He describes the micro-adjustments that he makes when his chisel slides from the wood, or when it jams. He explains that the knack for making such fine adjustments is something that "the mouth cannot put into words or theories (*yan* 言)." So, since the sages are not alive to transmit (*chuan* 傳) the direct pertinence of their sayings, to read them as the Duke reads them is like "consuming spent dregs."[50] In this episode, it is allowed that model sayings carry value and meaning, but they possess these only in some pertinent context. Having a sense for when a model saying is pertinent is like having the knack for making micro-adjustments in carving a wheel. Theories (*yan*) cannot be formulated in advance to tell us how to do this—it can only be directed by ordinary activity.

So, while concrete practice is primary in *dao* 道-activity, this does not mean that there is no generalized content involved. The point instead is that the *meaning* of the generalized content is found only in ordinary activity (*yong* 庸). Like the plumb line and the carpenter's square, general content is a "tool" of the master—but it does not impart mastery; only experience can do that. Cook Ding finds generalized content to be useful in the development of his own craft. For three years, he says, he saw nothing but the "entire ox" (*quanniu* 全牛)—and here, one might envision something like an anatomy chart. Eventually, Cook Ding settles into his *dao* and finds congruity (*he* 合) with the particularities of whatever ox is at hand. The generalized content is there, but only to be superseded in the achievement of his mastery.

From a Deweyan perspective, the Cook Ding episode illustrates the interplay between two kinds of method: the "general" and the "individual." The former consists of generic rules and the latter consists of site-specific adaptations in practice. For the pragmatic naturalist, the former method is instrumental in cultivating the latter. When overly prioritized and taught in isolation, general method is actually counterproductive to the achievement of individual mastery. As Dewey explains: "imposing an alleged uniform general method upon everybody breeds mediocrity in all but the very exceptional."[51] If there were but *one* way to carve all oxen, then there would be very few masters able to execute *that* particular procedure.

The core problem with over-emphasizing general method is that it creates a situation in which the powers that students bring to ordinary activities fail to be utilized. Suppose, Dewey writes:

> ... that [an] imaginary pupil works for and with a master carpenter who believes in only one kind of house with a fixed design, and his aim is not only to teach his apprentice to make just that one kind of house, but to accept it with all his soul, heart and mind as the only kind of house that should ever be built, the very type and standard model of all houses. Then it is easy to see that limitation of personal powers will surely result, not merely, moreover, limitation of technical skill but, what is more important, of his powers of observation, imagination, judgment, and even his emotions, since his appreciations will be warped to conform to the one preferred style.[52]

Accordingly, in order to cultivate the powers of observation, imagination, and judgment necessary to execute affairs intelligently (or *ming* 明), one cannot rely on general method *alone*. General method serves as a point of departure as one realizes, through experience, various individual methods for directing subject matters toward their proper ends. One might well begin with some generalized content, as Cook Ding does—but as the relative perfection of individual method becomes realized, general method is relied upon less and less.

In prioritizing individual over general method, Dewey intends to re-envision the meaning of method (*meta-hodos*) by subordinating the *meta-* and re-establishing the *hodos*, "road, path, way," as the primary element. The sense of *meta-* in the word "method," Dewey writes, "is *not* that of 'beyond,' [but rather] denotes a *with* and *after*." In other words, the *meta*- entails an "intrinsic connection with an activity directed towards bringing about *change*." Such change only registers upon the "road, path, or way" (*hodos*) of activity—in other words, *dao* 道. When the *meta*- is isolated from the activity to which it naturally belongs, "the original sense of *method* is unwittingly lost," Dewey writes. The prefix *meta*- "not only means *after* but means it only in the active sense of *coming* after, following from . . . [And] this sense when linked to *hodos* specifically indicates that to take a road is to pursue, engage in movement or change whose terminal point *differs* in one or more points from the point whence the movement sets out." As a result, "method" for Dewey becomes "an indissoluble union of the *what* and the *how*."[53]

Dewey never develops this reading of "method" to his own satisfaction; it remains suggested only in unpublished drafts of the 1949 "Re-Introduction" to *Experience and Nature*. It does, however, parallel the message of the Cook Ding episode. Cook Ding arrives at his own "road, path, or way" (*dao* 道) through an active process that initially involves generalized content but supersedes it as the unity of *what*-and-*how* is realized in his ox carving. Generalized content, for Cook Ding as for Dewey, remains operative—but it is transitional and subsidiary to the ultimate goal of *dao*-activity.

Thus, neither Cook Ding nor Dewey altogether repudiates generalization, nor does either fail to acknowledge the occasional bifurcation of thought and action that Dewey calls "so natural and so important" for certain purposes. Instead, each thinker restores generalized content to its proper role in perfecting a site-specific fit (*shi* 適) of method, subject matter, and activity in the process of reaching an end. If an antecedent, "complete" (*quan* 全) picture is necessary at all, it is either a preliminary or remedial tool in this process. Robert Eno recognizes that there are moments in the Cook Ding episode in which generalized content or "theory" is alluded to, and he worries that such moments are "not entirely consistent" with "On the Parity of Things."[54] They *are* consistent, however, if it is recognized that the generalized content of Cook Ding's *dao* 道-practice is strictly provisional and wholly instrumental to the recovery of the kind of union regarded as primary. After that, generalized method disappears and is forgotten (*wang* 忘). This should not come as any surprise. It never had any special ontological status apart from the arrangement of subject matter in the first place.

The Virtues of Individual Method

Dewey had an eclectic set of friends. One of them was W. R. Houston, a medical doctor and amateur Sinologist. After carefully reading Dewey's *The*

Quest for Certainty, Houston reported to him that his ideas about the relationship between general content and individual method were very Chinese. "Another note that I had jotted on the margin of [the text] was the Chinese word *guiju* 規矩 which means the carpenter's compass and square," Houston tells Dewey. "It is one of the commonest words in daily use and signifies habit, conventional practice, in a mildly honorific sense." Houston recognizes that Dewey's desire to subordinate general content to individual method was not really meant to "downgrade" general content, and that such a move already had its precedents in early Chinese thought. "Perhaps if we had such a word, we might have perceived the relationship more readily," he notes.[55]

Houston's observations are right on the mark. For Dewey, realigning general content and individual method is a positive reconstruction that does not wholly eliminate the role of general method. Moreover, his reconstruction carries positive moral dividends. Such features, properly understood, should help to mitigate the concerns of critics like Mumford, Hocking, and Hofstadter, and ease the "moral fear" of those like Robert Eno who worry that the subordination of theory knowledge in human conduct risks precipitating evil. For Dewey, prioritizing the "road, path, or way" (*hodos*) in relation to general method lends itself to the cultivation of distinct virtues. In *Democracy and Education* he articulates four such virtues: *directness, open-mindedness, single-mindedness* (or whole-heartedness), and *responsibility*.

Let us consider these in turn. *Directness*, says Dewey, is an immediate concern with subject matter. It is a "whole-souled relationship between a person and what [he or she] is dealing with." This is attended by humility because in order to be direct one must overcome the distraction of being unduly concerned with what others might think about one's performance. *Open-mindedness* is a habit of mind that "actively welcomes suggestions and relevant information from all sides."[56] In the development of individual method, one must remain flexible enough to change course as the situation demands. This is "very different from empty mindedness," explains Dewey. "While it *is* hospitality to new themes, ideas, facts, questions, it is not the kind of hospitality that would be indicated by hanging out a sign: 'Come right in, there is nobody at home.'" It is rather an "alert curiosity and spontaneous outreaching for the new which is the essence of the open mind." Dewey likens such open-mindedness to the "retention of a childlike attitude," which he contrasts with stubbornness of mind, prejudice, and "premature intellectual old age."[57]

Single-mindedness means being free of all "ulterior aims"—exhibiting "unity of purpose" and "mental integrity." Single-mindedness brings what is "native, spontaneous, and vital in mental reaction" to bear on the subject matter at hand. Also known as "whole-heartedness," it is nurtured by absorption and completeness of interest in what one is doing.[58] "When a person is absorbed the subject carries him on," Dewey writes.[59] Such completeness of interest leads naturally to the fourth virtue, *responsibility*. Dewey defines responsibility as "the disposition to consider in advance the probable consequences of any projected step and deliberately to accept them." Such acceptance does not amount to any lazy form of assent. It is marked instead by a complete "identification of the self" with what is done. As a trait of individual method, responsibility is likened to "seeing a thing through."[60]

Dewey maintains that, when individual method is the primary focus of instruction, the habits of *directness, open-mindedness, single-mindedness*, and *responsibility* are more easily cultivated. As he sees it, this most naturally occurs when students engage in ordinary activities (or *yong* 庸). There is no reason to limit such positive outcomes to four, and there is no reason to regard them as strictly "moral" in significance. While lecturing in Beijing on the virtue of planting trees with students, Dewey generates an alternative list of five traits that such activities help to cultivate: *experimentation, adventure, trial, aesthetics*, and *personal involvement*. These virtues, Dewey explains, constitute the foundation for scientifically oriented societies. "The development of science comes largely from the nurture of these natural dispositions," he tells his audience. "We know that classical Greek civilization reached a high level of development, but the Greeks did not develop science. Their mistake was that they studied things simply from the viewpoint of theory. They were unwilling to use their hands in actual experimentation, and did not utilize the instincts for natural activity."[61] Again, Dewey's concern is not only to recover the *virtues* that a more active, process-oriented outlook entails, but also to capitalize on the inescapable *facts* that it represents. Recall that the word "scientific," for Dewey, denotes practices in which "*process* is seen to be the 'universal' in nature and in life."[62] There is no avoiding the reality of changing conditions, and we must teach our children so as to cultivate their intellectual habits and instincts accordingly.

In addition to formulating a list of virtues, Dewey goes further in "The Nature of Method" to defend individual method by exploring the negative traits that result from an over-emphasis on general method. These are also four in number, and they can be treated under the following headings: *neglect of the concrete, falsity of interest, death of significance*, and the *deadening of activity*. These can be considered in turn. First, according to Dewey, "each individual has something characteristic in his way of going about things." General method, by its very nature, is in tension with this characteristic. If not used intelligently, it can retard the development of traits that emerge in response to concrete difficulties in their natural state. The result is *neglect of the concrete*. Such neglect triggers the second negative trait. When method is divorced from subject matter and considered "ready-made" apart from material, it is difficult to sustain interest in the respective activity. At that point, there are only three ways to remedy this in the learning environment: ignite some fleeting excitement, administer punishment for non-cooperation, or simply force the student to engage in the activity for no reason. Such tactics result in *falsity of interest*. Such falsity is detrimental to the goods associated with individual method; for once general method becomes the sole aim of learning, the natural rewards of contact with subject matter through ordinary activities become withheld.[63]

This leads to the third negative trait. Once learning becomes a list of procedures to complete rather than something achieved in the course of turning activity toward significant results, "real reasons or ends" dissolve and there is a resultant decrease in meaning. This results in the *death of significance*. Devoid of all marks of individual method, activity amounts to nothing more than "following mechanically prescribed steps." Having thus "[separated] mind from activity motivated by a purpose" activity becomes a "rigid woodenness." Such dead routine is anything but benign: it ultimately makes one *irresponsible*—it retards one's ability to discriminate the consequences of activities as they accrue. This results in the fourth and final negative trait, the *deadening of activity*. There are few things more dangerous to the public good than the irresponsibility that results from the deadening of meaningful engagement in what one is doing. Thus, *neglect of the concrete*, *falsity of interest*, *death of significance*, and the *deadening of activity* are the negative traits of general method improperly used.[64] Dewey invites us to weigh them against the virtues of individual method properly cultivated.

As Robert Eno observes, Zhuangzi does not provide any "theory" in support of Cook Ding's *dao* 道. In his estimation, Zhuangzi "*resists any temptation to lay groundwork for a theory that would allow us to transform this valuation of skill mastery into a coherent ethical theory.*"[65] It is easy to take Zhuangzi's side here. Note that Eno requires *two* theories: one theory to "allow" the other theory. The first step, however, is to "lay groundwork" for the first theory, which would presumably require a third theory. Must we really go down this road? The Cook Ding episode is *already* prescriptive. It is the centerpiece of a chapter on "Nurturing Life," and it elicits a joyous response in Wenhui, who exclaims: "How wonderful! From hearing the teachings of Cook Ding I have learned how to nourish life (*yangsheng* 養生)!" Clearly, there is something positive to be gleaned from the *dao*-activity of Cook Ding just as it stands. The traits of *directness*, *open-mindedness*, *single-mindedness*, and *responsibility* constitute a plausible set of *dao*-activity virtues.

Such virtues are not acquired through general method alone, but rather cultivated though ordinary activity (*yong* 庸) insofar that such activity trains one to become more aware of what one is doing. As Gregory Fernando Pappas reminds us: "To give each situation the attention and care that it deserves is the first imperative of Dewey's moral philosophy."[66] This imperative is one that A. C. Graham also identifies with the value of "spontaneity" in the *Zhuangzi*, the imperative to "Respond with awareness"—to which he adds the important corollary, "Prefer the response in fuller awareness."[67] Graham maintains that it is possible to build an entire ethics on this imperative alone.[68] For at its absolute limit, responding with awareness would mean "to attain full awareness from every viewpoint and react with (impartial) sympathies and antipathies."[69] One would thus perfect the virtues associated with *dao* 道 -activity and respond with perfect clarity (or *ming* 明) to the endless "ends" that arise in practice.

Of course, impartiality is hard to achieve in this world. One is always aware from *some* standpoint and disposed to preferences from that standpoint. "Humans eat meat, deer eat grass, snakes eat centipedes, and hawks eat mice," notes Wang Ni. "Of these four, which one knows how food *ought* to taste?"[70] The best one can do, Graham submits, is to "choose, in lesser or greater awareness, between goals towards which one is already spontaneously tending."[71]

Dewey would agree with Graham that choice always occurs in the midst of spontaneous tendencies. As Dewey writes: "It is a great error to suppose that we have no preferences until there is a choice. We are always biased beings, tending in one direction rather than another . . . Choice is not the emergence of preference out of indifference. It is the emergence of a unified preference out of competing preferences."[72] Within this unceasing stream of preferences, one *can* become more fully aware of the ramifications of competing interests and take the better course. It is conceivable that those who have cultivated the habits of *directness, open-mindedness, single-mindedness,* and *responsibility* are in a better position to choose well spontaneously. Getting there, however, requires experience. As Dewey observes, " 'spontaneity' is the result of long periods of activity, or else it is so empty as not to be an act of expression."[73] General method serves as an important tool in this process—but it cannot masquerade as a shortcut to mastery. In fact, the rigid adherence to fixed theories or rules in deliberation is a sure way of retarding one's ability to make the most sensitive decision in subsequent practice.

With respect to the negative traits of general method, it is important to recognize that these do not stem from *using* general method but rather from handling it improperly. *Neglect of the concrete, falsity of interest, death of significance,* and the *deadening of activity* only result when general method is misapplied or disproportionately valued in relation to ordinary activities and ends. The result is always the severance of aims from genuine interests, and the negative outcomes stem from this severance. Ethical theories and set moral maxims, Dewey warns, are particularly dangerous in this regard. As he relates in a talk at Shanxi University in Taiyuan: "Morality cannot be reduced to maxims; morality is a quality of living and a way of doing . . . Children develop moral insight naturally when they are helped to perceive the meanings in what they do and to discern the consequences of their actions."[74] The problem with abstract ethical theories, Dewey says, is that "they assume ends lying *outside* our activities; ends foreign to the concrete makeup of the situation; ends which issue from some outside source." This effects a "Means/End" bifurcation at the very outset of activity. The problem, then, is to "bring our activities to bear upon the realization of these externally supplied ends. They are something for which we *ought* to act."[75]

This echoes the apprehension felt by *dao* 道-practitioners in early China. They too express concern over the externally (*wai* 外) directed focus of the more doctrinaire thinkers. In the context of the knack passages, the concern over external ends is that they impede spontaneity, resulting in a kind of awkward fluster that is disruptive. In his encounter with the Cicada-Catching Hunchback, Confucius notes to his disciples that the key to "spirit-like" activity is not allowing one's efforts to become divided (*fen* 分). The division being referred to is that between ends *external* to activity and those that reside *within* ongoing activity (i.e., ends-in-view). Zhuangzi uses a gaming analogy to explain: "He who plays for a piece of tile displays his full skill (*qiao* 巧). He who plays for a belt buckle gets nervous. He who plays for gold gets flustered. The skill is the same, but since it attends to something else, what is given weight is external (*wai*). Whoever gives weight to what is external is clumsy within."[76] Such external distractions make it impossible to cultivate the kinds of habits that Dewey identifies with individual method. In fact, the more "externalized" ends become the more deleterious their consequences are. The "knack passages," accordingly, can be understood as taking a principled stand in opposition to any theoretical (*yan* 言) philosophy in early China that would formulate ends in isolation from ordinary activity (*yong* 庸).

It is technically correct to say, as Robert Eno does, that the *dao* 道 of Cook Ding is "not an ethical value."[77] We now see, however, that there are good reasons for that. Ethical theorizing by its very nature tends to divide the simple, unhewn (*pu* 樸) quality of *dao*-activity just as "moral language" in Daoist thinking operates as a "social technique for introducing distinctions," as Hans-Georg Moeller suggests.[78] Moeller is particularly adept at explaining why *a*-morality is a central value in Daoism, i.e., why "Daoists try to prevent the necessity of morality in the first place."[79] As he explains, moral evaluation lends itself to distinct pathologies, and often indicates the presence of such pathologies. As Chapter 18 of the *Daodejing* observes, moral language emerges only when *dao* has been abrogated (*fei* 廢). The ideal, as Zhuangzi says, is to be spontaneously good without "knowing it to be morally right" (*zhiyiweiyi* 知以為義).[80] Insisting that the moral status of activity be known (*zhi* 知), then, is not an unmitigated good. In addition to being, at the very least, "always rhetorical," moral language has a tendency to freeze complex problems into "black and white" and to produce dangerous forms of one-sidedness and self-righteousness.[81] This does not always happen, but it happens often enough that one must remain on guard when morality enters the picture. Moeller's basic point is that, from the Daoist perspective, there is no reason to assume that moral evaluation is always *good* and that its absence is always *bad*.

Moeller's work is upsetting to some readers.[82] Daoist *a*-morality seems to challenge something dear to us. Meanwhile, Eno's concern about the morality of Cook Ding's *dao* 道 strikes us as entirely sensible. But *is* it sensible? Logically, Eno's inference that *a*-morality translates into permissiveness with respect to mass killing is a *non sequitur*. Were a killer bear, for instance, to start marauding through a campground, it would immediately be judged as "bad" from the *a*-moral perspective. The bear would be stopped. But as Moeller explains: "We do not kill the bear because it is evil, but because it is dangerous."[83] Would the Daoist respond differently if the marauder were *human*? Distinctly human-level experiences indeed open space for moral considerations and evaluations to emerge, but do such elements *necessarily* add clarity to the situation?

Dewey shares Moeller's skepticism here. "Serious social troubles tend to be interpreted in *moral* terms," Dewey observes. However, "approach to human problems in terms of moral blame and moral approbation, of wickedness or righteousness, is probably the greatest single obstacle now existing to development of competent methods in the field of social subject-matter."[84] A better understanding of Dewey's thinking here might help us to absorb what Moeller and the Daoists are trying to tell us.

For Dewey, formulating problems in "moral" terms has the tendency to prejudice the manner in which they are presented, limit the data pertaining to their solutions, and restrict the methods considered in dealing with them. Once problems become distinctly "moral," ends in possession of some external justification are presumed to be governing their solutions already. Dewey understands that his objection to moral thinking will raise eyebrows. But as he observes, such concerns are based on an illegitimate inference: "The soundness of the principle that moral condemnation and approbation should be excluded" is "converted into the notion that all evaluations should be excluded." He identifies the error in such reasoning:

> [Such reasoning is] effected only through the intermediary of a thoroughly fallacious notion; the notion, namely, that the moral blames and approvals in question *are* evaluative and that they

exhaust the field of evaluation. For they are *not* evaluative in any logical sense of evaluation. They are not even judgments in the logical sense of judgment. For they rest upon some preconception of *ends* that *should* or *ought* to be attained. This preconception excludes ends (consequences) from the field of inquiry and reduces inquiry at its very best to the truncated and distorted business of finding out means for realizing objectives already settled upon.[85]

As Moeller observes, there is a peculiar "redundancy" to moral thinking. Somehow, it is not bad enough that something is *bad*—it must also be described as "evil." As he asks: "Is this extreme form of distinguishing between good and bad really desirable?"[86] Dewey goes further and asks whether such duplicate designations are even "evaluative" as judgments.

The question must be asked because judgment normally exhibits the use of intelligence (or *ming* 明). "Judgment which is actually judgment (that satisfies the logical conditions of judgment)," Dewey explains, "institutes means-consequences (ends) in *strict conjugate relation* to each other."[87] Such strict conjugation is the hallmark of *dao* 道-activity. Moral thinking, arguably by its very nature, reifies and externalizes (*wai* 外) the ends of human activity *as such*. Accordingly, as Zhuangzi says: "*Dao* is bifurcated (*li* 離) to make way for goodness."[88] When an already problematic situation is converted into a *moral* problem, what is further bifurcated is the continuity (*yi* 一) between means-and-ends—continuity the restoration of which is precisely what is desired. As Brook Ziporyn observes, moral thinking thus "possesses an overweening power to disrupt other processes which makes it intrinsically prone to misuse."[89] More pedestrian "Good/Bad" distinctions normally suffice for restoring equilibrium to ordinary *dao*-activities. Regrettably, "Good/Evil" distinctions sometimes prove necessary, but like any power tool they are rarely needed in the field. Daoists maintain that, generally speaking, "moral" evaluations *interfere* with the kind of clarity (*ming*) that resides at the "Pivot of *dao*."

Failing to recognize the value of the *a*-moral nature of Daoism prevents one from adequately understanding East Asian philosophies more generally. In succeeding centuries, the insights of philosophical Daoism would be absorbed into Zen Buddhism. The virtues implicit in Cook Ding's *dao* 道 then begin to surface more plainly. Tradition tells us that, like Lord Wenhui, the Japanese Zen Master, Dōgen 道元 also learned how to nurture life by observing the "ordinary practice" of the Cook. In his *Instructions for the Cook*, Dōgen explains that the vocation of the temple Cook represents a model of "wholehearted practice" and a "*dao*-seeking mind." According to Dōgen, the position of the Cook exemplifies humble dedication, devotion to one's practice, and an enormous degree of responsibility. For Dōgen, it is the Cook who serves as the exemplar of "Joyful Mind," "Kind Mind," and "Great Mind."[90]

Kōshō Uchiyama, in his commentary on the text, describes the ways in which the virtues of care, gratitude, and reverence relate not only to the activities of the Cook but to everything one does on an ordinary basis. Uchiyama describes the life of the Cook in terms of "making living calculations with your eyes open," remaining "unbiased and open," being "aware of the ramifications of your actions," and not "losing sight of the wholeness of life."[91] Such habits of mind do not need to be christened "moral virtues" in order to result in better people. As virtues of *dao* 道-activity, they call to mind the practical virtues of Dewey's individual method: *directness, open-mindedness, single-mindedness,* and *responsibility*.

Again, Dewey wished to see these habits cultivated in the schools. He thus regarded ordinary activities such as working with wood, weaving, sewing, and cooking, "as methods of living and learning." In the school setting, such activities result in a palpable "difference in motive, of spirit and atmosphere." Dewey reports that, "As one enters a busy kitchen in which a group of children are actively engaged in the preparation of food, the psychological difference, the change from more or less passive and inert recipiency and restraint to one of buoyant out-going energy, is so obvious as fairly to strike one in the face."[92] He understands such engagement to be permeated with the attitude of "play"—and for children, "there is no distinction of exclusive periods of play activity and work activity." The distinguishing mark of play, Dewey explains, is that it is activity with its own "directing idea." When young children play "doctor" or "house," for instance, "the activity is its own end, instead of its having an ulterior result."[93] Such activity is precisely that which retains the continuity (*yi* 一) of means-and-end.

This formula needs to be distinguished from that which normally informs moral theorizing in the Greek-medieval tradition. For Dewey, it would be a mistake—or more accurately, an *incoherency*—to associate "play" activity with what he calls "that strange thing," an end-in-itself.[94] The notion of end-in-itself, as Dewey sees it, amounts to a "contradictory term."[95] Really, what would an end "in itself" (*an sich*) actually *be*, and how would it operate in reality? How much conceptual sense does the notion of a non-instrumental "end" even make? Dewey instead identifies "play" as something that is "*good*-for-itself," and his description calls to mind *dao* 道-activity—i.e., that activity which operates not *for the sake* of anything else (*daochangwuwei* 道常無為).[96] Dewey explains:

> [As long as anything] makes an immediate appeal, it is not necessary to ask what it is good for. This is a question which can be asked only about instrumental value. Some goods are not

good *for* anything; they are just goods. Any other notion leads to an absurdity. For we cannot stop asking the question about an instrumental good, one whose value lies in its being good *for* something, unless there is at some point something intrinsically good, good for itself.[97]

Operationally speaking, the "good-for-itself" is not an "end" (*telos*) but simply a consummatory experience that is not instrumental.

Dewey regards this as an important corrective to Aristotle's thinking. Aristotle distinguishes ongoing activity (*praxis*) and production (*poiesis*) by noting that the "end" of the latter is not realized until the process is finished (e.g., building a house) while the former realizes its "end" while it is happening (e.g., watching a play).[98] To deny that activities of production realize any end as they are happening is but another instance of what Dewey calls "*the* philosophical fallacy"—the subordination of a process to its end. Because the ends of productive activity are not directly had, Aristotle effectively denies the possibility of there being meaning, fulfillment, enjoyment, etc. to productive activities *as such*. "When the difference is stated in this sharp fashion," Dewey observes, "there is almost always introduced a false, unnatural separation between process and product, between activity and its achieved outcome."[99]

By replacing the fixed and final "end" (*telos*) with the "end-in-view," Dewey collapses the "*Praxis/Poiesis*" distinction and restores continuity and meaning to ordinary activities (such as fashioning a bell-stand or carving an ox). His move thus sheds light on the meaning of the "knack passages" in the *Zhuangzi*. Dewey writes:

> To a person building a house, the end-in-view is not just a remote and final goal to be hit upon after a sufficiently great number of coerced motions have been duly performed. The end-in-view is a plan which is *contemporaneously* operative in selecting and arranging materials . . . The end-in-view is present at each stage of the process; it is present as the *meaning* of the materials used and the acts done . . . The case is still clearer, when instead of considering a process subject to as many rigid external considerations as building a house, we take for illustration a flexibly and freely moving process, such as painting a picture or thinking out a scientific process, when these operations are carried out artistically. Every process of free art proves that the difference between means and ends is analytic, formal, not material and chronological.[100]

In the freedom of "play," the genuinely operative end is the "end-in-view" that makes the activity worthwhile while it is happening. The postulation of an "end-in-itself" adds nothing to the picture—in fact, it only confuses it. Play is an active process undertaken *for its own sake*—not because it succeeds in realizing an "end-in-itself," but because it exhibits continuity between means-and-ends while it is happening. This is what Dewey means by saying that play is characterized by its own "directing idea." As he writes: "Persons who play are not just doing something (pure physical movement); they are *trying* to do or effect something." Such ends are coterminous with the means through which they are realized, and this is what gives play its free and plastic nature. Means-and-ends emerge *within* activity and remain integral to it as it unfolds. For children, simple imperatives like "Let's pretend . . . !" or "How about . . . !" are enough to render anything an end-in-view. Means are then directly at hand. A boy picks up a stick and says, "This is my fishing pole," and it becomes his fishing pole. Childhood play thus exemplifies the kind of activity in which means-and-ends are perfectly coterminous. As such, it is undivided in nature, "concerned primarily with *wholes*," and thus good-for-itself.[101]

The rationale for introducing ordinary activities like cooking into the curriculum is to integrate general content into education while preserving such wholeness. At the same time, such activities expose students to the integration of means-and-ends in more highly refined technological operations. "The final justification of shops, kitchens, and so on in the school is not just that they afford opportunity for activity," Dewey explains, "but that they provide opportunity for the *kind* of activity . . . which leads students to attend to the relation of means and ends. And then to consideration of the way things interact with one another to produce definite effects."[102] Such activities are different from playing "doctor" or "house" in that they employ technologies in reaching goals that are more sophisticated and remote. Such tools, however, are not introduced in isolation from genuine outcomes or ends. Thus, children engage in activities in ways that encourage the virtues that Dewey associates with individual method while having fun in the process. "[They have] a play-motive; [their] activity is essentially artistic in principle," Dewey explains. "What differentiates it from more spontaneous play is an *intellectual* quality; a remoter end in time serves to suggest and regulate a series of acts." The gradual "prolongation and postponement" introduced by more remote ends and the use of tools "requires an increasing use of intelligence."[103]

Again, the basic idea is to foster intelligence (or *ming* 明) by engaging students in occupations that concern themselves with undivided *wholes*—just as play naturally does. As Dewey says, "work which remains permeated with the play attitude is art."[104] Yet to be seen is where "knowledge" (*zhi* 知) fits into this picture. Its subordination to practice is what concerns Robert Eno most of all. The next experiment is to see how "knowledge" changes when Dewey and Daoism are juxtaposed alongside the Greek-medieval tradition.

Knowledge and Intelligence

Dewey's intellectual debts to the Greeks are plain to see, and his greatest debt is to Aristotle. As John Herman Randall observes, Dewey's naturalism, his pluralism, his realism, his functionalism, etc. "[are] nearer to the Stagirite than to any other philosopher." In Randall's estimation, by updating Aristotle's general approach in light of modern scientific understandings, Dewey becomes "more Aristotelian than Aristotle himself."[105]

While lecturing on Aristotle in China, Dewey's admiration shows. "Aristotle's thinking itself was extremely broad and deep," he tells his audience. "He was the first great systematic thinker in history, and still one of the greatest." Unfortunately, says Dewey, certain "warped versions of his ideas" became ingrained in medieval European thought, and these "became an obstacle to intellectual and cultural development for hundreds of years."[106] Dewey's generosity toward Aristotle comes from genuine respect. Aristotle worked within the science of his day, and his conceptual errors, while serious, were relatively few. Dewey identifies these errors in different iterations and in various contexts. Aristotle, he says, "never surrenders his bias in favor of the fixed, certain and finished."[107] Change, for Aristotle, "was simply the effort to realize a perfect or complete form."[108] Aristotle took "the universal which is instrumental as if it were final,"[109] and so on.

Dewey voices a certain regret with respect to Aristotle's out-sized contribution to Western civilization, as if it were an opportunity lost. "What if Aristotle had only assimilated his idea of theoretical to his notion of practical knowledge!" he laments.[110] "It is exasperating to imagine how completely different would have been Aristotle's valuation of 'experience' if he had but once employed the function of developing and perfecting value, [instead of] an unalterable object, as the standard by which to estimate and measure intelligence."[111] Given the depth of Aristotle's influence on Western thinking, Dewey understood that the only way forward for Western civilization was through a reconstruction of his ideas.

As J. E. Tiles observes, while Dewey works to amend the errors of Greek-medieval thinking, he does not always "fully [appreciate] the extent to which his own outlook is reflected in early Greek thought."[112] Aristotle, for instance, agrees with Dewey that "with a view to action, experience seems in no respect inferior to *technē*, and men of experience succeed even better than those who have theory without experience."[113] Aristotle knows that thought (*dianoia*) in isolation is inert—it "moves nothing." Only thought that "aims at an end and is practical" has any genuine consequence.[114] Dewey's understanding of the practical arts, in fact, closely resembles Aristotle's notion of *technē*, which the latter defines simply as a "productive habit [*hexis*] involving a course of reasoning."[115] As Aristotle understands it, *technē* relates directly to experience, and those without experience must consign themselves to luck (*tychē*).[116] Dewey understands the same. In coming to reconstruct the relation between means and ends, Dewey likewise observes that, in this respect, "Art is the sole alternative to luck."[117]

Given these broad similarities, the differences between Dewey and Aristotle are specific and immediately identifiable. Dewey's main problem with Aristotle is that, while he agrees that knowledge does not amount to anything in isolation, he still regards the objects of knowledge that inform practice to be both cognitively and metaphysically separate, fixed, and superior to the means employed in realizing them. Dewey appeals to the *Politics*, noting that for Aristotle, "When there is one thing that is means and another thing that is end, there is *nothing common* between them, except in so far as the one, the means, produces, and the other, the end, receives the product." As Dewey sees it, this is but a reflection of the social conditions in Athenian society at the time. Founded on servile labor, "there are classes of men who are necessary materials of society but are not integral parts of it."[118] Such a social organization enables a superior, more leisured class (the "Philosophers") to occupy themselves exclusively with *real* questions while the servile classes engage in *praxis*. According to such an arrangement, "the artisan is expert as long as purely limited technical questions arise, [but] is helpless when it comes to the only really important questions, the moral questions as to values." Consequently, Dewey says, "his type of knowledge is inherently inferior and needs to be controlled by a higher kind of knowledge which will reveal ultimate ends and purposes, and thus put and keep technical and mechanical knowledge in its proper place."[119]

Such a superior office is lacking in Cook Ding's *dao* 道-activity, and that is why Robert Eno regards it with suspicion. As he says, deprived of any faculty that takes "theoretical knowing to be the basis for wisdom and behavioral excellence," it lacks the "enterprise for knowledge acquisition characteristic of Greek philosophy."[120] For the Greeks, the faculty of "wisdom" (*sophia*) is solely concerned with such theoretical knowing, which Aristotle associates with the proper choice of ends. Wisdom involves the use of reason to apprehend universal truths about what things are and what one should be aiming at. For Aristotle, this faculty is completely separable from the granular vicissitudes of practical life. In fact, it is ideally enjoyed *as* separate from practical activities, since "[Wisdom] alone would seem to be loved for its own sake; for nothing arises from it apart from the contemplating, while from practical activities we gain more or less apart from the action."[121] Aristotle thus singles out contemplation of immutable truth as the most worthwhile of all human activities, even though he acknowledges that such contemplation produces nothing.[122] For Dewey, such mental indulgence "is neither practical nor social. Nothing is left but a self-revolving, self-sufficing thought engaged in contemplating its own sufficiency."[123] Aristotle insists, however, that such isolated contemplation is the happiest form of life for the human being, while the life devoted to ordinary activities is satisfying only to a "secondary degree."[124]

The postulation of "two lives," one contemplative and the other practical, has inspired numberless debates over their relative worth and compatibility. Commentators like Richard Kraut maintain that, according to Aristotle, the two lives "are not to be combined," and that the life of contemplation is simply the best kind of life for the human being.[125] Others, like C. D. C. Reeve, understand the "two lives" to be compatible by degrees, Aristotle's distinction between the two types referring to "the same person in both cases."[126] From Dewey's perspective, such debates are based on a false premise—namely, that human experience might actually be considered solely in terms of either ends *or* means, which is a formal rather than material distinction. Dewey summarizes in *Unmodern Philosophy* the errors that Aristotle's thinking on this topic have introduced into Western philosophy: "the isolation of knowledge from practice and the superiority of self-inclusive, self-revolving intellectual contemplation to any form of practical dealing with things," and "the first completely generalized statement of the idea that there is an inherent separation of means and ends."[127]

The Aristotle that Dewey is keen to rehabilitate is the one who takes "practical wisdom" (*phronēsis*) to be a central human virtue. It is *phronēsis* rather than *sophia* that is involved in proper deliberation with respect to human activity and its results. As such, *phronēsis* concerns itself not with "ends" in isolation from activity but with the "means" through which they are realized. Thus, it is not "concerned with universals only," explains Aristotle, "it must also recognize the particulars; for it is practical, and practice is concerned with particulars."[128] Aristotle suggests that the cultivation of practical wisdom in the ethically virtuous person is sufficient for a good type of life. As Jonathan Lear writes, it entails a "developed ability to judge the good and bad ends for [humans] and to choose the actions appropriate for securing those ends in the particular circumstances of life."[129]

As Lear observes, however, this also creates tension in light of Aristotle's "two lives" theory—for "if the ethical and contemplative describe two fundamentally different types of life, a serious question arises about the possibility of a coherent and harmonious life for [humans]."[130] If it is true, as Aristotle says, that "All humans by nature desire to know,"[131] then our signature desire compels us away from the practical life toward the contemplative. The practical life, however, is positively described as a "true state of capacity to act with regard to human goods."[132] It seems, then, that even if one is firmly and happily established in the practical life, one would still "have a conflicting desire in [the] soul: the desire to understand."[133]

Again, the commentarial tradition is replete with valiant attempts to reconcile Aristotle's "two lives" account. But as Dewey asks: "Why put upon thought the onus of introducing discrepancies into reality in order just to give itself exercise in the gymnastic of removing them?"[134] For Dewey, the signature human desire is not some peculiar state of static, isolated "knowing." Instead, "the characteristic human need is for possession and appreciation of the *meaning* of things," and this can only be realized when means-and-ends work together in ordinary activity.[135] For Dewey, as for all pragmatic naturalists, there is no state called "contemplation" that is divorced from all practical consequences, and there are no objects of "knowledge" that do not make some difference by virtue of being known.

Aristotle has insightful things to say about the proper relationship between means and ends in practical activity. His bifurcation of *sophia* and *phronēsis*, however, renders him a less than ideal avenue into early Chinese philosophy. Generally speaking, classical Chinese thinkers do not esteem the contemplation of abstract truths in isolation from practical activity. Likewise, Dewey initiates no separation between wisdom and practical activity. He thus provides a more reliable escort into Chinese ways of thinking.

There is, however, something called "wisdom" (*zhi* 智) in Chinese thought. How is this to be understood? Dewey, following convention, identifies "wisdom" with the proper formulation of ends: "Wisdom is the ability to foresee consequences in such a way that we form ends which grow into one another and reinforce one another."[136] But as we have seen, Dewey does not mean by "ends" objects that are fixed and finished in the nature of things. As Larry A. Hickman reminds us, ends for Dewey are always *ends-in-view*— "ends that are alive and active only as they exhibit continuous interplay with the means that are devised and tested in order to secure them." The resulting instrumentalism, Hickman explains, is not a "straight-line instrumentalism."[137] It stresses reciprocity and continuity between means-and-ends in ongoing experimentation and reflection.

Indeed, apart from contact with actual means, "wisdom" about ends is quite unreliable. "For wisdom as to ends depends upon acquaintance with conditions and means," writes Dewey, "and unless the acquaintance is adequate and fair, wisdom becomes a sublimated folly of self-deception."[138] For Dewey, "ends separated from means are either sentimental indulgences or if they happen to exist are merely accidental." The general ineffectiveness of our more lofty ends, he explains, is "due precisely to the supposition that means and ends are not on exactly the same level with respect to the attention and care they demand."[139] As we will see, "wisdom" in early China similarly involves the establishment of a *working* relationship between means-and-ends.

Perhaps due to its association with abstract contemplation, Dewey hardly ever uses the word "wisdom." He speaks more broadly about "intelligence." Intelligence, for Dewey is "active and planning thought within the very process of experience," providing activity with "concrete suggestions arising from past experiences, developed and matured in the light of the needs and deficiencies of the present."[140] The dynamic, temporal quality of such intelligence renders it distinct from the static, a-temporal nature of Greek wisdom (*sophia*), which fixes itself upon unchanging objects and then does nothing. Intelligence, by contrast, involves "the power of using past experience to shape and transform future experience. It is constructive and creative."[141]

This "constructive and creative" quality is what distinguishes intelligence (or *ming* 明) from Aristotle's practical wisdom (*phronēsis*), which focuses primarily on means. For "intelligence *as* intelligence is inherently forward-looking; only by ignoring its primary function does it become a mere means for an end already given," says Dewey. "A pragmatic intelligence is a creative intelligence, not a routine mechanic."[142] Unlike *sophia* and *phronēsis*, intelligence is not primarily identified with either ends *or* means—it is instead "associated with *judgment*; that is, with selection and arrangement of means to effect consequences and with choice of what we take as our ends." Intelligence is thus premised on an incontrovertible fact, one that Aristotle did not entirely fathom—namely, *that the world actually changes*. New technological means come into existence that enable us to reconsider future ends, and new ends come into existence (sometimes urgently) that require us to find effective ways of realizing them. To act with intelligence is to appreciate the existential relationship between means-and-ends as they currently stand and as they unfold, and to engage such realities creatively and constructively. It means, as Dewey says, to correctly "estimate the possibilities of a situation and to act in accordance with [this] estimate."[143]

Changing conditions regularly call for the redirection of activity, and for Dewey and Zhuangzi, intelligence (*ming* 明) is what detects and guides such "pivots." From a Daoist perspective, being open to changing course (*dao* 道) means reconstructing the coherence of means-ends relations as one moves along. Such flexibility preserves the wholeness of *dao*-activity in the midst of changing conditions. There are various ways that *ming* might be understood in this connection. Brook Ziporyn translates it as "illumination of the obvious," which in contrast to a more abstract "knowing" (*zhi* 知) involves "attentiveness to the surface," thus illuminating "varying perspectives and their transformations."¹⁴⁴ Steve Coutinho understands *ming* as "clarity" or "illumination" and presents it as a direct criticism of the Mohist distinction between "knowing" and "not knowing," which in the Mohist *Canons* is premised on the presumed "clarity" of knowing. Coutinho argues that Zhuangzi usurps the term and uses it to describe the "ever-present possibility of indeterminacy, of paradox and contradiction."¹⁴⁵

Both interpretations make good sense and together they underscore the idea that reality does not come with its objects of knowledge pre-established. Again, the Confucians and Mohists each claim to know (*zhi* 知) the proper ends for human life—they make or regard (*wei* 為) things to be a certain way. Their visions, however, logically contradict one another. If "X" is right, then "Y" is wrong and *vice versa*. "If, however, one wishes to affirm what is negated and negate what is affirmed," Zhuangzi says, "there is nothing like using intelligence (*ming* 明)." Zero-sum contests between theories (*yan* 言) only occur when they are treated in static abstraction as fixed objects of knowledge. In actual practice, "Nothing is [perfectly] completed or annihilated, each folds back and opens into the other to form a continuity (*yi* 一). There is no need to make (*wei*) things thus and so, and everything is entrusted to ordinary activity (*yong* 庸)." Guided by ordinary activity, one relies on the continuity between ideas to freely move between theories and draw from each whatever proves useful (*yong* 用) in the moment. As Zhuangzi explains: "To do this without realizing it is called *dao* 道."¹⁴⁶

This largely completes my response to critics. Lewis Mumford, Richard Hofstadter, and William Ernest Hocking maintain that Dewey's notion of "intelligence" does not provide enough guidance in the selection of ends and thus prevents us from *knowing* that our activities are the right ones. Robert Eno maintains that Zhuangzi does not provide sufficient theoretical assurance that things will not go horribly wrong, such that Cook Ding might become the prototype for serial killers. What my account suggests is that there are distinct virtues associated with Dewey's and Zhuangzi's approaches, and that the kind of moral "theory knowledge" that our critics desire can actually hamper the realization of such virtues. What arises here is not merely a "theoretical" disagreement. Recognizing *how* Dewey and Zhuangzi sustain their positions and *why* it is important to take them seriously means understanding how and why certain assumptions held by Eno et al. are "out of gear" with empirical reality and ought to be resisted.

Eno, of course, is not wrong in thinking that serial killers are bad. So we should ask: *do* the virtues of Cook Ding's *dao* 道—virtues like *directness, open-mindedness, single-mindedness,* and *responsibility*—guarantee that there will never be serial killers? No. But those who appeal to "theory knowledge" as the only remedy have a tendency to raise the bar unfairly high against natural intelligence. Eno, for instance, allows that "of course, [Zhuangzi] does not celebrate skilled killers: his exemplars are, from our point of view, benign, and it may be that [he] could have found a means to demonstrate that *dao*-mastery and evil were incommensurate, as I cannot."[147] Again, it is easy to take Zhuangzi's side here. To satisfy the criterion of being "incommensurate" with evil is an impossibly high bar to set for any generic approach to things. Eno cannot possibly be suggesting that "theory knowledge," generically speaking, is "incommensurate" with evil. As Dewey observes, in contrast with "experimental and re-adjusting intelligence, it must be said that Reason as employed by historic rationalism has tended to carelessness, conceit, irresponsibility, and rigidity—in short absolutism."[148] The world knows perfectly well that insensitive people can formulate theoretical justifications for genocide, racial inequality, injustice, and a host of lesser evils. Why not apply the "incommensurate" rule here? It can at least be argued that intelligence has positive moral value and that it prevents evil more often than it promotes it.

For this very reason, Dewey believes that ordinary activities (*yong* 庸) like cooking, planting, or raising silkworms help to develop good character. Teaching intelligence enables students "to formulate [their] experience more definitely and accurately." Such activities "involve ability to use tools" and to "pursue a continuous line of work until it accomplishes definite results."[149] Such practices require that students "attend to the relation of means and ends. And then [consider] the way things interact with one another to produce definite effects."[150] As in ancient Greece, there are debates in early China over the role that knowledge (*zhi* 知) properly plays in such processes. There are also disagreements over the status of the objects of knowledge and how they relate to more "primitive" (pre-theoretical) engagements with the world. Such topics call for another round of experiments, and these await us in chapter 6.

There remains, however, some unfinished business. We still ask after something called "wisdom" (*zhi* 智) in Chinese thought. What does this term mean? Since there is no clear Chinese analogue to "wisdom" (*sophia*) in the Greek sense—i.e., the inert contemplation of unchanging truths, *zhi* must mean something different. How does one go about defining what that is? As Plato teaches, "Those things that have an opposite must necessarily come to be from their opposite and from nowhere else."[151] Thus, one line of inquiry into Chinese "wisdom" would be through an analysis of what constitutes *unwise* behavior in early China. If enough examples of unwise behavior can be gathered from the tradition, then a positive account of *zhi* might be reverse engineered. Fortunately, the classical corpus provides plenty of material in the "examples of unwise behavior" department.

The Man from Song

It is unclear just how the "Man from Song" (*Songren* 宋人) acquired his reputation, but classical Chinese literature is replete with stories of his stupidity. These stories were commonly used in early China, as they appear in more than one text and serve more than one purpose. The story of the Man from Song who spent three years fashioning a mulberry leaf out of precious material, for instance, (some say ivory, some say jade) appears in the *Liezi* 列子, the *Hanfeizi* 韓非子, and the *Huainanzi*. The story relates that the end product was so delicate and life-like that it could not be distinguished from actual mulberry leaves. The Ruler of Song was so taken with this work that he granted the Man from Song royal patronage and a generous salary at public expense, allowing him to continue making his precious leaves. In the *Liezi*, this story illustrates how foolish it is for humans to waste time trying to replicate *dao* 道 through their own efforts.[152] In the *Hanfeizi*, the story illustrates the foolishness of a single person trying to produce a result unilaterally when such results emerge from a conglomerate of forces.[153] For *Huainanzi*, the story illustrates how oblivious humans can be to the relations of scale in the movements of Nature (*tian* 天).[154] For Mozi, the story would probably illustrate the foolishness of government waste.

The point is that any single Man from Song story can be used to make a variety of philosophical points. The same can be said for other literary allusions in early Chinese texts, such as those drawn from the *Songs* or the *History* (*Shujing* 書經). What is noteworthy about the Man from Song stories, however, is that everyone who uses them, regardless of philosophical perspective, agrees that the Man from Song is *stupid*. His stupidity is generic in nature, something that transcends different philosophical schools and their agendas. As a universal emblem of poor thinking, the Man from Song represents habits of thought that are *generally* frowned upon in early China. In this respect, he provides an ideal avenue through which to approach "wisdom" in the tradition. If wisdom represents anything in early China, it represents the opposite of whatever the Man from Song is doing.

On a practical level, to spend years fashioning an object out of ivory or jade only to have it become virtually identical to something that one can pick up off the ground is simply foolish. It is a purposeless waste of time. The Man of Song is known for engaging in such fruitless pursuits. Sometimes these take the form of failed business plans. In the *Zhuangzi*, we learn that the Man from Song invested all his money in caps to sell to the inhabitants of Yue, only to learn that the people in Yue do not wear caps. The inverse of such bad thinking is also his. We learn of the Song clan who sells their family hand lotion recipe to an anonymous itinerant for 100 pieces of gold.

The itinerant in turn presents the formula to the king and is rewarded with a fortune many times greater.[155] The stupidity lies in the foolishness of fixating on short-term ends, of not realizing opportunities to their full potential, and of losing sight of the big picture.

The Man from Song is routinely failing on such scores, oblivious to key features of his situation. Hanfei, for instance, tells the story of the Man from Song who struggles with a wine selling business. He has an excellent product, fair prices, conspicuous signage, and courteous service. Still, no one buys his wine. Having no idea what the problem is, he asks a village elder why his business fails to attract customers. The elder tells him that the problem is his dog. "He's too fierce," he says. "It bites children when they're sent to pick up wine for their parents."[156] The Man from Song had no idea what was happening right outside his shop door.

Generally speaking, the Man from Song lacks the ability to act in ways that are effective and productive. His failure, however, takes two forms. First, in carving jade leaves and selling his family hand lotion recipe, he fails to convert his energies into the means to some worthy end. Second, by ignoring his vicious dog and overlooking the aversion of certain people to wearing caps, he fails to achieve his ends by ignoring some inadequacy in their means. Instrumentally speaking, the Man from Song is a disaster case.

He will, for instance, rashly take hold of some goal as an end-in-itself and then force the issue, only to destroy any means by which to achieve that goal. In the *Annals of Lü Buwei*, we find the Man from Song wishing for his carriage to be pulled by a horse. When his horse does not pull the carriage, he cuts its head off it and casts it into a river. He proceeds to get another horse. When that horse does not pull his carriage, he cuts *its* head off. He gets a third horse, and does the same thing.[157] He also makes the inverse mistake. The Man from Song will take up some means and boldly proposes a fantastic end that cannot possibly be realized though their use. In *Hanfeizi* we find him promising a king that he will engrave a female ape on the edge of a thorn. The king supports him in this undertaking, but the product never materializes. A retainer finally reminds the King that: "As a rule, the instruments of engravers must always be smaller than their objects." In other words, there is no way that the means at his disposal can achieve the ends projected. This time, rather than a horse losing its head, the Man from Song is on the receiving end. The king executes him for not carving the ape.[158]

Structurally, the Man from Song stories point out types of stupidity that result when a working relationship between means-and-ends breaks down. This particular brand of stupidity is more suggestive of a lack of intelligencen (*ming* 明) than of Greek wisdom (*sophia*). Means and ends are always coming apart for the Man from Song, and this is the hallmark of behavior that lacks intelligence. As Dewey says: "The cases in which ends and means fall apart are the abnormal ones, the ones which deviate from activity which is intelligently conducted."[159] The Man from Song stories illustrate that the opposite of intelligence manifests itself in various ways. But again, such failures generally take two forms: *means separated from ends*, resulting in aimless and pointless behavior; and *ends separated from means*, resulting in heedless and abrupt behavior. Dewey recognized both. The Man from Song exemplifies each.

Consider the famous story of the rabbit and the stump. In Hanfei's telling, the Man from Song once found a rabbit in his field that had run into a stump. It broke its neck and died. "Free dinner," he thought. He then put all endeavors aside and passed his days watching the stump, waiting to obtain another rabbit by the same means.[160] In this case, the stupidity lies in fixating on *those* means without recognizing how disconnected they actually are from the desired end. "Stump watching" (*shouzhudaitu* 守株待兔) now stands as an idiom for idle and pointless behavior: the type that results from laziness of mind and unthinking routine. Meanwhile, at the other pole, we have the famous story in the *Mencius* of the Man from Song who wishes for his crops to grow. He is so eager to reach that specific end that he starts pulling on the shoots to help them grow more quickly. When his son learns of this practice, he rushes out to find that all of his father's crops have died.[161] "Shoot pulling" (*bamiaozhuzhang* 拔苗助長) now stands as an idiom for heedless and abrupt behavior: the type that results when ends are considered supreme and any means will do. Each type of behavior regards itself as intelligent, but wrongly, because each exhibits a fatal separation between means-and-ends. One half of what ought to be a whole is taken up and the other half is neglected.

For Dewey, "a man is stupid or blind or unintelligent" in activities in which "he does not know what he is about, namely, the probable consequences of his acts." Such intelligence requires a form of bidirectional thinking, one that involves both the relation of "present conditions to future results" (means-to-ends) and the "future consequences to present conditions" (ends-to-means). In Dewey's estimation, one is "imperfectly intelligent" (or marginally stupid) when one of two conditions obtain. First, one is content with "looser guesses about the outcome than is needful, just taking a chance with [one's] luck"—a good description of the "Stump watcher." Second, one is "[forming] plans apart from study of the actual conditions, including his own capacities"—a good description of the "Shoot puller." These are, for Dewey, two forms of the same basic stupidity. As he says: "the farmer who should passively accept things just as he finds them [i.e., the 'Stump watcher'] would make as great a mistake as he who framed his plans in complete disregard of what soil, climate, etc., permit [i.e., 'the Shoot puller']." In either case, Dewey advises:

You have to find out what your resources are, what conditions are at command, and what the difficulties and obstacles are. This foresight and this survey with reference to what is foreseen constitute mind. Action that does not involve such a forecast of results and such an examination of means and hindrances is either a matter of habit or else it is blind. In neither case is it intelligent. To be vague and uncertain as to what is intended and careless in observation of conditions of its realization is to be, in that degree, stupid or partially intelligent.[162]

In this connection, it is worth dwelling a little more on the "Shoot puller" episode. Exploring its context, it is possible to tease out an important issue in Chinese philosophy: namely, the relationship between enjoyment, the status of ends, and the contingencies of experience. Mencius uses the "Shoot puller" story in connection with his observation that Gaozi does not understand the virtue of appropriateness (*yi* 義) because he makes it "external" (*wai* 外). This foreshadows the first "Gaozi" chapter in the *Mencius*, where Gaozi claims that "respecting the elderly" is morally appropriate and that such appropriateness is "external" (*wai*). Mencius refutes this claim by suggesting that, if the moral appropriateness of "respecting the elderly" is external, then before long we will be respecting old horses. So it goes if "respecting the elderly" is a universal end-value to be realized by *every* possible means.

Resisted here is the postulation of "respecting the elderly" as a fixed, universal standard, external to any practical considerations that might pertain to its realization. Gaozi responds by doubling down, claiming that he treats elderly people from the state of Chu (i.e., strangers) exactly as he treats elderly people in his own family. Thus, he concludes: "Appropriateness is external." Mencius responds famously, but curiously: "Enjoying the roast meat of a person from Qin is no different from enjoying my own roast meat . . . is enjoying roast meat, then, also external (*wai* 外)?" As Mencius elsewhere observes, the enjoyment of roast meat is a common pleasure for humans.[163] The question he poses is whether or not this fact, and the fact that he would enjoy a roast from his own kitchen the same as from any another, means that "enjoying roast meat" (like "respecting the elderly") is an end-value that stands external to whatever circumstances are implicated in our desire for it. Mencius is suggesting here that it is *not*, and one is left to ponder what the "roast meat" analogy is all about.

As it happens, Dewey weighs in on the status of roast meat. As he observes: "The first time roast pork was enjoyed, it was *not* an end-value, since by description it was not the result of desire, foresight, and intent. Upon subsequent occasions it was, by description, the outcome of prior foresight, desire, and effort, and hence occupied the position of an end-in-view." These words, taken from *Theory of Valuation*, are written in response to Charles Lamb's 1888 essay, "A Dissertation Upon Roast Pig." This short work, an exquisite example of Victorian-era Orientalism, attributes to Chinese culinary history an obscure episode that sounds as if it could have featured the Man from Song.

Lamb relates a story (taken, he says, from a "Chinese manuscript") of one Ho-Ti and his foolish son, Bo-Bo. Born vegetarians, they peaceably cohabit with pigs. Playing with fire one day, Bo-Bo carelessly burns down their house, incinerating the pigs in the process. Dewey picks it up from there: "While searching in the ruins, the owners touched the pigs that had been roasted in the fire and scorched their fingers. Impulsively bringing their fingers to their mouths to cool them, they experienced a new taste. Enjoying the taste, they henceforth set themselves to building houses, enclosing pigs in them, and then burning the houses down." Dewey relishes the humor of Lamb's story in the same way that he would have loved the Man from Song stories. As John C. H. Wu observes, Lamb had a special knack for capturing Chinese humor.[164] Such humor is often a parable of stupidity born of a mismatch between means and ends.

Figures 5.1–5.4. L. J. Bridgman's original 1888 illustrations for Charles Lamb's *A Dissertation Upon Roast Pig*. Top (left to right): "Ye Delightful Pig" and "Bo-Bo Playeth with Fire." Bottom (left to right): "Ye First Taste" and "Ye Family Rejoiceth." Image source: http://www.gutenberg.org/ebooks/43566.

While such stories are funny, the lesson that Dewey draws from "A Dissertation Upon Roast Pig" is a serious one; and I am inclined to think that there is also something serious to draw from the Man from Song stories, and from Mencius' suggestion that our desire for roast meat is not "external" (*wai* 外). The challenge is to pull it all together.

The lesson that Dewey draws from Lamb's story is that the *value* of any given end is not an intrinsic, universal property. Sure, roast pork tastes wonderful, but it is not worth burning down houses in order to procure it. If it were, then the story of Ho-Ti and Bo-Bo would not be funny. The *worth* of roast pork as an end-value is relative to the *means* through which it is procured. Or, as Dewey explains: "The *value* of enjoyment of an object *as* an attained end is a value of something which in being an end, an outcome, stands in relation to the means of which it is a consequence."[165] This is an elaborate way of making the point that Mencius means to make in suggesting that our enjoyment of roast meat is not external. In the context of his debate with Gaozi, Mencius means to suggest that appropriateness (*yi* 義) is not an abstract value or property that transcends our desires, our histories, the means at our disposal, or the consequences of their use—in other words, it is not a property that simply *attaches* itself to ends (such as "respecting the elderly") and remains fixed and universal, everywhere and forever. If it did, then before long we would be respecting old horses.

Kim-chong Chong, I think, understands well what is going on in this debate. As he suggests, ripostes like the roast meat analogy are designed not to prove that appropriateness is internal (*nei* 內) but rather to annihilate the "Internal/External" (*neiwai* 內外) dualism altogether. Such exchanges "show that variation or non-variation in the circumstances has nothing to do with whether something is to be regarded as internal or external, in any sense of 'internal' or 'external.'"[166] Mencius' intention is to cut through the abstract ratiocination of such arguments and redirect attention back to the *wholeness* of the concrete situation. *Of course* "respecting the elderly" does not mean respecting old horses. Foremost and always, for Mencius as for Dewey, there are the lived situations that call for knowing what something like "appropriateness" really means. Such knowledge is neither *had* in some idle moment of abstract contemplation nor *reached* through logical dialectic—it is rather *acquired* in the process of transforming real situations from ones that are uncertain and unstable into ones that are settled and working. That is what Chinese "wisdom" (*zhi* 智) ultimately means. Theoretical knowing, as Dewey says, can "provide means for effecting [such changes] of condition," but in isolation from such processes it does nothing.[167]

Dewey liked to tell funny stories of his own about the sterility of abstract theory while lecturing in China.[168] The serious point of such stories is that, without experience actually *using* general method in practice, learning does not occur. This is what justifies the inclusion of ordinary, practical activities (*yong* 庸) in the school curriculum. As Dewey suggests, such active occupations enable students to attend to the working connections between means-and-ends and thereby cultivate both natural intelligence (*ming* 明) and wisdom (*zhi* 智) as character traits.

In chapter 6, we will be reminded that the exhibition of such working connections between means-and-ends is not something that humans are uniquely capable of realizing. Hardly. As we saw in part I of this volume, such continuity is the hallmark of organic form (*xing* 形) generally—a characteristic of all life that survives. Thus, in realizing means-end continuity, humans realize a more "primitive" mode of activity that long precedes the human species and its institutions. The ideals associated with such a mode of activity are celebrated in the *Zhuangzi* in teachings that commentators identify as "primitivist" in orientation. As we will see, knowledge (*zhi* 知) in the Daoist tradition is understood alongside such teachings as a human technology that can be mobilized in unique but not always intelligent ways.

As we turn to consider the hazards of knowledge and technology, it is important to keep the structural definition of stupidity in mind. Whenever means-and-ends get severed and become isolated foci of attention, the result is often behavior that is less than intelligent (*ming* 明). Such approaches tend to only *half* of what is supposed to be a *whole*. For Dewey and for Chinese thinkers, such "half-missing" approaches foster habits and attitudes that lend themselves to stupidity. This is nicely summarized in one last Man from Song story:

> Strolling along one morning, the Man from Song stumbled upon one half of a bank tally that someone had lost in the street. He took it home and carefully stored it away in a cabinet, taking it out occasionally to admire it and to count the indentations on its broken edge. "I'll be rich any day now," he told his neighbors. "I'll be rich any day now."[169]

6

Knowledge and Technology

> Long before humans appeared on the earth, their non-human ancestors developed eyes so that they could see and avoid dangers, protect themselves and their young, escape from their enemies and locate food. And just as the eye was an instrument for living, so were the ears, the nose, and the other sense organs. Even the brain had functions as an instrument of living, long before our ancestors began to use it for seeking knowledge and for forecasting and planning the future. [This] results in a drastic transformation in our concept of knowledge. Knowledge is not something apart from or added to life—it is a means of living.
>
> —John Dewey, Peking National University, November 1919

Knowledge Wanders North

Knowledge (*zhi* 知) wandered north to the remote shores of an obscure body of water wishing to better understand *dao* 道-activity. It climbed a jutting knoll into the mist above the banks. There, it encountered a mysterious entity, the "Mouthpiece for Not-Doing/Making" (*wuweiwei* 無為謂). Knowledge asked it three questions. "What should one think about and consider in order to know *dao*-activity? In what position and through what practice is it secured? Along what path and with what teaching is it obtained?" *Wuwei* just stood there. "It was not that it refused to answer," our narrator explains, "it was that it did not know how to answer." Receiving no reply, Knowledge departed and wandered southward to a shimmering body of water. It ascended a hill that offered a clear and unobstructed view. There it encountered another entity, "Wild-and-Twisty," and asked the same questions. "Ah! I *know* this," the entity shouted, "Let me tell you!" But just as "Wild-and-Twisty" was about to speak, he forgot (*wang* 忘) what he was going to say.

Knowledge returned to the Imperial Palace to consult with the Yellow Emperor. The emperor explained to Knowledge that, "Only through no-thinking and no-considering does one begin to know *dao* 道-activity. Only when there is no-position and no-practice does one begin to secure it. Only when there is no-path and no-teaching does one begin to obtain it." Knowledge then asked, "Since you and I *know* this, but the other two do not, who is right?" The Yellow Emperor replied: "The Mouthpiece of *wuwei* 無為 is actually right, Wild-and-Twisty only appears to be right, and you and I are not even close to being right. Those who *know* do not formulate theories (*yan* 言), and those who formulate theories do not know. Thus, the sage engages in teaching without the formulation of theories."[1]

Some commentators derive mystical insights from this story, which appears in the *Zhuangzi*. Its main point, however, can be understood on the ordinary plane. If *dao* 道-activity is spontaneous such that the end has gotten thoroughly organized into the means, then how (and what) does one "know" when one has arrived at such activity, and through what means is it obtained? The point of "Knowledge Wanders North" is that such questions are confused. The means-end aspect of such questions has already been considered as part of our analysis of the Cook Ding episode. Just as *dao*-activity cannot be treated as a *means* to some end outside (*wai* 外) its own activity, it cannot be treated as a *goal* toward which means are being instrumentally directed.[2] The question that Knowledge asks, however, is subtler. Through literary personification, Knowledge becomes the *subject* knower asking how to make *dao*-activity an *object* to itself—i.e., an object of knowledge. Being rehearsed here is a distinction, made elsewhere in the *Zhuangzi*, between a "knowing that knows" (*youzhizhi* 有知知) and a "knowing that does not know" (*wuzhizhi* 無知知).[3] "Knowledge" wanders north hoping to be directed toward the state in which it "*knows* that it knows."

This episode raises a number of questions with which to experiment in the present chapter. What exactly *is* knowledge (*episteme*)? How did it begin? What are its objects? Is there a "primitive" mode of *dao* 道-activity that comes before knowledge? Does knowledge relate to such primitive activity as an aid or as an impediment? Can one "know" too much? Here we approach such questions from the perspective of "primitivism," both as it appears in the *Zhuangzi* and as it appears in the writings of Dewey. The main experiment is to engage these versions of "primitivism" so as to observe connections and tensions between them, while also establishing an empirical context in which to assess the results.

Empirically speaking, it is highly plausible that knowledge did not (and does not) always "know that it knows." As Sing-nan Fen observes, "Human affairs are cognizable, but not therefore always cognitive."[4] As Dewey reminds us, "knowledge has evolved historically out of a state in which there was no mind."[5] Our pre-human ancestors had brains, but before their brains became organs for "knowing" they served to organize and coordinate their movements, sensations, memories, emotions, and other functions. Our brains still perform these functions. In the midst of such operations—coextensive, in fact, *with* such operations—"knowing" came to be. Between the first twinkling of knowledge and the advent of the modern epistemological question, "How does one *know* that one knows?" there is a vast spectrum covering 2.8 million years of the genus *Homo*. It strains credulity to think that knowledge sprang forth all-at-once aware of its own operations.

According to the *Zhuangzi*, our pre-historic ancestors indeed "knew things without knowing them" (*wuzhizhi* 無知知) and they were perfectly content in doing so. "The ancients who practiced *dao* 道-activity were contented in developing their knowledge," the *Zhuangzi* relates. "Knowledge was for the life-process (*sheng* 生), and they did not take it up in order to do or make (*wei* 為) anything with it. So, it might be said that through knowing they were developing their contentedness. Knowing and contentedness, interacting with one another, mutually developed. Thus, their harmony and coherence emerged from their natural dispositions (*xing* 性)."[6] Such an account agrees with Dewey's idea that knowing is not, as he says, "something apart from or added to life."[7] There is nothing unnatural about "knowledge" in its primitive form. Its operations retain continuity with the rest of Nature (*tian* 天). "The organs, instrumentalities and operations of knowing are *inside* nature," Dewey reminds us, "not outside."[8]

The "primitivist" viewpoint in the *Zhuangzi* is not a simple standpoint. Contemporary scholars understand the *Zhuangzi* to be a multi-authored text compromised of different philosophical viewpoints and orientations. In addition to the "Inner Chapters," which are generally believed to be authored by Zhuang Zhou 莊周, subsequent chapters feature the writings of authors commonly referred to as "Yangist," "primitivist," and "agriculturalist"—but the contours of these schools remain unclear.[9] Rather than determine the pedigree of any particular chapter of the *Zhuangzi*, the focus here is more on the general valuation of "primitivism" in the "Outer Chapters" and how this relates to "knowing" as a human enterprise. According to the *Zhuangzi*, while knowledge in its primitive form (i.e., *wuzhizhi* 無知知) is continuous with other life activities and with nature, operations of knowing *can* violate the continuity (*yi* 一) of things and become a disruptive force. The philosophically important distinction in the text is that between a "knowledge" that is disruptive and a "knowledge" that is not.

We are told, for instance, that in pre-historic times, "people had knowledge, but they had no use (*yong* 用) for it. This was called the state of utmost continuity (*yi* 一). At that time, no one did/made (*wei* 為) anything with it, and spontaneity (*ziran* 自然) was the norm." According to this narrative, our prehistoric ancestors *did* know things, but "they did not use logical dialectic (*bian* 辯) to ornament their knowledge; they did not try to use it to encompass the whole world; and they did not try to use it to encompass the character of things (*de* 德). They remained aloof and fell back upon their natural dispositions (*xing* 性)."[10] Rather than "wandering north" in order to confirm that they "knew" what they knew, our ancestors assumed the standpoint of the "Mouthpiece for *wuwei* 無為." Once humans departed from this standpoint, argues the "primitivist," things began to go wrong. The general concern is that the human obsession with knowing has resulted in impetuous action and overreaching hubris. Thus, as Chapter 3 of the *Daodejing* teaches: "The sage is one who compels those who know (*zhizhe* 知者) not to *make* things happen (*wei*)." This circles back to what Zhuangzi identifies as the disruptive enterprise of putting knowledge to "use" (*yong* 用).

As an alternative to such disruptive modes of knowing, the Daoist ideal of "primitive" knowledge is to exercise no-knowledge (*wuzhi* 無知), or what David L. Hall and Roger T. Ames call "unprincipled knowing." Hall and Ames do well in turning this negative phrase into a positive ideal. As they explain, *wuzhi* means "the absence of a certain kind of knowledge—the kind of knowledge that is dependent upon ontological presence: that is, the assumption that there is some unchanging reality behind appearance."[11]

In approaching what becomes a positive alternative, it is useful to remember Dewey's version of realism. Recall that, for Dewey, "realism is correct in insisting upon universals and upon the fact that they enter in some way into the determination of known and knowable existences."[12] The problem with realism, says Dewey, is that knowledge (*episteme*) is commonly understood as taking for its objects common nouns—fixed in language and presumably fixed in nature—whereas the content of universals are *ways* of changing and acting, designated by verb forms and variable over time. In *The Quest for Certainty*, and later in *Unmodern Philosophy*, Dewey reflects on how knowledge has evolved from its primitive, more dynamic state to one that is associated with fixed objects, those that Daoist philosophers refer to in terms of "Definitely So/Definitely Not" (*shi/fei* 是非). In order to appreciate Dewey's account of how knowledge came to be associated with such fixed objects, and how this connects with Daoist thinking, the Greek theory to which Dewey responds needs to be reviewed. Perhaps most readers are familiar with this heritage already.

For Plato, knowledge (*episteme*) is the highest function (*ergon*) of the mind. Like any function, it requires some object upon which to act. Plato's epistemology thus dovetails with his ontology, such that "different functions by nature deal with different things."[13] For each mental operation, there is a corresponding object with a specific grade of reality that serves as subject matter for that particular operation. This theory is most famously outlined in Plato's *Republic*. Socrates asks us to envision a "divided line" that is ultimately composed of five types of mental operation. On the very top is "knowledge," and on the very bottom is "ignorance." Socrates begins by asking the following: "Does someone who knows know something or nothing?"[14] The answer, obviously, is *something*. Knowledge is thus identified with *something* while ignorance, its complete opposite, is identified with *nothing*.

This makes good enough sense. Were one to ask, "What is the name of Confucius' pet turtle?" Only ignorance can be expected because such a thing does not exist. The object of one's ignorance is literally *no*-thing. One might, however, through imagination, generate an image of Confucius' pet turtle, its size, its color, its domestic accommodations, and so on. Such a mental object is not no-thing—it is *some*-thing—but on the scale of things, it is not very much. Still, imagination (*eikasia*) is one step above ignorance in terms of the ontological status of its objects.

One step above imagination is belief (*pistis*)—exactly midway between knowledge and ignorance on the ontological scale. For the Greeks, this is the middle ground between what "is" (i.e., *something*) and what "is not" (i.e., *nothing*) and thus the region of *change*. Accordingly, the objects of belief are things that undergo transformation over time. Confucius, for instance, believed that the Zhou dynasty was the pinnacle of human civilization. Twenty-five centuries later, things have changed—societies have come and gone, and even Confucius might change his assessment were he alive today. Thus, the truth of every belief is time-stamped, always provisional by virtue of the nature of its ontological conditions and the status of its objects.

The most important division in Plato's "divided line" is that which separates the next function, thought (*dianoia*), from belief—a division that marks a decisive split in Greek ontology. For Plato, the objects of thought are immune from change. He has in mind mathematical objects such as 2 + 2 = 4 and the Pythagorean Theorem. The signature feature of such objects is that they do not rely upon concrete things in order to be apprehended. Right triangles come and go—they can be carved into the dirt and then scrubbed away. The corresponding object, however, never comes or goes. Thus, the region in which the objects of thought exist is a region above physical things, above time, and above change. With this division, Plato establishes his "two world theory"—one world visible and changing and the other invisible and eternal. The highest mental function, knowledge (*episteme*), connects us to the objects of this invisible world. These are the unchanging forms (*eidos*) that stand waiting to be apprehended through dialectic (*elenchus*), the art of reasoning and logical argumentation.

While Aristotle disagrees with Plato about the degree to which forms are separable from particular things, he never doubts their ontological status as fixed and unchanging. Aristotle's gradation of three types of knowing: production (*poiesis*), activity (*praxis*), and theory (*theoria*), accords both with Plato's epistemic-ontology and with his preferences, such that "the theoretical sciences are more to be desired than the other sciences."[15] Again, Aristotle subordinates activity and production by noting that their "ends" are not realized apart from the processes that constitute them, locating them squarely in the realm of movement (*dunamis*): this being the bottom half of the "divided line." Alternately, the theoretical sciences deal with "things that have *in themselves* a principle of movement" and thus remain free from temporal passage and its contingencies: this being the top half of the "divided line."[16]

On the face of it, the association of knowledge with fixed, unchanging objects appears arbitrary. Why such an association? Dewey's account of how knowledge attained this connection traces back further than the Greeks, back to a primary distinction in human experience: that between "the ordinary and the extraordinary."[17] His account goes as follows. Not unlike ourselves, our primitive ancestors went about things in a matter-of-fact way and took daily enjoyment in doing so. There were tasks to be performed, and simple tools were fashioned to perform them. As a species, we have always used tools. The production and employment of stone implements is as old as the genus *Homo*. Recent archeological finds suggest that such tools were produced as long as 3.3 million years ago, predating our human ancestors by at least 700,000 years.[18] Primitive humans thus had prosaic knowledge about the properties of everyday things and they could foresee specific ends and plan accordingly. In short, they possessed sufficient intelligence (*ming* 明) to survive: an ability to coordinate means-and-ends creatively and productively.

Prehistoric humans, however, lived under conditions that rendered them "extraordinarily exposed to peril." Emotion and imagination transmuted such vulnerability into less prosaic beliefs about gods and other animistic forces beyond their control. "Herein is the source of the fundamental dualism of human attention and regard," writes Dewey. Two operative regions of activity emerged in human consciousness—one was a region of human undertakings that aimed to control the lived environment through simple technologies, and the other was a region of forces beyond such arts that stood apart from human beings and operated independently. "The philosophical tradition regarding knowledge and practice was not original and primitive," Dewey writes. "It had for its background the state of culture that has been sketched."[19]

Dewey maintains that this primitive state of culture, "the ordinary and the extraordinary," is a human universal, forming "the common matrix out of which emerged all the world's philosophies, Asiatic as well as European." Its two regions, he explains, marked out "by way of anticipation what are later called the natural and the supernatural." It would be a mistake, however, to read into these terms the connotations that they have for us today. For in the primitive mind, these two realms "overlapped and blended," such that there was "no sharp division between heaven and earth [as] separated sources or realms."[20] Of course, sharper separations between the "Natural/Supernatural" and "Material/Spiritual" would eventually develop. When they did, the region that continued to operate beyond the reach of human technology became the less transient realm toward which religious myths, rites, and ceremonies were directed. With the rise of pre-Socratic speculative cosmology in the Greek tradition (and its displacement of *nomos* with *phusis*), philosophy usurped this religious domain. "Philosophy," Dewey explains, "inherited the realm with which religion had been concerned."[21]

The previous mental distinction, with human arts on one side and divine forces on another, eventually became incorporated into Plato's "divided line." As Eric A. Havelock establishes, the concept of an "object" of knowledge that is "fiercely isolated from time, place and circumstance," had crystallized in Greek thinking following a lengthy process. Plato's audience "did not have to have the *Republic* written for them in order to arrive at these elementary and time-honored truths."[22] Still, it was with Plato that knowledge evacuated its humbler station explicitly to become a power separated from the simpler arts (*technē*) from which it arose. Its functions and objects no longer numbered among the tools that humans had fashioned for practical purposes since time immemorial. *Episteme* now operated in the realm of intransigent forces (i.e., fixed objects) that were distinct from human activities and purposes. This, in fact, had once been the region of the gods. As Dewey observes: "The change from religion to philosophy was so great in form that their identity as to content is easily lost from view."[23]

The story plays out somewhat differently in classical China, but the concept that knowledge (*zhi* 知) accesses fixed objects nevertheless arose. Like all human groups, the ancient Chinese exhibited a robust religious imagination, worshipping a variety of natural forces and spirits. During the Shang dynasty, worship coalesced around a primary deity, the "High Ancestor" (*shangdi* 上帝). As David N. Keightley explains, this deity "may have once been the progenitor of the Shang royal lineage," thus establishing a relationship between humans and deities that was "implicitly genealogical." Accordingly, "there was no sense of radical difference between spirits and humans" in early China.[24] Still, rituals were devised to negotiate two respective, and often antagonistic, fields of operation—tracking on to what Dewey calls "the ordinary and the extraordinary." Some Shang rituals (most notably human sacrifice) would suggest that Chinese divinities were as uncompromising as any other. The Chinese lived in fear of ghosts and spirits and in deference to forces beyond their control, which, as Dewey suggests, is consistent with the inherently precarious nature of primitive human experience.

With the advent of the Zhou dynasty, the "High Ancestor" of the Shang dynasty was displaced by a more generic force commonly translated as "Heaven" (*tian* 天). The meaning of *tian* would gradually evolve from a roughly anthropomorphic deity to the impersonal forces of "Nature," with texts often oscillating between one conception and the other. The key moment in the development of early Chinese religiousness, however, arrives when Confucius turns away from the spirit realm toward the human-centered world.[25] The Master would retain his fear and reverence for the inscrutable "mandates of Heaven" (*tianming* 天命), but he directs the use of ritual-custom (*li* 禮) away from divine propitiation to focus on its social and cultural dimensions.[26] As Michael J. Puett explains: "by decrying the instrumental use of sacrifices by ritual specialists, [Confucius] denied the powers that were used in the Bronze Age to mollify divine forces and to make them work for the living. Instead, he urged that we simply cultivate ourselves and accept whatever the divine powers do."[27] With this, the Confucian movement was born.

By revolutionizing the function of ritual-custom (*li* 禮) and relegating "extra-ordinary" matters to the inscrutable workings of fate (*ming* 命), Confucians trigger a highly organized, populist reaction led by Mozi. In his critiques of Confucianism, Mozi reasserts the supremacy of an anthropomorphic "Heaven" (*tian* 天) and chastises the Confucians for not believing in the spirit world. Presuming to have divine sanction, Mozi formulates a number of philosophical positions the veracity of which he refuses to doubt—he *knows* that he is right and that the Confucians are wrong. In showing how he "knows that he knows," Mozi becomes the first in China to use the tools of logical argumentation (*bian* 辯)—tools that win him a large number of devoted if not fanatical followers. His writings, in fact, assume the time-honored cadence of a mob rally.[28] The tools of analytic philosophy were refined, expanded, and used to defend positions on a range of issues with absolute confidence. With this, the Mohist movement was born.

Again, as Robert Eno observes, "Mohist teachings made it possible for China to embark on a philosophical enterprise similar to that of the Greeks."[29] In Mohist technical writings, knowledge (*zhi* 知) thus assumes a new status. "Knowing is a capacity," the *Canons* explain, and "with regard to the capacity of knowing, it is how one knows and knows with certainty."[30] This marks a departure from previous notions of knowledge in the Chinese tradition. As Eno says, the Mohists "claimed that what is so could be discovered through argument or through the processes of discursive thinking guided by rules that we call reason."[31]

As in the Greek world, the advent of "reason" in early China involved evacuating knowledge from the human realm and stationing it at a level once reserved for the gods. According to the Mohists, "Heaven's intention" (*tianzhi* 天志) furnishes us with unvarying "standards of rightness" (*yizhifa* 義之法) and such standards guarantee us absolute certainty. "I have Heaven's intention just like wheelwrights have compasses and carpenters have squares," declares Mozi. "What conforms to it is right. What does not conform to it is wrong." With such divine and permanent authorization, Mozi likens efforts to refute him to "throwing eggs against a rock."[32] He thus introduces into Chinese philosophy the notion of a "knowledge that knows" (*youzhizhi* 有知知). Such knowledge is what "Knowledge" wanders north hoping to validate. It is also that which Daoist primitivism encourages us to resist the urge to indulge.

The Primitive Mindset

While at Columbia, Dewey "co-taught" a seminar with his colleague, Franz Boas, one of the most highly regarded cultural anthropologists of his generation. It was noted that Dewey spoke only once during the entire semester. He interjected simply to indicate that he agreed with everything Professor Boas was saying.[33]

The appeal of Boas to Dewey is easy to understand. In keeping with his rejection of classical teleology, Dewey dismissed nineteenth-century anthropologies that regarded "primitive" phases of human development as preparatory for subsequent, "civilized" phases. He rejected Herbert Spencer's orthogenetic theory of cultural emergence as "automatic evolution."[34] As Dewey observes, the goal of evolution for Spencer "is a complete state of final adaptation in which all is peace and bliss and in which the pains of effort and of reconstruction are known no more."[35] Such end-driven notions, whereby cultural change unfolds "between a fixed origin and a fixed goal," suggested to Dewey that Spencer's mind "was never completely taken possession of by evolutionary conceptions."[36] Similarly, he had no use for Lewis Morgan's influential theory that human cultures exhibited "low, middle, and upper statuses," corresponding to the stages of "savagery," "barbarism," and "civilization," respectively.[37] As Alan Ryan observes, it was Boas who "appears to have exerted the greatest intellectual influence" on Dewey's thinking in the field of anthropology.[38] Dewey regarded Boas as an "anthropological authority of the very first rank," and he readily identifies with his view that "the difference between primitive beliefs and those of contemporary civilized man is due not to differences of inherent mental structure and capacity but to the cultural medium in which individuals think and act."[39]

Dewey thus distances himself from those who tend "to exaggerate the differences which mark off the more primitive cultures from those with which we are familiar today." He rejects the notion that whatever primitive habits we might exhibit are merely "survivals" or holdovers from phases that are now defunct or destined to be overcome. "As a matter of fact," Dewey argues, "there is hardly a phase of primitive culture which does not recur in some field or aspect of life today."[40] Primitive habits of mind, Dewey maintains, "are outgrowths which have entered decisively into further evolution, and as such form an integral part of the framework of present mental organization."[41] Like Boas, Dewey approaches the primitive mind on its *own terms*—not as an intermediate or subordinate phase for something else. As a result, he believes that we can learn a lot about ourselves from our prehistoric forerunners.

Dewey's openness to the primitive mind parallels his openness to the dependence and plasticity of childhood as a phase that is "good-for-itself" rather than one merely preparatory on the way to adult maturity. For Dewey, to think otherwise fails to appreciate the virtues inherent in immaturity, which again is a "positive force or ability—the *power* to grow."[42] He evokes the same line of reasoning in his defense of primitive humans. "The primitive mind is described in terms of 'lack,' 'absence': its traits are incapacities," Dewey complains.[43] In both cases, traits are being judged comparatively against a preconceived outcome or end.

As we saw in chapter 5, in treating childhood as a phase that is "good-for-itself," Dewey identifies a mindset permeated with the attitude of "play," wherein activity has its own "directing idea" such that "the activity is its own end, instead of its having an ulterior result."[44] In such a childlike attitude, Dewey recognizes parallels with the primitive mindset:

> Many anthropologists have told us there are certain identities in the child interests with those of primitive life. There is a sort of natural recurrence of the child mind to the typical activities of primitive peoples; witness the hut which the boy likes to build in the yard, playing hunt, with bows, arrows, spears, and so on. Again the question comes: What are we to do with this interest—are we to ignore it, or just excite and draw it out? Or shall we get hold of it and direct it to something ahead, something better?[45]

To repeat, Dewey does not see the childhood expression of primitive behavior as a phase in orthogenetic development. "Playing hunt" is not an instance of ontogeny recapitulating phylogeny. Instead, "playing hunt" is a plain expression of human nature; and as it happens, children, like our prehistoric ancestors, are closer to "raw" human nature than are civilized adults.

Dewey is careful here not to introduce sharp dualisms and thresholds. His basic argument: that a prehistoric human, "living in a primitive society, comes nearer to being a purely 'natural' human being than does civilized man," does not violate the principle of continuity. "Civilization itself is the product of altered human nature,"[46] writes Dewey, and this means that culture is something that grows from natural antecedents. The Daoist "primitivist" would partially agree with Dewey, stressing that our primitive ancestors, who more readily "fell back upon their natural dispositions (*xing* 性)," were more closely aligned with such uncorrupted antecedents.[47] Dewey, however, is not finished. He adds the following: "But even the [prehistoric human] is bound by a mass of tribal customs and transmitted beliefs that modify his original nature," meaning that a truly "pure," uncorrupted human nature is not there simply to be recovered.[48] Daoist "primitivists" are less univocal on this, but more needs to be said before we can assess the significance of the difference.

Without using higher civilization as a yardstick to measure what our early ancestors "lacked," Dewey wishes to present a *positive* account of how the primitive mind contributes to contemporary behavior. He felt it was naïve to assume that such a mindset was simply *there* to be reinstated. The word "mindset" (which is not one that Dewey uses) stands in for a range of conditions that Dewey sets in approaching the primitive. "If we search in any social group for the special functions to which mind is relative," he says: "occupations at once suggest themselves." More than anything, the things that early humans *did* determined their mindsets. By necessity, their mental habits and attitudes conformed to their dominant activities. Such activities furnished "the working classifications and definitions of value," and they decided "the sets of objects and relations that are important."[49] To study the mindset of earlier humans reveals the various ways that technologies sponsored the occupations that have brought us to where we are.

Accordingly, as a component in early childhood education, Dewey thought that it was important for children to "go on in imagination through the hunting to the semi-agricultural stage, and through the nomadic to the settled agricultural stage," so that the "interest of the child in people and their doings is carried on into the larger world of reality." Children should understand how stone tools facilitated the hunting life, how iron tools facilitated the agricultural life, and so on, in order to see how such objects "fused and welded with social conceptions regarding the life and progress of humanity."[50] Such studies teach us a lot about ourselves.

The insight gained, according to Dewey, is that the human experience exhibits forms of productive "wholeness" whenever unity is achieved between means-and-end (a.k.a., *dao* 道-activity). This can be appreciated most readily in the context of primitive times because there is less complexity and less "noise" obscuring the tool-end relation. The "primitive mind," however, is not one that resides uniquely or exclusively in the distant past. It resurfaces in all cultural times and places, whenever "occupations integrate special elements into a functional whole."[51] The knowing thus exemplified in the primitive mind is "practical" in every sense of the word: it is exacted by the surrounding environment, instrumental in effecting changes, and desirable in outcome.[52] The practicality of tool-knowledge in primitive times is thus the same practicality that we ask the tool of knowledge (*zhi* 知) to provide for us today. "If one looks at the history of knowledge," Dewey writes, "it is plain that at the beginning [humans] tried to know because they had to do so in order to live."[53]

Now what about that special "wholeness" that the primitive mind exhibits? What is its general antecedent in the species? Upon what is it modeled? In recovering the prehistoric structure of human knowledge, Dewey focuses on the "hunting vocation" as its prerequisite, probably because this connects us most closely to our animal ancestry. The distinguishing feature of hunting, Dewey explains, is its intimacy of means-and-ends and the wholeness of the situation in which it is carried out. His description is vivid:

> Want, effort, skill and satisfaction stand in the closest relation to one another. The ultimate aim and the urgent concern of the moment are identical; memory of the past and hope for the future meet and are lost in the stress of the present problem; tools, implements, weapons are not mechanical and objective means, but are part of the present activity, organic parts of personal skill and effort. The land is not a means to a result but an intimate and fused portion of life—a matter not of objective inspection and analysis, but of affectionate and sympathetic regard. The making of weapons is felt as a part of the exciting use of them. Plants and animals are not "things," but are factors in the display of energy and form the contents of [the] most intense satisfactions.[54]

Not surprisingly, given its status as a holistic activity "good-for-itself," the hunting vocation inspires the first known artistic expressions in human history: stunning images of running animals brought to life in remote caves, their rich pigments derived from ochre, hematite, charcoal, and other minerals of the earth. As Dewey observes, such vibrant works "kept alive to the senses experiences with the animals that were so closely bound with the lives of humans."[55] One can imagine the original viewers in these flame-lit spaces, responding vicariously as the objects of prey flickered before their eyes.

We have only recently learned how truly widespread and ancient such expressions are. The antiquity of European caves such as Altamira and Chauvet has now been surpassed by recent discoveries on the Indonesian island of Sulawesi. The oldest cave painting there is 40,000 years old, and there are 13,000 years' worth of images at the site. Researchers now conclude that the ubiquity of hunting-related cave painting suggests that it traces back to our common African origins. "The basis for this art was there 60,000 years ago; it may even have been there in Africa before 60,000 years ago," scholars now surmise.[56]

Ethnographic research also identifies early forms of dance with the hunting vocation, and to its closely related fighting vocation. As Dewey and James Tufts explain, "The hunting dance or the war dance represents, in dramatic form, all the processes of the hunt or fight . . . the dance or celebration after the chase or battle may give to the whole tribe the opportunity to repeat in vivid imagination the triumphs of the successful hunter or warrior, and thus to feel the thrill of victory and exult in common over the fallen prey."[57] Such activities, so closely associated with the primitive mind, furnish the original aesthetic subject matter for artistic expression in the human experience.

In *Unmodern Philosophy*, Dewey revisits the aesthetic dimension of primitive life and relates it directly to his theory of primitive knowledge. His account of this connection is quite illuminating when understood alongside Daoist-oriented primitivism. Dewey's focus on the hunting vocation, again, reconnects our behavior closely with that of our animal ancestors. Imagine, Dewey says, an animal watching the entrance-hole of its prey—"the whole *body* of the watching animal is *waiting* . . ." he writes. "If the hidden prey appears, then the body of the waiting animal comes into play as a whole." There exists in the animal predator a connected series of sensory-motor adjustments, a series that once executed "cannot be understood [in isolation] from the place it occupied, the function it [served], in the total life-behavior as an ongoing concern in space and time."[58]

As argued in chapter 2, it would violate the nature of organic form (*xing* 形) to regard such a series as anything less than a unit of behavior, to abstract it from its existential location and regard it as being for the sake (*wei* 為) of something else—even survival. *Animals hunt*—that is simply what they do. They do not hunt "in order" to survive. Given the strength and persistence of our teleological habits, this is a difficult insight to sustain. When discussing animal behavior, Dewey does his best to communicate its truth: "If the struggle for existence on the part of the wolf meant simply the struggle on his part to keep from dying, the sheep would have gladly compromised at any time upon the basis of furnishing him with the necessary food—including even an occasional bowl of mutton broth," he muses. But *no*, "the wolf asserted himself as a wolf," writes Dewey—"*It was not mere life he wished, but the life of the wolf.*"[59] Unfortunately for sheep, *wolves hunt*. Such is the *dao* 道 of wolves.

Again, to make the hunting of the wolf merely a *means* to some teleological end outside (*wai* 外) of itself is a "silly reduplication." It splits apart an organic unit of behavior only to evoke a final cause (*telos*) to pull it together again, an intellectual stunt "equally arbitrary and gratuitous."[60] It is, in fact, the striking quality and integrity (*de* 德) of animal behavior that explains why, for Dewey, it is "necessary to have recourse to animal life below the human scale" in order to "grasp the sources of aesthetic experience." Such animal behaviors "stand as reminders and symbols of that unity of experience which we so fractionize" when we bifurcate means-and-ends.[61]

The primitives who created those ancient cave paintings were themselves animal predators. The "unity of behavior" they exhibited in their hunting vocations points us toward the pre-human "ground pattern" of knowledge itself. It would be peculiar in colloquial speech to suggest that an apex predator like the African lioness does not *know* how to hunt. If anything, one would most emphatically stress the opposite—the African lioness knows *exactly* how to hunt. But does the lioness "know that she knows" (*youzhizhi* 有知知)? No. When it comes to hunting, she "knows without knowing" (*wuzhizhi* 無知知). Dewey locates this precursor to conscious knowing *inside* the behavioral sequence of the predator animal, which "in effect looks ahead" since "it gives readiness to meet future conditions." He argues that "*knowing with respect to its biotic aspect* as a form of behavior is an operation of surveying of existing conditions of a sort which interconnects with planning for future conditions and for behavior adapted to those conditions."[62]

The key word here is "interconnects." For the predator animal, there is no remote future that is planned *for*. Rather, the future *merges* into the present in which planning for it occurs. "The live animal is fully present," Dewey explains, "all there, in all of its actions: in its wary glances, its sharp sniffings, its abrupt cocking of the ears . . . What the live creature retains from the past and what it expects from the future operate as directions in the present."[63] As the *Zhuangzi* teaches, primitive knowledge is marked by such continuity (*yi* 一). Rather than being bifurcated into means in the present to be "used" (*yong* 用) for future ends, *dao* 道-activity is an entirely self-contained process. Again—in prehistoric times, "People had knowledge, but they had no use for it. This was called the state of utmost continuity. At that time, no one did/made (*wei* 為) anything with it."[64] For Dewey, once these holistic and essentially "aesthetic" features of primitive knowing are recognized and foregrounded, "we find that even on strictly biological grounds there is provision for development of knowing as a form of behavior as self-contained as is any other form of doing and making."[65]

This last point, however, sounds paradoxical. How is the primitive mind as "self-contained" as any other form of doing and making when "doing and making" routinely involve ends that are separable from our activities of doing and making? Can one do or make (*wei* 為) something *without* instrumentally "doing or making" it? This highlights a potential tension in Daoist thought. It surfaces, for instance, in Chapters 3 and 63 of the *Daodejing* where we are instructed to "*do/make* without doing/making" (*weiwuwei* 為無為). One feels compelled to ask: "How does one *do* that which consists of *not* doing?"

Edward Slingerland identifies this as the "paradox of *wuwei* 無為." *Wuwei* is portrayed as a state beyond external striving, but it is also a state that one *strives to realize*. How is it possible, Slingerland asks, "to *try* not to try?"[66] As Dewey sees it, what here seems like a paradox is resolved once one takes seriously the principle of continuity. For him, "biological operations have a double status." They are both means *and* ends when considered from one or another standpoint. There is nothing, Dewey says, "to prevent the eating of food, when obtained, [from being] immediately enjoyable as well as an indispensable means to keeping alive."[67] The former enjoyment is closer to the primitive mind, which resides with the animal standpoint; the latter is a simultaneous teleological interpretation that bifurcates the integration of means-and-ends through instrumental reasoning, which resides with the human standpoint.

Let us return to the wolf. As the sheep dog falls asleep, the wolf does not reflect upon the instrumental significance of this development in relation to its own survival prospects. *He is a wolf*—and he responds as any wolf would. "To animals to whom acts have no meaning, the change in the environment required to satisfy needs has no significance on its own account," explains Dewey. To recognize in reflective thought the *meaning* of the sleeping dog is to occupy a different standpoint. "When this estate is attained, we live on the human plane, responding to things in their meanings. A relationship of cause-effect has been transformed into one of means-consequence."[68] Humans "know" that the wolf has gained an advantage, whereas the wolf simply knows how to hunt. Both standpoints are practical and are continuous (*yi* 一) with one another. "In view of actual facts," Dewey writes, "a *generalized* distinction between *practical* in the sense of useful for something beyond itself and *practical* in the sense of an immediately enjoyed doing or making is *strictly conventional*."[69]

OK—but as Slingerland asks, how does one "*try* not to try?"[70] Observe that, in both form and substance, this is exactly the question with which "Knowledge" wanders north. Accordingly, the "Mouthpiece for *wuwei* 無為" has no response to it—and in fact, none needs to be given. Along with children, primitives, and brutes, gainfully employed adults do/make (*wei* 為) things without doing/making (*wei*) them all the time, whenever they engage in work holistically without treating each phase as a means to something else. Such activity expresses the "primitive mindset," and it is rather easy to lapse into. As Dewey suggests, such a mindset begins with childhood "play" and never wholly disappears.

One of the more substantive problems with Slingerland's "paradox" is its suggestion that *wuwei* 無為 is incompatible with "trying" as such. This is unfortunate. For Dewey, "play" activities are quite the opposite. "Persons who play are not just doing something," he writes, "they are *trying* to do or effect something, an attitude that involves anticipatory forecasts which stimulate their present responses."[71] Again, *dao* 道-activity is not activity that has no "end-in-view," it is simply activity in which means-and-ends are coterminous. Such activity is perfectly consistent with "trying," and even (as Philip J. Ivanhoe argues) "striving" to do something.[72] In fact, the Old French *trier*, from which the word "trying" is borrowed, means "to pick out, to cull, to separate off," suggesting undertakings that are isolated and self-contained, attempts at *doing* something that are experienced as wholes and thus "good-for-themselves."

Hunting is a kind of trying, and the fact of its wholeness is displayed even in the play of kittens and puppies. As Dewey notes, "modes of behavior which have to do [with] chasing or seizing prey, are engaged in under conditions in which there is no prey to hunt and in which hunger, the normal stimulus to the practical activity of searching for food, is absent."[73] The hunting vocation, closely related to animal play, is simply *fun*—which is exactly why it is done. As Dewey observes, hunting and fishing are among "the commonest forms of adult play."[74] The availability of seafood in our grocery stores does not eliminate the sport of fishing. The simple reason is that the process of *trying* to catch a fish is "good-for-itself."

Anyway, the point is that to raise the so-called "paradox" of *wuwei* 為無 signals that we have departed conceptually from *wuwei*. It involves "knowledge" formulating questions about *wuwei* in terms that are self-contradictory, e.g., "Through what practice is it secured?" and "How does one know when one achieves it?" As we learned from Robert Eno's critique of Cook Ding, such questions violate the essence of *dao* 道-activity in their very formulation. They misfire the moment they are asked. The predicament for knowledge (*zhi* 知), however, is not altogether hopeless. Remember that there is an intermediate position occupied by "Wild-and-Twisty." He once knew something about *dao*-activity but then he forgot about it (*wang* 忘). What can we learn from this character?

The ability to "forget" is highly esteemed in the *Zhuangzi*. We are told that the "genuine humans of primitive times" (*guzhizhenren* 古之真人) routinely forgot what they had verbally formulated (*yan* 言). They would sometimes know (*zhi* 知) something, but this "was a temporary expedient, arising only when the situation made it unavoidable."[75] Once they were finished knowing a thing, they would forget about it. Such a process of *un*-knowing could hardly be more different than what is celebrated in the Platonic tradition. Knowing (*episteme*) for Plato involves the "recollection" (*anamnesis*) of that which *had been* forgotten, not the forgetting of that which had come to be known.[76] Recollection, for Plato, is the process of remembering eternal objects of knowledge encountered prior to incarnation in the time-bound body. According to the *Phaedo*, such recollection proves that the soul (*psyche*) is immortal.[77] Zhuangzi's celebration of forgetting prompts us to wonder if such *psyches* exist at all.

In the mid-1920s, Dewey had an opportunity to reflect on the ontological difference between such approaches. He read the final draft of Boas' student Paul Radin's classic work, *Primitive Man as Philosopher* and composed the book's "Foreword." The main thrust of Radin's thesis was that substance ontologies and vocabularies hampered our ability to appreciate how our earliest ancestors experienced the world. Drawing on ethnographic studies from across the globe, Radin compared what he called the primitive "man of action" who "lives fairly exclusively to what might be called a motor level," to the more advanced "thinker." To the former, each object in the world is a "continually changing entity from which one is repeatedly subtracting and to which one is repeatedly adding." The outside world is one that is "dynamic and ever changing." When there is a static point identified for practical purposes, that point would fix not on an object as a static entity but "*in its effects.*" "Reality" for the primitive, explains Radin, "is pragmatic."[78] From Radin, Dewey came to understand that for primitive humans, "objects and nature were conceived dynamically; that change, transition, were primary, and transformation into stability something to be accounted for."[79]

In the *Zhuangzi*, the same rules apply. The primitives, we learn, held things in place by "using knowledge as a temporary expedient" (*yizhiweishi* 以知為時). Once they were finished using what they knew, they released it back into the wild by forgetting about it. Thus, knowledge was temporary, and so too the knower who knew. One thing to be said about the primitive notion of the "ego," Radin writes, is that it had "never fallen into the error of thinking of [itself] as a unified whole or of regarding [itself] as static."[80] In the primitive mind, ego and its objects would come together and disperse as new situations evolved. In the *Zhuangzi*, returning to the primitive mindset suggests the same: "To forget objects (*wu* 物) and to forget Nature (*tian* 天) is to be known as one who forgets oneself. One who has forgotten oneself is said to have entered completely into Nature (*ruyutian* 入於天)."[81]

Knowledge and Wholeness

To recalibrate knowledge by recovering the primitive mindset does not mean idealizing prehistoric times. Primitive humans, as Dewey notes, paid dearly for their inability to operate on the level of the "remote, generalized, objectified, [and] abstracted." Dewey's point is that we must "understand their incapacities only by seeing them as the obverse side of positively organized developments," and that "it is only by viewing them primarily in their positive aspect" that we "secure from its consideration assistance in comprehending the structure of present mind."[82] Teaching children about our primitive heritage is intended to serve as a "means of analyzing *present* life," says Dewey, so this must also "bring out its defects as well as its dramatic incidents, to see how and why [humans] worked their way out of it."[83]

The prehistoric mind, apart from simple tools, largely took things "as they are," says Dewey, leaving untouched manifold problems that modern technologies help us to mitigate.[84] Primitive humans "had none of the elaborate arts of protection and use which we now enjoy and no confidence in [their] own powers when they were reinforced by appliances of art."[85] The primitive hunting vocation, for instance, while highly practical, gave only sporadic satisfaction to our prehistoric ancestors. "Until agriculture and the higher industrial arts were developed, long periods of empty leisure alternated with comparatively short periods of energy put forth to secure food or safety from attack," notes Dewey.[86] Unlike Dewey's corpus, Daoist writings have a tendency to romanticize primitive times, portraying it as a golden age of perfect satisfaction before knowledge (*zhi* 知) came along to disrupt things. "People stayed at home without knowing what they were doing," we read, "they ventured out without knowing where they were going. Stuffing their mouths with food, they were happy; drumming on their bellies, they amused themselves."[87] Dewey had no such illusions.

Rather than idealize primitive life, Dewey sought to generate a positive account of its mindset in order to identify its most productive traits and consider how well these traits have passed over into present thinking. The most positive trait in the hunting vocation is the remarkable tightness that it exhibits in its means-and-ends—in other words, its *wholeness*. Again, for Dewey, the primitive mind is one whose "occupations integrate special elements into a functional whole."[88] Exhibiting continuity between means-and-ends is the foundation of all *dao* 道-activity and of intelligence (*ming* 明), including pre-human animal intelligence. The gradual "prolongation and postponement" of activity introduced by remoter ends "requires an increasing use of intelligence" in humans.[89] In all "post-hunting situations," Dewey explains, "the end is mentally apprehended and appreciated not as food satisfaction, but as a continuously ordered series of activities and of objective contents pertaining to them."⁹⁰ Dewey's appeal to the primitive mind, as Larry A. Hickman observes, "inverts the Victorian notion of technological progress." As Hickman writes: "Instead of looking among the 'savages' to find possible rudimentary traces of the 'superior' intelligence exhibited by industrial men and women, Dewey looks among the latter for vestiges of the particular intelligence of the former."⁹¹ Dewey thus recovers the primitive "ground pattern" upon which subsequent human technologies are built.

Surely there is something very powerful in the primitive mindset. Historically, it contributed to securing the genus *Homo* unparalleled success in adapting to myriad conditions and environments. *Homo erectus* migrated out of Africa two million years ago and reached as far as South-East Asia. *Homo sapiens* followed 100,000 years ago and now flourish in all corners of the earth. Understanding how the primitive mind became more technological—i.e., how it "ceased to be immediate and became loaded and surcharged with content which forced personal want, initiative, effort and satisfaction further and further apart"—is central to understanding who we are as a species. Such inquiry reveals how subsequent human interests emerged through "reconstruction and overlaying of the original hunting schema." Dewey explains:

> [By] these various agencies we have not so much destroyed or left behind the hunting structural arrangements of mind, as we have set free its constitutive psycho-physic factors so as to make them available and interesting in all kinds of objective and idealized pursuits—the hunt for truth, beauty, virtue, wealth, social well-being, and even of heaven and of God.⁹²

Such an attitude places Dewey in productive tension with Daoist-oriented primitivism. The latter tends to be skeptical of the idea that human arts and technologies can pursue higher things while preserving the integrity of *dao* 道-activity. Such skepticism ranges from benign mistrust to what Hagop Sarkissian notes are occasionally more radical suggestions, such as "destroying the compass and square" and "shackling the fingers" of technicians.⁹³ Such Daoists recognize primitive activity as pure and undivided in nature. Their reflex, then, is to regard such wholeness as incompatible with technological arts as such.

Eske Møllgaard, for instance, argues that in connection with its "critique of technical action . . . the *Zhuangzi* affirms an un-made 'ground' as the source of all authentic human action," one that is referred to as the "un-carved block" (*pu* 樸). This un-carved block, he notes, "is not a static substratum but an active force that moves human beings along together with everything else." This active, undivided force is *dao*-activity, and Møllgaard regards it as something original and pristine, violated the moment that humans subject it to technical action. As such, Møllgaard says, Zhuangzi is "the only major thinker in early China who is entirely beyond the technical."[94]

I resist such readings for a number of reasons. First, they strike me as obscurantist. Second, I don't think the *Zhuangzi* is univocally against technology. Third, I don't think such approaches are philosophically practical. More will be said about technology in chapter 7. For now, I note that there are better ways to reconcile the "un-carved block" (*pu* 樸) with the empirical fact that *Homo sapiens* (including Zhuangzi) always have been and always will be tool users. Dewey's version of the "primitive mind" and its signature vocation is more compatible with the existence of tools as such. The hunting vocation provides the primitive "ground pattern" upon which subsequent human arts and technologies are developed—and hardly does Dewey encourage completion and closure in these areas.

The tensions between Dewey and Daoist primitivism bring into focus a central concern in both philosophies: namely, the complex relationship between nature, innovation, and artifice. As we will see in chapter 7, Dewey and Zhuangzi have much to say about this relationship. At the end of the day, Dewey fits more comfortably alongside Confucian thinkers who maintain that the human experience, at its best, does not constitute any radical break from nonhuman Nature (*tian* 天). That said, as Michael J. Puett reminds us, the celebrated Confucian formula: the "continuity between Nature and the human" (*tianrenheyi* 天人合一) "only came to prominence at the end of a lengthy debate."[95] Primitivist discourse in the Daoist tradition contributes importantly to that outcome.

Turning to the "Inner Chapters" of the *Zhuangzi*, one finds a Daoist voice that sounds less hostile toward human activity and more constructive in its criticisms. It teaches that the optimal thing to know (*zhi* 知) is how Nature (*tian* 天) and the Human (*ren* 人) intersect and blend in our experience. The problem is that, once one is "human," it becomes difficult to ascertain this relation with any clarity. The text explains:

> Knowing what Nature does, and knowing what the Human does, is the optimal standpoint. One who knows what Nature does is natural and simply lives (*sheng* 生).[96] One who knows what the Human does can take that which such knowledge *knows* and use it to cultivate that which such knowledge does *not* know—thus living out the years that Nature affords without being cut off midway. This is the fullest knowledge. While this is so, there is a problem. This knowledge has something upon which it depends

before it becomes operative, and that upon which it depends is especially lacking in determination. How do we know that what we call "Nature" is not Human and that what we call "Human" is not Nature? If we posit a "genuine human" (*zhenren* 真人), then we can posit a genuine knowledge.⁹⁷

This passage is remarkable in a number of ways. First, it is quite contemporary in suggesting that elements in human-nature transactions are difficult to identify and observe once one is already "human." In the Western tradition, such insights rise to prominence in post-Kantian philosophies but hardly much before. Second, it provides warrant for the positing of a "genuine human" (*zhenren*) to serve as the prototype for primitive knowledge, thus sanctioning later "primitivist" authors to embellish on its nature. Third, it regards human knowledge as useful in distinguishing what it knows from what it does not know, regarding the cultivation (*yang* 養) of the latter as central to maximizing the lifespan of the knower.

This last point is important for rethinking the nature of human knowledge. As the *Zhuangzi* teaches, the actual scope of what humans know is extremely small. Wander far enough north, and one encounters the "God of the North Sea" (*beihairuo* 北海若). This god reminds us that: "One cannot discuss the ocean with a well frog, for he is limited to the space in which he lives." On the cosmic scale, the scope of the human experience is miniscule—like "a single fine hair on the body of a horse."⁹⁸ William James infuses American philosophy with a kindred epistemic humility. "Take our dogs and ourselves . . . how insensible, each of us, to all that makes life significant for the other!" he declares.⁹⁹ "We may be in the universe as dogs and cats are in our libraries, seeing the books and hearing the conversation, but having no inkling of the meaning of it all."¹⁰⁰ As the "God of the North Sea" reminds us, "what humans know is far less than what they do not know." The use of such a limited faculty carries special risks: "Our lives are limited, but what can be known is without limit. To use that which has limits to pursue that which has no limits is a perilous thing. One who responds to this peril by making (*wei* 為) knowledge do even more only compounds the peril!"¹⁰¹

Again, the Daoist solution is to exercise no-knowledge (*wuzhi* 無知), or what David L. Hall and Roger T. Ames call "unprincipled knowing,"—that which does not presume to lock onto objects with fixed ontological presence.¹⁰² By regarding the objects of knowledge as verb forms: *ways* of changing or acting, Dewey permits knowledge to track on to the results of transactions more fluidly and in all possible connections. Since Nature (*tian* 天) amounts to an immense (*da* 大) manifold of connections, including every possible transaction—physical, chemical, biological, subatomic, and so on—there is truly no limit to what can be known. James understands the world to be one of irreducible "noetic pluralism," impossible for any single knower to know completely all at once. For each knower, "the world hangs together from next to next in a variety of ways, so that when you are off of one thing you can always be on to something else, without ever dropping out of your world."[103] Thus, there is a "roaming" (*you* 遊) quality to human knowing for James. As Dewey writes, "to render experience in all its aspects richer and freer . . . [is] the central theme of James' account of the processes and operations by which knowledge is attained."[104] Knowledge affords humans such richness and freedom because beyond what we currently know there is always, as James liked to say, "MORE."[105]

As knowledge roams along, real connections are made between knowing and its objects. There are subtleties, however, to observe in the process. For Dewey, "knowing has to do with reorganizing activity, instead of being something isolated from all activity, complete on its own account."[106] Locating knowledge *in* activity results in a major reconstruction of the knower-known relationship. Knowledge and its objects are *themselves* transactions that occur across the knowing-known event. In their 1949 work, *Knowing and the Known*, Dewey and Arthur Bentley present their position in terms that strike the reader as boldly anti-realist and idealist: "We tolerate no 'entities' or 'realities' of any kind, intruding as if from behind or beyond the knowing-known events, with power to interfere, whether to distort or correct," they write.[107] Their position, however, is neither anti-realist nor idealist. As Larry A. Hickman explains, one of Dewey's primary tasks in his theory of knowledge is to overcome both realism and idealism as traditionally understood—a fact that Hickman finds to be "almost universally misunderstood" in Dewey scholarship.[108]

Hickman refers us to Dewey's own explanation: that the "key" to understanding the knowing-known relation is to appreciate the "temporal development of experience."[109] For Dewey, "the temporal quality of inquiry means . . . something quite other than that the process of inquiry takes time. It means that the objective subject-matter of inquiry undergoes temporal modification."[110] There is no eternal present in which objects stand apart from the knowing event. Also, there is no trans-temporal ego in which its subjects and objects are synthesized. There is *only* the event of knowing. As Dewey and Bentley explain:

> Since we are concerned with what is inquired into and is in process of knowing as cosmic event, we have no interest in any form of hypostatized underpinning. Any statement that is or can be made about a knower, self, mind, or subject—or about a known thing, an object, or a cosmos—must, so far as we are concerned,

be made on the basis, and in terms, of aspects of [an] event which inquiry, as itself a cosmic event, finds taking place.[111]

In world philosophy, the closest analogue to this is probably Buddhist.[112] In its actual inspiration, however, it lies closer to home in William James' identification of the "cognitive relation" with "pure experience."[113] In his 1943 article, "The Jamesian Datum," Bentley identifies the notion of "transaction" as a direct development of James' move to dissolve "independent subjectivities and objectivities" in the knowing relation.[114] James' thinking, incidentally, is immediately taken up into East Asian philosophy. Nishida Kitarō reads "A World of Pure Experience" in 1910 and finds that it bears "clear resemblance to Zen."[115]

Not unlike their Buddhist counterparts, Dewey and Bentley proceed to distinguish our more conventional, "interactional" accounts of knowing: those that posit ontologically separate entities, from our more thoroughly "transactional" accounts: those that note the dependent co-arising of each constituent in the event. The "knowing" event is thus similar to other complex events. They explain, for instance, that on conventional grounds it is fine to speak of someone called a "hunter" going into the woods to hunt. It is satisfactory enough "to report the shooting that follows in an interactional form in which rabbit and hunter and gun enter as separates and come together by way of cause and effect." Regarded as a "cosmic" event, however (i.e., factoring in "enough of the earth and enough thousands of years") one sees that only a "transactional" account covers the whole truth. One needs to factor in "history back into the pre-human" to account for what the hunter is doing, and the same for the rabbit and the gun—and still, the "hunting" is an irreducible unit composed exactly of its constituent elements. "No one would be able successfully to speak of the hunt*er* and the hunt*ed* as isolated with respect to hunt*ing*. Yet it is just as absurd to set up hunt*ing* as an event in isolation from the spatio-temporal connection of all the components."[116] Such a position is strikingly East Asian.[117]

Knowing and the Known argues that like any event, the knowing-known event is temporal, "transactional," and finite. Together, such features grant knowledge and its objects the flexibility to really change. Acknowledging that knowing-known events are finite in their scope of connections means that they can always be narrowed or enlarged to mobilize new and more productive (albeit limited) scales of wholeness. The positive side of accepting such finitude is the allowance that knowledge and its objects can always grow, thus "existing descriptions of events are accepted only as tentative and preliminary, so that new descriptions of the aspects and phases of events, whether in widened or narrowed form, may freely be made at any and all stages of inquiry."[118] This puts a finer point on the value of forgetting (*wang*

忘) in the *Zhuangzi*. If our predecessors were unable to periodically forget what they knew, then there would be no room for knowledge to actually grow. To "know" and to "forget" are thus two complementary aspects of a single dynamic: *the advancement of knowledge*.

Perhaps, as Thomas Kuhn suggests, "if we can learn to substitute evolution-from-what-we-do-know for evolution-toward-what-we-wish-to-know, a number of vexing problems may vanish."[119] The *Zhuangzi* seems already to have extinguished such problems. Rather than celebrate those who cling to and brandish what they know, the text celebrates individuals like Qu Boyu who at the age of sixty came to relinquish everything that he ever knew. He left his knowledge behind and *moved on*. "Humans all honor that which their knowledge knows, but no one knows enough to rely upon what knowledge does *not* know in order to later (*hou* 後) know."[120] For the primitive mind, as circumstances change there are different things to *do*—and as there are different things to do, there are different things to know.

The Tool of Knowing

Dewey and Zhuangzi each accept the idea that knowing *does* (*wei* 為) something to things. If we ever hope to get our thinking "back in gear," we need to understand this insight and to start taking it more seriously. As Dewey explains, there was bequeathed to generations of Western thinkers the idea that "knowledge is intrinsically a mere beholding or viewing of reality." At present, this is not assumed within the scientific community. If someone, "say a physicist or chemist," wants to *know* something she "proceeds to *do* something."[121] Knower-and-known emerge within a directed transactional whole. Dewey distinguishes this from what he calls the "spectator theory of knowledge," wherein "what is known is antecedent to the mental act of observation and inquiry, and is totally unaffected by these acts."[122] Such a theory tracks on to the Greek conception of thought (*dianoia*) and it no longer represents how we should understand our dealings with the world.

Dewey makes this point during his "Gifford Lectures" in 1928. Just prior to receiving this invitation, Jane Dewey was in Copenhagen testing Niels Bohr and Werner Heisenberg's predictions about the Stark effect in the helium spectra, which accounts for how its strings of atoms shift and divide in the presence of an electrical field.[123] Along with others, her findings contributed to the formulation of the "Uncertainty Principle" in 1927, which states that the more precisely one knows the position of a particle, the less precisely one knows its momentum. John Dewey immediately recognized the implications of this for theories of knowledge. During his "Gifford Lectures" (which became 1929's *The Quest for Certainty*) he explains that:

> The element of indeterminateness [in physics] is not connected with defect in the method of observation but is intrinsic. The particle observed does not *have* fixed position or velocity, for it is changing all the time because of interaction: specifically, in this case, interaction with the act of observing, or more strictly, with the conditions under which an observation is possible.[124]

Dewey would eventually shift his terminology from "interaction" to "transaction," making the ontological features of this insight more sophisticated.[125] This makes it even easier to appreciate how modern physics "presents itself as the final step in the dislodgement of the old spectator theory of knowledge."[126]

The idea that knowing is an act of doing/making (or *wei* 為) is one that Dewey maintained for quite some time. "Why should the idea that knowledge makes a difference to and in things be antecedently objectionable?" he asks in 1908.[127] Zhuangzi regards the notion as obvious: "Something is affirmed by *being* affirmed, something is negated by *being* negated. Paths are formed when someone walks on them. Things are so when someone refers to them as so. How is something so? Its' so-ness *becomes* so. How is something not so? Its' not-so-ness *becomes* not so." Like Dewey, Zhuangzi assumes such a position while fortifying himself against the charge of anti-realism: "Things certainly (*gu* 固) have that by which they become so, and they certainly have that by which they become affirmed. Non-entities (*wuwu* 無物) are not so, and non-entities are not affirmed."[128] As David L. Hall and Roger T. Ames observe, this view is one that "we in the West would term a realist perspective," but it is an "objectless" realism.[129] What *really* exist are not self-enclosed "objects," but *ways* of acting—and "concrete things," Dewey says, "have as many ways of acting as they have points of interaction with other things."[130] The object emerges as a result of transactions between knowers-and-the-known. As such, the "object of knowledge," Dewey writes, "is a constructed, existentially produced, object."[131] To know something as thus-and-so is to regard or make (*wei*) it thus-and-so in a transactional situation. Given that natural elements transact in an immense (*da* 大) variety of ways, the world is rich in logical and pragmatic space for overlapping objects to emerge.

Dewey understood that this complicated the relationship between the objects of science and those of common sense, but the problem is not one of "Realism/Anti-Realism." It is, for instance, simply wrong to ask whether the "water" of common sense (i.e., "the water we drink, wash with, sail boats upon, use to extinguish fires, etc.") is as *real* as the H_2O that is used in scientific inquiries. For Dewey, both are equally "real" objects that do different things.[132] Similarly for Zhuangzi, a bachelor might regard Xishi to be the most beautiful woman in the world and react accordingly—but when fishes see her they dart away, birds fly off, and deer bolt. Among these four, asks Zhuangzi, which one knows (*zhi* 知) the "right" way to apprehend her?[133] The connections that make up "Xishi"—physical, chemical, biological, subatomic, and so on—give rise to different "objects" that behave in different *real* ways when engaged by different knowers. All such objects are valid, viable, and practical, and each is irreducible to the other.

The pluralistic matrix in which such overlapping objects are sustained is one that Brook Ziporyn describes in terms of manifold "coherences" (*li* 理). As Dewey observes, "cherry trees will be differently grouped by woodworkers, orchardists, artists, scientists, and merry-makers."[134] The elements that comprise different "cherry trees" are neither unreal nor entirely separate from one another. They are, as Ziporyn would point out, different omnipresent coherences.[135] Remember that there is a Great Continuum (*taiyi* 太一) from which all "cherry trees" arise. Each version (or knowing-known event) realizes a distinct unit of possibility (*deyi* 得一), annulling its own potential state and distinguishing itself from other possibilities on the boundless spectrum. "Each division is a realization (*cheng* 成)," explains Zhuangzi, "and each realization is a kind of destruction" as each new annulment elbows itself into being. "But things in general (*fanwu* 凡物) are neither realized nor destroyed, and they revert to coming together again to form a continuum (*yi* 一)." Only those who are properly attuned to things, says Zhuangzi, "realize how they come together to form a continuum."[136]

There is a "mystical" dimension to such a realization if one is so inclined. The mystical vision here is one that David L. Hall calls "con-static," which differs from ecstatic (*out*-dwelling) and enstatic (*in*-dwelling) mystical experiences. "Con-stacy," for Hall, is an experience of "standing with" all things—having the sense that all objects stand together in a "felt unity."[137] Such a mystical vision is felt throughout the *Zhuangzi*, and there will be more to say about such feelings in chapter 8 of volume two.

Dewey says little about his own mystical leanings in his writings, but he was forthcoming in correspondence with one of his more eclectic acquaintances, Scudder Klyce. Klyce showered Dewey with details about his own metaphysical and mystical proclivities. Dewey's polite responses suggest that his own soul, in Steven C. Rockefeller's words, was one of "an infinite pluralist who emphasized the idea of continuity and interconnection leading to a sense of oneness and peace."[138] "I believe that the related many, the many in their relationships or continuity, when perceived as such, inevitably tend to make persons respond with a sense of One, God if you please," Dewey writes.¹³⁹ "Do the reality of the many—as continuous and interrelated—and of the one hang together? . . . I assert it."¹⁴⁰

Thus, from a mystical perspective, every version of the "cherry tree" stands together in "constancy." This does not mean, however, that one "cherry tree" is as good as the other. For Dewey, "there is a genuine objective standard for the goodness of special classifications [of the tree]. One will further the cabinetmaker in reaching his end while another will hamper him. One classification will assist the botanist in carrying on fruitfully his work of inquiry, and another will retard and confuse him."¹⁴¹ As Dewey says, "there will be as many kinds of known objects as there are kinds of effectively conducted operations of inquiry," and "the result of one operation will be as good and true an object of knowledge as is any other, provided it is good at all: provided, that is, it satisfies the conditions which induced the inquiry."¹⁴²

How does one navigate among such a multiplicity of objects, stacked as they are into a pluralistic manifold of coherences? Zhuangzi responds:

> Regarding any as definitely so (*shi* 是) is not helpful, so one should entrust it to ordinary activity (*yong* 庸). That which belongs to ordinary activity works in use (*yong* 用). That which works in use gets one through (*tong* 通). And that which gets one through achieves success (*de* 得). "Getting through and achieving success," that just about covers it—so just leave it at that. When it is left at that, and one does not know (*zhi* 知) how it is so, this is called *dao* 道-practice.¹⁴³

I agree with Robert Eno that "On the Parity of Things" downplays the value of theoretical knowing by "proposing an alternative route to certainty based on the potential of ordinary skill knowing." Such knowing, as he observes, "distinguishes [Zhuangzi's position] most essentially from Greek and subsequent Western traditions prior to the advent of the pragmatist schools."¹⁴⁴ When using the word "pragmatic," Dewey simply means "the doctrine that reality possesses practical character and that this character is most efficaciously expressed in the function of intelligence."¹⁴⁵ Whatever else Zhuangzi's understanding of knowing may be, it is certainly "pragmatic" in this respect. When confronted with conflicting theories, Zhuangzi grounds adjudication in ordinary practice (*yong* 庸) and subordinates "Definitely So/Definitely Not" (*shifei* 是非) designations to what actually works in use (*yong* 用). In sorting all of this out, "nothing matches intelligence (*ming* 明)."¹⁴⁶ Intelligence is the function by which theoretical formulations (*yan* 言), as Dewey says, are "accepted only as tentative and preliminary," such that necessary modifications to their character, "whether in widened or narrowed form, may freely be made at any and all stages of inquiry."[147] The power of intelligence thus exemplifies the positive "roaming" (*you* 遊) capacity of the human mind, which both James and Zhuangzi are so masterful at articulating.[148]

This raises a point. There is a pronounced tendency in Western scholarship to treat theoretical knowing as the default position in Chinese philosophy and to judge "On the Parity of Things" accordingly in terms of its comparative "skepticism" or "relativism."[149] Such readings, however, are not as sustainable in the Warring States context as they are in Western contexts. While the kind of static "knowing" (*zhi* 知) that Mohism represents is a target in the *Zhuangzi*, Mohist theories did not enjoy the same philosophical standing that Greek and early Modern theories of knowledge had in the West—theories that gave rise to "skepticism" and "relativism" as we know them. To suggest otherwise distorts the native context of Warring States discourse. The matrix of "the ordinary and the extraordinary," out of which Dewey says world philosophies emerged, became arrayed differently in China and the West.[150] For Daoist authors, a pre-philosophical humility before an un-domesticated "extraordinary" realm was not so difficult to recover. For more iconoclastic thinkers in the West—e.g., Sextus Empiricus, David Hume, or Friedrich Nietzsche—there stood more fortified Platonic or Aristotelian assumptions and/or Judeo-Christian theologies to contend with. Thus, philosophers such as Sextus, Hume, and Nietzsche tend to be regarded as derivative, "reactionary" thinkers rather than positive thinkers in their own right. Such thinkers are regarded not as genuine "realists" but rather, in one form or another, as "skeptics" or "relativists."

Pragmatists often receive the same negative reading. Dewey, however, has no qualms about asserting his positive credentials:

> If reality be itself in transition—and this doctrine originated not with the objectionable pragmatist but with the physicist and naturalist and historian—then the doctrine that knowledge *is* reality making a particular and specified sort of change in itself seems to have the best chance at maintaining a theory of knowing which is in wholesome touch with the genuine and valid.[151]

As Dewey sees it, the burden of proof needs to shift. Those who would assume, given all that we know in the physical and biological sciences, that the objects of knowledge are "unchangeable substances having properties fixed in isolation and unaffected by interactions" need to defend such claims.[152] In rejecting such a view, Zhuangzi is not exhibiting skepticism or relativism. Rather, as Steve Coutinho suggests, he is exhibiting a "nature-oriented form of pragmatism" while avoiding "the nihilistic extremes of relativism and skepticism."[153] Zhuangzi only becomes a "skeptic" or "relativist" in his encounter with our own Greek-medieval expectations.

To suggest that Zhuangzi's approach is "nature-oriented" entails that it is more than cultural in its origins. "Knowledge," as Zhuangzi reminds us, was originally for the life-process (*sheng* 生).[154] Thus, there must be a naturalistic account of knowledge—something like a "*dao* 道 of knowing"—from the Daoist perspective. For Dewey, the natural history of the knowing-known event "commits us to the conviction that mind, whatever else it may be, is at least an organ in service for the control of environment in relation to the ends of the life process."[155]

Where do we look for this pre-cultural dimension of knowing? One route would be to observe the characteristics of brain activity. "The brain," Dewey explains, "is essentially an organ for effecting the reciprocal adjustment to each other of the stimuli received from the environment and responses directed upon it." Brain activity, in this sense, is inherently *forward moving*. "While each motor response is adjusted to the state of affairs indicated through the sense-organs, that motor response shapes the next sensory stimulus." The function that the brain performs in sustaining the life process (*sheng* 生) is itself a form of *dao* 道-activity, such that it entails the "constant reorganization of activity so as to maintain its continuity; that is to say, to make such modifications in future action as are required because of what has already been done."[156] The kind of knowing that emerges from such processes recalls the faculty of knowledge (*guanzhi* 官知) that Cook Ding alludes to.[157] Such knowing amounts to *dao*-activity, which essentially involves three things: *continuity*, *novelty*, and *means-ends coordination*.

Empirical research concurs. Recent studies in primate behavior suggest that frequencies observed in these three areas: "social learning" (*continuity*), "innovation" (*novelty*), and "tool use" (*means-end coordination*) are "positively correlated with species' relative and absolute 'executive' brain volumes."[158] In keeping with the principle of continuity, it makes sense that there would evolve accordingly a "*dao* 道 of knowing" within Nature (*tian* 天) that is integral to sustaining life. "For if the brain is an organ of life," writes Dewey, "it would seem to be a truism that the experiences which are mediated by it, namely ideas and knowing, have something intrinsic to do with carrying on the life process."[159]

Daoism teaches us that knowledge (*zhi* 知) wrongly utilized bifurcates the qualities of *dao* 道-activity. The tradition also provides us, however, with a positive account of primitive knowing: a "knowing that does not know" (*wuzhizhi* 無知知). Such knowing preserves the wholeness of the knowing-known event without instrumentalizing the act itself. But here, almost by reflex, Edward Slingerland's "paradox" returns. If knowing (*zhi*) itself is a *tool*, then how does it not bifurcate activity in every instance of its use? Stubbornly, the human intellect asks how something as resolutely instrumental as "knowing" can be conceived as *not* striving to "do or make (*wei* 為) something happen."[160] As Slingerland insists: "It would seem that the very act of striving would inevitably 'contaminate' the end state."[161]

Preventing such cognitive mishandling of *dao* 道-activity requires steady philosophical vigilance. In his own attempt to overcome such errors in thinking, Dewey would (late in his career) eventually modify his own description of the knowing relation. This prompted him in *Unmodern Philosophy* to initiate another major shift in his vocabulary: replacing the word "instrumental" with the word "technological" to describe his theory of knowing. The problem with the word "instrumental," writes Dewey, is that it is "so linked with linguistic uses that give *instruments* a mechanical sense, which perforce renders knowledge subservient to ends externally set."[162] Dewey's position had always been that means-and-ends are ideally shaped reciprocally and that a pragmatic intelligence is thus *creative*—something more than a "routine mechanic."[163] Taking up tools as a *means*, then, is not merely instrumental in a mechanical sense, but "technological" in an artistic sense—"artistic" indicating the preservation of *wholeness*. Put another way, intelligence (or *ming* 明) does not simply take up tools in order to reach fixed goals; it also "perceives new possibilities of action" while "the discovery of objects not already used leads to suggestion of new ends."[164]

Given that "innovation" (*novelty*) is covariant with brain volume and inherent to its functioning, intelligence (or *ming* 明) so conceived amounts to an expression of the "*dao* 道 of knowing." Here, the inclusion of innovation tempers the anti-technology bias that lurks in Daoist primitivism while restoring the element of novelty that animates the bulk of the tradition. As Dewey reminds us: "Inventions of new agencies and instruments create new ends," initiating "new consequences which stir [humans] to form new purposes."[165] Objects of knowledge—theories, ideas, concepts, words, texts, etc.—are not inert "instruments" in such procedures. Regarding such things in this way, as Zhuangzi says, is like "consuming spent dregs." Within the framework of what Dewey calls "technology," such tools are a *means* to do or make something fresh and new in the moment. The key here is to allow ordinary activity (*yong* 庸) to furnish ends so that means-end continuity grows from within activity. Whenever this is achieved, knowing amounts to a "knowing that does not know" (*wuzhizhi* 無知知) and doing/making amounts to a "doing/making that does not do or make" (*weiwuwei* 為無為).

The Monopoly of Knowledge

As the *Zhuangzi* suggests, our primitive ancestors developed their knowledge sufficiently to be content. This was all-one with the life-process (*sheng* 生) and they did not take it up in order to do/make (*wei* 為) anything with it. In this way, their knowledge remained consistent with their natural dispositions (*xing* 性). This state of affairs, however, changed. As we read in the earliest Chinese treatise on technology, the *Artificer's Record* (*kaogongji* 考工記), the "knowers" (*zhizhe* 知者) would soon enough invent tools beyond those upon which our primitive ancestors relied.[166] As the Daoist observes, such mechanical contraptions (*ji* 機) transformed human activity. Most notably, as the *Zhuangzi* reminds us, such technologies significantly reconstructed the primitive hunting vocation. All of our "bows, crossbows, nets, stringed arrows, fishhooks, lures, seines, dragnets, trawls, weirs, pitfalls, snares, cages, traps, and gins" are presented as evidence of our "abundance of knowledge" (*zhiduo* 知多). Unfortunately for our terrestrial cousins, these tools caused them great befuddlement (*luan* 亂).

That is not all. The *Zhuangzi* draws an analogy between such hunting technologies and the fine machinery of analytic philosophy, which likewise has the power to trap and befuddle. "Hard and White" (*jianbai* 堅白) and "Sameness/Difference" (*tongyi* 同異) distinctions are tools of knowing that, when pushed too far, convert inquiries into puzzles and problems into paradoxes. Such philosophical instruments, like our fishing and hunting technologies, threaten to violate a more primitive form of activity and pose a threat to animals—but this time, *we* are the animals.

As suggested in chapter 1, comparative philosophy is not immune from the hazards of such technologies and the befuddlement that can result from their use. One recent example of a "Hard and White" question in comparative philosophy would be something like: "Is Confucianism a Virtue Ethics?" One presumes that it either "definitely is" (*shi* 是) or "definitely is not" (*fei* 非) and that the right answer will be known if opposing sides debate the question long enough. In truth, different parties in this debate approach the question with opposite presuppositions. Such a situation precludes finally "knowing" which side is right.

Henry Rosemont Jr. is noteworthy for recognizing this fact while remaining fully engaged in the debate. His insights are instructive. This debate (which is treated more extensively in chapter 5 of volume two) is one in which virtue ethicists like Philip J. Ivanhoe maintain that the "self" is the bearer of virtues while role-oriented ethicists like Rosemont and Roger T. Ames maintain that the "self" is a sum of its roles, thus denying that such autonomous, virtue-bearing "selves" exist. As Rosemont comes to realize, "One complication for dialogue or debate is that it is difficult to raise an objection to our position without begging the question against us. That is to say, reservations about role ethics are almost invariably grounded in a foundational individualistic framework." In other words, the "virtue ethics" side already assumes that there is an autonomous individual self that is the bearer of virtues. What are Ames and Rosemont supposed to say? "Our narrative problem is on all fours with anyone else who wants to claim the truth of a negative existential statement," Rosemont observes. "There seems to be, in short, no conceptual place where true *engagement* with our fellow philosophers might take place; both sides seem to have little choice but to be *confrontational*. We offer arguments on behalf of our claim that we believe are fairly strong, but admit straightaway that they are not, cannot be conclusive. It is difficult to ascertain how the dispute might be resolved because it is neither fully empirical nor *a-priori*. And there does not seem to be any vantage point from which to analyze and evaluate the two positions neutrally."[167] As Zhuangzi asks: what third party could possibly adjudicate such a debate—someone who agrees with one side, someone who agrees with the other, someone who agrees with neither side, someone who agrees with both?[168]

There are simply different ways of understanding Confucian ethics, and these ways have different practical results. The results are what actually matter. Like "Hard and White" debates, "Sameness/Difference" (*tongyi* 同異) debates proliferate in comparative philosophy and likewise cannot be resolved in neutral space. "Is Confucius similar to Dewey or to Aristotle?" Again, the real question is "Who is asking?" and "What difference would it make given the problems that concern the person asking?" Only when inquiries are grounded in actual problems rather than abstract assertions do tools for resolving them even present themselves. As Dewey says: "*the* problem of practice is what do we need to *know*, how shall we obtain that knowledge and how shall we apply it?"[169] Such considerations inform every comparative exercise.

From the standpoint of intra-cultural philosophy, philosophical inquiries that purport to be "comparative" are often framed in terms of trying (or claiming) to know something that does not really ask to be known—namely, the definitive "Sameness/Difference" relation between two block-like cultural objects. The practical applicability of having determined such relations is often treated "in conclusion" as a kind of felicitous by-product of having made an "objective comparison"—but this puts the cart before the horse. It overlooks the initial purpose that motivates such knowing in the first place: behaving as if Confucius himself maintains a position on whether he is properly or improperly classified as a "virtue ethicist" or should be located closer to Dewey or to Aristotle. Such questions matter to *us*, and frontloaded into any inquiry into them should be an honest and clear assessment as to *why* they matter. Providing such candid assessments is where philosophers like Henry Rosemont Jr. shine the brightest.

Pragmatic naturalists and Daoists agree that the number of things that matter enough to warrant inquiry is relatively small. There are vast regions of experience for which knowledge has no concern whatsoever: the great "North Sea" beyond our reach empirically and/or practically. Such regions, as Larry A. Hickman observes, "will never be the object of transformation by intelligent inquiry or the application of productive skill."[170] We must realize, however, that like any technology, knowledge falls under the Law of the Instrument: "When the only tool you have is a hammer, everything looks like a nail." Dewey and Daoism wish to remind us that knowledge by nature has its limits. Like the Daoist, Dewey maintains that knowledge "does not encompass the world as a whole," a fact that is neither "defect nor failure on its part." As a tool for inquiry, knowledge "attends strictly to its own business" and "not all existence asks to be known."[171]

Dewey traces our confusion about this back to "preconceived notions of knowledge and of 'reality' as a monopolistic possession of pure intellect."[172] Such a notion has manifold social consequences, not least of which is that it emboldens groups such as the Mohists (and legions of others) who claim to have a "monopoly of moral truth," should they begin to engage in the insensate and ruthless treatment of those who think otherwise.[173] This exposes a significant demerit in what will come (in volume two) to be critiqued as the "Heaven's plan" reading of Confucian philosophy. As Dewey reminds us: "History proves what a dangerous thing it has been for [human beings], when they try to impose their will upon other [human beings], to think of themselves as special instruments and organs of Deity."[174] It is easy to imagine that such unsavory tendencies, having been furniture in the human experience for so long, will never change. Dewey is realistic in his understanding that "the glorification of knowledge as the exclusive avenue of access to what is real is not going to give way soon nor all at once." But he is hopeful that "it can hardly endure indefinitely."[175] Let's hope that he's right.

In the meantime, the best we can do as progressive-minded philosophers is to continue reconstructing knowledge as a positive element in *dao* 道-practice. We should understand what human knowledge *does* so we can appreciate it for the positive tool that it is. No tool does everything. We thus rejoin Socrates, who understood the difference between a "*human* wisdom" that knows its limits and a "*super-human* wisdom" that thinks it knows what cannot be known.[176] Philosophers who automatically label those who point out the limits of knowledge as "skeptics" or "relativists" injure the human enterprise twice. First, they perpetuate a monopolistic conception of knowledge that fosters conflict and despair. Second, they negate the limited but positive qualities of our signature technology. Ideally, we could start over and positively reconstruct knowledge on the "ground pattern" of primitive intelligence, which bases itself on practical activity and reality. The long shadow of Greek-medieval thought, however, makes this difficult. For as Dewey sees it, "If it were not for the assumed monopolistic relation to reality of a knowledge disconnected from organic life, reference to action would cease to be a distorting, or even a limiting term with respect to knowledge. The reference would be wholly explanatory and clarifying."[177] The faculty of knowledge (*guanzhi* 官知) would then be returned to its native status and recognized for its natural powers as one among many functions in the life-process.

"I do not know when knowledge will become naturalized in the life of society," Dewey writes. "But when it is fully acclimatized, its instrumental, as distinct from its monopolistic role in approach to things of nature and society will be taken for granted without need for such arguments as I have been engaging in."[178] Until that day, we are left to monitor what the *Zhuangzi* calls the "crime that is over-fondness for knowledge (*zhi* 知)."[179] Indeed, as Aristotle observes: "All humans by nature desire to know."[180] Again, there is nothing inherently wrong with this desire. Knowing is an integral component of the life-process. In navigating reality, however, it has its limits. "In the absence of desire, one observes the mystery of things," says Chapter 1 of the *Daodejing*. When something goes unnamed (*wuming* 無名) and thus *un*-known, it is allowed to stand forth in its "thisness"—foregrounded in its sheer presence before nothing (*wu* 無). Again, things *are* knowable for the Daoist, but they are not primarily and exhaustively knowable. Each act of knowing does or makes (*wei* 為) something to be in some way, and once this happens there are practical consequences. Some of these consequences align with the *dao* 道 of knowing and some do not.

Of the latter, examples abound. As Chapter 2 warns: "Once everyone knows [the term] 'Beauty' (*mei* 美) to make (*wei* 為) beauty, then there is 'Ugliness.'" Indeed—is there really such a *thing* as "Beauty" that needs to be known? Plato worries that it might be the case that our "name-givers" are right, and that "everything is always moving and flowing," such that there is no standard (*fa* 法) for "whether a particular face or something of that sort is beautiful."[181] But let's be serious. When a father no longer knows that his daughter's face is beautiful, then I will worry. Until then, we can trust that there is a kind of knowing in Nature (*tian* 天) that "does not know that it knows" (*wuzhizhi* 無知知). When it starts "knowing" otherwise the situation turns pathological. Indeed, as Chapter 71 teaches: "Knowing without knowing is the best. But *not* knowing that you are 'knowing' is a kind of sickness. And only when we are sickened by the sickness can we be cured."

As Chapters 18 and 38 suggest, having to clarify the meaning of normative terms like "Beauty" is a sign that *dao* 道 has already broken down—or, as Dewey would say, there is a problem that requires technologies to restore wholeness to the situation. Ideally, such things as "Beauty" take care of themselves and do not need to be known. Intelligence (or *ming* 明) then, in its broad function as general manager of means-and-ends, is responsible in part for knowing when it is time to *stop* knowing. One needs to develop a feel for when to take up a tool and when to place it aside. The more that theories (*yan* 言) proliferate in abstraction from real problems, the more elusive such a primitive feel becomes—the more trapped and befuddled we are by the technological objects at our disposal. Some philosopher-types might even imagine that the proper way to *know* something like "Beauty" is to suspend judgment pending a critical survey of all existing theories. But, as Chapter 47 rightly suggests, it is sometimes the case that "the further one goes [in such a direction] the *less* one knows."

In the final analysis, Dewey and Zhuangzi turn Plato's "divided line" on its head. Rather than positing an eternal "world" that in its original state contains immutable objects (*eidos*) of knowledge (*episteme*), what precedes us is a real but "objectless" world in which objects are constructed and deconstructed. Like Radin's *Primitive Man as Philosopher*, the *Zhuangzi* envisions the primitive human (*guzhiren* 古之人) as living in a world devoid of fixed objects. In one sense, Radin writes, "It is quite erroneous to speak of the concept of the external *world* of the [primitive]," if by "world" we mean a domain that is populated with well-defined objects. "Strictly speaking," says Radin, "he has none."[182] Objects of knowledge do, however, gradually emerge in the human experience. Zhuangzi's "On the Parity of Things" traces the evolution of human cognition from such an "objectless" state to the present world in four distinct stages:

> [In the first stage] the knowing (*zhi* 知) of primitive people reached an ultimate point. What was this ultimate point? There were some for whom there had not yet begun to be objects. This is the ultimate point, the full measure, that which does not permit any increase. The second stage was that in which there were objects, but they had not yet begun to have definite boundaries. The third stage were those for whom [objects] had definite boundaries, but they had not yet begun to have "Definitely So/Definitely Not" (*shifei* 是非) distinctions. [In the fourth stage] the illumination of the "Definitely So/Definitely Not" distinction eclipsed *dao* 道.[183]

In Zhuangzi's account, cognitive activity at the first, second, and third stages exhibits the requisite flexibility to take up objects of knowledge for particular purposes and then to forget about them (*wang* 忘). We continue to do this all the time. Objects at the fourth level, however, since they are granted "Definitely So/Definitely Not" (*shifei* 是非) status, are dislodged from any particular activity or inquiry. For Plato, these are the objects of thought (*dianoia*). Rather than having superior ontological status, such objects in the *Zhuangzi* are regarded as detrimental to *dao* 道-activity. The worth of such objects is adjusted accordingly. As Dewey artfully puts it: "A reality which is not in any sort of use" in some particular activity or inquiry, "may go hang."[184] The situation changes, however, when such work-shy objects become employed dogmatically, blocking the road of inquiry or becoming tools of oppression or control. Logical debate (*bian* 辯) can be useful in resolving such situations, but not always. The ultimate tribunal in restoring *dao* is not logical but *empirical*—i.e., analyses that convert such theoretical objects (*yan* 言) back into their actual uses (*yong* 用) so that their consequences can be demonstrated and assessed in practice.

This last point is important in intra-cultural criticism. While much has been said already against conceptions that are "out of gear" with scientific understandings, it should be understood that the wholeness that *dao* 道-activity embodies is existential and not necessarily "logical." Personally, my objection to ideas like Creationism, final ends, essential natures, etc. is not that they are "illogical," but that they have grown ill effective in specific instances. My interest here is not in any fundamental sense rational *or* irrational. As Dewey reminds us, "rationality and irrationality are largely irrelevant and episodical in undisciplined human nature."[185] As he says: "Apart from the use made of it in knowing, [bare nature] exists in a dimension irrelevant to either attribution [i.e., "Rational/Irrational"], just as rivers inherently are neither located near cities nor are opposed to such location."[186] Logical sense can be made of *why* cities are next to rivers, but *that* rivers have cities next to them is a brute fact. Similarly, there are no strictly "logical" arguments for or against things like Creationism, final ends, and essential natures. People come to believe in such things, and that is all. One can only demonstrate alternative conceptions and assess the consequences of entertaining them—demonstrating *why* one should or should not embrace them.

As Brook Ziporyn suggests, the coherence (*li* 理) of particular objects of thought can be regarded both in terms of their intelligibility *and* their unintelligibility. Coherences are intelligible (or "non-ironic") whenever the "stability, balance, or equilibrium" they sustain is foregrounded and the "growth, continuance" that they sponsor is recognized. Alternately, coherences are unintelligible (or "ironic") when viewed within the context of their "indiscernible, not definitely identifiable" ontological conditions, i.e., the continuum (*yi* 一) in which they fuse with what they are not (*wu* 無) and that "entails an effacement of coherence in the sense of 'intelligibility.'"[187] What recommends one idea over another is not coherence *per se*—every idea that can be held has enough of *that*. What recommends one idea over another is the kind of "stability, balance, or equilibrium" that it sustains and the "growth, continuance" that it sponsors. Sometimes "logical" ideas perform better than "illogical" ideas, and sometimes it's the other way around. Creationism, for instance, is in some respects more "logical" than the theory of evolution. The trajectory that it puts us on, however, is a dead end.

Again, as Kurtis Hagen and Brook Ziporyn argue, the coherence (*li* 理) of Nature (*tian* 天) is not a single logical order in which fixed objects are destined to be realized.[188] It is a matrix in which natural transactions give rise to a plurality of coherent objects that do different things. Such a matrix, as Ziporyn puts it, is "*a harmony which, when harmonized with by a human being, leads to further harmonies.*" The way a coherent object takes shape is for "human beings to know it, to be aware of it, to pick it out and identify it, and for it to be intelligible."[189] For Dewey too, the point is that "nature is intellig*ible* and understand*able*. There are operations by means of which it *becomes* an object of knowledge, and is turned to human purposes."[190] For Ziporyn, the matrix in which such transactions occur has "the possibility of *establishing* real continuities by means of human actions and cognitions."[191] So too for Dewey: "Nature *has* intelligible order as its possession in the degree in which we by our own overt operations realize potentialities contained in it."[192] The "cherry trees" of the woodworkers, orchardists, artists, scientists, merrymakers, etc. are all coherent (*li*) objects. Each one is as "real" as anything that genuinely answers to some use. Thus, the uses (*yong* 用) that technological objects serve are the only criteria by which they can be judged better or worse.

Uses that work against the life-process (*sheng* 生) result in disharmony and disequilibrium, and these are valid grounds for resisting such instruments. Such "validity" is not grounded in logic, nor in some static "Definitely So/Definitely Not" (*shifei* 是非) object. Instead, such validity is grounded in *reality*—i.e., in the *dao* 道-activity that represents the concrete "need" of some living being some-*where* and some-*when*. Thus, while Robert Eno is correct to suggest that Zhuangzi's *dao* is "not an ethical value,"[193] this does not mean that it is incompatible with moral concerns altogether. The ethical vision perhaps most consistent with Daoist thinking is outlined in William James' short masterpiece, "The Moral Philosopher and the Moral Life." The aim of this essay, as James explains, is to demonstrate that there can be no such thing as "an ethical philosophy dogmatically made up in advance."[194] The reason is that the ontological status of moral obligation is always some concrete *demand*.

James asks us to imagine a universe in which there is but one sentient being in "moral solitude." There is now a chance for the good *really* to exist. Whatever that being desires is good—he *makes it good*, "for he is the sole creator of values in that universe, and outside of his opinion things have no moral character at all." Introduce a second being, and the situation becomes a "moral dualism." If the two disagree about what is "good," there is no possible ground upon which to say that one thinker's opinion is better than the other, and a third party is not going to help. Each party simply makes its claim to a different demand. How then does moral philosophy begin? James observes:

> [The] moment we take a steady look at the question, *we see not only that without a claim actually being made by some concrete person there can be no obligation, but that there is some obligation wherever there is a claim.* Claim and obligation are, in fact, coextensive terms; they cover each other exactly . . . Take any demand, however slight, which any creature, however weak, may make. Ought it not, for its own sole sake, to be satisfied? If not, prove why not. The only possible kind of proof you could adduce would be the exhibition of another creature who should make a demand that ran the other way.

Given that the good is grounded in concrete demands, the "guiding principle for ethical philosophy," James concludes, must be "simply to satisfy at all times *as many demands as we can*."[195]

Dewey is more careful than James not to conflate the "desired" with the "desirable," stressing that we learn from experience that some of our demands are better left *un*-satisfied. Still, he agrees that, "the object that *should* be desired (valued), does not descend out of the *a priori* blue nor descend as an imperative from a moral Mount Sinai."[196] Each value is concretely located. As Gregory Fernando Pappas observes, James and Dewey both hope that "the denial of a privileged universal standpoint [in ethics] . . . would lead to an appreciation of the particular and unique location [that] each of us inhabits in experience."[197]

With respect to Daoist sensibilities, an important corollary to such thinking is that each organic form (*xing* 形) has its own claim to existence *as such*. Recall that, for a living organism, attaining existence (*deyi* 得一) is not a static state of Being (*esse*) but rather a rhythmic event that takes place on the "Potter's Wheel of Nature." Each life-process is the expression of a "need," and thus becomes an existential *demand* that serves as the basis for moral obligation. Whatever the price of admission is to ride on this mad carousel we call "the world," that price is paid in full by everything that is "here" (*you* 有). Each being is whole and valid just as it is. In the Western tradition, Nicholas of Cusa arrives at such an insight only by breaking with Greek-medieval orthodoxy. As Ernst Cassirer notes, Nicholas turns away from Aristotelian thinking and rejects the idea that "all empirical being splits up into definite [genera] and species that stand in a definite relationship of super- or sub-ordination to each other."[198] As a result, Nicholas beholds the world in terms of parity (or *qi* 齊) rather than hierarchy, and thus in a more Daoist spirit. As he writes:

> Every creature is, as it were, "God-created" or "finite-infinity," with the result that no creature's existence could be better than it is . . . The inference from this is that every creature, as such, is perfect, though by comparison with others it may seem imperfect . . . (God) communicates being without distinction; and, since all receive being in accord with the demands of their contingent nature, every creature rests content in its own perfection, which God has freely bestowed upon it. None desires the greater perfection of any other; each loves by preference that perfection which God has given it and strives to develop and preserve it intact.[199]

So again—take any organic form, however slight, and any life-process, however weak: ought it not, for its own sole sake, be allowed to express its directional order (or *de* 德)? If not—*prove why not*. The only legitimate reason to disrupt the trajectory of a "God-created" life-process is that it presents a mortal threat or provides some needed food. Otherwise, "Leave it be!" (*zaiyou* 在宥). Or as James says, "Hands off: neither the whole of truth, nor the whole of good, is revealed to any single observer."[200]

We will continue to experiment with this line of inquiry in the next two chapters. For now, we have reviewed knowledge as a human technology and surveyed its pragmatic dimensions. In chapter 7, we will be approaching the relationship between primitive states and those represented by "knowing" from a different angle. What in the *Zhuangzi* is called our "over-fondness for knowledge" (*haozhi* 好知) is associated with the proliferation of tools—axes, saws, mallets, gouges, plumb lines, etc. These tools measure, tear, trim, and poke at us. Such instruments are useful (*yong* 用) but they also have the power to "cut away" at our natural dispositions (*xing* 性) and thus interfere with *dao* 道-activity.

In order to gain clarity on the nature and potential harm of such tools, we need to consider them in relation to bodily activities specifically. This is an important theme in the *Zhuangzi* and it represents a major topic of philosophical debate in Warring States China. Space will be devoted in chapter 7 to reconstructing this debate for present purposes. Foregrounded is the question of what distinguishes human beings from other animals. The answer is "technology" broadly construed, and this raises the question of whether and how our technologies are good or bad for our physical health.

Philosophically, this question extends deeply; because the technology that *really* distinguishes humans from other animals is that which Dewey calls the "tool of tools"—*language*.[201] Dewey benefits enormously from George Herbert Mead's naturalistic account of the emergence of language in the human animal, and this account will be considered at length in chapter 7. There will be a number of questions with which to experiment as "*specific philosophical relationships*" are made with early Chinese thinking on this issue. How does language relate to nonhuman experience? Does it alienate us from our animal bodies or grant us deeper access to them? Would the "Mouthpiece of *wuwei* 無為" even acknowledge such questions?

The problems that we encounter at the body-technology-language nexus are very important ones. Arguably, they are more acute today than they were in Warring States China. In the present age of social media and digital technologies, it is important to remain mindful of how such instruments affect our bodies-and-minds. As the *Zhuangzi* observes, it appears that we humans have committed ourselves to "using objects to alter our natural dispositions" (*yiwuyiqixing* 以物易其性).[202] Since there is no way back from here, we must reflect on what it means to adopt such technologies intelligently (*ming* 明). Experiments in chapter 7 will probe the insights of Dewey and Daoism on this pressing topic.

7

Bodies and Artifacts

> Human beings are not machines. Machines are cast in molds. They have no life, no individuality. One is exactly like all the others both in form and in function. But in the organic world there is no such complete similarity. Look at the plant life around you. Even the leaves on the same tree, though they look alike, are not precisely alike. Each, in one or another minute respect, is different from all the other leaves on the tree.
>
> —John Dewey, Hangzhou, June 1919

Dewey's Body-Practice

While visiting Japan, Dewey attended an exhibition of *Jūdō* 柔道, the martial arts tradition that translates as the "Gentle Way." He immediately appreciated what he saw. "I have yet to see a Japanese throw his head back when he rises," he observed. "The system . . . is based on the elementary laws of mechanics, a study of the equilibrium of the human body, the ways in which it is disturbed, how to recover your own and take advantage of the shifting of the center of gravity of the other person." *Jūdō* practitioners breathe "always from the abdomen," Dewey noted. "It really is an art."[1]

Dewey's insights into such body-practices were not primarily intellectual. He had by that time been a student of F. Matthias Alexander for over two years. From the time of his youth, Dewey had suffered from eyestrain, back pain, and a stiff neck, and these would flare up whenever he was under psychological stress.[2] During the First World War, when Dewey's support for American involvement was met with derision, he began feeling uneasy about his position and his stress intensified. As Max Eastman remembers, Dewey "got into a state of tension that in most people would have been an illness."[3] In 1916 a friend introduced him to Alexander, an Australian-born physical therapist and author who had developed an original and sophisticated approach to correcting such ailments. The method would come to be known as the "Alexander technique," and it would have a profound effect on Dewey's health. Dewey maintained that Alexander "had completely cured him, that he was able to read and to see and move his neck freely."[4] Friends noticed that Dewey, after becoming Alexander's student, had become "a radically changed person."[5] As Dewey would say: "I used to shuffle and sag. Now I hold myself up."[6]

Alexander came upon his technique by accident. As a young man, he was interested in Shakespearian theatre and studied elocution in the hope of making a career as an actor. Early in his training, however, he experienced tension in his vocal chords and had trouble breathing. He sought professional help, but nothing seemed to improve his condition. He decided to take matters into his own hands. Using an elaborate system of mirrors, he proceeded to observe himself in the act of speaking. He noticed that, just as he was about to speak, he would do three things. First, he would pull his head backwards and down. Second, he would depress his larynx. Third, he would suck air through his mouth. Upon further investigation, Alexander identified the latter two motor responses with his ailment and realized that by keeping his head forward and up they were prevented. So, he decided to keep his head "forward and up."

He focused on this very diligently, "forward and up," "forward and up," but his symptoms persisted. So, once again, he set up mirrors, and soon made a surprising discovery. While putting his mental energy into "forward and up," he reports, "I did not put my head forward and up as I intended, but actually put it back. Here, then, was startling proof that I was doing the opposite of what I believed I was doing and of what I decided I ought to do." The "backwards and down" habit was so strongly connected with the act of speaking that even when Alexander decided to *do* otherwise—and thought that he *was* doing otherwise—the act of speaking still triggered the old habit. He realized that the critical moment in the process, then, was "the moment when the giving of directions merged into 'doing' for the gaining of the end I had decided upon."[7] Alexander found that the actual first step to making the "forward and up" adjustment was to *do nothing*—thereby inhibiting the bad habit that was already integrated with the act. By shifting consciousness *away* from the end intended, he found it easier to reconstruct the *means* by which he spoke. If he focused instead on speaking as the *end*, it only reinforced the means by which he was habitually doing it.

Alexander coined the phrase "end-gaining" to describe the moment in which *doing* eclipses conscious awareness of the means by which something is done. He introduces the phrase "means whereby" to describe motor activities that through "conscious control" could be reconstructed along lines better suited to the optimal performance of the act. In the process of reeducating the body, "the 'means whereby' rather than the end should be held in mind. As long as the 'end' is held in mind instead of the 'means,' the muscular act, or series of acts, will always be performed in accordance with the old habits."[8] After extensive practice, "conscious control" itself became a habit, and Alexander experienced profound transformations in his physical health and mental outlook. He soon turned from acting to teaching, and before long he was living in London working with a number of students, including members of Sir Henry Irving's Queen's Theatre. Alexander eventually relocated to the United States, and Dewey became his pupil. Three decades after beginning his own body-practice, at the age of eighty-seven, Dewey remarked that, "My confidence in Alexander's work is unabated. He has made one of the most important discoveries that has been made in practical application of the unity of the mind-body principle. If it hadn't been for [his] treatment, I'd hardly be here today—as a personal matter."[9]

So in appreciating *Jūdō* and other Japanese arts, Dewey was identifying principles that he knew from his own body-practice. He even wrote to recommend a book on Japanese martial arts to Alexander. "I think a study ought to be made [in Japan] from the standpoint of conscious control," Dewey said.[10] "I think there can be no doubt that in these old ceremonies they had [conscious control] all right, abdominal breathing, lengthening of the spine, and absolute sureness of mental control before they move. I have an enormous respect now for the old etiquette and ceremonies regarded as physical culture," he wrote.[11] "Conscious control," Dewey concludes, "was certainly born and bred in Japan."[12]

Of course, Japanese martial arts are based on Daoist principles, so what Dewey was witnessing was originally born and bred in China. Alexander's technique, in fact, has a lot in common with Daoist practices.[13] The notion of "end-gaining" calls to mind the follies of the Man from Song, whose "shoot pulling" is a kind of heedless and abrupt *doing* that ignores its own means in the process. The notion of "means whereby" calls to mind Cook Ding, whose attentiveness to the intricacies of the ox bone is a kind of *not doing* that holds its end in suspension while caring for its means. Further resembling Daoism, Alexander moves in his philosophical writings beyond clinical application to address the nature of habits in civilized societies and how these relate to the inheritance we receive from our primitive and animal ancestors.

On this latter topic, there are striking parallels between Alexander's thought and the concerns of Daoist primitivism. Alexander believed that our technological environments have caused our native adaptive responses, accumulated over hundreds of thousands of years, to become displaced by less efficient, less healthy, and ultimately less intelligent patterns of behavior. Such distortions in our primitive somatic patterns, he believed, could be transmitted by heredity and thus threatened the ability of the human animal to survive. Impediments to the proper use of the human body, Alexander warned, now surround us—and the dangers are closer than one might think. Scholar and Alexander practitioner Galen Cranz, for instance, provides an eye-opening study of the chair—a common and seemingly innocent piece of furniture, but one that is surprisingly ill suited for maintaining proper posture and health in *Homo sapiens*. Sitting, as Cranz explains, is "hard work." Most chairs place 30 percent more pressure on spinal discs than standing. Even "well-designed" chairs strain the spinal column, back muscles, lower back nerves, and diaphragm.[14]

As Richard Shusterman explains, our modern torrent of somatic-psychic ailments—backaches, headaches, fatigue, tension, anxiety, etc.—"Alexander explained as resulting from a systematic mismatch between our somatic tendencies developed through slow processes of evolution and the very different modern conditions of life and work in which we are forced to function."[15] Alexander, like Dewey, did not envision any wholesale return to primitive life, but instead sought to develop methods by which we could "consciously control" our behavior and intelligently reconstruct our contemporary habits-and-habitats.

Alexander wrote four books, and Dewey provided "Introductions" to three of them. These writings are helpful in locating Dewey's thinking in relation to various tendencies in Daoist philosophy. Dewey agrees with Alexander that the proper reaction to maladjustments caused by civilization is not "a return to nature, a relapse to the simple life, or else flight to some mystic obscurity." Such responses, for Dewey, "represent an attempt at solution through abdication of intelligence." Dewey values spontaneity (or *ziran* 自然)—but he agrees with Alexander that once technology shapes our spontaneous responses it is impossible to recover what they originally were. "The spontaneity of childhood is a delightful and precious thing," Dewey writes, "but in its original and naïve form it is bound to disappear . . . True spontaneity is henceforth not a birth-right but the last term, the consummated conquest, of an art."[16]

Philip J. Ivanhoe writes insightfully on the distinction (but also continuity) between "untutored" and "cultivated" spontaneity in the Chinese tradition. He notes that both the spontaneity valued in Daoist primitivism and that which is valued in Confucianism "not only share a similar formal structure, but to some extent they also always partake of each other." It is not so easy, then, to consider them entirely separately. Given that human experience develops on a nature-culture continuum, one expects to find a single normative measure that enables us to "decide which [forms of spontaneity] are reasonable and good to pursue."[17] Dewey promotes "intelligence" for this office, and designates "art" as any activity that is simultaneously instrumental-and-consummatory (rather than either in alternation or displacement).[18] "Art" for Dewey thus exhibits the same basic feature of intelligence: the *continuity between means-and-end*. Habits *can* be reconstructed within artificial environments "artfully," thus recapturing the spontaneous harmony exhibited in non-human Nature (*tian* 天). The method is one whereby intelligence (*ming* 明) identifies and corrects maladjustments between means-and-ends in human activity. Without this, we risk losing touch with ourselves in the presence of our technologies.

Dewey regarded Alexander's discovery as one that was "necessary to complete the discoveries that have been made about non-human nature, if these discoveries and inventions are not to end by making us their servants and helpless tools."[19] Such concerns echo those of Daoist primitivism. For Dewey, the main question is "whether this physical mastery of physical energies is going to further human welfare, or whether human happiness is going to be wrecked by it." The danger is not merely, or even primarily, with the technologies themselves. The real question is whether or not we are able to preserve our own "wholeness"—i.e., to *use* ourselves in a manner that preserves *dao* 道-activity while taking up ends facilitated by technology. "In the present state of the world," Dewey writes, "it is evident that the control we have gained of physical energies, heat, light, electricity, etc., without having first secured control of our use of ourselves is a perilous affair. Without control of our use of ourselves, our use of other things is blind; it may lead to anything."[20]

Indeed. On February 1, 2012, a twenty-three-year-old man was found dead in an Internet café in Taiwan after ten straight hours of online gaming. The cause of death was sudden cardiac arrest. While his body was removed, the man's arms and fingers remained extended as if still playing at the keyboard. Five months later, another Taiwanese man was found dead after forty hours of continuous online gaming. In 2015, two more men died in Taiwanese Internet cafés, one after three straight days of online gaming and another after five straight days.[21]

These are tragic and extreme examples, but they illustrate how technologies can lure us into radical misuses of the body. Video games are an interesting case. They are a "playing" and a "trying," and as such they are extensions of the hunting vocation. Such games raise dopamine levels in the brain and provide a certain "wholeness" to experience—"They are immersive," explains Susan Greenfield, "offering not just strong sensory stimulation but 'flow,' or the capacity for a gamer to lose himself or herself in the game world and become utterly involved."[22] As Shusterman reminds us, even the "most advanced technologies of virtual reality are still experienced through the body's perceptual equipment and affective sounding board—our sensory organs, brain, glands, and nervous system."[23] These sounding boards, however, evolved in an altogether different reality. Recall the animal predator, whose *whole body* waits as it watches. Existing digital amusements stimulate only *parts* of our "affective sounding board" while leaving other parts idle—taste, smell, touch, and the vestibular system have little to do with the action.

Behavior in such environments, as Dewey would have guessed, turns out to be a "double-barreled" affair. Such "virtual" environments *act back* upon the human sensorium. Numerous studies have tracked brain structural alterations in adolescents who play video games excessively—changes in prefrontal cortex activity; abnormalities in the brain's white matter, affected emotional processing, attention, and decision-making; plus reductions in visual and auditory responsiveness.[24] On the flip side, there is evidence that some video games actually *improve* cognitive and perceptual functions.[25] The most noted improvements are in visual-spatial cognition.[26] As Greenfield reminds us, to "tease out a cause-and-effect sequence" between an individual brain and its environment is next to impossible.[27] What everyone agrees on, however, is that technological environments have the power to reconstruct our bodies-and-brains.

For Dewey and Alexander, each new technology calls for somatic awareness and conscious control of bodily use. Such practice becomes extremely important in times of rapid technological change. Those of us who hit "Send" for the first time in 1993 as adults remember the world before the arrival of the Digital Age. As children, our cognitive habits were shaped in environments that were markedly different from today's "digital natives." Is this a good thing? In the abstract, changes in technologically induced habits are neither better nor worse. As William James suggests, the only ground upon which any goodness rests is that of some concrete demand. Most organisms, in the process of carrying out their life-activities, demand to minimize difficulty and maximize ease and equilibrium. Tools can assist us—*or not*—depending on the situation that the organism and its technologies find themselves in. Judgment as to whether we are being helped or harmed by our technologies cannot be reached by looking at the technologies themselves or at the organism in isolation. Organism-technology relations index whole situations and such situations are the proper objects of critical inquiry.

There is a story in the *Zhuangzi* that helps to direct attention toward technological situations rather than their separate terms. Confucius' disciple, Zigong, was travelling in the south and came upon a peasant who had dug channels in the ground to transport water from his well. He used old jugs to lug the water up from the depths. "There is an instrument for that sort of thing," Zigong tells him. He proceeds to explain the principle of the well sweep (*gao* 槔), which uses a long pole anchored in the center to create a fulcrum to counter-balance the weight, making the retrieval of water easy. The farmer was unimpressed. "Where there are mechanical (*ji* 機) instruments, there are bound to be mechanical doings," he said, "and where there are mechanical doings, there are bound to be mechanical minds."²⁸

This story is generally used to illustrate what Joseph Needham calls Daoism's "anti-technology complex."²⁹ As Graham Parkes observes, however, while the story "is at first puzzling, since the gardener's rejection of such a benign labor-saving device seems uncharacteristically rigid and narrow," the farmer actually objects not to the well sweep *per se* but to a certain "frame of mind" that technological development encourages.³⁰ Such enthusiasm simply assumes that each new instrumentality improves a given situation.

We all have our own "well sweep" moments. Trustworthy people tell me that using an interactive, Internet-based calendar through my phone would make things easier for me and save me time. I believe them, but I continue to use the same (paper) calendar system that I have used for years. *Why?* The obvious reason is that it has become a habit. Not so evident, perhaps, is that in addition to working it provides me with a uniform physical archive (almost like a set of diaries), satisfies me emotionally (entries often resemble how I feel about them, and I enjoy scratching out disagreeable events when they are cancelled), works for me aesthetically (I write things in different sizes and in different colors according to whim), and it provides me with a sense of rhythm (with each full calendar one year ends, and with each fresh calendar another year begins). The digital calendar, I am sure, would be more efficient, save time, and provide a range of new instrumentalities—but only at the expense of these other virtues.

I have zero interest in switching to the digital calendar. Such resistance, I suspect, mirrors the kind of reaction that Dewey identifies with the primitive mind's "repugnance to what we term a higher plane of life," one that is "not due to stupidity or dullness or apathy—or to any other merely negative qualities," but instead "to the fact that in the new occupations [the primitive mind] does not have so clear or so intense a sphere for the display of intellectual and practical skill, or such opportunity for the dramatic play of emotion."³¹ Serious words for a personal calendar, but examples like the well sweep are similarly mundane. Even though the farmer exerts more energy and time *not* using the well sweep, he may have grown adept at pulling up the water, and perhaps he enjoys some private, untold pleasures in doing so. As William James would say: "Hands off."

Again, the argument for adopting or not adopting a particular technology is neither rational nor irrational. It rests instead on the concrete relation between specific body-mind habits in each human organism and the technologies in question. Dewey's own body-practice taught him that existential "wholeness," not detached reason, was the final arbiter of normative claims about particular technologies. In order to arrive at such claims, an analysis of how *we* are being used in the transaction needs to be included. In the modern age, humans have mastered the environment to a remarkable extent through tools. The problem, Dewey writes, is that "the one factor which is the primary tool in the use of all these other tools, namely ourselves . . . our own psycho-physical disposition, as the basic condition of our employment of all agencies and energies, has not even been studied as the central instrumentality."[32]

In early Chinese philosophy, the status of our psycho-physical dispositions (*xing* 性) becomes central in the debate over human technologies. This wide-ranging debate addresses the complex relationship between innovation, non-human nature, and artifice. What follows is an attempt to reconstruct some of the main points in this multifaceted debate, one that implicates nearly every major Warring States thinker. Once such points are articulated, they will serve as a productive basis on which to experiment with questions having to do with the relationship between technology and the body, the nature of the human self, and what makes humans distinct from other animals. Whatever digression the following requires will be worth it as we proceed.

Animal Bodies and Rival Anthropologies

Animals do not fare especially well in classical Confucianism. Zigong is chided for grudging the sacrificial sheep, Confucius neglects to ask about the horses when the stable catches fire, and Mencius advises those disturbed by animal suffering to steer clear of the kitchen.[33] If animals had a voice in Confucian literature, they might take issue with such indignities. True, Mencius advises "concern" for living creatures—but even then, what he really means to say is that "kindness" and "affection" should be reserved for those in the human world.[34] Humans come first in Confucianism, and animals are always on the outside. For Confucians, the term "animal" (*shou* 獸) is a boundary concept separating the qualitatively "human" (*ren* 人) from everything else.

While this preoccupation is widely recognized, not so widely recognized is how it reflects the ontological contingency of the "Human/Animal" distinction in early China. As John Knoblock observes:

> In Western thought the position of humanity is secure, having at creation been given dominion over the beasts, but in Chinese thought there is no such divinely sanctioned superiority. Thus, humanity's present position of superiority is attributable to the sages, who invented the various cultural objects that now give people superiority. The history of these sages is the story of the ascent of humanity from the level of the beasts.[35]

As Knoblock suggests, the Chinese world is not premised on any *essential* superiority of human nature over animal nature. Rather, it is premised on its *achieved* superiority.

The "Human/Animal" distinction is thus understood differently in early China than in the Greek-medieval tradition. As Roel Sterckx argues, the classification of animals into types (*lei* 類) did not involve an appeal to shared essences or natural kinds. Again, if anything, animals were classified according to the territories they inhabited. The "human" (*ren* 人) designation, similarly, was not understood as an "essential category that was ontologically differentiated from everything nonhuman."[36] Rather, humans were understood to be natural creatures whose moral and social achievements distinguished them from other animals. As Mencius understands it, this distinction is "slight" (*xi* 希) and could be lost.[37] The traits that now separate humans from animals are the result of the historical efforts of the sages: those who first established "human" practices in the distant past. The implication is that these achievements, if not sustained, could be reversed.

It is helpful to keep these developments in perspective. Current research in paleoanthropology suggests that separate hominid species survived alongside anatomically modern humans in East Asia much longer than we thought. The identification of the "Red Deer Cave people" (*maludongren* 馬鹿洞人) in 2008 confirmed through radiocarbon dating that there were creatures not "us" but like us right up until 11,500 BCE. The "Red Deer Cave" people, research suggests, "share no particular affinity with either Pleistocene East Asians [or] recent East Asians," indicating that "the evolutionary history of humans in East Asia is more complex than has been understood until now."[38] The "Red Deer Cave people" join the ranks of the Denisovans in Siberia and *Homo floresiensis* in Indonesia—the "Hobbit people" who averaged a diminutive 3-feet in stature and had no chins. These creatures were our terrestrial contemporaries.[39] By the age of the "Yellow Emperor" (*Huangdi* 黃帝), modern *Homo sapiens* had the line well secured—but this follows on a 1.8-million-year history of *Homo erectus*. Only fairly recently then did the historical sages embark upon the work that made us distinctly "human."

Across the classical literature, anthropological narratives identify specific sages with specific developments and invent the "Human/Animal" boundary in the process. As Mark Edward Lewis notes, these narratives are anything but objective. Accounts of how the sages separated humans from animals serve as rhetorical weapons in interschool debates. As Lewis observes, "each textual tradition identified its teachings with the essentials of civilization, and denounced rivals as later versions of a primitive bestiality."[40] The *Mencius* is especially explicit in using anthropological narratives to cast its opponents as nonhumans. In one instance, Mencius identifies the advent of the human experience with the reign of Yao and Shun and proceeds to explain how their Minister of Education, Xie, taught people human relationships (*renlun* 人倫)—thus separating humans from animals. Mencius' objection to the teachings of his rivals is that each fails to acknowledge one of the relationships that elevated humans from their animal-like condition. Mohism fails to acknowledge fathers, and Yangism fails to acknowledge rulers, and "without rulers and fathers, we are animals."[41]

In addition to animalizing Yangism and the Mohists,[42] the *Mencius* also de-humanizes various primitive-oriented positions. Again, the exact contours of "Yangism," "agriculturalism," and "primitivism" in the *Zhuangzi* remain unclear. Whatever the relationship is between these schools, however, in the larger polemical context they cooperate in criticizing Confucianism and the Confucians attack them in return. Mencius, for instance, takes aim at the "agriculturalist" position when discussing one of its patron sages, Hou Ji. While he "taught the people to sow and reap and to cultivate the five grains," the *dao* 道 of humans is such that if we are "well fed and warmly clothed but dwell idle without education, then we become little more than birds and animals."[43] Suggested here is that agricultural technologies and farming-based societies are not enough to sustain a qualitatively "human" experience. Social instruments of the type that Xie created are also required.

Mencius offers this lesson to a follower of Shennong, the sage most closely associated with the agriculturalist tradition. A. C. Graham identifies this obscure group (the *Nongjia* 農家) as the philosophical school about which "we know the least" in early China.[44] We do know that Confucians portrayed them in animal terms, not only in the *Mencius* but also in later strata of the *Analects*. Confucius and Zilu, we learn, once encountered two farmer-types yoked together pulling a plow. Zilu asks them where to ford the river, and they reply by asking, "Who is that holding the reins of your carriage?" In this scene, interlocutors already occupy the relative positions of animal and human. Plows were ox-drawn in China, and our two "agriculturalists" have harnessed themselves to a plow. Meanwhile, Confucius holds the reins of his carriage—controlling his own relation to his technology. From the Confucian perspective, the two animalized yokels disregard the "rightful social duties and the elaborations of culture [that] are part of any properly human life."[45] Disgusted, the Master remarks: "We cannot flock with the birds and animals (*niaoshou* 鳥獸). Am I not one among the humans of the world? If not with humans, then with whom should I associate?"[46]

Graham maintains that the cultivation of Shennong as a patron sage marked the first stage in a process that is "traced right through the classical age: the invention or adoption of prehistoric [sages] representing new philosophical or political ideals."[47] This process came to merge with the generation of anthropological narratives that identified patron sages with the advent of the "human" (ren 人) category. The "agriculturalist" tradition, however, suggests that these elements are separable. While its teachings are scattered and obscure, there is nothing to indicate that the Shennong movement was intent on identifying itself as "human" and casting its rivals as animals. In fact, the opposite is the case. By all accounts, the Shennong idealists were comfortable being associated with animals. In the "Robber Chi" (daozhi 盜跖) chapter of the Zhuangzi we read that: "In Shennong's time people laid down tired and got up wide-awake. They knew their mothers but not their fathers and lived together with the deer. They farmed their own food and wove their own clothes and had no idea of hurting each other. This was the high point of power (de 德)."[48]

As in the Book of Lord Shang (Shangjunshu 商君書), the narrative continues by associating the fall from this primitive state with the emergence of the "Yellow Emperor" who invented the quintessentially "human" (ren 人) institutions of State and Warfare. It teaches that the Confucian patron sages arose within this lamentable context only to further distance people from their innocent, animal origins. As Graham indicates, the state of "knowing mothers but not fathers" implies an "absolutely primitive existence."[49] At the very least it represents a stage prior to the advent of "fatherhood" (fu 父)—a social role that Confucians regard as absolutely indispensable to any qualitatively "human" experience.

The "agriculturalist" challenge is a provocative one. Like "primitivism" in general, the argument is that optimal power (de 德) is located in pre-human experience and that becoming human signals a decline from the apotheosis of natural efficacy. Cosmogonies such as the Hengxian underwrite such propositions. "Originally everything was good (shan 善)," we read, "there was order and no befuddlement. Once there were humans (ren 人), however, there was no-good (bushan 不善). Befuddlement emerges from human beings."[50]

Textual evidence makes it difficult to arrange moves in any chronological order, but we do see the Confucian tradition responding to such misanthropic assertions. The tradition begins to identify its ideals more closely with Nature (tian 天) and with our natural dispositions (xing 性) in their raw state. Mark Csikszentmihalyi argues that such responses result in a more "materialistic" conception of Confucian virtues, conceptions that associate Confucian ideals with bodily experiences generally.[51] The most familiar example is Mencius' claim that Confucian virtues are like four sprouts (siduan 四端), as integral to human nature as the four limbs (siti 四體).[52] As Csikszentmihalyi sees it, challenges in the Zhuangzi are not a "discrete catalyst" prompting such moves, but rather a "continuing process" driving the Confucian tradition to more and more forcefully materialize its virtues.[53] In whatever order this occurs, Confucians begin to appropriate physiology and physiognomy into their positions. Confucian moral character becomes increasingly connected to the body: to physical appearance and deportment, and Confucian virtues become correlated with specific bodily organs.

Marching in to disrupt this newly emerging Confucian picture is a parade of mutilated criminals and freaks—the *Zhuangzi*'s response to the equation of Confucian moral character with socially prescribed physical appearance and deportment. The title of the relevant chapter, "*De* Satisfies the Tally" (*dechongfu* 德充符), is a way of saying that one's native *de* is already whole and valid as it is—a kind of "claim tag" or "ticket" (*fu* 符). Again—the price of admission is paid in full by all who are "here" (*you* 有). The lesson is that even abnormal forms (*xing* 形) remain in full possession of their charisma or power (*de*) and that the derivative, moralized "virtues" (*de*) that Confucians add to the "tally" are superfluous and taxing.

Meanwhile, in pincer-like fashion, the "Webbed Toes" (*pianmu* 駢拇) chapter moves in to attack the Confucian appropriation of major bodily organs:

> Those who are crafty enough in their use of humanity (*ren* 仁) and appropriateness (*yi* 義) try to correlate them to the five vital organs, but this is not the correct approach to the proper way and power (*daode* 道德). To web toes together is to add a useless flap of flesh. To branch another finger off the hand is to sprout a useless digit. When craftiness webs or grafts something extra on to the five vital organs in their uncontrived state (*qing* 情), it makes for a distorted and perverse application of "humanity" and "appropriateness."[54]

Rather than being regarded as features that are integrally related to the body and to its native disposition (*xing* 性), Confucian virtue is presented here as extraneous to the body. However it might hurt to remove such alien appendages, they are useless from the bodily standpoint and serve no purpose (*wuyong* 無用).

At some juncture, Confucian narratives emerge to better bridge the divide between the human and pre-human realms. Sages are again evoked for this purpose. The sage Fuxi figures prominently in this context. He is recognized as the domesticator of animals, the inventor of hunting, and the compiler of the trigrams in the *Book of Changes*. The account of Fuxi's development of the latter represents a new approach. According to the "Appended Statements" (*Xicizhuan* 繫辭專) of the *Book of Changes*, the establishment of the trigram system preceded anthropogenic technologies in areas as diverse as hunting, agriculture, transportation, architecture, and funerary practices. Such developments, according to this account, were facilitated through reflection on the natural patterns exhibited in the trigrams themselves:

> In ancient times, Fuxi was ruler of everything under the sky. Looking up, he observed forms in the heavens. Looking down, he observed regularities on the land. He observed the patterns (*wen* 文) of the birds and animals, and how they adapted to the land. Close at hand, he considered his own body. From a distance, he considered other things. He then created (*zuo* 作) the eight trigrams in order to connect with the efficacious powers of spirit and intelligence (*ming* 明), using [the trigrams] to classify the qualities of the myriad things.[55]

Fuxi begins by observing other animals, as well as his own body. Each of these exhibits pre-human patterns and qualities, and these patterns and qualities inform the hexagram system. Subsequent human technologies are then correlated with the hexagrams that inspired them. The creation (*zuo*) of knotted fishing nets, for instance, becomes associated with the *li* 離 hexagram, and so on. In this way, anthropogenic technologies are presented as extensions of patterns (*wen*) latent in the pre-human world. According to this account, such patterns themselves indicate the underlying traits of nature.

In this narrative, the sagely creation of the "human" (*ren* 人) world does not constitute any severance from nonhuman Nature (*tian* 天). It marks instead an unbroken continuity—a seamless emergence. As Michael J. Puett argues, the glossing of *zuo* 作 as "rising up" (*qi* 起) in the *Shuowen* lexicon is a direct result of its usage in this context. The "term *zuo* is used for the act of lifting up natural patterns and bringing them to the realm of humanity," he writes, "a process that involves no sense of discontinuity from nature and hence no notion of artifice."[56]

With Confucians now more forcefully locating human ideals in pre-human Nature (*tian* 天) and in the animal body, critiques in the *Zhuangzi* take aim accordingly. Targeted are the anthropological narratives that celebrate the sagely act of lifting human culture from its animal origins and developing the native tendencies of the body in the process. Here, the "primitivist" view offers an alternative narrative of human emergence, one that defends the body by repudiating the sagely act of creation. As Harold D. Roth observes, this counter-narrative "looks back to a tribal Utopia in which [humans] lived as spontaneously as the animals."[57] These are the pre-human ancestors who "stayed home without knowing what they were doing" and "drummed on their bellies, amusing themselves." But not for long, because "along came the sages, who with the bending and twisting of ritual and music sought to correct the organic forms of the world." The disastrous result, we are told, is "entirely the fault of the sages." Noteworthy in this narrative is the suggestion that Confucian cultural instruments violate organic form (*xing* 形) itself. According to this line of reasoning, bodies were being used to the extent of their abilities (*neng* 能) in their native state. The sage arrives only to introduce additional operations associated with ritual and music, thereby "over-extending" these bodies. "[Yao and Shun] tormented the five organs in the service of humanity and appropriateness, and taxed the blood and energy (*qi* 氣) in establishing standards and measures."[58] Thus it is argued that Confucian-generated "humans" do not arise seamlessly from nonhuman nature. Rather, they violate bodies themselves.

Within this context, the organic body or form (*xing* 形) surfaces as a multidimensional standpoint in the *Zhuangzi*. As the substrate that humans and animals share, it becomes implicated in debates over how humans and animals both relate and differ. On the one hand, the body represents that which is uncontrived and genuine (*qing* 情). Here, we detect a more "Yangist" concern with nurturing its natural disposition (*xing* 性). On the other hand, the body stands in defiance of the anthropological narratives that presume that Confucian sages (especially Yao and Shun) introduced a qualitatively better, "human" experience through cultural instrumentation. Here, we detect a more "primitivist" or "agriculturalist" concern with restoring pre-human, animal-like *dao* 道-practices. These standpoints overlap, but they also function separately.

To clarify how, one can refer to the former, "Yangist" position as the "animal-body-*subject*" standpoint and to the latter, "primitivist" or "agricultural" position as the "animal-body-*object*" standpoint. To recognize the difference, consider the usefulness (*yong* 用) of anthropogenic technologies in relation to each. The "Webbed Toes" chapter assumes the standpoint of the animal-body-*subject* and declares that Confucian appendages serve no purpose (*wuyong* 無用)—like fleshy lumps, extra fingers, or warts. From another angle, however, "usefulness" or "purposefulness" is precisely what motivates the introduction of such appendages, which stand metaphorically for Confucian cultural instruments. From the animal-body-*object* standpoint, such accessories serve specifically *human* purposes—bridles, rings, and cruppers. Accordingly, Burton Watson detects that the "symbolism seems to shift" in these chapters, with the same bodily appendages representing both natural and anthropogenic features. He concludes that this "[does] some violence to the logic of the argument."[59] I disagree. The animal-body-*object* and animal-body-*subject* perspectives are meant to intersect in the *Zhuangzi*. The "logic" of the argument requires us to toggle between them.

The key difference between these positions is that, from the animal-body-*object* standpoint, the "Human/Animal" distinction has already been established—that is, the distinction between "human" features and the native genuineness (*qing* 情) of the primitive animal-body-*subject* has already been drawn. The "God of the North Sea" occupies such a standpoint, and from there looks back on the animal-body-*subject* as something that has been lost. "Cows and horses have four legs, this is called 'Natural' (*tian* 天). The bridle around the horse's head and the rings in the cow's nose, this is called 'Human,'" he explains. "Hence it is said, 'Do not use the Human to destroy the Natural. Do not use what is purposeful (*gu* 故) to destroy what is given . . . this is called returning to the genuine (*qing*).'"[60] From the animal-body-*object* standpoint, a bridle on a horse and rings on a cow are "useful" for human purposes, while from the animal-body-*subject* standpoint, such appendages are like extra fingers or warts—alien and "useless." Again, these two standpoints are perfectly coincident, but also distinct.

Critiques in the *Zhuangzi* are launched from both standpoints, and sometimes the same critique can be read from more than one standpoint. From the standpoint of the "Human/Animal" distinction, the *Zhuangzi* relates that when human purposes intervene to direct the activities of the animal-body-*object* the outcome is invariably bad for the animal. Consider the lesson from the "Horse's Hooves" (*mati* 馬蹄) chapter:

> As for Horses, their hooves are for treading on frost and snow. Their coats are for keeping out the wind and cold. They munch grass, drink from streams, and lift their feet to gallop. This is the genuine nature of horses. Even if they had fancy terraces and fine halls, they would find no use for them. But then along comes Bo Le, saying, "I'm good at managing horses." He proceeds to brand them, shave them, clip them, bridle them, fetter them with martingale and crupper, tie them up in stable and stall, until about a quarter of the horses have dropped dead. Then he proceeds to starve them, parch them, race them, gallop them, pull them into a line, torment them in the front with the bit and rein and from behind by the whip and spur. By that time, over half of the horses drop dead.[61]

So it is that human purposes destroy animal bodies. But how are we to read this? Remember, there are *two* standpoints to be taken here. In addition to the standpoint of the "Human/Animal" distinction, there is the standpoint of the animal-body-*subject*, prior to that distinction. Read from this perspective, humans *are* animals. Humans have animal bodies just as horses do. The appeal made on behalf of the horse-body is just as easily made on behalf of *our* bodies when our own technologies, as Dewey says, "end by making us their servants and helpless tools."[62]

Accordingly, the "Optimal Happiness" (*zhile* 至樂) chapter presents a list of uniquely "human" purposes and describes their effects in purely physical terms:

> People in the world honor the following: riches, eminence, legacy, and being good for something . . . If they do not obtain these things, they become greatly concerned and anxious. Is this not a stupid way to treat the *body*? . . . The wealthy are worn out with frantic work, they accumulate more stuff than they can possibly use. Treating the body this way only alienates it. The eminent worry day and night about whether they are good or not. Treating the body this way is to neglect it.[63]

In this instance, in what is likely a "Yangist" voice, we find an approach that caters to one "who prefers the comforts and limitations of private life to the prospects and dangers of office."[64] Typical of what A. C. Graham calls Yangism's "meticulous weighing of means and ends," the health of the body (*xing* 形) is deemed too valuable to sacrifice for Confucian ends.[65]

Here, Dewey would be more sympathetic with the Confucian side. Still, he would agree with the premise that the body provides a critical baseline and source for valuative reference—as such, it needs to be preserved for the normative insight that it gives. As Mark Johnson observes, although Dewey "did not have the benefit of the elaborate analyses from today's cognitive science," he understood that " 'higher' cognitive activities were grounded in, and shaped by, activities of bodily perception and movement."[66] As Dewey observes, such bodily experiences "give us our *sense* of rightness and wrongness."[67] From his own body practice, Dewey also knew, as the *Zhuangzi* teaches, that "knowing what Nature (*tian* 天) does, and knowing what the Human (*ren* 人) does, is the optimal standpoint."[68] Organically, the body performs myriad operations, and "we are not aware of the qualities of many or most of these acts; we do not objectively distinguish and identify them." Behaviors "acquired in connection with the use of tools and of language," however, "exercise a profound influence upon organic feelings." In this category, Dewey includes "*all* the consequences of tools and language—in short, [of] civilization." The behavior of civilized adults reflects organic modifications thus undergone, and "in so far as these involve mal-coordinations, fixations and segregations (as they assuredly come to do in a very short time for those living in complex 'artificial' conditions), sensory appreciation is confused, perverted and falsified."[69]

Dewey appeals directly to F. Matthias Alexander in noting that the resulting habits can "lose their immediate certainty and efficiency, and become subject to all kinds of aberrations."[70] He knew from personal experience that the Alexander technique could disrupt the "perverted consciousness" that "accompanies our wrongly-adjusted psycho-physical mechanisms," and thus afford us "new sensory observations," resulting in "new [and better] attitudes and habits."[71] Alexander taught Dewey to focus his awareness such that he could observe both the animal-body-*object* and the animal-body-*subject* standpoints—the "Human" (*ren* 人) and the "Natural" (*tian* 天)—in order to critically reflect on how these factors worked together in his experience. The continuity between technology and nature, for Dewey as for Alexander, was never in question. Transactions between them resulted not in any sharp bifurcation, but in habitual activities that were either well or poorly adjusted to specific situations.

"Only when organic activity achieves a conscious plane," Dewey writes, "shall we be adequately aware of what we are about." That is true, but it is difficult for most of us to occupy at length the standpoint of the animal-body-*subject* without practicing mindfulness meditation or other techniques in a serious way. Otherwise, we tend to recover our bodies only sporadically. Dewey was aware of this. As he says: "The occasions in which a human being responds to things as merely physical in purely physical ways are comparatively rare." He cites as examples jumping at a sudden noise, withdrawing our hand from heat, and our "animal-like basking in sunshine."[72] As we will see in chapter 1 of volume two, such experiences become enveloped in higher-order mental operations almost as soon as they happen.

Daoists also recognize that the animal-body-*subject* standpoint, which stands prior to the "Human/Animal" distinction, is not easily occupied. According to the *Zhuangzi*, the You Yu lineage that descends from Shun (thus representing Confucian anthropological narratives) is to blame for making it so difficult for us to recover this standpoint that we share with other animals. It is explained, however, that the mythical Tai lineage preserved this standpoint. In one of the most intriguing counter-narratives in the *Zhuangzi*, "Master Vine Clothes" (*puyizi* 蒲衣子) explains the difference:

> The You Yu lineage cannot touch the Tai lineage. The You Yu lineage still retains "humanity" in order to demand things of people and recruit them. It never happened that they began to extricate themselves from the "Not Human" (*feiren* 非人). The

Tai lineage, on the other hand, slept soundly and woke up fresh. One moment they regarded themselves as horses, and the next moment they regarded themselves as oxen. Their understanding was uncontrived and genuine (*qing* 情). It never happened that they entered the realm of "Not Human" to begin with.[73]

The standpoint preserved in the Tai lineage is prior to the "Human/Animal" distinction—prior, that is, to any move that construes animals as "other than human" (*feiren*). The "other than human" distinction is one that emerges only from the "human" (*ren*) side. In fact, the human standpoint emerges simultaneously *with* the distinction. It never occurred to the Tai lineage to draw this distinction. Thus, they never distinguished themselves as "Human" or "Not Human" in relation to it. In other words, they preserved without defilement the original animal-body-*subject* standpoint.

With respect to the aims and methods of intra-cultural philosophy, the treatment of the "Human/Animal" distinction in the *Zhuangzi* is particularly instructive. It models how one might toggle between nature and culture critically while avoiding the dualisms and reductionisms that often attend such inquiries. Plus, since the "Human/Animal" distinction is presumed to be neither ontologically fixed nor supernaturally sanctioned in early China, it affords ample critical space for intelligence (*ming* 明) to maneuver. With such a model in mind, we continue to inquire into what it is that distinguishes humans from other animals, and we do so interested in how this relates back to the animal-body standpoints presented in the *Zhuangzi*. Philosophers in early China as well as in the West converge in understanding the crucial difference between human and nonhuman animals to involve our signature technology: that which Dewey calls the "tool of tools."[74]

Language and the Human Difference

How does language relate to nonhuman experience? How does it emerge from nature? How does it act back upon nature? These are large questions that cut across multiple fields. Here, the most that will be attempted is to establish the continuity of language with nonhuman activity and to discuss some of its principle functions in human experience. Dewey benefitted so significantly from George Herbert Mead's naturalistic account of language that we will focus primarily on that. Mead's account is original and insightful, holds up well to contemporary scientific scrutiny, and is regularly misunderstood—all features that recommend it for further study. There are also "*specific* philosophical relationships" to observe between Mead and the Confucian thinker, Xunzi. Such connections are striking and will be explored.

While "Master Vine Clothes" disparages the You Yu lineage for inventing the "human" by making the "Human/Not Human" distinction, the idea that humans emerge in the act of making such distinctions is welcomed in the philosophy of Xunzi. Xunzi lives toward the end of the Warring States period, enabling him to assess the classical Confucian tradition fully and to respond to critiques made against it. He circumvents animal critiques in the *Zhuangzi* by simply accepting them. He affirms that Confucian innovations are artifices (*wei* 偽) added on to our original natures,[75] he rejects the increasingly tenuous claims of "material virtue" thinking,[76] and he abandons the claim that Confucian ideals are prefigured in Nature (*tian* 天).[77] Xunzi asserts instead that: "What makes humans 'Human' lies not in being featherless bipeds, but in having the ability to make distinctions (*bian* 辨)."[78] While continuing to possess their animal bodies, human beings are fundamentally *social* creatures with a unique ability to distinguish themselves from other animals on that basis. Xunzi writes:

> Fire and water possess energy (*qi* 氣) but have no life. Plants and trees have life, but lack awareness. Birds and animals have awareness, but lack any moral sense (*yi* 義). Humans possess energy, life, awareness, and a moral sense. This is why humans are the noblest beings in the world. In physical power, they are not as strong as oxen; and in swiftness, they cannot match the horse. But horses and oxen are put to use by humans. Why is this? Because humans have sociality (*qun* 群) and other animals do not.[79]

Xunzi acknowledges that other animals do "congregate" (*qun*) into groups. The distinctive feature of humans, however, is that we organize ourselves into ritually delineated social roles. Again, humans are those who make "distinctions," and as Xunzi sees it: "When it comes to distinctions, none are more important than social roles (*fen* 分); and in establishing social roles, nothing is more important than ritual-custom (*li* 禮)."[80]

The meaning of *fen* 分 in this context extends from "division," to "share," to "portion," to "role."[81] The modern notion of "personal identity" (*shenfen* 身份) can thus be understood as a function of one's "share" in the social order, facilitated by the conventions of ritual-custom and constituted by the roles one assumes. Human experience takes on its distinguishing moral features as a result of adopting such roles. As Kurtis Hagen observes, Xunzi's use of the binomial *liyi* 禮義 underscores the inseparability of ritual-custom and moral sense in his thinking.[82] It is not simply that human beings differ from animals in *having* a moral sense (*yi* 義). Rather, human beings organize themselves into societies in which roles and relationships give rise to selves that have a moral dimension. Since other animals do not organize themselves in such a way, Xunzi suggests that they lack both moral sense and personal selves.

By extension, nonhuman animals display little use of the means by which humans secure such features—namely, *language*. Like other Confucians, Xunzi regards the ancient sages as those who originally created (*zuo* 作) the human experience. The distinctions that they made in doing so were preserved in the form of names (名 *ming*) passed down from antiquity. While he does not mention language explicitly when distinguishing humans from other animals, it is difficult to imagine what "making distinctions" (*bian* 辨) would mean in the absence of language. Thus for Xunzi, the "Human" world is not simply a world of rituals, roles, and moral acts. It is also and more fundamentally a world of *meanings, names,* and *significant gestures*.

There are multiple connections to observe between Xunzi's thinking and that of George Herbert Mead. As Dewey's Chicago friend and colleague, Mead had a tremendous influence on Dewey's intellectual development. "I dislike to think what my own thinking might have been were it not for the seminal ideas which I derived from him," said Dewey. Mead's thought, he relates, "worked a revolution in my own thinking though I was slow in grasping anything like its full implications."[83] It has been observed elsewhere that Mead's philosophy resonates broadly with early Confucian thinking.[84] In the present context, it assists in the construction of a richer empirical framework in which to consider the "Human/Animal" distinction and how it relates back to the animal-body standpoints in the *Zhuangzi*.

Like Xunzi, Mead regards social distinctions as the key to the "Human/Animal" difference. He begins by considering organisms in general, finding that "the behavior of all living organisms has a basically social aspect." Mead continues:

> [Fundamental biological impulses] are social in character or have social implications, since they involve or require social situations and relations for their satisfaction by any given individual organism . . . All living organisms are bound up in a general social environment or situation, in a complex of social interrelations and interactions upon which their continued existence depends.

Beginning with insects, Mead observes that such creatures exhibit social organization and functional differentiation to an astonishing degree. Bees and ants maintain complex colonies with various functions performed by "queens," "drones," and "workers." Mead cautions, however, that we must avoid being "anthropomorphic in our accounts of the life of bees and ants." As he sees it, differentiation in insect societies has a fundamentally different cause than role differentiation in human societies. In insect societies, functional differentiation is the result of *physiological* differences. Members of insect societies are structurally different, resulting in the discharge of different functions in their social environments. Human societies are also physiologically divisible into male and female members, but "such differentiation is not the principle of organization in human society," submits Mead.[85] Human societies are instead organized as a result of "significant communication" in the form of human language and symbolic interaction.

It is tempting to read Mead as thus reifying the "Human/Animal" divide at the threshold of language. Indeed, some of Mead's students assert stridently that animals cannot possibly have language, despite evidence to the contrary.[86] Mead's own position on the matter is more nuanced. He is mindful of the perils of drawing sharp distinctions between humans and animals on language use. Even with respect to insects, he writes:

> [This distinction] still has to be made with reservations, because it may be that there will be some way of discovering in the future a language among the ants and bees. We do find, as I have said, a differentiation of physiological characters which so far explain the peculiar organization of these insect societies. Human society, then, is dependent upon the development of language for its own distinctive form of organization.[87]

Rhoda Wilkie and Andrew McKinnon help to correct the "myth" that Mead intends to divide humans and animals sharply in terms of language use, citing several ambiguities in his writings relating to the issue. As they see it: "Mead does clearly and repeatedly argue that human beings are distinctive *in the extent* to which they use significant gestures, and *in the extent* to which human social organization is dependent on significant gestures," but this is a matter of degree rather than an "absolute difference."[88]

In any case, as we will see, Mead locates the precursors of language deep in the animal world. His comment about insects demonstrates that he does not rule out the possibility of language at subhuman levels. For Mead, the existence of animal language is an empirical question, and definitive answers are not easy to come by. His main argument is that, empirically, there is a readily observable difference between the *primary* principles of organization operative in nonhuman and human societies respectively: one is primarily physiological and the other is primarily symbolic.

These basic principles also find expression in Xunzi's philosophy. Xunzi observes that animals can be differentiated into "male and female" (*pinmu* 牝牡) but cannot be differentiated into "man and woman" (*nannü* 男女). The first is a purely physiological difference, while the latter is wholly reliant on the ability to make distinctions (*bian* 辨). "Man and Woman" are names (*ming* 名) given to social roles (*fen* 分) constructed to delineate expectations in a humanly constructed social system. Other animals do not designate and rely upon such social roles.

To reiterate his point, Xunzi evokes the difference between simply fathering offspring and being a proper "father" (*fu* 父) to one's children, with all its responsibilities and special affections (*qin* 親).[89] This position is echoed in the "Summary of Ritual-Custom" (*Quli* 曲禮) chapter of the *Rituals*, which states: "Parrots can speak (*yan* 言), but this is not something that distinguishes them from other birds. Apes can speak, but this is not something that distinguishes them from other animals. When people today have no ritual-custom (*li* 禮) and yet speak, their minds (*xin* 心) are no different from such animals." Here, it is not just "speaking" that distinguishes humans—even parrots and apes can do that—more importantly it is the *distinctions* that humans make in terms of ritually delineated social roles *when* they speak. The passage continues: "Animals are those who are without ritual-custom, and that is why fathers and offspring share their female mates indiscriminately. Thus, the sages engaged in the act of creation (*zuo* 作)—making (*wei* 為) ritual-custom in order to instruct people. Having ritual-customs enables humans to recognize that only through *these* do they differ from other animals."[90]

What "speaking" (*yan* 言) means in this context is unclear. Does it mean language? Does it mean just making sounds? Likely something in the middle, if *yan* is something that parrots, apes, and other animals do. Human speaking is different for Xunzi only when it results in ritually delineated roles, which he associates with the act of naming (*ming* 名). His philosophy of naming is outlined in the "Rectification of Names" (*Zhengming* 正名) chapter of the *Xunzi*. Its most important passage is also its most controversial:

> Names (*ming* 名) have no intrinsic fit (*yi* 宜). Agreement is made and then a command (*ming* 命). Once agreement becomes set, a custom is established and [the name] is called "fit." What deviates from the agreed use is called "not fit." Names have no intrinsic actuality (*shi* 實). An agreement is made, and then there is a command [for] such actuality (*mingshi* 命實). Once agreement becomes set, a custom is established and this is called the name of the actuality. Names *do* have intrinsic goodness (*shan* 善). When they are direct, easy, and not at odds, then they are called good names.[91]

For obvious reasons, this passage triggers debates among scholars about whether or not Xunzi is a "realist." Kurtis Hagen carefully scrutinizes the most prominent realist positions and shows that they are untenable.[92] Such realist interpretations regard naming (*ming* 名) simply as tagging certain combinations of phonemes to objects already fixed in the world. Such approaches (Dewey calls them "bow-wow, pooh-pooh, and ding-dong" theories of language) tell us nothing about what language actually does.[93] In Hagen's assessment, the world for Xunzi "has regularities that may be patterned, categorized, and named based on [their] potential usefulness for human purposes." For Xunzi, "this process is an art."[94]

Along with Brook Ziporyn, I side with Hagen.[95] Hagen's reading enables us to place proper emphasis on the element of agreement (*yue* 約) in the act of naming, which is crucial to Xunzi's understanding. The *Shouwen* lexicon defines *yue* as "to wrap and bind together" (*chanshu* 纏束)—and the term here means "agreement" in the sense of binding treaty, mutual commitment, and covenant. This evokes a more solemn process than deciding that it's OK to call so-and-so a "ding-dong." When it comes to naming, the real question is normative: do we, as a group, "agree and commit ourselves" (*yue*) to "X" definition of something like "fatherhood" (*fu* 父)? If so, then it falls upon us to command (*ming* 命) into actuality "fathers" so defined and to withhold that term from those who are undeserving of the name (*ming* 名). Whatever nonhuman animals are doing with their vocal chords, it is not this. Other animals, in some sense, do "speak," but human animals are unique in determining social roles and norms through the use of language. This is what separates "humans" (*ren* 人) from other animals according to Xunzi. Ascribing "ding-dong" theories to him only obscures his position.

Fortunately, realists have better options. Alexus McLeod identifies Xunzi's position as what he calls a "semi-conventionalist realism," which means that establishing names is linked (as Xunzi says it is) to the ability to pick out or ostend (*zhi* 指) reality. As McLeod sees it: "an object *can* be part of reality . . . but reality is more than simply objects." According to him, the problem with most realist interpretations of Xunzi is that they ascribe to him a "substance-based metaphysics," thus obscuring the more dynamic registers of the real.[96]

As Dewey said, things have real *ways* of acting in transactional situations, and that includes transactions between parents-and-children. There are many coherent (*li* 理) concepts of what the term "fatherhood" (*fu* 父) might mean. There are, and historically have been, countless such concepts. The Platonic (i.e., realist) notion that somewhere out there (*where?*) floats an object (*eidos*) called "Fatherhood" is unhelpful. It only serves to downgrade the reality of all the world's "fatherhood" concepts. In any case, there is zero evidence that

Xunzi is a Platonist. His criteria for good (*shan* 善) names is clear: they should be direct, easy, and not in conflict with other names. This is consistent with "semi-conventionalist realism," an approach that if poorly executed results in objects that are indirect, difficult, and in conflict with each other.

The interesting thing, in any event, is not the ontological status of "fatherhood." The interesting thing is how distinctions pertaining to social roles (*fen* 分) emerge from pre-human vocalizations and how this gives rise to moral selves in the process. In order to get our social and moral reasoning "back in gear," we need to have a better understanding of how language operates in the brain and contributes to the advent of selfhood. Then, we need to understand what the moral features of selfhood are as a result.

For thinkers like Dewey and George Herbert Mead, selfhood is irreducibly social. If there were no selves-in-relation, then there would be no selves at all. Thus, selfhood represents the kind of situation that William James envisions in "The Moral Philosopher and the Moral Life"—one in which various agents negotiate desires in a value-laden "conversation" of gestures and actions. While such conversations take place on the "human" plane, they remain continuous with the biological activities of the body. Below the level of consciousness, the body grounds our sympathies over the course of social and moral transactions. The body is the "Great and Venerable Teacher" (*dazongshi* 大宗師) from which we learn to feel and to relate to one another. Common sense in this area remains in desperate need of philosophical reconstruction, and the remaining experiments in the present chapter will be devoted to testing alternative approaches to *bodies*, *selves*, and *moral experience*. Until philosophers establish more contemporary, naturalistic conceptions of how these three work together, we have little choice but to "wander" back into the Greek-medieval world.

Imitation and Human Selfhood

In the 1980s a team of Italian neurophysiologists began inserting electrodes into the skulls of macaque monkeys and presenting them with trays holding a single raisin. They were interested in mapping neural activity in the monkey's brains while they reached for the raisins, carefully picked them up, and brought them to their mouths. The monkey's brains were then observed as the researchers performed these same acts for the monkeys. Remarkably, a significant subset of the neurons activated when the monkeys performed specific acts were also activated when the researchers performed those same acts. "The responses evoked by these stimuli," it was determined, "are highly consistent and do not habituate." This marked the modern discovery of "mirror neurons." Based on these findings, researchers posited what they termed "resonance behaviors." These occur when "neural activity that is spontaneously generated during movements, gestures, or actions is also elicited when the individual observes another individual making similar movements, gestures and actions."[97] Subsequent research has shown the presence of neural mirroring systems in birds,[98] as well as in human beings.[99]

Both Mead and Dewey would have regarded the discovery of mirror neurons as a confirmation of their basic philosophical positions. As David D. Franks writes, "The current findings regarding mirror neurons add embodiment and thus refinement to Mead's 'theory of the act' as well as confirm the 'priority of action' which is the key to Chicago pragmatism." This is but another example, Franks explains, of how "almost a century later neuroscience and evolutionary findings have rediscovered the quintessential starting point of [the] early American pragmatists."[100]

Indeed. For Dewey, the essence of communication is that "something is literally made common in at least two different centers of behavior."[101] The outward manifestation of this is observed in the "signals" and "cues" through which animals communicate: "the most primitive language-behavior."[102] We now know that the bases for such activities are neural mirroring systems that enable imitation. Birds, for instance, imitate one another in their vocal gestures. When originally introducing the notion of "imitation," Mead never meant that birds simply copy one another. Imitation refers instead to the tendency of organisms in a social group to develop like responses to given stimuli. The "peculiar importance of the vocal gesture," Mead writes, is that "it is one of those social stimuli which affect the [animal] that makes it in the same fashion that it affects the [animal] when made by another."[103]

Birds hear themselves sing, and they hear other birds sing. Rather than copying one another, imitation is the one arousing in itself the "tendency to respond in the same way as the other" to the same vocal gesture, such that "the bird when singing is influenced by its *own* stimulus to a response which will be like that which is produced in another form." Ornithology teaches us that some bird vocalizations trigger mating responses; others elicit flights from danger. Parrots repeat human sentences the meanings of which completely elude them. In such instances, phonetic elements stimulate the bird to simply respond in a like manner—i.e., *phonetically*, while it repeats them. The tendency to imitate vocal gestures is an essential condition for the emergence of language. It develops within the organism sets of coordinated responses to shared stimuli, responses upon which all meaning will depend.

Imitation, as such, is a social process. It can only occur within the context of social interaction among organisms. Mead refers to this social context as a "conversation of gestures," and his favorite example is the dogfight. As he explains, "the very fact that the dog is ready to attack another becomes a stimulus to the other dog to change his own position or his own attitude. He has no sooner done this than the change of attitude in the second dog in turn causes the first dog to change his attitude. We have here a conversation of gestures."[104] Such animal signals, as Dewey explains, are the "material condition of language," but such responses are not yet *significant* in that "only from an external standpoint is the original action even a signal; the response of other animals to it is not to a sign, but, by some preformed mechanism, to a direct stimulus."[105] Mead continues: "We do not assume that the dog says to himself, 'If the animal comes from this direction he is going to spring at my throat and I will turn in such a way.' What does take place is an actual change in his own position due to the direction of the approach of the other dog."[106] Mead here indicates both the preliminary social conditions for language as well as the cognitive threshold that characterizes the "significant gesture."

In living organisms, such "conversations of gestures" take place below the level of consciousness all the time. Consciousness emerges as a feature of such conversations, and its emergence initiates meaning as well as moral sense. The reason is this: the moment that one organism consciously *anticipates* the response of another to a given gesture in a conversation, that gesture takes on *significance*. The degree of its significance depends on the *extent* to which two or more organisms have imitated one another in their responses to it and have become aware of the consequences of those responses. Here we glimpse simultaneously the raw foundations of language: *meaning* and *reference* alongside those of morality: *sympathy* and *responsibility*. As imitation and response-awareness increase in extent, gestures operate more fully and effectively as signs indicating their own meanings in relation to social acts. Coextensive, then, with the dawn of consciousness, language begins. It immediately becomes and remains the "tool of tools" for managing social relations including our moral relations.

Again, there is nothing that precludes language at the subhuman level. There are, however, two features that distinguish human language in Mead's account: the *extent* to which our languages have developed, and the *extent* to which our imitative responses anticipate the responses of others. It is the latter feature that most clearly distinguishes humans. According to Mead, this is implicated not only in the development of language but also in the emergence of selfhood in the human animal. In addition to enabling language, Mead teaches that our imitative capacities allow us to become "what we are in relationship to other individuals through taking the attitude of the [other] towards ourselves so that we stimulate ourselves by our own gesture." By assuming the attitude of the other, we become, as Mead says, "doubles" to ourselves. The "Me" that is implicated in the attitude of others becomes an object to the "I" engaged in conversation with them.[107] We thus distinguish ourselves as objective "selves" who have roles in a "conversation of gestures" with others.

Lawrence E. Cahoone recognizes this reflexive capacity rather than language *per se* to be the strongest candidate for what distinguishes humans from other animals. As Cahoone sees it, Mead is essentially correct in suggesting that the "human individual's very thought process and self are social and hence communicative. For *the others are in my head* . . . my mind represents them, and I incorporate and think from their perspectives, take on their roles, converse with them internally, and exchange signs with them that arouse the same response in myself, a self that emerges out of my relations to them."[108] Born through reciprocal role taking and assuming the attitudes of others, the emergence of the social self is the signature human achievement. As Xunzi suggests, the emergence of robust social distinctions (*fen* 分) and their resultant identities is what really sets humans apart.

Even here, however, the difference is best understood as one of degree. Insects do not have such personal selves, obviously. The "high degree of physiological differentiation" among insects, Mead writes, "precludes [them] from reaching self-consciousness."[109] Each insect performs its specialized function, never entering into activities that require it to incorporate the attitudes of others and thus to objectify itself. More to the point is that insects lack the brain physiology required for such operations in the first place. Such capacities are witnessed only in vertebrates with well-developed central nervous systems. These systems, Mead submits, are "too minute" to pinpoint precisely the structures that enable the advent of selfhood.

Today, the science on this remains imprecise. Recent studies, however, have implicated two areas of activity: mirror-neuron areas in the frontoparietal lobes, which establish the "physical self" (the "I") and cortical midline structures, which process the self in "more abstract, evaluative terms" (the "Me"). Researchers affirm Mead's basic hypothesis, reporting that, "self and other are two sides of the same coin."[110] Whatever the precise mechanism, Mead observes that "selves have appeared late in vertebrate evolution" and he maintains that it is "only in the behavior of the human animal that we can trace this evolution."[111] The precursors to selfhood are there, however, in pre-human behavior. To some extent, animals do become *in part* objectified within their own environments. Specifically, "with the emergence of what we call consciousness we find the animal entering in part into its own environment."[112] As Mead observes: "Our bodies are parts of our environment; and it is possible for the individual to experience and be conscious of his body, and of bodily sensations, without being conscious or aware of himself—without, in other words, taking the attitude of the other toward himself." With a suitably evolved central nervous system, an organism will not only need water but also *get thirsty*. Such organisms experience their own bodily states, but not to such an extent that an awareness of "themselves" emerges. Until the social process resulting in selfhood takes place, "the individual experiences his body—its feelings and sensations—merely as an immediate part of his environment, not as his own, not in terms of self-consciousness."[113]

The strength of this position is that it introduces no sharp divisions or dualisms into what is a seamless range of organic experiences. Such an approach is helpful in understanding the Chinese tradition which, as John Knoblock reminds us, does not regard the "human" (*ren* 人) as a category "ontologically differentiated from everything nonhuman."[114] Like Ziqi at the opening of "On the Parity of Things," the human animal can slide back into the pre-human standpoint when conditions are right. "Staring up at the sky and sighing—absently, as if he had just lost his counterpart (*ou* 耦) . . . [Ziqi said]: 'Just now the "I" (*wu* 吾) lost the "Me" (*wo* 我). Can you understand that?'"[115] Ziqi stopped for a moment being his own object. There are times when one is so "intensely preoccupied with the objective world," Mead writes, that the "accompanying awareness [of the "Me"] disappears."[116] In such moments, human selfhood recedes and bodily experiences become "partially a portion" of our lived environment. We recover the standpoint that we share with other animals. Before long, however, the "Me" (*wo*) resurfaces to claim ownership and eclipses the animal-body-*subject*.

For Mead, the apex of self-consciousness is exhibited in human societies whenever individuals enter as selves into social environments in which the animal-body-*subject* standpoint is entirely overwritten by ideational meanings. Mead thus recognizes that human selfhood invites some degree of estrangement from the animal body. One might look upon one's own feet as "strange things," and just as quickly look away and forget about them. The body, as Mead observes, "can be there and can operate in a very intelligent fashion without there being a self involved in the experience."[117]

Given this position, some commentators regard Mead as being somehow dismissive of the body. Wimal Dissanayake, for instance, maintains that "Symbolic Interactionism," and Mead by association, provide a "telling example of how the body came to be marginalized in modern social theory," in that "the somaticity of the self is ignored in favor of its sociality."[118] There is a more charitable way of understanding Mead on this issue. Granted, he focuses on the "sociality" of the self. For Mead, all selves are social selves. Physiological activity, however, is also "social in character" for Mead.[119] The social nature of selfhood does not marginalize or ignore the body automatically or by definition. While Mead identifies selfhood in social terms, he recognizes that "it remains for a human social individual to distinguish itself as a physical being, as a living being, as an animal, [and] as a self-conscious social individual," *all at once*. Human selves retain membership in all of these "systems," and the "[occupation] of two or more systems carries with it no conflict between the systems."[120]

So, while recognizing that there can be estrangement between self and body at the phenomenological level, Mead affirms their continuity and parity at the ontological level. Rather than marginalize the body, he identifies conditions in experience that threaten to disrupt the integration of the two in behavior. While Mead does not devote much discussion to the recovery of self-body integration, this is not because he thought that it was impossible—rather, it was because he was unsure how to proceed. "The legitimate basis of distinction between [self] and body is between the social patterns and the patterns of the organism itself. Education must bring the two closely together," he writes. "We have, as yet, *no comprehending category*. This does not mean to say that there is anything logically against it; it is merely a lack of our apparatus or knowledge."[121]

Dewey found in the Alexander technique a kind of apparatus that could help him bridge the disconnection between social patterns and the patterns of organic form. "With adults the integration which is accomplished by the technique at Mr. Alexander's command is obviously a re-education that is at best remedial and more or less palliative," suggests Dewey; adding that, "With subsequent generations it can, to the degree in which it is utilized with children, become positive and constructive."[122] Through such practices, Dewey believed that humans could recover somatic awareness and learn directly from their animal bodies.

The Great and Venerable Teacher

Once again, "Knowledge" wanders north above the banks of an obscure body of water to stand before the "Mouthpiece of *wuwei* 無為." Knowledge asks: "How does one *learn* from one's animal body?" There is no reply. To respond would be to objectify the body, and thus dissolve the very standpoint in question. The so-called "paradox of *wuwei*" returns. If the animal body cannot be made an object of knowledge for educational purposes without being eclipsed, then how does one *learn* anything from it?

Irving Goh advances this point in his reading of the *Zhuangzi*. Recovering the animal standpoint, he writes, demands our "rejection of the very concept of the human [in order] to avoid appropriating the animal or the knowledge of it within the limits of human knowledge and understanding," thus making it an "object of utility." Animals in the *Zhuangzi* are not there to educate the human knower—they are *simply there*. "One must not take stock at any particular point and seek to make animal philosophy useful for the human," Goh warns. The lesson of the animal (if there is any lesson) is that not everything *has* a lesson. "With regard to human education and human politics," Goh writes, "Zhuangzi's animal philosophy can be regarded as useless." The animal experience is precisely that which regards human tools, such as bridles and rings, as nothing more than useless flaps or warts. The animal insists that we *stop* instrumental thinking altogether—*stop knowing*. Thus, Goh maintains that, "any discourse on the animal must *not* be recuperated as a reflection on the state of human knowledge or ignorance."[123]

This last admonition breaks a path forward. The states of knowledge and ignorance are the binary states established with Socrates' question in the *Republic*: "Does someone who knows know something or nothing?"[124] Knowledge is thus identified with *something* and ignorance with *nothing*. By making the animal a *nothing* to human knowledge, Goh slips into such binary thinking. "One can never understand the animal," he argues, "one can never know what it thinks or how it thinks."[125] This is what Plato calls "ignorance," the opposite of which is knowledge (*episteme*). Such thinking, however, obliterates the vast territory between "Being" and "Not-Being," the realm of becoming that is canvassed by practical activity and experience. This is the land of "Wild and Twisty," where knowledge (*zhi* 知) and forgetting (*wang* 忘) are two aspects of the same process and forgetting at the age of sixty is good thing.[126]

Dewey was approaching sixty when he became Alexander's student. One of the first things he discovered was that he had to *un*-learn how to *sit down*. "I had the most humiliating experience in my life, intellectually speaking," he writes. "For to find that one is unable to execute directions, including inhibitory ones, in doing such a seemingly simple act as to sit down, when one is using all the mental capacity which one prides himself upon possessing, is not an experience congenial to one's vanity."[127] What Dewey learned from his own body-practice through the Alexander technique was difficult to verbally formulate (*yan* 言). He says of his practice that, "it is difficult for anyone to grasp its full force without having actual demonstration of the principle in operation. And even then, as I know from personal experience, its full meaning dawns upon one only slowly and with new meanings continually opening up."[128]

As Mead suggests, we have no comprehending category that encompasses both the physical "body" and the mental "self," and thus no over-arching context in which to consider cultural technologies that steer their integration. Dewey regards this as an intellectual travesty, for the category that eludes us is that of human life itself. "We have no word by which to name mind-body in a unified wholeness of operation," Dewey writes. "For if we said 'human life' few would recognize that it is precisely the unity of mind and body in action to which we were referring."[129] The Alexander technique enabled Dewey to reconnect with the wholeness of human life. This changed both *what* he

Figure 7.1. F. Matthias Alexander works on John Dewey's posture, date unknown. John Dewey collection, Special Collections Research Center, Morris Library, Southern Illinois University–Carbondale.

knew and *how* he knew it. "I found the things which I had 'known'—in the sense of theoretical belief—in philosophy and psychology, changed into vital experiences which gave a new meaning to knowledge of them."[130] Again, it was *practice* that afforded Dewey such growth in experience. As he reports: "In just the degree in which action, behavior, is made central, the traditional barriers between mind and body break down and dissolve."[131]

The stubbornness with which "Knowledge wanders north" is the stubbornness with which such *episteme* insists on displacing *praxis*. Dewey witnessed such stubbornness in those who were dismissive of his own body-practice. "Dewey was smiled at in some circles for his adherence to this amateur art of healing," reports Max Eastman.[132] JoAnn Boydston, general editor of the *Collected Works of John Dewey* and herself an Alexander practitioner, notes how scholars have continued to downplay the importance of Dewey's practice of the Alexander technique. In a keynote address before an international meeting of Alexander teachers in 1986, Boydston characterizes this general attitude as, "Oh, yes! Alexander was an Australian doctor who helped Dewey once when he had a stiff neck."[133] The fact that Dewey's practice is overlooked only underscores how unfortunate it is that common sense lacks a comprehending category with which to refer to his body-mind experience.

From a scholarly perspective, to regard Dewey's body-practice as a mere sidebar to his philosophy is a serious error. Quite to the contrary, F. Matthais

Alexander's influence on Dewey was penetrating and extensive, and it did not stop at the boundaries of the philosopher's body. In a superb dissertation on Dewey, *Frederick Matthias Alexander and John Dewey: A Neglected Influence*, Fr. Eric McCormack demonstrates that Dewey's body-practice found its way "into the heart of his philosophical thinking." Alexander's theories are so influential in *Human Nature and Conduct* and *Experience and Nature*, argues McCormack, that the full importance of each work "cannot be grasped until its reader is acquainted with its Alexandrian background."[134] The evidence that McCormack assembles is clearly organized and basically overwhelming. Even Dewey acknowledges the influence of Alexander on his philosophy: "My theories of mind-body, of the coordination of the active elements of the self and of the place of ideas in inhibition and control of overt action required contact with the work of [Alexander] to transform them into realities."[135]

The lesson here is that "human life" is the comprehending mode in which we act with body-and-mind, and much of our life activity is concerned with sustaining and growing its wholeness. Chinese thought can help to remedy the regrettable fact that common sense lacks such a comprehending category. In classical Chinese, the term *shen* 身 can mean both "body" and "self." As Roger T. Ames observes, the term refers to "one's entire psychosomatic person."[136] *Shen*, as Ames says, is "at once the self-conscious 'I' as the existential experience and the embedded 'me' as 'my living body for other subjects'—[it] is an indissoluble continuity between self and world."[137] As a general category or mode, *shen* resists both "Mind/Body" and "Subject/Object" dualisms.[138] As Yao Xinzhong explains, the term "refers to the self understood as the whole of one's existence and especially as the unity between one's mind and body . . . the whole existence of a person."[139]

Despite what some "primitivists" might imagine, cultivating human life (*xiushen* 修身) requires taking up tools. Granted, the *non*-instrumental standpoint of the *non*-human animal remains valid. As the *Zhuangzi* says, such animals have as much interest in the plumb line (*shengmo* 繩墨) and carpenter's square (*guiju* 規矩) as does clay or wood.[140] Humans, however, are not *non*-human animals. "Any notion that human action is identical with that of non-living things or with that of the 'lower' animals is silly," Dewey writes. "It is contradicted by the fact that behavior is so *organized* in human beings as to have for its consequences all that we call civilization, culture, law, arts—fine and industrial, language, morals, institutions, science itself. And by its fruits we know it."[141]

The "Great and Venerable Teacher" instructs us that the optimal standpoint is one that remains cognizant of how Nature (*tian* 天) and the Human (*ren* 人) meet and become organized in human life. For this purpose, the notion of a "genuine human of primitive times" (*guzhizhenren* 古之真人) is a useful tool. But make no mistake: there is no such thing as the technologically innocent *zhenren* 真人. Our African ancestors who migrated off the continent 60,000 years ago had *always* been tool users—there never were *Homo sapiens* who were not. "Observed and observable facts," Dewey reminds us, "make it evident that all distinctively human intelligent behavior is attended with use of artifacts, appliances, implements, tools, weapons, head- and foot-gears, etc."[142] By constructing the "genuine human" along with various anthropological (or anti-anthropological) narratives, Daoist thinkers were able to reflect intelligently on the consequences of certain instrumentalities of civilization—not only social tools, but material implements as well. It should be remembered that the Warring States period covers the Iron Age in China almost exactly. This was a period of significant social and material change and a variety of positions on human technologies emerged as a result: "Yangist," "agriculturalist," "primitivist," and so on. We have here partially reconstructed these debates as they relate to Daoist philosophy more generally.

Rather than dwell on the past, however, more pressing for us is to *use* Daoist teachings to reflect critically and constructively on our Digital Age. It is a mistake, I believe, to overstate the "anti-technology complex" in Daoism. Cook Ding, after all, cherishes his knife (*dao* 刀) and Wheelwright Bian his chisel (*zao* 鑿)—each of these are technologies by which their problems are brought to solution. Again, the role of any tool—from the stone axe to the semi-conductor—is to achieve a site-specific fit (*shi* 適) of method, subject matter, and activity in the process of reaching an end-in-view. Since the knife and chisel are primitive tools, virtually extensions of the hands that hold them, "fit" can be readily and immediately controlled. As Dewey says, however, the expansion of tool use "has made possible, both in the history of the race and of the individual, complicated activities of long duration—that is, with results that are long postponed [and] it is this prolongation and postponement which requires an increasing use of intelligence."[143] The key is to recognize that the durations that require increased intelligence (*ming* 明) are the same durations that create space for stupidity to manifest itself.

As we have seen, intelligence (*ming* 明) involves the coordination of two complimentary functions: means-to-ends and ends-to-means. The first function involves engineering means to achieve remote ends in the most direct way possible. With this, we cross easily from hand tools to machines (*ji* 機). As Barry Allen says, "Machines teach people that they can *make* things happen and need not wait for things." This, he observes, is partly why the well sweep alarms the peasant farmer. As Allen asks: "A well sweep is a fairly primitive machine; simple, not without elegance, and obviously more efficient than drawing water by hand . . . [But] why should people want to be more efficient in this or any task? And more efficient for whom, themselves or others?"[144]

This evokes the second function of intelligence: matching ends-to-means. The well sweep is indeed innocent. As the *Zhuangzi* says, "Pull it down, and it sinks down. Pull it up, and it swings up. Humans pull it, and it does not pull them. So, whether it is up or down, it commits no crime (*zui* 罪) against humans."[145] When technologies lead to harm, says Dewey, "it is hard to think of anything more childish than the animism that puts the blame on machinery."[146] Machines are nothing but supplementations of energy to human nerve and muscle. "The only basis on which the machine can be condemned logically," Dewey suggests, "is that of a passive and pessimistic philosophy which regards all exercise of energy as intrinsically evil."[147]

As Graham Parkes suggests, the peasant farmer is not objecting to the *machine*. Rather, he objects to the frame of mind that uncritically adopts each new technology that comes along. The rationale for adopting the well sweep is that it can "irrigate a hundred fields in one day."[148] *That's great*—but are there commensurate technologies being developed for those who wish to irrigate only one field a day? Are such technologies more rare and expensive because they *do* less? "The problem," Barry Allen submits, "is not the machines but the ethics of the engineers," those whose contrivances are designed upon "despotic ideas of efficiency and profit."[149] As Nathan Sivin observes: "To a greater extent than we generally realize, [technology's] strength emerges in application to needs and expectations that do not exist until it generates them."[150]

This brings us to the heart of Daoism's critique of technology. To *use* a machine is often to be *used* by the forces that drive its industry. One becomes *useful* in the process. As the Madman teaches Confucius, "Everyone knows the use of being useful, but no one knows the use of being useless (*wuyong* 無用)." For Zhuangzi, in order to live a genuine human life, to grow sufficiently and to see out one's years, it is important not to become *too* useful. As catalpa, cypress, and mulberry trees know, there is danger in that.[151] The danger lies in being used as a *means* to some end other than those that emerge in one's own *dao* 道-activity.

For Dewey, the careless bifurcation of means-and-ends gives rise to nearly every anthropogenic malady that besets human life. In addition to being the definition of stupidity, it perpetuates the distinction between the "theoretical" and "practical" arts and reinforces the outmoded ontology that fortifies it. Among all the calamities that this has caused, nothing, Dewey writes, has been "so disastrously affected by the tradition of separation and isolation" as the "Body/Mind" dualism.[152] This issue bears directly on the question of technology. As Dewey writes in "Dualism and the Split Atom," we are "out of gear" in that our technological advances have been "superimposed as external strata upon institutions and habits so old as to be established beyond the reach of easy and fundamental transformation." This is the *tragic split*—the assumption that there is "a split in the very nature of things, and hence not to be overcome, between what is 'material' [on the one hand] and what is moral and ideal . . . 'spiritual' [on the other]."[153] Such a split negates the wholeness of human life (*shen* 身). Thus, for Dewey, the degree to which the "Body/Mind" dualism is dissolved measures the degree to which culture results in experience that is truly "human." As he writes: "The more *human* [humankind] becomes, the more civilized it is, the less is there some behavior which is purely physical and some other purely mental. So true is this statement that we may use the amount of distance which separates them in our society as a test of the lack of human development in that community."[154]

In communities that do poorly by this standard, it is difficult to sustain what Larry A. Hickman calls "responsible technology."[155] Technology fails when means-and-ends become dissociated. When this happens, rather than inquiry and experimentation giving birth to means-and-ends together the latter are determined by fixed political, religious, or economic ideologies and the former are dictated by habit and unthinking routine. Each tendency is well represented in consumer-driven capitalist systems. In the separations that result, there grow activities "almost exclusively mechanical" and others in which "the physical factor is at a minimum [and is] regretted as a deplorable necessity." Each extreme signals alienation, marking "an approximation to the pathological, a departure from that wholeness which is health."[156]

Recovering the "wholeness which is health" requires care with respect to how we utilize the "primary tool in the use of all [our] other tools, namely ourselves . . . our own psycho-physical disposition [or *xing* 性]."[157] We must not lose sight of this truth. Never in history have there been more "gadgets" available to human groups than are available to the denizens of modern industrialized societies. As Chapter 57 of the *Daodejing* observes: "The more technologically savvy (*jiqiao* 技巧) we become, the more weird things pop up." Human beings, however, as Dewey told his audience in Hangzhou, are not machines among the machines. No two human bodies are exactly alike, just as no two leaves on a tree are identical.[158] The responsibility for managing one's relation to technology is a resolutely personal one—and it is primarily *physical* rather than logical or illogical.

Heeding the "Great and Venerable Teacher," we begin to explore how Nature (*tian* 天) and the Human (*ren* 人) are organized in our experience. This opens up a boundless field for experimental inquiry, one in which there is always more to learn. "Our feet tread upon a small area of ground, but in treading we rely upon ground un-trodden to later make good on the distance we cover," the *Zhuangzi* teaches. "Human knowledge is also very small, but in knowing we rely on what is unknown to later know what Nature means."[159] The process of realizing (*zhi* 知) how Nature (*tian* 天) relates to human life (*shen* 身) never ends, because its terminus is an active disposition (*xing* 性) that cannot be objectified. Dewey embarked on this journey the only way possible: through his own body-practice. The present age requires that each of us tread such steps for ourselves—lest we unwittingly become "useful tools" for ends other than our own. "Each lesson carries the process somewhat further," Dewey promises. "As one goes on, new areas are opened, new possibilities are seen and then realized; one finds [oneself] continually growing, and realizes that there is an endless process of growth initiated."[160]

How "progress" is made along this path depends on how value registers in Nature (*tian* 天) more generally. How is improvement measured? Is value intrinsic to things or do sentient beings introduce value instrumentally? What determines better and worse with respect to nature? Such are the questions that vex philosophers—especially environmental philosophers, for whom the category of "intrinsic" value is paramount. As we will see, for Dewey and the Daoists, such approaches risk introducing a false dichotomy. Views that begin with transactional assumptions tend not to resort to dualisms like "Intrinsic/Instrumental" in subsequent analyses. How value resides in nature, however, stands to be better understood non-dualistically. Daoist philosophy suffers when commentators insist that it either has an "inherent" value scheme or else is "relativistic." It also suffers at the hands of those who would equate it with the kind of *laissez-faire* mentality that presumes that value "naturally" prevails so long as one does nothing to interfere with things. These are serious misunderstandings of Daoist thinking, and they prevent Daoism from fully contributing itself as a viable philosophical resource for us today. Chapter 8 will address such problems.

8

Values and Inquiry

New ways of thinking and new commitments are not yet evolved to replace the ones that are being discarded. In this generation we must formulate new ways of thinking, and make decisions about principles to which we will give our loyalty. This is why we say that the world stands at the crossroads of change, with regard both to knowledge and to modes of thought.

—John Dewey, National Peking University, October 1919

Autumn Floods

The story of Planet Earth is told in eons, eras, periods, and epochs. As the "Autumn Floods" chapter of the *Zhuangzi* reminds us, the scope of the human experience is miniscule—like "a single fine hair on the body of a horse."[1] In geological time, humans are only recently introduced players in the Phanerozoic eon, occupying less than one-twentieth of 1 percent of its duration. The prelude to the Phanerozoic (meaning "appearance of life" in Greek) was composed some 540 million years ago when the fossil record blooms into an array of novel organic forms. This follows the climax of the "Cambrian explosion," a twenty-million-year period during which single-celled organisms evolved into more complex organisms at a rate never before seen. We are already three eras into the current eon. The Paleozoic or "early life" era tells the story of creatures bellying up from the waters to dry land to breathe. The Mesozoic or "middle life" era tells of birds and reptiles evolving in tandem, from flying lizards to the mighty *Sauroposeidon*.

The third and current era began with the cataclysm that doomed the dinosaurs. The Cenozoic or "new life" era ushered in conditions more favorable to mammals like ourselves. We are now in the third period of this era, one marked by radical swings in global temperature. The current period has two epochs. The first, the Pleistocene, lasted from 2.5 million years ago to about 9,000 BCE. Also known as the "Ice Age," at its crescent the landmass of what is now Canada south to Chicago and east to Boston was under a thick sheet of ice. Our hunter-gatherer ancestors evolved during the last few hundred thousand years of this epoch, which overlaps with the Paleolithic period in Anthropology.

Ninety-five percent of human technological history lies in the Paleolithic—in stone, wood, bone, fiber, leather, and fire. The use of the latter led to cooked foods, softer to chew and easier to digest than raw foods. As a result, our jaws decreased in capacity and our teeth and digestive systems became smaller. Some propose that changes in caloric intake related to cooking technologies were responsible for the rapid growth in human brain size, although evidence for this is not definitive.[2] The Pleistocene epoch and the Paleolithic period ended together around 9,000 BCE, when the planet entered the Holocene epoch, meaning "wholly recent." Warming temperatures marked its beginnings, as the planet entered its current interglacial period—one that may persist for another 80,000 years before the next ice age begins. For now, glaciers have receded, forests have replaced tundra, and conditions have become optimal for the proliferation and expansion of the human race. Within the Holocene, major stages in human technological development have succeeded one another in the blink of an eye: the last phase of the Stone age, the Bronze age, the Iron age, the Agricultural revolution, the Industrial revolution, and now the Digital age.

As emerging technologies change our bodies-and-brains, they also transact with the environmental and atmospheric conditions that support life on the planet. Scientists are nearing consensus that the time has come to call the Holocene to an early close and to name its successor. Recent human activities related to the burning of fossil fuels, intensive farming, and the use of industrial chemicals have so altered the Earth's biosphere and atmosphere that we find ourselves thrust into another planetary epoch—one that is now called the "Anthropocene," or the "Human Age."[3]

Perhaps readers of this volume need little persuading that Zhuangzi has something to teach us about ourselves in this new epoch. Then again, there are Sinologists who resist such ideas. Paul R. Goldin, for instance, in an article entitled "Why Daoism is Not Environmentalism," alerts us that, "nowhere in [the *Zhuangzi*] is there any discussion of pollution, the extinction of species, soil erosion, ecology, or the concrete consequences of environmental mismanagement," and that, "we cannot ask thinkers of the past to help us with issues that they themselves never imagined."[4] Really? If this is correct, then it is hard to see how a commentarial tradition like the Chinese ever amounted to anything. The fact that Mencius never knew Buddhism did not prevent later Chinese thinkers from using his insights to debate Buddhism. Were such thinkers wrong to do so?

The challenge assumed by intra-cultural philosophers in every age is to imagine for past thinkers how their teachings might speak to contemporary issues. As Dewey tells his audience at Nanjing in 1920, "We must not forget that the main reason we want to conserve and teach the culture of the past is that we need to relive it, to infuse life into it, to use it, and make it applicable to present day social situations and conditions."[5] Ideally, one does not distort the past by reading the present into it. But the process of encountering past ideas is never wholly separate from the process of applying them to some present concern, and intra-cultural philosophers acknowledge that the process of doing so is largely imaginative and always situated. As Dewey says: "The philosopher is first and last a human being with his own intellectual and emotional habits who is involved in a concrete scene."[6] We do not suspend our own predilections, passions, and biases in order to study Chinese philosophy—in fact, we do not suspend our predilections, passions, and biases while doing anything.

This fact calls to mind an episode in Aldo Leopold's *Sand County Almanac*. It takes place in the "November" chapter and is entitled "Axe-in-Hand." Being a "conservationist," according to Leopold, is a matter of what a person thinks about while chopping or deciding what to chop. On this November morning, heading out into the crunchy snow axe-in-hand, Leopold decides to chop the red birch trees to favor the pine. *Why?* He admits to finding it disconcerting to analyze after the fact the reason for his decision. He planted that pine himself. Is that why he favors it? Birch is abundant, while pine is scarce. Is that the reason? Further north, the opposite is true. Would he still favor the pine further north? He doesn't know. The pine will shelter a grouse; but on the other hand, the birch will feed him. Does he value lodging more than board? Pine is more lucrative than birch; does he have an eye on his bank account? He notes that the pine braves the winter winds. "Does the pine stimulate my imagination and my hopes more deeply than the birch does?" he wonders. "If so, is the difference in the trees, or in me?"[7]

In the final analysis, Leopold concludes: "I love all trees, but I am in love with pines," and he refers to this love as a *bias*. "The wielder of an axe," he writes, "has as many biases as there are species of trees on his farm." Leopold compares his own biases to those of his neighbors, and they differ. "Our biases are indeed a sensitive index to our affections, our tastes, our loyalties, our generosities, and our manner of wasting weekends."[8] If one could only eradicate all biases and recover some underlying, clear directive—then exercising "Axe-in-Hand" judgments would be easy. But Nature (*tian* 天) doesn't work that way. If anything is true in Sand County, it is that living things (or *wu* 物) are biased all the way down.

Does *dao* 道 respect our biases? China's Yellow River (*Huanghe* 黃河) is the most heavily silted river on earth, and also the deadliest. Before dikes were completed in 1946–1947, the river would regularly overflow its banks with horrific consequences. Dewey wrote to his children about the flooding while he visited China in 1919. "The Yellow river is known as the curse of China, so much damage is done," he writes.[9] In 1931, flooding inundated 34,000 square miles of land and left 80 million people homeless. The flooding, along with disease and famine, killed between one and four million people that year, making it the deadliest natural disaster in recorded history.

The Yellow River had been flooding for millennia, and at one point the "Lord of the River" consulted with the "God of the North Sea." The swollen River was not sure how it *should* be acting. "Well then, what should I do and what should I not do?" he asked the North Sea. "How do I decide what to accept and reject, what to pursue and avoid?" The North Sea responded: "From the standpoint of *dao* 道, what is valuable and what is worthless? These designations are always changing places." The North Sea continued, "[*Dao*] is broad and expansive, like the limitlessness of the four directions—nothing bounds or encloses it. It includes all living things. Nothing receives special protection. This is called having no leanings (*fang* 方)." The Lord of the River was confused. "In that case," it asked, "what is the value of *dao*?" The North Sea answered: "One who understands *dao* is sure to reach through to the coherence of things (*li* 理). One who reaches through to the coherence of things is sure to act intelligently (*ming* 明) in weighing things up (*quan* 權). One who acts intelligently in weighing things up will not allow things to harm him."[10]

Vexed by modern suggestions that Zhuangzi is a "relativist," some seek out elements suited to challenge such interpretations. Such commentators approach the *Zhuangzi* with what is aptly called a "moral fear."[11] Statements that appear to support relativism are recast as a kind of "spiritual therapy," intended to liberate us from parochial views so we can begin to see things from the "proper perspective: the Heavenly view of the world."[12] Zhuangzi is reimagined as a "therapeutic mystic" whose purpose is "to help us follow the Way."[13] Such therapy enables one to "feel the beat of the *dao* 道," and thus "to perceive and accord with an ethical scheme inherent in the world."[14]

Such readings, while soothing, are unhelpful. They frustrate efforts to free common sense from Greek-medieval assumptions by perpetuating the notion that behind appearances there stands a readymade, normative order to things. They offer something akin to the "coherent, luminous, intellectually secure and dependable world" afforded by the "Great Chain of Being" in the West.[15] Philip J. Ivanhoe regards Chinese philosophy as sponsoring such a vision. Like the "Great Chain of Being," he explains, the "grand scheme" in Chinese thought is one in which "the place and function of each thing provides both justification and a normative standard for how it ought to be." Such a framework, says Ivanhoe, presents "a view about the nature of the world and the self that entails a corresponding moral vision."[16]

Applying such a reading to the *Zhuangzi* is problematic. For starters, the "God of the North Sea" refutes it squarely: "From the standpoint of *dao* 道, things are neither valuable nor worthless. From the standpoint of things, each thing values itself and regards others as worthless. From the standpoint of [human] convention, such value is 'objective' (*buzaiji* 不在己)."[17] The message here is that the "value" of things *seems* to be objective from the standpoint of human convention, but from the so-called "Heavenly view of the world," no such values exist. Accordingly, there is no "ethical scheme" inherent in the world.[18] This is why Kim-chong Chong maintains that "Heaven" is an inapt English translation for *tian* 天 in the *Zhuangzi*. It really ought to be "Nature," since by that we mean "authenticity, genuineness, spontaneity, or an original state of primitive innocence." As Chong notes, "there is no unique moral relationship between *tian* and human beings" in the text. "There is no normative order that is laid down by *tian*," and "no universal principle or principles governing human affairs."[19] Nature (*tian*) is a resolutely *a*-moral force in the *Zhuangzi*.

This is not terribly disturbing to those who accept the theory of evolution. The Phanerozoic eon has not been particularly kind. Legions of blameless species have perished into dirt. *Dao* 道 has indeed maintained its essence throughout—but it is more aligned with ruthlessness than with any tender cosmic bosom or "ethical scheme." As Eske Møllgaard says, it is the "uncarved block" (*pu* 樸), which is "not a static substratum but an active force that moves human beings along together with everything else."[20] *Dao*-activity proceeds wherever continuity between means-and-ends is achieved, and as such it "has an essence and can be trusted, although it has no purpose (*wuwei* 無為) and takes no form."[21] The cholera germ is granted clearance to thrive just as the human being is, and *dao* will yield its power to the bacteria when the situation is right. As Chapter 5 of the *Daodejing* reminds us: "Heaven and Earth are not humane (*ren* 仁), they treat the myriad beings as straw dogs." Ivanhoe's moral/therapeutic vision (one in which we snuggle up "safe and welcome within the bosom of *dao*")[22] is not representative of early Daoist thinking. Given its sheer neutrality and indiscriminate generosity, there is no superordinate plan to the direction that *dao* will take—no "inherent ethical scheme" for humans to apprehend and then "follow." In fact, such thinking is the antithesis of early Daoism.

Zhuangzi gets described as a "relativist" because he adopts a meta-level perspective on the situation, one that in the abstract is "large and useless" like an oversized gourd. From this meta-perspective, he sees the use of various biases and realizes how they link up with one another. This enables him to occupy the "Pivot of *dao* 道," a position from which he can respond intelligently (*ming* 明) to the endless "ends" that arise in practical activity. Zhuangzi affirms that there is a plurality of perspectives, and he does not seek to go around them. After all, any one of them might become good in the context of *dao*-activity when a situation arises to determine its pertinence. As long as such standpoints remain subordinate to practice, their theoretical content fits (*shi* 適) coherently.[23] This is not "relativism," and it does not require the reactionary postulation of an empirically unverifiable "ethical scheme inherent in the world" to counter it.

Besides—relativism poses no real threat. Philosophers keen on defeating it are tilting at windmills. Richard Rorty was right when he observed:

> "Relativism" is the view that every belief on a certain topic, or perhaps on *any* topic, is as good as every other. No one holds this view. Except for the occasional cooperative freshman, one cannot find anybody who says that two incompatible opinions on an important topic are equally good. The philosophers who get *called* "relativists" are those who say that the grounds for choosing between such opinions are less algorithmic than had been thought.[24]

Between the two extremes of "relativism" and the "ethical scheme inherent in the world" lies the ground wherein serious reflection on the intelligence (*ming* 明) of competing measures takes place. We badly need to recover this ground and to establish ourselves there as philosophers.

When the "God of the North Sea" tells the Yellow River that understanding *dao* 道 enables one to apprehend coherence (*li* 理), the North Sea is not suggesting that one thereby sees how all values register in some inherent normative scheme nor is he suggesting that everything swings free of everything else. Rather, one is seeing, in the words of Brook Ziporyn, "the way things fit together," seeing the "lines according to which one may divide things up so as to make them cohere into a desired whole," and "what patterns of action are workable with respect to [a] thing."[25] As the North Sea explains, one who apprehends this is able to act intelligently (*ming* 明) in weighing things up, and to escape from being harmed. By a similar process, the blade of Cook Ding's knife never dulls, because it accords with the natural patterns (*tianli* 天理) of the ox that it carves. Its cutting edge is one that emerges unscathed because things are taken as they actually are.

How, then, do we move forward? As we saw in chapter 5, *dao* 道-activity can help us to find the way. Ordinary practice (*yong* 庸) helps to cultivate the habits of *directness, open-mindedness, single-mindedness,* and *responsibility,* and this puts us in a better position to choose well. As A. C. Graham argues, spontaneity lends itself to the imperative to "respond with awareness," and one can base an ethics on this imperative alone.[26] At its ideal limit, responding with awareness means "[attaining] full awareness from every viewpoint and [reacting] with (impartial) sympathies and antipathies."[27] This would mean realizing the virtues of Cook Ding's *dao* perfectly and thus exhibiting perfect clarity and intelligence (*ming* 明) in judgment.

But as Aldo Leopold asks: can such an ideal be realized in the snowy Wisconsin winter, "Axe-in-Hand"? Can one ever become *perfectly* clear? Such a conundrum helps to foreground the kind of stalemate that prevents us from formulating ethical approaches adequate to the environmental crises that we face. We have, it seems, a strong bias against all bias, and we will not rest until objectivity is secured. Properly understood, however, the Daoist ideal of perfect clarity is just that—*an ideal.* Organic form (*xing* 形) cannot be expected to completely transcend its own biases. Every ethical question involves how value is negotiated between competing biases, and the Daoist way is to negotiate such "difficult parts" with the spontaneity of Cook Ding. Such a way invites further experimentation.

Nature and Valuation

To have a bias is to engage in the act of valuation, to become inclined for or against something in relation to something else. In having no organic form (*xing* 形) and behaving without doing/making (*wuwei* 無為), it is plain that *dao* 道 does not have such biases. Again, as Edward Slingerland explains, the term *wei* 為 has a broad semantic range in classical Chinese. In addition to "doing" something it also means "taking" things to be a certain way, "regarding" things to be such or so.[28] To "act without regard" (*wuwei* 無為) or "non-regarding" (*wuyiwei* 無以為) is to resist attributing undue value to things. This means *not*-making things into what they are not, and thus not being motivated by erroneous estimations of worth. As the "God of the North Sea" explains, from the standpoint of *dao* things are neither valuable nor worthless. It is a standpoint of sheer indifference.

As we have seen, William James provides a starting point for understanding how such impartiality gives birth to a moral world, a world in which values and obligations have genuine ontological standing. Recall that, for James, moral obligation is grounded in some concrete *demand.* Were the universe to have but one sentient being in moral solitude, the good would really exist—whatever that being desires would be good. As James observes, demand and obligation are thus coextensive and overlap exactly. "Take any demand, however slight, which any creature, however weak, may make. Ought it not, for its own sole sake, to be satisfied? If not, prove why not."[29] In Daoist terms, each organic form (*xing* 形) similarly has its own claim to existence. Each organism is the expression of a "need," and to paraphrase James again: take any life-form, however slight, and any life-process, however weak—ought it not, for its own sole sake, be allowed to express its "quality" and directional order (*de* 德)? Such generosity is what *dao* 道 facilitates so perfectly through the "Piping of Nature." It honors each and allows the diversity of living things (*wu* 物) to emerge and simply be themselves (*ziyi* 自已).[30]

Suggested here is a point of departure congenial to some of the earliest forms of environmental ethics. All living things have equal status. Thinkers like Peter Singer evoke the principle of equality when properties and rules apply across cases. Nonhuman animals, for instance, feel pain. Thus, the burden is on those who would deny nonhuman animals equality of consideration under relevant rules that govern the treatment of humans in similar cases. The aim should be to reduce as much pain as possible—if not, *prove why not*.

Foregoing Singer's utilitarian approach, Tom Regan seeks to ground animal rights in the intrinsic value of the organism. Like humans, the nonhuman animal is alive and is the subject of a life/growth process (or *sheng* 生). Life is self-justified; it expresses its own value. The aim should be to allow each life to continue—if not, *prove why not*.

Bio-centric vs. Holistic debates ensue. The Holist argues that it is permissible (even praise-worthy) to hunt and kill whitetail deer because periodically culling this population is good for the species, good for the ecosystem, and better for the planet than raising more cows. This introduces values not easily scaled within a bio-centric model. As Holmes Rolston argues, the value of a "species" does not reduce to the intrinsic values of its members, and entities like "ecosystems" make no demands or claims. How does one defend the "intrinsic value" of a coastline? Thus, Rolston argues that in addition to intrinsic value ("for itself") and instrumental value ("for others") philosophy must develop the notion of systematic value ("for the whole").[31] J. Baird Callicott makes advancements in this direction and argues that a "lasting alliance" between Bio-centrism and Holism waits upon the emergence of a "Meta-Human Moral Community," a theory that provides principles for weighing the intrinsic value of individual organisms against values in things like ecosystems.[32]

The history of environmental ethics reveals, as much as anything, the difficulty that traditional moral theory encounters in dealing effectively with environmental issues. The magnitude and complexity of the problems expose theoretical inadequacies quickly. James' "moral monism," for instance—as cogent an axiological theory as one is likely to find—fails to be sufficient for environmental purposes. Like every so-called "thought experiment," it suffers from its own abstraction. James' "moral monism" provides a useful basis for reflection, but things never happened that way. There never was a sentient being suddenly introduced into a valueless world, then another, and so on. Rather, sentience emerged *from* the world, and its biological and physical antecedents have always conditioned its claims and demands. Collapsing demand and obligation does align James with many environmental philosophers—but as Anthony Weston argues, the notion of "intrinsic value" that unites them is fraught with assumptions inconsistent with pragmatic naturalism more generally. To qualify as "intrinsic," a value must be self-sufficient such that it would be retained in isolation. This evokes *substance ontology*. To be "intrinsic," it must operate as an end-in-itself and have no instrumental character. This evokes *final cause*. To be "intrinsic," it must have some special justification or status that involves no contingency. This evokes *essentialism*. In sum, the idea of "intrinsic value" is completely "out of gear."

Dewey, accordingly, rejects the notion as unscientific. Every notion of "values-in-themselves," he argues, perpetuates outmoded, absolutistic thinking. "The necessity of employing the phrase 'in-themselves' shows that the absolutistic retention is *more* than attenuated," he writes. " 'In-themselves' is always a sure sign of denial of *connections*, and hence is proof of an affirmation of an absolute. As long as this continues, discussion of valuings-values will remain in its present backward state."[33] Dewey regards "intrinsic value" to be an extreme form of non-naturalism. "The extreme instance of the view that to be intrinsic is to be out of any relation is found in those writers who hold that, since values *are* intrinsic, they cannot depend on *any* relation whatever, and certainly not upon a relation to human beings."[34] As Dewey sees it, the whole notion of "intrinsic value" is riddled with ambiguity.[35]

As Hugh P. McDonald explains, environmental ethicists line up to denounce Dewey on this point. Denying "intrinsic value" undermines what is considered to be one of the cornerstones of environmental philosophy. Dewey's "pragmatism," accordingly, is understood as inescapably anthropocentric and subjectivist in its value theory. Lacking any notion of "intrinsic value," Dewey's instrumentalism is regarded as a warrant for humans to use nature for their own purposes virtually unchecked.[36] As environmental philosophers like Eric Katz see it: "Pragmatism and environmental ethics must part company over the role of human interests in the determination of value."[37]

Such criticisms reveal serious misunderstandings of Dewey's philosophy while also reflecting how radical it actually is. Dewey understood that "every error is attended with a contrary and compensatory error, for otherwise it would soon be self-revealing." The dualism in which environmental ethics is trapped is that between "Instrumental/Intrinsic" values. This dualism tracts on to the Greek-medieval bifurcation of reality into two separate domains: the "Materialistic vs. Ethical," resulting in "the division of arts into those concerned with mere means and those concerned with ends in themselves." The more primary function of intelligence (or *ming* 明) "easily slips through such course meshes, [meaning that] by far the greater part of life goes on in a darkness un-illuminated by thoughtful inquiry."[38]

Like *dao* 道-activity, every "art" or technical operation is ideally intelligent (*ming* 明)—marked by the continuity between means-and-ends. Thus, it is both instrumental *and* final. As means and ends become separated from one another, the possibility for stupidity increases—and this is plainly apparent in our stewardship of the planet. We have failed to realize that the goal of *every* intellectual separation between means-and-ends is to reinstate their continuity at a more sustainable level—in other words, to restore *dao*-activity. For Dewey, "means and ends are two names for the same reality."[39] While they can be distinguished in thought, they must not be ontologically severed. When value becomes splintered into two wholly separate domains: the "instrumental" (*mere means*) and the "intrinsic" (*ends in themselves*), this is a sure sign that *dao* has been lost.

How then is value distributed for Dewey and for Daoism? The short answer is that it is distributed across situations. The limits of James' "moral monism" are revealed once one takes a steady look at what "demands" really look like in nature. As the *Hengxian* teaches, living things are engendered "according to what they *desire* (*yu* 欲)."[40] Dewey also identifies need as "the most obvious difference between living and non-living things."[41] For living things, "There are needs (in the sense of existential tensions); [and] these needs can be satisfied only through institution of a changed objective state of affairs."[42] Plant life provides the model. The directional order (*de* 德) of a plant is not something that is simply "intrinsic" to the plant. Rather, the *de* of the plant in being itself (*ziyi* 自己) activates kinetic phases that *use* the environment to its own advantage, converting potential energies into means for its own growth. Thus, the plant is engaged in an "instrumental" relation with its environment *already*. Since every organism as such is embedded in an environment, humans are hardly unique in behaving instrumentally. As McDonald reminds us: "All organisms create an altered environment, not just humans . . . Plants root themselves by penetrating into the soil, taking nutrients from it and leaving behind their by-products." In doing so, "the organism alters the environment to enhance valued outcomes and bring about what is prized."[43] As Dewey observes, "There is no difference between the growth of a plant and the prosperous development of [any] experience."[44] The growth of a plant *is* experience (*dao* 道) in one of its manifold expressions—the historical result of a life-process exhibiting continuity between means-and-end in activity.

In its generosity, *dao* 道 sponsors all experience. It does not, however, *have* experience. This explains its value neutrality. Wherever experience *does* occur, it is shot-through with value. Such value does not reduce to "intrinsic" or "instrumental" forms—it is always *both*. Where James' analysis is most important is in its suggestion that the challenge that ethical philosophy faces is not the prospect of nihilism. Hardly. The problem of ethics is the *superabundance of value*. Plants literally grab onto the soil with their roots in a greedy clump (which also prevents soil erosion). Such is their *demand*, their "need" (*yu* 欲), and it is a claim that asks for recognition. What Dewey adds to James' analysis is a notion of "demand" that is not reliant on sentience (as it is for James) and thus not as prone to anthropocentric reductionism. For Dewey, all things are *in* Nature (*tian* 天), "not as marbles are in a box but as events are in a history, in a moving, growing never finished process."[45]

Here, we do well to remember our cosmological suppositions. From the Peircean perspective, even inorganic phenomena exhibit a basic feature: *the tendency of nature to form habits*. All things are similar in "[tending] asymptotically toward bringing about an ultimate state of things."[46] As Dewey observes, "In this fact, taken by itself, there is nothing which marks off the plant from the physico-chemical activity of inanimate bodies." Each is subject to conditions of disturbed inner equilibrium, "which lead to activity in relation to surrounding things, and which terminate after a cycle of changes—a terminus termed saturation, corresponding to satisfaction in organic bodies." What distinguishes organic from inorganic form is its *organization*—its bias toward a more generic end-state and its valuation of its environment as a means to do so. Such "bias" however, *precedes* organic life—even chemicals exhibit such habits and tendencies. "Iron as such exhibits characteristics of bias or selective reactions," Dewey observes, "but it shows no bias in favor of remaining simple iron; it had just as soon, so to speak, become iron-oxide."[47] Thus, the precursors to what we think of as valuation (i.e., values) lie deep in Nature (*tian* 天) and do not await sentience to make their claims.

That said—there is a significant degree of organization involved in the emergence of valuation-propositions, passing from inorganic "biases," through organic "needs/demands," on up through sentient "desires." Animals, at some point, do go from "needing water" to "being thirsty." Dewey does maintain (and this is a debatable point) that humans are the only creatures to make valuation-propositions, because "ends-in-view as anticipated results reacting upon a given desire are *ideational* by definition or tautologically," thus "desire, having ends-in-view, and hence involving valuations, is the characteristic that marks off human from nonhuman behavior."[48] The accuracy of this would depend on whether or not nonhuman animals actually *have* sentient desires and ideas, which is unclear. But no matter—as biases evolve into needs, and needs into desires, and desires into valuations, and valuations into moral obligations—there is no moment or phase in which this process is *not* embedded in a Nature (or *tian* 天) replete with value. As Hugh P. McDonald observes in assessing Dewey's position: "If this is anthropocentric, I do not know what a non-anthropocentric position would be."⁴⁹

Dewey has utter respect for the environment in his ethics. "To get a rational basis for moral discussion," he writes, "we must begin by recognizing that functions and habits are ways of using and incorporating the environment in which the latter has its say as surely as the former."⁵⁰ Such an approach is not only *compatible* with environmental ethics—it is *paradigmatic* for such an enterprise. Dewey's philosophy "does not have to be reworked," McDonald argues. "It is already naturalistic, organic, and environmentally minded."⁵¹ As Dewey's thinking becomes more transactional over time, it becomes even *more* environmentally minded. "A behavior is always to be taken transactionally; i.e., never as *of* the organism alone, any more than *of* the environment alone, but always as of the organic-environmental situation, with organisms and environmental objects taken as equally its aspects."⁵² This, Dewey argues, is the most scientifically warranted perspective from which to assess values in nature. Philosophical theories that bifurcate value into separate domains, e.g., "Means/Ends," or "Instrumental/Intrinsic" can be useful tools in reflection and criticism, but they must not impede or obscure our more comprehensive appraisals. Dewey and Daoism might not provide explicit treatments of problems like pollution, soil erosion, or climate change—but these philosophies do something more. They provide a standpoint in which environmental awareness is *central*. Such an ethics, by default, is an "environmental ethics," such a logic is an "environmental logic," and such an aesthetics is an "environmental aesthetics," and so on. These are philosophies that are already reconstructed to meet our most urgent needs.

Daoist philosophy augments Dewey's approach in important ways. It is unrelentingly pluralistic in its appraisal of value. As Wang Ni reminds us, "Sleeping in damp places, humans would wake up sick and with a backache; but this is not so for the eel. Living in trees, humans would tremble and shake in terror, but this is not so for the monkey. Of these three creatures, which one knows the right place to live?"⁵³ Values are always posited *somewhere*—i.e., they are distributed across situations while *dao* 道 remains neutral. Sing-nan Fen offers insight into the importance of this fact for the possibility of criticism. "If values are already good or bad in themselves there is nothing we can do about them," he writes: "If a value is good, we need not change it. If it is bad, we are unable to change it." This reveals the importance, and in fact the *advantage*, of the neutrality of *dao*. "Only when we look on [a] value situation as originally neutral are we furnished with a material condition for criticism or evaluation," Fen explains. "From a cosmological point of view, therefore, neutrality . . . indicates that events are running their course in as natural a manner as it would without restraint." Thus, "the possibility of criticism or appraisal with respect to [a] value situation is [assured] so long as we take [the] value situation as neutral and as non-teleological as we take any other kind of natural event."[54] By deferring value *to* situations, *dao* enables those of us who are *in* them to critically appraise and actually modify and improve them. Again—this is not "relativism."

From what standpoint, however, does one make such evaluative judgments and thus manage situations? Should humans govern from the "human" (*ren* 人) standpoint? As Franklin Perkins argues, there is a significant line of thinking in the *Zhuangzi* that disrupts the coherence of such a standpoint, and thus "weakens anthropocentrism by attacking the unity of *anthropos*."[55] From what ideal standpoint, then, should those who assume "control" manage things in the world? Daoism answers the question this way:

> If the exemplary person finds that there is no choice but to oversee the world, nothing is as good as not doing/making (*wuwei* 無為). By not doing/making, one can rest in the sensibilities of one's disposition and life-allotment (*xingmingzhiqing* 性命之情). If one values the world as one values one's own human life (*shen* 身), then one can be entrusted with the world. If one cares for the world as one cares for one's own human life, then one can be given the world.[56]

Again, human life (*shen*) is the context in which we act with body-and-mind, a term in classical Chinese that means both "body" and "self." Being in touch with human life is to recognize how Nature (*tian* 天) and the Human (*ren*) intersect in lived experience, and thus to remain optimally aware of how human technologies, artifacts, and biases operate in the world and impact relations between ourselves and the nonhuman environment. This is the optimal standpoint from which to "govern" the world.

The second component in intelligent (*ming* 明) governance is *wuwei* 無為: not doing/making things to be thus or so. Again, Dewey offers a nuanced interpretation of this concept. "It is something more than mere inactivity," he explains, "it is a kind of rule of moral doing, a doctrine of active patience, endurance, persistence while Nature [*tian* 天] has time to do her work."[57] "Active patience," as Dewey calls it, recovers the element of *timing*—which results in action that is elegant, efficacious, and hardly noticed. Again, Daoism is not about having *no* objectives or goals. It teaches instead that great achievements are only incrementally secured. As Chapter 63 says: "The greatest things in the world can only arise from what is small. Thus, ultimately, sages do not make (*wei* 為) great things happen. This is why they can bring great things to fruition (*cheng* 成)." In actual practice, *wuwei* means being attentive to minute opportunities and changing course as needed in the midst of an ongoing process. In this way, the process is not subordinated to any preconceived end. This is known as "observing the small" (*jianxiao* 見小)—and as Chapter 52 teaches: "To observe the small is called intelligence (*ming*)."

Unfortunately, *wuwei* 無為 has been subjected to serious distortion by commentators who equate it with a kind of *laissez-faire* attitude toward governance, that which Dewey identifies as the "[denial] of the possibility of radical intervention of intelligence in the conduct of human life."[58] *Laissez-faire*, explains Dewey, "trusts the direction of human affairs to nature, or providence, or evolution, or manifest destiny—that is to say, to accident—rather than to a contriving and constructive intelligence."[59] Since *laissez-faire* thinking is implicated in the most pressing issues of our time, namely, those of environmental and economic justice, it is worth considerable digression at this juncture to explain why our free-market, libertarian friends are so thoroughly wrong to equate the Daoist ideal of *wuwei* with the concept of *laissez-faire*.

Dismissing Market Daoism

Libertarians and free-market theorists routinely claim Laozi as one of their own. David Boaz for instance, in his reader on Libertarianism, features selections "*from Lao-tzu to Milton Friedman*," reflecting his belief that Laozi was the "first known libertarian."[60] Even Ronald Reagan quoted the *Daodejing* in support of government deregulation during a State of the Union address.[61] Such statements are based on the perception that notions of nonintervention and spontaneous order in the *Daodejing* are identical to those in the writings of thinkers like Adam Smith and Friedrich A. Hayek. Ken McCormick, for instance, treats such notions as equivalent. In his article, "The Tao of Laissez-Faire," he writes:

> *Laissez-faire* is simply an extension of *wuwei* 無為 to government policy. Harmonizing with the *dao* 道, which is universal and whose power extends everywhere, even to the social realm, allows a beneficent natural order to emerge. Moreover, this natural order is superior to any order which human beings could create because human knowledge is partial and fragmented. In order to take

advantage of this natural order, the ruler must seek stillness. By following a course of non-action, the natural order will emerge on its own, with beneficial results for the society."[62]

To illustrate that Laozi's advocacy of *laissez-faire* is explicit, McCormick quotes Chapter 57 of the *Daodejing*. The chapter reads: "I take no action and the people are transformed of themselves. I prefer stillness and the people are rectified of themselves. I am not meddlesome and the people prosper of themselves."[63]

From here, the logic proceeds as follows. Daoists advocate nonintervention in the form of *wuwei* 無為. Free-market capitalists advocate that government interference in markets be reduced to a bare minimum: *laissez-faire*. The two ideas (*wuwei* and *laissez-faire*) are identical. Thus, Daoism provides further philosophical justification for free-market capitalism. McCormick finds it exciting that *laissez-faire* was, as he sees it: "independently developed in China, in such a different culture, time, and place." This, he says, enables free-market advocates to "call upon another, quite powerful, philosophical tradition for help" in promoting their economic vision. He continues: "Daoism has existed for more than two millennia, and it is not a philosophy that can be easily dismissed . . . It is a tradition which is unmistakably different from classical liberalism, but on the very important subject of the propriety of a policy of *laissez-faire*, there is complete agreement."[64]

McCormick interprets free-market reforms in China accordingly. Such reforms are "not so much [an] importation of a foreign ideology, but [rather the] reawakening of a home-grown concept."[65] James A. Dorn, Vice President for Academic Affairs at the conservative Cato Institute, echoes McCormick's enthusiasm in his own article, "China's Future: Market Socialism or Market Taoism?" As Dorn sees it: "The market-liberal vision is not new to China; it was inherent in the Daoist doctrine of *wuwei* 無為 developed by Laozi and his disciples. China's leaders need only let the Chinese people return to their roots to see the wisdom of letting the spontaneous market process organize economic life, while limiting government to the protection of life, liberty, and prosperity."[66]

Based on the perceived equivalence of *wuwei* 無為 and *laissez-faire*, Market Daoism assumes that the former, like the latter, must lend support to market liberalism. Such a brisk inference, however, bypasses some important questions. Was *wuwei* originally connected to an economic ideal in early Daoism? Was that ideal one of market liberalism? If not, were there features of that ideal that would preclude market liberalism? Coming at Daoism as they invariably do, not as scholars of Chinese thought but as free-market advocates, Market Daoists seldom ask such questions. They do need to be asked, however, if Daoism is to be legitimately enlisted on behalf of market capitalism.

Consider, for instance, the ideal society envisioned in Chapter 80 of the *Daodejing*. It is hardly a scene of robust commercial activity. Rather, it is a society in which people will "find relish in their food, and beauty in their clothes. Will be content in their abode, and happy in the way they live. Adjoining states are within sight of one another, and the sounds of dogs barking and cocks crowing in one state can be heard in another, yet the people of one state will grow old and die without having had any dealings with those of another."

The absence of contact with adjoining states does not preclude basic economic activity within the confines of a state. But as Karl Polanyi argues, primitive localism of the type envisioned here does not suggest activities consistent with the emergence of full-scale market mechanisms. Contrary to the logic of classical economic theory, Polanyi argues that markets are not institutions "functioning mainly within" economies, but rather among economies.[67] Markets, he argues, are primarily and originally the result of distance contact. Even if markets are understood instead as the result of some innate desire to trade, as they are in classical liberal theory,[68] the vision in the *Daodejing* is one in which such a desire is ignored. Thus, it is not at all clear that Laozi's ideal community is consistent with even the most rudimentary notion of a market—let alone free-market capitalism.

Be that as it may, there were of course markets in ancient China. Trade was an indispensable and closely monitored component of social life. The *advent* of market exchange, however, like the advent of every social innovation in China, is not attributed to the essence of "human nature." Rather, it traces its origin to the ingenuity (*zuo* 作) of the ancient sages. According to the cultural history sketched in the "Great Appendix" in the *Book of Changes*, it was Shennong who first inaugurated markets. According to this account: "He made it such that markets were held at midday. He brought it about that all the people would assemble their goods, exchange them, and withdraw, each securing that which they obtained."[69] Noteworthy in this passage are the active verbs. The market system was something that was originally "done" (*wei* 為) by Shennong. It was something "brought about" (*zhi* 致) by his policies. In other words, markets did not pop up spontaneously. Once markets gained momentum in early China, they were carefully regulated by the state. During the western Zhou dynasty, market frequency, location, hours of operation; the arrangement of goods, products made available, and prices, were all subject to state control.[70] As the quality of handicrafts gradually improved, the market economy expanded, and the strictly controlled markets of the western Zhou gave way to freer systems of exchange. This process eventually gave birth to an independent merchant class.

Merchants have historically been held in low esteem in China. In the social hierarchy, they occupied a place below the royal, civil, military, intellectual, agricultural, and artisan classes. As Romeyn Taylor explains, this new class was immediately regarded as a threat:

> Although the orthodox social order comfortably accommodated the concept of economy as livelihood, the emergence of an autonomous market system on a significant scale in the late Zhou and Han presented a fundamental threat in the form of a flourishing merchant class ambitious for higher status. In the former Han the battle was joined. Merchants were forbidden by law to buy land or hold office and, continuing Zhou practice, trade was confined to officially administered urban markets. Government monopolies were established in some commodities in order to divert commercial profits from private to public hands.[71]

Confucians taught that it was important for wealth not to accumulate in the hands of any elite group, whether state or commercial. The Confucian ideal of governing was to act as a "Parent of the People" (*minzhifumu* 民之父母). As the *Great Learning* (*Daxue* 大學) explains, this required that virtue be prioritized over profit and that wealth be widely distributed. As the text says: "Virtue is primary. Getting rich is secondary. If virtue becomes an afterthought and getting rich is foremost, [the ruler] will compete with the people and engage in theft. Hence, to gather riches is to scatter the people. To scatter the wealth is to draw the people to you." While most of the prescriptions in the *Great Learning* are addressed to rulers rather than to private citizens, its principles regarding the accumulation of wealth applied across all social classes. As the text observes: "Head of a state or head of a household, anyone devoted to wealth and its use must be under the influence of a petty person (*xiaoren* 小人)"[72]

Then as now, the primary source of income for early Chinese states was tax revenue, and a common grievance among people was lavish state spending. Mozi represents the populist sentiment in this regard. He advocates for moderation in state expenditures, and identifies and criticizes the insufficient production of such basic goods as housing, clothing, food, and transportation—production that needed to be met if the population of the state was to increase. Mencius was also interested in expanding the size of the state, and he pushes for broad-based tax reductions: the elimination of duties at border stations, the remittance of property tax on local merchants, and relief for those working public lands into production.[73]

Before Mencius gets branded the first "business-friendly" Confucian, one should recognize that he endorses a standard set of limited stimulus measures. The measures that he proposes are outlined in the "Monthly Government Orders" (*Yueling* 月令) chapter of the *Rituals* as well as in the *Annals of Lü Buwei*, and rather than being prescribed as general government policy, these measures were understood to be only periodically appropriate—specifically, for the second month of autumn and in some cases the first month of summer.[74] The *permanent* elimination of taxes and border tariffs is not endorsed in the ancient records. Rather, what is advised is the periodical modification (*yi* 易) of taxes and border tariffs. Such adjustments are indicative of continued state control, and there is nothing to indicate that Mencius was unorthodox in this respect.

It is clear, in any case, that Mencius had no problem taxing the merchants. In fact, it is in the *Mencius* that we learn of the original rationale for doing so. As the text relates:

> In ancient times, markets were instituted so that people could exchange what they had for what they did not have. Officials were there just to keep order. But then came some despicable people who sought out a "high mound" and scaled it. They looked left and right and monopolized the market profits. The people all recognized them as despicable, so they went ahead and taxed them. The practice of taxing merchants originated with such despicable people.[75]

There were good reasons for Chinese thinkers to be wary of this emerging class. One of the primary economic concerns in early China was that heightened commercial activity would have a detrimental effect on the production and distribution of basic necessities, especially food. Xunzi thus recommends that the state "keep statistical records to reduce the number of merchants and traders" in order to prevent farmers and craftspeople from abandoning their vocations in pursuit of greater profits. Xunzi describes such restrictions as "allowing the people a generous living through the exercise of government."[76] Across the board, Chinese philosophers advise government intervention to limit and control the expansion of market activity and to mitigate the problems that it generates.

The proponents of Market Daoism would have us believe that Laozi was profoundly different in this regard. For Murray N. Rothbard, co-founder of the Cato Institute, Laozi was the "first political economist to discern the systemic effects of government intervention." The early Daoists (again, in his estimation, "the world's first libertarians") advocated "virtually no interference by the state in economy or society."⁷⁷

There is, in fact, zero textual evidence that Laozi envisioned *wuwei* 無為 as applicable to economies specifically. Instead, a careful reading of the *Daodejing* suggests similar concerns, if not the advocacy of similar policies, current in the period. Like Xunzi, the *Daodejing* is concerned with certain vocations becoming too profitable and having a detrimental impact on vital industries. As Chapter 53 says: when "robbers" possess too much wealth, the fields become overgrown with weeds and granaries stand empty. Like Mencius, the *Daodejing* is concerned with despicable agents who thrive where profits are easily made. As Chapter 19 says: "discard profit" and thereby get rid of thieves and bandits. Like Mozi, the *Daodejing* is concerned that profligate state spending, especially on the military, misallocates treasure. As Chapter 46 says: when *dao* 道 prevails in the land, the best horses are found working the field rather than being diverted by the state for military use. And like everyone, the *Daodejing* is interested in targeted tax relief. As Chapter 75 says: people are hungry because those in power eat up too much in taxes.

One might derive from this some kind of "Daoist economic theory," or not. That's not the point. The point is that, with respect to economic concerns, the *Daodejing* is not so different from other Chinese philosophical schools. It shares the same basic concerns: a distrust of the profit motive, and concerns about vital industries, unfair taxation, and the misallocation of state treasure. There is, however, one *key* difference between Laozi and other philosophers. Laozi never appeals to the standard list of market-friendly policies outlined in the "Monthly Government Orders" and elsewhere. Why? Because the lowering of border tariffs, remittance of taxes on merchants, and the incentives for commercial development were motivated by the desire to *increase the size of the state*. But unlike other philosophers, Laozi did not wish to increase the size of the state. As Chapter 80 plainly says: "Reduce the size and population of the state (*guo* 國)." According to Daoism, the best way to survive geopolitical instability is to maintain a low demographic profile. The growth of the state, the only goal that ever motivated early Chinese thinkers to adopt pro-market policies, was something that Laozi wished to avoid. Not *wanting* to facilitate economic growth, he had no interest in developing interstate commerce and thus expansive markets. This being so, to casually assert as the Market Daoists do that Laozi represents the "market-liberal vision" in China is not only unsubstantiated, it is positively contradicted by the facts.⁷⁸

Turning to philosophical considerations, we again find Market Daoism disregarding important dimensions of its subject. Daoist teachings on human desire and human nature are largely ignored in Market Daoist treatments. Not surprisingly, proponents of Market Daoism approach the tradition already committed to theories of human nature that support their capitalist views. As if by reflex, when they encounter appeals to "nature" in the *Daodejing*, such preferences inform their interpretations of the text. Flagrant omissions, equivocations, and distortions are the result.

McCormick, for instance, regards Adam Smith and Daoism as identical in that both maintain "that we must not interfere with the natural order of things," and both believe "[that] it is not proper to *force* people to oppose their own natural inclinations."[79] He never once considers that one's view of "nature" might imply something other than a free-market system. Dorn is equally neglectful in this regard. He asserts that alternative economic systems are "contrary to human nature," and that if people are simply left alone to find their way (i.e., *wuwei* 無為), "a spontaneous market order will arise."[80] It never enters his mind that Daoism might have its own ideas about "human nature" and that those ideas might be antithetical to the emergence of a market order.[81] Such oversights need to be addressed.

It is true that Daoism advocates *wuwei* 無為 as a strategy for governance. Chapter 57 of the *Daodejing* is a clear illustration of this, and it is the darling passage of Market Daoism. It is noteworthy, however, that in the works of Rothbard, McCormick, and Dorn the concluding line of this passage is routinely edited out. The full passage reads as follows: "I take no action and the people are transformed of themselves. I prefer stillness and the people are rectified of themselves. I am not meddlesome and the people prosper of themselves. *I am free from desire and the people of themselves become simple like the un-carved block.*"

Market Daoists regard Laozi's teachings on desire (*yu* 欲), here restored, to be irrelevant to his teachings on *wuwei* 無為—hence their systematic removal of the last line. Rothbard, for instance, suggests that it was only after "seeing no hope for a mass movement" in support of *laissez-faire* that Laozi turned to "[counseling] the now familiar Daoist path of withdrawal, retreat, and limitations of one's desires."[82] This is pure speculation on Rothbard's part—a wild guess. McCormick is more explicit in arguing that the topic of desire *should* be severed from *wuwei* for philosophical reasons. As he sees it: "One must not confound [Daoist] moral arguments regarding proper individual behavior with [its] policy recommendations." For McCormick, Daoist teachings on desire operate on a different level than its teachings on *wuwei*. His argument:

> The fact that [Daoists] do not think that wealth brings contentment does not change the fact that [they do not advocate] a policy to stop people from pursuing what they want. Wise people will

learn on their own that riches do not bring contentment. The fact that other people may not understand this does not justify economic restrictions. One cannot force people to be virtuous.[83]

This is a classic red herring. The question is not whether one can force another to be virtuous. The question is whether desire is a good thing according to Daoism. McCormick's premise here is false anyway. The *Daodejing* does not expect us to "learn on our own" that rampant desire and the accumulation of material goods do not bring contentment. To the contrary, the text tells us so over and over again. Let Chapter 46 suffice: "There is no crime greater than having too many desires. There is no disaster greater than not being content. There is no misfortune greater than being covetous. Hence, in being content, one will always have enough."

However Market Daoism tries to reconcile or conceal the issue,[84] the fact remains that *wuwei* 無為 and desire are closely related topics in the *Daodejing*. In fact, the widespread reduction of desire is precisely the type of transformation that government by *wuwei* is intended to effect. In Chapter 37, the outcome of such governing is presented in terms of desire explicitly: "The myriad beings will be transformed of their own accord. After they are transformed, should desire raise its head, I shall press it down with the weight of the nameless un-carved block (*pu* 樸). The nameless un-carved block is freedom from desire. And if I cease to desire and remain still, the empire will be at peace of its own accord."

Market Daoists feel safe ignoring the link between *wuwei* 無為 and desire for the simple reason that the Western idea of *laissez-faire* has nothing to do with the psychology of desire. McCormick argues exactly that. At precisely this juncture, however, a more critical scholar would pause to inquire into the differences between *wuwei* and *laissez-faire*. As we have seen, the term *wei* 為 has a broad semantic range in classical Chinese. In addition to meaning "not doing," *wuwei* also means "not taking" things to be a certain way—"not regarding" things to be such or so. As Edward Slingerland explains, such "non-regarding" is a central theme in the *Daodejing*:

> [In] Laozi's view desire is merely a symptom of a deeper malaise: knowledge, or the "regarding" (*wei*) that springs from knowledge. "Regarding" in the sense that is criticized by Laozi refers to making normative, not merely definitional, distinctions—to hold something in (high) regard. Such regarding causes a person to value one thing over another, and therefore provides ulterior motives for action.[85]

Such "ulterior motives," in the form of desires, can lead to misguided government policies, and this illuminates an important dimension of Laozi's advocacy of *wuwei*. Chapter 75 explains that difficulties in governing emerge when those in power "have regard" (*youwei* 有為). D. C. Lau's translation, however, offers a different gloss. He suggests that such difficulties result from government action *itself*. His rendition: "The people are difficult to govern. It is because those in authority are too fond of action [*wei* 為] that the people are difficult to govern." Relying on Lau's translation, Market Daoism seizes on this passage. It appears to advocate for European-style *laissez-faire*. But *pace* Lau, the *wei* spoken of in this passage is something that rulers "have" (*you* 有). It is not something that they "do," nor is it something they are unusually "fond" of doing. Slingerland's understanding of *wei* as "regard" is a more adequate translation of the term in this instance.[86]

With such an adjustment, the meaning of the passage might be paraphrased as follows: "Difficulties in governing are a result of those in charge having special regard for some particular outcome or interest."[87] Such an observation does not lead to a prescription for doing literally nothing, *laissez-faire*. Rather, it advises that those in government not subordinate the actual process of governing to a fixed end that is held in higher regard (*wei* 為). This means that governing should remain intelligent (*ming* 明)—flexible, "observing the small" (*jianxiao* 見小), and "actively patient," as Dewey would say—like "cooking a small fish" (Chapter 60). The Daoist ideal, accordingly, is one in which government does not hastily impose its own design on the social order. This much Market Daoism understands. What it fails to understand, however, is that such non-regard (*wuwei* 無為) is both a means-and-end to an ideal social order. As Chapter 37 relates, the aim of governing "without regard" is that people return to the state of the un-carved block (*pu* 樸), free from desire themselves. As Lau explains, the un-carved block is "a symbol for the original state of [humans] before desire is produced in [them] by artificial means."[88]

Here it becomes important to recognize the difference between "nature" as conceived in Daoism and "human nature" as conceived in classical liberal economics. For Daoism, the human being is not primordially driven by the desire to profit, to acquire, to barter, or to trade. Such desires are the result of a regard (*wei* 為) for things that comes not from our "nature" but from its perversion. Government may instigate such inclinations by acting perversely itself—desiring to grow the state beyond its natural limits and wanting to acquire the goods of its neighbor. Such perversion was commonplace in the Warring States period. The ideal Daoist state is posited as an antidote to this tendency. It rejects economic expansion and interstate commerce, which together increase the desire for material goods and trigger an unremitting cycle of acquisition and exchange. According to the logic of Daoism, this is precisely the spiraling dynamic that makes populations difficult to manage. Thus, to have "as few desires as possible" is the aim of Daoism, both individually and communally (Chapter 19). Only with this will "peace of its own accord" be achieved (Chapter 37). Hence, as Hu Jichuang explains, early Daoism was "indifferent to, if not disdainful of human economic activities."[89] Robust commercial activities, if anything, make society *more difficult* to govern according to its logic.

This is where Market Daoism fails to recognize its own self-refutation: the very antipathy between markets and Daoism. This fatal error becomes all the more egregious as their argument is mobilized in support of modern consumer capitalism. In modern parlance, the word "market" is a verb as well as a noun. Hundreds of billions of dollars are spent each year on commercial advertising worldwide. In such a hyper-commercial environment, attention itself becomes a commodity. Gimmicks are developed to excite and absorb attention, and then markets are created to redistribute it for the sole purpose of creating desire where it does not exist. Hans-Georg Moeller recognizes straight away the manner in which such a system is utterly out of synch with classical Daoism. "Obviously [Laozi] did not envision a capitalist market economy with its culture of creating demand and desires through advertising and a public ideal of ever-increasing prosperity," he observes. "The early Daoists, it seems, were not interested in 'heating up' the economy by stimulating the acquiring of goods and possessions."[90] As D. C. Lau contends, there is "no doubt" that Laozi would recognize commercial advertising as one of the "banes of modern life," a practice that "creates new desires for objects [that] no one would have missed if they had not been invented."[91] Nothing is more antithetical to Daoism than the creation of such desires.

The degree to which Market Daoism ignores this fact is stunning. In "The Case for Market Taoism," Dorn claims that the good Daoist government (i.e., one by *wuwei* 無為) acts "in harmony with each person's desire to prosper and to expand the range of choice."[92] Positively omitted is the fact that Daoism stands totally opposed to feeding such desire and expanding the range of choice. As Chapter 12 teaches: "The five colors blind the eyes. The five tones deafen the ears. The five flavors destroy the palate. Racing and hunting make a mind wild and crazy. Rare and expensive things make people lose their way." Such a colossal oversight is the result of two philosophical errors. The first is the severing of *wuwei* from the topic of desire. This results in a distortion of the meaning of the idea and thus a failure to recognize its psychological dimension. The second error is ignoring the fact that Daoism has a conception of "nature" distinct from that of classical liberalism. At crucial junctures, Market Daoism conflates the teachings of Daoism with classical liberalism, and thus fails to detect the relevant and distinguishing features of Daoist philosophy. Taken together, these two errors leave Market Daoism with little philosophical credence.

Intelligence and Prognostication

Even with better scholarship, however, we should not expect to find classical Daoism univocally endorsing or disavowing our modern economic practices. The historical divergences are too wide, and the contemporary world is too complex. Consider again the ideal Daoist society. Here, adjoining states are "within sight of one another," hearing "the sounds of dogs barking and cocks crowing," yet their populations have no substantive dealings with one another. Such a vision is naïve in our globalized world. El Paso, Texas, and Juárez, Mexico, for instance, are technically neighboring cities separated by national borders, but they are integrated by larger global systems creating relationships that cannot be ignored.

Dewey would recognize the same. While in China, he travelled to China's southeastern Fujian province in May of 1921, and upon returning he spoke of the detrimental effects of its isolation from other parts of China (Fujian is coastal and surrounded by mountains). "Inhabitants of villages only a few miles apart do not understand each other," he reported, thus "people do not comprehend situations outside the area where they live." To live in such a state today is not a virtue but an impediment to meaningful participation in larger discussions that impact everyone. Given the condition of the Fujian inhabitants, "it is not to be wondered at that their interests are so often strictly limited to affairs of their own locality."[93] In the modern world, primitive localism of the type advocated in the *Daodejing* does not really fit (*shi* 適) our circumstances or our needs.

There are, however, other contemporary practices the intelligence of which can be assessed in Daoist terms. Our desire for "rare and expensive things," for instance, today creates markets for exotic foods in all seasons and in defiance of any natural geographical limits. Most lamb meat, for instance, comes from New Zealand. Once it is raised and transported to foreign markets, it is estimated that for every two pounds of lamb 2,300 gallons of water are used and 20 kilograms of CO_2 released into the atmosphere. Yet, demand is on the rise in China. Lamb imports increased 18 percent in 2016, reaching 27,000 tons of meat.[94] Here, Daoist teachings speak cogently to our situation. Sometimes we desire wrongly, and we fail to realize how such desires negatively impact the world around us.

Such philosophical analysis is not complex, and any number of ethical theories might be evoked to reach the same conclusion. This is what Zhuangzi means by remaining centered on the "Pivot of *dao* 道." Daoism is not a "block-like" object whose truth table reveals once and for all whether something is "Definitely So/Definitely Not" (*shifei* 是非). Its ideas are *tools* through which real situations can be assessed. The notion that one accepts or rejects "Daoism," or any philosophy wholesale, would be antithetical to Zhuangzi's critique of his more doctrinaire contemporaries. Remember that such schools claim to know (*zhi* 知) the absolute truth—they make or regard (*wei* 為) things to be a certain way. Their visions, however, sometimes contradict each other. If "X" is right, then "Y" is wrong, and *vice versa*. Thus, in order to affirm what is negated and negate what is affirmed, "there is nothing like using intelligence (*ming* 明)." Again, zero-sum contests between theories (*yan* 言) occur only when they are treated in static abstraction as fixed objects. In actual practice, "nothing is [perfectly] completed or annihilated, each folds back and opens into the other to form a continuity (*yi* 一). There is no need to make (*wei*) things thus and so, and everything is entrusted to ordinary activity (*yong* 庸)." Guided by actual problems, one relies on the continuity between ideas to move freely from one theory to another and to draw from each whatever proves useful (*yong* 用) in the immediate context. As Zhuangzi explains, "to do this without realizing it is called *dao*."[95]

Environmental ethicists are beginning to realize that such an approach is more promising than arguing for consensus on any single philosophical framework. Indeed, at this stage of the game, there are more than enough theories (*yan* 言) on the table. Arguing (*bian* 辯) over their relative supremacy while the planet burns may not be the best use of our intellectual energies. A Daoist-oriented environmental ethics approaches the objects of knowledge pragmatically. As tools, theories are instrumental in removing obstacles to the restoration of *dao* 道-activity. Unfortunately, what contemporary philosophers call "applied ethics"—a weird designation suggesting that ethics in its original state is "detached"—introduces obstacles as often as it removes them. It is not especially good at locating the kinds of values that practitioners of ordinary activities (*yong* 庸) normally adjudicate. The problem is that, as the description suggests, applied ethics begins with the prioritization of theory (which it then "applies"). Such an approach has the tendency to lock positions into place from the top-down, whereas desires and biases in their natural state are more fluid.

Paul B. Thompson's analysis of the "Chatham River" case study, a heuristic model that is used for teaching students about water policy disputes,[96] reveals vividly the limits of applied ethics in resolving real-world problems. The "Chatham River" model provides a snapshot of a "typical" water use dispute. In the fictional town of Springfield, wells are producing at their limit and the economy is sagging. The town borders the Chatham River, and the town council proposes diverting some of its waters for residential and light industrial use. Riparian rights-holders object to the proposal, as do sportsmen and environmentalists. That is the "situation."

From the standpoint of philosophical ethics, it is easy enough to formulate the rationales involved. Riparian rights-holders adopt a basically "libertarian" position, sportsmen a basically "anthropocentric" position, environmentalists a basically "bio-centric" position, and the town council a basically "utilitarian" position. Thompson, however, asks whether such philosophical analysis actually clarifies anything. "It is questionable whether we are really better off than we were when disputants had vague, intuitive understandings of their own rationale," he writes. Indeed, once the situation is imbued with the spirit of philosophical ethics, it arguably becomes *worse*. The newly introduced foundational approach now requires that each of these theoretical positions (*yan* 言) defend themselves *theoretically*, and this "beckons disputants into the academy" where they can watch philosophers do battle on behalf of each theory—awaiting the victor to be declared so they can know who is right. As Thompson observes: "The availability of incompatible moral justifications for each position can form the basis for a brand of self-righteousness on the part of each interest that bodes ill for a consensus solution to the problem."[97] The truth of the matter in environmental philosophy, as Emery N. Castle argues, is that "no single environmental ethic or philosophic system exists nor is one likely to be discovered that will guide natural resource and environmental policy."[98] Thus we are left, as William James says, to "invent some manner" of solving such problems.

So, are we doomed? Thompson gives us hope by analyzing the Chatham River model alongside actual, real-time problems with the Edwards Aquifer in Texas, one of the most dynamic artesian aquifers in the world. It supplies two million people with drinking water, feeds springs, provides spring flow for downstream recreational activities, and is home to several unique and endangered species. The first thing that Thompson notes is that, when problems arise, "arguments offered by each group of disputants are more complicated" than the simpler positions back in Springfield. Environmentalists, he notes, often usurp libertarian arguments with their own well-developed economic valuation models. Given changes in agriculture, some riparian rights-holders make more money selling water to the Sea World amusement park than using it to grow crops, and such economic realities become factors in adjudication and persuasion. Changing demographics means that social justice issues are often implicated in Texas water disputes, such that egalitarian rationales weave in and out among the more conventional theoretical rhetoric.[99] The truth is that moral situations are complex and always changing, and they are not so easily captured in the "thought experiments" so loved by analytic philosophers.

Real-world problems do call for abstract philosophical thinking. The question is one of *how* theories (*yan* 言) as tools are best used in converting problematic situations into those that are more steady and sure. This is a complex question, and in order to address it we must have a clear view of what theories are. Plato remains helpful here. Taken in the abstract, theories are neither true nor false—i.e., they do not fit into the rubric of "Definitely So/Definitely Not" (*shifei* 是非). For Plato, objects that function in thought (*dianoia*) are not true but *intelligible*. "2 + 2 = 4" is intelligible: a tautological formulation given the meaning of its terms. Any *truth* that it might have is of the synthetic variety. It is true, for instance, that 2 oranges + 2 oranges = 4 oranges; thus, "2 + 2 = 4" is true *of oranges*. The objects about which truth is concerned, i.e. the oranges, are located squarely in the *visible* (i.e., empirical) world: the one in which science operates and change is supreme. Accordingly, in Plato's "divided line," the true applies not to thought (*dianoia*) but to belief (*pistis*). Belief is the only cognitive power (*dunamis*) to which truth attributions apply.

The virtue of knowledge (*episteme*) is different. Its presumed object is not the true but the good. The fact that the good is "higher" than truth is what fuels arguments over the merits of censorship and "noble lies" in the *Republic*. One might object to Dewey's "back in gear" thesis based on a rationale similar to one forwarded by Socrates in this connection. Might it not be *better* to preserve concepts that are not "in gear" with empirical reality (i.e., literally true) if they are *good* to believe for therapeutic or other reasons? Here, Philip J. Ivanhoe argues in the affirmative. He presumes, for instance, that there are versions of the so-called "oneness hypothesis" in world philosophy that "modern people will find difficult to embrace, as [they are] clearly inconsistent with the best science of the day." According to him, however, one should consider embracing such hypotheses anyway. For, "by immersing oneself in such a form of life, by embracing what one at least initially regards as improbable, impossible, or even a hallucination, one will over time come to *feel* it as true and act accordingly, perhaps forgetting why one ever worried so much about whether or not it was literally true."[100]

Students of American philosophy will immediately distinguish Ivanhoe's approach from that which William James adopts in his famous article, "The Will to Believe" (and it is significant that Ivanhoe evokes Blaise Pascal and not James in his discussion). For James, one cannot *will* oneself to embrace a proposition that is "impossible." Rather, it must be a "live option."[101] Plus, in keeping with the more rigorous standards of pragmatism, the consequences of any hypothesis must run the gamut of whatever else one currently takes to be *true*, i.e., not clashing with other beliefs of vital benefit.[102] Thus, from both the classical Greek and the American pragmatic perspectives, Ivanhoe's approach to truth is problematic.

It is similar, however, to an indulgence that is rampant among anti-scientifically-minded people today. The cultural thrust against the theory of evolution in the United States, for instance, is not empirical but *moral*. The driving cultural objection to evolution by natural selection is not that it is empirically "false" but that it is perceived as "bad" for human beings to regard themselves as products of blind natural forces—it just doesn't "feel" right. Such properly *theoretical* arguments against evolution are far more effective in popular culture than empirical arguments, because against the evidence (e.g., the fossil record, carbon dating, genetics, etc.) Creationism doesn't stand a chance. The question, however, is not a theoretical one but a *factual* one. In such cases, it matters greatly whether or not something is "literally true."

The problem with telling our selves "noble lies" is that belief is a power (*dunamis*) and as such it has a good way to be (*arete*). Because they are rules for action, the beliefs that one holds *ought* to be true. Properly speaking, since theories themselves are neither true nor false, the "Philosopher King" rises above them and judges their relative goodness in various applications. To do so requires going "back into the cave," deep among the time-bound objects upon which theories will have practical consequences. While this is the realm of flux and change, at any given time-space location propositions about such objects do have truth values. Ideally, the "Philosopher King" refuses to ignore such facts in favor of any theoretical commitment. Minds like that of the Creationist, however, stop short of rising to this level of cognition—they stall at the level of thought (*dianoia*) and thus exhibit tendencies of the "Timocratic" character. They are myopic, dogmatic, and prone to conflict.[103] Having only a partial glimpse of the good, they tolerate lapses in intellectual virtue (i.e., they are willing to believe falsely) in order to maintain their cherished theories. The "Philosopher King," however, is beholden to no particular theory but only to knowing "the Good." Thus, he is prepared to relinquish any doctrine if its application becomes detrimental to the Soul/City as a whole or to the proper functioning (*ergon*) of any part—including that of belief (*pistis*).

Had Plato simply relinquished the idea that "the Good" is a static object removed from time-and-space and developed instead the idea that goodness is an immanent function of the harmony (*he* 和) sustained in an irreducibly dynamic and integrated world, Athens would have delivered to us a pragmatist for the ages. In that case, in place of the "Philosopher King" with his "Sun" eternally shining, we would have received a figure more like the Daoist sage whose luminous intelligence (*ming* 明) shines within the world and waxes-and-wanes upon the Pivot of *dao* 道.[104]

Again, Dewey and Chinese thought are powerful resources for reconstructing the outmoded elements that have attached themselves to the Greek-medieval framework. Just as we need to make adjustments to Aristotle's system, adjustments need to be made to Plato's "divided line." Empirical philosophies approach the good in terms of concrete, melioristic improvements. For Dewey, the goal of any practical inquiry is to remove impediments, clear up confusions, and restore smooth-running activity in a positive direction. While pragmatic naturalists reject the notion of transcendent "forms" (*eidos*), abstraction remains central to "inquiry" so understood. Since there is normally more than one solution to any given problem, different theoretical tools (*yan* 言) need to be considered to direct situations toward desirable ends. The generation and use of such abstract conceptual tools, for Dewey, relies on "operations of both observation and ideation," as these cooperate in generating symbols through which problems are then managed.[105] Morris S. Eames provides a good summary of how pragmatic naturalists understand such a process:

> Observations cannot be made without the use of symbols, for symbols allow us to assimilate one event to another, to record observations made only a moment or even years ago, and to imagine observations of the same kind in future situations. Groupings of observations around specific problems, as these *kinds* of problems recur from time to time, show us that many of them can be treated generically.[106]

In coming to understand what such generic "tools" look like in cultures that organize themselves in a process-oriented fashion, one turns naturally to early China. Here, the *Book of Changes* is the place to start. Scholars are unsure when the earliest strata of this text was composed. At its core, however, it is a system of symbols: 64 hexagrams (*gua* 卦) composed of broken and unbroken lines with short descriptive statements (*tuan* 彖). To this is added more elaborate, interpretive images (*xiang* 象) and a series of judgments corresponding to dynamic variations made possible through each "change" line. When one consults the text, one uses a method (traditionally involving the tossing of yarrow sticks) to generate one of 4,096 possible combinations of the 64 hexagrams (64^2). Each outcome is understood to represent one type (*lei* 類) of dynamic situation or "change" that regularly occurs in nature.

The core text accrues commentary, the most important being the "Great Appendix" which emerges toward the end of the Warring States period. This text explains that trends (*fang* 方) in nature can be sorted according to types, and events can be distinguished according to groups. Here, we find Fuxi generating the hexagrams in the distant past through observing (*guan* 觀) patterns and relations operative in nature. Observing such changes (*yi* 易) reveals the coherence (*li* 理) of the world and enables one to position oneself at its center (*zhong* 中).[107]

The art of prognostication in China is ancient. There is evidence of practices involving "oracle bones" and tortoise shells that date back to the Shang dynasty. Such practices, however, differ from those associated with the *Book of Changes*. As David N. Keightley explains, divination practice during the Shang was mostly "black-and-white," more like fortune telling than prognostication. The more "enigmatic aphorisms" of the *Book of Changes*, however, were developed to cope with the "greys" of experience.[108] The text does not provide its readers with *answers*—it provides *symbols* through which problematic situations can be reconstructed into unified wholes. These symbols are not divine revelations; they are instead the results of empirical observations processed through human imagination. Nature (*tian* 天) is replete with patterns, habits, and regularities, and once these are formulated abstractly they become "tools" (*qi* 器) in coping with future situations. Such tools are what the text provides.

Assumptions about human cognition in the *Book of Changes* are consistent with classical American pragmatism. As Charles Sanders Peirce teaches, inquiry emerges from a state of doubt that follows upon some problematic situation. Where there is no problem, there is no inquiry. Likewise in the *Book of Changes*—if there is no problem, there is no point to consulting the text. Its oracular function is premised on the fact that inquiry arises from some problematic situation. Early Chinese thinkers understood that such situations issue from crises in interpretation—one simply does not know what is happening. As Cheng Chung-ying explains, to consult the *Book of Changes* is "to find a point of contact with reality so that one may make a relevant decision in light of some induced interpretation of a situation."[109] This involves reintegrating the immediacy of a problematic situation with elements that define and shape its emergence. We *must* perceive the world in some determinate way if we are to manage things at all. Otherwise, experience is nothing but a flood of discontinuous stimuli before which we lose all bearing. The *Book of Changes* works because those who consult it already find themselves in a problematic situation—they have *ipso facto* surrendered certainty as to their interpretation of events. Cognitively, this constitutes a crisis in what Alfred North Whitehead calls "symbolic reference," and its resolution demands a further act of symbolic reference.[110] The *Book of Changes* serves this purpose. The hexagrams invite us to re-orient perception by stimulating the reconstruction of a problematic situation.

Images (*xiang* 象) work like "ideas," and as such are "tools" that operate in restoring coherence (*li* 理) to our experience. As Dewey explains: "Ideas are operational in that they instigate and direct further operations of observation; they are proposals and plans for acting upon existing conditions to bring new facts to light and to organize all the selected facts into a coherent whole."[111] The accuracy of ideas is measured by how well they organize facts and guide one's action in a satisfactory direction. What working ideas reveal, and this is especially true in the *Book of Changes*, is not the static properties of a situation but the dynamic *relations* that are at play within it. "Knowledge which is merely a reduplication in ideas of what exists already in the world may afford us the satisfaction of a photograph," Dewey writes, "but that is all."[112] Images in the *Book of Changes* are hardly photograph representations, and such *non*-representation is fundamental to how they operate. As A. C. Graham explains:

> If (the hexagrams) meaning were unambiguous, the overwhelming probability would be that the prognostications would be either obviously inapplicable or grossly misleading. Since on the contrary the hexagrams open up an indefinite range of patterns for correlation . . . the effect is to free the mind to take account of all information whether or not it conflicts with preconceptions, awaken it to unnoticed similarities and connections, and guide it to a settled decision adequate to the complexity of factors.[113]

Charles Sanders Peirce would have appreciated this semiotic function immediately. In Peirce's terminology, the image (*xiang* 象) takes the form of a "Third." Thus, "It is general. It is potential. It is vague, but yet with such a vagueness as permits of its accurate determination in regard to any particular object proposed for examination."[114] The image thus awaits articulation in concrete situations in order to take on meaning, and such vagueness is essential to its function. Once meaning becomes restored, one's purposes and intentions are reformulated according to the reconfiguration of elements that constitute the newly clarified situation.

The *Book of Changes* is regarded as an oracle in that it speaks for *dao* 道, but it does not change the situation *objectively* (magic) or deliver insights *subjectively* (revelation). Rather, it works on behalf of *dao* by reintegrating situations into novel existential unities in which means-and-ends regain continuity. Remember, *dao* itself has no leanings (*fang* 方)—but things in the world do. Organized forms (*xing* 形) with their directional biases (*de* 德) appear before a formless and purposeless *dao* and exhibit genuine "ways of behaving" that our intellectual "tools" (*qi* 器) attempt to capture in some revealing fashion. Thus, as the "God of the North Sea" explains: "One who understands *dao* is sure to reach through to the coherence of things (*li* 理). One who reaches through to the coherence of things is sure to act intelligently (*ming* 明) in weighing things up."[115]

The *Book of Changes* suggests to us how this is done, and it is important to recognize that it is an active process. As Dewey says, inquiry is an overt doing, thereby *changing* our relation to the objects that we apprehend in thought and action. Thus, "the outcome of the directed activity is the construction of a new empirical situation in which objects are differently related to one another, and such that the *consequences* of directed operations form the objects that have the property of being *known*."[116] Prognostication (*prognosticare*) means to "know before," but in actual practice its infinitive operates as a past participle: to *prognosticate* is to *have prognosticated*, resulting in objects that come to have the property of being *known*. Such "knowing before" knows the world into stability in the present and sets forth from there to see what happens next. There is no "telling the future" implied in the *Book of Changes*. The future cannot be foretold.

Destiny Unbound

In July of 1896, Dewey delivered a lecture at the famous Chautauqua Institution in upstate New York. The center of the growing Chautauqua movement, the Institution aimed to bring education, culture, and spiritual connectedness to adult learners each summer in a kind of utopian "vacation school" atmosphere. During his visit, Dewey spoke on "Imagination in Education," and William James attended the talk.[117] James also delivered his own talk, and he decided to linger for a week at the camp. He leaves behind some vivid impressions:

> Sobriety and industry, intelligence and goodness, orderliness and ideality, prosperity and cheerfulness, pervade the air . . . You have the best of company, and yet no effort. You have no zymotic diseases, no poverty, no drunkenness, no crime, no police. You have culture, you have kindness . . . you have the best fruits of what mankind has fought and bled and striven for under the name of civilization . . . You have, in short, a foretaste of what human society might be, were it all in the light, with no suffering and no dark corners . . . the middle-class paradise, without a sin, without a victim, without a blot, without a tear.[118]

The scene got under James' skin. "Through the whole place there is an atmosphere of happiness and *success*," he wrote to his wife. "The charmless goodness and seriousness of the place grows."[119] Looking back weeks later, James describes Chautauqua as "10,000 people with no wilder excess to tempt them than 'ice cream soda.'"[120] When he finally left the grounds, he found himself "quite unexpectedly and involuntarily saying: 'Ouf! What a relief!'"[121] He felt that he needed time to recalibrate to the real world. "The flash of a pistol, a dagger, or a devilish eye, anything to break the unlovely level of 10,000 good people, a crime, murder, rape, elopement, anything would do."¹²² What for others was a "therapeutic" interval of spiritual replenishment for James was a kind of saccharine torture.

On later reflection, James observes that what he missed at Chautauqua was "the element of precipitousness, so to call it, of strength and strenuousness, intensity, and danger." What the human spirit requires is not therapeutic reassurance but "the sight of the struggle going on."¹²³ By evoking Laozi in *Experience and Nature*, Dewey means to affirm such precipitousness, which he refers to as the irreducible mixture of the "stable and precarious" in experience.¹²⁴ As Chapter 2 of the *Daodejing* says, one cannot have the easy without the difficult—the two are mutual (*xiang* 相). When such inseparables are bifurcated (*li* 離) in thought, utopian notions of a kind of moral perfection become conceptually possible: e.g., the perfectly virtuous life in line with an "ethical scheme inherent in the world."

It is easy to mistake *wuwei* 無為 for a state of utopian bliss or moral perfection, but this ignores the fact that it is an ideal derived from Nature (*tian* 天) and from *life*—the defining adventure of which is the constant need to adjust means-and-ends in the process of staying alive. As Dewey understood: "Because the success of any particular struggle is measured by reaching a point of frictionless action, therefore there is [projected] such a thing as an all-inclusive end of effortless smooth activity endlessly maintained."¹²⁵ *Wuwei*, however, is not such a state of sitting back and no longer having to "try" to do anything. That, in fact, is the straight path to extinction. Still less is *wuwei* a kind of *laissez-faire* attitude that entrusts everything to "God's will," "Heaven's plan," or the "Invisible hand." Such approaches are "too easy," says Dewey. In the human world, they leave things "just about as they were before; that is, sufficiently bad so that there is additional support for the idea that only supernatural aid can better them." For Dewey, "the position of natural intelligence is that there exists a *mixture* of good and evil," and for him, "reconstruction in the direction of the good which is indicated by ideal ends, must take place, if at all, through continued cooperative effort."¹²⁶

What Daoism provides is insight into what it means for our efforts to be *cooperative* as opposed to *coercive*—that is, "co-working" (co-*operari*) as opposed to "co-restricting" (co-*arcēre*). What Dewey describes as "active patience" (*wuwei* 無為) works *with* existing conditions in realizing ends incrementally alongside other processes in Nature (*tian* 天); whereas overt doing/making (*wei* 為) works *against* Nature (*tian*) in order to realize its goals all at once. The former approach is consistent with natural growth, while the latter is not.

Growth, for Dewey, is its own norm. "The question is whether growth in this direction promotes or retards growth in general," he explains. "Does this form of growth create conditions for further growth, or does it set up conditions that shut off the person who has growth in this particular direction from the occasions, stimuli, and opportunities for continuing growth in new directions?" *Forcing* growth limits the furthering (*yuan* 遠) of things by restricting their freedom to annul (*fan* 反) their own possibilities as they go along. As the *Daodejing* explains, those who govern with "profound" *de* 德 refuse to set fixed ends for this reason. As Chapter 65 explains: "Those who consistently realize this style [of governance] are said to be profoundly *de*. Profound *de* goes deeper and advances further. It goes with things as they annul (*fan*). Only when this happens is the great flowing accordance (*dashun* 大順) reached." Again, this is not *laissez-faire* or "not trying." Instead, it is intelligent (*ming* 明) activity that pays careful attention to means-and-ends. Such growth, as Dewey explains, "is one exemplification of the principle of continuity."[127]

It is a formidable challenge to build a world in which demands for growth are optimally realized. As Dewey points out, the basis of organic life is "need"—and as William James asks, ought not *every* demand by *every* living thing be satisfied for its own sake? In concluding that, "*the essence of good is simply to satisfy demand*," James establishes that the "guiding principle for ethical philosophy" is the obligation "simply to satisfy at all times *as many demands as we can*." Neither James nor Dewey, however, is sanguine at the prospect. First, as James observes, the perfect world would be one "in which every demand was gratified as soon as it was made," but this is logically impossible. "Spending our money, yet growing rich; taking our holiday, yet getting ahead with our work; shooting and fishing, yet doing no hurt to the beasts."[128] Such demands cannot be simultaneously fulfilled.

Dewey understands that human desires conflict by virtue of their ends-in-view. There are conflicts that involve "desire which wants a near-by object and a desire which wants an object which is seen by thought to occur in consequence of an intervening series of conditions, or in the 'long run.'"[129] The need to register this difference is precisely why axiological theories need to overcome the "Instrumental/Intrinsic" dualism and realize that the unit of value is a specific means-end relationship *as a whole*. This is the lesson that Dewey draws from Charles Lamb's essay, "A Dissertation Upon Roast Pig," i.e., that the value of any given end is not a property "intrinsic" to its elements nor is there an "end in itself" to which means are merely subordinate considerations. Yes, roast pork tastes wonderful, and so too does New Zealand lamb—each is desirable, but is it really worth burning down the house in order to procure them? Such are the important questions.

The Daoist approach to satisfying desire (*yu* 欲) is relevant here, and it connects in important ways to Dewey's treatment of "Epicureanism." The Epicurean focuses on securing enjoyment in the *present* with the awareness that the future is uncertain. "If it were possible to isolate the present from the future," Dewey observes, "perhaps no better working rule for attaining happiness could be found." But the future *does* come, thus Epicureanism proves insufficient as a general approach. However, as Dewey says, "this emphasis upon the conditions of security of *present* enjoyment is at once the strong and the weak point in the Epicurean doctrine."[130]

Daoists agree. The *Daodejing*, as Hans-Georg Moeller explains, favors "'immediate' and present satisfaction, and it argues that such immediate satisfaction is only possible if no desires exist that violate a perfect contentment with the present."[131] Epicureanism's "strong point," according to Dewey, is that it *does* recognize "the importance of nurturing the *present* enjoyment of things worth while," instead of sacrificing such value to some remote (*wai* 外) end. This reinforces recognition of "the need of fostering at every opportunity direct enjoyment of the kind of goods [that] reflection approves."[132] The key here is that the "goods [that] reflection approves" are ideally those in which the bifurcation between *means*-value and *ends*-value has been eradicated. The activity in such cases, regardless of duration, is a "good-in-itself" at every phase. As Moeller explains, desire (*yu* 欲) in its pathological sense presupposes "that true satisfaction is possible only in the near future," and too often that future never comes.[133] The only antidote to this pathology, as Chapter 37 of the *Daodejing* teaches, is to overcome it with the un-carved block (*pu* 樸). This is to restore the primitive non-dualism of means-and-ends (i.e., *dao* 道). Only then is desire eliminated and equilibrium (*jing* 靜) reached. With this, the world achieves stability on its own accord.

Much of the responsibility for this lies with the individual. Should one find upon reflection that certain desires are causing misery, then those desires need to be overcome and the continuity between means-and-ends restored. Such is doable. "Nothing more contrary to common sense can be imagined than the notion that we are incapable of changing our desires and interests by means of learning what the consequences of acting upon them are," writes Dewey.[134] Such personal responsibility extends, as we have seen, to one's use of technologies. By their very nature, tools open up space between the primitive simplicity of means-and-ends. In fact, this is precisely how Chapter 28 of the *Daodejing* defines technology. "When the un-carved block (*pu* 樸) is divided," we read, "then tools (*qi* 器) come into being." Each of us must monitor our own (and increasingly, our children's) physical relationship to such tools and we cannot rely on others to do this for us.

In large part, however, the onus for restoring stability to the world does lie with those in positions of power and influence; for they must use such leverage to secure conditions under which legitimate desires can be satisfied without undue sacrifice or drudgery. For Dewey, "drudgery" is a technical term. He defines it as an "extreme form" of work that "involves subordination of an activity to an ulterior material result."[135] This mode of activity, wherein "Means/Ends" are completely severed, is anathema to Daoist thinking. Accordingly, as a political philosophy, Daoism stands for its elimination.

State intervention in industry and economics is thus warranted from the Daoist perspective, since such forces have the tendency to create unnatural desires and to foster conditions in which "Means/Ends" are manipulated for nothing but pecuniary gain. This lends a philosophical rationale for intelligent intervention that aims to restore wholeness where systemic drudgery exists. Daoism adds to this rationale the practical fact that governing unhappy people is simply more difficult. Restoring the un-carved block (*pu* 樸) amounts to creating a society in which means-end wholeness (which is the key to happiness) is easier to come by. As Chapter 32 suggests, in such a state the people become satisfied on their own.

While *dao* 道 provides norms for realizing such "goods-in-themselves," it does not proactively assist us in achieving such things for ourselves or for the planet. The cholera germ and the "Autumn Floods" are also driven by *dao* and we must reserve our biases against them. Not every demand in Nature (*tian* 天) can be respected. Once William James came to realize that a world in which *every* demand is satisfied is not logically possible, he concluded that the ethical situation is "tragically practical." There is no way to satisfy all obligations, and in the moral life "some part of the ideal must be butchered, and [one] needs to know which part." We thus stand with Aldo Leopold upon the snowy plain, "Axe-in-Hand" with all of our biases intact. There is little to guide us here except our instincts and an over-stuffed toolbox of rules and theories, none of which give us general satisfaction. The only way forward, as James teaches, is to "invent some manner" of satisfying as many demands as possible, while adopting the "strenuous mood" of faith in the ultimate desirability of our efforts.[136] This is the actual purpose of moral philosophy—the best that it can do.

Pragmatic naturalism, in this respect, is neither pessimistic nor optimistic; rather, it is "melioristic," according to which the improvement of things is "neither necessary nor impossible."[137] This restores the struggle, uncertainty, and precipitousness that James had been missing at Chautauqua and puts destiny unbound into our hands. James' response to the fact that the universe offers us no guarantee of success is to assert that we must boldly philosophize with *faith*. As Dewey reflects in his memorial dedication to James: "Our greatest act of piety to [William James] to whom we owe so much is to accept from him some rekindling of a human faith in the human significance of philosophy."[138] For "the work of philosophy," as Sing-nan Fen writes, "should be to help bring into existence a desired future."[139]

Dewey's talk at Chautauqua hints perhaps at the spirit in which we ought to proceed. His paper was likely a version of the paper that he would publish two months later on a related topic, "Imagination and Expression." This paper focuses on pedagogy in the visual arts among kindergarten students. The dualism at which Dewey takes aim in this paper is that of "Imagination/Technique," imagination being "mental-spiritual" and technique being "physical-mechanical." For young children, Dewey argues, the "idea" being expressed is never bifurcated into such dualisms because it is not disconnected from their lived reality—"it is not something which [the child] thinks about or looks at; it is something in which he lives. In other words, it is his whole self, his whole life, for the time."[140] This is why children, in the spirit of play, are so often good at what they spontaneously do.

In the field of Chinese philosophy, Hans-Georg Moeller and Paul J. D'Ambrosio do a splendid job of articulating the notion of what they call "genuine pretending" in the *Zhuangzi*. Such "childhood play," they explain, exhibits an "impersonal attitude toward the tasks [one happens] to face," such that one becomes "genuinely or spontaneously skillful at them."[141] Such "smooth operators" remain open to changing circumstances and produce results with a vivid sense of rightness and fit.

For Dewey, the fact that imagination is expressed through motor channels together with artistic technique is what accounts for the "spontaneous grace and beauty" of young children, as well as for the rightness and fit of their artwork.[142] Less than a year after Dewey's essay appeared, Franz Cižek initiated the "Child Art Movement" in Vienna, opening classes to children and touring exhibitions so that adults could learn from the remarkable artistic talents of children. The movement would impact Modernist aesthetics in Europe.[143] Years later, Dewey visited a Cižek classroom.[144] He voiced reservations, however, with what he encountered there. The children were encouraged to exercise "free expression," Dewey notes. "It is found that children at first are then much happier in their work—anyone who has seen Cižek's class will testify to the wholesome air of cheerfulness, even of joy, which pervades the room—but gradually [they] tend to become listless and finally bored, while there is an absence of cumulative, progressive development of power and of actual achievement in results."[145]

Dewey diagnoses the problem in terms of a "Means/Ends" severance. The Cižek approach was to "surround pupils with certain materials, tools, appliances, etc." and then *let them go*. "Above all let us not suggest any end or plan to the students" was the idea.[146] It was presumed that they would spontaneously express what Moeller and D'Ambrosio keenly identify as a form of "authenticity." But ignored was the fact that such "authenticity" is hollow apart from some role or function to "go by" (*dai* 待). One *must* perform some role or function or *end*, for this is what invites genuineness (*zhen* 真) to emerge in the free play of doing so.[147] Cižek wrongly expected "authenticity" to surface without such formal assignments.

"Such a method is really stupid," Dewey writes. "For it attempts the impossible, which is always stupid."[148] Imagination, for Dewey, works *within* the means-end continuum, and guiding ideas are crucial in establishing "ends" that are actually *working*—ends the finality of which may be vague but that will be determined in the intervening process of spontaneously adapting means to them. This is the only way that "means" in activity take on any significance. "The consciousness of technique must grow up out of and within this expression, having its own meaning within itself," Dewey explains. "Every gain in technique must be at once utilized for a further and richer imaginative expression."[149] In minds that are animated by imagination, means-and-ends are discovered together, and changes in one term mean adjustment in the other. "Play" is what enables this to happen. Intelligence (or *ming* 明) follows imagination closely, ready to pivot among the myriad combinations that it spontaneously envisions.

When William James calls on us to "invent some manner" of making the world a better place, the idea is not that we start from zero and that anything goes. Such an idea is stupid. Rather, there are ideals that we cherish, roles that we assume, methods that we trust, and conditions in place that can be reconstructed to better realize our aims. Imagination is the medium through which such amelioration is made possible. The severance of "Imagination/Technique" obscures the fact that imagination operates *within* the existential coordination of means-and-ends, working with the world as we actually find it and live within it. "The aims and ideals that move us are generated through imagination," Dewey writes, "but they are not made of imaginary stuff. They are made out of the hard stuff of the world of physical and social experience." Dewey's idea of a "moral faith" is one that transforms ideals into *ends-in-view*, the realization of which require our persistent and creative efforts. The same kind of effort that goes into artistic creation can be realized in making the world a better place than it currently is.

Because we cherish our ideals, the "hypostatization of them into an existence . . . into an antecedent reality" is always a temptation.[150] We succumb to this temptation whenever we convert Nature (*tian* 天) into an "inherent ethical scheme." To thus hypostasize the *objects* of faith, however, actually weakens the operations of faith. For faith is the substance (*hypostasis*) of things hoped for, the evidence of things not seen—the hypostatized *objects* of faith are not the substance. Dewey understood accordingly that, without sustaining faith in the possibility of making *this* imperfect world a better place, there is nothing to hope for. Dewey's own hope was sustained by his faith in the possibilities of human nature, education, and culture. In this respect, his philosophy parallels and intersects with Confucianism in important ways. Volume two in this series will be devoted to exploring how this is so.

༄

In volume one, we have established intra-cultural philosophy as a general method that seeks to foreground the various contexts in which cross-cultural philosophy occurs and the purposes for which it is carried out. The overarching purpose of the present work is to recover ways of thinking that are more "in gear" with contemporary scientific understandings, thus making us less beholden to outdated Greek-medieval patterns of thought. To that end, part I made connections between Dewey's thought and early Chinese natural philosophy, especially as it relates to teleology and to the nature of organic form (*xing* 形). The Chinese tradition, as we have seen, stands up well alongside contemporary understandings of the natural world, especially in fields like biology and systems theory. On this basis, inquiry was extended in part II to include Daoist approaches to knowledge, the body, technology, and intelligence. The hope is that such inquiries might help us to recover such approaches and assimilate them to present needs and purposes.

Contemporary textual and philosophical analyses suggest that ascribing strong essentialist and/or teleological assumptions to early Daoist philosophies obfuscates what these traditions have to teach us. Daoist teachings are not alone, however, in suffering at the hands of our Greek-medieval categories. Arguably, distortion has been even greater in the case of early Confucian thought, especially given the popularity of Greek-medieval "virtue ethics" as a comparative *tertium* in the Western academy. In volume two, we will be especially interested in scrutinizing arguments that support such readings. It will be argued in part II of volume two that, in texts like the *Analects* and the *Mencius*, support for such readings is not very strong and in some respects quite negligible. While it is easy to see *how* Greek-medieval inferences are made when reading early Confucian texts, it is more difficult to see *why* the Chinese texts warrant such inferences.

Of primary concern will be the so-called "Heaven's plan" reading of early Confucianism. This particular reading, as we will see, is thinly defended—and as Donald J. Munro advises, it is one that should be retired sooner rather than later.[151] Abandoning this reading, however, is not primarily a deconstructive exercise. Rather, it is a *reconstructive* exercise in recovering the meanings of early Confucianism while developing a normative framework that more plausibly illuminates early Confucian thinking. Questions regarding this reconstructed framework will be raised and addressed throughout part II of the next volume as we experiment with topics such as ethics, human nature (*renxing* 人性), and religiousness.

Before addressing such topics, however, we will explore Dewey's visit to China in greater detail and look into how his experiences there influenced his own social and political philosophy. Part I of volume two will be devoted to such inquiries. As we will see, Dewey's philosophy changed demonstrably before and after his exposure to East Asian civilizations. Connections between Dewey and Confucius will be explored in relation to such changes. Here, there are several "*specific* philosophical relationships" to observe. Both Dewey and Confucius are distinguished by their shared interest in education and in the broader technologies of culture. One way to understand how these philosophies connect is to study such thinking alongside more hardline conservative approaches. As it happens, Chinese students who studied in the United States and then returned to China during the Republican era became implicated in debates between Dewey and his conservative critics in the American academy. Such debates still reverberate a century later, as the field of Chinese philosophy continues to wrangle over how to best understand Confucius—is he "conservative" or "progressive"? Now as then, the terms of such debates mirror cultural trends in North America more than anything that occurred in early China. The warp-and-weft of such historico-cultural strands needs to be recognized in order to understand what the Dewey-Confucius encounter meant a century ago and what it means today.

So there is much that lies ahead. For now, let us leave volume one with an image. About midway through his China trip, Dewey travelled through Shandong province on his way from Beijing to Nanjing. There, he had the experience of ascending China's sacred Mount Tai (*Taishan* 泰山). Taishan is the easternmost of the "Five Great Mountains" in China and the foremost in cultural importance—especially for Daoism. According to Han mythology, Taishan is the head of the god Pangu 盤古. As Dewey notes, "The mountain is over 5,000 feet high, straight up from the almost sea level plain." It is the oldest and most unusual geological formation in eastern China. Pangu's head is composed of the Earth's crust and the magma plume that began lifting it 2,700 million years ago. 2,000 million years later, the "God of the North Sea" arrived and slowly covered it with a blanket of salt water. Five hundred million years after that, Pangu's head began to resurface faulted and eroded, wearing a 2,000-meter-thick layer of limestone and shale. Today, this coating is rich in fossilized Trilobite, an extinct form of marine life that flourished for 275 million years and splintered into 17,000 known species before dying out.

The Taishan range began to take its present form 70 million years ago, with the gradual subduction of the Pacific plate. Uplift continues on Taishan, gently and imperceptibly. Vegetation covers 80 percent of the mountain, and given its unique climactic profile (ocean climate to the east, dry conditions to the west) it has become home to a diverse range of plants—1,858 species in 645 genera. *Homo sapiens* inhabited the area since Paleolithic times, 40,000 years and counting, and there was never a time in Chinese history when the mountain was not sacred. Religious worship can be traced back 3,000 years to the Shang dynasty, but rituals surely preceded that. There are numerous ancient and famous trees on the mountain, including 2,100-year-old cypress trees planted by the Han Emperor Wu Di 武帝. Temples and ruins of great historical significance rest on site, along with hundreds of stone tablets and cliff inscriptions celebrating the many treasures of Chinese culture. There are 6,600 stone steps from the base to the summit.

As Dewey reminds us: "Mountain peaks do not float unsupported; they do not even just rest on the earth. They *are* the earth in one of its manifest operations."[152] The same can be said about Taishan and its heritage. The cultural deposits that have accumulated on Taishan do not float unsupported. Nor are they simply piled on nature as on a platform. Taishan's cultural heritage *is* nature in one of its manifold operations—operations that began with an initial upsurge 2,700 million years ago and that continue to this day. Having reconstructed some of the early Chinese debates regarding the relationship between human-level operations and Nature (*tian* 天)—debates involving knowledge, technology, language, and so on, we are in a good position to appreciate the philosophical conviction that finally comes to define the Confucian tradition: namely, "continuity between Nature and the human" (*tianrenheyi* 天人合一). Accordingly, as we move in these volumes from "natural" to more "cultural" concerns, we are not entering some "other world." We continue to explore operations of the world already described in these pages.

6,600 steps is a serious climb. "We were six hours going up, and three down," Dewey reports. He enjoyed the natural beauty along the way. "In the lower reaches there are cedars along the path and above wonderful pines." When his party set out, there was "not much prospect of a view," but as they ascended, the winds lifted so that "at the top it was clear but with a soft mist effect over everything."[153]

The last leg of the climb would be the most dramatic. "Toward the end it is almost all steps," Dewey writes, "and the view from below looking up to a red gate at the top of the gorge is a sight for a lifetime." *Up, and up, and up*—inscriptions of poetry encouraging every step. As Dewey remembers: "Hear the running water, or the waterfall, see the color of the sky . . . hear the whistling of the pines . . . we are coming to better places." *Up, and up, and up*. Everything starts to float and become dreamlike. As Dewey recalls, the steepness of the climb is what gives one "the feeling that the mountain is going up to meet heaven."[154]

Notes

Prelude/Acknowledgments

1. *Correspondence* (14627), John Dewey to Delbert Ames, Jr., March 4, 1949.
2. "Life with 'Father,'" by Sing-nan Fen, March 19, 1985. Included in folder, *Correspondence* (13804), John Dewey to Sing-nan Fen, March 22, 1949.
3. Sing-nan Fen, "An Examination of the Socio-Individual Dichotomy as it Relates to Educational Theory." PhD Dissertation, Columbia University Rare Book and Manuscript Library, Butler Library, New York, NY (1949): 1.
4. *Correspondence* (13804), John Dewey to Sing-nan Fen, March 22, 1949.
5. *John Dewey Papers*, Mina H. Adlerblum, "Transcription of Tape on John Dewey," 71/3: 12.
6. *Correspondence* (17984), Shao Chang Lee to Roberta Lowitz Grant Dewey, November 12, 1959.
7. *John Dewey Papers*, "Reminiscences of Dewey: Mrs. C. W. Leung," 81/14, audio recording.
8. *John Dewey Papers*, "Reminiscences of Dewey: C. S. Tsang," 81/14, audio recording.
9. "Biography of John Dewey," Schilpp and Hahn (1989): 42.
10. Meng (1981): 141–42.
11. He would, for instance, offer Chinese associates practical advice, draft statements of support for Chinese causes, and serve on the Advisory Board of the "East and West Association" at the request of Pearl S. Buck. See: *Correspondence* (09749), Kang-cheng Tuan to John Dewey, June 21, 1941; *Correspondence* (15852), John Dewey to Kang-cheng Tuan, August 9, 1941; *Correspondence* (21773), Maurice William to John Dewey, March 6, 1934; *Correspondence* (21774), John Dewey to Maurice William, March 21, 1934; and *Correspondence* (09794), Pearl S. Buck to John Dewey, January 20, 1942 and Conn (1998): 245.
12. Dewey arrived in Shanghai in the spring of 1919, visited Jiangsu and made his way from there to Nanjing, Tianjin, and then to Beijing were he settled. In October of that year, he paid a visit to Taiyuan, the capital of Shanxi province. In December, he visited Shandong province, but "didn't go to the tomb of Confucius [in Qufu], as the connections were bad." He returned to Beijing and remained there through the winter before heading out in April 1920 for Nanjing and then Shanghai.

During May and June of that year he travelled extensively—Hangzhou, Zhenjiang, Yangzhou, Changzhou, Nantong, Jiaxing, Xuzhou, Wuxi, and Suzhou. By July, he was back in Beijing. In the autumn of 1920, he travelled south to Changsha, the capital of Hunan province, and then to Hankou, the capital of Hubei. From there, he went to Jiujiang in Jiangxi province, on the southern shores of the Yangzi River. He then travelled by boat through Anhui province. He returned to Beijing to spend the winter of 1920–1921. In April 1921, he set off again—southeast to sail into the port city of Xiamen in Fujian province *via* Shanghai, and then cruised along the coastline to Fuzhou and Guangzhou, with further excursions inland into Guangdong province. He returned to Beijing in May. His final trip was eastward to Qingdao in July 1921 to catch his connection back to Japan for his journey home. At this juncture, Dewey again passed through Shandong province, stopping in Jinan. He was then able to make the 75-mile passage to the tomb of Confucius in Qufu, which he visited on July 13, 1921. After that, he proceeded to Qingdao, thus concluding his China trip. For more on Dewey's initially aborted trip to Qufu, see: *Correspondence* (03578), John Dewey to Dewey Children, January 1, 2, 4, 1920.

13. *Correspondence* (04068), John Dewey to Nicholas Burry Butler, May 3, 1919.
14. *Walter Lippman Papers*, Walter Lippman to John Dewey, June 14, 1921. Special Collections, Yale University Library, New Haven, CT.
15. Wang (2007): 65.
16. See: *Correspondence* (10461), Yu-lan Fung to John Dewey, December 20, 1946, note, and *Correspondence*, "Research Tools," Hu Shih.
17. Munro (2002): 305–07.
18. Boisvert (1988): 49–50.
19. Alexander (1959): 59.
20. Slingerland (2019): 29.
21. Van Norden (1993): 342.
22. Whitehead and Price (1954): 276.

Chapter 1

1. Chan (1988): 230.
2. Moore (1951): 3.
3. Deutsch and Larson (1988): 230.
4. *Correspondence* (10717): Arthur F. Bentley to John Dewey, April 20, 1948.
5. *Correspondence* (20269): Walter Fales to Albert C. Barnes, October 5, 1947.
6. *Correspondence* (13802): John Dewey to Sing-nan Fen, March 22, 1949.
7. This letter, which according to Moore was dated October 6, 1950, is no longer extant.
8. *Correspondence* (12377): Charles A. Moore to John Dewey, December 6, 1950.
9. *The Honolulu Advertiser* (January 18, 1951): 5.
10. *Correspondence* (19138): Charles A. Moore to Roberta Dewey, February 10, 1965.

11. "On Philosophical Synthesis," LW 17: 35–36.

12. As Dewey wrote that same year, "The troubles that now plague the world are exhibited on the largest scale in tensions due to the splitting of the peoples of one globe into two *human* worlds." See: "Contribution to *Democracy in a World of Tensions*," LW 16: 405.

13. "The Unfinished Introduction to *Experience and Nature*," LW 1: 363.

14. Dewey and Deen (2012). This work is referred to as *Unmodern Philosophy* hereafter.

15. Corliss Lamont relates the famous story of the manuscript's 1947 disappearance. "He and Mrs. Dewey came back one summer from Nova Scotia—they drove—and pulled up in front of their apartment house at Fifth Avenue and 97th Street. They left their bags with the doorman to bring up, and went upstairs in the elevator. When the doorman had brought up the baggage, Dewey looked around and said to Roberta, 'My heavens, my briefcase isn't here.' Mrs. Dewey immediately rushed downstairs. The briefcase *had* been taken out of the car, they knew; but it had disappeared. And in that briefcase was the manuscript of Dewey's almost completed book summarizing his whole philosophy. There was no carbon copy." As Phillip Deen explains, the manuscript may never have been lost—it may have been left behind in Nova Scotia and discovered years later, or there may have been extant drafts that Dewey did not know about that were archived after his death. In any event, the work has largely been recovered. See: Lamont and Farrell (1959): 50–51, and *Unmodern Philosophy*, Dewey and Deen (2012): xv–xvii.

16. *Unmodern Philosophy*, Dewey and Deen (2012): xiv, xv, xix, 305.

17. *John Dewey Papers*, "Philosophy: Its Relation to Common Sense and Science," 102/56/7: 9.

18. *Unmodern Philosophy*, Dewey and Deen (2012): 8, 78.

19. Creel (1953): 74.

20. Moore (1951): 5.

21. See: *Proceedings* (1979): 378–80. On March 9, 1961, a local newspaper in Glens Falls, New York announced a talk by Krusé entitled "What Did John Dewey Say?" reporting that, "Dr. Krusé has been told by Chinese friends that John Dewey sounded like Confucius—a counterpart he plans to present to his audience." The talk was delivered to the Glens Falls Teachers Association in a local high school.

22. Moore (1951): 393, 4, italics added.

23. As Moore reported following the 1959 meeting: "We are now convinced that there is no simple or single 'East' or 'West'—and that even within each of the many cultures and philosophical traditions, East and West, there is wide variety as well as historical variation." See: Moore (1962): 701.

24. "The Unfinished Introduction to *Experience and Nature*," LW 1: 361, 331–33.

25. "Modern Philosophy" was originally written in 1947, but then held up in press. See: "Modern Philosophy," LW 16: 417, 558–67.

26. *Unmodern Philosophy*, Dewey and Deen (2012): 129.

27. "The Unfinished Introduction to *Experience and Nature*," LW 1: 345–46, italics added.

28. *Unmodern Philosophy*, Dewey and Deen (2012): 107–08, 111.

29. "Modern Philosophy," LW 16: 418, italics added.
30. *Correspondence* (09404): John Dewey to Corrine Chisholm Frost, June 27, 1941.
31. *Unmodern Philosophy*, Dewey and Deen (2012): 129.
32. "Modern Philosophy," LW 16: 413.
33. Bernstein (1991): 93.
34. *Experience and Nature*, LW 1: 28.
35. Hall and Ames (1995): 174.
36. Nussbaum (1997): 118.
37. Slingerland (2013): 6–10.
38. E.g., Richey (2003): 580–81.
39. E.g., Van Norden (2007): 16.
40. See: Cline (2013a): 289 and Cline (2013b): 52.
41. Cline (2004): 232n.59.
42. Zhang (2010): 93.
43. *Timaeus* 36a–d, Plato and Cooper (1997): 1239–240.
44. Gerson (2004): 305, 310–11.
45. Zhang (2010): 93.
46. Zhang (2010): 90, 94, 96.
47. "Contributions to *Cyclopedia of Education*," MW 6: 389.
48. *Democracy and Education*, MW 9: 206, 207.
49. As Zhang puts it, situations consist of the "non-objectifiable stream of space-time experience . . . the inner and exterior lived region accompanying every experience." Their terms are "the manifested or prominent parts of this anonymously functioning horizon." For Dewey, situations are located "in the temporal continuum constituting life-experience," and they "cannot be stated or made explicit" but "[form] the universe of discourse of whatever is expressly stated or of what appears as a term in a proposition." See: Zhang (2010): 96, "Experience, Knowledge and Value: A Rejoinder," LW 14: 30 and "Qualitative Thought," LW 5: 247, respectively.
50. *Logic: A Theory of Inquiry*, LW 12: 126.
51. See: Shusterman (1999): 199–201.
52. "Qualitative Thought," LW 5: 247.
53. Jackson (1998): 17.
54. Shusterman (1999): 202.
55. *Logic: The Theory of Inquiry*, LW 12: 72.
56. *Experience and Education*, LW 13: 25.
57. Fen (1951): 560, italics added.
58. "Qualitative Thought," LW 5: 247.
59. Hall and Ames (1987): 11.
60. Møllgaard (1998): 332.
61. Sing-nan Fen, "John Dewey's Theory of Situation," *John Dewey Papers*, 102/72/6: 16–17.
62. Smid (2009): 204.
63. Johnson (2010): 134, 135.

64. Berthrong (2001): 243.
65. *Experience and Nature*, LW 1: 40.
66. *Unmodern Philosophy*, Dewey and Deen (2012): 33–34. I have taken the liberty of changing the comma to a colon after the word "variables" in the above quote.
67. As Dewey commented elsewhere during this period: "I have moved myself progressively in the direction of using such terms as *Life-behavior* or *Life-activities*, with the understanding of course that, in the case of philosophy, the behavior and/or activities involved are those of *human* beings and hence are *culturally* affected throughout." See: "Experience and Existence: A Comment," LW 16: 387.
68. *Unmodern Philosophy*, Dewey and Deen (2012): 316.
69. "Whitehead's Philosophy," LW 11: 152.
70. *Unmodern Philosophy*, Dewey and Deen (2012): 331.
71. *John Dewey Papers*, "Manuscripts Undated: Assorted," 102/61/14: 4–5.
72. *Unmodern Philosophy*, Dewey and Deen (2012): 331, 334, italics added.
73. *John Dewey Papers*, "Manuscripts Undated: Assorted," 102/61/14: 5.
74. *Unmodern Philosophy*, Dewey and Deen (2012): 33, 329, 336, 337.
75. Weber (2014): 162, italics added.
76. *The Quest for Certainty*, LW 4: 150.
77. Weber (2014): 166, 168–69, italics added.
78. "On Philosophical Synthesis," LW 17: 35–36.
79. Škof (2012): 21. This tradition of "intercultural philosophy" is associated with the work of philosophers like Ram Adhar Mall and others who work in the Indian philosophical and hermeneutic traditions in the German-speaking world. Mall (2000) provides a good introduction to this tradition. Eric S. Nelson has recently expanded this tradition by showcasing the breadth, depth, and considerable sophistication of "intercultural philosophy" in Weimar Germany, focusing on Buddhist and Chinese traditions. See: Nelson (2017).
80. Smid (2009) provides an account of the history of this tradition, which includes treatments of William Ernest Hocking, F. S. C. Northrop, David L. Hall and Roger T. Ames, and Robert C. Neville.
81. The tide, however, continues to turn. Such realignment is advanced by Bryan W. Van Norden's recent book, *Taking Back Philosophy: A Multicultural Manifesto*. Working within the framework of Western virtue ethics, analytic philosophers at Stanford University began engaging Chinese philosophy seriously during the period of the 1980s resurgence. These figures—pioneers, really—played an important role in elevating the status of Chinese philosophy in analytic circles. See: Nivison and Van Norden (1996): 2–5, *Proceedings and Addresses of the American Philosophical Association*, 70: 2 (November, 1996): 161–63, and Van Norden (2017).
82. "The Unfinished Introduction to *Experience and Nature*," LW 1: 339.
83. *The Quest for Certainty*, LW 4: 99, italics added.
84. *Democracy and Education*, MW 9: 207.
85. I have in mind Sim (2012), Hall and Ames (1999), Cline (2013b), and Peterman (2015), respectively.
86. *Logic: The Theory of Inquiry*, LW 12: 74.

87. "The American Scholar," 1837. Emerson and Ziff (1982): 90.

88. Such a view is operative early in Chinese philosophy, exhibited most clearly in Confucius' own attitude toward the canonical *Songs* (*Shijing* 詩經). This attitude, central to the Chinese commentarial tradition, will be discussed in chapter 2 of volume two. At the start of the Han dynasty, Yang Xiong 揚雄 expresses this long-standing spirit through his comparison of philosophical texts to elements like water and fire: "Like water—fathom them and they increase in depth; follow them to the end and they increase in distance. Like fire—use them and they increase in luminosity, contain them and they increase in intensity." See: Bullock (2011): 73, *Yangzi* 楊子 (1983): 卷四.三.

89. *Unmodern Philosophy*, Dewey and Deen (2012): 33, 336.

90. *The Quest for Certainty*, LW 4: 70.

91. This is a central component in Dewey's theory of inquiry and variations are seen elsewhere in the American tradition. As Alfred North Whitehead says, "It is more important that a proposition be interesting than that it be true. The importance of truth is that it adds to the interest." Whitehead's point is that there are numberless true propositions. Most of them, however, are entirely irrelevant. As William James observes, "if you ask me what o'clock it is and I tell you that I live at 95 Irving Street," a *true* proposition is delivered but it is one that carries no interest to the inquirer. Thus, it is indeed more important that a proposition be interesting than that it be true. The importance of *truth*, however, as Whitehead suggests, is that it *adds* to the interest—and thus to the *importance*—of propositions that interest us. Dewey offers similar insights with respect to the relationship between truth and meaning. "Meaning is wider in scope as well as more precious in value than is truth," he writes, "and philosophy is occupied with meaning rather than with truth." Truth is "infinitely important when it is important at all," but "meaning is the wider category." We do not, for instance, "inquire whether Greek civilization was true or false," Dewey notes, "but we are immensely concerned to penetrate its meaning." See: *Process and Reality*, Whitehead (1929): 259, *Pragmatism*, James and Kuklick (1987): 588, "Philosophy and Civilization," LW 3: 4–5.

92. *Art as Experience*, LW 10: 330, italics added.

93. *Pragmatism*, James and Kuklick (1987): 488–89.

94. *Art as Experience*, LW 10: 275, 334.

95. "Qualitative Thought," LW 5: 261.

96. Dewey defines "*an* experience" as one in which "the material experienced runs its course to fulfillment." See: *Art as Experience*, LW 10: 42.

97. "Qualitative Thought," LW 5: 261.

98. With respect to artworks, Dewey says, such experiences "are not the same in any literal sense" as those had by the original producer or other beholders. See: *Art as Experience*, LW 10: 60.

99. Fen (1951): 559.

100. "Qualitative Thought," LW 5: 261.

101. On the broader American scene, figures like Thomas Merton practice assimilation. Merton was not attempting to approach non-Western traditions "coldly and objectively from the outside." He hoped, instead, "in some measure at least, to try to share in the values and the experience which they embody." He wished to make them, "as far as possible, 'his own.'" See: Merton (1967): ix.

102. Fen (1957): 555.
103. *Art as Experience*, LW 10: 336–37.
104. *Art as Experience*, LW 10: 9.
105. *Democracy and Education*, MW 9: 147 and *Art as Experience*, LW 10: 50–51.
106. *Art as Experience*, LW 10: 51.
107. *Democracy and Education*, MW 9: 146.
108. *Art as Experience*, LW 10: 58–60.
109. Fen (1957): 558.
110. Hall and Ames (1995): 166, 169.
111. When Dewey speaks of common elements in aesthetic experience he speaks of "potential common material" rather than "common potential material," which is a non-trivial distinction. The difference is one between a vague field of *potentially* common elements on the one hand, and a standing field of *common* elements in potential on the other. In the first formulation, the possibilities are limitless and grow as novel individuals enter the field. In the latter, the possibilities are finite and shrink as common elements become realized. In Dewey's mind, what is suggested here would hold for cultural elements in general. "Anything in the world," Dewey writes, "no matter how individual in its own existence, is potentially common." See: *Art as Experience*, LW 10: 291.
112. *Art as Experience*, LW 10: 333, 338.
113. Margolis (2011): 212, 214.
114. Pryba (2011): 226, 235.
115. "Philosophy and Civilization," LW 3: 7–8.
116. *Experience and Nature*, LW 1: 118.
117. *Art as Experience*, LW 10: 338.
118. "On Philosophical Synthesis," LW 17: 35–36.
119. *Unmodern Philosophy*, Dewey and Deen (2012): 334–35.
120. As Sing-nan Fen explains, "the block universe monism view neglects selective interest," which is fundamental to the generation of dynamic cultural situations. See: Sing-nan Fen, "John Dewey's Theory of Situation," *John Dewey Papers*, 102/72/6: 24.
121. Hall and Ames (1995): 178.
122. *Unmodern Philosophy*, Dewey and Deen (2012): 335.
123. "Philosophy," LW 8: 38.
124. Clopton and Ou (1973): 210–12.
125. *A Common Faith*, LW 9: 30.
126. In critiquing pseudo-translations of the *Daodejing*, for instance, Russell Kirkland describes them as "imagined—and I emphasize the word 'imagined,'" suggesting distrust with imagination *per se*. See: Kirkland (1997): 1.
127. *How We Think*, MW 6: 310–11.
128. Ziporyn (2018): 114–15.
129. Welch (1966): 182.
130. See: "'Philosophy' in Contributions to *Encyclopedia of the Social Sciences*," LW 8: 38–39 and *Quest for Certainty*, LW 4: 248.
131. *Experience and Nature*, LW 1: 274.
132. *Art as Experience*, LW 10: 66.

133. "Philosophy and Civilization," LW 3: 7.

134. "The Future of Philosophy," LW 17: 467.

135. *John Dewey Papers*, 59/10, Assorted Manuscripts, 2 pp. holo notes, green ink, 2/19/51.

136. *Plenary Session Remarks*, Eleventh East-West Philosophers' Conference, Honolulu, May 25, 2016.

137. Dewey began using hyphens with increasing frequency in his late-period works. He stressed that it was something that "stands for inherent connection, in *both* directions, between what the two terms stand for." See: *Unmodern Philosophy*, Dewey and Deen (2012): 325.

138. Clopton and Ou (1970): 1–2.

139. "On Philosophical Synthesis," LW 17: 36.

Chapter 2

1. *Unmodern Philosophy*, Dewey and Deen (2012): 129.

2. See: "Dualism and the Split Atom: Science and Morals in the Atomic Age," LW 15: 200.

3. Clopton and Ou (1970): 44.

4. *A Common Faith*, LW 9: 42–43.

5. *How We Think*, LW 8: 138.

6. *Experience and Education*, LW 13: 26.

7. *A Common Faith*, LW 9: 23.

8. *Individualism Old and New*, LW 5: 115.

9. "Dualism and the Split Atom: Science and Morals in the Atomic Age," LW 15: 202,

10. In polls conducted in 2009 and 2014, the Pew Research Center reports sizable divergences between public opinion and scientific consensus in the United States on a host of issues: the reality and threat of climate change; the safety of nuclear power, vaccinations, genetically modified foods, pesticides; and the evidence for evolution. See: Pew (2015).

11. Norgaard (2009): 31. "Ontological security" is Anthony Gidden's phrase for "the continuity of self-identity and the constancy of the surrounding social and material environments of action." See: Giddens (1991): 92.

12. With respect to Earth's climate, Aristotle taught that variations occur, but they are so gradual that they "are not observed" on the human scale. See: *Meteorology* 351b.10–11, Aristotle and Ross (1931a): 351. With respect to Nature more broadly, Aristotle maintained that forms (*eidos*) and their teleological ends are never subject to change.

13. "The Future of Philosophy," LW 17: 469.

14. "1948 Introduction to *Reconstruction in Philosophy*," MW 12: 257.

15. "Dualism and the Split Atom: Science and Morals in the Atomic Age," LW 15: 203.

16. For an introduction to the possible renderings and misunderstandings of this integration, see: Pappas (2008): 17–20.
17. "1948 Introduction to *Reconstruction in Philosophy*," MW 12: 260–61.
18. "Modern Philosophy," LW 16: 413.
19. *Freedom and Culture*, LW 13: 172.
20. "The Influence of Darwinism on Philosophy," MW 4: 11.
21. *Reconstruction of Philosophy*, MW 12: 123.
22. *A Common Faith*, LW 9: 43.
23. "John Dewey's Aims Held Un-American," *New York Times*, October 27, 1939.
24. Lamont and Farrell (1959): 76.
25. *Correspondence* (12750), John D. Graves to Roberta Lowitz Dewey, October 3, 1951.
26. *Correspondence* (21078), Unknown to John Dewey, July 2, 1951 and *Correspondence* (15853), Faye Cummins to John Dewey, Date Unknown, 1950–1952.
27. *Correspondence* (14249), John Dewey to Harold Taylor, January 1, 1950.
28. Alan Phillips' article, "John Dewey and His Religious Critics" (2002) provides considerable insight into the negative attitudes toward Dewey by this group, including reflections on Dewey from two prominent, contemporary fundamentalist figures, Pat Robertson and Charles Colson.
29. *German Philosophy and Politics*, MW 8: 139.
30. Kelemen (2004): 295.
31. Kelemen (1999): 244–46.
32. Gelman finds, for instance, that preschool children tend to predict that a child switched at birth will speak the language of the birth parents rather than that of the adopting parents, suggesting that innate potential and structure are untaught components of essentialist thinking. See: Gelman (2004): 405–06.
33. Slingerland (2008): 26.
34. Parkes (2013): 67.
35. For further discussion, see: Marshall (2014).
36. *Dialogues Concerning Natural Religion*, Hume and Popkin (1998): 7.
37. *Critique of Pure Reason*, Kant and Smith (1965): 384–86.
38. *Reconstruction in Philosophy*, MW 12: 137.
39. Rottman et al. (2015).
40. Bloom and Weisberg (2007).
41. Pusey (1998): x.
42. Grieder (1970): 27.
43. Kwok (1965) and Hu (1965): 87–88. Controversies in China were not over the *fact* of evolution by natural selection, but rather over its implications with respect to China's perceived backwardness. See: Pusey (1983).
44. Grieder (1970): 26.
45. Ipsos (2011) and Ipsos (2014).
46. Kim (2013).
47. Olivola and Machery (2016): 499.
48. Clopton and Ou (1970): 37, 45.

49. "The Sentiment of Rationality," James and Myers (1992): 979.

50. *Some Problems in Philosophy*, James and Kuklick (1987): 1002–003.

51. *On the Heavens*, 301b.34–35, Aristotle and McKeon (2001): 444.

52. "Every realm of nature is marvelous," Aristotle writes in *The Parts of Animals*, and "we should venture on the study of every kind of animal without distaste; for each and all will reveal to us something natural and something beautiful. Absence of haphazard and conduciveness of everything to an end are to be found in nature's works in the highest degree, and the resultant end of her generations and combinations is a form of the beautiful." See: *The Parts of Animals*, 645a.17–26, Aristotle and Ross (1931b): 644.

53. In the Wang Bi version of the *Daodejing* one can either take *ming* 名 as a verb or not, resulting in these two complimentary understandings. In the earlier, Mawangdui version the ambiguity is resolved in favor of the nominative. I remain fond of the grammatical ambiguity of the Wang Bi version.

54. *Metaphysics*, 980a.1, Aristotle and McKeon (2001): 689.

55. *Human Nature and Conduct*, MW 14: 46.

56. "Time and Individuality," LW 14: 112.

57. In his article, "Soul and Body," Dewey observes that, with respect to the powers of mind, "there is just the same mystery about it that there is about every fact in the universe, the mystery that there should be such a fact at all." See: "Soul and Body," EW 1: 106.

58. *Unmodern Philosophy*, Dewey and Deen (2012): 218–19.

59. *Physics*, 196a.20 and 196b.5, Aristotle and McKeon (2001): 243–44.

60. *Physics*, 198a.14–199b.33, Aristotle and McKeon (2001): 248–51.

61. *Physics*, 199b.32–33, Aristotle and McKeon (2001): 251.

62. Mayr (1988): 49.

63. Mayr refers to these as "closed" and "open" programs, respectively.

64. Often this is done by translating teleological statements into function statements that are then more easily reduced to "physico-chemical explanations." See: Mayr (1992): 123–24.

65. Such arguments rely on variations of "eliminative materialism." E.g., Churchland (1981).

66. Perlman (2004): 4.

67. Grene (1972): 408.

68. For Mayr, "the conceptual framework of biology is entirely different from that of the physical sciences and cannot be reduced to it." See: Mayr (1988): 18. Among philosophers of biology, it is Mayr who has "most strenuously defended this view." See: Grene and Depew (2004): 265.

69. Mayr (1974): 102.

70. Mayr (1988): 45.

71. Hulswit (2004): 94.

72. The word "teleology" is modern, coined by Christian Wolff in the eighteenth century to designate that part of natural philosophy "which sets forth the purposes (*fines*) of things." See: Owens (1968): 159n.1.

73. Drawn from: *The Encyclopedia of Philosophy*, Edwards (1967).

74. Mayr (1988) 44–48.

75. As Menno Hulswit explains: "According to Mayr, nature is split up into two realms of 'an entirely different nature:' the realm of genuinely goal-directed processes [i.e., teleonomic], and the realm of seemingly goal-directed processes [i.e., teleomatic]. But even the genuinely goal-directed processes can entirely be explained by efficient causation." See Hulswit (2004): 91.

76. *Democracy and Education*, MW 9: 107–09.

77. *Physics*, 199a 32–33, Aristotle and McKeon (2001): 250.

78. *Summa Theologica*, I. 5.4 and I–II. 1.8. See: Aquinas (1981), Vol. 1: 26 and Vol. 2: 589.

79. *Experience and Nature*, LW 1: 86.

80. *Experience and Nature*, LW 1: 84–85.

81. *Experience and Nature*, LW 1: 83–84.

82. The crucial shift is in the status of ends. Since organic forms evolve continuously, there will be no fixed ends that define an organism once and for all. As Dewey writes, "While Existence as process and as history involves 'ends,' the change from ancient to modern science compels us to interpret ends relatively and pluralistically, because as limits of specifiable histories." See: "Nature in Experience," LW 14: 146.

83. *Experience and Nature*, LW 1: 84.

84. Understanding how this is so awaits a fuller account of how continuity (*yi* 一) operates. For now, as Dewey notes: "Nature and life manifest not flux but continuity, and continuity involves forces and structures that endure through change; at least when they [do] change, they do so more slowly than do surface incidents, and thus are, relatively, constant." See: *Art as Experience*, LW 10: 326, 327.

85. "Time and Individuality," LW 14: 112.

86. *Experience and Nature*, LW 1: 210–11.

87. "Qualitative Thought," LW 5: 247, 250, 259.

88. *Experience and Nature*, LW 1: 195.

89. Fen (1948): 716.

90. As Dewey explains: "Quality is quality, direct, immediate and un-definable. Order is a matter of relation, of definition, dating, placing and describing." See: *Experience and Nature*, LW 1: 92.

91. Whitman (2007): 40.

92. Alexander (2004): 248.

93. *Experience and Nature*, LW 1: 16–17.

94. "The Postulate of Immediate Empiricism," MW 3: 158–64, italics added.

95. "Experience and Philosophical Method," LW 1: 377.

96. This tendency mirrors that which William James identifies as "The Psychologist's Fallacy." See: James (1890): 196–98.

97. *Experience and Nature*, LW 1: 196.

98. "Qualitative Thought," LW 5: 261–62.

99. Dalton (2002): 204–26.

100. See: "Textual Commentary," LW 12: 539–41 and Dalton (2002): 237, 333–34n.28.

101. *Logic: A Theory of Inquiry*, LW 12: 203.

102. *Logic: A Theory of Inquiry*, LW 12: 203.
103. "Qualitative Thought," LW 5: 261.
104. *Logic: A Theory of Inquiry*, LW 12: 205.
105. Dalton (2002): 226–29.
106. *Logic: A Theory of Inquiry*, LW 13: 211, 215.
107. Whitehead (1925) and (1933) each offer penetrating historico-cultural analyses of the "Qualitative/Quantitative" distinction, and Pirsig (1974) offers an insightful cultural analysis of its effects.
108. Dalton (2002): 227.
109. *Logic: A Theory of Inquiry*, LW 13: 404–05.
110. *Logic: A Theory of Inquiry*, LW 13: 206–07, 219.
111. Winchester (2008): 172, 259–60.
112. Sivin (1990): 169.
113. Raphals (2015): 549.
114. "World's Oldest Decimal Times Table Found in China," *National Geographic*, April 5, 2014.
115. "Time and Individuality," LW 14: 112.
116. *Daodejing*, Ch. 2, 10, 51, 77.
117. *Daodejing*, Ch. 37.
118. The Mawangdui version of this chapter (and others) omit *de* 德, suggesting that *dao* 道 is what "rears, grows, nurtures . . ." the living thing. While there is sense to be made of such versions, the chapter states at the very beginning that *de* is what "rears" a living thing. Thus, I retain the Wang Bi version.
119. It should be noted that *de* 德 is a particularly rich term in classical Chinese philosophy, one that carries various metaphysical and ethical connotations in different contexts. This is a preliminary discussion of the metaphysical connotations of *de* in the *Daodejing*. There will be opportunities to discuss the term in other contexts later on.
120. See: Dennett (1995): 104–23.
121. Dawkins (2014): 1.
122. "Events and the Future," LW 2: 62.
123. *Art as Experience*, LW 10: 62.
124. *Experience and Nature*, LW 1: 75.
125. *Art as Experience*, LW 10: 62.
126. *Experience and Nature*, LW 1: 74, 82.
127. "Context and Thought," LW 6: 9–10.
128. There are tens of billions of *other* solar systems, but they do not concern us here. Also, there are other planets in our solar system that might have harbored life before Earth did.
129. The *Hengxian* 恆先 is one of several recently unearthed documents that are revolutionizing our study of pre-Qin philosophy. This particular text was released in 2004.
130. For a recent translation of the entire text, see: Brindley et al. (2013): 145–51.
131. Brindley et al. (2013): 147.
132. Brindley et al. (2013): 147.

133. Brindley (2013): 201–02.
134. *Experience and Nature*, LW 1: 194.
135. *Logic: The Theory of Inquiry*, LW 12: 385.
136. *Experience and Nature*, LW 1: 210.
137. *Experience and Nature*, LW 1: 195, 196.
138. The meaning of *de* 德 is often glossed with the homophone *de* 得, "to attain."
139. "The Reflex Arc Concept in Psychology," EW 5: 99.
140. "The Reflex Arc Concept in Psychology," EW 5: 104, 105n.5, italics added.
141. "The Reflex Arc Concept in Psychology," EW 5: 104–105, italics added.
142. *Democracy and Education*, MW 9: 15, 174.
143. *Democracy and Education*, MW 9: 29–30, 51.
144. "Habit," James and Myers (1992): 142. The science of habit formation is much better understood since James wrote. The formation of habits relies on a superabundance of neural connections at birth and eventual synaptic pruning. James was the first to label this organic condition one of "plasticity."
145. "The Reflex Arc Concept in Psychology," EW 5: 104.
146. *Experience and Nature*, LW 1: 82.
147. *Art as Experience*, LW 10: 61.
148. It would require advanced exegesis to speculate on Aristotle's exact view of final causality, if indeed it is possible to determine his exact view. In lecturing on Aristotle to a Chinese audience in 1920, Dewey relates his own view that Aristotle suffered a "monumental misunderstanding and misinterpretation" in the medieval period. See: Dewey and Meyer (1984): 251.
149. *Experience and Nature*, LW 1: 224.
150. Lear (1988): 25.
151. At the time of writing, the National Oceanic and Atmospheric Administration maintains an online database tracking fish migrations. See: Press (2014).
152. Chen, Hill et al. (2011): 1024.
153. Hoffman and Sgrò (2011): 480.
154. "Jim Inhofe's Snowball has Disproven Climate Change Once and For All," *The Washington Post*, February 26, 2015.
155. "Contributions to *Cyclopedia of Education*," MW 6: 438.
156. *Logic: The Theory of Inquiry*, LW 12: 244.
157. *Reconstruction in Philosophy*, MW 12: 128.
158. Kolbert (2014): 23.
159. As Nancy Ross-Flanigan suggests, in order for biologists to properly understand the impact of climate change, an even more expansive transactional approach is required, one that "takes into account interacting environmental pressures, interconnected species and the varied sensitivities of different species to changing conditions." Today the latter element is becoming increasingly important, meaning "there are plenty more interactions to factor in." See: Ross-Flanigan (2012): 21.
160. *Analects* 17.9, Ames and Rosemont (1998): 206.
161. The text becomes an important source for later works that establish botanical and zoological nomenclature. See: Sterckx (2005): 26n.2.

162. Legge (2000) vol. 4: 116, 137–38, 147, 176–77, 190–91, 201, 213–14, 217, 271–73, 334, 359, 414.

163. Allan (1997): 95.

164. See: Sterckx (2002): 101–10.

165. As Roel Sterckx reports: "Early Chinese writings rarely classify the animal world and its members as individuals and classes [and] none of these sources are concerned with the systematic description of animal life and morphology." See: Sterckx (2005): 27.

166. As John Major relates, this chapter "emphasizes that physical features of terrain interact in important ways with plants, animals, and people." The actual title of the chapter uses the more obscure allograph, *di* 墜 rather than the more common character, *di* 地. See: Major et al. (2010): 149.

167. 土地各以其類生. See: Major et al. (2010): 160, Huainanzi 淮南子 (1936), 卷4: 27.

168. 萬物之生而各異類. See: Major et al. (2010): 162, Huainanzi 淮南子 (1936), 卷4: 27.

169. 五類雜種興乎外肖形而蕃. See: Major et al. (2010): 169, 170, Huainanzi 淮南子 (1936), 卷4: 30.

170. Major et al. (2010): 152.

171. Watson (1968): 195–96, Zhuangzi 莊子 (1994) 上: 505. Watson's translation of this passage is here used.

172. Graham (2001): 286.

173. Allan (1997): 106.

174. See: Ames (1989): 124–31.

175. Barnwell (2013): 9.

176. See: Karlgren (1964): 242–43, entry 919a.

177. See: Jullien (1995) and Jullien (2004).

178. Jullien (1995): 13, 17.

179. Ames (1993a): 114–20.

180. Jullien (2004): 17.

181. Jun (2013): 144–45n.28.

182. *Democracy and Education*, MW 9: 15.

183. Longo and Montévil (2014): 3.

184. Major et al. (2010): 162, Huaiainanzi 淮南子 (1936), 卷4: 27.

Chapter 3

1. "The American Scholar," Emerson and Ziff (1982): 86.

2. *Experience and Nature*, LW 1: 12.

3. "The American Scholar," Emerson and Ziff (1982): 85–86.

4. *Experience and Nature*, LW 1: 11, 14.

5. In terms of its cogency, the first important critique is George Santayana's review of *Experience and Nature*, in which he labels "naturalistic metaphysics" a

contradiction in terms. Dewey responds by defending his understanding of what naturalistic metaphysics entails. See: Morgenbesser (1977): 337–66. Another pivotal moment is when Richard Rorty rejects the role of metaphysics in Dewey's work and is roundly criticized as a result. See: Rorty (1982a), Alexander (1987): 67, Boisvert (1988): 3–9, and Stuhr (1992). In terms of its purview, some commentators maintain that Dewey's metaphysics pertains to "existence" as a whole (e.g., R. W. Sleeper) while others maintain that it relates more exclusively to "experience" (e.g., Sidney Hook and John Stuhr). Thomas Gardner provides a helpful overview of this disagreement and argues persuasively, in my opinion, that Dewey would have rejected the terms of this debate, concluding that, "those who argue that the subject matter of [Dewey's] metaphysics must be *either* existence *or* experience are drawing a distinction between the two that Dewey does not accept." See: Gardner (2000): 401.

6. Watson (1968): 292, Zhuangzi 莊子 (1994) 下: 758. I use Brook Ziporyn's translation in rendering the final line.

7. Watson (1968): 183, Zhuangzi 莊子 (1994) 上: 472.

8. Wang (2016): 169–70.

9. Dewey follows Kant in encouraging metaphysics to overcome such tendencies by dropping assertions whose "truth or falsity cannot be discovered or confirmed by any experience." See: *Prolegomena to Any Future Metaphysics*, Kant and Beck (1997): 75–80. For a summary comparison of Dewey and Kant, see: Boisvert (1988): 116–21.

10. "Time and Individuality," LW 14: 112.

11. *Prolegomena to Any Future Metaphysics*, Kant and Beck (1997): 40.

12. "The Subject Matter of Metaphysics," MW 8: 4, 15 italics added.

13. Sleeper (1986): 96.

14. "The Subject Matter of Metaphysics," MW 8: 6–7.

15. "Nominalism," Peirce and Hartshorne et al. (1931): 1.25.

16. "A Guess at the Riddle," Peirce and Hauser et al. (2000): 6.170, 181, italics added.

17. Hausman (1993): 128.

18. "Sundry Logical Conceptions," Peirce and Hauser et al. (1998) vol. 2: 268.

19. See: "A Guess at the Riddle," Peirce and Hauser et al. (2000): 6.206.

20. "One, Two, Three," Peirce and Hauser et al. (1993): 5.293.

21. "Nominalism," Peirce and Hartshorne et al. (1931): 1.26.

22. *Correspondence* (13259): John Dewey to Sing-nan Fen, November 10, 1946.

23. "Experience and Existence: A Comment," LW 16: 387–88.

24. "The Subject Matter of Metaphysics," MW 8: 4–6.

25. "The Subject Matter of Metaphysics," MW 8: 13.

26. See: "Nature and Humanity," LW 11: 432. Elsewhere, Dewey identifies cosmology with a "theory of nature" along similar lines. See: "Nature in Experience," LW 14: 145.

27. Neville (1981): 34, 66.

28. Many of these pertain to our understanding of the *Daodejing*. In the final months of 1973, a collection of texts written mostly on silk was discovered in a Han-era tomb (c. 168 BCE) in the village of Mawangdui 馬王堆 in China's southern Hunan province. Included in this collection were two different versions of the *Daodejing* and a number of documents associated with the syncretic philosophical movement known as "Huang-Lao" 黃老. In October 1993, archeologists in the village of Guodian 郭店 in China's Hubei province excavated a tomb containing 731 bamboo strips with writing on them. This cache also contained an early version of the *Daodejing* in addition to various unknown writings. It has been determined that this tomb was sealed around 300 BCE, prior to the infamous literary purge undertaken during the Qin dynasty (220–210 BCE) when many philosophical works fell out of circulation. Months later, in early 1994, a collection of around 400 bamboo strips still encased in mud appeared mysteriously on the Hong Kong antiquities market. These were purchased by the Shanghai Museum, followed by another purchase of around 800 strips. The museum has since embarked on the arduous task of organizing, reading, and redacting these materials. The first volume of texts was released in 2001, and subsequent volumes have appeared steadily since. Many new and unknown writings have emerged from this collection. The Shanghai Museum, however, is not the only institution currently engaged in restoring lost documents. In 2008, a donor wishing to remain anonymous presented Qinghua University with a staggering 2,500 bamboo strips, none of which can be positively sourced but which have been carbon-dated to around 300 BCE. See: Hendricks (1989): xii–xviii, Yates (1997): 3–43, Cook (2012) Vol. 1: 1–18, Shaughnessy (2014): 37–38 and "Rare Record of Chinese Classics Discovered," *New York Times*, July 10, 2013.

29. *Unmodern Philosophy*, Dewey and Deen (2012): 33, 336.

30. Burns (1982): 44.

31. The earliest known commentary on the *Daodejing* was written by the Legalist thinker, Hanfei 韓非 (280–233 BCE), indicating that the text was mobilized for diverse purposes early in its history.

32. Roth (1999): 150.

33. *Mencius* 7A.26, Bloom (2009): 150, Mengzi 孟子 (1995): 358.

34. *Daodejing*, Ch. 29, 64.

35. Note that the silk manuscripts discovered at Mawangdui include several Huang-Lao texts along with its version of the *Daodejing*.

36. Hendricks (1989): 232.

37. Knoblock and Riegel (2000): 404, 434. My translation differs only slightly. According to Knoblock and Riegel, this chapter represents teachings "characteristic of the various branches of the Legalist school."

38. The "Inner Training" (*Neiye* 內業), for instance, relates that "holding to the one" (*zhiyi* 執一) enables one to "master the myriad things," and thereby "act upon them without being acted upon *by* them." See: Roth (1999): 62–63.

39. Peerenboom (1993): 33. See also: Hall and Ames (1987): 16, 131–38, and Ames (1989): 115–19.

40. Peerenboom (1993): 35–36.

41. Tu (1979): 103.

42. Peerenboom (1993): 34, 196, italics added.

43. Girardot (1983): 57.

44. In the Mawangdui materials, the opening "Chapter 42" lines consist of lacunae in the "A" version and flow seamlessly from "Chapter 40" in the "B" version. In the latter, the wording varies slightly from the Wang Bi edition, reading: 道生一生二生三生 . . . [lacunae]. Clearly, this formulation was not editorially fixed and its meanings were open to readers' interpretations. How the editor of Mawangdui "B" would have understood its particular version is unclear to me. See: Hendricks (1989): 107.

45. Chan (1991): 125.

46. Complete, annotated translations as well as insightful commentaries on this document can be found in Hendricks (2000): 122–29, Hall and Ames (2003): 225–31, Cook (2012): 323–54, and Wang (2016): 165–67.

47. Hendricks (2000): 124.

48. Positions on this issue are reported and attributed in the proceedings of the International Conference on the Guodian 郭店 *Laozi* and re-stated in Hendricks (2000): 124–25. See also: Allan and Williams (2000): 162–71.

49. Cook (2012): 323.

50. My translation is similar to both Hendricks (2000): 123, and Hall and Ames (2003): 230.

51. Robinet (1999): 132.

52. *Dao* 道 is generally understood in process-oriented terms. Citing the pervasive association of *dao* with water imagery, Sarah Allan submits that *dao* behaves "like the water that comes from a deep spring, ceaselessly emerging from the depths of the earth," Steve Coutinho notes that the term is presented in "dynamic, processive terms," David L. Hall and Roger T. Ames demonstrate that "the character [itself] is primarily gerundive, processional, and dynamic," and Hans-Georg Moeller, citing the wheel motif, argues that *dao* is best understood as "something that moves," literally a process of "going forwards." Such process-oriented readings make little sense unless what is generated *in* the process is something perpetually new, other, and different. See: Allan (1997): 76, Coutinho (2014): 52, Hall and Ames (2004): 57, and Moeller (2004): 27.

53. Ryden (2008): 89.

54. The formula reads: "一生兩, 兩生參, 參生母, 母成結." See: Wang (2016): 173.

55. Perkins (2015): 217.

56. Yates (1997): 50–51, 80–81.

57. Wang (2015): 144, 151.

58. Major et al. (2010): 50n.6, 51.

59. Moeller (2006): 40.

60. As Dewey states: "I hold that nature has both an irreducible brute unique 'itselfness' in everything which exists and also a connection of each thing (which is just what *it* is) with other things such that without them it can neither be nor be conceived." See: "Half-Hearted Naturalism," LW 3: 80.

61. The *Huainanzi* affirms this traditional understanding. See: Major et al. (2010): 133.

62. Seasonal regularities listed in the text are manifold: e.g., in spring, "hibernating creatures begin to stir and revive . . . fishes rise and rub their backs on the ice . . . duckweed begins to sprout;" in summer, "crickets and tree frogs sing on the hillsides . . . bitter herbs flourish . . . cicadas begin to sing;" in autumn, "swallows return . . . hoarfrost begins to descend . . . plants and trees turn yellow and fall;" and in winter, "lychee buds stand out . . . wild geese head north . . . and the year is about to begin again."

63. Chen (2011): 160.

64. "The Origin of the Universe," Peirce and Hartshorne et al. (1935): 6.217, 219–20.

65. "Ideals of Conduct," Peirce and Hartshorne et al. (1931): 1.615.

66. Isabelle Robinet's understanding of the Lu Xisheng 陸希聲 and Wang Bi 王弼 commentaries supports the understanding that *fan* 反 refers to the "positive value of indeterminacy" and the manner that "form begins from the formless." See: Robinet (1999): 146.

67. D. C. Lau's translation captures the sense equally well: "Being great it is further described as receding. Receding, it is described as far away. Being far away, it is described as turning back." See: Lau (1963): 82.

68. "A Guess at the Riddle," Peirce and Hartshorne et al. (1931): 1.412.

69. "The Logic of the Universe," Peirce and Hartshorne et al. (1935): 6.203.

70. *Parmenides* 137c–155e, Plato and Cooper (1997): 371–87.

71. This is argued in Behuniak (2009b).

72. Peirce articulates his own view on this matter in a letter to the editor of the journal *Science*, dated March 16, 1900. He writes: "[Points on a line] do form a collection; but ever a greater collection remains determinable upon the line. *All* the determinable points cannot form a collection, since, by the postulate, if they did, the multitude of that collection would not be less than another multitude. The explanation of their not forming a collection is that all the determinable points are not individuals, distinct, each from all the rest. For individuals can only be distinct from one another in three ways: First, by acts of reaction, immediate or mediate, upon one another; second by having *per se* different qualities; and third, by being in one-to-one correspondence to individuals that are distinct from one another in one of the first two ways. Now the points on a line not yet actually determined are mere potentialities, and, as such, cannot react upon one another actually; and *per se*, they are all exactly alike; and they cannot be in one-to-one correspondence to any collection, since the multitude of that collection would require to be a maximum multitude." See: "Infinitesimals," Peirce and Hartshorne et al. (1933): 3.568. As Peirce later observes: "A true continuum is something whose possibilities of determination no multitude of individuals can exhaust." See: "Synechism," Peirce and Hartshorne et al. (1935): 6.170.

73. *On Knowing Ignorance*, Popkin and Edwards (1969): 460–61. Note that the "movement" of beings, according to Nicholas, amounts to "rest drawn out in an orderly series." Such an idea is more in line with Dewey's notion of non-teleological units of directional order than with conventional Aristotelian understandings.

74. Again, alternative punctuation in this line would read: "The 'nameless' (*wuming* 無名) is the beginning of the myriad beings, and the named (*youming* 有名) is the mother of the myriad beings."
75. Cook (2012): 346, 348.
76. Dennett (1995): 105.
77. Knoblock and Riegal (2000): 106–07.
78. Hendricks (1989): 100–01.
79. "The Origin of the Universe," Peirce and Hartshorne et al. (1935): 6.219–20.
80. As Scott Barnwell observes, the Heshanggong 阿上公 commentary to Chapter 51 makes sense in this context by equating *de* 德 with the "one" (*deyiye* 德一也). See Barnwell (2013): 47. The identification of *de* as that which is "attained" (*de* 得) in order to live is also stated in the *Zhuangzi* (*wudeyisheng weizhide* 物得以生謂之德). See: Watson (1968): 131, Zhuangzi 莊子 (1994) 上: 341.
81. Ivanhoe (1999): 248.
82. "The Subject Matter of Metaphysics," MW 8: 13, italics added.
83. "Review of *Collected Papers of Charles Sanders Peirce*, Vol. 1," LW 6: 277.
84. "Peirce's Theory of Linguistic Signs, Thought, and Meaning," LW 15: 151.
85. "A Guess at the Riddle," Peirce and Hartshorne et al. (1931): 6.207.
86. "The Physiology of Habit," Peirce and Hartshorne et el. (1935): 6.262.
87. "The Logic of the Universe," Peirce and Hartshorne et al. (1935): 6.204, italics added.
88. "A Guess at the Riddle," Peirce and Hartshorne et al. (1931): 1.409.
89. *Experience and Nature*, LW 1: 83–84.
90. It is "simple" because one can start anywhere. Even rolling a stone down a hill amounts to "genuine change in a specific direction" and exhibits organization as such. "The stone starts from somewhere," Dewey observes, "and moves, as consistently as conditions permit, toward a place and state where it will be at rest—toward an end." The degree to which this event expresses an "aim" is a matter of its organization, and in this instance organization is insufficient to support an aim. "Let us add, by imagination," Dewey suggests, ". . . that [the stone] looks forward with desire to the final outcome." Then there would be the conditions for an aim. The point is that the rolling *as such* is already marked by chance, efficient causality, and goal-directedness to *some* degree, and that "aim" is the higher-order organization of these existing characteristics. In a related context, Dewey maintains that inorganic processes display "biases," and "with organization, bias becomes interest." Accordingly for Dewey, "the distinction between physical, psycho-physical, and mental is thus one of levels of increasing complexity and intimacy of interaction among natural events." See: *Art as Experience*, LW 10: 46, *Experience and Nature*, LW 1: 197, 200.
91. Dewey admits as late as 1935 that "I do not think that I have fully mastered [Peirce's system]." See: "Peirce's Theory of Quality," LW 11: 94.
92. "Natural Classes," Peirce and Hartshorne et al. (1931): 1.211, 220.
93. For discussion of Peirce's observations and their relation to final causality, see: Short (1981).
94. "Non-Conservative Action," Peirce and Burks (1958): 7.471.

95. "Peirce's Theory of Linguistic Signs, Thought, and Meaning," LW 15: 151.
96. *Mencius* 6B.11 and 6A.2, Bloom (2009): 141, 121, Mengzi 孟子 (1995): 282–83, 328.
97. Major et al. (2010): 56.
98. "Review, *Collected Papers of Charles Sanders Peirce*, Vol. 1," LW 6: 275–76.
99. "One, Two, Three: An Evolutionist Speculation," Peirce and Kloesel (1993): 300–01, italics added.
100. Kauffman (1993): 8.
101. "Review, *Collected Papers of Charles Sanders Peirce*, Vol. 1," LW 6: 276.
102. "The Triad in Physics," Peirce and Houser et al. (2000): 204.
103. Kauffman also begins with statistical mechanics with respect to gases at thermodynamic equilibrium confined to a box, and proposes a model of self-organization in complex systems that directs us toward the "ensemble" that characterizes "the *typical, average*, or, more generally, *generic* features of such systems." With respect to biological order, Kauffman predicts that, "it will become natural to think of evolution as exploring such an ensemble, as mutations drive populations through neighborhood volumes of the ensemble." See: Kauffman (1993): 22–25.
104. *Experience and Education*, LW 13: 30.
105. *Art as Experience*, LW 10: 62–63.
106. "Review, *Collected Papers of Charles Sanders Peirce*, Vol. 1," LW 6: 276.
107. "The Reflex Arc Concept in Psychology," EW 5: 105–06.
108. *Experience and Nature*, LW 1: 34, 200, 352, 389.
109. Hickman (1990): 125–26.
110. *Physics* 199b.34–200b.9, Aristotle and McKeon (2001): 251–52.
111. *The Parts of Animals* 642a.10–15, Aristotle and Ross (1931b): 642.
112. *The Generation of Animals*, 715a 5–6, Aristotle and Ross (1931b): 715.
113. W. D. Ross is quoted here. See: Aristotle and Ross (1936): 526.
114. Rosen (2014): 76, 79.
115. *Physics* 192b.8–193b.22, Aristotle and McKeon (2001): 236–38.
116. "Contributions to *Cyclopedia of Education*," MW 6: 444.
117. Ariew (2007): 173, 177–78.
118. *Reconstruction in Philosophy*, MW 12: 113.
119. Sterckx (2005): 29n.14.
120. Major et al. (2010): 908 and Hall and Ames (1995): 262.
121. Wilhelm (1967): 280, 328, Zhouyi 周易 (1999): 387, 414.
122. Major et al. (2010): 876–77.
123. No fewer than twenty-two separate "species" accounts have been identified. See: Grene and Depew (2004): 292.
124. See: Ghiselin (1974) and Hull (1976).
125. Hull (1987): 168.
126. Kearney (2007): 224.
127. Mayr (1988): 350–51.
128. Hansen (1983): 30–31.
129. Hansen (1992): 240–41.

130. Graham (1989): 418.
131. Graham (1978): 36–37, 169.
132. Graham (1989): 148.
133. Although for Graham as well, "stuff" (*shi* 實) will "enforce on us a priority over divisions we can make as we please." See: Graham (1986): 383.
134. Graham (1989): 148.
135. Hagen (2007): 41, 154.
136. Some key readings in this debate are Harbsmeier (1989), Graham (1991): 274–78, and Robins (2000). In the latter, Dan Robins refutes Christoph Harbsmeier's objection to the "mass-noun" hypothesis but also offers his own objections, leading him to revise the hypothesis, claiming only that "all classical Chinese nouns are free to function as mass-nouns," that they "vary in their freedom" to do so, and that ultimately it is "never necessary to know" whether nouns are "count-nouns" or "mass-nouns" when reading classical Chinese.
137. Fraser (2007): 421, 431, 438–39.
138. *Parmenides* 135b.6–135c.3, Plato, Cooper, and Hutchison (1997): 369.
139. Fraser (2007): 421, 429, 431, 440.
140. Hall and Ames (1987): 262–64.
141. Hall and Ames (1995): 253, 273.
142. Ziporyn (2012): 44–45, 56, 59.
143. Larry A. Hickman and Thomas Alexander specifically note the "difference between [Dewey's position] and both the realism of Peirce and the nominalism of James" in their introduction to Dewey's work. See: Hickman and Alexander (1998): xi. J. E. Tiles notes that Dewey's Hegelian training positioned him "directly opposed to nominalism" from the very beginning; and while Dewey moves away from Hegel, that "did not alter this orientation." See: Tiles (1988): 84.
144. *Experience and Nature*, LW 1: 145.
145. Ziporyn (2012): 59, 76.
146. "What Are Universals?" LW 11: 109.
147. Fraser (2007): 444.
148. "The American Scholar," Emerson and Ziff (1982): 86.
149. *Experience and Nature*, LW 1: 11.
150. Chang (1963): 56 and Chan (1963): 262.
151. See: Hall and Ames (1995) and (1998).
152. Fen (1961): 86.

Chapter 4

1. *Correspondence* (05030): K. J. Koo to Bertrand Russell, October 17, 1920.
2. *Correspondence* (05018): John Dewey to K. J. Koo, May 14, 1919.
3. See: *Correspondence* (03959–03962): M. D. Lu to John Dewey, July 8, 1921. The current whereabouts of this painting is unknown.
4. Zou (2010): 48.

5. *Correspondence* (04091): John Dewey to Albert C. Barnes, January 15, 1920.
6. *Correspondence* (04082): John Dewey to Albert C. Barnes, January 9, 1919.
7. *Correspondence* (04123): John Dewey to Albert C. Barnes, March 28, 1920.
8. "John Dewey Surveys the Nation's Ills," LW 6: 411.
9. "Tribute to S. J. Woolf," LW 17: 526.
10. "A Philosopher's Philosophy: Interview by S. J. Woolf," Supplementary Vol. 1: 1884–951: 230.
11. *Correspondence* (15925): Ella Christiansen to Roberta Lowitz Grant Dewey, June 2, 1952.
12. *Correspondence* (08103): John Dewey to Agnes E. Meyer, November 11, 1935.
13. *Logic: A Theory of Inquiry*, LW 12: 247.
14. *Art as Experience*, LW 10: 147.
15. Clopton and Ou (1970): 223.
16. *Art as Experience*, LW 10: 213 and *Outlines of a Critical Theory of Ethics*, EW 3: 256.
17. Brindley et al. (2013): 146–47, 146n.4.
18. Liu (2016).
19. Watson (1968): 178, Zhuangzi 莊子 (1994) 上: 458.
20. This is an important point to relate. The present world realizes itself entirely within open space. Its "spontaneity" (*ziran* 自然) and sheer novelty become dimmer to perception as we grow increasingly familiar with what we take to be its proximate stock of possibilities. It is, however, essentially a wide-open affair.
21. *Metaphysics* 1069a.6–8, Aristotle and Hope (1952): 247.
22. Tsung (1995): 33, 52.
23. Lee (1982): 344, 346–47.
24. "Years ago I had a copy of Maxwell's little book, *Matter in Motion* [1892]—I think when I was at Ann Arbor. I remember thinking it was the only thing on physical science principles I could understand." See: *Correspondence* (15545) John Dewey to Arthur Bentley, January 22, 1946.
25. Dalton (2002): 54–57.
26. *Knowing and the Known*, LW 16: 100.
27. *John Dewey Papers*, Ernest Nagel interviewed by Kenneth Duckett, New York City on October 10, 1966, 102/17, see also: Dalton (2002): 321n.74.
28. Dalton (2002): 151, 168–72.
29. *Freedom and Culture*, LW 13: 166.
30. *Knowing and the Known*, LW 16: 278.
31. *Art as Experience*, LW 10: 340, 343.
32. Nor does it preclude it. For, "it is possible that there may come a day in which subject matter that now exists only for laborious [scientific] reflection . . . will become the substance of poetry, and thereby be the matter of enjoyed perception." See: *Art as Experience*, LW 10: 154.
33. *Art as Experience*, LW 10: 154.
34. *Art as Experience*, LW 10: 187, 189.
35. *Human Nature and Culture*, MW 14: 113.

36. *Art as Experience*, LW 10: 189.
37. Legge (2000) vol. 5: 573, 580–81.
38. Shun (2004): 184.
39. Mencius, for instance, speaks of the effects of "calm morning *qi* 氣" and "evening *qi*" on one's emotional temperament. See: *Mencius*, 6A: 8, Bloom (2009): 126, Mengzi 孟子 (1995): 295.
40. See: Watson (1968): 32, 87, 121, 236, Zhuangzi 莊子 (1994) 上: 16, 213, 312, 611.
41. Major et al. (2010): 883.
42. Geaney (2002): 9–10.
43. Farquhar (1994): 34.
44. The *Hengxian*, for instance, maintains that *qi* 氣 was spontaneously generated in the beginning phases of the universe, which is an unverifiable metaphysical claim.
45. *Freedom and Culture*, LW 13: 123.
46. Roth (1999): 42.
47. *Freedom and Culture*, LW 13: 123–24.
48. See: "How to Make Our Ideas Clear," Peirce and Buchler (1955): 35–36. The text is here paraphrased.
49. *Pragmatism*, James and Kuklick (1987): 580.
50. *Freedom and Culture*, LW 13: 123–24.
51. As Feynman explains, the conservation of energy "states that there is a certain quantity, which we call energy, that does not change in the manifold changes which nature undergoes. That is a most abstract idea, because it is a mathematical principle; it says that there is a numerical quantity which does not change when something happens. It is not a description of a mechanism, or anything concrete; it is just a strange fact that we can calculate some number and when we finish watching nature go through her tricks and calculate the number again, it is the same." See: Feynman (1963): 4.1.
52. Clopton and Ou (1973): 231–32.
53. "Liberty and Social Control," LW 11: 361.
54. "Syllabus for 'Social Institutions and the Study of Morals,'" MW 15: 247, italics added.
55. *Physics* 257b.8, McKeon (2001): 253.
56. *Nicomachean Ethics* 1174a.18–24, McKeon (2001): 1098.
57. *Physics* 201b.33, McKeon (2001): 255.
58. "Syllabus for 'Social Institutions and the Study of Morals,'" MW 15: 247.
59. Coutinho (2014): 43.
60. *Art as Experience*, LW 10: 184.
61. *Art as Experience*, LW 10: 158–59.
62. *Logic: The Theory of Inquiry*, LW 12: 34.
63. "The Need for a Recovery of Philosophy," MW 10: 7.
64. *Art as Experience*, LW 10: 22.
65. "The Need for a Recovery of Philosophy," MW 10: 7.
66. Clopton and Ou (1970): 383.

67. *Experience and Nature*, LW 1: 47.
68. *Experience and Nature*, LW 1: 47.
69. *Correspondence* (11524): Felix Frankfurter to Dewey 90th Birthday Committee, October 20, 1949.
70. *Correspondence* (05264): W. W. Norton to Oliver Wendell Holmes, Jr., March 6, 1929.
71. *Correspondence* (17036): Oliver Wendell Holmes, Jr. to John C. H. Wu, February 20, 1927.
72. *Experience and Nature*, LW 1: 47–48.
73. *Experience and Nature*, LW 1: 49.
74. "Context and Thought," LW 6: 10.
75. It is regularly pointed out, however, that there is a significant degree of asymmetry in the treatment of complementary notions in the *Daodejing*. The female, for instance, is preferred over the male, the soft over the hard, and the weak over the strong. This is true. Such philosophical preferences, however, are not inconsistent with the position that such notions are mutually entailing and ontologically on par. I disagree with Benjamin Schwartz's suggestion that the former terms enjoy "a higher 'ontological' status" than the latter terms in Daoist philosophy. See: Schwartz (1985): 203.
76. *Art as Experience*, LW 10: 20, 161, italics added.
77. Watson (1968): 304–305, Zhuangzi 莊子 (1994) 下: 792.
78. Ziporyn (2009): 14n.16.
79. *Art as Experience*, LW 10: 22, 171, 174, 183.
80. Dennett (1995): 69.
81. Rickett (1985): 216.
82. *Art as Experience*, LW 10: 173.
83. *Logic: The Theory of Inquiry*, LW 12: 42.
84. *Art as Experience*, LW 10: 184.
85. Major et al. (2005): 116, 160, 875.
86. Major maintains that its assumptions trace back to the *Jixia* 稷下 academy in the third century BCE. See: Major (1993): 30.
87. *Physics* 199b 16 and 201a 10–11, Aristotle and McKeon (2001): 251, 254.
88. *Metaphysics* 1050a 2, Aristotle and McKeon (2001): 829.
89. *Physics* 202a 13–202b 29, Aristotle and McKeon (2001): 256–57.
90. Major et al. (2005): 116.
91. Defoort (1997): 167.
92. Joseph Needham, for instance, finds that Chinese causal thinking is "reticular and hierarchically fluctuating," rather than "singly catenarian and particulate." Cheng Chung-ying describes Chinese thinking as "holistic," "internalistic," and "organistic," and thus "quite unlike" standard Western models of causality. Joseph S. Wu regards mechanistic causality to be "totally alien to Chinese metaphysics," which treats events as "organically interrelated," a "comprehensive continuum" that exhibits a "process of never-ceasing growth." In articulating this vision, he appeals to Dewey's idea that "the antecedent and the consequent are not two distinct events but are two integral constituents of the same event." See: Needham (1956): 289, Cheng (1967): 13, Wu (1975) 19, 14.

93. Norenzayan and Nisbett (2000).
94. Russell (1945): 167.
95. Waley (1958): 31–32.
96. "The Subject Matter of Metaphysical Inquiry," MW 8: 11, italics added.
97. Hall and Ames (2003): 60–61.
98. *Democracy and Education*, MW 9: 46–47.
99. Stevenson and Lamb (1979).
100. *Democracy and Education*, MW 9: 48.
101. "Contribution to *Encyclopedia and Dictionary of Education*," MW 13: 402.
102. *Democracy and Education*, MW 9: 48–49, see also: James and Myers (1992): 137–40.
103. I follow John C. H. Wu's rendition of the standard version here, as it captures the botanical sense of *bi* 蔽, which in the *Shuowen* lexicon is defined as "little blades of grass" (*xiaocao* 小艸).
104. "Contributions to *Cyclopedia of Education*," MW 7: 246.
105. *Daodejing*, Ch. 52.
106. "The Subject Matter of Metaphysical Inquiry," MW 8: 11.
107. *Logic: The Theory of Inquiry*, LW 12: 386.
108. *Physics* 201b.9–12, Aristotle and McKeon (2001): 255.
109. *Physics* 202b.12–13, 202b.6–8, Aristotle and McKeon (2001): 257. J. L. Ackrill's translation is partially relied upon here. See: Aristotle and Ackrill (1987): 115.
110. *Experience and Education*, LW 13: 25.
111. *Logic: The Theory of Inquiry*, LW 12: 452–53.
112. Ziporyn (2012): 43.
113. "Review, *Collected Papers of Charles Sanders Peirce*, Vol. 1," LW 6: 276.
114. "Peirce's Theory of Quality," LW 11: 89.
115. "What Are Universals?" LW 11: 111.
116. *Logic: The Theory of Inquiry*, LW 12: 249.
117. "Characteristics and Characters: Kinds and Classes," LW 11: 97–99.
118. "What Are Universals?" LW 11: 112.
119. *Logic: The Theory of Inquiry*, LW 12: 261.
120. *Logic: The Theory of Inquiry*, LW 12: 255. It should be noted that Dewey's nomenclature differs from that being used here. Dewey uses the word "kind" to denote the "classes" that such characteristic traits determine. The word "class," for Dewey, is used "to designate both kinds and the different ways of being universal." See: *Logic: The Theory of Inquiry*, LW 12: 258–59. It is not necessary to over-analyze Dewey's word choices here.
121. *Reconstruction in Philosophy*, MW 12: 167.
122. "Time and Individuality," LW 14: 109.
123. "The Subject Matter of Metaphysical Inquiry," MW 8: 11.
124. *Logic: The Theory of Inquiry*, LW 12: 440.
125. Major et al. (2010): 216.
126. Such thinking is suggested, for instance, in the intriguing but little understood practice of military divination through sonic instrumentation. It was thought that sound could reveal features of the terrain on which enemy forces were stationed, thus

helping to forecast how events might unfold on the battlefield. Pipes were sounded, and their reverberations used in prognostication. Like all such practices, sonic divination was not based on linear, "Cause/Effect" thinking, but rather on the assumption that potential energies were shored up in configurative distributions over entire fields. It was assumed that the propensity of the whole field would be implicated in the outcome of any action taken, and that changes in one region would alter the configuration of energies throughout. Thus, as Léon Vandermeersch observes: "from one event to another, the relation revealed by the science of [such] divination was not presented as a chain of intermediate causes and effects, but as changes in diagrammatic configuration." See: Vandermeersch (1988): 27 and Brindley (2012): 69–73.

127. Longo and Montévil (2014): 174–75. To understand the term "generic" in this context, recall Peirce's notion of the "general." As Stuart Kauffman explains, the "generic" is the "*typical, average*" which represents an "ensemble" range of outcomes.

128. "The Subject Matter of Metaphysics," MW 8: 13, italics added.

129. Longo and Montévil (2014): 75.

130. *Art as Experience*, LW 10: 174.

131. Longo and Montévil (2014): 76.

132. Longo and Montévil (2014): 138.

133. *Art as Experience*, LW 10: 183.

134. Longo and Montévil (2014): 18, 162.

135. Ziporyn (2012): 53.

136. Longo and Montévil (2014): 18.

137. Kuhn (1962): 43–51.

138. Longo and Montévil (2014): 191.

139. Ziporyn (2012): 49–63.

140. Ziporyn (2012): 56, 59.

141. *Experience and Nature*, LW 1: 10, 30–31.

142. *Quest for Certainty*, LW 4: 172.

143. Longo and Montévil (2014): 205.

144. Longo and Montévil (2014): 62.

145. Fen (1961): 86.

146. "1948 Introduction to *Reconstruction in Philosophy*," MW 12: 260–61.

147. Ziporyn (2012): 21–22. For a general introduction to "process philosophy," see: Rescher (1996).

148. Longo and Montévil (2014): 195, 218.

149. Chin and Freeman (1990): 113.

150. *Mencius* 7A.30, Bloom (2009): 151, Mengzi 孟子 (1995): 361.

151. Watson (1968): 204–05, Zhuangzi 莊子 (1994) 上: 533.

152. Taxonomically, oaks are notoriously difficult to sort out. As Kelleher et al. (2005) finds in its study of Irish oaks, "molecular variation is partitioned more strongly between populations than between species."

153. Knoblock and Riegel (2000): 64–65.

154. Robins (2011): 33.

155. Watson (1968): 169, Zhuangzi 莊子 (1994) 上: 439.

156. Robins (2011): 48n.30.

157. *Mencius* 6A.7, Bloom (2009): 125, Mengzi 孟子 (1995): 292.
158. Robins (2011): 32.
159. Graham (1989): 136 and Graham (1990a): 7.
160. Graham (1990a): 8.
161. Graham (1991): 287–88.
162. Ames explains that "Graham offers us what we would call a 'narrative' understanding of *xing* 性 in which person and world evolve together in a dynamic, contrapuntal relationship." Graham "did not come to the narrative understanding of *xing* 性 easily," however, and "in his later writings becomes dissatisfied with and indeed repudiates his earlier essentialist reading of *xing* 性." See Ames (2018): 190–96.
163. Robins (2011): 37, italics added.
164. Graham (1990a): 7. For a discussion of how recent archeological finds add to our understanding of the close relationship between these terms, see: Cook (2012): 697n.3.
165. *Mencius* 6A.2, Bloom (2009): 121, Mengzi 孟子 (1995): 282–83.
166. Knoblock (1994): 127.
167. See: Robins (2011): 37 and Hutton (2011).
168. One would imagine, for instance, that vestigial reflexes such as the plantar grasp reflex, important for the survival of our arboreal (and hairy) ancestors, might someday cease to be an infant-stage reflex for us. But who knows.
169. "The Reflex Arc Concept in Psychology," EW 5: 104.
170. *Human Nature and Conduct*, MW 14: 65, italics added.
171. "Brigham Young Educational Lectures," LW 17: 215.
172. *Human Nature and Conduct*, MW 14: 65.
173. "Brigham Young Educational Lectures," LW 17: 305, 306.
174. Hall and Ames (2001): 89.
175. Raphals (2005): 76–77.
176. Legge (2000) vol. 4: 64–65. This account comes from a commentary on three songs, each of which is missing from the received text.
177. Later in the tradition, Wang Chong 王充 (27–ca. 97) ascribes one's *ming* 命 to the configuration of "cosmic energies" (*tianqi* 天氣) and "astral potencies" (*xingjing* 星精) that prevail at the moment of conception. Such beliefs continue to be held in China today and surely preceded Wang Chong.
178. *On the Soul* 415b.15–20, Aristotle and McKeon (2001): 562.
179. *Daodejing*, Ch. 2, 10, 37, 51, 77.
180. In translating *zuo* 作 as "arise" in this context, I follow Brindley, Goldin, and Klein in their understanding of non-anthropogenic emergence in the *Hengxian* 恆先. See: Brindley et al. (2013): 149n.19.
181. Ivanhoe's translation of Chapter 16 enables him to gloss its meaning as follows: "By following the *dao* 道, everything will return to its root and proper destiny." This establishes *dao* 道 as a superordinate entity that governs the proper ends of things. See: Ivanhoe (2002): xxvi, 16.
182. Relying on recently unearthed materials, Xing Wen documents how *fu* 復 comes to mean a kind of "returning that starts a new cycle of *sheng* 生 generation,"

resulting in a "new generation from existing generations," which indicates a process of growth. See: Xing (2015): 117–23.

183. *Experience and Nature*, LW 1: 194.

184. Moeller (2006): 92.

185. "Syllabus for 'Social Institutions and the Study of Morals,'" MW 15: 249, italics added.

186. Moeller (2006): 94.

187. The degree to which nonhuman animals and infants possess this ability, as well as how one might go about testing it, is discussed in McCormack and Hoerl (2011).

188. Campbell (1994).

189. Slingerland (2003): 78–84, 303n.4.

190. Van Norden (1999): 203.

191. "As the Chinese Think," MW 13: 222.

192. *Mengzi* 2A.1, Bloom (2009): 28, Mengzi 孟子 (1995): 53–54.

193. "As the Chinese Think," MW 13: 222–23.

194. Van Els (2011): 327.

195. Cleary (1991): 40.

196. This is especially true with respect to its philosophy of law (*fa* 法). The author states that: "Rigid laws and harsh punishments are not the work of great leaders," and "law does not descend from heaven, nor does it emerge from earth; it is invented through human self-reflection and self-correction." See: Cleary (1991): 15, 161.

197. Waley (1958): 154.

198. This line is sometimes parsed another way, obscuring the fact that it involves discussion of "embracing the one" (*baoyi* 抱一). See: Behuniak (2009a): 373–74 for an argument in support of the current punctuation.

199. This recension is based on both the *textus receptus* and Wang Bi's commentary. Amended here is the line "can you play the part of the female," which is negatively formed in the received version but interpreted as positive in Wang Bi's commentary as well as in the Mawangdui. The Mawangdui version of Chapter 10 differs grammatically from the Wang Bi in other respects: it replaces all the *wu* 無 forms with alternate negatives. It also differs substantively by omitting the phrase "Act, but do not be presumptuous." The significance of these variants, if any, is not entirely clear to me. See: Wagner (2003): 146–53.

200. *Art as Experience*, LW 10: 58, 213.

Chapter 5

1. Watson (1968): 42, Zhuangzi 莊子 (1994) 上: 75.
2. Needham (1956): 121.
3. Watson (1968): 50–51, Zhuangzi 莊子 (1994) 上: 106.
4. Watson (1968): 51, Zhuangzi 莊子 (1994) 上: 106.
5. Eno (1996): 131, 134, 136.
6. See: Eno (1996): 142.

Notes to Chapter 5 / 339

7. Eno (1991): 24, 25n.43.
8. Eno (1996): 139, 142–43.
9. Moeller (2009): 32.
10. Quoted in Westbrook (1991): 382.
11. Hofstadter (1962): 375, italics added.
12. *The Quest for Certainty*, LW 4: 37–38.
13. Hocking (1930), see also: LW 5: 475.
14. Eno (1991): 25n.43.
15. *Gorgias* 464b–66a, 500b, Plato and Cooper (1997): 808–09, 844.
16. *Philebus* 56b–c, Plato and Cooper (1997): 445–46.
17. *Mencius* 6A.20, Bloom (2009): 131, Mengzi 孟子 (1995): 309.
18. Major et al. (2010): 417, Huainanzi 淮南子 (1936), 卷11: 78.
19. *Mencius* 7B.5, Bloom (2009): 157, Mengzi 孟子 (1995): 381.
20. Major et al. (2010): 416, Huainanzi 淮南子 (1936), 卷11: 78.
21. "Individuality and Experience," LW 2: 57.
22. Major et al. (2010): 415, Huainanzi 淮南子 (1936), 卷11: 77–78.
23. *Euthydemus* 290b, Plato and Cooper (1997): 728.
24. "The University Elementary School: History and Character," MW 1: 331.
25. Menand (2001): 323.
26. *The School and Society*, MW 1: 50–51.
27. *Experience and Nature*, LW 1: 105.
28. Eno (1996): 131.
29. "The Influence of Darwinism on Philosophy," MW 4: 3, 9, italics added.
30. "The Influence of Darwinism on Philosophy," MW 4: 6.
31. *Democracy and Education*, MW 9: 172–73.
32. *Logic: The Theory of Inquiry*, LW 12: 109.
33. Eno (1996): 135.
34. Watson (1968): 205–06, Zhuangzi 莊子 (1994) 上: 536, 540.
35. *Human Nature and Conduct*, MW 14: 133, 134, 139.
36. "Introduction to *Essays in Experimental Logic*," MW 10: 328, 328n.3.
37. Graham (2001): 6–8.
38. Graham (1983): 10–11.
39. *Experience and Nature*, LW 1: 142.
40. Watson (1968): 206–07, Zhuangzi 莊子 (1994) 上: 540.
41. Eno (1996): 142.
42. *Human Nature and Conduct*, MW 14: 154–55.
43. *Art as Experience*, LW 10: 201.
44. Eno (1996): 136.
45. *Reconstruction in Philosophy*, MW 12: 131.
46. Watson (1968): 40, Zhuangzi 莊子 (1994) 上: 61.
47. *Human Nature and Conduct*, MW 14: 232.
48. Clopton and Ou (1970): 285.
49. Watson (1968): 152–53, Zhuangzi 莊子 (1994) 上: 393-94. Here, "pertinence" is a shorthand translation of the more complex phrase, *yizhisuosuizhe* 意之所隨者.

50. Watson (1968): 152–53, Zhuangzi 莊子 (1994) 上: 393–94.
51. *Democracy and Education,* MW 9: 173.
52. "Individuality and Experience," LW 2: 57.
53. "*Experience and Nature,* Scattered Drafts, June 1949," *John Dewey Papers,* 102/56/13.
54. Eno (1996): 148n.33.
55. *Correspondence* (10300), W. R. Houston to John Dewey, April 12, 1946.
56. *Democracy and Education,* MW 9: 180–82.
57. *How We Think,* LW 8: 136–37.
58. *Democracy and Education,* MW 9: 182–85.
59. *How We Think,* LW 8: 137.
60. *Democracy and Education,* MW 9: 185–86.
61. Clopton and Ou (1970): 150–51.
62. "Modern Philosophy," LW 16: 413.
63. *Democracy and Education,* MW 9: 175–76.
64. *Democracy and Education,* MW 9: 176–77.
65. See: Eno (1996): 142, italics added.
66. Pappas (1998): 114–15.
67. See: Graham (1983): 15. This imperative is also presented as "Be aware of everything relevant to the issue," "Respond with awareness (of what is objectively so)," and "Face facts." For Graham, "awareness" is superior to knowing as a guide to living. In using the term, he refers to a "highly variable capacity to take facts, sensations, and inclinations into account, by no means guaranteed by knowing in the abstract." See: Graham (1983): 13–15, and Graham (1992): 17, 21, 27n.1.
68. Graham (1992): 17–27. See also n.67 above.
69. Graham (1983): 14, 18.
70. Watson (1968): 45–46, Zhuangzi 莊子 (1994) 上: 89.
71. Graham (1983): 18.
72. *Human Nature and Conduct,* MW 14: 134.
73. *Art as Experience,* LW 10: 79.
74. Clopton and Ou (1970): 175.
75. *Democracy and Education,* MW 9: 111.
76. Watson (1968): 201, Zhuangzi 莊子 (1994) 上: 519–20.
77. Eno (1991): 24.
78. Moeller (2009): 25.
79. Moeller (2004): 116–20.
80. Watson (1968): 138, Zhuangzi 莊子 (1994) 上: 359.
81. Moeller (2009): 34–35.
82. The range of sentiments observed in response to his book, *The Moral Fool: A Case for Amorality* (2009) is noteworthy, however, for its correlation between expertise in Daoist philosophy and general receptivity to the argument. At one end of the spectrum lies someone like Brook Ziporyn, who understands the *Zhuangzi* as well as any scholar working today. Ziporyn praises Moeller's book—"I wish I had written it," he says. His review adds considerably to the strength and persuasiveness of Moeller's

thesis. On the other end lies someone like Michael R. Slater, whose expertise is not in Chinese philosophy. He receives Moeller's book with complete disapproval—citing its "overall failure to substantiate its major claims." See: Ziporyn (2010) and Slater (2010).
  83. Moeller (2009): 21.
  84. *Logic: The Theory of Inquiry*, LW 12: 488–89.
  85. *Logic: The Theory of Inquiry*, LW 12: 489–90.
  86. Moeller (2009): 21, 43–52.
  87. *Logic: The Theory of Inquiry*, LW 12: 490.
  88. Watson (1968): 172, Zhuangzi 莊子 (1994) 上: 445.
  89. Ziporyn (2010): 482.
  90. *Tenzo Kyōkun* 典坐教訓, Tanahashi (1985): 53, 64–66.
  91. Uchiyama and Wright (2005): 39, 58, 73–74.
  92. *The School and Society*, MW 1: 10.
  93. *Democracy and Education*, MW 9: 210-11.
  94. *Experience and Nature*, LW 1: 274.
  95. *Theory of Valuation*, LW 13: 228.
  96. *Daodejing*, Ch. 37.
  97. *Democracy and Education*, MW 9: 250.
  98. *Nicomachean Ethics* 1094a 3–5, Aristotle and McKeon (2001): 935.
  99. *How We Think*, LW 8: 287.
  100. *Experience and Nature*, LW 1: 280.
  101. *Democracy and Education*, MW 9: 206, 210, 211.
  102. *Experience and Education*, LW 13: 57.
  103. *Interest and Effort in Education*, MW 7: 188, 190.
  104. *Democracy and Education*, MW 9: 214.
  105. Randall (1989): 101–02.
  106. Dewey and Meyer (1984): 251.
  107. *Experience and Nature*, LW 1: 47.
  108. *Human Nature and Conduct*, MW 14: 154.
  109. *Experience and Nature*, LW 1: 96.
  110. "Beliefs and Existences," MW 3: 89.
  111. "Experience and Objective Idealism," MW 3: 142.
  112. Tiles (1988): 126.
  113. *Metaphysics* 981a 12–15, Aristotle and McKeon (2001): 689-90.
  114. *Nicomachean Ethics* 1039a 36-37, Aristotle and McKeon (2001): 1024.
  115. *Nicomachean Ethics* 1040a 10, Aristotle and McKeon (2001): 1025; Tiles' simpler translation is here adopted. See: Tiles (1988): 188.
  116. *Metaphysics* 981a 4–5, Aristotle and McKeon (2001): 689.
  117. *Experience and Nature*, LW 1: 279.
  118. *Experience and Nature*, LW 1: 277. See also: *Politics* 1328a 28–30, Aristotle and McKeon (2001): 1287.
  119. *Reconstruction in Philosophy*, MW 12: 88.
  120. Eno (1996): 131.
  121. *Nicomachean Ethics*, 1177b 2–4, Aristotle and McKeon (2001): 1104.

122. Urmson (1988): 18, cf. *Nicomachean Ethics* 1039a 36–37, Aristotle and McKeon (2001): 1024.
123. *Human Nature and Conduct*, MW 14: 122.
124. *Nicomachean Ethics*, 1077a 1–1179a 33, Aristotle and McKeon (2001): 1104–108.
125. Kraut (1991): 28.
126. Reeve (2006): 63.
127. Dewey and Deen (2012): 45, 297.
128. *Nicomachean Ethics*, 1141b 14–16, Aristotle and McKeon (2001): 1028.
129. Lear (1988): 173.
130. Lear (1988): 173.
131. *Metaphysics*, 980a.1, Aristotle and McKeon (2001): 689.
132. *Nicomachean Ethics*, 1140b 20–21, Aristotle and McKeon (2001): 1027.
133. Lear (1988): 173.
134. "The Intellectualist Criterion for Truth," MW 4: 63.
135. *Experience and Nature*, LW 1: 272, italics added.
136. *Ethics*, LW 7: 210.
137. Hickman (1992): 12–13.
138. *Experience and Nature*, LW 1: 50.
139. *The Quest for Certainty*, LW 4: 223.
140. *Reconstruction in Philosophy*, MW 12: 134.
141. Syllabus for "Problems of Philosophical Reconstruction," MW 11: 346.
142. "The Need for a Recovery of Philosophy," MW 10: 45.
143. *The Quest for Certainty*, LW 4: 170.
144. Ziporyn (2009): 217–18.
145. Coutinho (2004): 90–93, 153–56.
146. Watson (1968): 39–41, Zhuangzi 莊子 (1994) 上: 56, 61, 69.
147. Eno (1996): 150n.49.
148. *Reconstruction in Philosophy*, MW 12: 135.
149. "The University Elementary School: History and Character," MW 1: 331.
150. *Experience and Education*, LW 13: 57.
151. *Phaedo* 70e, Plato and Cooper (1997): 61.
152. Graham (1960): 161.
153. Liao (1959): 220–21.
154. Major et al. (2010): 798.
155. Watson (1968): 34–35, Zhuangzi 莊子 (1994) 上: 30.
156. Liao (1959): 105.
157. Knoblock and Riegal (2001): 491–92.
158. Liao (1959): 35–36.
159. *Theory of Valuation*, LW 13: 235.
160. Liao (1959): 276.
161. *Mencius* 2A.2, Bloom (2009): 30–31, Mengzi 孟子 (1995): 57–59.
162. *Democracy and Education*, MW 9: 110, 112, 138.

163. *Mencius* 7B.36, Bloom (2009): 164, Mengzi 孟子 (1995): 409.
164. Wu (1951): 221.
165. *Theory of Valuation*, LW 13: 227.
166. Chong (2002): 111.
167. *Logic: The Theory of Inquiry*, LW 12: 121.
168. One of Dewey's favorite stories, which he started telling in 1897, goes as follows:

> I am told that there is a swimming school in the city of Chicago where youth are taught to swim without going into the water, being repeatedly drilled in the various movements which are necessary for swimming. When one of the young men so trained was asked what he did when he got into the water, he laconically replied, "Sunk."

Dewey insists that the story "happens to be true." There is an independent telling in an article in *The Country Gentleman* magazine dated Sept. 14, 1912. It is difficult to say if this corroborates the story's veracity or is simply lifted from Dewey's own telling. The *Country Gentleman* version goes:

> There is a swimming school in one town I know about, where the boys are taught to swim without going near the water. Very diligently their teacher makes them go through and learn the various movements of swimming—out of the water. One of these boys was asked what he did when he got into the water. In a matter-of-course tone he replied, "Sunk."

While lecturing in China, Dewey would revisit (and revise) the story on at least four occasions. The most embellished telling is June 1919 in Beijing:

> I have heard that there is a correspondence school in the United States which advertises that it will teach students to swim by mail. People send payments to the school every month, and the school sends them mimeographed materials on swimming—materials in which there are pictures showing proper swimming postures, directions for the movements of hands and feet, and so on. The student goes into his room, lies on the floor, and following the directions in the mimeographed material, goes through the motions of swimming. After several months of this, when the student has read through all the materials and has attained satisfactory scores on examinations, the school issues him a "Swimming Diploma." But when the student actually dives into the swimming pool, the techniques which he has "learned" fail to function, and he sinks to the bottom!

Whether the "Swimming School" story is true or not, it certainly drives the point home. See: "Ethical Principles Underlying Education," EW 5: 61, Clopton and Ou (1970): 32.

Chapter 6

1. Watson (1968): 234–36, Zhuangzi 莊子 (1994) 上: 610–11.
2. The error made by "Knowledge" in this episode is thus the same error that Robert Eno makes in treating *dao* 道-learning as a means only. This time, the error is made from the other direction.
3. Watson (1968): 58, Zhuangzi 莊子 (1994) 上: 127.
4. Sing-nan Fen, "John Dewey's Theory of Values," *John Dewey Papers*, 102/72/7: 11.
5. "Brief Studies in Realism," MW 6: 115.
6. Watson (1968): 171, Zhuangzi 莊子 (1994) 上: 442.
7. Dewey and Meyer (1983): 115.
8. *The Quest for Certainty*, LW 4: 168, italics added.
9. See: Roth (2003): 194, 201, 205–06 for an analysis of contrary findings.
10. Watson (1968): 172–74, Zhuangzi 莊子 (1994) 上: 445, 448–49.
11. Hall and Ames (2003): 40.
12. "What are Universals?" LW 11: 111.
13. *Republic* 478a.11–12, Plato and Cooper (1997): 1104–105, translation adjusted.
14. *Republic* 476e.7–8, Plato and Cooper (1997): 1103.
15. *Metaphysics* 1026a.21–22, Aristotle and McKeon (2001): 779.
16. *Metaphysics* 1064a.16, Aristotle and McKeon (2001): 861.
17. *Unmodern Philosophy*, Dewey and Deen (2012): 4.
18. Morelle (2015): 1.
19. *The Quest for Certainty*, LW 4: 11.
20. *Unmodern Philosophy*, Dewey and Deen (2012): 4.
21. *The Quest for Certainty*, LW 4: 11.
22. Havelock (1963): 223–24.
23. *The Quest for Certainty*, LW 4: 12.
24. Keightley (2014): 63.
25. *Analects* 3.12, 6.22, 7.21, 11.12, Ames and Rosemont (1998): 85, 108, 115, 144.
26. *Analects* 16.8, 20.3, Ames and Rosemont (1998): 198, 229.
27. Puett (2002): 98.
28. Chris Fraser (2016) argues rightfully that the Mohist movement is unfairly maligned in Chinese history and that their philosophical positions are far more sophisticated than is generally recognized. This does not, however, change the tenor of their discourse.
29. Eno (1996): 131.
30. Mozi and Johnston (2010): 376–77. The translation is Johnston's.
31. Eno (1996): 131.
32. Mozi and Johnston (2010): 159-61, 241–43, 673. Johnston's translations are largely relied upon.
33. Lamont and Farrell (1959): 55–56.
34. "Time and Individuality," LW 14: 100.

35. "Evolution and Ethics," EW 5: 47.
36. "Contributions to *Cyclopdia of Education*," MW 6: 444–45.
37. This theory was made popular in Morgan's 1877 work, *Ancient Society*. See: Weiner (1949): 147.
38. Ryan (1995): 166.
39. "Some Connections of Science and Philosophy," LW 17: 404–05.
40. "Anthropology and Ethics," LW 3: 11.
41. "Interpretation of Savage Mind," MW 2: 39.
42. *Democracy and Education*, MW 9: 47.
43. "Interpretation of Savage Mind," MW 2: 40.
44. *Democracy and Education*, MW 9: 210–11.
45. *The School and Society*, MW 1: 31.
46. "Does Human Nature Change?" LW 13: 291.
47. Watson (1968): 172–74, Zhuangzi 莊子 (1994) 上: 445, 448–49.
48. "Does Human Nature Change?" LW 13: 291.
49. "Interpretation of Savage Mind," MW 2: 41.
50. *The School and Society*, MW 1: 32.
51. "Interpretation of Savage Mind," MW 2: 42.
52. See: "What Pragmatism Means By Practical," MW 4: 103–04.
53. *The Quest for Certainty*, LW 4: 30.
54. "Interpretation of Savage Mind," MW 2: 44.
55. *Art as Experience*, LW 10: 13.
56. Ghosh (2014): 1.
57. *Ethics*, LW 7: 45–46.
58. *Unmodern Philosophy*, Dewey and Deen (2012): 281.
59. "Evolution and Ethics," EW 5: 45, italics added.
60. *Experience and Nature*, LW 1: 210.
61. *Art as Experience*, LW 10: 24.
62. *Unmodern Philosophy*, Dewey and Deen (2012): 281–82.
63. *Art as Experience*, LW 10: 24.
64. Watson (1968): 172, Zhuangzi 莊子 (1994) 上: 445.
65. *Unmodern Philosophy*, Dewey and Deen (2012): 282.
66. Slingerland (2003): 6.
67. *Unmodern Philosophy*, Dewey and Deen (2012): 282.
68. *Experience and Nature*, LW 1: 276, 278.
69. *Unmodern Philosophy*, Dewey and Deen (2012): 282–83, italics added.
70. Slingerland (2003): 6.
71. *Democracy and Education*, MW 9: 211.
72. In his critique of Slingerland's "paradox of *wu-wei* 無為," Ivanhoe notes that "neither early Confucians nor early Daoists reject striving *per se*; both traditions manifest a profound and enduring concern with how to improve oneself." See: Ivanhoe (2007): 281.
73. *Unmodern Philosophy*, Dewey and Deen (2012): 282.

74. *Democracy and Education*, MW 9: 210.
75. Watson (1968): 79, Zhuangzi 莊子 (1994) 上: 186–87. Translation is Brook Ziporyn's.
76. *Meno* 85d.5–8, Plato and Cooper (1997): 886.
77. *Phaedo* 92a, Plato and Cooper (1997): 79.
78. Radin (1927): 230, 243–44.
79. "Foreword in Paul Radin's *Primitive Man as Philosopher*," LW 3: 337.
80. Radin (1927): 259.
81. Watson (1968): 133, Zhuangzi 莊子 (1994) 上: 344.
82. "Interpretation of Savage Mind," MW 2: 48.
83. "Group IV. Historical Development of Inventions and Occupations," MW 1: 223–24.
84. *Reconstruction of Philosophy*, MW 12: 128–29.
85. *The Quest for Certainty*, LW 4: 8.
86. *Reconstruction in Philosophy*, MW 12: 81–82.
87. Watson (1968): 106, Zhuangzi 莊子 (1994) 上: 275.
88. "Interpretation of Savage Mind," MW 2: 42.
89. *Interest and Effort in Education*, MW 7: 188, 190.
90. "Interpretation of Savage Mind," MW 2: 43.
91. Hickman (1990): 89.
92. "Interpretation of Primitive Mind," MW 2: 51–52.
93. See: Watson (1968): 111, Zhuangzi 莊子 (1994) 上: 286, and Sarkissian (2010): 323.
94. Møllgaard (2007): 31–32, 46.
95. Puett (2001): 3.
96. As Brook Ziporyn notes, this line, *tianershengye* 天而生也, is "extremely rich with ambiguities." My translation is meant to retain its simplicity and ambiguity. See: Ziporyn (2009): 39n.2.
97. Watson (1968): 77, Zhuangzi 莊子 (1994) 上: 185–86.
98. Watson (1968): 175, 177, Zhuangzi 莊子 (1994) 上: 452, 453.
99. "On a Certain Blindness in Human Beings," James and Myers (1992): 841.
100. *A Pluralistic Universe*, James and Kuklick (1987): 771.
101. Watson (1968): 50, 177, Zhuangzi 莊子 (1994) 上: 104, 458.
102. Hall and Ames (2003): 40.
103. *Some Problems of Philosophy*, James and Kuklick (1987): 1048.
104. "William James as Empiricist," LW 15: 11.
105. *Varieties of Religious Experience*, James and Kuklick (1987): 454.
106. *Democracy and Education*, MW 9: 347.
107. *Knowing and the Known*, LW 16: 111.
108. Hickman (1990): 31.
109. "'Introduction to *Essays in Experimental Logic*," MW 10: 320.
110. *Logic: The Theory of Inquiry*, LW 12: 121–22.
111. *Knowing and the Known*, LW 16: 112.

112. In early Buddhism, the irreducible term in the transaction between sense faculties, sensory objects, and consciousness is termed "contact" (*phassa*). Entailing no self-subsisting "entities" or "realities," *phassa* is one instance in the process of "dependent co-arising" (*paticcasamupāda*). See: Holder (2006): 203.

113. "A World of Pure Experience," James and Kuklick (1987): 1164–165.

114. See: "Introduction," LW 16: xxviii, n.55.

115. Kitarō (1955): 132.

116. *Knowing and the Known*, LW 16: 125.

117. It calls to mind the Buddhist philosophy of Dushun 杜順 whose "Four-fold *Dharmadhātu*" includes the "non-obstruction of wholeness and events" (*lishiwuai* 理事無礙). From such a perspective, each constituent of the "hunting" is without ontological own-being, and even the act of "knowing" the event factors into what amounts to a transactional whole. See: Chang (1971): 141–71.

118. *Knowing and the Known*, LW 16: 113.

119. Kuhn (1962): 171.

120. Watson (1968): 288, Zhuangzi 莊子 (1994) 下: 748.

121. *Reconstruction in Philosophy*, MW 12: 144.

122. *The Quest for Certainty*, LW 4: 19.

123. Dalton (2002): 170–74.

124. *The Quest for Certainty*, LW 4: 162.

125. The shift can be traced throughout *The Knowing and the Known*, LW 16: 3–4, 66–68, 71, 96–130, 242–44, 272, and 472–73, and also in the Dewey-Bentley correspondence. See: Dewey and Bentley (1964).

126. *The Quest for Certainty*, LW 4: 163.

127. "Does Reality Possess Practical Character?" MW 4: 127.

128. Watson (1968): 40, Zhuangzi 莊子 (1994) 上: 69.

129. Hall and Ames (1998): 55–56.

130. *Reconstruction in Philosophy*, MW 12: 167.

131. *The Quest for Certainty*, LW 4: 168.

132. "Dewey's Reply to Albert G. A. Balz," LW 16: 280.

133. Watson (1968): 46, Zhuangzi 莊子 (1994) 上: 89–90.

134. *Reconstruction in Philosophy*, MW 12: 168.

135. Ziporyn (2012): 61.

136. Watson (1968): 41, Zhuangzi 莊子 (1994) 上: 69.

137. Hall (1982): 247.

138. Rockefeller (1991): 494.

139. *Correspondence* (04751), John Dewey to Scudder Klyce, October 21, 1927.

140. *Correspondence* (04690), John Dewey to Scudder Klyce, April 30, 1927.

141. *Reconstruction in Philosophy*, MW 12: 168.

142. *The Quest for Certainty*, LW 4: 157.

143. Watson (1968): 41, Zhuangzi 莊子 (1994) 上: 69.

144. Eno (1996): 128, 134.

145. "Does Reality Possess Practical Character?" MW 4: 128.

146. Watson (1968): 39, Zhuangzi 莊子 (1994) 上: 61.

147. *Knowing and the Known*, LW 16: 113.

148. Charles Sanders Peirce joins this list. As Peirce saw it, "Our knowledge is never absolute but always swims, as it were, in a continuum of uncertainty and of indeterminacy. Now the doctrine of continuity is that *all things* so swim in continua." See: "Fallibilism, Continuity, and Evolution," Peirce and Hartshorne et al. (1931) 1: 171.

149. Kjellberg and Ivanhoe (1996) provides evidence of this tendency.

150. *Unmodern Philosophy*, Dewey and Deen (2012): 4.

151. "Does Reality Possess Practical Character?" MW 4: 129.

152. *The Quest for Certainty*, LW 4: 103.

153. Coutinho (2014): 83, 121.

154. Watson (1968): 171, Zhuangzi 莊子 (1994) 上: 442.

155. "Interpretation of Savage Mind," MW 2: 41.

156. *Democracy and Education*, MW 9: 346.

157. Watson (1968): 51, Zhuangzi 莊子 (1994) 上: 106.

158. Reader and Laland (2002): 4436.

159. "William James as Empiricist," LW 15: 14.

160. Watson (1968): 171, Zhuangzi 莊子 (1994) 上: 442.

161. Slingerland (2003): 6.

162. *Unmodern Philosophy*, Dewey and Deen (2012): 242.

163. "The Need for a Recovery of Philosophy," MW 10: 45.

164. *Democracy and Education*, MW 9: 231.

165. *Logic: The Theory of Inquiry*, LW 12: 83.

166. Jun (2013): 3, 120.

167. Rosemont (2018): 233, 235.

168. Watson (1968): 48, Zhuangzi 莊子 (1994) 上: 98.

169. *The Quest for Certainty*, LW 4: 30.

170. Hickman (1990): 75.

171. *The Quest for Certainty*, LW 4: 236.

172. "Beliefs and Existences," MW 3: 97.

173. See: "Religion and Morality in a Free Society," LW 15: 178.

174. *German Philosophy and Politics*, MW 8: 159.

175. *The Quest for Certainty*, LW 4: 237.

176. *Apology* 20d.5-20e.4, Plato and Cooper (1997): 20–21.

177. "Perception and Organic Action," MW 7: 6.

178. *The Quest for Certainty*, LW 4: 238, comma removed after "monopolistic."

179. 罪在於好知. Watson (1968): 113, Zhuangzi 莊子 (1994) 上: 291.

180. *Metaphysics*, 980a.1, Aristotle and McKeon (2001): 689.

181. *Cratylus* 439c, Plato and Cooper (1997): 154–55.

182. Radin (1927): 241–42, italics added.

183. Watson (1968): 41, Zhuangzi 莊子 (1994) 上: 74–75.

184. "Does Reality Possess Practical Character?" MW 4: 130.

185. *Reconstruction in Philosophy*, MW 12: 83.

186. *The Quest for Certainty*, LW 4: 168.

187. Ziporyn (2012): 84, 87.

188. Hagen thus translates *li* 理 as "constructive patterns," in order to underscore that "these patterns are picked out for their positive effect, not for their representing exclusive ontological truth." See: Hagen (2007): 56.

189. Ziporyn (2013): 45.

190. *The Quest for Certainty*, LW 4: 168.

191. Ziporyn (2012): 59.

192. *The Quest for Certainty*, LW 4: 172.

193. Eno (1991): 24.

194. "The Moral Philosopher and Moral Life," James and Myers (1992): 595.

195. "The Moral Philosopher and Moral Life," James and Myers (1992): 600, 602–03, 610.

196. "Theory of Valuation," LW 13: 219.

197. Pappas (2008): 225.

198. Cassirer (1963): 12.

199. *On Knowing Ignorance*, Edwards and Popkin (1969): 460.

200. "On a Certain Blindness in Human Beings," James and Myers (1992): 860.

201. *Experience and Nature*, LW 1: 134.

202. Watson (1968): 101, Zhuangzi 莊子 (1994) 上: 264.

Chapter 7

1. *Correspondence* (10746): John Dewey to Dewey Children, April 1, 1919.

2. Martin (2002): 285.

3. Eastman (1959): 285.

4. Lamont and Farrell (1959): 27.

5. Martin (2002): 286.

6. Eastman (1959): 286.

7. Alexander (1910): 10, 32.

8. Alexander (1932): 81.

9. *Correspondence* (07140), John Dewey to Joseph Ratner, July 24, 1946.

10. *Correspondence* (10746), John Dewey to Dewey Children, April 1, 1919.

11. *Correspondence* (03877), John Dewey to Dewey Children, February 22, 1919.

12. *Correspondence* (10750), John Dewey to Dewey Children, March 3, 1919.

13. One can find in North America serious teachers trained in one tradition who also train in the other. Shoko Zama at the Taoist Studies Institute in Seattle, Washington, for instance, is one. Several sources report that Aldous Huxley, one of Alexander's students in London, referred to Alexander as the "First Western Daoist." I have been unable to locate a reliable citation for this widely circulated quote.

14. Cranz (2000): 97.

15. Shusterman (2008): 192–93.

16. "Introductory Word to *Man's Supreme Inheritance*," MW 11: 351–52.

17. Ivanhoe (2010): 194, 199.

18. *Experience and Nature*, LW 1: 271.

19. "Introduction to *Constructive Conscious Control of the Individual*," MW 15: 313.
20. "Introduction to *The Use of the Self*," LW 6: 315, 318.
21. *Taipei Times* (Feb. 4, 2012): 1, *Taipei Times* (Jan. 17, 2015): 3.
22. Greenfield (2015): 160–62.
23. Shusterman (2008): 12.
24. See: Greenfield (2015): 198.
25. See: Boot et al. (2011).
26. See: Ferguson (2007).
27. Greenfield (2015): 161.
28. Watson (1968): 134, Zhuangzi 莊子 (1994) 上: 350.
29. Needham (1965): 332.
30. Parkes (1987): 129–30.
31. "Interpretation of Savage Mind," MW 2: 45.
32. "Introduction to *Constructive Conscious Control of the Individual*," MW 15: 315.
33. *Analects* 3.17 and 10.17, Ames and Rosemont (1998): 86, 138–39; *Mencius* 1A.7, Bloom (2009): 8, Mengzi 孟子 (1995): 14.
34. *Mencius* 7A.45, Bloom (2009): 155, Mengzi 孟子 (1995): 375.
35. Knoblock (1990): 5.
36. Sterckx (2002): 81, 101–10.
37. *Mencius* 4B.19, Bloom (2009): 89, Mengzi 孟子 (1995): 314.
38. Curnoe et al. (2012): 20, 24.
39. See: "Scientists Stumped by Prehistoric Human whose Face doesn't Fit," *Brisbane Times*, March 15, 2012, and "The Mystery of Red Deer Cave," *Popular Archeology*, 20 (Fall, 2015).
40. Lewis (1999): 129.
41. *Mencius* 3B.9, Bloom (2009): 70, Mengzi 孟子 (1995): 154–55.
42. To be fair, Mozi animalizes the Confucians first. His narrative is less direct, but equally de-humanizing. As Mozi sees it, animals are born with all their needs provided: warm coats, adequate footwear, and ready-made food. Humans are different in needing to put forth effort to secure such things. The sages did the original work to procure these needs, enabling humans to survive. Hence, what separates humans from other animals is "exertion" (*li* 力). Confucians, according to Mozi, are lazy and parasitical scholars—knowing nothing about basic labors and industries. Thus, they resemble animals in being similarly oblivious to any need for exerting themselves. "They turn their backs on what is fundamental and abandon their duties, finding contentment in idleness and pride . . . They are indolent in carrying out their responsibilities and fall into hunger and cold . . . They have no way of avoiding these things." By lacking "exertion," Confucians become like animals. They "hoard food like field mice, stare like he-goats, and walk about like castrated pigs." See: Mozi and Johnston (2010): 41–45, 313, 355.
43. *Mencius* 3A.4, Bloom (2009): 56, Mengzi 孟子 (1995): 122.

44. Graham (1990b): 67. The school was important enough to have nine titles catalogued in the Imperial Han Library, but all of these books are lost.
45. Slingerland (2003): 217.
46. *Analects* 18.6, Ames and Rosemont (1998): 214–15.
47. Graham (1989): 65. As Lewis observes, Shennong was "virtually the invention of one school and the embodiment of its program." See: Lewis (1999): 127.
48. Watson (1968): 327, Zhuangzi 莊子 (1994) 下: 847.
49. Graham (1990b): 99.
50. Brindley et al. (2013): 148.
51. See: Csikszentmihalyi (2004).
52. *Mencius* 2A.6, Bloom (2009): 35, Mengzi 孟子 (1995): 74.
53. Csikszentmihalyi (2004): 254.
54. Watson (1968): 98, Zhuangzi 莊子 (1994) 上: 255.
55. Wilhelm (1967): 328–29, Zhouyi 周易 (1999): 414.
56. Puett (1997): 507.
57. Roth (2003): 83.
58. Watson (1968): 116–17, Zhuangzi 莊子 (1994) 上: 302.
59. Watson (1968): 99n.9.
60. Watson (1968): 183, Zhuangzi 莊子 (1994) 上: 470.
61. Watson (1968): 104, Zhuangzi 莊子 (1994) 上: 269–70.
62. "Introduction to *Constructive Conscious Control of the Individual*," MW 15: 313.
63. Watson (1968): 190, Zhuangzi 莊子 (1994) 上: 490.
64. Graham (2001): 221.
65. Graham (1989): 58.
66. Johnson (2007): 140.
67. *Experience and Nature*, LW 1: 227.
68. Watson (1968): 77, Zhuangzi 莊子 (1994) 上: 185.
69. *Experience and Nature*, LW 1: 227–28.
70. *Experience and Nature*, LW 1: 229.
71. "Introduction to *Constructive Conscious Control of the Individual*," MW 15: 308, 314.
72. *Experience and Nature*, LW 1: 48, 239.
73. Watson (1968): 92, Zhuangzi 莊子 (1994) 上: 232.
74. *Experience and Nature*, LW 1: 134.
75. See: Knoblock (1994): 143, 150.
76. He critiques physiognomy in several forms. See: Knoblock (1988): 196–211 and Csikszentmihalyi (2004): 136–37.
77. See: Knoblock (1994): 3–22.
78. Knoblock (1988): 206, Xunzi 荀子 (1995): 71.
79. Knoblock (1990): 104, Xunzi 荀子 (1995): 164.
80. Knoblock (1988): 206, Xunzi 荀子 (1995): 71.
81. Karlgren (1957): 130–31.

82. Hagen (2007): 56, 155–56.
83. "George Herbert Mead as I Knew Him," LW 6: 24, 27.
84. This has been noted by Hall and Ames (1987): 80–84 and Odin (1996): 271–80.
85. Mead (1934): 227–28, 230–32.
86. Miller (1973): 85–87.
87. Mead (1934): 235.
88. Wilkie and McKinnon (2013): 3.13, 4.1.
89. Knoblock (1988): 206, Xunzi 荀子 (1995): 71.
90. Legge (1967) vol. 1: 64–65, Liji 禮記 (1998) 上: 6.
91. Knoblock (1994): 130–31, Xunzi 荀子 (1995): 458.
92. Hagen (2007): 61–84.
93. *Experience and Nature*, LW 1: 139.
94. Hagen (2007): 75–76.
95. Ziporyn (2012): 205–06.
96. McLeod (2016): 96–99.
97. Rizzolatti et al. (1999): 88, 91.
98. Prather et al. (2008).
99. Molenberghs et al. (2009).
100. Franks (2010): 86.
101. *Experience and Nature*, LW 1: 141.
102. *Knowing and the Known*, LW 16: 143.
103. Mead (1934): 62. Mead uses the word "form" in this context rather than "animal." He means, in any case, the organism in question.
104. Mead (1934): 63–64, 359–60.
105. *Experience and Nature*, LW 1: 140, comma removed after "standpoint."
106. Mead (1934): 43.
107. Mead (1934): 42–43, 149, 173–78, 279.
108. Cahoone (2013): 13.
109. Mead (2002): 83.
110. Uddin et al. (2007).
111. Mead (2002): 184.
112. Mead (1964): 555.
113. Mead (1934): 171–72.
114. Knoblock (1988): 81.
115. Watson (1968): 36, Zhuangzi 莊子 (1994) 上: 37.
116. "The Social Self," Mead and Reck (1964): 145.
117. Mead (1934): 136.
118. Dissanayake (1993): 23.
119. Mead (1934): 227–28.
120. Mead (1964): 555, 556.
121. Mead (1934): 186–187n.17, italics added. For purposes of consistency and clarity, I have taken the liberty of substituting the word "self" for "mind" in the second sentence. Mead uses the words interchangeably in this passage.
122. "Reply to a Reviewer," MW 11: 354.

123. Goh (2011): 121–24.
124. *Republic* 476e.7–8, Plato and Cooper (1997): 1103.
125. Goh (2011): 124.
126. Watson (1968): 288, Zhuangzi 莊子 (1994) 下: 748.
127. "Introduction to *The Use of the Self*," LW 6: 318.
128. "Introduction to *Constructive Conscious Control of the Individual*," MW 15: 308.
129. "Body and Mind," LW 3: 27.
130. "Introduction to *The Use of the Self*," LW 6: 318.
131. "Body and Mind," LW 3: 28.
132. Eastman (1941): 683.
133. Boydston (1986): 1.
134. McCormack (1958): 159.
135. "Biography of John Dewey," Schilpp and Hahn (1989): 44–45.
136. Ames (1993b): 165.
137. Ames (2011): 59.
138. See: Zhang (2007): 36.
139. Yao (1996): 181.
140. Watson (1968): 104, Zhuangzi 莊子 (1994) 上: 270.
141. "Body and Mind," LW 3: 31–32.
142. "Importance, Significance, and Meaning," LW 16: 326–27.
143. *Interest and Effort in Education*, MW 7: 188.
144. Allen (2015): 110, 114.
145. Watson (1968): 160, Zhuangzi 莊子 (1994) 上: 410.
146. *Individualism Old and New*, LW 5: 87.
147. "Contributions to *The Educational Frontier*," LW 8: 68.
148. Watson (1968): 134, Zhuangzi 莊子 (1994) 上: 350.
149. Allen (2015): 115.
150. Sivin (2005): 8.
151. Watson (1968): 65, Zhuangzi 莊子 (1994) 上: 149.
152. "Body and Mind," LW 3: 27.
153. "Dualism and the Split Atom," LW 15: 200–01.
154. "Body and Mind," LW 3: 29, italics added.
155. Hickman (1990): 202–03.
156. "Body and Mind," LW 3: 29.
157. "Introduction to *Constructive Conscious Control of the Individual*," MW 15: 315.
158. Clopton and Ou (1970): 116.
159. Watson (1968): 278, Zhuangzi 莊子 (1994) 下: 721.
160. "Introduction to *The Use of the Self*," LW 6: 317.

Chapter 8

1. Watson (1968): 176–77, Zhuangzi 莊子 (1994) 上: 453.

2. Adler (2013): 1.
3. "Signs of the 'Human Age,'" *New York Times*, January 11, 2016.
4. Goldin (2005): 82–83.
5. Clopton and Ou (1973): 212.
6. *Unmodern Philosophy*, Dewey and Deen (2012): 33. I have taken the liberty of changing the comma to a colon after the word "variables" in this quote.
7. Leopold (1949): 126–28.
8. Leopold (1949): 128–30.
9. *Correspondence* (10776), John Dewey to Dewey Children, July 19, 1919.
10. Watson (1968): 181–82, Zhuangzi 莊子 (1994) 上: 466–67, 469.
11. Moeller and D'Ambrosio (2017): 75.
12. Ivanhoe (1993): 646, 652.
13. Van Norden (2011): 154.
14. Ivanhoe (1993): 646–47.
15. Lovejoy (1960): 328.
16. Ivanhoe (2017): 16.
17. Watson (1968): 179, Zhuangzi 莊子 (1994) 上: 462.
18. Ivanhoe sometimes appears to understand this, but then he makes assertions and inferences that reinforce the "inherent ethical scheme." He observes, for instance, that from the perspective of *dao* 道 in the *Zhuangzi*, humans "are simply things among things; like the tiny figures in later landscape paintings." Then, however, he reads the text as affirming a "deep structure to the cosmos which unites it together as a systematic whole," one that "defines the proper structure and function of each and every thing in the universe." Such a single, inherent, structural, and normative order becomes the "inherent ethical scheme" the moment one presses into it. See: Ivanhoe (1997): 157–158.
19. Chong (2016): xii, 11, 139.
20. Møllgaard (2007): 31–32.
21. Watson (1968): 81, Zhuangzi 莊子 (1994) 上: 199.
22. Ivanhoe (2017): 138.
23. One is reminded of Edward Abbey's proclamation in the *Monkey Wrench Gang*: "Do we know what we are doing and why? No. Do we care? We'll work it out as we go along. Let our practice form our doctrine, thus assuring precise theoretical coherence." See: Abbey (1999): 68.
24. Rorty (1982b): 166.
25. Ziporyn (2009): 215.
26. Graham (1983): 15 and Graham (1992): 17–27.
27. Graham (1983): 14, 18.
28. Slingerland (2003): 78–84, 303n.4.
29. "The Moral Philosopher and Moral Life," James and Myers (1992): 603.
30. Watson (1968): 37, Zhuangzi 莊子 (1994) 上: 37–38.
31. Rolston (2005): 91–101.
32. Callicott (2005): 130–38.
33. "The Field of 'Value,'" LW 16: 349.

34. *Theory of Valuation*, LW 13: 216.
35. "The Ambiguity of 'Intrinsic Good,'" LW 15: 42–45.
36. See discussion in McDonald (2004): 57–65.
37. Katz (1996): 313.
38. *Experience and Nature*, LW 1: 286–87.
39. *Human Nature and Conduct*, MW 14: 28.
40. Brindley et al. (2013): 147.
41. *Experience and Nature*, LW 1: 194.
42. *Logic: The Theory of Inquiry*, LW 12: 385.
43. McDonald (2004): 78.
44. *Democracy and Education*, MW 9: 174.
45. *Experience and Nature*, LW 1: 224.
46. "Non-Conservative Actions," Peirce and Burks (1958): 7.471.
47. *Experience and Nature*, LW 1: 195.
48. *Theory of Valuation*, LW 13: 250.
49. McDonald (2004): 83.
50. *Human Nature and Conduct*, MW 14: 15.
51. McDonald (2004): 79, 141.
52. *Knowing and the Known*, LW 16: 260.
53. Watson (1968): 45, Zhuangzi 莊子 (1994) 上: 89–90.
54. Sing-nan Fen, "John Dewey's Theory of Values," *John Dewey Papers*, 102/72/7: 17–18, 20.
55. Perkins (2014): 165.
56. Watson (1968): 116, Zhuangzi 莊子 (1994) 上: 299, cf. *Daodejing*, Ch. 13.
57. "As the Chinese Think," MW 13: 222, "Nature" capitalized.
58. *A Common Faith*, LW 9: 52.
59. "Progress," MW 10: 240.
60. Boaz (1997): 27.
61. See: Van Norden (2017): 169n.62.
62. McCormick (1999): 334.
63. McCormick uses D. C. Lau's translation of the *Daodejing*. For the sake of consistency, I do the same.
64. McCormick (1999): 339.
65. McCormick (1999): 339.
66. Dorn (1989): 144.
67. Polanyi (1944): 61.
68. Such as Adam Smith's postulation of the human being's innate "propensity to truck, barter, and exchange one thing for another," in *Wealth of Nations*, Pt. 1. ii. 1, Smith (1849): 6.
69. Wilhelm (1967): 331, Zhouyi 周易 (1999): 415.
70. Hu (1988): 7–10.
71. Talyor (1989): 500.
72. Chan (1963): 92–94.
73. *Mencius*, 2A.5, Bloom (2009): 34–35, Mengzi 孟子 (1995): 72.

74. Legge (1967): Vol. 1, 274, 289 (Legge's translation of the *Liji* is relied upon here), and Knoblock and Riegal (2000): 134, 192.

75. *Mencius*, 2B.10, Bloom (2009): 46, Mengzi 孟子 (1995): 100.

76. Knoblock (1990): 123, Xunzi 荀子 (1995): 179–80.

77. Rothbard (1995): 23.

78. Elizabeth Economy's recent study of Chinese policies under Xi Jinping does an excellent job of explaining how China's state-owned enterprises "continue to play a dominant role and limit the impact of the market." Most importantly, she locates this in the context of China's long-standing aversion to market mechanisms, an aversion that is displayed throughout Chinese history. See: Economy (2018): 100–104, 118–120.

79. McCormick (1999): 338–39.

80. Dorn (1989): 135, 143.

81. Dorn repeats this error in Dorn (2003): 492–93.

82. Rothbard (1995): 23.

83. McCormick (1999): 338, 339.

84. Dorn simply suppresses the evidence.

85. Slingerland (2003): 79.

86. In addition to its grammatical advantages, this rendition is more thematically consistent with the chapter's subsequent, parallel discussion of "regard" (為 *wei*) for life (*yishengwei* 以生為).

87. Or, as in John C. H. Wu's rendition, the people are difficult to govern "because those above them are fussy and have private ends to serve."

88. Lau (1963): xxxii.

89. Hu (1988): 209.

90. Moeller (2006): 91.

91. Lau (1963): xxxi.

92. Dorn (2007): 1.

93. Clopton and Ou (1970): 67–68.

94. Rousseau (2016): 1.

95. Watson (1968): 39–41, Zhuangzi 莊子 (1994) 上: 61, 69.

96. Wilson and Morren (1990): 309–26.

97. Thompson (1996): 191, 200, 204.

98. Castle (1996): 247.

99. Thompson (1996): 188–93.

100. Ivanhoe (2017): 56, 74, italics added.

101. "The Will to Believe," James and Myers (1992): 458.

102. *Pragmatism*, James and Kuklick (1987): 521.

103. *Republic* 544d–547a, Plato and Cooper (1997): 1156–159.

104. The term "intelligence" (*ming* 明) is composed of both "sun" (*ri* 日) and "moon" (*yue* 月).

105. *Logic: The Theory of Inquiry*, LW 12: 108, 136.

106. Eames (1977): 100–01.

107. Wilhelm (1967): 280, 328–29, Zhouyi 周易 (1999): 387, 414.

108. Keightley (2014): 106–07.

109. Cheng (2003): 44.
110. The central readings are *Process and Reality*, Whitehead (1929): 168–83 and *Symbolism: Its Meaning and Effect*, Whitehead (1927): 18–19. In these passages, Whitehead explains that "symbolic reference" reintegrates "presentational immediacy" and "causal efficacy" in a novel perceptual situation.
111. *Logic: The Theory of Inquiry*, LW 12: 116.
112. *The Quest for Certainty*, LW 4: 110.
113. Graham (1989): 367–68.
114. "Potential Aggregates," Peirce and Hartshorne et al. (1935): 6.186.
115. Watson (1968): 181–82, Zhuangzi 莊子 (1994) 上: 466–67, 469.
116. *The Quest for Certainty*, LW 4: 70.
117. Richardson (2006): 366.
119. "What Makes a Life Significant?" James and Myers (1992): 863.
119. William James to Alice James, July 24–27, 1896, Skrupskelis and Berkeley (2000), vol. 8: 172–74.
120. William James to Henry James, August 15, 1896, Skrupskelis and Berkeley (1993), vol. 2: 406.
121. "What Makes a Life Significant?" James and Myers (1992): 863.
122. William James to Alice James, July 24–27, 1896, Skrupskelis and Berkeley (2000), vol. 8: 177.
123. "What Makes a Life Significant?" James and Myers (1992): 864.
124. *Experience and Nature*, LW 1: 47.
125. *Human Nature and Conduct*, MW 14: 123.
126. *A Common Faith*, LW 9: 32.
127. *Experience and Education*, LW 13: 19.
128. "The Moral Philosopher and the Moral Life," James and Myers (1992): 607, 608, 610.
129. *Ethics*, LW 7: 187.
130. *Ethics*, LW 7: 201.
131. Moeller (2006): 94.
132. *Ethics*, LW 7: 210.
133. Moeller (2006): 94.
134. *Theory of Valuation*, LW 13: 218.
135. *Democracy and Education*, MW 9: 212, see also: *How We Think*, LW 8: 346–47.
136. "The Moral Philosopher and the Moral Life," James and Myers (1992): 607, 608–609, 610, 615.
137. *Pragmatism*, James and Kuklick (1987): 612.
138. "William James," MW 6: 102.
139. Sing-nan Fen, "John Dewey's Theory of Values," *John Dewey Papers*, 102/72/7: 3.
140. "Imagination and Expression," EW 5: 196.
141. Moeller and D'Ambrosio (2017): 71, 163.
142. "Imagination and Expression," EW 5: 196.

143. Kelly (2004): 82–83.
144. *Correspondence* (04215), John Dewey to Albert C. Barnes, December 4, 1925.
145. "Individuality and Experience," LW 2: 55.
146. "Individuality and Experience," LW 2: 58.
147. Moeller and D'Ambrosio (2017): 85, 125–26.
148. "Individuality and Experience," LW 2: 59.
149. "Imagination and Expression," EW 5: 198.
150. *A Common Faith*, LW 9: 30, 33.
151. Munro (2002): 305–07.
152. *Art as Experience*, LW 10: 9.
153. *Correspondence* (03595), John Dewey to Dewey Children, April 5, 1920.
154. *Correspondence* (03595), John Dewey to Dewey Children, April 5, 1920.

Works Cited

Abbey, Edward (1999). *The Monkey Wrench Gang*. Salt Lake City: Dream Garden Press.
Adler, Jerry (2013). "Why Fire Makes Us Human," *Smithsonian Magazine*, June 2013. http://www.smithsonianmag.com/science-nature/why-fire-makes-us-human-72989884/.
Alexander, Matthias F. (1910). *Man's Supreme Inheritance*. Whitefish: Kessinger Publishing.
——— (1932). *The Use of the Self*. Long Beach, CA: Centerline Press.
Alexander, Thomas M. (1987). *John Dewey's Theory of Art, Experience, and Nature: The Horizons of Feeling*. Albany: State University of New York Press.
——— (2004). "Dewey's Denotative-Empirical Method: A Thread Through the Labyrinth." In *The Journal of Speculative Philosophy* (18.3): 248–56.
Allan, Sarah (1997). *The Way of Water and Sprouts of Virtue*. Albany: State University of New York Press.
Allan, Sarah, and Crispin Williams (2000). *The Guodian Laozi: Proceedings of the International Conference, Dartmouth College, May 1998*. Early China Special Monograph Series No. 5. The Institute of East Asian Studies, University of California, Berkeley.
Allen, Barry (2015). *Vanishing Into Things: Knowledge in Chinese Tradition*. Cambridge: Harvard University Press.
Ames, Roger T. (1989). "Putting the *Te* Back in Taoism." In *Nature in Asian Traditions of Thought: Essays in Environmental Philosophy*. Edited by Roger T. Ames and J. Baird Callicott. Albany: State University of New York, 113–44.
——— (1993a). *Sun-Tzu: The Art of Warfare*. New York: Ballantine Books.
——— (1993b). "The Meaning of Body in Classical Chinese Philosophy." In *Self as Body in Asian Theory and Practice*. Edited by Roger T. Ames and Wimal Dissanayake. Albany: State University of New York Press, 157–77.
——— (2011). *Confucian Role Ethics: A Vocabulary*. Honolulu: University of Hawai'i Press.
——— (2018). "Reconstructing A. C. Graham's Reading of Mencius on *Xing* 性: A Coda to "The Background of the Mencian Theory of Human Nature" (1967)." In *Having a Word with Angus Graham at Twenty-Five Years into his Immortality*. Edited by Carine Defoort and Roger T. Ames. Albany: State University of New York Press, 185–213.

Ames, Roger T., and Henry Rosemont, Jr. (1998). *The Analects of Confucius: A Philosophical Translation*. New York: Ballantine Books.
Aquinas, St. Thomas. (1981). *Summa Theologica*. Vol. 1–5. Allen, TX: Christian Classics.
Ariew, André (2007). "Teleology." In *The Cambridge Companion to The Philosophy of Biology*. Edited by David L. David and Michael Ruse. Cambridge: Cambridge University Press, 160–81.
Aristotle, and Ackrill, J. L. (1987). *A New Aristotle Reader*. Princeton, NJ: Princeton University Press.
Aristotle, and Hope, Richard (1952). *Aristotle: Metaphysics*. Ann Arbor, MI: University of Michigan Press.
Aristotle, and McKeon, Richard (2001). *The Basic Works of Aristotle*. New York: Modern Library.
Aristotle, and Ross, W. D. (1931a). *The Works of Aristotle*. Vol. 3. Oxford: Clarendon Press.
——— (1931b). *The Works of Aristotle*. Vol. 6. Oxford: Clarendon Press.
——— (1936). *Aristotle's Physics*. Oxford: Clarendon Press.
Barnwell, Scott. A. (2013). "The Evolution of the Concept of *De* 德 in Early China." *Sino-Platonic Papers* 235: 1–83.
Behuniak, James, Jr. (2009a). "Embracing the 'One' in the *Daodejing*." *Philosophy East and West* 59(3): 364–81.
——— (2009b). "*Li* in East Asian Buddhism: One Approach from Plato's *Parmenides*." *Asian Philosophy* 19(1): 31–49.
——— (2010). "John Dewey and the Virtue of Cook Ding's *Dao*," *Dao: a Journal of Comparative Philosophy* 9(2): 161–74.
——— (2015). "Two Challenges to Market Daoism," In *Value and Values: Economics and Justice in an Age of Global Interdependence*. Edited by Roger T. Ames and Peter D. Hershock. Honolulu: University of Hawai'i Press, 283–95.
Behuniak, Jim. (2016). "Lessons from Stupidity: Wisdom and the Man from Song." In *Wisdom and Philosophy: Contemporary and Comparative Approaches*. Edited by Hans-Georg Moeller and Andrew Whitehead. New York: Bloomsbury, 15–24.
——— (2017). "John Dewey and East-West Philosophy," *Philosophy East and West* 67(3): 908–16.
Bernstein, Richard (1991). "Incommensurability and Otherness Revisited." In *Culture and Modernity: East-West Philosophic Perspectives*. Edited by Eliot Deutsch. Honolulu: University of Hawai'i Press, 85–103.
Berthrong, John (2001). "The Idea of Categories in Historical Comparative Philosophy." In *Ultimate Realities*. Edited by Robert C. Neville. Albany: State University of New York Press, 237–60.
Bloom, Irene (2009). *Mencius*. New York: Columbia University Press.
Bloom, P., and D. S. Weisberg (2007). "Childhood Origins of Adult Resistance to Science." *Science* 316(5827): 996–97.
Boaz, David (1997). *The Libertarian Reader: Classic and Contemporary Writings from Lao-tzu to Milton Friedman*. New York: Free Press.
Boisvert, Raymond D. (1988). *Dewey's Metaphysics*. New York: Fordham University Press.

Boot, Walter R. et al. (2011). "Do Action Video Games improve Perception and Cognition?" *Frontiers in Psychology*, Sept. 13, 2011. https://doi.org/10.3389/fpsyg.2011.00226.
Boydston, Jo Ann (1986). "John Dewey and the Alexander technique: Text of Keynote Address at the International Congress of Teachers of the Alexander technique." http://www.alexandercenter.com/jd/deweyalexanderboydston.html.
Brindley, Erica F. (2013). "The Cosmos as Creative Mind: Spontaneous Arising, Generating, and Creating in the *Heng Xian*." *Dao* 12(2): 189–206.
Brindley, Erica F., Paul R. Goldin, and Esther S. Klein (2103). "A Philosophical Translation of the *Heng Xian*." *Dao* 12(2): 145–51.
Brindley, Erica Fox (2012). *Music, Cosmology, and the Politics of Harmony in Early China*. Albany, State University of New York Press.
Bullock, Jeffrey S. (2011). *Yang Xiong: Philosophy of the Fa Yan, A Confucian Hermit in the Han Imperial Court*. Highlands: Mountain Mind Press.
Burns, Gerald (1982). *Inventions: Writing, Textuality, and Understanding in Literary History*. New Haven, CT: Yale University Press.
Cahoone, Lawrence (2013). "Mead, Joint Attention, and the Human Difference." *The Pluralist*, 8(2): 1–25.
Callicott, J. Baird (2005). "Animal Liberation and Environmental Ethics: Back Together Again." In *Environmental Philosophy: From Animal Rights to Radical Ecology*, Fourth Edition. Edited by Michael E. Zimmerman et al. Upper Saddle River, NJ: Pearson Prentice Hall, 130–38.
Campbell, John (1994). *Past, Space, and Self*. Cambridge, MA: The MIT Press.
Cassirer, Ernst (1963). *The Individual and the Cosmos in Renaissance Philosophy*. Mineola, NY: Dover Publications.
Castle, Emery N. (1996). "A Pluralistic, Pragmatic and Evolutionary Approach to Natural Resource Management." In *Environmental Pragmatism*. Edited by Andrew Light and Eric Katz. New York: Routledge, 231–50.
Chan, Alan (1991). *Two Visions of the Way: A Study of the Wang Pi and Ho-shang Kung Commentaries on the Lao-Tzu*. Albany: State University of New York Press.
Chan, Wing-Tsit (1963). *A Source Book in Chinese Philosophy*. Princeton, NJ: Princeton University Press.
——— (1988). "Chu His and World Philosophy." In *Interpreting across Boundaries: New Essays in Comparative Philosophy*. Edited by Gerald Larson and Eliot Deutsch. Princeton, NJ: Princeton University Press, 230–64.
Chang, Chung-yuan (1963). *Creativity and Taoism: A Study of Chinese Philosophy, Art, and Poetry*. New York: The Julian Press, Inc.
Chang, Garma C. C. (1971). *The Buddhist Teaching of Totality: The Philosophy of Hwa Yen Buddhism*. University Park: Pennsylvania University Press.
Chen, Ellen M. (2011). *In Praise of Nothing: An Exploration of Daoist Fundamental Ontology*. Bloomington, IN: Xlibris.
Chen, I. C., J. K. Hill, R. Ohlemuller, D. B. Roy et al. (2011). "Rapid Range Shifts of Species Associated with High Levels of Climate Warming." *Science* 333(6045): 1024–026.

Cheng, Chung-ying (1976). "Model of Causality in Chinese philosophy: A Comparative Study." *Philosophy East and West* 26(1): 3–20.

——— (2003). "Inquiring Into the Primary Model: *Yi-Jing* and Chinese Ontological Hermeneutics." In *Comparative Approaches to Chinese Philosophy*. Edited by Bo Mou. Burlington: Ashgate, 33–59.

Chin, Ann-ping, and Mansfield Freeman (1990). *Tai Chen on Mencius: Explorations in Words and Meaning*. New Haven, CT: Yale University Press.

Chong, Kim-chong (2002). "Mengzi and Gaozi on *Nei* and *Wai*." In *Mencius: Contexts and Interpretations*. Edited by Alan K. L. Chan. Honolulu: University of Hawai'i Press, 103–25.

——— (2016). *Zhuangzi's Critique of the Confucians: Blinded by the Human*. Albany: State University of New York Press.

Churchland, Paul (1981). "Eliminative Materialism and the Propositional Attitude." *Journal of Philosophy* 78(2): 67–90.

Cleary, Thomas (1992). *Wen-Tzu: Further Teachings of Lao-Tzu*. Boston: Shambhala.

Cline, Erin M. (2004). "Two Interpretations of *De* in the *Daodejing*." *Journal of Chinese Philosophy* 31(2): 219–33.

——— (2013a). "Religious Thought and Practice in the *Analects*." In *Dao Companion to the Analects*. Edited by Amy Olberding. Dordrecht: Springer, 259–91.

——— (2013b). *Confucius, Rawls, and the Sense of Justice*. New York: Fordham University Press.

Clopton, Robert, and Tsuin-Chen Ou (1970). *John Dewey: Additional Lectures in China, 1919–1921*. Special Collections, Hamilton Library, University of Hawai'i.

——— (1973). *John Dewey: Lectures in China, 1919–1920*. Honolulu: University of Hawai'i Press.

——— (1985). *John Dewey: Lectures in China, 1919–1920, On Logic, Ethics, Education, and Democracy*. Taipei: Chinese Culture University Press.

Clutton-Brock, T. H. (1989). "Mammalian Mating Systems." *Proceedings of the Royal Society of London*, B (236): 339–72.

Cook, Scott (2012). *The Bamboo Texts of the Guodian: A Study*, Vol. 1 and 2. Ithaca, NY: Cornell University East Asian Program.

Correspondence of John Dewey, 1871–1952 (I–V), Electronic edition. InteLex Past Masters. Charlottesville, VA: InteLex Corporation.

Coutinho, Steve (2004). *Zhuangzi and Early Chinese Philosophy: Vagueness, Transformation, and Paradox*. Burlington, VT: Ashgate Publishing Company.

——— (2014). *An Introduction to Daoist Philosophies*. New York: Columbia University Press.

Cranz, Galen (2000). *The Chair*. New York: W. W. Norton and Company.

Creel, H. G. (1953). "Chinese Philosophy and the Second East-West Philosophers' Conference." *Philosophy East and West* 3(1): 73–80.

Csikszentmihalyi, M., and P. J. Ivanhoe (1999). *Religious and Philosophical Aspects of the Laozi*. Albany: State University of New York Press.

Csikszentmihalyi, Mark (2004). *Material Virtue: Ethics and the Body in Early China*. Leiden: Brill.

Curnoe, Darren, Ji Xueping et al. (2012). "Human Remains from the Pleistocene-Holocene Transition of Southwest China Suggest a Complex Evolutionary History for East Asians. *PLoS ONE* 7(3): 1–28.
Dalton, Thomas C. (2002). *Becoming John Dewey: Dilemmas of a Philosopher and Naturalist.* Bloomington: Indiana University Press.
Dawkins, Richard. (2014). "The Origin of Life in the Universe." http://www.dailygalaxy.com/my_weblog/2014/06/richard-dawkins-on-the-origin-of-life-in-the-universe.html.
Defoort, Carine. (1997). "Causation in Chinese Philosophy." In *A Companion to World Philosophies.* Edited by Eliot Deutsch and Ronald Bontekoe. London: Blackwell Press, 165–73.
Dennett, Daniel (1995). *Darwin's Dangerous Idea: Evolution and the Meanings of Life.* New York: Simon & Schuster.
Deutsch, Eliot (1991). *Culture and Modernity: East-West Philosophic Perspectives.* Honolulu: University of Hawai'i Press.
Dewey, John, and Arthur F. Bentley (1964). *John Dewey and Arthur F. Bentley: A Philosophical Correspondence, 1932–1951.* Edited by Sidney and Jules Altman. New Brunswick, NJ: Rutgers University Press.
Dewey, John, and Samuel Myer (1984). *Types of Thinking: Including A Survey of Greek Philosophy.* New York: Philosophical Library.
Dewey, John, and Philip Deen (2012). *Unmodern Philosophy and Modern Philosophy.* Carbondale: Southern Illinois University Press.
Dewey, John, Jo Ann Boydston et al. (2008). *The Collected Works of John Dewey, Early Works*, Vols. 1–4. *Middle Works*, Vols. 1–15. *Late Works*, Vol. 1–17. Carbondale: Southern Illinois University Press.
Dissanayake, Wimal (1993). "Body in Social Theory." In *Self as Body in Asian Theory and Practice.* Edited by Roger T. Ames and Wimal Dissanayake. Albany: State University of New York Press, 21–36.
Dorn, James A. (1989). "China's Future: Market Socialism or Market Taoism?" *Cato Journal*, 18(1): 131–46.
——— (2003). "The Primacy of Property in a Liberal Constitutional Order: Lessons for China." *The Independent Review*, 7(4): 485–501.
——— (2007). "The Case for Market Taoism." *The American Spectator*, Sept. 24, 2007. http://spectator.org/archives/2007/09/24/the-case-for-market-taoism#.
Eames, S. Morris (1977). *Pragmatic Naturalism: An Introduction.* Carbondale: Southern Illinois University Press.
Eastman, Max (1941). "John Dewey." *The Atlantic Monthly*, Dec. 1941: 671–84.
——— (1949). *Great Companions: Critical Memoirs of Some Famous Friends.* New York: Farrar, Straus, and Cudahy.
Economy, Elizabeth C. (2018). *The Third Revolution: Xi Jinping and the New Chinese State.* Oxford: Oxford University Press.
Edwards, Paul (1967). *The Encyclopedia of Philosophy.* New York: Macmillan.
Edwards, Paul, and Richard H. Popkin, ed. (1969). *Medieval Philosophy: From St. Augustine to Nicholas of Cusa.* New York: The Free Press.

Emerson, Ralph Waldo, and Larzer Ziff (1982). *Ralph Waldo Emerson: Selected Essays*. Harmondsworth, Middlesex, UK: Penguin Press.
Eno, Robert (1991). "Creating Nature: Juist and Taoist Approaches." In *Chuang Tzu: Rationality, Interpretation: Essays from the 1991 New England Symposium on Chinese Thought*. Edited by Kidder Smith. Brunswick: Breckenridge Public Affairs Center, 3–28.
——— (1996). "Cook Ding's Dao and the Limits of Philosophy." In *Essays on Skepticism, Relativism, and Ethics in the Zhuangzi*. Edited by Paul Kjellberg and Philip Ivanhoe. Albany: State University of New York Press, 127–51.
Farquhar, Judith (1994). *Knowing Practice: The Clinical Encounter of Chinese Medicine*. Boulder, CO: Westview Press.
Fen, Sing-nan (1948). "A Transactional Conception of Experience as Art." *The Journal of Philosophy* 45(26): 712.
——— (1951). "Situation as an Existential Unit of Experience." *Philosophy and Phenomenological Research* 11(4): 555–60.
——— (1957). "On Appreciation." *The Journal of Philosophy* 54(18): 550.
——— (1961). "Education as Growth of Environmental Consciousness." *Educational Theory* 11(2): 85–92.
Ferguson, C. J. (2007). "The Good, the Bad, and the Ugly: A Meta-analytic Review of Positive and Negative Effects of Violent Video Games." *Psychiatric Quarterly*, 78(4): 309–16.
Feynman, Richard P. (1963). *The Feynman Lectures on Physics: New Millennium Edition*, Vol. 1. New York: Basic Books.
Franks, David D. (2010). *Neurosociology: The Nexus Between Neuroscience and Social Psychology*. Dordrecht: Springer.
Fraser, Chris (2007). "Language and Ontology in Early Chinese Thought." *Philosophy East and West* 57(4): 420–56.
——— (2016). *The Philosophy of the Mozi: The First Consequentialists*. New York: Columbia University Press.
Gardner, Thomas (2000). "The Subject Matter of Dewey's Metaphysics." *Transactions of the Charles S. Peirce Society* 36(3): 393–405.
Geaney, Jane (2002). *On the Epistemology of the Senses in Early Chinese Thought*. Honolulu: University of Hawai`i Press.
Gelman, Susan (2004). "Psychological Essentialism in Children." *Trends in Cognitive Sciences* 8(9): 404–09.
Gerson, Lloyd P. (2004). "Plato on Identity, Sameness, and Difference." *The Review of Metaphysics* 58(2): 305–22.
Ghiselin, M. T. (1974). "A Radical Solution to the Species Problem." *Systematic Zoology* 23: 536–44.
Ghosh, Pallab (2014). "Cave Paintings Change Ideas about Origins of Art." BBC News, October 8, 2014. http://www.bbc.com/news/science-environment-29415716.
Giddens, Anthony (1991). *Modernity and Self-identity: Self and Society in the Late Modern Age*. Stanford, CA: Stanford University Press.
Girardot, Norman J. (1983). *Myth and Meaning in Early Taoism: The Theme of Chaos, Hun-Tun*. Berkeley: University of California Press.

Goh, Irving (2011). "Chuang Tzu's Becoming Animal." *Philosophy East and West* 61(1): 110–33.
Goldin, Paul R. (2005). "Why Daoism is not Environmentalism," *Journal of Chinese Philosophy* 32(1): 75–87.
Graham, A. C. (1960). *The Book of Lieh-tzu: A Classic of Tao*. New York: Columbia University Press.
——— (1978). *Later Mohist Logic, Ethics and Science*. Hong Kong: The Chinese University of Hong Kong Press.
——— (1983). "Taoist Spontaneity and the Dichotomy of 'Is' and 'Ought.'" In *Experimental Essays on Chuang Tzu*, edited by Victor H. Mair. Honolulu: University of Hawai'i Press, 3–23.
——— (1989). *Disputers of the Tao: Philosophical Argument in Ancient China*. La Salle, IL: Open Court.
——— (1990a). "The Background of the Mencian Theory of Human Nature." In *Studies in Chinese Philosophy and Philosophical Literature*. Albany: State University of New York Press, 7–66.
——— (1990b). "The Nung-Chia 'School of the Tillers' and the Origins of Peasant Utopianism in China." In *Studies in Chinese Philosophy and Philosophical Literature*. Albany: State University of New York Press, 67–110.
——— (1991). "Reflections and Replies." In *Chinese Texts and Philosophical Contexts: Essays Dedicated to Angus C. Graham*. Edited by Henry Rosemont, Jr. La Salle, IL: Open Court, 267–322.
——— (1992). *Unreason Within Reason: Essays on the Outskirts of Rationality*. La Salle, IL: Open Court.
——— (2001). *Chuang-tzŭ: The Inner Chapters*. Indianapolis: Hackett Publishers.
Greenfield, Susan (2015). *Mind Change: How Digital Technologies are Leaving their Mark on our Brains*. New York: Random House Publishers.
Grene, Marjorie (1972). "Aristotle and Modern Biology." *Journal of the History of Ideas* 33(3): 395–424.
Grene, Marjorie, and David J. Depew (2004). *The Philosophy of Biology: An Episodic History*. Cambridge: Cambridge University Press.
Grieder, Jerome (1970). *Hu Shih and the Chinese Renaissance*. Cambridge, MA: Harvard University Press.
Hagen, Kurtis. (2007). *The Philosophy of Xunzi: A Reconstruction*. Chicago: Open Court.
Hall, David L. (1982). *The Uncertain Phoenix: Adventures Towards a Post-Cultural Sensibility*. New York: Fordham University Press.
Hall, David L., and Roger T. Ames (1987). *Thinking Through Confucius*. Albany: State University of New York Press.
——— (1995). *Anticipating China: Thinking through the Narratives of Chinese and Western Culture*. Albany: State University of New York Press.
——— (1999). *The Democracy of the Dead: Dewey, Confucius, and the Hope for Democracy in China*. Chicago: Open Court.
——— (2001). *Focusing the Familiar: A Translation and Philosophical Interpretation of the Zhongyong*. Honolulu: University of Hawai'i Press.

———— (2003). *Dao De Jing: A Philosophical Translation: "Making this Life Significant."* New York: Ballantine Books.
Hansen, Chad (1983). *Language and Logic in Ancient China.* Michigan Studies on China. Ann Arbor: Center for Chinese Studies of the University of Michigan.
———— (1992). *A Daoist Theory of Chinese Thought: A Philosophical Interpretation.* Oxford, UK: Oxford University Press.
Harbsmeier, Christoph (1989). "Marginalia Sino-logica." In *Understanding the Chinese Mind: The Philosophical Roots.* Edited by Robert Allison. Oxford, UK: Oxford University Press, 125–66.
Hausman, Carl R. (1993). *Charles S. Peirce's Evolutionary Philosophy.* Cambridge: Cambridge University Press.
Havelock, Eric A. (1963). *Preface to Plato.* Cambridge, MA: Harvard University Press.
Hendricks, Robert G. (1989). *Lao-Tzu Te-Tao Ching: A New Translation Based on the Recently Discovered Ma-wang-tui Texts.* New York: Ballantine.
———— (2000). *Lao Tzu's Tao Te Ching: A Translation of the Startling New Documents Found at Guodian.* New York: Ballantine.
Hickman, Larry (1990). *John Dewey's Pragmatic Technology.* Bloomington: Indiana University Press.
Hocking, William Ernest (1930). "Action and Certainty." *Journal of Philosophy* 27: 225–38.
Hoffmann, Ary A., and Carla M. Sgrò (2011). "Climate Change and Evolutionary Adaptation." *Nature* 470(7335): 479–85.
Hofstadter, Richard (1962). *Anti-Intellectualism in American Life.* New York: Vintage Press.
Holder, John J. (2006). *Early Buddhist Discourses.* Indianapolis, IN: Hackett Publishers.
Hu, Jichuang (1988). *A Concise History of Chinese Economic Thought.* Beijing: Foreign Languages Press.
Hu, Shih (2013). *English Writings of Hu Shih: Literature and Society (Volume One).* New York, NY: Springer.
Huainanzi 淮南子 (1936). *Huainanzi Ershiyijuan* 淮南子二十一卷. Shanghai: The Commercial Press.
Hull, David L. (1976). "Are Species Really Individuals?" *Systematic Zoology* 25: 174–91.
———— (1987). "Genealogical Actors in Ecological Roles." *Biology and Philosophy* 2(2): 168–83.
Hulswit, Menno (2002). *From Cause to Causation: A Peircean Perspective.* Dordrecht: Kluwer Academic.
Hume, David, and Richard H. Popkin (1998). *Dialogues Concerning Natural Religion.* Second Edition. Indianapolis, IN: Hackett Publishers.
Hutton, Eric (2011). "A Note on the Xunzi's Explanation of *Xing*." *Dao: A Journal of Comparative Philosophy* 10(4): 527–30.
Ipsos (2011). "Ipsos Global Advisory: Supreme Being(s), the Afterlife, and Evolution," http://www.ipsos-na.com/news-polls/pressrelease.aspx?id=5217.
———— (2014). "Global Trends 2014: Environment," http://www.ipsosglobaltrends.com/environment.html.

Ivanhoe, Philip J. (1993). "Skepticism, Skill and the Ineffable Tao." *Journal of the American Academy of Religions* 61(4): 639–54.

——— (1997). "Human Beings and Nature in Chinese Thought." In *A Companion to World Philosophies*. Edited by Eliot Deutsch and Ron Bontekoe. Oxford: Blackwell Publishing, 155–64.

——— (1999). "The Concept of *De* ('Virtue') in the *Laozi*." In *Religious and Philosophical Aspects of Laozi*. Edited by Mark Csikszentmihalyi and Philip J. Ivanhoe. Albany: State University of New York Press, 239–57.

——— (2002). *The Daodejing of Laozi*. Translation and commentary by Philip J. Ivanhoe. Indianapolis, IN: Hackett Press.

——— (2007). "The Paradox of *Wuwei*?" *Journal of Chinese Philosophy* 34(2): 277–87.

——— (2010). "The Values of Spontaneity." In *Taking Confucian Ethics Seriously: Contemporary Theories and Approaches*. Edited by Kam-por Yu, Julia Tao, and Philip J. Ivanhoe. Albany: State University of New York Press, 183–207.

——— (2017). *Oneness: East Asian Conceptions of Virtue, Happiness, & How We Are All Connected*. Oxford: Oxford University Press.

Jackson, Philip. W. (1998). *John Dewey and the Lessons of Art*. New Haven, CT: Yale University Press.

James, William (1890). *The Principles of Psychology*. Vol. 1. New York: Dover Publications.

James, William, and Bruce Kuklick (1987). *William James: Writings, 1902–1910*. New York: The Library of America.

James, William, and Gerald E. Myers (1992). *William James: Writings 1878–1899*. New York: The Library of America.

John Dewey Papers, 1858–1970. Special Collections, Morris Library. Southern Illinois University, Carbondale.

Johnson, Mark (2007). *The Meaning of the Body: Aesthetics of Human Understanding*. Chicago: University of Chicago Press.

——— (2010). "Cognitive Science and Dewey's Theory of Mind." In *The Cambridge Companion to Dewey*. Edited by Molly Cochran. Cambridge: Cambridge University Press, 123–44.

Jullien, François (1995). *The Propensity of Things: Toward a History of Efficacy in China*. New York: Zone.

——— (2004). *A Treatise on Efficacy: Between Western and Chinese Thinking*. Honolulu: University of Hawai`i Press.

Jun, Wenren (2013). *Ancient Chinese Encyclopedia of Technology: Translation and Annotation of the* Kaogong ji *(The Artificer's Record)*. London: Routledge.

Kant, Immanuel, and Lewis White Beck (1997). *Prolegomena to Any Future Metaphysics*. Upper Saddle River, NJ: Prentice Hall.

Kant, Immanuel, and Norman Kemp Smith (1965). *Immanuel Kant's Critique of Pure Reason*. New York: St. Martin's Press, 1965.

Karlgren, Bernhard (1964). *Grammata Serica Recensa*. Stockholm: Museum of Far Eastern Antiquities.

Katz, Eric (1996). "Searching for Intrinsic Value: Pragmatism and Despair in Environmental Ethics." In *Environmental Pragmatism*. Edited by Eric Katz and Andrew Light. New York: Routledge, 307–18.

Kauffman, S. A. (1993). *The Origins of Order: Self-Organization and Selection in Evolution*. New York: Oxford University Press.

Kearney, Maureen (2007). "Philosophy and Phylogenetics: Historical and Current Connections." In *The Cambridge Companion to The Philosophy of Biology*. Edited by David L. David and Michael Ruse. Cambridge: Cambridge University Press, 211–32.

Keightley, David N. (2014). *These Bones Shall Rise Again: Selected Writings on Early China*. Edited by Henry Rosemont, Jr. Albany: State University of New York Press.

Kelemen, Deborah (1999). "The Scope of Teleological Thinking in Preschool Children." *Cognition* 70(3): 241–72.

——— (2004). "Are Children 'Intuitive Theists'? Reasoning About Purpose and Design in Nature." *Psychological Science* 15(5): 295–301.

Kelleher, Colin T. et al. (2005). "Species Distinctions in Irish Populations of *Quercus petraea* and *Q robur*: Morphological versus Molecular Analysis." *Annals of Botany*, 96(7): 1237–246.

Kelly, Donna Darling (2004). *Uncovering the History of Children's Drawing and Art*. Westport: Praegar Publishing.

Kim, Geunyoung (2013). "Psychological Essentialism among Korean Children and Adults: A Modified Replication Study." *International Journal of Psychology* 48(5): 809–17.

Kirkland, Russell (1997). "The Taoism of the Western Imagination and the Taoism of China: De-Colonizing the Exotic Teachings of the East." Public talk presented at the University of Tennessee, Oct. 20, 1997.

Kitarō, Nishida (1955). *Nishida Kitarō Zenshu (The Complete Works of Nishida Kitarō)*, Vol. 19. Tokyo: Iwanami Shoten.

Kjellberg, Paul, and Philip J. Ivanhoe, ed. (1996). *Essays on Skepticism, Relativism, and Ethics in the Zhuangzi*. Albany: State University of New York Press.

Knoblock, John (1988). *Xunzi: A Translation and Study of the Complete Works*. Vol. 1. Stanford, CA: Stanford University Press.

——— (1990). *Xunzi: A Translation and Study of the Complete Works*. Vol. 2. Stanford, CA: Stanford University Press.

——— (1994). *Xunzi: A Translation and Study of the Complete Works*. Vol. 3. Stanford, CA: Stanford University Press.

Knoblock, John, and Riegel, Jeffrey (2000). *The Annals of Lü Buwei*. Stanford, CA: Stanford University Press.

Kolbert, Elizabeth (2014). *The Sixth Extinction: An Unnatural History*. New York: Henry Holt and Company.

Kraut, Richard (1991). *Aristotle on the Human Good*. Princeton: Princeton University Press.

Kuhn, Thomas S. (1962). *The Structure of Scientific Revolutions*. Chicago: University of Chicago Press.

Kwok, D. W. Y. (1965). *Scientism in Chinese Thought: 1900–1950*. New Haven, CT: Yale University Press.
Lamont, Corliss, and James T. Farrell (1959). *Dialogue on John Dewey*. New York: Horizon Press.
Lau, D. C. (1963). *Tao Te Ching*. London: Penguin Books.
Lear, Jonathan (1988). *Aristotle: The Desire to Understand*. Cambridge: Cambridge University Press.
Lee, Sherman E. (1982). *A History of Far Eastern Art*. Englewood Cliffs, NJ: Prentice-Hall, Inc.
Legge, James (1967). *Li Chi: Book of Rites*, Vol. 1 and 2. New Hyde Park, NY: University Books.
——— (2000). *The Chinese Classics*, Vol. 1–5. Taipei: SMC Publishing Inc.
Leopold, Aldo (1949). *A Sand County Almanac: With Essays on Conservation*. New York: Oxford University Press.
Lewis, Mark Edward (1999). *Writing and Authority in Early China*. Albany: State University of New York Press.
Li, Ling (2002). *Guodian Chujian Jiaoduji* 郭店楚簡校讀記. Beijing: Beijing University Press.
Liao, W. K. (1959). *The Complete Works of Han Fei Tzu: A Classic of Chinese Political Science*, Vol. 1. London: Arthur Probsthain Publishers.
Liezi 列子 (1987). *Liezi Jishi* 列子集釋. Taipei: Hwa Cheng Publishing Company, Ltd.
Liji 禮記 (1998). *Liji Jinzhujinyi* 禮記今註今譯, Vol. 1 (上) and Vol. 2 (下). Taipei: The Commercial Press, Ltd.
Liu, Jing (2016). "Ziran: The Place of Dao." Public talk delivered at Eleventh East-West Philosophers' Conference, Honolulu, HI. May 25, 2016.
Longo, Giuseppe, and Maël Montévil (2014). *Perspectives on Organisms: Biological Time, Symmetries, and Singularities*. Springer: Lecture Notes on Morphogenesis.
Lovejoy, Arthur O. (1960). *The Great Chain of Being: A Study of the History of an Idea*. New York: Harper and Row Publishers.
Major, John S. (1993). *Heaven and Earth in Early Han Thought: Chapters three, four and five of the* Huainanzi. Albany: State University of New York Press.
Major, John S., Sarah A. Queen et al. (2010). *The Huainanzi: A Guide to the Theory and Practice of Government in Early Han China*. New York: Columbia University Press.
Mall, Ram Adhar (2000). *Intercultural Philosophy*. Lanham, MD: Rowman & Littlefield Press.
Margolis, Joseph (2011). "Re-Reading Dewey's *Art as Experience*." In *Dewey's Enduring Impact: Essays on America's Philosopher*. Edited by John R. Shook and Paul Kurtz. Amherst: Prometheus Press, 207–18.
Marshall, George (2014). "Hear No Climate Evil." *New Scientist* 223(2982): 24–25.
Martin, Jay (2002). *The Education of John Dewey: A Biography*. New York: Columbia University Press.
Mayr, Ernst (1974). "Teleological and Teleonomic, a New Analysis." *Methodological and Historical Essays in the Natural and Social Sciences Boston Studies in the Philosophy of Science*: 91–117.

——— (1988). *Towards a New Philosophy of Biology*. Cambridge, MA: Harvard University Press.

——— (1992). "The Idea of Teleology." *Journal of the History of Ideas*, 53(1): 117–35.

McCormack, Fr. Eric (1958). "Fredrick Matthias Alexander and John Dewey: A Neglected Influence." PhD Thesis, University of Toronto, 1958.

McCormack, Teresa, and Hoerl, Christoph (2011). "Tool Use, Planning and Future Thinking in Children and Animals." In *Tool Use and Causal Cognition*. Edited by Teresa McCormack et al. Oxford: Oxford University Press, 129–47.

McCormick, Ken (1999). "The Tao of Laissez-Faire." *Eastern Economic Journal* 25(3): 334–41.

McDonald, Hugh P. (2004). *John Dewey and Environmental Philosophy*. Albany: State University of New York Press.

McLeod, Alexus (2016). *Theories of Truth in Chinese Philosophy: A Comparative Approach*. New York: Rowman and Littlefield.

Mead, George Herbert (1932). *Works of George Herbert Mead, Vol. 1: Mind, Self, and Society*. Edited by Charles W. Morris. Chicago: University of Chicago Press.

——— (1964) "Metaphysics." *The Review of Metaphysics*, 17(4): 536–56.

——— (2002). *The Philosophy of the Present*. Amherst: Prometheus Books.

Mead, George Herbert, and Andrew J. Reck (1964). *Selected Writings: George Herbert Mead*. New York: The Bobbs-Merrill Company, Inc.

Menand, Louis (2001). *The Metaphysical Club: A Story of Ideas in America*. New York: Farrar, Straus, and Giroux.

Meng, Chih (1981). *Chinese American Understanding: A Sixty-Year Search*. New York: China Institute of America.

Mengzi 孟子 (1995). *Mengzi Jinzhujinyi 孟子今註今譯*. Taipei: The Commercial Press, Ltd.

Merton, Thomas (1967). *Mystics and Zen Masters*. New York: Farrar, Strauss and Giroux Press.

Miller, David L. (1973). *George Herbert Mead: Self, Language, and the World*. Chicago: University of Chicago Press.

Moeller, Hans-Georg (2004). *Daoism Explained: From the Dream of the Butterfly to the Fishnet Allegory*. Chicago: Open Court.

——— (2006). *The Philosophy of the Daodejing*. New York: Columbia University Press.

——— (2009). *The Moral Fool: A Case for Amorality*. New York: Columbia University Press.

Moeller, Hans-Georg, and Paul J. D'Ambrosio (2017). *Genuine Pretending: On the Philosophy of the Zhuangzi*. New York: Columbia University Press.

Molenberghs, P. et al. (2009). "Is the Mirror Neuron System Involved in Imitation? A Short Review and Meta-Analysis." *Neuroscience and Biobehavioral Reviews* 33(7): 975–80.

Møllgaard, Eske (1998). *Anticipating China: Thinking Through the Narratives of Chinese and Western Culture* by David L. Hall and Roger T. Ames. *The Journal of Religion* 78(2): 331–32.

——— (2007). *An Introduction to Daoist Thought: Action, Language, and Ethics in Zhuangzi*. New York: Routledge.

Moore, Charles A. (1951). *Essays in East-West Philosophy: An Attempt at World Philosophical Synthesis*. Honolulu: University of Hawai`i Press.

——— (1962). *Philosophy and Culture-East and West: East-West Philosophy in Practical Perspective*. Honolulu: University of Hawai`i Press.

Morelle, Rebecca (2015). "Oldest Stone Tools Pre-date Earliest Humans." BBC News, May 20, 2015. http://www.bbc.com/news/science-environment-32804177.

Morgenbesser, Sidney (1977). *Dewey and His Critics: Essays from the Journal of Philosophy*. New York: Journal of Philosophy.

Mozi, and Ian Johnston (2010). *The Mozi: A Complete Translation*. New York: Columbia University Press.

Munro, Donald J. (2002). "Mencius and an Ethics of the New Century." In *Mencius: Contexts and Interpretations*. Edited by Alan K. L. Chan. Honolulu: University of Hawai`i Press, 305–15.

Nagel, Ernest (1961). *The Structure of Science; Problems in the Logic of Scientific Explanation*. New York: Harcourt, Brace & World Press.

Needham, Joseph (1956). *Science and Civilization in China*. Vol. 2. Cambridge: Cambridge University Press.

——— (1965). *Science and Civilization in China*. Vol. 4. Cambridge: Cambridge University Press.

Nelson, Eric S. (2017). *Chinese and Buddhist Philosophy in Early Twentieth Century German Thought*. London: Bloomsbury Press.

Neville, Robert C. (1981). *Reconstruction of Thinking*. Albany: State University of New York Press.

Nivison, David S. (1996). *The Ways of Confucianism: Investigations in Chinese Philosophy*. Edited by Bryan W. Van Norden. Chicago: Open Court.

Norenzayan, A., and R. E. Nisbett (2000). "Culture and Causal Cognition." *Current Directions in Psychological Science*, 9: 132–35.

Norgaard, Kari Marie (2009). "Cognitive and Behavioral Challenges in Responding to Climate Change." The World Bank: *Policy Research Working Papers*.

Nussbaum, Martha C. (1997). *Cultivating Humanity: A Classical Defense of Reform in Liberal Education*. Cambridge, MA: Harvard University Press.

Odin, Steve (1996). *The Social Self in Zen and American Pragmatism*. Albany: State University of New York Press.

Olivola, Christopher Y., and Edouard Machery (2016). "Is Psychological Essentialism an Inherent Feature of Human Cognition?" *Behavioral and Brain Sciences* 37(5): 499.

Owens, Joseph (1968). "Teleology of Nature in Aristotle." *Monist* 52(2): 159–73.

Pappas, Gregory F. (2008). *John Dewey's Ethics: Democracy as Experience*. Bloomington: Indiana University Press.

Parkes, Graham (1987). "Thoughts on the Way: *Being and Time* via Lao-Chuang." In *Heidegger and Asian Thought*. Edited by Graham Parkes. Honolulu: University of Hawai`i Press, 105–44.

——— (2013). "The Politics of Global Warming (1): Climate Science and Skepticism." In *Environmental Philosophy: The Art of Life in a World of Limits Advances in Sustainability and Environmental Justice*. Edited by Liam Leonard et al. Bingley, UK: Emerald Group Publishing, 51–80.

Peerenboom, Randall P. (1993). *Law and Morality in Ancient China: The Silk Manuscripts of Huang-Lao*. Albany: State University of New York Press.

Peirce, Charles S., and Justus Buchler (1955). *Philosophical Writings of Peirce*. New York: Dover Publications, Inc.

Peirce, Charles S., and Arthur W. Burks (1958). *Collected Papers of Charles Sanders Peirce*. Vol. 7. Cambridge, MA: Harvard University Press.

Peirce, Charles S., and Nathan Houser (2000). *Writings of Charles S. Peirce: A Chronological Edition*, Vol. 6. Bloomington: Indiana University Press.

Peirce, Charles S., and Christian J. W. Kloesel (1993). *Writings of Charles S. Peirce: A Chronological Edition*. Vol. 5. Bloomington: Indiana University Press.

Peirce, Charles S., Charles Hartshorne, and Paul Weiss (1931). *Collected Papers of Charles Sanders Peirce*. Vol. 1. Cambridge, MA: Harvard University Press.

——— (1933). *Collected Papers of Charles Sanders Peirce*. Vol. 3. Cambridge, MA: Harvard University Press.

——— (1935). *Collected Papers of Charles Sanders Peirce*. Vol. 6. Cambridge, MA: Harvard University Press.

Peirce, Charles S., Nathan Houser, and Christian J. W. Kloesel (1998). *The Essential Peirce: Selected Philosophical Writings*. Vol. 2. Bloomington: Indiana University Press.

Perkins, Franklin (2014). *Heaven and Earth are not Humane: The Problem of Evil in Classical Chinese Philosophy*. Bloomington: Indiana University Press.

——— (2015). "Fanwuliuxing ('All Things Flow Into Form') and the 'One' in the Laozi." *Early China*, 38: 195–232.

Perlman, Mark (2004). "The Modern Philosophical Resurrection of Teleology." *Monist* 87(1): 3–51.

Peterman, James F. (2015). *Whose Tradition? Which Dao?: Confucius and Wittgenstein on Moral Learning and Reflection*. Albany: State University of New York Press.

Pew (2015). "Public and Scientists' Views on Science and Society." *Pew Research Center Internet Science Tech RSS*, 29 Jan. 2015.

Phillips, Alan G. (2002). "John Dewey and His Religious Critics." *Religion & Education* 29(1): 31–40.

Pirsig, Robert (1974). *Zen and the Art of Motorcycle Maintenance*. New York: William Morrow and Company.

Plato, John M. Cooper (1997). *Plato: Complete Works*. Indianapolis, IN: Hackett Publishers.

Polanyi, Karl (1944). *The Great Transformation: The Political and Economic Origins of Our Time*. Boston: Beacon Press.

Prather, J. F. et al. (2008). "Precise Auditory-Vocal Mirroring in Neurons for Learned Vocal Communication." *Nature* 451: 305–10.

Press, Rich (2014). "The Ocean Adapt Website: Tracking Fish Populations as the Climate Changes." *NOAA Fisheries*. http://www.nmfs.noaa.gov/stories/2014/12/oceanadapt_trackingfish.html.

Proceedings (1979). *Proceedings and Addresses of the American Philosophical Association*, 52(3): 378–80.
Pryba, Russell (2011). "John Dewey and the Ontology of Art." In *Dewey's Enduring Impact: Essays on America's Philosopher*. Edited by John R. Shook and Paul Kurtz. Amherst, MA: Prometheus Press, 219–35.
Puett, Michael (1997). "Nature and Artifice: Debates in Late Warring States China Concerning the Creation of Culture." *Harvard Journal of Asiatic Studies* 57(2): 471–518.
——— (2001). *Ambivalence of Creation: Debates Concerning Innovation and Artifice in Early China*. Stanford, CA: Stanford University Press.
——— (2002). *To Become a God: Cosmology, Sacrifice, and Self-Divinization in Early China*. Harvard University Asia Center. Cambridge, MA: Harvard University Press.
Pusey, James R. (1983). *China and Charles Darwin*. Cambridge, MA: Council on East Asian Studies, Harvard University.
——— (1998). *Lu Xun and Evolution*. Albany: State University of New York Press.
Radin, Paul (1927). *Primitive Man as Philosopher*. New York: Dover Publications.
Randall, John Herman, Jr. (1989). "Dewey's Interpretation of the Philosophy of History." In *The Philosophy of John Dewey*. Edited by Paul Schilpp. La Salle, IL: Open Court, 77–102.
Raphals, Lisa (2005). "Languages of Fate: Semantic Fields in Chinese and Greek." In *The Mandate of Ming: Command, Allotment, and Fate in Chinese Culture*. Edited by Christopher Lupke. Honolulu: University of Hawai`i Press, 70–106.
——— (2015). "Daoism and Science." In *Dao Companion to Daoism Philosophy*. Edited by Liu Xiaogan. Dordrecht: Springer, 539–50.
Reader, S. M., and K. N. Laland (2002). "Social Intelligence, Innovation, and Enhanced Brain Size in Primates." *Proceedings of the National Academy of Sciences USA*, 99(7): 4436–441.
Reeve, C.D.C. (2006). "Aristotle on the Virtues of Thought." In *The Blackwell Guide to Aristotle's Nicomachean Ethics*. Edited by Richard Kraut. Oxford, UK: Blackwell Publishers, 198–217.
Rescher, Nicolas (1996). *Process Metaphysics: An Introduction to Process Philosophy*. Albany: State University of New York Press.
Richardson, Robert D. (2006). *William James: In the Maelstrom of American Modernism*. Boston: Houghton Mifflin Company.
Richey, Jeffrey (2003). "Review of *Mencius: Context and Interpretation*." *Journal of Asian Studies*, 6(2): 580–81.
Rickett, Allyn W. (1985). *Guanzi: Political, Economic, and Philosophical Essays from Early China: A Study and Translation*. Princeton, NJ: Princeton University Press.
Rizzolatti, G. et al. (1999). "Resonance Behaviors and Mirror Neurons." *Archives italiennes de biologie* 137(2–3): 85–100.
Robinet, Isabelle (1999). "The Diverse Interpretations of the *Laozi*." In *Religious and Philosophical Aspects of Laozi*. Edited by Mark Csikszentmihalyi and Philip J. Ivanhoe. Albany: State University of New York Press, 127–59.

Robins, Dan (2000). "Mass Nouns and Count Nouns in Classical Chinese." *Early China* 25: 147–84.

——— (2011). "The Warring States Concept of *Xing*." *Dao: A Journal of Comparative Philosophy* 10(1): 31–51.

Rockefeller, Steven C. (1991). *John Dewey: Religious Faith and Democratic Humanism*. New York: Columbia University Press.

Rolston, Holmes III (2005). "Challenges in Environmental Ethics." In *Environmental Philosophy: From Animal Rights to Radical Ecology*, Fourth Edition. Edited by Michael E. Zimmerman et al. Upper Saddle River, NJ: Pearson Prentice Hall, 82–101.

Rorty, Richard (1982a). "Dewey's Metaphysics." In *Consequences of Pragmatism: Essays, 1972–1980*. Minneapolis: University of Minnesota Press, 72–89.

——— (1982b). "Pragmatism, Relativism, and Irrationalism." In *Consequences of Pragmatism: Essays, 1972–1980*. Minneapolis: University of Minnesota Press, 160–75.

Rosemont, Henry, Jr. (2018). "Role Ethics: Problems and Promise." In *Appreciating the Chinese Difference: Engaging Roger T. Ames on Methods, Issues, and Roles*. Edited by Jim Behuniak. Albany: State University of New York Press, 229–46.

Rosen, Jacob (2014). "Essence and End in Aristotle." *Oxford Studies in Ancient Philosophy*, Vol. XLVI: 73–107.

Ross-Flanigan, Nancy (2012). "Animals on the Move: A Warming Climate Means Shifting Ranges and Mixed-up Relationships for a Lot of Species." *Science News* 181(13): 16–21.

Roth, Harold D. (1999). *Original Tao: Inward Training and the Foundations of Taoist Mysticism*. New York: Columbia University Press.

——— (2003). *A Companion to Angus C. Graham's* Chuang Tzu. Honolulu: University of Hawai`i Press.

Rothbard, Murray N. (1995). *Economic Thought before Adam Smith*, Vol. 1 of *An Austrian Perspective on the History of Economic Thought*. Cheltenham, UK: Edward Elgar.

Rottman, J., L. Zhu et al. (2016). "Cultural Influences on the Teleological Stance: Evidence from China." *Religion, Brain & Behavior*. 7(1): 17–26.

Rousseau, Oscar (2016). "Demand for Lamb Rises in China," *Global Meat News*, June 29, 2016. http://www.globalmeatnews.com/Industry-Markets/Demand-for-lamb-rises-in-China.

Russell, Bertrand (1945). *A History of Western Philosophy*. New York: Simon and Schuster.

Ryan, Alan (1995). *John Dewey and the High Tide of American Liberalism*. New York: W. W. Norton Company.

Ryden, Edmund (2008). *Laozi: Daodejing, A New Translation by Edmund Ryden*. Oxford: Oxford World Classics, Oxford University Press.

Sarkissian, Hagop (2010). "The Darker Side of Daoist Primitivism." *Journal of Chinese Philosophy* 37(2): 312–29.

Schilpp, Paul Arthur, and Lewis Edwin Hahn (1989). *The Philosophy of John Dewey*. La Salle, IL: Open Court.

Schwartz, Benjamin I. (1985). *The World of Thought in Ancient China*. Cambridge, MA: Harvard University Press.

Shaughnessy, Edward (2006). *Rewriting Early Chinese Texts*. Albany: State University of New York Press.
Shaughnessy, Edward L. (2014). *Unearthing the Changes: Recently Discovered Manuscripts of the Yijing and Related Texts*. New York: Columbia University Press.
Short, Thomas L. (1981). "Peirce's Conception of Final Causation." *Transactions of the Charles S. Peirce Society*, 17: 369–82.
Shun, Kwong-loi (2004). "Conception of Person in Early Confucian Thought." In *Confucian Ethics: A Comparative Study of Self, Autonomy, and Community*. Edited by Kwong-loi Shun and David B. Wong. Cambridge: Cambridge University Press, 183–99.
Shusterman, Richard (1998). "Dewey on Experience: Foundation or Reconstruction?" In *Dewey Reconfigured: Essays on Deweyan Pragmatism*. Edited by Casey Haskins and David I. Seiple. Albany: State University of New York Press, 193–219.
——— (2008). *Body Consciousness: A Philosophy of Mindfulness and Somaesthetics*. Cambridge: Cambridge University Press.
Sim, May (2012). *Remastering Morals with Aristotle and Confucius*. Cambridge: Cambridge University Press.
Sivin, Nathan (1990). "Science and Medicine in Chinese History." In *Heritage of China: Contemporary Perspectives on Chinese Civilization*. Edited by Paul S. Ropp. Berkeley: University of California Press, 164–96.
——— (2005). "Why the Scientific Revolution Did Not Take Place in China—Or Didn't It?" Revised version of 1982 article first published in *Chinese Science* 5: 45–66.http://ccat.sas.upenn.edu/~nsivin/scirev.pdf.
Škof, Lenart (2012). *Pragmatist Variations on Ethical and Intercultural Life*. Lanham, MD: Lexington Press.
Skrupskelis, Ignas K., and Elizabeth M. Berkeley (1993). *The Correspondence of William James*. Vol. 2. Charlottesville: University of Virginia Press.
——— (2000). *The Correspondence of William James*. Vol. 8. Charlottesville: University of Virginia Press.
Slater, Michael R. (2010). "Moeller, Hans-Georg, *The Moral Fool: A Case for Amorality*." *Notre Dame Philosophical Reviews*, http://ndpr.nd.edu/news/the-moral-fool-a-case-for-amorality/, Feb. 19, 2010.
Sleeper, Ralph (1986). *The Necessity of Pragmatism: John Dewey's Conception of Philosophy*. New Haven, CT: Yale University Press.
Slingerland, Edward (2003). *Effortless Action: Wu-Wei as Conceptual Metaphor and Spiritual Ideal in Early China*. Oxford: Oxford University Press.
——— (2008). *What Science Offers the Humanities: Integrating Body and Culture*. Cambridge: Cambridge University Press.
——— (2013). "Body and Mind in Early China: An Integrated Humanities-Science Approach." *Journal of the American Academy of Religion* 81(1): 6–55.
——— (2019). *Mind and Body in Early China: Beyond Orientalism and the Myth of Holism*. Oxford: Oxford University Press.
Smid, Robert (2009). *Methodologies of Comparative Philosophy: The Pragmatist and Process Traditions*. Albany: State University of New York Press.

Smith, Adam (1849). *An Inquiry into the Nature and Causes of the Wealth of Nations*. Edinburgh: Adam and Charles Black.
Sterckx, Roel (2002). *The Animal and the Daemon in Early China*. Albany: State University of New York Press.
——— (2005). "Animal Classification in Ancient China." *East Asian Science, Technology, and Medicine* 23: 26–53.
Stevenson, Marguerite B., and Michael E. Lamb (1979). "Effects of Infant Sociability and the Caretaking Environment on Infant Cognitive Performance." *Child Development* 50(2): 340–49.
Stuhr, John (1992). "Dewey's Reconstruction of Metaphysics." *Transactions of the Charles S. Peirce Society* 28(2): 161–76.
Talyor, Romeyn (1989). "Chinese Hierarchy in Comparative Perspective." *The Journal of Asian Studies* 48(3): 490–511.
Tanahashi, Kazuaki (1985). *Moon in a Dewdrop*. New York: North Point Press.
Thompson, Paul B. (1996). "Pragmatism and Policy: The Case of Water." In *Environmental Pragmatism*. Edited by Andrew Light and Eric Katz. New York: Routledge, 187–208.
Tiles, Jim (1988). *Dewey*. London: Routledge.
Tsung, Paihua (1995). "Space-Consciousness in Chinese Art." In *Contemporary Chinese Aesthetics*. Edited by Zuo Liyuan and Gene Blocker. New York: Peter Lang, 49–54.
Tu, Weiming (1979). "The Thought of Huang-Lao: A Reflection on the *Lao Tzu* and *Huang Ti* Texts in the Silk Manuscripts of the Ma-wang-tui." *Journal of Asian Studies* 39(1): 95–110.
Uchiyama, Kōshō, and Thomas Wright (2005). *How to Cook Your Life: From the Zen Kitchen to Enlightenment*. Boston: Shambhala
Uddin, Lucina Q. et al. (2007). "The Self and Social Cognition: The Role of Cortical Midline Structures and Mirror Neurons." *Trends in Cognitive Sciences*, 11(4): 153–57.
Urmson, J. O. (1988). *Aristotle's Ethics*. Oxford: Basil Blackwell.
Van Els, Paul (2011). "The Philosophy of the Proto-*Wenzi*." In *Dao Companion to Daoist Philosophy*. Edited by Liu Xiaogan. Dordrecht: Springer, 325–40.
Van Norden, Bryan W. (1993). "Book Review: *John Dewey and American Philosophy*." *Philosophy East and West* 43(2): 341–43.
——— (1999). "Method in the Madness of the *Laozi*." In *Religious and Philosophical Aspects of Laozi*. Edited by Mark Csikszentmihalyi and Philip J. Ivanhoe. Albany: State University of New York Press, 187–210.
——— (2007). *Virtue Ethics and Consequentialism in Early Chinese Philosophy*. Cambridge: Cambridge University Press.
——— (2011). *Introduction to Classical Chinese Philosophy*. Indianapolis, IN: Hackett Publishers.
Vandermeersch, Léon (1988). "Tradition chinoise et religion." In *Catholicisme et Sociétés asiatiques*. Paris: L'Harmattan.
Wagner, Rudolf G. (2003). *A Chinese Reading of the* Daodejing. Albany: State University of New York Press.

Waley, Arthur (1958). *The Way and its Power: A study of the* Tao Tê Ching *and its Place in Chinese Thought*. London: G. Allen & Unwin Publishers.
Wang, Jessica Ching-Sze (2007). *John Dewey in China: To Teach and to Learn*. Albany: State University of New York Press.
Wang, Zhongjiang (2015). *Daoism Excavated: Cosmos and Humanity in Early Manuscripts*. Center for Daoist Studies, Peking University. St. Petersburg, FL: Three Pines Press.
——— (2016). *Order in Early Chinese Excavated Texts: Natural, Supernatural, and Legal Approaches*. Translated by Misha Tadd. New York: Palgrave Macmillan.
Watson, Burton (1968). *The Complete Works of Chuang Tzu*. New York: Columbia University Press.
Weber, Ralph (2014). "Comparative Philosophy and the Tertium: Comparing What with What, and in What Respect?" *Dao* 13(2): 151–71.
Welch, Holmes (1966). *Taoism: The Parting of the Ways*. New York: Beacon Press.
Westbrook, Robert B. (1991). *John Dewey and American Democracy*. Ithaca, NY: Cornell University Press.
Whitehead, Alfred North (1925). *Science and the Modern World*. New York: Free Press.
——— (1927). *Symbolism: Its Meaning and Effect*. New York: Fordham University Press.
——— (1929). *Process and Reality: Corrected Edition*. New York: Free Press.
——— (1933). *Adventures of Ideas*. New York: Free Press.
Whitehead, Alfred North, and Lucien Price (1954). *Dialogues of Alfred North Whitehead*. Boston: Little, Brown Publishers.
Whitman, Walt (2007). *Leaves of Grass: The Original 1855 Edition*. Mineola, NY: Dover Publications.
Wiener, Philip P. (1949). *Evolution and the Founders of Pragmatism*. New York: Harper and Row, Publishers.
Wilhelm, Richard, and Cary Baynes (1967). *The I Ching or Book of Changes*. Princeton, NJ: Princeton University Press.
Wilkie, Rhoda, and Andrew McKinnon (2013). "George Herbert Mead on Humans and Other Animals: Social Relations after Human-Animals Studies." *Sociological Research* 18(4): 1–13.
Wilson, Kathleen Karah, and George E. B. Morren (1990). *Systems Approach for Improvement in Agriculture and Resource Management*. London: MacMillan Publishing Company.
Winchester, Simon (2008). *The Man Who Loved China*. New York: Harper Collins.
Wu, John C. H. (1951). *Beyond East and West*. New York: Sheed and Ward.
Wu, Joseph S. (1975). "Causality: Confucianism and Pragmatism." *Philosophy East and West* 25(1): 13–22.
Xing, Wen (2015). "Early Daoism Thought in Excavated Bamboo Strips." In *Dao Companion to Daoism Philosophy*. Edited by Liu Xiaogan. Dordrecht: Springer, 101–26.
Xunzi 荀子 (1995). *Xunzi Jinzhujinyi* 荀子今註今譯. Taipei: The Commercial Press, Ltd.
Yangzi 揚子 (1983). *Yangzi Fayan* 揚子法言. Taipei: Chung Hwa Book Company, Ltd.
Yao, Xinzhong (1996). "Self-Construction and Identity: The Confucian Self in Relation to Some Western Perceptions." *Asian Philosophy* 6(3): 179–95.

Yates, Robin (1997). *Five Lost Classics: Tao, Huang-Lao, and Yin-Yang in Han China.* New York: Ballantine.
Zhang, Xianglong (2010). "Comparison Paradox, Comparative Situation and Inter-paradigmaticy: a Methodological Reflection on Cross-Cultural Philosophical Comparison." *Comparative Philosophy* 1(1): 90–105.
Zhang, Yanhua (2007). *Transforming Emotions with Chinese Medicine: An Ethnographic Account from Contemporary China.* Albany: State University of New York Press.
Zhuangzi 莊子 (1994). *Zhuangzi Jinzhujinyi* 莊子今註今譯, Vol. 1 (上) and Vol. 2 (下). Taipei: The Commercial Press, Ltd.
Zhouyi 周易 (1999). *Zhouyi Jinzhujinyi* 周易今註今譯. Taipei: The Commercial Press, Ltd.
Ziporyn, Brook (2009). *Zhuangzi: The Essential Writings.* Indianapolis: Hackett Publishing Company.
——— (2010). "Moeller, Hans-Georg, *The Moral Fool: A Case for Amorality*." *Dao* 9(4): 481–85.
——— (2012). *Ironies of Oneness and Difference: Coherence in Early Chinese Thought; Prolegomena to the Study of Li.* Albany: State University of New York Press.
——— (2013). *Beyond Oneness and Difference: Li and Coherence in Chinese Buddhist Thought and its Antecedent.* Albany: State University of New York Press.
——— (2018). "Vast Continuity versus the One: Thoughts on *Daodejing* 42, *Taiyishengshui*, and the Legacy of Roger T. Ames." In *Appreciating the Chinese Difference: Engaging Roger T. Ames on Methods, Issues, and Roles.* Edited by Jim Behuniak. Albany: State University of New York Press, 111–32.
Zou, Zhenhuan (2010). "The 'Dewey Fever' in Jiangsu and Zhejiang During the May Fourth Movement and its Relation to the Cultural Tradition in Jiangnan." *Chinese Studies in History* 43(4): 43–62.

Index

Abbey, Edward
  and theoretical coherence, 354n.23
Acorns to Oak Trees
  and its status as if-then proposition, 131–132
  and the naturalistic account, 137–138
Aesthetic Perception
  and recognition, 28
Agriculturalism
  and ancient China, 242
  and Confucianism, 242–250
Aims
  and Dewey, 49–51
Alexander, F. Matthias
  biographical, 234–235
  and the Alexander technique, 233–235, 236–237, 249, 261, 262–264
  and Dewey's encounter with, 233–234, 262–264
  and his influence on Dewey's philosophy, 263–264
Alexander, Thomas M.
  and the denotative method, 53
  and Dewey and nominalism, 331n.143
  and Dewey and Western philosophy, xvi
All Things Flow in Form
  and living things, 77
  and pre-established order, 86
Allan, Sarah
  and *dao* 道, 327n.52
  and *de* 德, 72
  and living things in early China, 71

Allen, Barry
  and Daoism and technology, 266
Ames, Roger T. *See also* Hall, David L. and Roger T. Ames
  and assumptions, 15–16
  and comparative philosophy, 10–11
  and *de* 德, 72, 127
  and Graham on *xing* 性, 139, 337n.162
  and *shen* 身, 264
  and virtue ethics vs. role ethics debate, 223–224
Amorality
  and Daoism, 173–176, 272–275
Analytic Philosophy
  and Daoist concern with, 224
  and intra-cultural philosophy, 22–23
  and non-Western traditions, 315n.81
  and thought experiments, 294
Animals
  and animal activity, 205–207
  and animal body standpoints in the *Zhuangzi*, 245–250
  and Confucianism, 240–241
  and language, 253–254, 258–259
  and selfhood, 259–260
  and the *Zhuangzi* on animal behavior, 76–77, 99, 206
Annals of Lü Buwei
  and attaining the one, 93
  and government action, 286
  and holding to the one, 82
  and the Man from Song, 187

Annals of Master Yan
  and form-environment continuity, 73–74
Anthropocene, 270
Aquinas, St. Thomas
  and teleology and God, 50
Archeological finds
  and Chinese philosophy, 24–25, 80–87, 147, 322n.129, 326n.28
Ariew, Andre
  and Aristotle's formal and final causes, 101–102
Aristotle, xvii
  and the beauty of nature, 320n.52
  and chance, 47
  and change and motion, 125–126
  and continuity, 113
  and Darwinian theory, 48
  and Dewey, 179–180
  and Earth's climate, 318n.12
  and energy and motion, 118–119
  and formal and final cause, 101–102
  and hypothetical necessity, 101
  and influence on Western thought, 37
  and knowledge, 46, 198, 226
  and potentiality, 125–126, 129
  and *praxis* and *poiesis*, 177, 198
  and *techne*, 180
  and teleology, 47, 50, 101–102, 142–143, 323n.148
  and thisness, 45
  and the two lives thesis, 181–182
  and wisdom, 180–181
Art
  and aesthetic perception, 28
  and the children's art movement, 305–306
  and Chinese landscape painting, 109–113
  and Dewey and Chinese art, 109–110
  and experience, 25–28
  and means-end continuity, 237, 278
  and quality, 25–28

Art of War
  and form and propensity, 73
  and sonic divination, 335–336n.126
Artificer's Record
  and knowledge and tools, 223
Assimilation
  and aesthetic experience, 26–28
  and individualized cultures, 28–31

Balance. *See* Rhythm
Barnwell, Scott
  and *de* 德, 72, 329n.80
Bentley, Arthur
  and Dewey on knowledge, 214–215
Bergson, Henri
  and change, 122
Bernstein, Richard J.
  and East and West, 9
Berthrong, John H.
  and comparative philosophy, 16
Bias
  and form, 275
  and inorganic matter, 279–280
  and valuation, 271–272, 275, 304
Boaz, David
  and Daoism and libertarianism, 282
Boaz, Franz
  and influence on Dewey, 201–202
Body
  and the Alexander technique, 234–236
  and animal body standpoints in the *Zhuangzi*, 245–250
  and Confucian debates, 243–244
  and knowledge, 261–263
  and moral sensibility, 248, 256
  and the organism-technology circuit, 238–240, 270
  and selfhood, 261, 262–263, 264
  and technology, 235–236
Bohr, Niels, 114, 216
Boisvert, Raymond D.
  and Dewey on Greek-medieval thought, xvi

Book of Changes
 and advent of markets, 284
 and human emergence, 244–245
 and natural philosophy, 102
 and prognostication, 297–300
Book of Lord Shang
 and human emergence, 243
Boydston, JoAnn
 and Dewey and the Alexander technique, 263
Brain activity
 and digital amusements, 237–238
 and the emergence of selfhood, 259–260
 and forward movement, 221
 and mirror neurons, 256–257
Brindley, Erica Fox
 and desire in the *Hengxian*, 63
Bruns, Gerald L.
 and manuscript *vs.* print cultures, 81
Buck, Pearl S.
 and Dewey, 311n.11
Buddhism. *See also* Zen Buddhism
 and contact (*phassa*), 347n.112
 and the knowing relation, 215
 and Mencius, 270–271

Cage, John, 22
Cahoone, Lawrence E.
 and Mead on selfhood, 259
Callicott, J. Baird
 and environmental values, 276
Cambrian Explosion, 269
Campbell, John
 and animal cognition, 145
Carpenter's Square
 and Dewey's philosophy, 168–169
 and Chinese philosophy, 159, 166, 264
Cassier, Ernst
 and Nicolas of Cusa, 231
Castle, Emery N.
 and environmental pragmatism, 294

Causality
 and Chinese and Western thinking, 126
 and early Chinese thought, 126–127
 and ordered sequence, 129
 and systems theory, 132–135
Cave Painting
 and the hunting vocation, 204–205
Chan, K. L.
 and Chapter 42 of the *Daodejing*, 84
Chatham River Case Study. *See* Thompson, Paul B.
Chautauqua Institution
 and Dewey's talk, 300, 305
 and James, 300–301, 304
Chen, Ellen M.
 and Peirce and the *Daodejing*, 89
Cheng, Chung-ying
 and causality in early China, 334n.92
 and prognostication in the *Book of Changes*, 298
Children's Art Movement, 305–306
China Institute
 and Dewey, xiv
China Lectures (Dewey)
 and their number and scope, xiv
 and citation, xviii–xix
Chong, Kim-chong
 and inner/outer distinction in the *Mencius*, 191
 and *tian* 天 as Nature, 273
Cižek, Franz
 and the children's art movement, 305–306
Classic on the Pulse
 and system-level diagnostics, 135
Climate Change
 and climate tracking, 69
 and climate change denial, 39–40, 44
Cline, Erin M.
 and her critique of Ames, 10–11
Coherence
 and Chinese cosmology, 88–89, 274
 and Chinese painting, 110–112

Coherence *(continued)*
    and intelligibility, 228–229
    and realism, 134, 218, 274
    and types, 105–106
Colson, Charles
    and his critique of Dewey, 319n.28
Common Sense
    and philosophy, 42–43
Communication
    and Dewey, 34, 257
    and across and over cultures, 34–36
Comparison
    and the comparative situation, 10–17, 313n.49
    and the comparison paradox, 11–13
    and Dewey, 13–14, 54–55
Confucius
    and ritual-custom, 200
Continuity
    and means-and-ends, 67, 96–97
    and mysticism, 218–219
    and Nature-and-the-human, 212, 309
    and objects of knowledge, 217–220
    and organic form, 51
    and self-and-body, 261, 262, 264, 267
Cook Ding. See also *Zhuangzi*
    And the *Huainanzi* on, 159
Cook, Scott
    and *Great Continuum Produces the Waters*, 85
Cosmogony
    defined, 80
Cosmology
    defined, 80
    and the *Daodejing*, 83–93, 110–112
Coutinho, Steve
    and balance in Daoism, 119–120
    and *dao* 道, 327n.52
    and *ming* 明, 184
    and the *Zhuangzi* and relativism, 220–221
Cranz, Galen
    and the chair, 236

Creel, Herrlee C.
    and the East-West Philosophers' Conference, 6
Csikszentmihalyi, Mark
    and material virtues in Confucianism, 243–244
Culture
    and Dewey, 6, 20–22, xv
    and individual cultures, 29–32
    and nature, 203, 240–250, 309
D'Ambrosio, Paul J.
    and genuine pretending, 305–306
Dai, Zhen
    and *xing* 性, 137
Dalton, Thomas C.
    and quality and quantitative measurement, 55
Dao 道-Activity
    and adaptation, 66–67
    and amorality, 173–176, 273
    and the logical or illogical, 228–229
    and brain activity, 221
    and domain distinctions, 98
    and Eno's critique of Cook Ding, 157–158, 161
    and external ends, 173, 175–176, 208, 266
    and form, 73–74
    and generalized content, 166–167
    and habit, 64–70
    and intelligence, 210, 237, 275, 278
    and knowledge, 194–196, 221–222, 228
    and mechanical *vs.* teleological activity, 67–68, 165
    and primitivism, 203–204, 210
    and theory, 159–160
    and *xing* 性, 140–141
Daodejing 道德經
    and amorality, 173–174
    and attaining the one, 94
    and cosmology, 83–93, 110–112

and creativity and ontology, 90
and desire, 144, 145, 288–290, 291, 302–303
and desire and naming, 46, 226
and governance, 95, 281–282, 282–292, 287, 302, 304
and growth, 143
and incremental achievement, 146
and knowledge, 196, 226–227
and lack of teleology, 57–58, 94, 207, 273
and localism, 292
and market activity, 284
and mutuality of opposites, 88, 301
and mutual generation of opposites, 88, 121
and the mystery of things, 45–46
and observing the small, 146, 282, 290
and organic form, 58, 72
and Peirce's categories, 89
and its prescriptive stance, 147–148
and recent archeological finds, 80–87
and softness and pliancy, 128
and space, 113
and systems theory, 136
and technology, 267, 303
and things as straw dogs, 142
Darwinism. See also Evolution
and China, 43, 319n.43
and Chinese vs. American culture, 43–44
and common sense, 41
Dawkins, Richard
and the possibility of animal life, 60
Daxue 大學. See Great Learning
De 德
and animal behavior, 206
and attaining the one, 96
and dao 道, 58–59
and de 得, 64
and directional order, 59–60
and growth, 72
and the newborn infant, 127
and potentiality, 126–127
and power, 87
and pre-human experience, 243
and spontaneity, 94
Defoort, Carine
and causality in Chinese thought, 126
Denisovans, 241
Dennett, Daniel C.
and animal life and its possibility, 60, 93
and life and the law of entropy, 124
Denotative Method
and Dewey, 53
and quantitative inquiry, 53–57
Dewey, Jane
and her research in theoretical physics, 114, 216
Digital Age. See Technology
Directional Order
and attaining the one, 96
and de 德, 59–60
and environment, 74, 278
and growth, 51, 278–279
and teleology, 65–66
Dissanayake, Wimal
and symbolic interactionism and the body, 260
Dissertation Upon Roast Pig, 190–191
Dōgen
and the dao 道-seeking mind, 175–176
Dorn, James A.
and Daoism and libertarianism, 283, 288, 291
Drudgery
and Dewey, 303–304
Dushun
and the four-fold dharmadhātu, 347n.117

Eames, Morris S.
and pragmatic naturalism and symbols, 297

East-West Philosophers' Conference, 3, 6–7, 9, 29, 313n.23
Eastman, Max
  and Dewey and the Alexander technique, 263
Economy, Elizabeth
  and state-owned enterprises, 356n.78
Edwards Aquifer, 194
Embracing the One
  and the Daoist ideal, 80–81
  and observing the small, 147–148
Emerson, Ralph Waldo
  and nature and mind, 75
  and reading, 24
Ends
  and the end-in-itself, 176
  and ends-in-view, 164–165, 177, 182–183
  and being external to activity, 172–173, 189–192
Energy. *See also* Qi 氣
  and conservation, 333n.51
  and Dewey's aesthetics, 114–116
  and Maxwell's work, 114, 117–118
  and rhythm, 119–120
Eno, Robert
  and his critique of Cook Ding, 156–159, 164–165, 169, 171, 173–174, 180, 184–185, 208, 229
  and Greek assumptions, 162, 184
  and knowledge and Mohism, 200
  and theory in the *Zhuangzi*, 157, 168, 171, 180, 219
Environmental Ethics. *See* Morality
Epicureanism
  and Dewey, 302–303
Eriugena, John Scotus, xvii
Essentialism
  and common sense, 42, 44
Ethics. *See* Morality
Events
  and Dewey, 61–62, 122
Evolution. *See also* Darwinism
  and anthropology, 201–202
  and creationism, 38–39, 296
  and early Chinese thought, 43, 71–72
  and Greek-medieval assumptions, 161–162
  and the *Huainanzi*, 102
  and morality, 161–162
  and Peirce's cosmology, 98
Evolution and Ethics, 43
Experience
  and artworks, 25–28
  and Dewey, 19, 28, 75
Experimental Inquiry
  and Dewey, 23, 25

Faith
  and imagination, 306
Fanwuliuxing 凡物流形. *See All Things Flow in Form*
Farquhar, Judith
  and *qi* 氣, 117
Fen, Sing-nan
  biographical, xi–xii
  and cultural assimilation, 28
  and culture and nature, xii
  and the purpose of philosophy, 304
  and quality, 27
  and science and the philosopher, 107–108
  and situations, 15, 317n.120
  and universes of discourse, 16
  and values in nature, 280–281
Feng, Youlan
  biographical, xiii
Feynman, Richard
  and energy, 118, 333n.51
Focusing the Familiar
  and *ming* 命 and *xing* 性, 141
Forgetting
  and knowledge, 208–209, 215–216, 228, 262
  and method, 168
  and wild and twisty, 193, 208, 262
Form
  and bias, 275, 276

and the Chinese militarist tradition, 73
and Confucian-Daoist debates, 244–250
and directional order, 57–60
and ends, 68, 205–206
and environment, 69–70, 70–74
and events, 61–62
and evolution, 102
and habit, 99
and moral obligation, 230–231, 276
and need, 63–64, 276
and organization, 52–53, 66–67
and the potential to change, 100
and quality, 53
Franks, David D.
and neuroscience and American pragmatism, 257
Fraser, Chris
and the mass-noun hypothesis, 104–105
and Mohism, 344n.28
and Mohist mereology, 107

Ganying 感應. *See* Resonance
Gardner, Thomas
and Dewey and metaphysics, 325n.5
Geaney, Jane
and *qi* 氣, 116
Gelman, Susan
and essentialist assumptions, 42, 319n.32
Genetic-Functional, 18–19
Gerson, Lloyd P.
and identity and difference, 11
Ghiselin, M. T. and David L. Hull
and species as individuals, 103
Gidden, Anthony
and ontological security, 318n.11
Goh, Irving
and animals in the *Zhuangzi*, 261–262
Goldin, Paul R.
and Daoism and environmentalism, 270–271

Graham, A. C.
and agriculturism, 242–243
and *ji* 機, 72
and names, objects, and types, 104
and primitivism, 243
and prognostication in the *Book of Changes*, 299
and spontaneity, 164, 172, 275, 340n.67
and *xing* 性, 139, 141, 337n.162
and Yangism, 248
Great Chain of Being
and ascribed to Chinese thought, 272–273
Great Continuum Produces the Waters
and cosmogony, 84–93
and primordial continuity, 90–91
Great Learning
and profit and virtue, 285
Green Ink Pages, 34–36
Greenfield, Susan
and video gaming, 237–238
Grene, Marjorie
and the rejection of teleology, 48
Growth
and the 1-2-3 cosmology, 98
and *de* 德, 72
and dependence, 127
and directional order, 51
and organic form, 99
and its status as a norm, 301–302
and plasticity, 127–128
and softness and pliancy, 128, 301
Guanzi 管子
and life, 124
and *qi* 氣 and systemic integration, 117

Habit
and *dao* 道-activity, 64–70
and Dewey, 66–67, 140–141
and environment, 66–67
and form, 99, 279
and James, 67, 323n.144
and Peirce, 96, 98, 279

Hagen, Kurtis
  and coherence, 229, 349n.187
  and names, objects, and types, 104
  and realism in the *Xunzi*, 255
  and the *Xunzi* and morality, 251–252
Hall, David L.
  and mysticism, 218
Hall, David L. and Roger T. Ames
  and aesthetic *vs.* logical order, 82–83
  and cultural vagueness, 29, 31–32
  and *dao* 道, 327n.52
  and the focus/field model, 105, 107
  and objectless realism in the *Zhuangzi*, 217
  and the rejection of incommensurability, 10
  and unprincipled knowing, 196, 213
Hanfei
  and the *Daodejing*, 326n.31
  and the Man from Song, 186, 187
Hansen, Chad
  and the mass-noun hypothesis, 103–105
Harbsmeier, Christoph
  and the mass-noun hypothesis, 331n.136
Harmony
  and the *Daodejing*, 89
Havelock, Eric A.
  and objects for Plato, 199
Hayek, Friedrich A., 282
He 和. *See* Harmony
Heaven's Plan
  and the monopoly of moral truth, 225
  and the understanding of early Confucianism, 307, xvi
Heisenberg, Werner, 114, 216
Hemholtz, Hermann von, 114
Hendricks, Robert G.
  and holding to the one, 82
Hengxian 恆先
  and cosmogony, 62–63
  and human goodness, 243
  and organic life, 63, 278

Heraclitus, xvii
Hermeneutics
  and intra-cultural philosophy, 24–25
Hershock, Peter D.
  and East-West philosophy, 36
Hickman, Larry A.
  and culture and technology, 211
  and Dewey and nominalism, 331n.143
  and Dewey's theory of knowledge, 214
  and ends-in-view, 182–183
  and the limits of knowledge, 225
  and responsible technology, 267
  and the philosophical fallacy, 100
Hobbit People, 241
Hocking, William Ernest
  and his critique of Dewey, 158, 161, 169, 184
Hofstadter, Richard
  and his critique of Dewey, 158, 161, 169, 184
Holmes, Oliver Wendell
  and *Experience and Nature*, 121
Honeybees
  and ends *vs.* aims, 49–50
Houston, W. R.
  and Dewey on general content, 168–169
Hu, Jichuang
  and Daoism and economic activity, 291
Hu, Shih
  biographical, 43, xiii
Huainanzi 淮南子
  and Cook Ding, 159
  and *dao* 道 as source, 87
  and evolution, 102
  and learning, 159–160
  and living things, 71, 74
  and the Man from Song, 186
  and spontaneity, 98
  and types, 104, 125, 132
Huang-Lao 黃老
  and top down order, 82–83

Hulswit, Menno
  and his critique of Mayr, 49, 321n.75
Human Nature
  and animal nature in China, 240–250
  and the hunting vocation, 202–203
Human Universals
  and Dewey, 198–199
Hume, David
  and philosophical skepticism, 42
  and his status as positive thinker, 220
Hunting Vocation. *See also* Play
  and human nature, 202–203
  and primitivism, 204–209
  and technology, 223
  and wholeness, 204, 210–211
Hutton, Eric L.
  and *xing* 性, 140–141
Huxley, Aldous
  and the Alexander technique, 349n.13
Huxley, T. H., 43
Hyphens
  and Dewey, 36, 318n.137

Imagination
  and Dewey, 32
  and intra-cultural philosophy, 32–33, 271
  and Sinology, 32–33, 317n.126
  and technique, 305–306
Imitation
  and Mead, 257–258
Incommensurability, 9
  and Bernstein, 9
  and Hall and Ames, 10
Inherent Ethical Scheme
  and Daoism, 273, 354n.18
  and hypostatization, 306
  and philosophy, 274
  and its status as therapeutic, 301
Instrumentalism
  and artworks, 26, 33
  and ends for Dewey, 182–183
  and the human animal, 264–265
  and knowledge, 199, 204, 216–218, 222

  and organisms, 278
  and the primitive mind, 211–212
  and theories, 25, 166–168
Intelligence
  and coherence, 272
  and the *dao* 道 of knowing, 222
  and *dao-*道 activity, 210
  and general method, 167
  and governing, 290
  and imagination, 306
  and judgment, 175, 274, 278
  and knowledge, 179–185, 219–220, 227
  and the pivot of *dao* 道, 165, 183, 274, 293
  and stupidity, 187–188, 265
  and technology, 222, 237, 265–268
  and wisdom, 183–184
Intra-cultural philosophy, 3–36, 21–22
  and assimilation, 26–28
  and communication, 34–36
  and comparison, 21, 224–225
  and its status as experimental, 27–28
  and hermeneutics, 24–25
  and the human/animal distinction, 250
  and imagination, 32–33, 271
  and importance, 25
  and individualized cultures, 29–31
  and instrumentalism, 25
Ivanhoe, Philip J.
  and *de* 德 and spontaneity, 94
  and the grand scheme in Chinese thought, 273, 354n.18
  and Heaven's plan, xvi
  and the paradox of *wu-wei* 無為, 208, 345n.72
  and spontaneity, 236
  and the teleological reading of the *Daodejing*, 143, 337n.181
  and the therapeutic reading of Daoism, 272–273
  and truth, 295
  and the virtue ethics *vs.* role ethics debate, 223

Jackson, Philip W.
  and situations, 14
James, William
  and the Chautauqua Institution,
    300–301, 304
  and energy, 118
  and epistemic humility, 213–214
  and faith and philosophy, 304
  and habit, 67
  and moral philosophy, 229–230, 238,
    239, 256, 275–277, 278–279, 294,
    302, 304, 306
  and the mystery of fact, 45–46
  and the ontological question, 45
  and pure experience, 215
  and truth, 316n.91
  and the will to believe, 295
Ji 機
  and animal behavior, 76–77
  and mechanical contraption, 223,
    265–266
  and militarist thought, 73
  and organic form, 71–72
Jingfa 經法. See Mawangdui 馬王堆
    Canon Law
John Dewey in China: To Teach and to
    Learn, xiv
Johnson, Mark
  and Dewey's somatic awareness, 248
  and situations, 16
Jūdō
  and Dewey, 233, 235
Jullien, François
  and shi 勢, 72–73

Kant, Immanuel
  and cognitive limits, 42
  and metaphysics, 77
Kaogongji 考工記. See Artificer's Record
Katz, Eric
  and Dewey and environmental ethics,
    277
Kauffman, Stuart A.
  and emergent order, 99, 330n.103,
    336n.127

Kearney, Maureen
  and species as individuals, 103
Keightley, David N.
  and Chinese religion, 199
  and divination in early China, 298
Keleman, Barbara
  and teleology and common sense, 42
Kirkland, Russell
  and imagination in Sinology,
    317n.126
Kitarō, Nishida
  and Zen and pure experience, 215
Klyce, Scudder
  and correspondence with Dewey,
    218
Knack Passages. See Zhuangzi
Knoblock, John
  and humans and animals in China,
    240–241
Knowledge
  and the animal body, 261–263
  and Chinese thought, 199–201
  and continuity, 217–218, 221
  and dao 道-activity, 194–196,
    221–222
  and its status as instrumental, 204,
    216–218, 222
  and intelligence, 219–220, 227
  and its limits, 223–227
  and its scope, 213–214
  and Mohism, 200–201
  and its status as monopolistic,
    223–228
  and Plato, 196–197
  and the Zhuangzi, 227–228
  and technology, 223
  and transaction, 214–215
  and the uncertainty principle,
    216–217
Kolbert, Elizabeth
  and Aristotle on animals, 70
Koo, K. J.
  biographical, 109
Kraut, Richard
  and Aristotle's two lives thesis, 181

Kruse, Cornelius
    and Dewey and Chinese thought,
    6–7, 313n.21
Kuhn, Thomas
    and the advancement of knowledge,
    216
    and paradigms, 134

Laissez-faire
    and Daoism, 268, 282–292, 301
Lamb Meat
    and environmental cost, 292, 302
Lamb, Charles
    Dissertation Upon Roast Pig, 190–191,
    302
Lamont, Corliss
    and Dewey's missing manuscript,
    313n.15
Language
    and animals, 253–254
    and human uniqueness, 250–256
    and imitation, 257–258
    and its status as the tool of tools,
    232, 250, 258
Laozi 老子
    and *Experience and Nature*, 121–122
Lau, D. C.
    and Daoism and economic activity,
    291
    and *wuwei* 無為, 290
Lear, Jonathan
    and Aristotle and environment, 68
    and Aristotle's two lives thesis,
    181–182
Lee, Sherman E.
    and landscape paintings, 113
Legalism
    and holding to the one, 82–83
Leopold, Aldo
    and axe-in-hand judgments, 271–272,
    275, 304
Lewis, Mark Edward
    and anthropological narratives in
    China, 241
Li 理. *See* Coherence

Libertarianism
    and Daoism, 282–283
Liezi 列子
    and the Man from Song, 186
Life
    and the planet Earth, 62, 269–270,
    322n.128
    and its status as infinitesimal
    possibility, 60, 92–93
    and the law of entropy, 124
    and *qi* 氣, 116, 124, 142
    and the systems theory of organism,
    132–135
    and *wuwei* 無為, 301
Liji 禮記. *See Rituals*
Lippman, Walter
    and Dewey and China, xiv
Longo, Giuseppe and Maël Montévil
    and the systems theory of organism,
    74, 132–135
Lüshichunqiu 呂氏春秋. *See Annals of
    Lü Buwei*

Maijing 脈經. *See Classic on the Pulse*
Major, John S.
    and the *Huainanzi*, 71
    and resonance, 125, 323n.166
Mall, Ram Adhar
    and intercultural philosophy, 315n.79
Margolis, Joseph
    and culture in *Art as Experience*, 30
Mass-Noun Hypothesis
    and types, 103–105
Mawangdui 馬王堆 *Canon Law*
    and top-down order, 86
Maxwell, James Clerk
    and energy and transactions, 114
Mayr, Ernst
    and programs, 47–49, 98
    and species as individuals, 103
    and the teleomatic/teleonomic
    distinction, 49, 98
McCormack, Fr. Eric
    and Dewey and the Alexander
    technique, 264

McCormick, Ken
  and Daoism and libertarianism, 282–283, 288–289
McDonald, Hugh P.
  and Dewey and environmental ethics, 277, 280
  and organisms and growth, 278
McKinnon, Andrew
  and readings of Mead, 253
McLeod, Alexus
  and realism in the *Xunzi*, 255
Mead, George Herbert
  and body and selfhood, 261, 262
  and human language, 250, 252–253, 257–259
  and imitation, 257–258
  and his influence on Dewey, 232, 252
  and social self, 256, 259–261
Meliorism
  and pessimism *vs.* optimism, 304
Menand, Louis
  and Dewey's lab school, 160
Mencius 孟子
  and animals, 240, 241
  and Buddhism, 270–271
  and the *dao* 道 of water, 98
  and ends as external, 191
  and the four sprouts, 243
  and government action, 285–286
  and human emergence, 241–242
  and learning, 159
  and the Man from Song, 188
  and *qi* 氣, 333n.39
  and *xing* 性, 137
Meng, Chih
  and Dewey and China, xiv
Merton, Thomas, 22
  and cultural assimilation, 316n.101
Metaphysics
  and Dewey, 75–80, 95, 324–325n.5, 325n.9
  and energy, 118–119
Method
  and its status as general and individual, 167–168

  and *meta-hodos*, 167–168
  and the negative traits of general method, 170–171, 172–173
  and subject matter, 162–163
  and the virtues of individual method, 169–171, 172, 176, 184–185
Ming 明. See Intelligence
Mirror Neurons
  and brain research, 256–257
Moeller, Hans-Georg
  and Chapter 42 of the *Daodejing*, 87–88
  and *dao* 道, 327n.52
  and Daoism and economic activity, 291
  and Daoist amorality, 157, 173–175, 340–341n.82
  and desire in the *Daodejing*, 144, 303
  and genuine pretending, 305–306
Mohism, 225, 344n.28
  and the animalization of Confucianism, 350n.42
  and government action, 285
  and knowledge, 184, 200–201, 220
  and Mencius' critique, 242
  and mereology, 107
  and names, objects, and types, 104
  and rational argumentation, 156, 161, 200–201
Møllgaard, Eske
  and his critique of Ames, 16
  and the uncarved block, 211–212, 273
  and the *Zhuangzi* on technology, 211–212
Monkey Wrench Gang, 254n.23
Montévil, Maël. See Longo, Giuseppe and Maël Montévil
Moore, Charles A.
  and East and West, 313n.23
  and *Philosophy East and West*, 3–4
Morality. See also Amorality, Inherent Ethical Scheme
  and Cook Ding's *dao* 道, 156–157
  and Daoism, 157–158, 173–175, 229, 276

and Darwinian theory, 161–162
and environmental ethics, 276–277, 280, 293, 294
and general method or maxims, 172–173
and the good in Greek thought, 158–159
and human language, 258
and James' moral philosophy, 229–230
and the monopoly of knowledge, 225
and moral faith, 306
and the purpose of moral philosophy, 304
and its status as redundant, 175
and scientific understandings, 39–41
and spontaneity, 172, 275
and the virtues of individual method, 169–170, 184–185
Morgan, Lewis
and cultural evolution, 201
Mozi 墨子. *See* Mohism
Mumford, Lewis
and his critique of Dewey, 158, 161, 169, 184
Munro, Donald J.
and filtering out Heaven, 307, xvi
Mystery
and Dewey, 46–47
and form, 60
and quality, 51
Mysticism
and continuity, 218–219
and Dewey, 218–219

Nagel, Ernest
and Dewey, 54
and Dewey and physics, 114
Need
and demand and obligation, 230–231, 276, 302
and organic form, 63–64, 276, 278
and rhythmic adjustment, 144
Needham, Joseph
and the "Needham Question," 56
and causality in early China, 334n.92

and the knack passages, 155
and technology and Daoism, 239
Nelson, Eric S.
and intercultural philosophy, 315n.79
Neville, Robert C.
and cosmology, 80
Nicolas of Cusa, xvii
and God-created creatures, 231
and the maximum, 91
Nietzsche, Friedrich
and his status as positive thinker, 220
Norenzayan, Ara and Richard E. Nisbett
and causal reasoning and culture, 126
Norgaard, Kari Marie
and climate change denial, 39–40
Northrop, F. S. C.
and dualistic approach, 56
and East and West, 3
Nussbaum, Martha C.
and descriptive chauvinism, 10

Observing the Small
and the Daoist ideal, 146–148
"On Philosophical Synthesis," 4–5, 10, 21–22, 29, 32, 34, 148–149
One
and its different senses, 80–88, 93–94, 112, 147, 326n.38
Orange Trees
and form-environment continuity, 73–74
Ordinary activity
and the classroom, 160–161, 176, 178, 185, 192
and *dao* 道-activity, 184, 275
and external ends, 173, 222
and generalized content, 166–167
and knowledge, 222, 293
and the virtues of individual method, 170–171, 275
and the wholeness of play, 178
Organization. *See* Form

Painterly Traditions
and Europe and China, 112
and the use of space, 112–113

Pappas, Gregory Fernando
  and Dewey on moral philosophy,
    171–172, 230
Paradox of *Wuwei* 無為. *See* Slingerland,
  Edward
Parkes, Graham
  and climate change denial, 42
  and Daoism and technology, 239, 266
Pascal, Blaise, 295
Peirce, Charles Sanders
  and the chalk line on the board, 91
  and continuity and world order,
    95–96, 348n.148
  and creativity and ontology, 90, 94
  and doubt and inquiry, 298
  and final and efficient causality,
    97–98
  and firstness, secondness, thirdness,
    78–79, 89, 91, 97, 99
  and generals/universals, 99–100, 130
  and habit, 96
  and infinitesimals, 328n.72
  and pure zero, 89–90
  and vagueness, 97, 299
Perenboom, R. P.
  and Huang-Lao, 82–83
Perkins, Franklin
  and the human standpoint in the
    Zhuangzi, 281
  and novelty in the *Daodejing*, 86
Perlman, Mark
  and the rejection of teleology, 48
Phillips, Alan
  and religious critiques of Dewey,
    319n.28
Philosophical Fallacy, The
  defined, 100
  and Aristotle, 101
  and Daoism, 146
  and the historical fallacy, 100
  and the *praxis/poiesis* dualism, 177
Philosophy
  and common sense, 42–43
  and Dewey's definition, 17–19

  and its status as genetic-functional,
    18–19
Philosophy East and West, 10
Pivot of *Dao* 道. *See Zhuangzi*
Plank Epoch, 96, 141
Plato, xvii
  and the divided line, 197, 199, 227,
    295–296
  and the good, 295–296
  and knowing beauty, 226
  and knowledge, 196–197, 199, 209,
    262
  and sameness and difference, 11–12
  and *techne vs. empeiria*, 158–159,
    160
  and theories, 295
  and true belief, 296
  and the two-world theory, 197
Play
  and children's art, 305–306
  and its status as good-for-itself,
    176–177, 178, 202
  and the hunting vocation, 202–205
  and wholeness, 178
Plumb Line. *See* Carpenter's Square
Polanyi, Karl
  and market economies, 284
Potentiality
  and Aristotle, 125–126
  and *de* 德, 127, 132
  and Dewey, 128–130
Potter's Wheel of Nature. *See Zhuangzi*
Primitivism. *See also Zhuangzi*
  and the body, 235–236
  and Confucian debates, 242–250
  and knowledge, 194–196, 198, 227
  and modern thought patterns,
    201–209, 210
  and *Primitive Man as Philosopher*,
    209, 227
  and romanticism, 210, 211–212
  and technology, 211–212, 222, 239,
    264–265
  and the *Zhuangzi*, 195

Principles
  and philosophy, 17
Process Philosophy
  and Chinese thought, 136
  and responsibility, 170
Prognostication. See *Book of Changes*
Progressivism
  and instrumental knowledge, 225
Pryba, Russell
  and culture in *Art as Experience*, 30
Puett, Michael J.
  and Confucius on ritual, 200
  and continuity between Nature-and-human, 212
  and culture and nature in early China, 245
Pusey, James Reeve
  and Darwinism in China, 43

Qi 氣
  and Chinese thought, 116–121, 333n.39
  and life, 124
  as prenatal allocation, 142
Quality (and Qualitative Thought)
  and its status as feature of artworks, 25–28
  and form, 52–53, 321n.90
  and quantitative inquiry, 54–57

Radin, Paul
  and primitive humans, 209
Randall, John Herman
  and Dewey and Aristotle, 179
Raphals, Lisa
  and *ming* 命, 141
  and science and Daoism, 57
Ratner, Joseph, xi
Reagan, Ronald
  and the *Daodejing*, 282
Realism
  and Chinese thought, 105–107, 217–218
  and Dewey's thought, 106, 130–132, 196

  and objectless realism, 217–218
  and the philosophy of the *Xunzi*, 254–256
Red Deer Cave People, 241
Reeve, C. D. C.
  and Aristotle's two lives thesis, 181
Regan, Tom
  and animal rights, 276
Relativism
  and the limits of knowledge, 225–226
  and the *Zhuangzi*, 220–221, 272–275
Religious Fundamentalism
  and its anti-scientific bias, 149, 296
  and creationism, 38–39, 296
  and its critique of Dewey, 41, 319n.28
  and the tragic split, 38
  and truth, 296
Renaissance, European
  and painterly traditions, 112
Resonance
  and causality, 126
  and *qi* 氣, 125
Return Wave
  and aesthetic experience, 27
Rhythm
  and clock time, 133–134
  and energy, 119–120
  and the potter's wheel of nature, 123–124
Rituals
  and government action, 286
Robertson, Pat
  and his critique of Dewey, 319n.28
Robinet, Isabelle, 328n.66
  and *dao* 道, 85
Robins, Dan
  and the mass-noun hypothesis, 331n.136
  and *xing* 性, 138–141
Rockefeller, Steven C.
  and Dewey's mysticism, 218
Role Ethics
  and its debate with virtue ethics, 223–224

Rolston, Holmes
    and environmental values, 276
Romantic Approach
    and Chinese thought, 56
Rorty, Richard
    and relativism, 274
Rosemont Jr., Henry
    and the role ethics *vs.* virtue ethics debate, 223–225
Rosen, Jacob
    and Aristotle's formal and final causes, 101
Ross-Flanigan, Nancy
    and organic interaction, 323n.159
Roth, Harold D.
    and Daoist primitivism, 245
    and embracing the one, 81–82
    and the power of *dao* 道, 87
    and *qi* 氣 and systemic integration, 117
Rothbard, Murray N.
    and Daoism and libertarianism, 286–287, 288
Russell, Bertrand
    and potentiality, 126
Ryan, Alan
    and Boas and Dewey, 201
Ryden, Edmund
    and Chapter 42 of the *Daodejing*, 86

Sagehood
    and cultural creation, 241–245
Schrödinger, Erwin, 114
Schwartz, Benjamin
    and complements in the *Daodejing*, 334n.75
Science
    and China, 56–57
    and Dewey's aesthetic theory, 114–116
    and philosophy, 135–136, 149
    and *qi* 氣 energies, 117–118
    and science denial, 37–45, 318n.10
Sextus Empiricus
    and his status as positive thinker, 220

Shangjunshu 商君書. See *Book of Lord Shang*
Shen 身
    and the body-self relation, 264, 267
Shen, Kuo
    and landscape paintings, 113
Shoko Zama
    and the Alexander technique, 349n.13
Shoot Pulling
    and the Alexander technique, 235
    and its status as form of stupidity, 188–189
Short Preface to the Songs
    and organic form, 142
Shusterman, Richard
    and digital amusements, 237–238
    and situations, 14–15
    and somatic-psychic ailments, 236
Singer, Peter
    and animal rights, 276
Situations
    definition of, 14–15
    and the limits on measurement, 55–56
    and value distribution, 278
Sivin, Nathan
    and science in China, 56
    and technology, 266
Škof, Lenart
    and intercultural philosophy, 22
Slater, Michael R.
    and his critique of Moeller, 340–341n.82
Sleeper, R. W.
    and Dewey and metaphysics, 78, 325n.5
Slingerland, Edward
    and evolution and common sense, 42
    and neo-Orientalism, xvii, 10
    and the paradox of *wuwei* 無為, 207–208, 222
    and *wuwei* 無為, 145, 275, 289–290
Smid, Robert W.
    and comparative philosophy, 22

Smith, Adam, 282
  and his comparison with the
    Daodejing, 288
  and human nature, 355n.68
Snyder, Gary, 22
Socrates
  and human *vs.* super-human wisdom,
    225
Space
  and the *Hengxian*, 112–113
  and space-time, 115
Species. *See* Types (Species)
Spencer, Herbert
  and cultural evolution, 201
Sterckx, Roel
  and animals in early China, 102, 241,
    323n.165
Stuhr, John
  and Dewey and metaphysics, 325n.5
Stump Watching
  and its status as form of stupidity,
    188
Stupidity
  definition of, 187–188, 192
  and Dewey, 188–189
  and environmental stewardship, 278
  and the Man from Song, 186–192
  and shoot pulling, 188–189
  and stump watching, 188
Sturgeon, Donald
  and the Chinese Text Project, xviii
Sunzibingfa 孫子兵法. *See Art of War*
Swimming School, 343n.168
Symbolic Interactionism. *See* George
    Herbert Mead
Systems Theory
  and the organism, 74, 132–135

Taishan 泰山, 308–309
  and Dewey's visit, 308–309
Taiyishengshui 太一生水. *See Great
    Continuum Produces the Waters*
*Taking Back Philosophy: A Multicultural
    Manifesto*, 315n.81

Taxonomy
  and early China, 70–71, 102, 241,
    323n.165
  and oak trees, 336n.152
  and types in early China, 102–103,
    241
Taylor, Romeyn
  and markets in early China, 285
Technology
  and the body, 235–236, 237, 245–250
  and the *Daodejing*, 303
  and the instrumental, 222
  and the hunting vocation, 211
  and intelligence, 237, 265–268
  and knowledge, 223
  and the organism-technology circuit,
    238–240, 265–268
  and primitivism, 198, 203, 211–213,
    239
  and the rise of digital age, 238,
    265–268, 270
Teleology
  and Aristotle, 101–102, 142–143
  and Chinese *vs.* American culture,
    43–44
  and common sense, 42, 96–97
  and cultural evolution, 201
  and directional order, 65–66
  and Greek-medieval thought, 50
  and habit, 65–66
  and mechanical *vs. dao* 道-activity,
    67–68
  and the origin of the term, 320n.72
  and stag's legs, 52, 68
  and teleomatic/teleomatic processes, 49
Thompson, Paul B.
  and Chatham river case study,
    293–294
Tian 天
  and the evolution of the term, 200
  and its definition as Nature, 273
Tianrenheyi 天人合一. *See* Continuity
Tiles, J. E.
  and Dewey and the Greeks, 179

Togetherness
  and Dewey, 31
Tradition
  and Dewey, 33–34
Tragic Split
  defined, 37–38, 266–267
Transaction
  and environmental value, 280
  and Maxwell's work, 114
  and the theory of knowledge, 214–217
Truth
  and Dewey, 39
  and Ivanhoe, 295
  and James, 316n.91
  and Plato, 296
  and Whitehead, 316n.91
Tsung, Pai-hwa
  and Shen Kuo's art criticism, 113
Types (Species)
  and Dewey, 130–132
  and early China, 102–103
  and the *Huainanzi*, 125
  and if-then propositions, 131–132
  and individuals, 103
  and potentials, 125–136
  and resonance, 125

Uchiyama, Kōshō
  and *Instructions for the Cook*, 176
Uncertainty Principle
  and the theory of knowledge, 216–217
University of Hawai`i
  and Dewey's 1951 visit to Hawai`i, 4
  and its doctoral program, 36
Unmodern Philosophy and Modern Philosophy, 5–8, 17–18, 21
  and the loss of the manuscript, 313n.15

Vagueness
  and cultures, 29, 31–32

Value
  and bias, 271–272, 275
  and its status as intrinsic, 268, 277–279, 302
  and nature, 275–282
  and valuation, 272–275, 279–280, 302
Van Norden, Bryan W.
  and comparative philosophy, 315n.81
  and Daoist utopia, 145
  and Dewey and Chinese thought, xvii
Video Gaming
  and the body, 237–238
  and deaths associated with, 237
Virtue Ethics
  and early Confucianism, 307, xvi
  and its debate with role ethics, 223–224

Waley, Arthur
  and *baoyi* 抱一 and *zhiyi* 執一, 147
  and *de* 德, 126
Wang 忘. *See* Forgetting
Wang Chong
  and *ming* 命, 337n.177
Wang, Jessica Ching-Sze
  and Dewey and China, xiv–xv
Wang, Zhongjiang
  and the generosity of *dao* 道, 87
Watson, Burton
  and animal standpoints in the *Zhuangzi*, 246
Weber, Ralph
  and the *tertium comparationis*, 20–21, 29
Welch, Holmes
  and imagination in Sinology, 33
Well Sweep
  and the technological attitude, 238–239, 265–268
Wenzi 文子
  and observing the small, 147
Weston, Anthony
  and intrinsic value, 277

Whitehead, Alfred North
  and doing philosophy, xxi
  and symbolic reference, 298
  and truth and importance, 316n.91
Wilkie, Rhoda
  and misreadings of Mead, 253
Wisdom
  and Dewey, 182–183
  and its Greek sense, 180–181, 185
  and intelligence, 183
  and the Man from Song, 186–192
  and *phronesis*, 181–182
Woolf, S. J.
  and Dewey and Chinese art, 110
Wu, John C. H.
  and Chinese humor, 190
  and *Experience and Nature*, 121
Wu, Joseph S.
  and causality in early China, 334n.92

Xi, Jinping
  and state-owned enterprises, 356n.78
Xiaoxu 小序. See *Short Preface to the Songs*
Xing 性
  and Daoist primitivism, 195–196, 203, 223
  and early Chinese thinking, 136–142
  and technology, 231–232, 240, 244–245
  and teleology, 136–137, 138
Xing Wen
  and *fu* 復, 337–338n.182
Xunzi 荀子
  and government action, 286
  and the human difference, 251–252, 254, 259
  and moral thought, 251–252
  and realism, 254–256
  and *xing* 性, 140

Yang Xiong
  and reading texts, 316n.88

Yangism
  and the animal standpoint, 246
  and the body, 248
  and Mencius' critique, 242
Yanzi Chunqiu 晏子春秋. See *Annals of Master Yan*
Yao, Xinzhong
  and *shen* 身, 264
Yellow River
  and natural disasters, 272
Yi 一. See One
Yijing 易經. See *Book of Changes*
Yin-Yang 陰陽
  and Chinese cosmology, 88
  and *qi* 氣, 116, 119, 121
Yong 庸. See *Zhuangzi*

Zen Buddhism
  and the *dao* 道-seeking mind, 175–176
  and James' pure experience, 215
Zhang, Xianglong
  and the bamboo rod example, 12, 55
  and the comparative situation, 10–17, 313n.49
  and the comparison paradox, 11–13
Zhi 知. See *Mozi*, *Zhuangzi*
Zhongyong 中庸. See *Focusing the Familiar*
Zhuangzi 莊子
  and amorality, 173–176, 272–275
  and animal behavior, 76–77, 99, 206, 264
  and Artisan Chui, 164
  and the body, 244–250
  and Carver Qing, 163
  and continuity, 218
  and Cook Ding, 155–156, 163–164, 166–168, 171, 194, 265, 275
  and environmental philosophy, 270–271, 280
  and evolution, 71–72
  and forgetting, 208–209, 215–216
  and generalized content, 166–168

Zhuangzi 莊子 *(continued)*
   and the genuine human of primitive times, 208–209, 213, 227, 264–265
   and genuine pretending, 305–306
   and intelligence and *dao* 道, 184
   and the knack passages, 155–157, 163–164, 166, 173, 265
   and knowledge, 155, 193–196, 206, 213, 217, 226, 227, 267–268
   and the Man from Song, 186–187
   and moral concerns, 229, 272–275, 280
   and the optimal human standpoint, 212, 248–249
   and ordinary activity, 155, 184
   and the pivot of *dao* 道, 165–166, 183, 274, 293
   and the potter's wheel of nature, 123–124, 128, 133, 143, 230
   and its status as pragmatic, 219, 220–221
   and primitivism, 195, 210, 243, 264–265
   and *qi* 氣, 116
   and relativism, 220–221, 272–275
   and space, 112–113
   and technology, 211–213, 223, 238–239, 264–266
   as therapeutic mystic, 272
   ans *tian* 天, 273
   and valuation, 272–275, 280
   ans *xing* 性, 137, 138

Ziporyn, Brook
   and Chinese thought as process-oriented, 136
   and coherence, 134, 218, 228–229, 274
   and coherence *vs.* realism/nominalism, 105–106
   and Daoist amorality, 175
   and Dewey and nominalism, 106, 130–131
   and imagination in Sinology, 33
   and *ming* 明, 183–184
   and Moeller's moral fool, 340–341n.82
   and realism in the *Xunzi*, 255

Zuozhuan 左傳
   and *qi* 氣, 116

www.ingramcontent.com/pod-product-compliance
Lightning Source LLC
Chambersburg PA
CBHW020119240426
43673CB00038B/533